We Americans

We Americans

WE AMERICANS
A VOLUME IN THE STORY OF MAN LIBRARY
PUBLISHED BY
THE NATIONAL GEOGRAPHIC SOCIETY
Gilbert M. Grosvenor, *President
and Chairman of the Board*
Owen R. Anderson, *Executive Vice President*
Robert L. Breeden, *Senior Vice President,
Publications and Educational Media*

Editorial Consultant
DANIEL J. BOORSTIN
Librarian of Congress 1975-1987

Chapters by Dr. Boorstin and
JOHN R. ALDEN
Author of *A History of the American Revolution*

ERIK BARNOUW
Author of *Tube of Plenty: The Evolution of American Television*

RAY ALLEN BILLINGTON
Author of *Westward Expansion*

DAVID HERBERT DONALD
Professor of American History, Harvard University

FRANK FREIDEL
Author of *Over There*

WILLIAM H. GOETZMANN
Professor of History, University of Texas

RUSSELL LYNES
Author of *The Domesticated Americans*

BLAKE McKELVEY
Author of *The City in American History*

EDMUND S. MORGAN
Author of *Inventing the People*

ELTING E. MORISON
Author of *Men, Machines, and Modern Times*

ANN NOVOTNY
Author of *Strangers at the Door*

WILLIAM PEIRCE RANDEL
Author of *Centennial: American Life in 1876*

RICHARD SCHICKEL
Film critic, author of *The Men Who Made the Movies*

WILLIAM V. SHANNON
Professor of History and Journalism, Boston University

BEN J. WATTENBERG
Political advisor, author of *The Real America*

BERNARD A. WEISBERGER
Author of *The New Industrial Society*

GORDON S. WOOD
Professor of History, Brown University

LOUIS B. WRIGHT
Author of *Cultural Life of the American Colonies*

Folklore panels by **RICHARD M. DORSON**
Author of *American Folklore*

659 illustrations, including 439 photographs

First edition 600,000 copies. Second printing, 1976, 175,000 copies. Third printing, 1981, 280,000 copies. Revised edition, 1988, 170,000 copies.
Library of Congress CIP data page 456

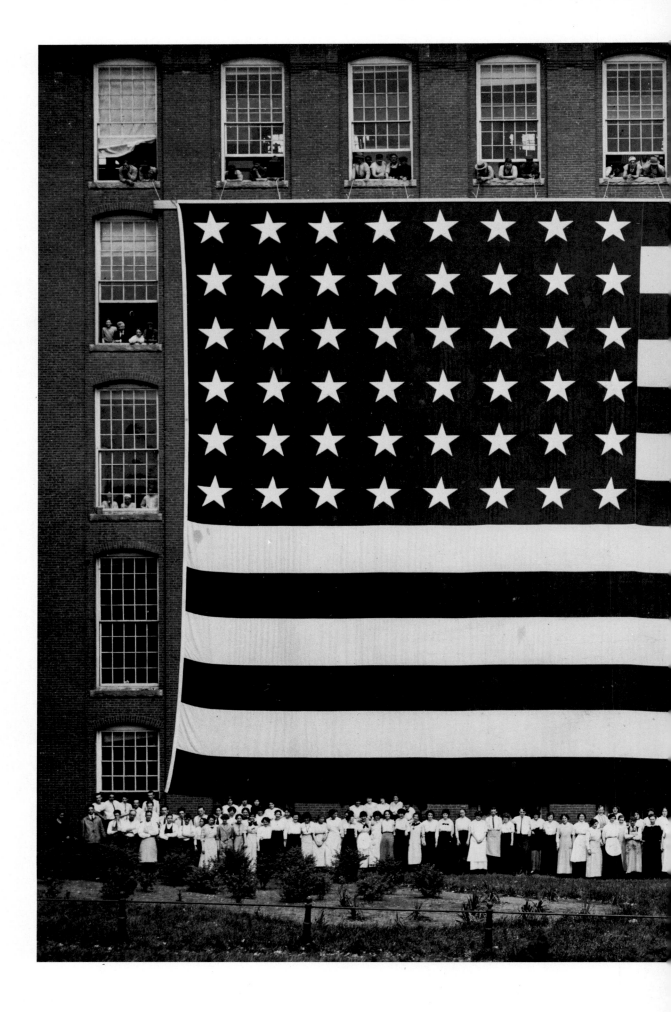

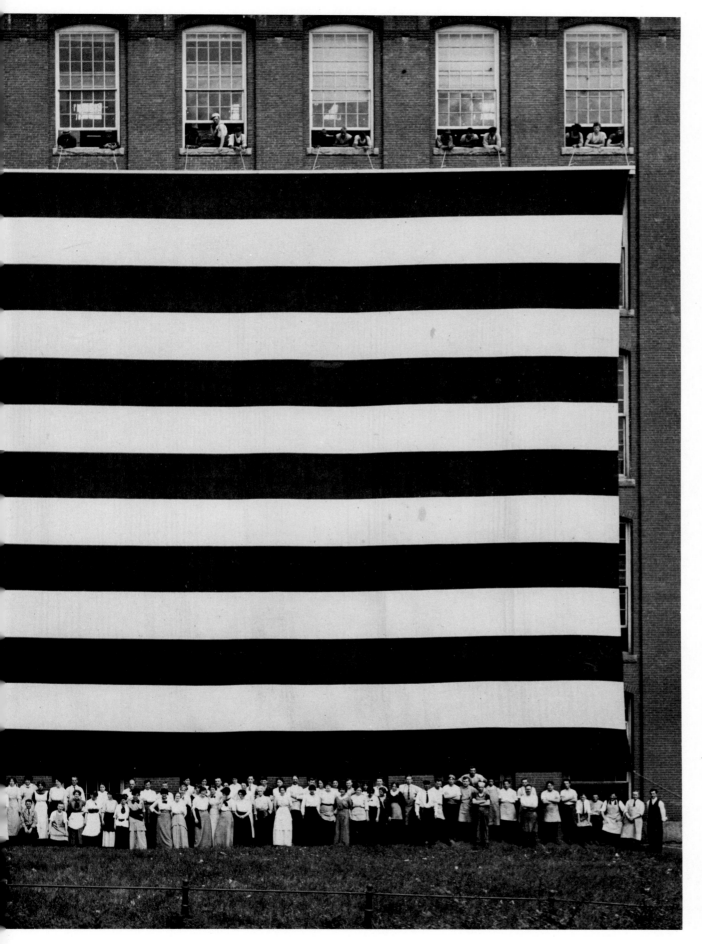

PREPARED BY
NATIONAL GEOGRAPHIC BOOK SERVICE

THOMAS B. ALLEN
Editor

CHARLES O. HYMAN
Art Director

ANNE DIRKES KOBOR
Illustrations Editor

WILHELM R. SAAKE
Production Manager

CAROL BITTIG LUTYK
Chief Researcher

ROSS BENNETT
JULES B. BILLARD
MARY B. DICKINSON
SEYMOUR L. FISHBEIN
MARY SWAIN HOOVER
EDWARD LANOUETTE
PAMELA MUCCI
DAVID F. ROBINSON
SHIRLEY L. SCOTT
MARGARET SEDEEN
VERLA LEE SMITH
ELIZABETH L. WAGLEY
ANNABELLE WITHERS
Editorial Staff

CONNIE BROWN
Design

KAREN F. EDWARDS
Production

LINDA BRUMBACH MEYERRIECKS
BARBARA G. STEWART
KAREN VOLLMER
Illustrations Research

JOHN R. METCALFE
WILLIAM W. SMITH
JAMES R. WHITNEY
Engraving and Printing

WERNER JANNEY
Style

BARBARA L. KLEIN, ANNE K. McCAIN,
BRIT AABAKKEN PETERSON
Index

JOAN PERRY, SARAH L. ROBINSON,
ELIZABETH S. WOOSTER
Assistants

With contributions by
MIKE W. EDWARDS, ROBERT C.
RADCLIFFE, PAUL SAMPSON, *and* PAUL A.
SCARAMAZZA, *National Geographic Staff,*
and DIANE S. MARTON, PATRICIA RAYMER

For the revised edition:
MARY B. DICKINSON
Editor

SUSAN C. ECKERT
KIMBERLY I. STEERE
Research

RICHARD S. WAIN
ANDREA CROSMAN
Production

JOHN T. DUNN
DAVID V. EVANS
Quality Control

Old Glory, displayed by patriotic textile workers during World War I, bedecks the Amoskeag Mill in Manchester, N.H. One of the largest flags of its time, it measured 50 by 95 feet and weighed 200 pounds; each star spanned a yard.

Contents

Picturing Our Past 8

From the Land to the Machine 23

Voyage to Eden 37

Working the American Land 49

The Planting of Cities 73

Living Through a Revolution 93

★1776★ Birth of the Nation 107

A New World of Learning 117

Americans on the Move 133

Tying the Nation Together 163

The People's Choice 185

Living Through a Civil War 201

★1876★ Centennial! 223

New Ways of Working 235

The World Enters America 259

Cities in the Machine Age 279

The Automobile Arrives 303

Americans at Play 331

Gone to the Movies 351

On the Home front 379

In Everybody's Living Room 415

An American Inventory 433

The Fertile Machine 443

Folklore Panels 44/60/78/120/150/270/317   Picture Credits 450   Biographical and Reference Notes 451   Index 452

Picturing Our Past

"To catch hold of and encompass in words — to describe exactly — the life of a single people, much less of humanity, would appear impossible," grumbled Leo Tolstoy in *War and Peace* more than a century ago. Fortunately, to our great enrichment, historians have kept trying. Their latest triumph is the volume in your hands — the product of 20 distinguished authors, among them recipients of the prestigious Bancroft, Parkman, and Pulitzer awards for history. Despite Count Tolstoy's gloomy pronouncement, they have managed superbly "to catch hold of and encompass in words" the life of this vastly varied, marvelously mingled people we call Americans.

But gifted writing alone could not make *We Americans* what it is. As you leaf its richly illustrated pages you will be struck by the realization that the United States is the world's most photographed country; fully two-thirds of our national adventure has been chronicled on film and tucked away in archives across the country.

The earliest daguerreotype practitioners committed the image of a people to a sensitized copper plate — and found they had captured their character, too. The camera, we know now, can be more precise than words, and just as powerful. Portraitist Mathew B. Brady undertook to record the Civil War by sending teams of photographers to almost every battlefield. "Let him who wishes to know what war is look at this series of illustrations," wrote Oliver Wendell Holmes of Brady's work. By contrast, glance at the "Little Lord Fauntleroy" in the following "series of illustrations" and wonder at a fad that put a nation's boys in velvet suits and curls. Or turn to the photograph of a migrant-worker mother and find a full textbook on the despair that stalked America during the Great Depression of the '30's — and the grit that pulled its people through.

"History is the essence of innumerable biographies," wrote Thomas Carlyle. People have always been the true stuff of history. Yet the greatest events and struggles often are shaped by the nameless ones. A score of Africans — forgotten now — brought to Jamestown in 1619 foreshadowed momentous tides across this land: a vast, foredoomed plantation economy; a tragic fratricidal war; a long, painful groping toward equality and dignity; racial resentments that still smolder. In one of those oddly interweaving currents of history, another ship in 1619 delivered to Jamestown some 90 "young maids to make wives" — and another American struggle for parity was ordained. That battle continues as a campaign for women's rights.

We Americans include history-makers whose names survive, but whose impact has been dimmed by time. Samuel Slater, for example. In 1789 *(continued on page 20)*

Jacob Byerly in 1842 opened a gallery as one of America's first daguerreotypists. Hardly a decade later 10,000 others were producing the same "remarkable objects of curiosity and admiration." Thus sprouted the nation's fascination with the camera — and the rich harvest arrayed on these pages.

The strong mothers pulling them
    from a dark sea, a great prairie,
a long mountain. . . . The strong men
    keep coming on.   Carl Sandburg, *Upstream*

They were going to look at war,
the red animal—war, the blood-swollen
god. Stephen Crane, *The Red Badge of Courage*

Where today is the Pequot? Where are the Narragansetts,
the Mohawks, the Pokanoket . . . ? They have vanished . . .
as snow before a summer sun. Tecumseh, Shawnee chief

Other old-timers have told all about stampedes and swimming rivers
and what a terrible time we had, but they never put in any of the fun,
and fun was at least half of it.   E. C. Abbott, *We Pointed Them North*

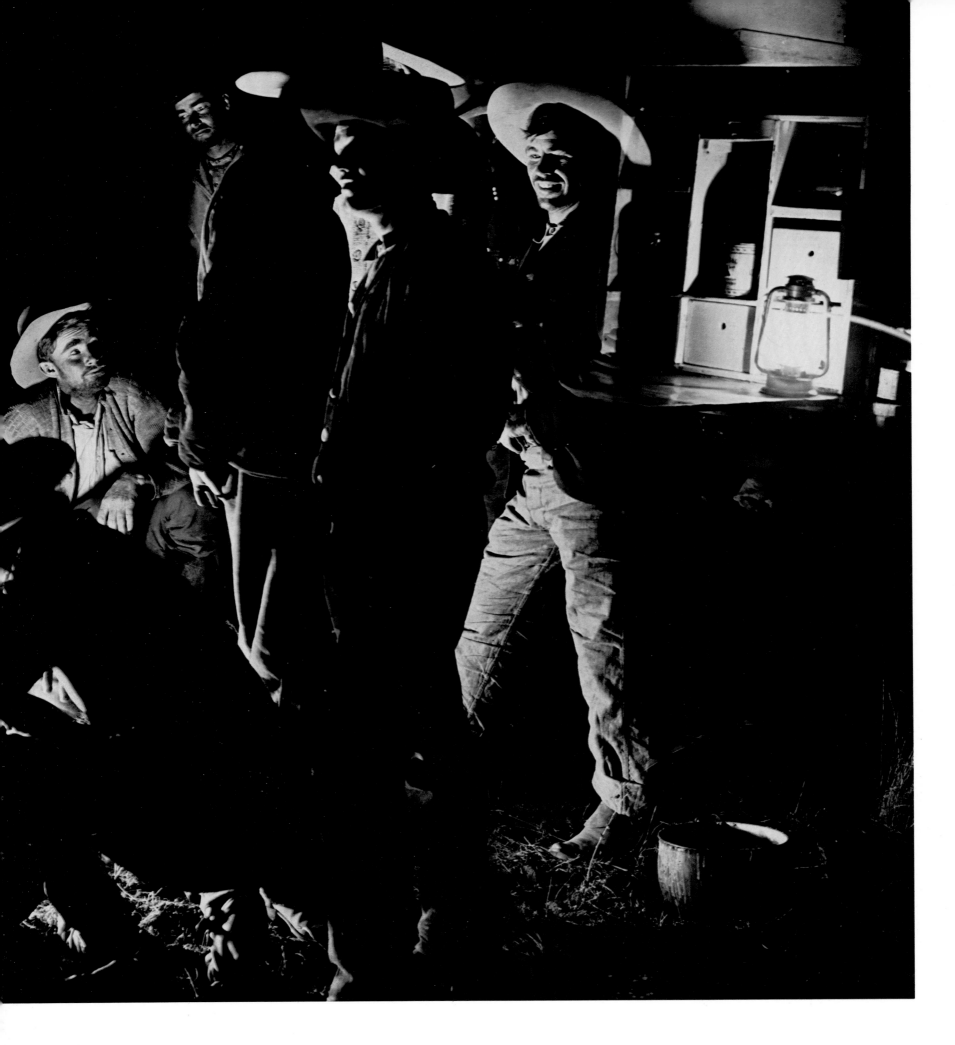

"Oh, Dearest," he said [to his mother], "I should rather not be an earl. None of the boys are earls. Can't I *not* be one?"   Frances Hodgson Burnett, *Little Lord Fauntleroy*

Who knows/ What strange, multi-fathered child will come Out of the nervous travail of these bloods/ To fashion in a new world . . . A newer breed of men?   Paul Engle, *America Remembers*

It was an age of miracles, it was an age of art,
it was an age of excess, and it was an age
of satire.   F. Scott Fitzgerald, *Echoes of the Jazz Age*

They had been living on [unmarketable] vegetables from the . . . fields,
and birds that the children killed. She had just sold the tires from
her car to buy food.   Dorothea Lange, a photographer's recollections, 1936

It was as if joy had been rationed and saved up
for the three years, eight months and seven days since
Sunday, Dec. 7, 1941.   *Life* magazine, report on VJ Day, 1945

Now, since my baby left me I've found a new place to
dwell, down at the end of Lonely street. . . . I'm so lonely . . .
I'm so lonely, that I could die.   M. Axton, T. Durden, E. Presley, *Heartbreak Hotel*

he came to New York, his head crammed with the secret mechanical details of an English spinning mill. From these mentally pirated blueprints grew a New England textile industry that was to outstrip its parent, decline, and find rebirth in the South. Similarly, Elisha Otis is hardly a household name today, but he stood our great cities on end: They had to await his safety elevator before they could—literally—grow up.

The more familiar names are here too, of course—Whitney, Edison, Bell, Wright, and others. One could hardly ignore the peculiar American genius for tinkering that evolved so awesomely into assembly lines, automation, computerization. But this book is no dry catalog of technological triumphs. Its words and pictures are dramatic and emotional; the social history of a nation, told through its people, could not be otherwise. We Americans are tycoons—Vanderbilts, Astors, Morgans, Fords, Rockefellers—and we are their hard-knuckled adversaries, too: Samuel Gompers; John L. Lewis; formidable negotiators named Reuther, Meany, Dubinsky.

We Americans seem always to have been on the brink of one revolution or another: political, industrial, social, even agricultural. In less than 200 years unexplored America became the world's breadbasket—the most fruitful, highly mechanized agricultural nation on this planet. It began with the vision of Thomas Jefferson, who couldn't resist a bargain when Napoleon put sprawling Louisiana up for sale. The broad land lured "men with the West in their eyes," as historian Ray Allen Billington calls them.

By itself that epic westward movement made the United States unique. Where else could so many pack their few possessions and pursue a dream across countless miles— and never leave the country? Sodbusters, gold hunters, glory-seekers by the thousand headed for the sunset. Many found home, and a few even found gold. And some found eternal shame, for the relentless westering drove even older Americans from their ancestral plains, and buried a culture that had flourished for centuries.

In the last great Indian "battle," some 200 Sioux were massacred, in 1890 at Wounded Knee, South Dakota. Today we mourn them (when we think about it), for we are capable of the deepest compassion and kindness. Yet, for the world's foremost nation of laws, we can be astonishingly lawless. We Americans include not only a John Marshall, an Oliver Wendell Holmes, and a trust-busting Teddy Roosevelt; we are also robber barons, Jesse James, John Dillinger, and the Godfather. Epic romance with the frontiersman's rifle and tawdry affair with the Saturday Night Special—they are both part of a fixation with firearms which many other nations find difficult to comprehend.

We Americans are not basically an aggressive people. We are, however, probably the world's most competitive. We show it in our broad-ranging passion for sports, and the royal esteem we accord our champions. No other country has spawned a Babe Ruth, a Bobby Jones, and a Bill Tilden in the same generation—or a Billie Jean King, a Sonny Jurgensen, and a Muhammad Ali. A talented American athlete can go from poverty to instant wealth in the flick of a basketball. And there perhaps is the essence of America: For all its problems, it is still the land of greatest hope.

Among the millions who have come in pursuit of that hope, one, German immigrant Carl Schurz, rose to be a noted editor and a U. S. Senator. On its hundredth birthday in 1876 he gave his adopted homeland a trenchant task. "Our generation has to open the second century of our National Life, as the Fathers opened the first," he said. "Theirs was the work of independence, ours is the work of reformation."

More than another hundred years have passed, and our generation has embarked on the third century of our national life. It seems to me that our work, too, is clear. It is not so much the work of heads, as confronted the authors of our political system, or of hands, as faced the builders of city, railroad, and highway—but of hearts. A just, open, and compassionate society would be the most enduring monument to the labor of those who came before us.

Gilbert M Grosvenor

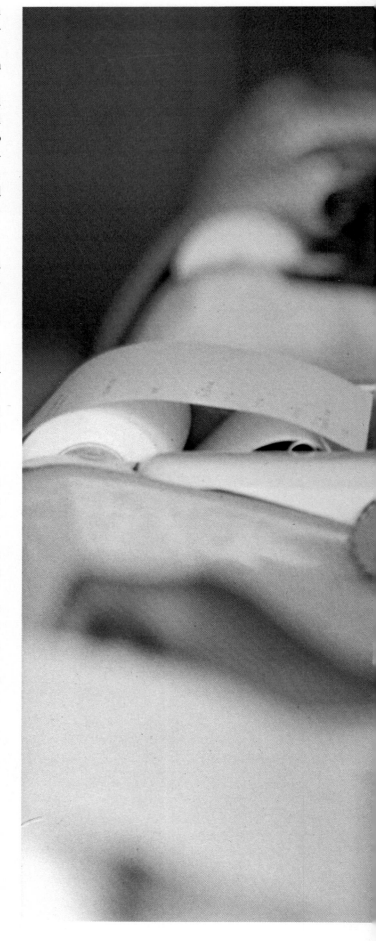

O, let America be America again—
The land that never has been yet—
And yet must be.   Langston Hughes, *Let America Be America Again*

From the Land to the Machine

Daniel J. Boorstin

When the seafaring Pilgrim Fathers disembarked from the *Mayflower* on November 21, 1620, and stepped out on their new home country, "they fell upon their knees and blessed the God of Heaven who had brought them over the vast and furious ocean, and delivered them from all the periles and miseries thereof, againe to set their feete on the firme and stable earth, their proper elemente." They were on their way to discovering, and inventing, a New World. They had committed themselves to a country that their fellow Europeans had not even imagined scarcely a century before. This might have been called The Impossible Land, for the American Continent had no place in the European's tradition. In the later Middle Ages the best authorities on the shape and extent of the known world had described a three-part planet of Europe-Asia-Africa. Their *mappae mundi* placed Jerusalem at the center and filled the rest with settled lands, real or imagined. There was no room on their map—and hardly any in their thinking, or in their history or travel literature—for a fourth continent.

By the time the Pilgrim Fathers landed, Europeans were painfully and reluctantly discovering that these shores were not part of Asia, that the Great Khan would probably not be encountered, and that the Emperor of Cipangu (Japan) would not be met on the next island. Much of what explorers had learned in the century before the Pilgrims arrived was negative. The bold settlers knew they were coming to a New World unspoiled and mostly uninhabited. But they did not yet know how new their New World might be. Despite the strenuous, nostalgic efforts of several generations of colonials and "New Englanders," America would not become a New Europe.

The American experience would be different. Here men would discover new possibilities in the land, man's "proper elemente." In Europe man had shaped his notions of himself—of what he could and could not do—by his experience on familiar lands. Grandchildren and great-grandchildren usually relived their traditional experience on a friendly landscape. America offered a landscape strange and not always friendly.

There had been migrations before: the ancestors of American Indians across the Bering land bridge from Asia; the Normans into Britain, Sicily, and the Middle East; the Crusaders and their followers toward the Holy Land; the Mongols and the Turks into Eastern Europe. But most such migrations had been crusades or invasions. The ebb and flow of soldiers, nomads, bedouins, and traders had touched many lands without occupying them. The Great Atlantic Migration—in only the century and a half between 1820 and 1970—would bring some 36 million Europeans to the United States.

"Where industry has sunk its steel into the plains country," Thomas Hart Benton painted a landscape changed by Man and Machine.

The American settlers came to take and shape the land. The first occupants of the land — the "Indians" whom the European migrants encountered — would not be treated, in the pattern of the Romans, as people to be incorporated into an empire. Instead, they were treated as part of the landscape. Most of them were simply cleared away, like the forests, or pushed back, like the wilderness.

By an oddity of history one large portion of the temperate regions of the planet, the heart of North America, had remained sparsely settled. When the Europeans came in the late 15th and 16th centuries, there were perhaps 2 or 3 million Indians scattered over an area about twice the size of Europe — which then had a population estimated at about 100 million. The pre-Columbian Americans had spread so thinly across North America that they had made little impression upon the land — cliff-cut pueblos in the Southwest, the tipi encampment, the occasional village. So the continent which the English and French settlers saw was almost untouched by human hand. An explorer could walk for miles through the American wilderness, or float for days down one of the broad rivers, without once seeing a sign of humankind.

Just as the Indians lacked the technology to drive off the European settlers, they also lacked the technology to change the face of the land. The land was virginal too because people elsewhere, especially Europeans, had remained so long ignorant of this part of the world. The common phrase, "The Discovery of America," tells volumes about how Europeans thought — their unashamed provincialism, their isolation, the self-imprisonment of the Old World imagination.

The European encounter with the land was shaped not only by what had not happened to America but also by what had been happening in Europe. The Renaissance in Europe was an Age of Discoveries, of which the discovery of America was only one. The foundations of modern science were being laid while the Pilgrims landed at Plymouth. Francis Bacon's *Novum Organum* persuaded men to turn from the authority of Aristotle to the evidence of their senses. Settlers who came during the 17th and 18th centuries not only possessed firearms and the knowledge to navigate thousands of miles at sea but also were beginning to chart the flow of blood through the human body and to trace the planets in their orbits around the sun.

When these European settlers came to North America, there was a new kind of encounter, one that could not have happened before and which would never happen again. The encounter of people possessing the accumulated cultures of Western Europe, the inheritance of much of Arabic learning, the traditions and literatures of the classical world, the institutions, theologies, and philosophies of Judaism and Christianity, and the experience of a passage across a perilous ocean. A rare opportunity! "Civilized" people seeking their God and their Fortunes in a raw and savage land.

The Puritans, who were adept at finding God's purpose in everything, explained that Divine Providence had for centuries kept this New World secret from mankind. New England, they believed, had thus been held in reserve until, at last, these English Protestants could fill it with their Puritanized religion. The Indians, then, were God's Custodians, unwittingly assigned to hold the land until the Puritans arrived.

The discovery of America did not end with the arrival of the Pilgrims. Settlers from Europe and elsewhere continued their collaborative voyages of discovery in and around and across a continent. American history, for at least a full century after the Declaration of Independence, could be summed up as a continuing discovery of America — a discovery at great cost and with great rewards — of what the land held, what people could make of the land, and how its resources could remake people's lives. This strangely American encounter with the raw land left its birthmarks on American civilization at least into the later 20th century.

Paul Bunyan, invented hero, through Carl Sandburg: "Paul logged . . . in Oregon one winter. The cook stove . . . covered an acre. . . . They fastened the side of a hog on each snowshoe and four men used to skate on the griddle while the cook flipped the pancakes."

As a consequence of the variety of the land, this was to be a *federal* nation. This was not a homogeneous land, but a land—even leaving out Alaska and Hawaii—that spread across nearly 25 degrees of latitude and nearly 58 degrees of longitude, with a Death Valley reaching 282 feet below sea level and a Mount Whitney reaching 14,494 feet above sea level, with cypress swamps, sand dunes, subtropical everglades, and pine forests along with alpine tundra and glaciers, a land that could produce cotton and tobacco, mink and beaver. The awkwardness of the nation's name remained a living symbol that—as the engrossed final version of the Declaration of Independence read—this was to be the thirteen united (with a small *u*) States of America.

This variety of land—of geology, of climate, of topography, of seacoast and river, of mountains and prairies—made a seafaring New England, a plantation South, a Middle West of wheat fields and corn, a Far West of mines and cattle ranges, a Northwest of lumber and fisheries. And geographic variety, reinforced by varieties of history, religion, and national origins, made the States. This explained the rewards of free trade among the States. There were unexampled opportunities for a citizenry that could select from so large a catalog. There would be something here for *every* variety of human hope and skill and talent.

The American Encounter would produce what Walt Whitman called "Man in the Open Air." The European peasant had brought his cattle indoors to live with his family through the winter. In the American West the cowboy went outdoors: He bred his cattle for the fenceless range and learned to live out there with them. The West became the symbolic American land and even into the late 20th century remained a relic of primitive America. The "Wild" West was not wild in the style of an Old World rooted in feudalism, a world of frustrated crusades and inquisitions, of contesting duchies and invading hordes. The American West was wild in its own outdoor way. To conquer a raw land, you needed athletic virtues, stamina to survive long treks, courage to tackle unknown and unseen enemies. These had little in common with the peasant virtues of docility, dogged persistence, and reverence for ancient ways.

The Westward movement required virtues that were not merely intellectual or moral. The proverbial survivor was not the crafty Ulysses but the ripsnorting Davy Crockett, Mike Fink, or Daniel Boone—the man who was a crack shot and could rassle a bear. Unlike the Cyclops, Circe, or the Sirens, nature could not be outwitted. It had to be stood up against. No wonder that here the athlete would have a special heroic appeal.

Without the vastness and emptiness of the land, Americans could hardly have become what they proved to be: the movingest people of modern times. They would translate the ways of the nomad into the vernacular of advanced European civilization. This nation was not shaped by possessing so much "free" land, for if there ever was land that was not free, it was the land of the American West. It had to be bought not by the Old World transactions of feudal vassalage or loyalty in battle but by life-risking struggles against the perils of weather and insect, mountain steepness, river rapids, or desert drought—all shrouded in a fog of myth and ignorance. Men prepared to find a Great American Desert also had to be ready to discover that this very land could be made into the Great American Breadbasket.

Still, the crucial fact was not whether the land was friendly or hostile, charted or mysterious. The overwhelming fact was that the land—uncleared, untilled—was *there*. And in such vast quantities! The mere existence of so much land out there gave men in the East a new kind of feeling—a feeling of independence, a belief that if they did not find their America near the settled seaboard, they could move on. For disappointed Americans, the West was a New America, a place with opportunities yet undiscovered, a place with antidotes for the present.

Edwin Aldrin, American hero on the moon, through electronics: "The rocks are rather slippery. . . . Have to be careful that you are leaning in the direction you want to go. . . . You have to cross your foot over to stay underneath where your center of mass is."

Machines, more than years or miles, separate a Nebraska homestead of a century ago and the here-to-horizon sweep of Montana wheat fields today (overleaf). Once sweating settlers barely wrested a living from 160-acre claims in arid plains then called the Great American Desert. Necessity mothered inventions to make farming pay: plows, reapers — and combines that now gobble grain in mile-long strips.

This mystery-laden faith in the future was, for much of American history, a faith in the land. The gradual unfolding of the wonders of the continent, of what could be grown on it, of what might be found under it, of how one could move up and down and across it, reinforced faith that this country was a treasure-house of the unexpected. An early surprise came in the Old Northwest, the still unmapped regions around the Great Lakes between the Ohio and Mississippi rivers, ceded to the United States by the Treaty of Paris in 1783. This was not (as many imagined) a land of swamps and deserts but a domain of well-watered plains and fertile valleys.

And the surprises multiplied. Who could have guessed that in 1848 the streams in northern California's foothills would prove to be gold mines? Or that eleven years later there would be found in the mountains of western Nevada silver deposits rich beyond dreams of avarice? Or that the "folly" of Edwin Drake, a vagrant ex-railroad conductor, would turn out to be a strangely flowing black mineral underneath the soil of western Pennsylvania? Who could imagine where there might be copper, coal, iron — or uranium? Who could predict where a farmer could grow sugar beets, soybeans, oranges, peanuts? Where a rancher could raise cattle for beef, sheep for wool — even alligators for luggage? Such surprising qualities of the land were not the only shaping facts of the first American centuries. But they did dominate the lives and open and define the opportunities for millions of Americans.

As the unexpected treasures of the continent-nation were revealed, as every generation uncovered some astonishing new resource, Americans quite naturally created the legend that this was a Golden Land. This legend — perhaps an overstatement but never a lie — brought more and more settlers. And Americans naturally enough believed that a God who had provided such riches for the people of His New World Nation must surely have assigned them some special mission. All these once-hidden resources somehow helped persuade Americans that they had a destiny which was "manifest." Their destiny was clear, obvious, even "self-evident" — like the rights enumerated in the Declaration of Independence. Americans, then, had the further duty of discovering for all mankind all the promises still hidden in the New World.

Much of the special character of American life and American civilization, at least until the Centennial of 1876, came from the continuing encounter of post-Renaissance Europeans with pre-Iron Age America. Here was the first surprising promise of the New World, a promise that would be fulfilled in many ways: Americans would find new ways to work the land. They would build new kinds of cities — cities in a wilderness — and new kinds of schools and colleges, a new democratic world of learning. The promise — that civilization could transform the raw land — would explain why so many Americans were on the move, why they were so energetic at building canals, so precocious at laying railroads and at making their own kind of steamboats and locomotives. It explained the special opportunities for Americans to better their lot and rise in the world.

The rich variety of the land also explained why there would be a Civil War. Out of this variety would emerge problems, tragedies, and a new sense of nationhood. The Civil War, which stained with blood the first century of national life, was a conflict between opposing views of freedom, contrasting ways of life, and contrasting regions.

In the second century of national life, the land remained, and the landscape of the continent-nation still inspired wonder. But the special qualities of American civilization were no longer the result of the encounter of sophisticated men and women with a raw continent. Now there was another, no less dramatic and no less characteristic: the encounter of Man and the Machine.

Like the other, this encounter was remarkable for its anachronism, its scale, and its

Manhattan's skyline — 1906, 1933, 1974 — graphs the surge of an American idea: Land does not confine a city; it can soar on steel.

speed. The new nation somehow compressed the history that Europe had experienced through two thousand years into a compact century or two. Here appeared some of the relics — slavery in the South, trial by personal combat in the West — of earlier stages of European civilization. America, though, could skip some of those stages on its way to becoming a modern nation. Moving along with unprecedented haste, America did not have to go through feudalism — with its fragmentation of loyalties, its creation of aristocracies. History here, compared to the history of Western Europe, was like a fast-motion movie, speeded up to be shown at five times the normal rate. And in the American version, many of the episodes in the original European story were left out.

The United States never had a Middle Ages. The nation's great commercial cities — Boston, Philadelphia, Chicago, Pittsburgh — had no "city companies" or powerful, monopolizing craft guilds of the kind that had grown up over the centuries in London. In the 19th century this nation, by contrast with England, France, or Germany, had unexpected industrial advantages, similar to those of the bombed-out nations after World War II. The Americans could build an industrial plant from scratch. The United States, for example, astonished the world by the pace and style of its railroad-building. Railways were laid more speedily — and often more flimsily — than elsewhere, and the young United States fast outdistanced the world in railroad mileage. In Great Britain the railways grew in laborious competition with ancient roads. Foreign visitors, especially the British, marveled at how American railroads stretched from "Nowhere-in-Particular to Nowhere-at-All." This was accomplished not in spite of — but because of — the "primitiveness" of the land. In half-wild America, today's technology did not have to compete with yesterday's technology.

The United States was still only half-explored when it entered the Machine Age. Even before the nation had ceased its encounter with the land, the special qualities of the machine began to put their lasting mark on American civilization. The tone and rhythm of American life — no longer the humble refrain of "Only God can make a Tree" — became "Only Man can make a Machine." Americans lived in a world that every year became more man-made.

While the Machine made man feel himself master of his world, it also changed the feeling of the world that he had mastered. The Machine was a homogenizing device. The Machine tended to make everything — products, times, places, people — more alike. In the pre-Machine Age, man's life had been controlled by the weather, the landscape, the distances between places. His diet was confined by the season. In winter his house was cold; in summer it was hot. Much of what he bought was made in his

Rube Goldberg's cartoon inventions, like funhouse mirrors, gave Americans a look at themselves and their love of zany gadgets. They laughed at one in 1928 that showed a complex way to open a garage door. Who would ever need a machine to do that?

PROFESSOR BUTTS WALKS IN HIS SLEEP, STROLLS THROUGH A CACTUS FIELD IN HIS BARE FEET, AND SCREAMS OUT AN IDEA FOR A SELF-OPERATING NAPKIN.
AS YOU RAISE SPOON OF SOUP(A) TO YOUR MOUTH IT PULLS STRING(B),THEREBY JERKING LADLE(C) WHICH THROWS CRACKER (D) PAST PARROT(E). PARROT JUMPS AFTER CRACKER AND PERCH(F) TILTS, UPSETTING SEEDS(G) INTO PAIL(H). EXTRA WEIGHT IN PAIL PULLS CORD(I) WHICH OPENS AND LIGHTS AUTOMATIC CIGAR LIGHTER(J), SETTING OFF SKY-ROCKET(K) WHICH CAUSES SICKLE(L) TO CUT STRING(M) AND ALLOW PENDULUM WITH ATTACHED NAPKIN TO SWING BACK AND FORTH THEREBY WIPING OFF YOUR CHIN.
AFTER THE MEAL, SUBSTITUTE A HARMONICA FOR THE NAPKIN AND YOU'LL BE ABLE TO ENTERTAIN THE GUESTS WITH A LITTLE MUSIC.

neighborhood and by his neighbors. His ability to witness events was limited by the narrow range of his own eyesight. Visits to distant parts of the nation required weeks or even months, and travel was uncertain or dangerous.

The Machine changed all this. Central heating became so widespread by the mid-20th century that most middle-class Americans never even thought of it as an American peculiarity. Nor did they realize that central heating was a way of mastering the weather, of transforming the indoor climate from winter into summer. By the later 20th century air conditioning completed man's mastery of the indoor climate.

Before the end of the 19th century the American diet had begun to be shaped by the Machine. The railroad refrigerator car brought fresh meat and milk to the cities. Canning, then refrigeration in the home, and finally quick-freezing and dehydration, made winter and summer diets more alike. By the mid-20th century the "TV dinners" that Americans ate were as unregional and as homogeneous as the network programs they watched in their living rooms. Continental distances had a new meaninglessness. The automobile had brought the city to the farmer; the airplane projected the Chicago businessman into easy reach of New York City or San Francisco. Thousands of Americans now visited Paris or Tokyo during their two-week vacations.

While this machine-mastery of the world simplified and enriched the lives of Americans in many ways, there was always a price. The golf carts that carried sedentary Americans around the courses deprived them of the pleasure of walking—and made golf a hurried, automotive sport. The snowmobile that took hordes of unskiworthy Americans across the virgin snow polluted the mountain air and shattered the mountain silence. (Perhaps the special appeal of baseball, basketball, and football was their inability to be mechanized.) Even the national parks were not immune. This characteristic American institution became frustrated by its success. Despite the efforts of the National Park Service, some of the nation's most beautiful camping grounds were made into rural slums as cars and motorcycles brought millions to the "wilderness."

The very wonders of American democracy, which aimed to bring everything to everybody, brought new complications and confusion. Nearly everybody had more things; nearly everybody ate better, had an opportunity for more education, the chance for a better life. But were these benefits less enjoyed? Less appreciated?

The relations of Americans to their elected officials and to their governments had somehow changed. When President Thomas Jefferson received a letter, it was placed on his desk. He very likely would have opened it himself. If it merited his attention, he would have written his reply. By the middle of the 20th century, letters directed to the

Electronic chip, brain of computers, contains circuitry that required hundreds of transistors in the 1960's, thousands of grid vacuum tubes in the 1950's—all American inventions. A better way to make potash won patent No. 1 in 1790; by 1988 patents totaled 4.7 million.

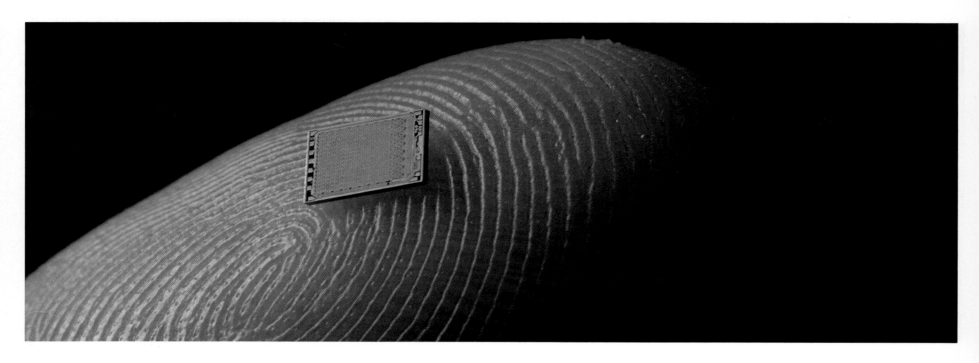

President of the United States were being "processed" in the White House Mail Room, opened by an electric letter-opener, and routed to one of the thousands of workers "in the White House." The few letters that reached the President's attention would get a dictated reply, probably by one of the President's assistants. The letter might appear to be signed by the President. But a signature-machine affixed the President's signature —or, rather, a facsimile thereof—not only to that letter but also to most of the documents that he appeared to have signed.

The factitious and the real overlapped. Not only in the White House was there a merging of the artificial and the authentic. Americans watching television were often puzzled about when and where the visible events had occured. They wondered whether what they saw in "living color" was indeed happening then at all, whether it was "simulated" or real, fact or fiction, history or fantasy.

The Machine brought endless novelty into the world. There was hardly an activity of daily life that some device could not make more interesting—or more complicated. The carving knife and the toothbrush were simple tools long in use. But American inventiveness and American love of novelty would produce in time the electric knife and the electric toothbrush. And what would come next?

In the early 20th century a philosophical American humorist, Rube Goldberg, had entertained Americans by caricaturing their love of the Machine. He also gave them an ironic motto for modern times: "Do it the hard way!" When he first began illustrating the motto in cartoons of impossible mechanisms, Americans had become newly infatuated with complicated ways of simplifying everyday life. Why walk if you could ride? Why use a wooden pencil if you could use a metal pencil with retractable lead— including many colored leads that you did not need? Or why not a ball-point pen that could write underwater? Why write with a pencil or pen if you could use a typewriter? And why use a simple hand-operated typewriter when you could use a much more complicated electric machine? Why write it yourself at all, if you could first dictate it into a machine that recorded your voice on some sort of tape, which would be put into another machine to be played back to a person who would transcribe the words on an electric typewriter or computerized word processor? And so it went.

Just as the American's love affair with his land produced pioneering adventures and unceasing excitement in the conquest of the continent, so too his latter-day romance with the Machine produced pioneering adventures—of a new kind. There seemed to have been an end to the exploration of the landed continent—and an end to the traversing of deserts, the climbing of mountains, the discovery of new minerals. But there were no boundaries to a machine-made world. The New World of Machines was of man's own making. No one could predict where the boundaries might be or what his technology might make possible. To keep the Machine going, the American advanced from horse power to steam power to electrical power to internal-combustion power to nuclear power—to who could guess what.

The challenge of the Machine was as open-ended as the human spirit. Americans in the latter part of the 20th century, in defiance of some fashionable woe-sayers, had more chance than ever before to do the unprecedented. Their problem was not the lack of opportunity for adventure but the depth of their human satisfaction and human fulfillment. The American challenge was how to keep alive the sense of quest which had brought the nation into being. How to discover the endless novelties of the Machine, how to make new plastics, devise television in living color and three dimensions, explore the moon and planets. How to do a thousand still unimagined works of machine-magic without becoming the servant of the Machine or allowing the sense of novelty to pall or the quest for the new to lose its charm.

Charlie Chaplin, in the teeth of hungry gears, depicts the plight of man made servant of the Machine. Early prophets had feared that workers transplanted from the land to the factory would become robots and then "fall to pieces at death." When labor unions organized, leaders such as Samuel Gompers put the machine in its place: "You can't weigh the soul of a man with a bar of pig iron."

Voyage to Eden

Louis B. Wright

Adrift on a tide of mariner's gear, a model of the Mayflower *calls to mind the bold men and frail ships that challenged the unknown to map the New World. The 180-ton bark, so nondescript in her day that scant record of her actual appearance exists, sailed from Plymouth, England, in September 1620. She carried 101 Pilgrims—men, women, and children seeking religious freedom on little-known shores. After a 67-day voyage, buffeted by "cross winds . . . and many feirce stormes," the ship anchored off Cape Cod, far north of her intended destination in Virginia.*

Skippers later navigated with better equipment than the primitive charts and cross staffs available in the Mayflower's *day. Nicholas de Fer's 1705 map depicts the Western Hemisphere with fair accuracy. The 18th-century brass-and-rosewood quadrant measured sun angles to determine latitude. The 14-second sandglass timed the rate at which a knotted line, fastened to a log, ran out over a ship's side, thereby gauging speed—in knots.*

A new land. A strange land. And to a Europe venturing from the confines of medieval geography and thought, a new world that held the promise of an earthly paradise scarcely less fruitful than Eden itself. When Columbus returned from his first journey across the Western Sea, he brought reports of gold and spices and pearls, of a realm "more richly endowed than I have skill and power to say." He described timid, kindly islanders who "go as naked as when their mothers bore them," and he told of women warriors garbed in "plates of copper" and of people utterly without hair. His men, like sailors of every age, spread tales made believable by the Admiral's exotic cargo of parrots, monkeys, and scantily clad natives; strange herbs and fruits; pearls and ornaments of gold. Columbus's account of Cuban natives smoking an aromatic weed rolled into tubes—the first Havana cigars—presaged Europe's use of tobacco, a source of wealth that would ultimately exceed all the treasures of the Indies.

Spanish colonists journeying to Hispaniola (now Haiti and the Dominican Republic) found gold in the sands of rivers. The discovery touched off feverish exploration that lured succeeding waves of settlers and adventurers. The conquests of Mexico and Peru added credence to stories of riches to be wrested from the New World. Within three or four decades after Columbus's voyage of 1492 Europeans had gleaned enough solid information about America to excite their imaginations and stimulate their desire to benefit from its promise. Already the American Dream had begun.

Early descriptions of the New World, though seldom deliberately exaggerated, were often vague or inaccurate. Misconceptions lingered. Columbus himself died believing he had found not a new continent but a new route to fabled Cathay and the riches of the East. In 1608, more than a century after Columbus's voyages, Capt. Christopher Newport brought to Jamestown Colony a knocked-down barge. He intended to carry it over the Appalachian Mountains, expecting to find on the other side a waterway to the Great South Sea, as the Pacific then was known. As late as 1803 Thomas Jefferson hoped that Lewis and Clark would find in the Northwest a short portage leading to a stream navigable to the Pacific. It would take generations of explorers to make known the nature and vast sweep of the North American continent.

In 1497 John Cabot, a Venetian mariner licensed by Henry VII of England, led an expedition to the northern reaches of America and took possession of "unknown islands" his royal patron later called "the newe founde lande." Upon that mysterious voyage Britain later based her claims to whatever territory she could seize from her rivals. France in 1524 enlisted another Italian mariner, Giovanni da Verrazzano, a Florentine who sailed from Rouen on a voyage that took him to the Carolinas, then along the coast to Cape Breton Island and Newfoundland. He probably made his first landfall near what is now Cape Fear, North Carolina. Here Verrazzano met a "great store of people. . . . not much unlike the Saracens." Some wore bird-feather garlands and "showed us by sundry signs where we might most commodiously come aland with our boat, offering us also of their victuals to eat."

Verrazzano and his men tarried awhile, then sailed northward. Like others before him, he sought a passage to Asia and suspected that the sandy reaches of the Outer Banks were barrier islands off China. Although muddled in his geography, Verrazzano accurately described the land and its people: "We found certain small rivers and arms of the sea that enter at certain creeks," he reported of the Carolina coast. "And beyond this we saw the open country rising in height above the sandy shore, with many fair fields and plains, full of mighty great woods . . . of palm trees [palmettos], bay trees, and high cypress trees, and many other sorts of trees unknown in Europe which yield most sweet savors far from the shore."

Coasting present-day Virginia or Maryland, Verrazzano noted "many [grape] vines growing naturally . . . which, if by husbandmen they were dressed in good order, without all doubt they would yield excellent wines." The hope of profitable wine production would persist many years after England gained a foothold on the continent. But it was a vain hope. Soil and weather conspired against establishment of a viable colonial wine industry, despite royal edicts and repeated attempts.

At one point a sailor bearing trinkets for the Indians attempted to swim ashore, but great combers hurled him onto the beach "so bruised that he lay there almost dead." The Indians dragged him out of the water and carried him "a little way off from the sea. The young man . . . began then greatly to fear and cried out piteously." Standing helplessly offshore in a small boat, the mariner's companions grew dismayed when the Indians stripped off his clothes and started a roaring fire. Were they cannibals? Would he be roasted? But the Indians proved friendly. They dried and warmed the youth and accompanied him to the water's edge "clapping him fast about with many embracings." (On a subsequent voyage to the Caribbean, Verrazzano himself was killed and eaten "down to the smallest bone" by cannibals.)

Verrazzano sailed past the mouth of Chesapeake Bay without suspecting the presence of that great body of water. But he discovered New York's harbor, reporting its entrance "a very pleasant place situated amongst certain little steep hills." Between the hills, "there ran down into the sea a great stream of water, which within the mouth was very deep." He wished to linger on the Hudson, but a storm drove him back to sea.

In New England waters, Verrazzano reported the Indians of Narragansett Bay and Newport's harbor "the goodliest people, and of the fairest conditions, that we have found in this our voyage. They exceed us in bigness," he wrote, describing the men as "of comely visage" and the women as "very handsome and well-favored." The land itself he adjudged "pleasant as is possible to declare, very apt for any kind of husbandry of corn, wine, and oil." Verrazzano—the first Newport tourist—put into Narragansett Bay in late April 1524. Many explorers of these shores, arriving in spring or summer, assumed the weather would always be pleasant and that the land would yield tropical products—a delusion that brought much future disappointment.

Threading the coast of Maine in mid-May, Verrazzano "found another land: high, full of thick woods." Rocky channels full of "turnings and windings" laced the island-studded waters of Penobscot Bay. "Barbarous" Indians here lowered ropes from the craggy rocks to waiting boat crews, trading "what it pleased them to give us" for

Fancied beasts in a sea cruelly real

Wind and waves pummel a shoreline nearly as wild today as when 16th-century explorers roved these waters. Mariners rightly feared the fury of gales such as this one pounding the coast near Charleston, South Carolina. Early narratives describe monstrous swells beating against low, shelterless shores, and "the terrible cries and murmurs of the winds." One account tells of finding strewn on a Florida beach masts "which were wrecks of Spaniards coming from Mexico."

Nature's ferocity sometimes altered the course of history. A 1565 hurricane demolished French ships sent to attack the Spanish outpost at St. Augustine, Florida, thereby wrecking plans to set up Huguenot colonies in territory claimed by Spain. In 1609 a "dreadful storm . . . swelling and roaring" led to the discovery of Bermuda by an English ship driven aground there—and provided inspiration for Shakespeare's *The Tempest*.

No less fearsome to seafarers of Columbus's time were monsters of the deep: gigantic serpents reputed to be especially troublesome in north winds, and fanged creatures like the "physeter" that, by spouting water through its forehead, could swamp a ship.

fishhooks and knives. After touching at Cape Breton Island and taking on fresh stores in Newfoundland, Verrazzano returned to France. Through him Europe got its earliest detailed account of North America and its inhabitants. His report spun no fanciful tales. He described what he himself had observed: a varied land of stately forests and open fields ready to be planted, a land populated mostly by friendly people.

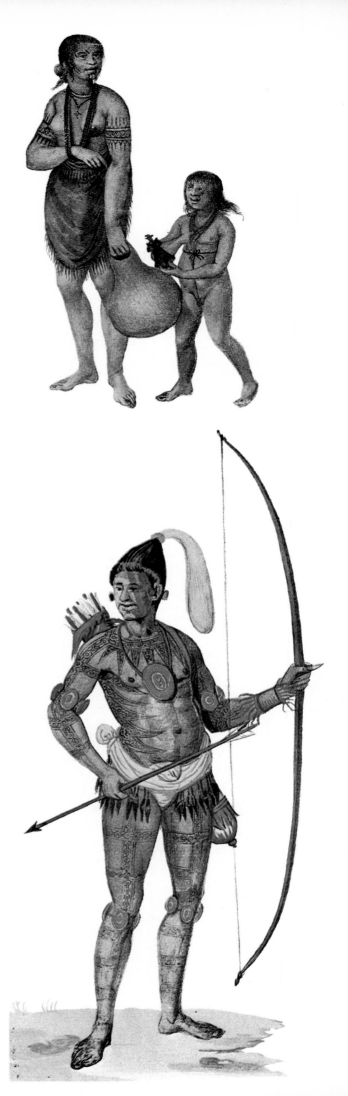

Far to the south, meanwhile, Spain had taken possession of Florida as early as the spring of 1513. ("Florida" in those days extended northward beyond Virginia.) In the summer of 1526 Vásquez de Ayllón established the first mainland settlement north of Mexico, probably near today's Georgetown, South Carolina. Disease, mutiny, and Indian hostility eventually destroyed the colony, discouraging further Spanish attempts to settle—but not to explore.

Hernando de Soto, an adventurer and conquistador with Pizarro in Peru, led the first extensive expedition into the continent's interior. Landing in the Tampa Bay area in May 1539, with some 600 men and more than 100 horses, he began a three-year search for silver and gold that took him north into present-day Tennessee and as far west as Oklahoma. Knowing he would be beyond reach of supplies, de Soto brought with him an ambulatory commissariat: a number of hogs from Cuba that increased to several hundred along the way. Escapees from his herd may be the ancestors of the razorbacks that to this day roam Florida's woodlands.

At Silver Bluff on the Savannah River, de Soto captured a woman chieftain, the "Queen of Cofitachequi," along with several female attendants and a hamper of pearls (a freshwater variety worth little by European standards). But deep in the forests of piedmont South Carolina the queen and her party escaped with the pearls—and with a paramour, a slave attached to de Soto's party.

Somewhere in eastern Louisiana, sick and despondent from a "putrid fever," de Soto died. To keep hostile Indians from learning of his death, his men secretly committed his body to the waters of the Mississippi.

An anonymous Portuguese adventurer who accompanied de Soto, a "gentleman of Elvas," eventually published an account of the trek. The author's narrative gives us one of the first European glimpses of the Mississippi, near present-day Memphis: "The river was almost half a league broad. If a man stood still on the other side, it could not be discerned whether he were a man or not. The river was of great depth and of a strong current; the water was always muddy." Mississippi catfish particularly impressed the traveler: "There was a fish which they [the Indians] call *bagres*. The third part of it was head, and it had on both sides . . . great pricks like very sharp awls; those of this kind . . . in the river . . . were some an hundred and an hundred and fifty pounds weight. . . ." He described an Indian village in Arkansas "which was inhabited for the space of a quarter of a league; and within a league and a half-a-league were other great towns wherein was great store of maize, of French beans, of walnuts, and prunes."

Twenty years after de Soto's death, Jean Ribaut, a French sea captain seeking a refuge for Protestant Huguenots along the southern shores of the continent, landed at the mouth of the St. Johns River in Florida. He met friendly Indians, then sailed along the coast to South Carolina and attempted to establish a colony at what we now know as Parris Island. This and a subsequent colonization effort on the St. Johns came to nothing. Settlers abandoned Charlesfort in South Carolina; Spanish soldiers from St. Augustine slaughtered the colonists at Fort Caroline in Florida.

But Ribaut's account renewed England's interest in the New World. John Sparke, a gentleman-adventurer who accompanied John Hawkins on a cruise to Florida shortly before the destruction of Fort Caroline, described a land "marvelously sweet, with both marsh and meadow ground and goodly woods among." Here sorrel grew "as

A people "so handsome . . . as I have seen"

"The Indians . . . are all archers," ruefully reported a survivor of the 1528 Spanish march into northwestern Florida. "They . . . appear at a distance like giants. . . . The bows they use are as thick as the arm . . . they will discharge [them] at 200 paces with so great precision that they miss nothing."

Pánfilo de Narváez's 300-man expedition had reason to be impressed with the Timucuan warriors (opposite) they encountered. Slogging through snake-infested swamps and forests in search of gold, the Spaniards kidnaped guides and looted food supplies. Timucuan bowmen, nearly invisible behind trees, retaliated, firing at stragglers with deadly effect. Their reed arrows, tipped with snake teeth, bone, or flint, penetrated six inches of wood — or skewered "from side to side" soldiers in chain mail. One of the few survivors of Narváez's expedition, Alvar Nuñez Cabeza de Vaca, crossed the continent to a Spanish outpost on Mexico's Pacific coast after an eight-year odyssey by boat and on foot.

Meeting Timucuan tribesmen (left) at the mouth of the St. Johns River in Florida some 35 years later, French explorer Jean Ribaut described them as "very gentle, courteous, and good natured."

"On landing," wrote expedition artist Jacques Le Moyne, "our men saw many Indians, who came on purpose to give them a most kind and friendly reception. . . . Some of them gave their own skin garments to the commander," and pointed out their chief, "who did not rise up, but remained sitting on boughs of laurel and palm."

Each woman wore a single garment of Spanish moss, Ribaut noted; the men were clad in breechclouts of painted deerskin, hung with jingling metal strips. Both sexes tattooed themselves "with pretty devices in azure, red, and black," and ornamented their pierced ears with "little inflated fish-bladders, shining like pearls."

Indians of Virginia and the Carolinas "are generally tall of stature . . . of comely proportions," wrote a colonist in 1612, "and the women have handsome limbs . . . and pretty hands. . . . When they sing they have a delightful and pleasant tang in their voices."

The wife and daughter of an Algonquian chief (opposite) wear the dress of tidewater Indian aristocrats. The woman carries a gourd "full of . . . pleasant liquor"; the child's doll is the gift of an English settler.

Atlantic loggerhead turtle

Sharp-nosed sturgeon

Red-breasted merganser

"All these and diverse other good things . . ."

Florida Indians "have a way of hunting deer which we never saw before," Le Moyne wrote. "They . . . put on the skins of the largest [deer] which have before been taken . . . so that they can see out through the eyes as through a mask. . . . They take advantage of the time when the animals come to drink at the river, and . . . easily shoot them, as they are very plentiful in [these] regions."

Nature's bounty in the New World awed early chroniclers. Many of them reported an abundance of wildlife ("Deere . . . Beares, Foxes, Otters, Beuers [Beavers], Muskats, and wild beasts unknowne"). Coastal waters provided ample sustenance: sturgeon so large and "so numerous, that it is hazardous for canoes and . . . small vessels to pass"; sea turtles that "feasted well a dozen messes"; and ducks and other waterfowl in such numbers that to one watcher the thunder of their wings sounded like "the desolution of Nature."

A settler described the fish of Chesapeake Bay as "lying so thick with their heads above the water, as for want of nets . . . we attempted to catch them with a frying pan." Off New England, Capt. Bartholomew Gosnold in five or six hours of fishing "took more Cod than we knew what to do with." Wild turkeys, hunted in the southern woodlands, amazed those who encountered them, especially at dawn during the mating season. An 18th-century naturalist wrote: "The high forests ring with the noise . . . for hundreds of miles around; insomuch that the whole country is for an hour or more in a universal shout."

Strange and wondrous creatures—some real, some imagined—prowled the wilderness. At Fort Caroline, the French outpost in Florida, a credulous visitor reported "it is thought that there are lions and tigers as well as unicorns, lions especially. . . . The captain of the Frenchmen saw also a serpent with three heads and four feet . . . which for want of a harquebus he durst not . . . slay." Equally astounding to him were "venomous beasts, as crocodiles, whereof there is great abundance [and] adders of great bigness."

In Virginia, a traveler noted winged "Glow-worms" in such multitudes "I thought the whole Heavens had been on fire." Capt. John Smith described flying squirrels able to glide 30 or 40 yards, and the opossum, with "a head like a swine, and a tail like a rat. . . . Under her belly she hath a bag, wherein she lodgeth, carrieth, and sucketh her young."

abundantly as grass" and the Indians stored great quantities of "maize and mill [millet], and grapes of great bigness but of taste much like our English grapes."

Hawkins, sometimes credited with introducing smoking tobacco to England, observed Indian pipes with interest. He and Sparke noted that the natives "do suck through the cane the smoke thereof, which smoke satisfieth their hunger and therewith they live four or five days without meat or drink." Europe soon hailed tobacco as a cure-all. Its powdered leaves supposedly healed fresh wounds, cured old sores, and brought "an injured man to perfect health." Boiled into syrup, the plant relieved chest congestions; its smoke, inhaled, alleviated shortness of breath. Other tobacco concoctions soothed toothaches, chilblains, swellings and pains in the joints, and banished weariness. Physicians prescribed pipe smoking to ward off plague.

In 1577 Francis Drake set sail from England on a voyage that took him around the globe. He cruised the west coasts of South and North America, looting Spanish gold wherever he could and searching for the mythical Strait of Anian, then believed to be the western terminus of the legendary Northwest Passage. In June 1579 he arrived in the vicinity of what would become San Francisco and promptly claimed "New Albion" for Queen Elizabeth. Drake's description of the cold weather during his two-month stay has long puzzled historians—but not modern Californians familiar with the area's chill summer fogs. An account of the expedition described the Indians, their houses partially dug into the hills, their virtual nakedness, and their delight at the sailors' singing of psalms. "Inland we found to be far different from the shore," the author wrote, "a goodly country and fruitful soil, stored with many blessings fit for the use of man." He also expressed astonishment at the multitudes of deer and at "a strange kind of conies" (rabbits), with long tails and paws like moles'—probably gophers.

Reports such as these eventually prompted England to try colonizing the New World. Spurred by glowing accounts, Sir Walter Raleigh in 1587 sought to establish a settlement on Roanoke Island off the coast of North Carolina. The attempt failed, and to this day the fate of Raleigh's "Lost Colony" remains one of history's enigmas. But the effort resulted in the most extensive description of the region recorded to that time—a book by naturalist Thomas Hariot entitled *A Brief and True Report of the New Found Land of Virginia*. Hariot's work contained a wealth of factual, detailed, and interesting information about the country and its aboriginal inhabitants, as well as propaganda designed to foster colonization. John White, an artist who served briefly as governor of the ill-fated colony, brought back the first pictorial record of the area and its exotic wonders.

Early narratives invariably spoke well of North America. And in 1602 Bartholomew Gosnold brought a small group of men to settle "North Virginia," as New England then was known. But after loading their ship with cod, bartered pelts, and sassafras, a plant esteemed as a "sovereign remedy for the French poxe," they packed up and sailed home again. Thus failed the first English attempt to settle New England.

The first successful English colony—Jamestown, settled in 1607—marked a new era for British overseas expansion. The expedition to establish Jamestown was saved by an enterprising explorer and administrator, Capt. John Smith. A vain man who may have invented the story of his rescue by Pocahontas, Smith nevertheless recorded much truthful information about the Chesapeake Bay region. He mapped the 200-mile-long body of water as accurately as he described the area and its variable weather: hot in summer, cold in winter, but "no extreme long continueth." Open fields and forests abounding with deer and other game impressed him. Smith, especially pleased with the seafood, reported that at a place he called Cedar Isle, "we lived ten weeks upon oysters." Near Jamestown "in summer no place affordeth more plenty of sturgeon, nor in winter more abundance of fowl." His report makes all the more puzzling the virtual starvation of the Jamestown settlers during the winter of 1609. Perhaps the reason was that Smith by that time had returned to England.

The first permanent New England settlement, the little Pilgrim colony at Plymouth, originally was destined for "Virginia," which then extended to Pennsylvania. But bad weather blew the *Mayflower* far off her intended course and, in late November, the sea-weary voyagers rounded Cape Cod. They found the sight of land so inviting—and an attempt to sail south around the cape over Pollock Rip shoals so harrowing—that they decided to settle in New England, though they had no legal warrant to be there. The Pilgrims found a haven in the harbor at Plymouth and built their homes in an abandoned Indian cornfield nearby. They met few hostile red men, but did find several Indian graves. A plague had nearly annihilated the coastal tribes. William Bradford, later governor of the colony, described the terrible effects of smallpox on the natives: "They that have this disease . . . fall into a lamentable condition . . . their skin cleaving . . . to the mats they lie on. When they turn . . . a whole side will flay off at once . . . and they will be all of a gore blood, most fearful to behold. And then being very sore, what with cold and other distempers, they die like rotten sheep."

In April 1609 Henry Hudson, an intrepid English navigator then employed by the Dutch East India Company, set sail from Amsterdam on a mission to find a northeast or a northwest passage to Asia. His ship, the *Half Moon,* carried a crew of English and Dutch seamen. After a valiant but futile attempt to break through heavy ice in the Barents Sea east of Norway, Hudson turned back, resolved to seek a northwest route in the New World. He arrived off the coast of Maine and, finding no passage there, headed south. On September 2, after a cruise that took him as far as North Carolina before doubling back up the coast, he hove into sight of New York harbor near the mouth of the great stream that today bears his name. The wide, deep channel looked as though it might provide a passageway to the Pacific. Steep little hills and heavily timbered forests rose on either side. The natives appeared friendly and eager to trade furs and foodstuffs for beads, knives, and hatchets.

The *Half Moon* sailed serenely up the river until shoal water near Albany stopped her. Disappointed, Hudson started back down the river. All went well until, somewhere below the Catskill Mountains, an Indian broke into an officer's cabin and stole his pillow, two shirts, and two belts. A mate who witnessed the theft shot and killed the Indian. Crewmen launched a ship's boat in the midst of other Indians who were paddling or swimming away. When a swimmer tried to overturn the boat, the ship's cook lopped off one of the Indian's hands and he drowned. The next day a band of warriors attempted to storm the *Half Moon,* but blistering fusillades drove them off—and several Indians were killed. The incident would be long remembered by the natives and would haunt the Dutch when they settled Manhattan several years later.

By the time the Pilgrims had established themselves at Plymouth, most of the eastern seaboard from Virginia to Maine had been explored. By 1630 English Puritans were pouring into the Massachusetts Bay region in search of a way of life better than they had known in the Old World—and a place where they could remain uncontaminated by other faiths. But soon dissidents led by Roger Williams were driven to settle in Rhode Island. The Dutch occupied Manhattan and began to spread out along the upper Hudson River Valley. In 1638 Sweden chartered a company to establish a colony of Swedes and Dutch on the Delaware River. They built their first base, Fort Christina, where Wilmington, Delaware, stands today. Because so few Swedes wanted to leave their homeland, the company had to recruit a number of Finns. North America was already becoming a polyglot land.

The meaning of folklore

Much of America's folklore springs from reports of explorers and early travelers who described the New World and its marvels in glowing terms. These chroniclers often had competing motives: to regale the stay-at-homes with stories of serpents and cannibals and to promote colonization and investment with "relations" of lush soil and abundant game. Eventually, many accounts of the newly discovered continent's people, plants, animals, and the land itself came to be known as travelers' tales—or travel lies.

Bears and b'ar hunts inspired tales from the beginning. In time hunting stories verged on the fabulous, as in the exploit of the wonderful hunt: a great bag of game obtained with a single shot. Like many American tall tales, it can be traced to Europe. Yet the boast of the wonderful hunt took on an especially American flavor. Unlike European fairy tales of bounty bestowed by magic rings and amulets, the American whopper tells of nature's abundance yielding to the hunter's skill and luck. Because survival might depend on the huntsman's success, the hunting theme lies deep in the American imagination.

The folklorist finds such themes and moods in tall tales, jokes, anecdotes, ballads, and legends. His province includes folktales, not literature; folk

history, not documentary history; folk arts (the making of objects, from bowls to cabins), not the fine arts.

Folklore takes the form of tales, songs, sayings, and beliefs that enjoy a traditional life of their own. "The Star-Spangled Banner" is not a folk song because it is sung in one fixed version written by a known author. "Barbara Allen" is a folk ballad, since a singer often introduces his own words and may even use a different tune. "Casey Jones" leads a double life as a folk ballad and a copyrighted popular song.

No pure oral tradition exists in the United States, for printed, mass media, and verbal streams of lore intermingle. To preserve oral lore, modern folklorists tape-record the words, intonations, and inflections of the "informant," as the carrier of tradition is called. "Motifs," recurrent elements in oral tradition, and "types," traditional plot formulas, are minutely indexed to identify folklore.

Examples of folklore, set off in panels like this one, appear in several chapters. They illustrate how folklore reflects ideas and values of different historical periods: Legends of witches give way to anecdotes of oil drillers.

Early scholars of folklore thought that it was found chiefly among peasants. But today's folklorists have learned that oral traditions live in the city, that a car can become a subject of legends, a telephone the instrument for spreading a folktale. Whether the emphasis be on the land or on the machine, in all of American history folklore has lived on the lips of the people, telling of their joys, hopes, fears, and fun.

RICHARD M. DORSON

Virginia, in the meantime, had grown rapidly, with plantations scattered along the rivers, each with its own dock where ships loaded tobacco for London and brought back everything the planters needed. London was Virginia's market town; the colony developed no commercial centers of its own.

On the east side of the Potomac River, Maryland's first settlers arrived in March 1634. Lord Proprietor Cecil Calvert, second Baron Baltimore, wanted his colony to become a refuge for persecuted Roman Catholics, but he also guaranteed religious toleration to people of all faiths. Maryland planters, like those of Virginia, settled initially near the coast, but soon spread out along the multitudinous waterways—and learned to relish the area's oysters, crabs, and terrapins.

English colonies also flourished in the Caribbean, especially on the island of Barbados, where sugarcane grew luxuriantly and brought wealth to many a planter. Some of the first Carolina settlers came from Barbados, arriving in 1670 and establishing themselves on the west bank of the Ashley River. Promoters lured many with advertisements praising the region's fertile soil and "clear and sweet" air. Ten years after the first colonists landed they moved downstream to the peninsula between the Ashley and Cooper rivers and there established Charles Town, later Charleston. Within a few years planters had learned to grow rice in the swamps beyond reach of the salt tides and along rivers where dams and canals impounded the water needed to flood the rice fields.

Although South Carolina never produced all the commodities that backers in London hoped for, rice and indigo crops eventually proved extremely profitable. French and Swiss immigrants, encouraged to start a silk industry, actually produced some silk, but lack of skilled labor kept that commodity from becoming commercially significant. Olive and orange trees planted by early Charles Town settlers grew to productive size, but a cold spell killed the trees, and the effort was abandoned.

William Penn, a Quaker who became by far the most successful promoter of North American colonization, wanted his colony to welcome Christians of all denominations. His advertisements emphasized the fact and also subtly appealed to women. A pamphlet published in London in 1681 noted that in Pennsylvania, men who "could not only not marry here [in England], but hardly live and allow themselves clothes, do marry there, and bestow thrice more in all necessaries and conveniencies . . . for themselves, their wives and children, both as to apparel and household-stuff."

Here was the promise of the American Dream—and it proved phenomenally successful. Immigrants poured by hundreds and then by thousands through the port of Philadelphia: Quakers and Baptists from Wales and England; Presbyterian Scots from Ulster in Ireland; Mennonite Germans and Swiss from the Rhineland; and a variety of other German-speaking people, including, eventually, many Lutherans.

Unlike the promises held out by many other promotional tracts, most of those made by Penn actually did come true. To ensure peace with the Indians, Penn made numerous treaties with them and bought their land for fair prices. His policy paid off. Pennsylvania prospered as no other colony. Voltaire later commented that Penn's treaties were the only ones made without an oath—and the only ones never broken.

Georgia, the last colony settled, started as the most utopian. A visionary Scot, Sir Robert Montgomery of Skelmorly, as early as 1717 concocted a plan to establish an earthly paradise between the Savannah and Altamaha rivers. He persuaded the lords proprietors of Carolina to authorize a feudal principality in the wilderness, to be called the Margravate of Azilia. Montgomery described his woodland realm as "our future Eden." So blessed was it by nature, he said, "that Paradise, with all her virgin beauties, may be modestly suppos'd at most but equal to [Azilia's] native excellencies." Prospective colonists were assured that the new Eden would produce unlimited quantities of "coffee, tea, figs, raisins, currants, almonds, olives, silk, wine, cochineal [a red dyestuff], and a great variety of still more rich commodities." But Montgomery's plan came to naught. A severe depression in the 1720's—brought on by wild stock speculation—discouraged Englishmen from seeking even Eden.

When Georgia actually was established in 1732 as a haven for the destitute, Montgomery's glittering hopes took on new luster. Colonial trustees in London required land recipients to plant mulberry trees for silkworms—typically, 100 trees for every 50-acre grant. They also sought skilled silk workers from Switzerland and northern Italy. By 1735 the colony's entire silk output, shipped to England, made a single gown for the queen. By 1764 some 15,000 pounds of cocoons reached a silk-winding works in Savannah. But once again sericulture died out. Georgia obstinately refused to become a tropical paradise. Even so, the dream died hard. As late as the beginning of the present century a few growers attempted to revive the state's silk industry.

Most of our ancestors came to North America with high hopes for bettering their condition. First they wanted land, hard to come by in Europe, and the independence, prosperity, and prestige that land could ensure. Many also sought freedom from old tyrannies, political and religious. They dreamed, if not of an earthly paradise, at least of a better life than they had known.

Only one group came without hope: slaves from Africa, bartered for rum and gewgaws by tribal kings of Guinea, Sierra Leone, and adjacent regions. The growing of rice, tobacco, and indigo required an ample supply of unskilled labor. Through most of the 17th century, field hands were white workers who indentured themselves in return for passage to America. But in 1619 a nameless Dutch warship brought 20 Africans to Jamestown, foreshadowing a traffic in black humanity that increased as the demand for labor grew. Nor were slaves owned only in the South. Planters in Rhode Island and New Jersey used them as well. Even pious preachers like Cotton Mather of Boston kept black slaves as household servants.

Not all white colonists found what they were looking for in the New World. Many succumbed to disease, despite sometimes exaggerated claims of "health-giving climates" in their new homeland. Some fell to Indian tomahawks. Others grew discouraged and returned to Europe, or lapsed into poverty.

Even though North America did not lie on the threshold of the Orient, and did not produce the exotic commodities anticipated, other crops and other products in the long run far outweighed in value the glittering wealth that had drawn the earliest explorers. Beginning about 1614, John Rolfe's experiments with sweet tobacco grown from Caribbean seed opened the door to fortunes greater than any the Spaniards had ever dug from their mines. Soon after Rolfe's first shipment to London, the price of tobacco shot so high that Jamestown settlers began planting it to their very doorsteps. Tobacco culture threatened to curtail the growing of food. Other colonies prospered too: New England with codfish and with ships' timbers from the oak forests of Massachusetts; Pennsylvania with vast quantities of farm produce; and the southern settlements with rice, indigo, and naval stores from the piney woods of the Carolinas.

The American people, even early in the colonial period, revealed qualities of self-assertiveness and independence that later made it difficult for Great Britain to impose arbitrary laws. When the lords proprietors of Carolina rejected laws requested by the colonists and failed to protect them from pirate and Indian raids, the Carolinians in 1719 declared their independence from proprietory rule, demanding and receiving the status of a royal colony. In every colony citizens gained experience in self-government, especially at the local level. Consequently by the end of the colonial era, they knew what they wanted and had acquired the wisdom to create a new nation of free men.

Whistling swans, scudding before a setting sun at Back Bay National Wildlife Refuge near Jamestown, recall the vast flocks that wintered along these shores in colonial times. A "fruit-full and delightsome land," wrote John Smith of the fertile, well-watered hills and valleys of southeastern Virginia's Chesapeake Bay area. "Heaven and earth never agreed better to frame a place for mans habitation."

Working the American Land

Edmund S. Morgan

Golden bounty rewarded New World planters for a season's investment of toil in soils some rated the "most plentiful, sweet, and wholesome in all the world." Seaboard settlers had the tutelage of local Indians to thank for the "aboundant encrease of corne" that "proves this countrey to be a wonderment" — and that spelled survival for some. Capt. John Smith ordered every man in hardpressed Jamestown to grow the natives' staple as a hedge against starvation. Squash, "pompions," and gourds twined among hills of maize in Indian-style gardens.

While the newcomers learned from the Indians, they also grew familiar foods. "Our English seeds thrive very well here, as peas, onions, turnips . . . and many other," said Alexander Whitaker's Good News from Virginia *in 1613. Other good news — the endless forests — yielded wood for dwellings and furniture, utensils, and tools such as the wood-handled sickle and rake with wooden wedges riveted between its wooden tines.*

Becoming an American has never been easy. The Englishmen who first tried it, at Jamestown and Plymouth and Massachusetts Bay, found that they had much to learn and more to unlearn. Whether they came looking for a way to wealth or a way to righteousness, they had to begin by staying alive, by making a living. And making a living in the New World required a whole new set of ideas and attitudes.

The England that the settlers left behind had become a puzzle to its inhabitants. For a century people had been multiplying at a rate that almost surpassed the capacity of the island to support them. Jobs were scarce; the cost of food had soared. The government did what it could to spread work around. To hold down the number of artisans so that each would have business to support him, laws required young men to serve long apprenticeships before setting up in trade for themselves. Employers had to hire by the year, not by the day or hour or job. It was illegal to practice more than one trade. Labor was divided, not for efficiency's sake but to multiply jobs. The making of a bow and arrow, for example, was shared by four workers: one who rough-hewed bow staves, a bowyer who finished them, an arrowhead maker, and a fletcher.

Some farming tasks, too, became the preserve of specialists. Many villages had but one plow and one team to pull it, and only after the plowman had done his work could the ordinary farmer or "husbandman" plant his fields. Whether a man tilled his own land or labored for someone else, he had to coordinate his tasks with those assigned to others. They would resent, and perhaps even prosecute, an over-eager individualist who tried to do for himself a job that rightly belonged to another.

Farmland, like work, was scarce in England; it had to be used continuously and intensively in order to nurse from it as much food as possible. And few men could afford farmland. The island also had hilly, wooded lands too rough to till. To these wastelands, especially in the north and west, drifted men and women who could find no land or work elsewhere. They squatted and made do, living from scrawny gardens, wild nuts and roots, and animals that foraged in the woods. Not wild animals — only aristocrats could hunt — but the cows and pigs that an ordinary man might raise on the common land. At best he went hungry much of the time; at worst, he turned to thieving and ended up on the gallows. The number of thieves, rogues, and tramps rose ever higher. It seemed to John Winthrop, future governor of Massachusetts Bay, that the land "growes wearye of her Inhabitants." He and other gentlemen looked to America to provide room for England's miserable surplus — as well as room at the top for themselves.

The drifters, used to a hand-to-mouth existence, were better prepared to cope with life in the New World wilderness than were the well-fed owners of English farms and manors. But to get here poor emigrants had to sign on as servants, indentured to work several years for "the better sort" to repay the cost of passage. Masters and servants alike, whether set down on New England's rocky shores or Virginia's fertile tidewater, confronted a country where past experience was a poor guide.

The English found a vast land thinly peopled by the native Indians. The first Spanish conquerors in Mexico had faced a country of 25 million people with an intensive agriculture; by contrast, the English encountered only 8,000 or 10,000 Indians in the Virginia area and probably no more than twice that many in all New England. The settlers quickly outnumbered the native peoples, whose small tribes, already reduced from the onslaught of European diseases and firearms, became rapidly smaller.

For land-hungry Englishmen the new, almost-empty continent seemed an answer to prayer, and in the end it proved so to be. The ambition of the ordinary Englishman was to own his land, and by the end of the colonial period most English settlers in America had achieved or were achieving that goal. In 1776 approximately 90 percent of the 2.5 million Americans lived on farms, and most families owned their land. But in becoming Americans, the colonists had had to learn to use their lands and their hands in ways that would have seemed immoral, if not illegal, in England. The scarcity of people made it necessary to husband labor, not land. Specialization seldom proved feasible. The average farmer had to be a jack-of-all-trades, doing nearly everything for himself— however crudely—yet conserving his precious labor.

Fortunately teachers were at hand. The Indians had long since devised ways of making a living from the continent with a minimum of labor. One way was to treat land as a natural food preserve. Eastern tribes subsisted partly from hunting, and on large

Grubbing out a dream with ax and hoe

Worm fences scrawl bleak beauty on a simple farmstead in northern Virginia, a reconstruction of life in the late colonial era. The man who began his American venture owing service to a wealthier planter worked off his debt and took up his own land. Putting his back and crude tools to the task, he hewed out a home and livelihood for his family: a patch of corn and vegetables, animals for meat and leather, an acre or two of sotweed—tobacco —for barter. Neighbors might join for the backbreak of harvest or house-raising.

Timber felled in clearing fields framed a one-room dwelling, often dirt floored. Though meager the house, hospitality usually ruled. Any traveler might warm at the fire. While alien visitors doing a grand tour of the outlands often decried the "miserable huts" and the "wan looks and ragged garments," the farmer took a more positive view. Retorted a 17th-century Marylander still indentured: Servants here ". . . stigmatiz'd for Slaves by the clappermouth jaws of the vulgar in England, live more like Freemen than the most Mechanick Apprentices in London."

Morning shadow of Shirley manor greets the tranquil James, a watery way to distant markets for colonial products. Sweet-scented tobacco — often labeled with drawings of Indians — made prosperity and gracious living more than a pipe dream for planters. The ninth and tenth generations of the Hill and Carter families preserve this showplace, tangible link to an all but vanished style of life.

areas they let the game grow, harvesting animals as needed by stalking with bow and arrow, or sometimes by firing forests and encircling deer as they ran from the flames. Burned-over tracts sprang up with wild nut trees, berries, and edible roots.

But most of what the Indians ate came from patches of land they tilled. In the forest near a village families would girdle the trees on a few acres and perhaps build fires around the trunks to hasten their death. Then, without removing the trees, they scraped up the ground between and planted maize. All the Indians on the Atlantic Coast had acquired this plant, which had been developed in the more advanced Indian civilizations to the south. Corn is still perhaps the most sophisticated, highly bred grain that man possesses (so highly bred that it does not survive by itself in the wild). An acre or two planted to it, with beans and squash mixed in, could sustain a man for the better part of a year. The tribe would abandon a patch when its fertility gave out after a few years. It was easy to "clear" another one, Indian style.

The technique is still in use today in parts of the world where small groups of "primitive" people have an abundance of land. To observers used to the intensive farming needed for dense populations, this "shifting" agriculture has always seemed lazy and wasteful. But economists and anthropologists have recently taken another look and discovered that it offers the maximum crop for the minimum of labor. Not only does preparing the land require no plows and no draft animals, but in virgin soil weeds are few so that crops need little care.

Few white Americans became full-time hunters, and they did not copy the Indian hunter's method of firing forests. But early settlers often treated the cattle and hogs brought from England almost like game. Turned loose to fend for themselves, the animals sometimes grew as wild as the deer they supplanted. Hogs especially multiplied rapidly, feeding on acorns. Wolves thrived too, preying on the new delicacies, but the colonies paid bounties to Indian and white hunters to keep them in check. Virginians even built a palisade between the James and York rivers near the present site of Williamsburg and thereby gained a whole wolfproof peninsula for a cattle range. Cattle and hogs, the colonists' game, provided a more reliable meat supply than deer. But the Indian's corn proved a more effective way of getting bread than the Englishman's wheat. Everywhere the settlers grew corn. An acre or two in corn and a few hogs in the woods gave a man enough to eat and time to grow something else for sale.

In Virginia and Maryland the land proved ideal for a crop that brought high prices in the Old World—tobacco, which produced the first American boom. In 1619, two years after the initial shipment to London, the secretary of Jamestown Colony observed that "one man by his owne labour hath in one yeare raised to himselfe to the value of £200 sterling"—ten or twenty times what a farmer could expect to make in England. The price collapsed in 1629, but settlers continued to come and to plant tobacco. Throughout the colonial period the annual crop was worth as much as all other American exports combined. A coarse variety of tobacco was native to Virginia and Maryland; but Europeans preferred—and were willing to pay more for—a variety that had originated in the West Indies, and so the colonists grew that.

Tobacco required a longer growing season and much more attention than corn. You sowed the seeds—so tiny that 10,000 fit in a teaspoon—in special beds sometime

53

Blessed with a fecund sea and "excellent good woods for building . . . Boats, Barks, or Ships," New Englanders seemed predestined mariners. They sought the prolific, protein-rich cod from its namesake cape in Massachusetts to the icy waters of the Grand Banks off Nova Scotia. At a shore stage for drying and salting, cannon guard the valuable catch from raids by Indians or boatmen of rival nations.

after the middle of January, transplanting the seedlings to the field in May or June. Thereafter you had to pick over the plants for worms. June was weeding time. When stalks grew a foot or more high, you topped each plant; and to secure maximum growth of the remaining leaves, you snipped the suckers as they appeared. Harvesting began in late August. Plants were cut, wilted to limpness, then hung in open sheds to cure for several weeks. Finally, you packed the leaves tightly in hogsheads.

The crop demanded such close attention that one man could tend only a few acres. But a tobacco planter still needed a lot of land, for the plants required rich soil and lowered its fertility rapidly. After three or four crops of tobacco, a field still might grow passable corn for a few years. Then it was allowed to return to forest.

When clearing new fields, tidy planters cut the trees and burned them, but no one removed stumps. The hoe was the usual tool of cultivation; it was useless to think of pulling a plow through the tree roots. By the time the roots rotted, the plot would have been abandoned and would again be growing trees. Eventually, fertility returned to the worn land. The cycle might take 20 or 30 years. By the usual calculation, a tobacco plantation to stay in continuous operation required 50 acres of land for each working hand, though only 2 or 3 acres per hand was under tobacco at any one time.

Primitive agriculture, yes—but profitable. As tobacco profits rolled in, planters invested in more labor, and the family farm grew into the plantation. In the early period planters bought English, Irish, Welsh, and Scottish servants. Increasingly after the 1680's they bought slaves from Africa. By the end of the colonial period, 40 percent of Virginia's population consisted of slaves. The most profitable plantations, on Virginia's broad rivers, had direct access to the London market through ocean-going ships that docked at their doorsteps. Their owners frequently marketed the crops of inland planters and imported and sold them manufactured goods. Great mansions facing the James, York, Rappahannock, and Potomac rivers still bespeak the elegance which primitive agriculture, abundant land, and a supply of forced labor brought to the lives of the first gentlemen of Virginia.

For every big riverside plantation, there were dozens with no river land and only 100 or 200 acres. On them lived the ordinary men and women, raising their families, helped out by the children as they grew old enough. At first they built crude houses by simply placing posts in the ground, attaching boards to them, and throwing up a roof and chimney. Inside would be one or two rooms, with a loft for storing corn and tobacco. Later they learned to use timber they cut in clearing to make equally crude log cabins. Living with plenty to eat, if not in comfort, they shocked European visitors by their uncouth manners, surly independence, and slovenly farming methods.

Tobacco also grew fairly well in part of the Carolinas adjacent to Virginia. Farther south, the settlers found stands of pine growing in a soil that would support little more than a meager food supply. But they could tap the pines for sap, which was crude turpentine. After the wounded trees died, in about three years, the wood, processed in a kiln, yielded tar and pitch, valued for keeping ships tight and dry.

The vast swamplands of coastal South Carolina at first seemed worthless and were bypassed for pinelands. Among the early settlers of the area during the 1680's were sugar planters from Barbados. Sugarcane had been even more of a bonanza in Barbados than tobacco in Virginia, and by the 1640's sugar planters had already turned to slave labor to exploit it. As large Barbados planters expanded, smaller ones were forced out; many took ship for South Carolina, bringing their slaves. When South Carolina proved unsuited to sugarcane, they set the slaves to making tar and pitch. Then someone had the notion of trying rice in swamps. Since rice was a common crop on the west coast of Africa, from which many slaves came, it seems likely the slaves first taught

Plowing the ocean to harvest the whale

Nantucket folk were "not famous for tracing the fragrant furrow on the plain," wrote J. Hector St. John (Crèvecoeur) in *Letters from an American Farmer*. But "they plough the rougher ocean, they gather ... with Herculean labours, the riches it affords; they go to hunt and catch that huge fish which ... ought to be beyond the reach of man."

Unruly seas that washed whales onto the beaches launched the bold saga of Yankee vs. Leviathan. From tame onshore salvage of gamy carcasses for oil and the whalebone used in collars and corsets, skippers moved to the mildly risky pursuit of right whales that in winter fed close to the coast.

In a third—most dangerous, most profitable —phase, New England sloops and schooners braved the breadth of the seas chasing "sparm," Ahab's quarry in *Moby Dick*. The 60-foot sperm whale yielded ambergris used in perfume, waxy spermaceti for candles, oil for the lamps of America and Europe. The mammal did not give them up without a fight.

Even the sluggish right whale could easily swamp a boat with a sideswipe of its flukes; the sperm whale "fights at both ends" and had a mouth big enough to swallow Jonah. One Boston whaler in 1766 sailed home with this distressing tale: "A Spermaceti Whale ... coming up with her Jaws against the Bow of the Boat struck it with such Violence that it threw a Son of the Captain's ... a considerable Height from the Boat, and when he fell the Whale turned with her devouring Jaws opened, and caught him: He was heard to scream, when she closed her Jaws. . . ."

In its heyday, the 1840's, American whaling had 736 vessels plying the seas. *Charles W. Morgan,* last of the wooden blubber-hunters, closed her log in 1921 after 80 years of plowing the ocean; she now bobs in Connecticut's Mystic River, serving as a museum.

their masters to grow and process rice. Rice culture was probably America's most intensive agriculture, for waters that fed the swamps apparently renewed their fertility, and they could be cropped continuously. But rice never rivaled tobacco in value.

In the 1740's Carolinians discovered they could also grow indigo, a plant then prized as a source of blue dye. An English traveler described their farming methods in 1776: "They take a piece of fresh land, and plant it perhaps with indigo, which it yields as long as any heart remains sufficient in the soil for that exhausting crop; then they plant it with wheat or Indian corn and afterwards with barley; and when it will yield nothing any longer, they leave it to itself, and treat other pieces in succession in the same manner." This, he said, was the way they farmed from New England to Florida, "a system from which they will all by and by feel the most monstrous inconvenience." *By and by* seemed a long way off for the colonial farmer who had a continent spread before him. He used the land, used it up, and left it to recover by itself.

North of Virginia where the climate, soil, or terrain did not favor crops that Europeans craved, such as indigo or rice or tobacco, the use of servants and slaves on a large scale was unprofitable, and no one made a fortune from farming. But there, as in the South, land shaped people's lives, giving thousands of ordinary men a security and independence few of their ancestors could have known. They paid something in neighborliness, for the American farm was large enough to isolate a man and his family from casual daily contacts with neighbors. Some binding customs and rituals that had punctuated country life in the Old World did not survive transplantation to the wilderness. In New England a unique religious dedication combined with a stubborn, rocky soil to keep people living and working together for a time in tightly knit villages. Gradually, though, the endless land drew families away to farms remote from the village. Self-sufficient, they produced a small surplus of cattle and hogs, dairy products, corn, and wheat to take to market. Though lonelier than his European counterpart, a man could well "rest satisfied, and thank God that my lot is to be an American farmer, instead of a Russian boor, or an Hungarian peasant."

Most of the artisans who came to the New World quickly shifted to farming. Some of the best, however, stuck to their hard-learned skills and clustered together in the towns and cities that gradually grew up along the coast. Although not numerous, American craftsmen turned out ironware, silverware, and fine furniture that still command admiration. They also built the houses of men who had earned enough to pay for more than a cabin. They made barrels for shipping rice and tobacco, they fashioned wheels for carts and harness for horses, and they carved gravestones.

A number of men, hardier than most, had no taste for the farm and took to the sea. The eastern continental shelf, especially the Grand Banks off Nova Scotia, teemed with fish. Indeed, for a century before the Atlantic coast of North America attracted any settlers, fishermen had sailed there in the spring from England, France, Spain, and Portugal—to return in the fall loaded with well-salted cod for the tables of their less daring countrymen. The settlers of New England first had in mind a colony close to the fishing grounds so that men could combine farming and fishing. The combination never worked very well, for good fishermen made poor farmers and vice versa.

New England fishermen led a grueling life, fishing with hand lines in the icy waters of the Gulf of Maine in winter and the Banks in summer. They could reach the fishing grounds in smaller ships than the French and English who had to make the Atlantic voyage, and the smaller size made it easier for New Englanders to maneuver on the Banks and to bring the daily catch ashore to be dried and salted. As a result they were able to take over a large share of the "dry" fishery in summer as well as to supply the local market with fresh fish in winter.

Plying a lucrative if sometimes illegal West Indies trade, New England ships freighted food to the islands and Dutch-held Surinam, onloading sugar and molasses, sweet genitor of Yankee rum. An expatriate artist from Boston portrayed these high-spirited captains carousing in a Surinam tavern. One of them later became commander of the Continental navy, another the governor of Rhode Island.

"The soul shall have a Glorious Convoy"

The early American way of death included as lavish a send-off for the loved one as survivors could manage. Even no-nonsense Puritans who trod a prim path in life wanted their bodies bedded in the churchyard and their souls cheered heavenward—with fanfare. Elaborate funerals with endless corteges and costly "gloves, scarfs, and scutcheons" for mourners got so extravagant that they were banned in Boston and elsewhere in the 1700's.

Tilted stones in New England's old burying grounds shadow the dust of a democratic assemblage: infant and octogenarian, the rich

Feathers suggest a soul's flight.   *Emblem of a Massachusetts carver*

*Garlands, rosettes, and winged cherub
adorn the grave of a woman, dead at 33.*

and not-so-rich. Plain letters or grim symbols —coffin, pick, spade, hourglass, death's head —mark early monuments Later carvers fleshed out the bare bones, especially the face, "seat of the soul." Skilled stonecutters sculptured human features—a likeness of the dead person or an idealized "soul effigy," framed with wings to speed its flight.

Most carvers kept a stock of ready-made stones complete with design and sentiments, needing only names and dates. Serving two ends, many epitaphs not only mourn the dead but also warn the living to mind his own piety:

> *Behold and see all that pass by*
> *As you are now so once was I*
> *As I am now so you must be*
> *Prepare for Death and follow me*

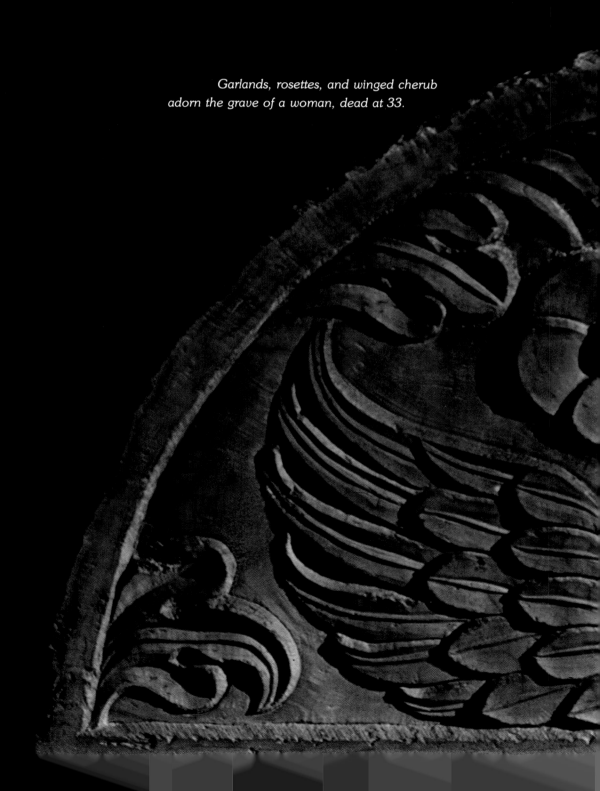

Stark symbols of a 1680 gravestone

Detail from an 18th-century memorial

Death is a passageway, arch implies.

Yarns of the soil

The richness of America's soil proved a source of wonder to early settlers, many of whom had left Old World farmlands that were exhausted by overuse. True, some of the earliest colonists did starve, but, as one 17th-century visitor pointed out, "if men be neither industrious nor provident, they may starve in the best place of the world."

A more typical comment was the glowing report about the land, such as this one penned in 1630 by a clergyman soon after arriving in Boston: "The fertility of the soil is to be admired at," he wrote. "Yea Joseph's increase in Egypt is outstripped here with us. Credible persons have assured me . . . that of the setting of thirteen gallons of corn [they have] had increase of it fifty-two hogsheads, every hogshead holding seven bushels of London measure."

Two centuries later the traveler's tale of natural history had swelled into the tall tale and contributed to America's frontier humor. Boasting to a Yankee about Indiana's fertile soil, a Hoosier asserts, "If a farmer in our country plants his ground with corn and takes first-rate care of it, he'll git a hundred bushels to the acre; if he takes middlin' care of it, he'll git seventy-five bushels to the acre; and if he don't plant at all, he'll git fifty.

"The beets grow so large," he continues, "that it takes three yoke of oxen to pull a full-sized one; and then it leaves a hole so large, that I once knew a family of five . . . who all tumbled in a beet hole . . . and they all perished."

Ohio parsnips, he adds, grow "clean through the earth, and have been pulled through by the people on t'other side."

Working the sea was no more a way to wealth than working the land. Most fishermen died poor. Inventories of the estates they left in coastal towns list fewer of the world's goods than those of neighbors who stuck to the farm. Even whalers who logged thousands of miles for their more valuable prey seldom died rich. Nor did the young men who manned ships carrying commodities between the colonies and Europe.

Yet it was the sea and ships that offered men in America the greatest opportunity for profit. Even in tobacco country, the biggest profits came not from growing the crop but from marketing it. Virginia's great planters were as much merchants as planters. In South Carolina the large rice and indigo planters, also doubling as merchants, made Charleston the only commercial city of any size south of Maryland.

Trade had been one reason for founding colonies in America. Until Europeans discovered how few the natives were and how little they had to offer in trade, many thought of the colonies simply as trading posts. The Dutch in New Netherland saw the Hudson and Mohawk rivers—and the chain of lakes that ran northward—as floating access to Indian tribes beyond the Appalachians. When the Indians found that the white man would exchange blankets, guns, hatchets, and rum for the skins of beaver, they filled canoes with pelts and brought them down the lakes and rivers in sufficient quantity to make the fur trade a principal activity on the Hudson. From beaver pelts Europeans made felt hats. New York continued as a center of the fur trade long after the English took over the colony from the Dutch in 1664; for beaver, though widely available in America, were most plentiful in the interior. In New England, where no easy waterway led to the interior, the fur trade flourished only briefly.

But New England was not short on good harbors and trees for building ships, huge oaks for timbers and white pine for masts and spars. Abundant raw materials made it possible to build ships for half what they cost in old England; here a man could acquire one, or an interest in one, with far less capital. New Englanders had hardly arrived before they began building not merely small fishing boats but also ocean-going vessels. Captains in the growing seaboard cities often turned merchant and sent off younger men to peddle their wares around the globe.

Merchants found their best commercial opportunities in the sugar plantations of the West Indies, which began to flourish about the time New England colonies were getting established. It was sugar, not, as so often supposed, the slave trade that attracted the New England merchants to the islands. Not that their principles precluded human cargo. In the 17th century the Dutch and the English Royal African Company monopolized the trade. During the 18th century New England merchants did deal in slaves on a small scale, but the principal carriers operated out of Bristol and Liverpool. The slave trade amounted to only a small fraction of New England's commerce.

New England supplied the sugar islands with wood staves and headings for their sugar casks, with horses and oxen to turn the sugar mills, and with food for both slaves and their masters. Land in the islands was too valuable to be used for much besides sugar. New England's small farmers contributed salted beef and pork as well as live animals and corn. New England fishermen specialized in "refuse fish," the poorer grades that sugar planters wanted for slave food. On the return voyage the New Englanders brought back molasses, the syrup left over from the first crystallization of sugar. They thus traded refuse fish for refuse syrup, and they distilled that into a rum which many people considered refuse too! New England rum sold—for pennies that the poorest man could afford—in enormous quantity throughout the mainland colonies.

Yankees, though notoriously aggressive traders, did not dominate colonial commerce. The merchants of New York and Philadelphia were an equally numerous and ubiquitous tribe. And they all had to compete with English merchants. *(continued on page 68)*

Making iron bend to a master's will

Spree of sparks and the ring of hammer on anvil attend the act of forge-welding an iron tool. To produce an intense "sparkling" heat —hotter than red hot—the smith's helper has pumped the leathern lung of the bellows, forcing air through the fire bed until the implement on the forge reaches the necessary 2,100° F. Then at the anvil the blows of the artisan's hammer seal the iron seam.

The colonial blacksmith practiced one of the key crafts of his time, making tools for other artisans and workmen: hoes, axes, hooks, blades, harness fittings, and hinges. A town craftsman might double as gunsmith, a country one as farrier, a shoer of horses.

People in a land abuilding discarded no metal item that could be mended or recycled. A planter leaving a worn-out tobacco plot for a new one might burn the old sheds to reclaim the nails. Large plantations had their own forges, manned by skilled servants.

Women looked to the blacksmith instead of a store to deck the hearth with hooks and skewers and long-handled trivets—and even luxuries, such as a toaster that swiveled to brown both sides of the bread.

Always a pillar of the community, the village smith perhaps tamed his own personal demons with blows in his workaday inferno.

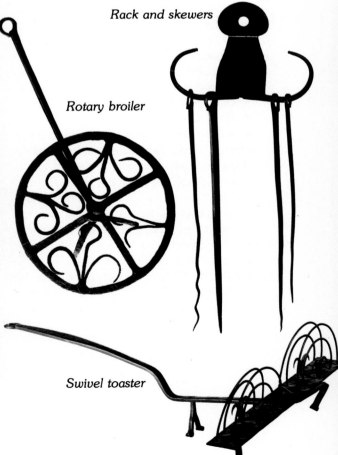

Rack and skewers

Rotary broiler

Swivel toaster

The barrel: It held the New World's fate

Hewing to the line in his mind's practiced eye, the cooper made the wooden containers that New World settlers needed—half-ton tobacco hogsheads to tiny piggins used as ladles.

Every farm and home put to use a wide array of staved products: tubs and butter churns, kegs and oaken well-buckets. Coopers worked mainly in port towns and on river-front plantations, shaping casks for storing and shipping the yearly yield of tobacco, fish, grain, and naval stores from the colonies. In 1735 alone Charleston, South Carolina, exported 37,000 barrels of turpentine, tar, and pitch and 44,400 barrels of rice. That year, the Chesapeake Bay colonies shipped 40,000 hogsheads of tobacco to England.

For tobacco, America's biggest cash crop, hogsheads had to be sturdy enough to be rolled over washboard roads to the nearest landing and to protect the tightly packed contents during a long sea voyage. While the best cask could be re-used indefinitely, one poorly made would shatter or be stove in, at substantial loss to the planter. Tobacco sold by the pound; shipping and handling fees were levied by the hogshead. The bigger the cask, the bigger the margin of profit. Competing growers in Virginia and Maryland waged a hogshead war for half a century, successively ballooning the size until in the mid-1700's inspectors enforced a uniform size set by the Crown: 48 inches high, 30 across the head.

By 1771, American exports filled a quarter million barrels a year of varying sizes; tobacco alone took some 100,000 hogsheads. As the Revolution brought commerce with England to a standstill, the coopers' output carried food, clothes, and ammunition.

Early in 1776, barrels went to war in an unorthodox role. Gen. George Washington planned to fortify Dorchester Heights, within artillery range of British-occupied Boston. On March 3, he wrote to Gen. Artemas Ward: "As I have a very high opinion of the defense which may be made with Barrels . . . have a number [sent] over. . . . the Hoops should be well Naild or else they will soon fly, and the Casks fall to Pieces." On another letter he anxiously appended, "Remember—Barrels."

Working swiftly while a diversionary battle raged in the harbor, the Continentals hauled timbers up the hills, raised a fort, placed cannon, and set earth-filled barrels outside the breastworks—not needed, as it happened. The British left the city without a fight.

Eye judgment and precise use of a hollowing knife shape the inner curve of an oak stave.

Craftsmen "raise the cask," fitting beveled staves into an end truss. Then hoops of varying sizes will be forced on to shape bulge.

Fire and moisture steam-soften the wood.

Dowels will join boards to shape the head.

After heads are set in place, the temporary wooden trusses will be replaced with iron ones.

Exemplar of tight cooperage, this 36-gallon barrel is beerproof and good for a century.

George Pettengell, master cooper at Colonial Williamsburg, uses only traditional 18th-century hand tools such as the cooper's hatchet (opposite, lower). A bucksaw (above) trims circle scribed with a compass. Both top and bottom pieces of a barrel are called heads.

Hypnotic hum of the spinning wheel makes hearth music. The need to keep their families clothed inspired deft womenfolk to artistic handiwork. Said a Boston official in 1718, "Scarce a Country man comes to town, or woman, but are clothed in their own spinning."

Jill-of-all-trades, mistress of some

Lack of womanpower made a New World manpower shortage more acute. Needing a stabilizing influence to "fix the people on the Soyle," Jamestown Colony in 1619 imported 90 "young maids to make wives," each at a shipping cost of 120 pounds of choice tobacco to the swain who wooed and won her. For decades men outnumbered women; most girls who wanted to wed could find husbands.

No lilies-of-the-field but partners in a struggle, colonial women did toil and spin. And garden, cook, bake, brew, preserve and pickle, make soap and candles, knit, sew, mend, quilt, and embroider—all while caring for the many children they were blessed with.

The wives of wealthy planters imported English goods; others short of cash and remote from shipping points were on their own. New England colonies encouraged settlers to grow flax and raise sheep, boys and girls to spin. Households needed stacks of linens. Before 1750 few people had forks, and eating with the fingers required napkins; washday came only once a month in some homes.

Making a virtue of necessity, many women found a creative outlet in the textile arts. "The yarn is fine," sang poet Edward Taylor, "Then dy the same in Heavenly Colours Choice, All pinkt with Varnish't Flowers of Paradise." Not as addicted to dull dress as people imagine, even Puritans dyed wool and linen in hues as joyful as they could concoct with goldenrod or bloodroot or imported indigo.

As in every age and milieu, early American women took an interest in fashion, limited by their purse and sometimes by social dictum. Pennsylvania Quaker fathers in 1726 officially frowned on the wearing of striped shoes, the "immodest fashion of hooped petticoats," and gowns with too-low necklines.

The male-dominated society thought that book learning would overburden women's minds and that politics was "too Difficult and Knotty for the fair Sex." Yet women could rise to challenge in other than domestic areas. A widow sometimes kept her husband's business going; in 1696 Dinah Nuthead was operating a printing press in Annapolis, first of many successful women publishers.

In wartime Daughters of Liberty not only held spinning bees such as one in Newport that set "sixty-four spinning wheels going," but in Virginia "very spiritedly attended at the Gunnery and assisted to make up already above 20,000 Cartridges with Bullets."

A daughter's duty, making butter, means plying a dasher up and down, up and down.

Butter's up. An eternity of churning brings golden globs to the top, leaving buttermilk.

A cheese press at Old Sturbridge Village in Massachusetts squeezes whey from milk curds.

A miss in 19th-century-style dress takes the cheese from the hoop to be mellowed.

The American rifle, a hunter's right arm

Born in Pennsylvania, raised all along the moving frontier from Kentucky to California, the long rifle ranked with ax and hoe as basic equipment for pioneers. Wrote Crèvecoeur: "The deer often come to eat their grain, the wolves to destroy their sheep, the bears to kill their hogs . . . . by defending their property, they soon become professed hunters. . . . once hunters, farewell to the plough."

Like many men who used it, the gun was a reconstructed immigrant. German settlers in the early 1700's began lengthening and lightening a short-barreled Bavarian hunting rifle into the sleek and deadly handmaiden of future Daniel Boones. It weighed less than ten pounds, took less lead and powder; a hunter could trek the woods for weeks loaded for bear without breaking his back. In Pennsylvania *Schützenfests,* a good man with a good gun could hit the bobbing head of a tethered turkey at 100 yards. In the privacy of the wilds the range grew and targets shrank with the retelling. One sharpshooter had to salt his bullets, he boasted, to keep the game from spoiling before he reached it.

Spiral grooves inside a rifle barrel put a spin on the ball, making the air pressure uniform, giving truer flight at longer range than a smoothbore. But the rifle was slow to load. When a bull's-eye meant life or breakfast, riflemen aimed with care. A wild turkey would fly, a deer flee, or an enemy shoot back in the time it took to measure a charge of powder, pour it down the barrel, lick a cloth patch and lay it over the muzzle, put a bullet on top, ram it down on the powder, lower the rifle, prime the pan, set the steel, raise the gun into position, sight, and fire.

Handcrafting firearms—rifle or smoothbore —took the skills of blacksmith, foundryman, machinist, woodworker, engraver. Few men could do it all—or had the time in a raw America. A need for men to make and fix guns grew more vital in the Revolution. In the ten months before July 1776, Virginia bought 3,325 muskets and 2,098 rifles and contracted for more. One contractor, owner of one of America's biggest iron works, advertised in the *Virginia Gazette:* "Wanted, at Hunter's Iron Works, the Falls of Rappahannock River, . . . a Number of Hands who understand the File." After supplying part of Virginia's needs for small arms for more than a year, Hunter closed his armory for lack of workmen—lost, ironically, to militia duty and the draft.

Trial by fire: Master gunsmith Gary Brumfield at Colonial Williamsburg sights-in a new rifle.

Exploding powder gets the lead out of the muzzle at about 2,000 feet per second.

Forge-welding a rifle barrel entails wrapping a heated flat bar around a cylindrical core.

A hand-cranked reamer opens up the barrel; rifling—spiral grooves—improves accuracy.

To cast trigger guards, imprints are made in fine, damp sand held in a wooden flask.

Brass, hot from the crucible, flows through ducts in the sand to fill the impressions.

Securing the flintlock completes an American long rifle: lock and barrel of iron, stock of curly maple. When made entirely by hand, it takes some 300 hours of precision work. An engraved brass plate frames the hinged lid of a patchbox recessed into the stock.

Moreover, British policy limited the markets open to the colonists. Under the Navigation Acts of 1660 and 1663, tobacco and other "enumerated" products could be carried only to England or to another British colony. European goods could be bought only in England, which meant that English merchants and manufacturers had a virtual monopoly of the expanding American market. But colonial ships were given parity with English ships in imperial trade, while foreign ships were excluded. Colonial merchants were therefore able to compete with merchants of the mother country in carrying goods everywhere that the laws permitted—and sometimes where they did not permit. Colonial captains bought and sold goods of every kind in ports all over the world, from Surinam to Istanbul. And merchants sometimes realized tremendous profits.

By the mid-18th century, Americans other than slaves enjoyed a degree of prosperity that would have been hard to match most places in the world. It gave them not only confidence in themselves but a strong attachment to the mother country under whose auspices they had achieved it. They were content to buy from England whatever manufactured goods they needed, as the laws required, for English workers made the kinds of cloth and clothing and hardware the colonists wanted, and made them as cheaply as other European workers, if not cheaper. Just as the sugar planters found it better to buy food from New England than to divert land and labor from sugar, so the mainland planters found it better to buy manufactures from England than to divert their own labor from the profitable exploitation of the American soil.

The British imperial system worked because it seemed well suited to the needs of people who lived in the different interdependent parts of it. It was not a perfect system. The interests of one part were sometimes sacrificed to those of another, and the interests of all the colonies were subordinated to those of England. But the laws were not too strictly enforced; they could be bent to prevent serious inequities.

In 1764 the system began to come apart. England had hitherto borne the brunt of the expenses of administering and protecting the empire, and during the Seven Years War with France, which had just ended, those costs had helped to double the national debt. In that war England had wrested Canada and the eastern Mississippi Valley from France. The colonists would benefit; they were prosperous. And it seemed reasonable, at least in England, to make them pay by levying taxes.

But taxation was one form of subordination to England that the Americans refused to accept. Their view of the matter was that English customs duties and trade restrictions already exacted a fair contribution from them. They insisted that they could be taxed only through their own representative assemblies. They had in Parliament no representatives who would know how large a tax burden they could bear, who would themselves have to pay the taxes levied, and who could affect decisions with their votes. If Parliament could tax the colonists a little, it could tax them a lot. It might take as much from them as they took from their slaves!

Denying that Parliament had any right to tax them, the colonists tried to make the members change their minds. To reinforce their assemblies' protests, they decided to bring pressure on English merchants and manufacturers. So many English workers got a living out of making goods for export to the colonies that an American boycott of those goods might seriously impress the mother country. And so it did.

In response to Parliament's Revenue Act of 1764 and the Stamp Act of 1765, merchants of the several colonial cities agreed not to import English goods until the acts were repealed. The Stamp Act *was* repealed and the Revenue Act modified. Yet Parliament did not give up. Neither did the colonists. Between 1767 and 1773 when Parliament levied taxes on tea, glass, paint, and paper, the colonists responded with agreements not to import these products. And when Americans finally created the

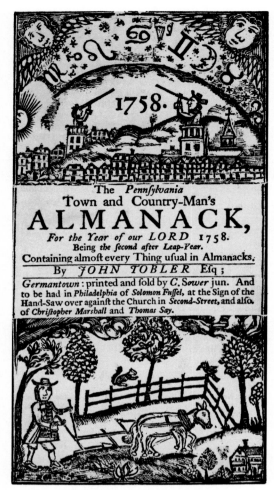

Everything you always wanted to know . . .

"COURTEOUS READER, I might . . . attempt to gain thy favor by declaring that I write almanacs with no other view than that of the public good. . . . The plain truth of the matter is, I am excessive poor." Thus Poor Richard Saunders, alias Ben Franklin, introduced his *Almanack,* most famous of its kind but not first. Nearly a century earlier, in 1639, Massachusetts folk who needed to know what time the sun rose and set—or tides peaked and ebbed or when to plant crops—could consult an almanac printed at Cambridge.

Soon nearly every colonial press was turning out a yearly almanac at a tidy profit. Philadelphia printers gained an edge with the first paper mill in 1690. Pleas for rags to make into paper took a place in the columns along with timetables and weather predictions, notes on dog days, court schedules, maxims, diatribes, and recipes for eyewash.

Astrology was pooh-poohed but popular. The ancient Man of the Signs in 1760 began doing his bit to intrigue the readers and bulge the purse of not-so-poor Richard (opposite).

Continental Congress to coordinate their continuing struggle against Parliament, the delegates adopted an even broader agreement against trade with England. And local vigilance committees enforced it.

The boycotting of British goods turned out to be the first step toward a fundamental change in the way Americans made a living. Until the boycotts, they had generally avoided manufacturing on any extensive scale except for products requiring heavy raw materials which they possessed in abundance. They built ships and they smelted iron, for they had both ore and the large quantities of wood needed for smelting it. The colonies in 1776 were actually producing one-seventh of the world's iron. But apart from iron, ships, and rum, they considered manufacturing a poor way to use their time. Parliament's attempts to tax them made them begin to wonder about that.

Americans accepted the idea that until their point was won they must be prepared to do without some things they had hitherto bought from abroad. It became patriotic for the well-to-do to do without: "Save your money and save your country." But some things you could not do without for very long. So why not do for yourself instead? Along with the non-importation agreements, people formed societies to promote manufacturing. A New York society for that purpose offered bounties for the production of textiles and other necessaries. College gentlemen made a show of appearing at commencements in homespun. Ladies held spinning bees.

Once the war with Britain began, Americans had to make their own clothes and tools and weapons or else find a new source of supply. In total output these efforts at manufacturing were small, but they fixed in the American mind the need to be more self-sufficient, not simply as individuals but as a nation. The Declaration of Independence was a proud gesture; but when the military and political battles had been won, would Americans be able to sustain independence against a hostile world? Unless they had the means to make for themselves the goods they had formerly bought from abroad, might they not be held in economic, and perhaps ultimately political, bondage?

The question of manufacturing agitated Americans in the years just after the winning of independence. In college halls, in newspapers, in pamphlets, and in legislative assemblies men debated whether the people of the United States should devote themselves to agriculture and commerce as in the past or should also take up manufacturing. Advocates of manufacturing saw it as the only way out of a perpetual dependence on England or Europe. It might cost more to make hardware and textiles than to buy them abroad, but the price of buying might be loss of independence.

The argument gained weight from the fact that Americans had gone on a buying spree after the war, indulging themselves in the "baubles of Britain"—goods they had done without as long as the war lasted. British merchants, happy to recover old customers, extended credit liberally. Americans found themselves heavily in debt to the people from whom they had just broken loose. No-import movements bloomed anew, along with societies to promote domestic manufacturing. But what Americans needed most was a stronger central government to keep them from the folly of falling into debt and dependence on England or any other country.

The adoption of the federal Constitution of 1787, establishing a strong new national government, did not in itself guarantee a more independent economy. There were still those who thought that America could make her way in the world most effectively by concentrating on what was economically most profitable—agriculture. The author of the Declaration of Independence himself, Thomas Jefferson, was convinced of this. He grudgingly acknowledged that Americans were too addicted to commerce to think of forgoing it, but he believed that manufacturing would weaken the country by creating a class of men who were dependent on "the casualties and caprice of customers."

The Anatomy of Man's Body as govern'd by the Twelve-Constellations.

Aries The Head and Face.

Gemini Arms

Leo Heart

Libra Reins

Sagittarius Thighs

Aquarius Legs

Taurus Neck

Cancer Breast

Virgo Bowels

Scorpio Secrets

Capricorn Knees

Pisces The Feet.

To know where the Sign is.
First Find the Day of the Month, and against the Day you have the Sign or Place of the Moon in the 6th Column. Then finding the Sign here, it shews the Part of the Body it governs.

The Names and Characters of the Seven Planets.
☉ Sol, ♄ Saturn, ♃ Jupiter, ♂ Mars, ♀ Venus, ☿ Mercury, ☽ Luna, ☊ Dragons Head and ☋ Tail.

The Five Aspects.
☌ Conjunction,   ☍ Opposition,   ✶ Sextile.
△ Trine,   □ Quartile.

Trouble springs from Idleness, and grievous Toil from needless Ease. Many without Labour, would live by their Wits only, but they break for want of Stock.

Plough deep, while Sluggards sleep, and you shall have Corn to sell and to keep. He that riseth late, must trot all Day.

A Ploughman on his Legs is higher than a Gentleman on his Knees.

'Tis hard for an empty Bag to stand upright.

Many Estates are spent in the Getting, Since Women for Tea forsook Spinning and Knitting, and Men for Punch forsook Hewing and Splitting.

If you would know the Value of Money, go and try to borrow some.

Sloth, like Rust, consumes faster than Labour wears, while the used Key is always Bright.

The Borrower is a Slave to the Lender, and the Debtor to the Creditor, disdain the Chain, preserve your Freedom.

Experience keeps a dear School, but Fools will learn in no other, and scarce in that.

—WISDOM FROM "POOR RICHARD'S ALMANACK"

Though Jefferson himself was a man of exquisite tastes, his ideal was the self-sufficient farmer, who neither needed nor wanted baubles of Britain or of anywhere else. Whatever manufactured goods Americans needed they could get in exchange for agricultural produce. And the demand for what they produced from the rich American land would give the United States all the bargaining power it needed to stay independent. Other nations of the world, teeming with people and short on land, would vie with one another to sell their goods for American rice, cotton, corn, wheat, and tobacco.

Alexander Hamilton, however, felt that the country must make its own goods, even if these cost more than goods purchased abroad. Disagreements over this and other matters split George Washington's cabinet and split the country into opposing political parties. But while politicians and the rest of the country argued, a new element had entered the picture, an element that changed the meaning of manufacturing.

The word "manufacture" is today indelibly associated with machinery. In 1780 the word still meant what its roots imply, to make by hand. When Americans argued about manufacturing for themselves, they were talking about making things by hand. But in England an inventor, Richard Arkwright, had devised a way of spinning cotton into thread that was stronger than cotton thread spun by hand. Strong enough so that cloth could be made entirely of cotton (hitherto it had to be mixed with linen). The invention was a closely guarded secret, for it enabled England—and England alone—to produce cotton cloth that was light, cheap, and strong. But such secrets do not keep indefinitely. In 1789 a young Englishman named Samuel Slater, who had worked for six years with Arkwright's machine, arrived in New York posing as a farm laborer. He carried details of the machine in his head, and in Pawtucket, Rhode Island, he built one for a firm started by the Brown family, the state's wealthiest clan of merchants.

Thus with an idea stolen from the old mother country, the American industrial revolution began, hard on the heels of the political revolution. The introduction of Arkwright's machine was a minute but momentous beginning. It produced only thread, not cloth, and it did not replace hand labor, for it did what could not be done effectively by hand. But what it did was done so well that it suggested the possibility that machines might also do better other things normally done by hand. And it brought in such profits that merchants who had made fortunes in overseas trade began to think of investing in machinery rather than ships. What Slater had done once he could do again, and others could copy him. The Browns' spinning mill in Pawtucket became the nursery of a host of others in Rhode Island, Massachusetts, and Connecticut; weaving machines and mills would follow. Overseas commerce would continue to attract American entrepreneurs in the years ahead. But the debate whether the United States should devote any of its energies to manufacturing was settled by the threads that wound out of Samuel Slater's machine.

For machinery would reverse the forces that had dictated American addiction to the land. Since hands were scarce, it had always made sense to use them where their work would bring the greatest profit, in extracting the riches of field and forest. But with machinery that could do the work of hands and do it better, human labor could extract more profit from a machine than it could from the soil.

It would take time to invent the machines and to build them. It would take some assistance from the new federal government. And it would be many years before manufacturing took the place of agriculture as the principal way to make a living in America. The very invention of cotton-spinning machinery would turn the Southern states not to manufacturing but to growing cotton. But in the end machines would triumph, even on the farm itself. As the 19th century opened, ten years after Samuel Slater built his first mill, the transformation had already begun.

Industry flowers by the old mill stream

Harnessed energy of swift-flowing streams powered the mills that ground grain into meal, sawed logs into boards, and pounded homespuns into firm-textured cloth. The steep gradient that made New England rivers unfit for navigation made them ideal for gristmills.

The stream's current, directed against and under the slanted boards, set in motion this undershot wheel of Dexter's Mill in Sandwich, Massachusetts, dating to 1654. Through gears, the revolving shaft of the wheel drives a vertical spindle that turns the top stone of a pair in the mill above. Grooves indent both the lower face of the revolving top stone and the upper face of a stationary bed stone. As grain feeds in from a hopper, opposing grooves scissor the hulls and pulverize the kernels. A slow stream of whole-grain meal flows to a bin below.

Milling took both precision and muscle. Stones had to be balanced and "dressed"—furrows cleaned and chiseled deeper—as they wore dull. It took the miller a full day or more to remove hopper, casing, and top stone, regroove the stones, and reassemble.

Millers took a toll for their services, perhaps every tenth bushel. Selling off the surplus, some became rich merchants. The early mills set the stage for America's machine age and, as natural gathering places, became the hub of many a bustling new town.

The Planting of Cities

Blake McKelvey

Streets on paper became streets of stone as planned towns emerged from the wilderness. A map of New Haven in 1748 shows its plan intact a century after founding; a grid of blocks, each 825 feet square, surrounds public buildings on a central green. Most towns sprawled, their muddy roads following builders' whims. Then paving inscribed the pattern of streets—in naturally rounded "cobbles" or in hewn stones. These neat, closely arrayed Belgian blocks (named for the source of the style, not the granite) gave horses solid footing as they clattered in Washington, D. C. In time, progress in paving—and automobiles—made cobblestones and blocks relics.

As cities changed, so did ways to save them from fire. Volunteers, manning hand pumps, heard commands boomed through their foreman's gleaming fire horn (which, when corked, doubled as a tankard). Cherishing tradition, some firemen resented steam pumpers. But when the fire engine matured to such magnificence as an Amoskeag of 1873, modeled here, neither firemen nor fire could resist it.

Aboard the good ship *Arbella* as she headed for New England in the spring of 1630, the Puritan leader John Winthrop composed a sermon for his fellow passengers —the ladies and gentlemen, artisans and their families, yeomen farmers and servants who would establish the Massachusetts Bay Colony. To them, and to posterity, he gave an image: "Wee shall be as a Citty upon a Hill." In his warning that what they built would stand as a model before "the eies of all people," he chose a religious symbol taken from the Gospel of Matthew. But in evoking an urban rather than a rural image, John Winthrop foretold the enduring importance of the city in America.

As Spain, France, England, and Holland expanded their mercantile empires during the 16th and 17th centuries, they founded frontier outposts in the New World—a dozen ports that would become thriving towns by 1700. But the towns were not alike. From Spain's Santo Domingo in the West Indies to France's Montreal in Canada, the ports reflected the strikingly different colonial attitudes of the rival European powers. The Spanish towns, whose patterns dated to Greek and Roman times, were built as strongholds to impress the native peoples. The Dutch in New Amsterdam, like the French in Quebec, Montreal, and elsewhere in the St. Lawrence and Mississippi valleys, erected walls not only for defense against natives but also to repel European invaders. The British planned and built towns that resembled the towns of home. William Penn's plan for Philadelphia was adapted from one proposed for London after the Great Fire of 1666. Carolina's Charles Town, "famous for the regularity of its streets," was laid out along the lines of Londonderry in northern Ireland.

The British ports became commercial, cultural, and administrative centers of prosperous colonies—and a source of the empire's strength. Charles Town failed to produce the silks, oils, wines, and olives called for in its mercantile charter of 1663. But the Carolina port began to ship deerskins, naval stores, rice, and later indigo, to the profit of its backers and to the benefit of planters who built summer homes in town to escape the humid rice fields. The Dutch in New Amsterdam had been content to anchor ships off the strand at the foot of Manhattan Island and to off-load and onload with the aid of lighters. The British who took over the port developed a more active commerce. They assessed the merchants of the town to raise funds for a substantial dock in 1676. Some 18,000 cartloads of rock went into its construction.

While the imperial strongholds of Mexico, South America, and the West Indies grew rich on the tribute and labor extracted from suppressed natives and the slaves of mines

73

Telltale fashions
of a changing society

Though we know them only as "Mrs. Freake and Baby Mary," the colonial mother and daughter reveal themselves in what they wear.

The portrait, done about 1674, itself bespeaks wealth; only the rich posed – and they wore their best. The pair's look-alike finery reflects the custom of dressing children as adults. Their clothes would have appalled some earlier Puritans whose dress code forbade wearing apparel "with any lace."

Bostonians strolling the Common in 1768 mirrored the styles of a revolutionary era: some in "Genteelest fashion," many "indifferently cloathed." Dress then prompted epithets: big-wig, laced-coat, silk-stockinged – and, in that "Metropolis of Sedition," one that signified much more than dress: redcoat. The 29th Regiment, denied quarters, tent here on the Common, near John Hancock's mansion. In 1770 victims of the Boston Massacre would fall before the guns of the 29th.

Ornament for a lady:
a servant in livery

Dressed for work: ample
skirt and short sleeves

Apron and cleaver
proclaim a butcher.

Boston, 1801: The Old State House, built to serve the Crown, looks down upon a democratic street whose name-change capsules history: King to State. Merchant and banking houses cluster here, hard by the sea that enriched — but hemmed — the city. Land-hungry developers in 1811 took bites of Beacon Hill, near the new State House (opposite). Hauled off in tipcarts, the 60-foot hill filled in a pond.

and plantations, the British ports promoted settlements peopled mostly by fellow Englishmen and European immigrants. Each British colony had such autonomy that its leaders could develop it in ways fitted to its situation. The diversity that resulted was destined to be a prominent characteristic of American cities. Leaders of every colony—merchants, craftsmen, clergymen, lawyers, landowners, and land promoters—lived in the principal towns. Intermediaries between the New World and the mother country, the local leaders became the spokesmen and champions of the colonies.

As governor of the Massachusetts Bay Colony, John Winthrop approved the site for Boston, planting his city not on one hill but on a rugged, hilly peninsula jutting into a spacious bay. Most of the hills eventually were leveled off to fill in adjoining marshes and expand the city. Along the narrow neck connecting with the mainland ran a road that intersected King Street, a broad approach to the most convenient docking area. As the town grew, its promoters extended more streets into other parts of the sprawling piece of land. Several early roads led to a 45-acre plot purchased by the town in 1634 as a military training field and common pasture. It also became a site for executions of witches and criminals. Long called Boston Common, it is the nation's oldest park.

Boston's meandering streets resembled those of Salem, an older town. But the irregular layout gave walkers access to all parts of the growing city and encouraged the building of compact arrays of commercial structures and homes.

By 1674 the city had the air of London. "The houses," a resident wrote, "are . . . raised on the sea-banks . . . many of them standing upon piles, close together on each side of the streets as in *London* and furnished with many fair shops . . . with three meeting Houses or Churches, and a Town-house built upon pillars where merchants may confer. . . . Their streets are many and large, paved with pebble stone."

From the beginning Boston served as the administrative and commercial capital of the colony. The city was also a religious center from which groups of settlers went forth. Typically, they would be banded together by formal covenant and led by a minister. Such migrants established "covenanted" towns throughout New England. Most were to be rural hamlets or villages. But a few, such as Newport in Rhode Island and New Haven in Connecticut, aspired to become self-contained colonies.

No offshoot rivaled the ambition or enterprise of Boston. Merchants there not only strove to serve the needs of the expanding colony but also reached out to develop trade elsewhere. Bostonians handled the catch of fishing villages and the produce of inland rural areas. They shipped foodstuffs to slave plantations—to Virginia for tobacco, to the West Indies for sugar and molasses. Then Boston ships carried these products and others, including lumber, furs, and naval stores, to Britain in exchange for supplies that the colonists needed—and luxury goods they could be enticed to buy.

More and more sailing craft crowded the harbor. Merchants and property owners joined to develop two coves as inner harbors. Private wharves appeared. And in 1710 "Gentlemen" promoters received permission to build the Long Wharf, which would extend almost half a mile from the foot of King Street.

New Amsterdam, founded by the Dutch five years before the establishment of Boston, had been slow in exploiting its great harbor. But soon after the port became New York, it began to flourish. The British stepped up the already profitable trade in furs

Slickers and bumpkins

Encounters between the country bumpkin and the city slicker have provided endless story fare. A diarist in 1688 recorded an exchange between "a hectoring debauchee" from Boston and "an honest, ingenious countryman."

"What news, countryman?" asks the Bostonian, to which the country dweller replies, "I know none."

"I'll tell you then, son," says the city man. "The Devil is dead."

"How?" replies the countryman. "I believe not that."

"Yes. He is dead for certain."

"Well, then," allows the countryman, "if he be dead, he hath left many fatherless children in Boston."

But when the countryman ventured into the city, he often became a target for city slickers. In an 1851 yarn, Nehemiah Flufkins comes to Boston to see the sights. He is promptly spotted by a sharper who charges him an "entrance fee" to stroll on the public common.

On Tremont Street, a second sharpy "fines" him 50 cents for failing to doff his hat before the "mayor's house" — actually the home of a greengrocer.

And so it goes. Nehemiah is "fined," "taxed," and otherwise fleeced at every turn until, shaken, he stumbles into a tobacco shop and buys a cigar.

His troubles deepen. On Washington Street a policeman stops him for smoking on the street and fines him $5. Nehemiah pays. Now down to his last dollar and deathly afraid lest he "break some other unknown law," he bolts for the station. In his flight Nehemiah bumps into another newcomer to Boston, who tries to ask directions. Terrified, Nehemiah breaks loose, shouting, "Can't help it if 'tis a fine to run. I haven't got no money."

with the Indians and expanded harbor facilities. Quays fringed the East River, which was less exposed to the sea than was the Hudson. The provisioning of foreign ships became a business. Wind-powered mills, first erected by the Dutch, ground the grain of neighboring farms into flour. A cluster of bakeries converted the flour into hardtack for outbound voyages. The British extended the three principal streets of the small Dutch settlement beyond its "good stiff Fence," the protecting wall where Wall Street runs today. By 1710 the entire southern tip of Manhattan was occupied, and the population approached 6,000. But already a rival city, founded by William Penn on the lower Delaware in 1682, had more people. Penn's Philadelphia—the capital of his "holy experiment"—had become second only to Boston in size and commercial vitality.

Philadelphia was the first large city in the British colonies to be laid out on a gridiron pattern. The design by Penn's surveyor, Thomas Holme, projected a mile-wide city stretching for two miles between the Delaware and Schuylkill rivers. The checkerboard plan reserved five spacious squares for public use and provided ample water frontage for both seagoing and coastal shipping. Though some of the first settlers lived in "holes digged in the Ground, Covered with Earth," Penn had induced artisans to make the voyage, and building soon began.

Making bricks from the local clay and harvesting wood from surrounding forests, the settlers so transformed the wilderness that a former resident could write in 1698, "the Industrious (nay Indefatigable) Inhabitants have built a *Noble* and *Beautiful* City . . . which contains above two thousand Houses, all Inhabited; and most of them Stately, and of Brick, generally three Stories high, after the Mode in *London,* and as many as several Families in each. . . . Here is lately built a Noble Town-House or Guild-Hall, also a Handsom Market-House, and a convenient Prison."

The building splurge created a demand for imports, and the "Industrious Inhabitants" raised meat and surpluses of produce for export. Such commerce promoted a rate of growth unmatched by the older ports. With the building of wharves, warehouses, and a flour mill, Philadelphia began competing with New York for the ship-provisioning trade and with Boston for intercolonial trade. There was enough business to assure the healthy growth of all three cities and of the lesser ports, Newport and Charles Town.

Of the three major cities only Boston had the right to hold a town meeting and choose its own selectmen; other New England communities had similar rights. But in the colonial hierarchy local officials had relatively limited powers. The leaders could extend their authority by responding to a crisis. A frequent one was fire.

After its first "great fire" in 1653, Boston adopted a fire code that required every householder to have a 12-foot pole "with a good large swob at the end of it" and a ladder long enough to reach the ridge of his house. Crude, self-help methods of fire fighting continued until 1676 when "a Taylour Boy, who arising alone and early to work, fell asleep and let his light fire the House, which gave fire to the next, so that about fifty Landlords were despoyled of their Housing." The selectmen sent an order to London for America's first fire engine, which arrived in 1679. That year another "great fire" consumed 80 houses and 70 warehouses.

Fires in other towns—and reaction to the Great London Fire—prompted the widespread adoption of numerous local ordinances. Major towns required the replacement of thatch roofs with tile or slate and the lining of mud-daubed chimneys with brick or stone. Boston, New York, and Philadelphia ordered the use of brick or stone in new construction. After Boston's 1679 fire, city leaders, assuming more powers, divided the city into quarters and appointed a fire marshal for each district. Ladders, buckets, and other equipment were assembled. After a conflagration in 1682 eight men were hired to replace the volunteers who had manned the fire engine's hand pump.

The fireman's art

Flames threaten to sweep a New York block as helping hands render the "voluntary aid" proclaimed on an 18th-century fireman's certificate. Working in teams, some volunteers haul valuables from imperiled buildings, while others pump handles on "engines" pulled to the blaze. One pumper jets water spouting from a public well. The other, filled by a bucket brigade, stands closer so a man can climb with the "hoase"—leather, like Thomas Hazard's bucket at right. Slogans also adorned buckets; one boasted: "VENI, VIDI, VICI."

Heroism earned admiration: The silver pitcher went to a Bostonian whose "intrepid . . . exhertions" helped save Old South Church in 1810. Ben Franklin, realizing that organization mattered more than valor in putting out —and paying for—fires, had set up Philadelphia's first volunteer brigade in 1736 and promoted what is now America's oldest fire insurance company. "Fire mark" 861, put on a Philadelphia house in 1798, told firemen it was insured. Marked houses got priority.

The fire fighters' need for water increased the demand for public wells. Officials in Boston and other towns issued permits to enterprising residents, giving them permission to dig wells and sell water at moderate rates to their neighbors. Towns provided public wells and maintained underground cisterns in strategic locations for fire fighters. The public pumps became popular meeting places, especially on washdays. Laws prohibited the spilling of slops near wells, but sparklingly pure water was not always the reward. It was so bad in New York that "Tea-Water Men" readily found customers for water hauled in from out of town. Philadelphians quenched their thirst from the best water-supply system in the colonies, if not the British Empire. "They are stocked with plenty of excellent water in this city," a traveler reported in 1744, "there being a pump att almost every 50 paces distance." And nearly every house had a well.

Each town started its own public market. As the towns grew, the markets became the principal suppliers of food. New York officials opened a "Butcher's Shamble" and markets for meat, fish, and vegetables three mornings a week; no one could sell produce anywhere else while the market was open. No retailer could buy until the markets had been opened for two hours. In Philadelphia public-market butchers slaughtered "above Twenty Fat Bullocks . . . besides many Sheep, Calves and Hogs" a week. Boston's Town House, built in 1657 with a merchant's bequest and citizens' contributions, had a ground-floor market. Town meetings were held in the hall above.

Private shopkeepers, on the rise in every town, were enraged at public supervision of food selling. So were "hucksters," who hawked produce in the streets. When a fire destroyed Boston's Town House in 1711, the shopkeepers and hucksters blocked the re-establishing of a public market. They held out for 29 years until, after a heated debate, the town meeting voted to accept the offer of Peter Faneuil, a prosperous merchant who wanted to build a new market house. Opened in 1742, Faneuil Hall was gutted by fire in 1761. When it was restored two years later, James Otis, Royal official turned rebel, made a dedication speech; prophetically, he called the hall "The Cradle of Liberty." Indeed, its great room above the market soon became a meeting place for colonists plotting independence.

The selectmen of Boston and local officials elsewhere assumed responsibility for the laying out and care of streets. Most of the streets rambled, following the whims of their private developers—and the lay of the land. But in the wake of the great fires in Boston, the selectmen's surveyors of highways seized the opportunity to widen and straighten the streets of the burned-out neighborhoods before new buildings went up. New York tried to keep up with the demand for new streets by appointing six overseers of roads and fences. Philadelphia relied mainly on its original plan to regulate development. In the beginning, every able-bodied man in most towns was required to work one to three days a year on street maintenance. Later, when cities began paving their streets, citizens contributed money instead of muscle.

Boston paved strips 24 feet wide down the center of main thoroughfares; owners of property along the streets supplied bordering blocks of paving stones. The streets were said to be surpassed only by those of London. And Boston took pride in keeping them clean. The selectmen appointed "scavangers," authorizing them to hire "at the cheapest rates they can" men with horses and carts to remove accumulated dirt. Later, all householders were ordered to sweep the streets in front of their residences once a week; the piles were hauled away at public expense. Boston also banished the "noisome smell" of slaughtering to an isolated area, fined litterers who threw "any intralls of beast or fowles or stinkeing thing, in any hie way or dich or Common," and ordered that privies, or "necessaries," be at least 40 feet from any street, shop, or well. Such regulations achieved sanitation standards unmatched anywhere.

A "most regular, neat, and convenient city"

That tourist, so pleased in 1776, would still find cobbled streets and "brave Brick houses" in Philadelphia, which preserves a past other cities have lost. Under its graceful cupola stands Carpenters' Hall (opposite), meeting place of the First Continental Congress, a monument to freedom—and to the art of fine building. Its owner, the Carpenters' Company, promoted "the science of architecture" and aided members and their families. During the city's 18th-century building boom, most carpenters did not belong to the guild-like Company. But its members usually served as "Measurers," who figured—for a 3 percent fee—the cost of a job. Such costs in effect set a Company-backed wage scale.

A pushcart vendor sells oysters on the half shell across from a theater in the early 1800's. "Comedy" and "Tragedy" look down from niches, finally secure in a city where Quaker opposition to "prophane stage plays" kept theater illegitimate until 1789. Drama—including Shakespeare—was so popular that one playhouse kept going through a hot spell in 1791 by "air conditioning": Fire engines sprayed water on its roof and walls.

"I shall be killed with the kindness . . ."

Abigail Adams need not have worried when she read those words; John survived the hospitality of Philadelphia while attending the First Continental Congress in 1774. A dinner he described began at 4 p.m. with "Turtle and every other thing," proceeded through "flummery, jellies, sweetmeats, of 20 sorts," and ended with "fruits, raisens, almonds, pears, peaches, wines most excellent & admirable." His host for that feast was Benjamin Chew, head of Pennsylvania's judiciary system, who also had a country house, Cliveden, in Germantown, then six miles out of town.

Elegance burnished by time still reigns there (opposite). The table set for tea offers two sweets: jumbles—cookies laced with brandy—and a pound cake whose ingredients include a pound of butter, eight eggs, and a good measure of brandy. Cliveden's early furnishings mirror an age when artisans built to English design, using how-to books from London and experimenting with native wood, such as wild cherry. Cabinetmakers who left the city after learning the art advertised themselves as "From Philadelphia."

William Penn had planned a "green countrie towne which will never be burnt, and always be wholesome." Each house would stand amid its own fields, orchards, or gardens. But by 1698 promoters were subdividing lots. In the 1770's Philadelphians lived at three levels: "the better sort," the rich gentry; "the middling sort," tradesmen and men like Ben Franklin; "the meaner sort," the unskilled who in bad times might enter the Bettering House, a name for the almshouse.

Housing for the middling sort ranged from row houses on narrow streets to quarters in alleys, formed when owners sold off the back sections of deep lots. Elfreth's Alley (below), reputed to be the oldest continuously occupied street in the nation, has a house that dates to 1694. The mirror, dubbed a "busybody," gives a peeker a look at the alley without being seen at the window. A gutter, now covered, runs down the middle of the Belgian block pavement.

Spiral staircases in narrow houses hampered casket-bearers. So they passed their burden through a second-floor "coffin door." Sand, swept into designs, carpeted the lower floor. Meals were cooked over an open hearth in the kitchen. A favorite: planked shad or sturgeon broiled with johnnycake.

A rooming house at No. 114 did its part to bolster Philadelphia's claim as the City of Brotherly Love. One group of roomers there included a rabbi, a Catholic priest, a Quaker, and a French refugee.

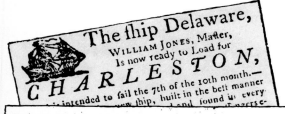

In 1697 New York became the first city in the colonies to light its streets. Officials ordered that on winter nights a lantern or candle be hung before the door of every seventh house. In 1751 Philadelphia lighted up by erecting whale-oil lamps and hiring lamplighters. Boston relied on private lanterns until 1773, when a committee headed by John Hancock recommended public lighting. The following winter the city installed 310 lamps imported from London.

Soon after its founding each town appointed one or more constables to maintain law and order. Equipped with long black staves, these officials, generally one to a ward, patrolled the streets during the day, enforced numerous regulations, and supervised the night watch. In Massachusetts constables had to "make, signe, & put forth pursuits, or hues & cries, after murthrers, manslayrs, peace breakrs, theeves, robers, burglarers . . . also to apphend without warrant such as are ovr taken with drinke, swearing, breaking ye Saboth, lying, vagrant psons, night walkers. . . ." Peace officers also rounded up sailors brawling in taverns or on the streets; caught runaway apprentices, indentured servants, or slaves; and tracked down arsonists who set fires to cover up burglaries. Boston and several other towns instituted a night watch; each male inhabitant took his turn patrolling the streets after dark. But so many residents refused to serve their turn as constable or watchman—preferring to pay fines instead—that the towns voted small payments to the men willing to serve.

Every town had a place for public punishment. A man or a woman might be given a specific number of lashes at the whipping post. Or a constable might put an offender (typically, a town drunk) in stocks, where he sat with his legs or hands—or both— clamped between notched timbers; sentenced to a pillory, he stood, head and hands projecting through a pair of notched boards on a post. Hanging was such a relatively

rare spectacle that when two pirates were hanged in Newport, Rhode Island, in 1760, more than 5,000 people gathered to watch. Piracy once had been winked at. But merchants, prospering on legitimate trade, could no longer tolerate buccaneering.

The port cities provided the headquarters for the colonial governors and courts and the seats for other colonial or Royal functions. During England's protracted hostilities with France and Spain, when the ports served as bases for privateers foraying against the enemy, the cities acquired a sense of self-reliance and a need for better ways to keep in touch with each other. Andrew Hamilton of New Jersey, a colonial official of the king's post, had established a postal link between New York and Philadelphia in 1693; soon other towns pressed for an extension of this service by coastal packet north to Boston and Portsmouth, New Hampshire, and south to Charles Town.

Regular stage service between Boston and Newport began in 1736. Within two decades a similar service of stages and post riders had supplied the last links in an overland communications system south to Charles Town. Philadelphia, which promoted more interior roads than any other city, pressed for the construction by the colony of the Great Philadelphia Wagon Road; by the early 1750's it reached 60 miles to Lancaster. Townsmen helped extend the road southwestward into the Carolina piedmont, forming a route for migration and trade between Philadelphia and the frontier.

The urban terminals for these highways and stage routes were the principal taverns or public houses, which had become important meeting places in every port city. Boston, whose first tavern opened in 1634, had 54 by 1690. Most "ordinaries" provided lodgings for travelers, as well as food, liquor, coffee, tea, and amusements, such as ninepins, billiards, and cards. The King's Arms, overlooking Boston's market square, offered elegant fare. Besides a public room and bar for strangers, it had a large chamber

"A genteel Appearance," a traffic in tragedy

Charles Town posed for her portrait in 1774 and conjured up an American Venice — one of the many compliments paid to a city "as elegant and urbane as the best . . . in the Old World." A British ship of the line sails into a harbor dominated by the newly built Exchange; like the city, it mixed business (a merchants' hall) with pleasure (a ballroom).

Charleston — the name changed in 1783 — reigned over a rice and indigo empire. Wealthy planters built town houses there, enhancing them with gardens of camellias, jasmine, even fig trees. The city lured ships from other ports and fostered a trade in slaves. Henry Laurens, the *Laurens* on the ad (opposite), took a 10 percent commission on slaves, twice his charge for other goods. Black cargo was perishable; two out of ten usually died on a slave ship's voyage. Often those who survived, as Laurens complained, "seemed past all hopes of recovery. . . . a most scabby lot. . . ." He later quit the trade. By 1770 half the city's people were slaves.

called the Exchange, where merchants gathered. Its success prompted the opening of two rival coffeehouses that also catered to merchants. Similar public houses played an even larger role in the social life of New York, which had 166 by 1744. Philadelphia, whose population was increasing more rapidly than either of its rivals in the mid-18th century, had about 100 taverns and many boardinghouses. Some of the taverns specialized as stage depots, some as home ports for sailors, some as genteel coffeehouses, where ladies could gather to sip tea in separate parlors.

In New England hamlets and towns founded under religious covenant, the church held the commanding position, usually on the village green. The white, steepled church generally overshadowed all dwellings and commercial structures—including, of course, any taverns. But the colonial ports quickly outgrew their church-dominated era, as public buildings, warehouses, and the inevitable taverns increased in number and size. And rival religious congregations appeared, depriving any single church or minister of undisputed leadership. Above all, the diversity of inhabitants distinguished the growing cities from the more homogeneous villages. To New York came enough Dutch Calvinists, French Huguenots, British adherents of the Church of England, Quakers, Anabaptists, and Jews to give the city its lasting cosmopolitan character. The Puritans, who for several decades dominated Boston, were not able to check the influx of settlers of different faiths. The Quakers of Philadelphia sought out potential immigrants, especially in Germany. Both cities came to realize that their economic fortunes depended on their ability to attract and absorb newcomers with needed skills and resources. Both increasingly accepted immigrants from Scotland and Ireland; Philadelphia and New York gave haven to German Lutherans and French Huguenots.

The flow of newcomers also brought an enduring urban problem: the care of the poor. English law held the local community responsible for its poor. But when neither town nor countryside could support them, people in need usually drifted into the cities. There officials had to develop welfare and educational institutions unknown in rural areas. Boston's early solutions reveal the emergence of two distinct patterns of urban charity: private, as in the organization in 1657 of the Scot's Charitable Society by 27 Bostonians of that nationality; and public, as in the opening of an almshouse by the city in 1665. Some self-help groups, such as the Society of Friends in Philadelphia, developed institutions that the city later maintained. Church and fraternal groups, though, chose to provide for their own needy; these included Boston's Episcopal Charitable Society and Charitable Irish Society and Philadelphia's Carpenters' Company. Widows of sailors, soldiers, and other townsmen needed the most help; in 1751 alone, widows made up 7 percent of Boston's population. And, as the number of orphans exceeded the ready adoptions, the plight of children worsened.

"I have often beheld with Concern," a Bostonian wrote in 1748, "the Swarms of Children of both Sexes, that are continually strolling and playing about the Streets of our Metropolis, cloathed in Rags, and brought up in Idleness and Ignorance. . . ." He wrote in support of the establishment of the "Manufactory House," where children eight or over could help produce linen. That was one solution. An almshouse was another. But the cities also had to take care of children in other ways.

In towns as well as in rural areas of the North and South, children were taught to read and write in "dame schools" run by women in their own homes. These had to be supplemented in the growing towns by private and charity schools. Boston parents who could afford the small fee, for example, sent their children to the "five free schools." To learn a trade youngsters were apprenticed to craftsmen who cared for and instructed them. In the leading towns this early educational system evolved into one that included secondary schools, academies, and colleges.

They built fortunes —and New York City

"From eleven to two o'clock, the merchants, brokers, &c. meet at the Tontine coffee-house . . . where, they transact all their concerns in a large way," a New York visitor wrote in 1793. Men of commerce had already made the city "the great commercial emporium of America," and the Tontine was its flag-flying nerve center. It housed the stock exchange, insurance offices, a ship's registry—and it loomed over a place even then famed for finance: Wall Street. Prospective buyers look over cargo deposited there. The street, which began as a wooden stockade across Manhattan, witnessed sharp trading—often by merchants who outfitted pirates and shared their booty; smugglers also prospered. A leading citizen was Captain Kidd, hanged in England in 1701 for piracy and murder.

In the Revolutionary War era merchants such as Elijah Boardman of Connecticut became more than moneygrubbers—and less than what the Pennsylvania Constitution of 1776 called "an inconvenient aristocracy." Proud of the fine bolts of cloth that enriched him and the books that reflect his tutored learning, he shows the poise that won him seats in the state legislature and U. S. Senate.

Boston had its first bookstore by 1647, and in the next four decades 19 others opened. The city's first Town House sheltered a public library as well as a market. When a fire destroyed that structure—and more than a dozen nearby bookstores—merchants ordered new books from London. They were sold in the first of a series of book auctions usually held at a tavern or a coffeehouse like Mr. Selby's, which became the center of a cluster of bookstores and printing shops. Gentlemen in New York and Philadelphia acquired large private libraries, and numerous booksellers and subscription libraries appeared in those cities. A clergyman's bequest of about 1,000 books formed the nucleus of a public library that opened in New York's City Hall in 1730.

Leading printers in each city were achieving positions of influence. Stephen Daye for a decade operated the first press brought to the colonies. Set up near Harvard College, the press produced the *Bay Psalm Book,* a speller, official broadsides, and the colonies' first annual almanac. Samuel Green, who succeeded Daye in 1649, published several religious books, including a translation of the Bible into an Indian language. In 1704 Bartholomew Green, a son of Samuel, began printing the *Boston News-Letter.* Philadelphia got its first almanac in 1685, the product of William Bradford's press. But after the Quakers tried to censor his work, he moved to New York. In 1719 his son Andrew launched the *American Weekly Mercury* in Philadelphia, where a decade later Benjamin Franklin acquired the *Pennsylvania Gazette.* Andrew Bradford and Franklin began short-lived magazines in 1741, nine years after Franklin started his phenomenally successful *Poor Richard's Almanack.*

By 1760 people in every port were reading weeklies—including one in German. From the presses came a steady stream of almanacs, sermons, and substantial volumes —3,666 titles between 1743 and 1760. Printers developed communication between the colonial ports and between the ports and their hinterlands. The migration of the youthful Franklin from Boston to Philadelphia and of Andrew Bradford from New York to Philadelphia was characteristic of a movement of apprentices and sons of the press pioneers not only to distant ports but also to inland towns ready to support an enterprising man with a press. Printers were among the most active advocates of the extension of the postal service and the opening of new stage routes. The arrival of a printer frequently brought a revival of activity to an old settlement, such as Salem, where three weeklies appeared in quick succession on the eve of the Revolution. New Haven, Albany, and Newport attracted printers and saw the establishment of weeklies and a rebirth of vitality. A promotional and advertising journal in Baltimore helped to boost the port into ninth place in population among American cities in 1775.

By that time, many secondary towns—such as Savannah, Lancaster, Hartford, Portsmouth, and Providence—had urban aspirations and potentialities. New Haven, the commercial port for Connecticut, could boast of a college (though it was named after a native of Boston, Elihu Yale). Salem was a fish-marketing and shipbuilding center second only to Boston. Albany held command over the fur trade on the New York frontier, as Lancaster in some respects did in Pennsylvania. The frontier was in fact becoming a major interest of both land speculators and potential emigrants in the colonial ports. Boston merchants and craftsmen moved north to Portsmouth and Portland and west to Worcester. Newport sent whaling vessels into the Gulf of St. Lawrence. Philadelphia reaped the rewards of earlier efforts as hundreds of the great Conestoga wagons built in Lancaster County rumbled in with produce from the west to be reloaded with merchandise for the distant frontier. Rafts—more easily built and propelled than wagons—gave Baltimore a way to compete with Philadelphia. The laden rafts were floated down rivers emptying into Chesapeake Bay, which Baltimore ships plied in coastal commerce. The trade brought the Maryland city vigorous, if tardy, growth.

"For a Publick Good, to give a true Account . . ."

With that purpose, the *Boston News-Letter,* the first regular colonial newspaper, began publishing in 1704—"by Authority," the customary gag on colonial papers. But defiance flared in the *New-York Weekly Journal.* Its printer, John Peter Zenger, was arrested in 1734 for seditious libel and tried after spending nine months in jail. A jury, ignoring precedent, acquitted him. The case is a landmark on the long way toward freedom of the press.

The Stamp Act in 1765 inspired attack by newspapers—23 by then. The *Pennsylvania Journal,* in deadly symbols, suspended publication. The *Massachusetts Spy* in 1774 uncoiled a "Join or Die" snake. A severed one had appeared 20 years earlier—heralding American political cartoons—in the *Pennsylvania Gazette,* Ben Franklin's "good News-Paper." Apprenticed at 12, he later practiced his trade in London on this press (opposite). He signed himself "B Franklin, Printer."

The secondary towns shared the urban concerns of the leading colonial cities. Each was linked with a principal port. Boston sent not only printers and clergymen but also merchants to its New England neighbors; Philadelphia did the same for Lancaster and even Baltimore. Yet every secondary city acquired self-confidence as it filled the marketing and cultural needs of its region.

The secondary cities diffused urban development and pointed it westward. The Great Philadelphia Wagon Road to Lancaster continued on a southwesterly course through Virginia. In 1775 the Transylvania Company, composed of land speculators from North Carolina, engaged Daniel Boone to cut a way westward—the famous Wilderness Road—through Cumberland Gap into the Kentucky country. There, after independence, a stream of migrants settled in Lexington and Boonesborough. A western branch of the Pennsylvania road wound over the mountains to the site of Pittsburgh, which soon displaced Lancaster as Philadelphia's western outpost. Some migrants pushed on to Cincinnati, Louisville, and St. Louis in the early 1800's. Others journeying westward from Albany established Utica, Rochester, and Buffalo, then pressed on to Cleveland, Detroit, and Chicago. The new nation, meanwhile, had purchased the vast Louisiana Territory and acquired New Orleans.

Like the colonial ports, these new urban settlements first served as marketing centers and promoters of a rapidly developing region. Each attracted leaders and artisans from Eastern cities, drew its inhabitants from many districts and from abroad, and developed a keen sense of autonomy. Each prospered by processing the products of its region—rope walks and hemp factories at Lexington, ironmongering and glass-making at Pittsburgh, brewing and meat-curing at Cincinnati, the milling of flour at Rochester. Each faced the traditional concerns of towns: fire, crime, a safe water supply, schools, adequate streets, and a public market.

Colonial cities had lacked an adequate currency and a system of credit. "Gold is very scarce here and I believe at Philadelphia too," a New York merchant complained in 1762. There were no banks in the colonies until after the Revolution. The new federal government created a national currency and a national bank. The venturesome enterprise of groups of investors in Philadelphia, New York, and Boston developed the private and state banking systems that gave unprecedented flexibility to the economy. By the 1820's there were banks in every city and growing town.

Technological advances would also aid urban development. The steamboat would revolutionize commerce on rivers and lakes—and eventually on the ocean. New inventions would provide incentive for the founding of industrial cities and for the emergence of a factory-based economy in such old colonial cities as Hartford and New Haven. In the West, rapidly growing cities would achieve a feeling of independence comparable to that experienced by colonial cities in the 1760's. The federal government would recognize urban leadership and admit the cities' territories into the Union.

The colonial cities had not been so treated. When they had displayed self-confidence, the mother country had tried to suppress them. But it was too late. In those vigorous cities lived people who would kindle revolution: the disgruntled merchants and lawyers gathering in coffeehouses; the restless craftsmen thronging the taverns; the newspaper printers railing against taxation; the clergymen in their pulpits joining in the clamor for independence. A city man would become our symbol for the call to arms. He was a craftsman who etched *Liberty* on silver and engraved "The Bloody Massacre" drawing that inflamed Boston. His art emblazoned incendiary broadsides attacking British control over the colonies. The "shot heard round the world" was fired by farmers on a rural green. But the signal was flashed from the steeple of a city church. And the warning was spread by that city man, Paul Revere.

Pulling for independence on July 9, 1776, New Yorkers topple King George III. His statue's gilt went to the Patriots' coffers, the lead to their guns—as 42,000 bullets. Acts of protest had worried British officials for years. One even feared the rise of "Ochlocracy, or government by a mob." But a Baltimorean, writing in 1773, had a more hopeful vision: "Free cities" are "nurseries of . . . liberty."

Living Through a Revolution

John R. Alden

Articles of war, plucked from time's corrosive clutches, keep alive the memory of mortals who employed them in immortal days. Jonathan Pettibone, a colonel of Connecticut militia in '76, wore this felt tricorn—a civilian style that served the military as well. Sam Davis spent his spare hours at Fort Ontario in 1762 scrimshawing his powder horn. Many a Patriot began the Revolution with leftovers from the French and Indian War, including the British musket he mustered out with. In time lighter and sturdier French imports, like this model 1763 Charleville, gained greater favor.

A false start toward national coinage survives in a pewter prototype. Instead of coin, the Continental Congress printed paper bills, some with bold mottoes, all offering to redeem in metal—empty promises that eventually made the paper worthless. "Sic Floret Respublica—Thus Flourishes the Nation," proclaimed the $45 bill. More fittingly, the $3 note tendered: "Exitus in Dubio Est—The Outcome is in Doubt."

Entrenched in Boston with a small army, Gen. Thomas Gage reported ominous news to his London superiors in the autumn of 1774: British authority had collapsed outside his lines. No longer was New England's resistance to Parliament's taxes and controls confined to city rioters. Now the country folk were equally determined to fight rather than bend the knee. Moreover, wrote the commander of British land forces, the Yankees would fight very well. If England decided to enforce obedience with troops, she must send many thousands of them across the Atlantic. "Affairs are at a crisis," Gage declared, "and if you give way it is for ever."

The spreading defiance beyond the cities was ominous because 90 percent of the 2.5 million colonists lived in the countryside. Only five places along the seaboard—Boston, Newport, New York, Philadelphia, and Charleston—could be described as cities. At a time when wagon tracks passed for roads, when travelers crossed rivers by wading, by swimming, or by ferry, many Americans had never seen a city. The typical colonist was a homestead farmer, and in the main a self-sufficient one. He saved his money, acquired more land, and helped his sons to get farms. Fathers and sons fished nearby waters, hunted ducks, turkeys, quail, geese, deer, bear, and opossum. They were taller and stronger than their relatives in Europe. And most took the Patriot side.

The first days of the war justified Gage's forebodings. On April 18, 1775, under prodding from London, he sent troops to destroy Patriot supplies at Concord. Minutemen—militia members specially chosen to guard against such a move—quickly responded to the alarm spread by Paul Revere and others. More important, other Massachusetts militiamen also took up arms and drove the British back into Boston. Then militia from all New England took the field. Gage soon was penned against the sea.

Tens of thousands of militiamen served in the long war, boys and men, 16 to 65. They were ill-trained, led by officers sometimes elected for their popularity rather than selected for their competence. The troops were prone to panic under attack. Subjected to cold, hunger, and homesickness, they sometimes headed home even before the few months of service required of them ended. A British surgeon viewed the militiamen outside Boston after the battle of Lexington and Concord as "a drunken, canting, lying, praying, hypocritical rabble." Nonetheless, when led by a Benedict Arnold, a Daniel Morgan, or an Andrew Pickens—an officer who could inspire them—the part-time soldiers could mount a formidable attack. Acquiring experience and steadiness, they became quite valuable to the Patriot cause. Even so, to check the thrusts of the Royal

Prelude to war

While London waffled, now stern, now relenting, the colonies set a defiant course for freedom. Taxation without representation spurred them on. A stamp tax on documents? Not a stamp was sold in 12 colonies. Duties on lead, glass, tea? "Sons and Daughters of LIBERTY" boycotted the importers. "Tea parties" ranged from the fracas in Boston to the sedate gathering in Edenton, North Carolina (below), where 51 women vowed total abstinence from tea while the tax was in effect.

The sight of hated redcoats roused city folk. "Lobster-backs," goaded by a jeering mob, fired on it in 1770; the five dead of that "Boston Massacre" became martyrs. New York hailed "Patriotick Barber" Jacob Vredenburgh, who, upon learning a patron was a British officer, hustled him out half-shaved.

armies, especially in battle on open ground, the Patriots needed disciplined, skillful, and reliable troops who would not return home at a critical time. Late in 1775, several months after George Washington took command of the American armies, the Continental Congress authorized one-year enlistments, which marked the appearance of the soldiers called Continentals. A year later Congress undertook to raise and maintain 88 regiments and other troops, for a total of 75,000, that would serve for three years or the duration of the war. It was a large order, never fully met. Yet many rallied to arms, some perhaps encouraged by a ballad sung by American girls:

Our country's call, arouses all   My love shall crown the youth alone,
Who dare to be brave and free!   Who saves himself and me.

Bounties helped fill the ranks, though the $20 and 100 acres of land promised by Congress was topped by some states — and state enlistees could serve near home. Men from all sections of the Old Thirteen, and even a few from Britain, went into the Continental army. Richard Montgomery was a British officer until 1772; in '75 he died a Continental brigadier in the assault on Quebec. Most of the recruits were of good stuff, though not every one was a splendid specimen. Alexander Graydon, a Continental officer, told of one prospect described as a fellow who "would do to stop a bullet as well as a better man . . . a truly worthless dog."

Musketmen, riflemen, cannoneers, and cavalrymen, the Continentals came to form the hard core of the Patriot armies. At the center of the core stood the musketman. A long-persisting myth alleges that the Patriots and their Pennsylvania rifles had the advantage over the British and their inefficient muskets. True, a rifleman could aim at an individual, could concentrate on hitting officers, or could bring down an enemy at 200 yards. The long-barreled rifle proved effective in skirmishing, in forest fighting, and against Indians. Against a charge of Royal infantry across an open field, however, the musket was much more deadly. Its one-ounce pellet, about twice the weight of the rifle bullet, could smash as well as penetrate. The musket took half the time to reload — and, unlike the rifles of that time, it had a bayonet. After getting off one or two shots at charging musketmen, the riflemen had to face "the white weapon" — the bayonet, against which knives, hatchets, or clubbed rifles were hopeless.

British generals knew much about the art of war and military traditions, sometimes to their cost. As winter came, European generals headed for the warmth of towns and forts, to relax until battle resumed in spring; the soldiers sang, "And when in quarters we shall be, Oh! how I'll kiss my landlady." The Patriots, unhampered by such traditions, could move to the attack in winter, as Benedict Arnold and Richard Montgomery did at Quebec, as Washington did at Boston and Trenton.

We see pictures of Continentals in resplendent uniforms, and there were well-dressed men among them, especially at time of enlistment. But uniforms wore out and could not be replaced. The soldier of the United States more often fought in a hunting shirt and pants that had not received the attention of a tailor. Marching ruined his shoes, and it is literally true that his steps could at times be traced by the bloodstains from his bare feet. His blanket, if he had not lost it, was likely to be sleazy, of "baize thin enough to have straws shot through without discommoding the threads."

Continental soldier Joseph Plumb Martin recalled that he had been promised for each year of service: "One uniform coat, a woolen and a linen waistcoat, four shirts, four pairs of shoes, a pair of woolen, and a pair of linen overalls, a hat or a leather cap, a stock for the neck, a hunting shirt, a pair of shoe buckles, and a blanket." Usually Martin received the coat, one or two shirts, and shoes and stockings. Washington's troops, encamping at freezing Valley Forge, could hardly have appreciated a New Jersey newspaper's little joke. The paper suggested that women, who had "worn the

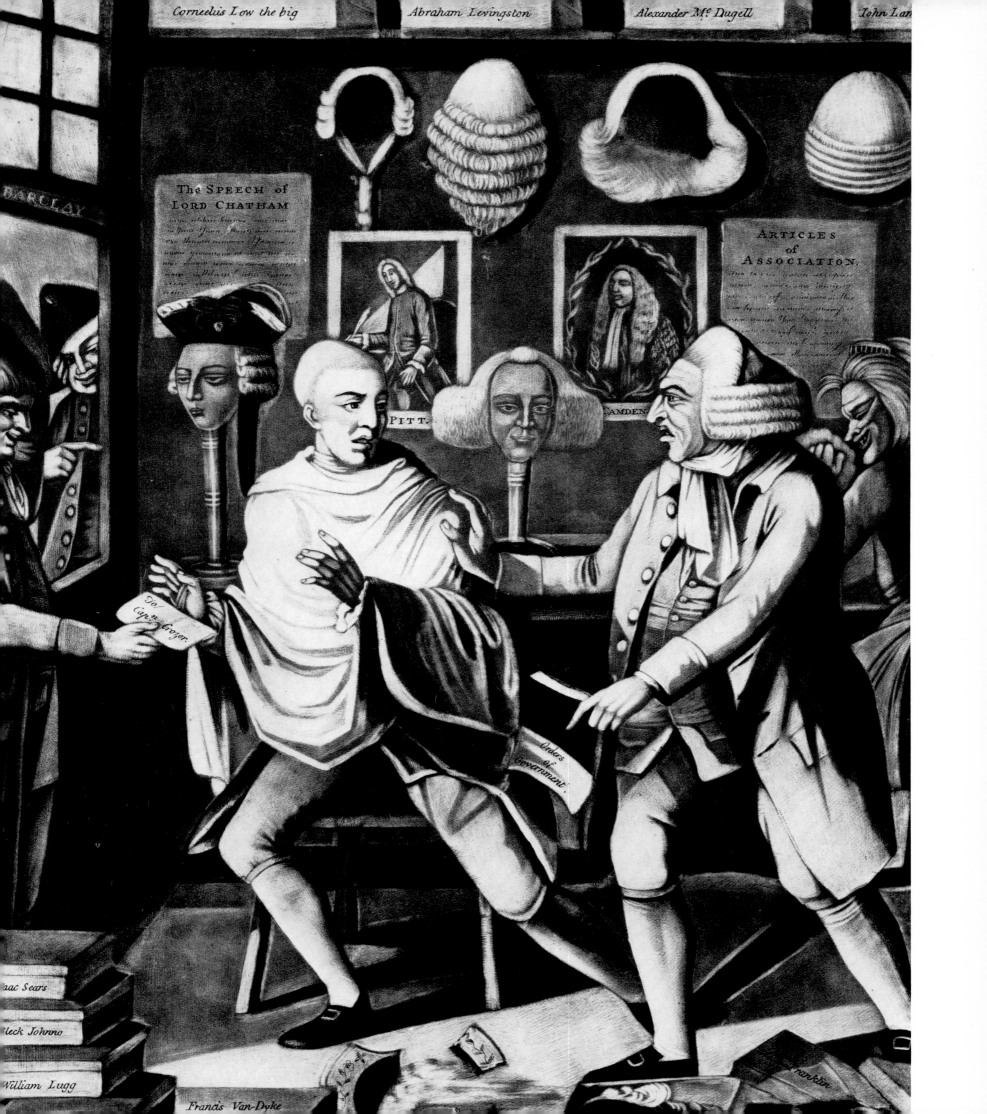

"In CONGRESS, July 4, 1776."

The war had sputtered for 14 months. Two days earlier the Continental Congress had formally resolved to cut all ties to Britain, but few would remember that fateful act. Now on the mild evening of July 4 the delegates in Philadelphia's State House approved Jefferson's amended draft of a public statement: "That these United Colonies are, and of Right ought to be Free and Independent States." It was signed by John Hancock, president, and attested by Charles Thomson, secretary. This was the moment history calls the "signing"— though the delegates did not sign the Declaration until August 2 and later.

Congress ordered copies sent forth for public reading, and printer John Dunlap labored all that night and half the next day. First news of independence appeared on July 5 in the *Pennsylvanischer Staatsbote*—in German. Three days later a third of the townsfolk (not the most respectable class, claimed one hostile observer) jammed the State House green for the reading. Bells clanged (including the Liberty Bell) far into the night, and bonfires flickered across the city.

So it went throughout colonies about to become states, as post rider (above), coach, packet, and coastal vessel carried forth the Declaration. Wagon road and wilderness being what they were, it took more than a month to reach the hundred or so hamlets and cities.

Apparently no one told the courier to New Hampshire that the capital had moved from Portsmouth. By the time he arrived in Exeter on July 16 with the "wished for news" he had ridden 30 extra miles. Abigail Adams listened with a vast crowd as the document was read in Boston on July 18. Around that time a child named Independence was baptized in Connecticut, and an innkeeper was jailed for declaring against the Declaration. In New York, an express rider delivered copies to General Washington on the 9th; at six that evening some 15,000 troops lined up in hollow-square formation to hear the announcement in sight of the enemy fleet.

Charleston, South Carolina, recovering from a British assault by sea, staged a grand independence day August 5. Savannah, southernmost town of the Old Thirteen, took the news with mixed solemnity and joy.

Engrossed on parchment, the original Declaration accompanied the wanderings of the government until both found a permanent home in Washington, D. C. Few outside the Continental Congress knew the author was Thomas Jefferson until the fact appeared in a newspaper in 1784. He had lived through all the bellringing and speechmaking without any personal commendation from the press.

Britain in late '76 saw its colonies intact, Quebec reaching to the mouth of the Ohio. The vastness of North America was scarcely comprehensible to folk of a tight little isle whose length spanned about half the distance shown between Boston and Savannah.

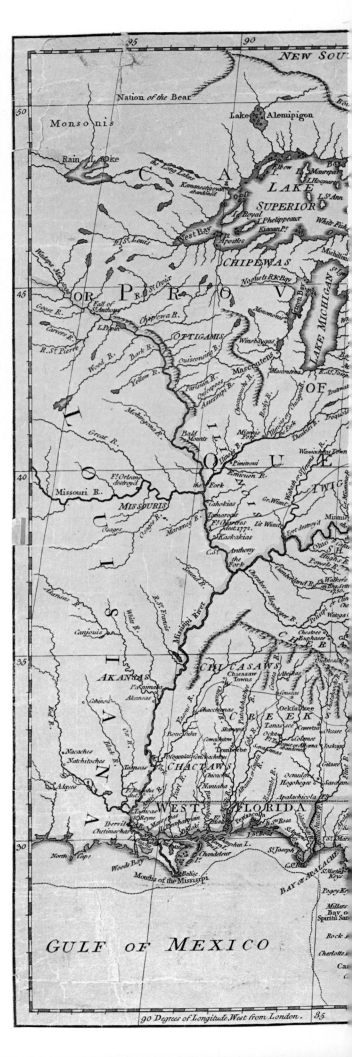

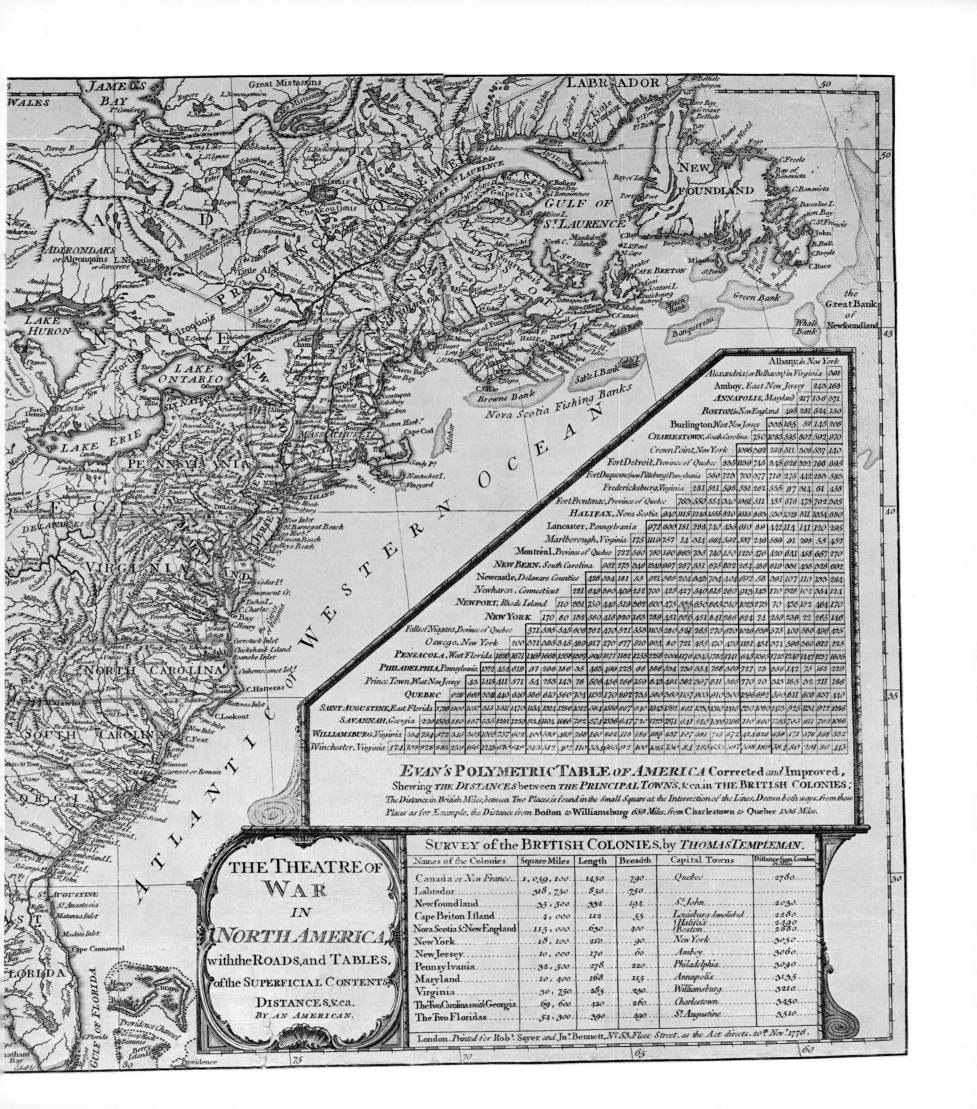

Light infantryman

Musketman

French soldier

Rifleman

A pickup army that won

As varied as the land it fought over, the Patriot army included backwoodsmen, northerners in the Second Canadian Regiment (top), freedmen in the First Rhode Island (at left) who fought with "desperate valor." Louis XVI sent seasoned troops, a glittering contrast to their ill-clad allies ("Falstaff's army, poor and bare," jibed a Tory). At Yorktown threadbare Continentals, splendidly arrayed Frenchmen, and riflemen in fringed hunting shirts blended in triumph.

breeches" for over a century, should donate their petticoats to be made into waistcoats and breeches for the soldiers.

The militiaman might shelter from heavy storms at his home; the Continental who had fought beside him suffered through the humid heat of southern summers, the frigid northern winters. He seldom had a tent and commonly spent the winter in wind-beaten cabins in camps near towns and cities where Royal forces were comfortably quartered. Martin remembered a night in the open when rain doused campfires and "we had to lie and 'weather it out.'" Later, "we joined the grand army near Philadelphia, and . . . we were obliged to put us up huts by laying up poles and covering them with leaves, a capital shelter from winter storms."

Ill-clothed and ill-housed, the Americans were also ill-fed. Militiamen who marched with Arnold ate candles and a dog. In New York, soldiers heading for the ferry to Brooklyn and the battlefield loaded up on "sea-bread," or hardtack, "nearly hard enough for musket flints." At times the Continentals received fresh bread, beef, and rum, but they often ate salt pork and hardtack, washed down by whatever water was available. Not infrequently the commissary issued only flour, which was moistened and cooked over an open fire. On the march soldiers might help themselves to fruit, vegetables, poultry, and nuts. In desperation famished troops on both sides ate green corn with predictable results: diarrhea. As Washington's troops hungered through the bitter winter at Valley Forge, farmers took their cattle and grain to the British in Philadelphia, preferring hard cash to depreciating Continental currency. Patriot foragers forced the paper money on the farmers, or gave them proof that the products had been requisitioned, or simply made off with what the army needed.

Fighting was preferable to such hardships. Once, when the British sortied from Philadelphia, wrote Martin, "we . . . wished nothing more than to have them engage us, for we were sure of giving them a drubbing, being in excellent fighting trim, as we were starved and . . . ill-natured as curs."

Eventually the spring run of shad up the Schuylkill revived the troops at Valley Forge. Soldiers leaped into the stream with shovels, tree limbs, anything they could find to land the fish. Horsemen clattered in to hem the shad with a living fence. The troops ate their fill of fresh fish, and salted down others by the barrel. At the Morristown, New Jersey, camp two years later, the Patriot army spent an even harsher winter; the weather was the worst that anyone could remember.

Some 6,000 Patriots died in battles on land. John Adams probably exaggerated when he claimed that ten times that many died in hospitals, but it is certain that more men died of sickness than were killed in combat. Typhoid fever, typhus, yellow fever, smallpox, and the "bloody flux" (dysentery) took an enormous toll. Inoculation checked the ravages of smallpox to a degree; Washington, who had survived an attack of smallpox in his youth, ordered the inoculation of every soldier with him at Morristown in 1777. But the army medical service lacked competence and was weakened by discord. (Dr. Benjamin Church, first director general of the Continental medical department, was a British spy.) Perhaps 200 of the 3,500 doctors practicing in America at the time held medical degrees. Among regimental surgeons Washington found "very great rascals" who let soldiers off duty on "sham complaints" and took bribes "to certify indispositions with a view to procure discharges or furloughs." Hospitals—crowded, filthy, their medicine chests empty—offered little succor to the sick or wounded; reportedly, 60 percent of the men sent to one hospital in New Jersey died. Camp hygiene was often neglected. At King's Bridge on Spuyten Duyvil Creek in New York, Dr. James Tilton found "excrementitious matter . . . scattered indiscriminately. . . . A putrid diarrhoea was the consequence. Many died, melting as it were and running off at the bowels. Medicine answered little or no purpose."

The soldier taken prisoner endured an especially hard lot. After seizing New York in 1776, the British found themselves with large numbers of captives, little food, and a housing shortage in the fire-wracked city. Confined to prison ships in New York harbor, Patriots died by the hundreds. Their plight was worsened by callous keepers headed by a vicious provost marshal, William Cunningham, whose grafting ways "starved the living and fed the dead." According to report, he later hung from the gallows in Britain for the minor crime of forgery.

Failure of the government regularly to pay its soldiers exaggerated the privations of war. Even worse, the paper money that was paid out steadily lost value. As early as 1779 a soldier could buy no more than a bottle of rum for his month's pay. Hardly surprising, then, that desertion was common. Late in the war Gen. Nathanael Greene quipped that both his army and the one he opposed were composed of the other's deserters. Nor is it strange that the Continentals rebelled more than once. In sore distress, soldiers in New Jersey mutinied on New Year's Day, 1781. Their enlistment terms, three years or the duration of the war, meant to them "whichever came first" —and their three years were up. They were not disloyal; they promptly imprisoned two British agents seeking to lead them into British lines. After much cajoling the mutiny came to an end; some 1,250 soldiers won discharges—though a high proportion re-enlisted. The British agents went to the gallows.

Men who fought on year after year were not liberally compensated for their bravery and constancy after independence had been won. Many were crippled, broken in health, ill-fitted for civilian pursuits. The veteran received neither medical care nor money to resume his education. If a man obtained a grant of 100 acres of land beyond the Appalachians, as many did, he commonly sold it to a speculator for cash. At last, in 1818, Congress voted a pension of $8 per month to destitute "old soldiers." By that time not a few of the fighting men had gone to their heavenly reward.

Patriots who fought on the seas fared much better than the soldiers. Sailors had more cover and lived closer to the kitchen, though not all returned home safely. An estimated 832 Patriots died in sea battles. Congress, the states, and even General Washington built "navies," and balladeers sang hopefully of sea power "Wide o'er the ocean spread." But the total of American war-ships remained small compared to the British navy, which blockaded the Atlantic Coast. Many a Patriot sailor went to sea in a privateer. Unable to challenge Britain's mighty ships-of-the-line, the privateers stalked her merchant ships instead. Privateering offered the lure of prize money and less discipline. In Boston an enlisting officer enticed men with a song:

> All you that have bad masters   Come, come my brave boys,
> And cannot get your due   And join with our ship's crew.

At one time there were more privateersmen on the Atlantic than there were Continentals with Washington. While the infant navy sank or captured 200 British ships, the privateers accounted for 600. A few who owned privateers prospered, as did the merchants whose vessels ran the blockade. A merchant could lose half the ships he sent to sea and still grow rich. Thus the Cabots of Beverly, Massachusetts, gained

For king, coin . . . and ancestral land

British commissions were bought and sold, soldiers recruited with liquor and fast talk. Yet courage, a fighting tradition, and experience welded an infantry second to none, though small in numbers. To swell the thin red line, Britain hired men from Hesse-Cassel and other German states, and "Hessian" became a synonym for hated mercenary. Indians, defending their sacred soil, sought to roll back the defiling colonial tide. Like Joseph Brant and his Iroquois, many sided with the king, and the frontiers ran red.

British officer

German grenadier

Chief Joseph Brant

enough wealth to move to Boston and eventually join its aristocracy. And William Bingham of Philadelphia, while a young Continental agent in the West Indies, piled up a fortune that would make him the richest man in postwar America.

Not all Americans struggled on the side of independence; perhaps one of every four white colonists remained loyal to the king. Holders of royal offices, latecomers from Europe, individuals of Highland Scottish background, and Anglican clergymen were all especially likely to support the British, but Loyalists came from every element in society. Loyalists, or Tories (from the name given to British politicians especially attached to the Crown), acted as guides and spies for Royal forces, fitted out privateers to prey on Patriot ships, counterfeited Continental currency, and put forth royalist propaganda. No fewer than 30,000 took up arms. Late in the war, at battles such as Hanging Rock and Rocky Mount, near Camden, South Carolina, the contestants were nearly all Americans. Patriots detested the Tories, the more so because they had

earlier been neighbors and friends; some were relatives. In consequence the Tories became the greatest sufferers from the war. Mob action against them began years before fighting broke out. Tory Edward Stow found his Massachusetts home befouled with feces and feathers in 1770 and again the next year. Filer Dibblee of Connecticut, reportedly victimized four times by Patriot plunderers, slit his own throat. Tories were denied the vote, subjected to heavy taxes, forbidden to move about, and barred from the professions. As Cornwallis's southern campaigns of 1780-81 spread turmoil through Virginia, Charles Lynch, a justice of the peace whose family gave its name to Lynchburg, convened an extralegal court which dealt harsh punishments to Tory "conspirators." The term "lynch law" apparently derives from these activities. After Cornwallis was trapped at Yorktown and it became evident that Britain had lost the war, Patriots sang a song, to the tune of "Yankee Doodle":

> Now Tories all what can ye say? That while your hopes are danced away,
> Come—is not this a griper, Tis you must pay the piper.

They continued to pay dearly long after the war ended. Every state undertook to expropriate Tory lands, houses, and shops. Some families sought safety in hedging; they agreed, for example, that a pair of brothers would take opposing sides, and that title to their property would pass to the partner who had stood with the winner. There are indications that the wealthy Dulanys of Maryland and the Gardiners of Long Island employed such strategy. Though most Tories remained in the new republic, perhaps 75,000 went into exile, the majority to Canada, others to England and Caribbean islands. Britain rewarded their loyalty with money and land grants, but the uprooting was not without pain. A Tory wife recalled her arrival in Nova Scotia: "I climbed to the top of Chipman's Hill and watched the sails disappear in the distance, and such a feeling of loneliness came over me that though I had not shed a tear through all the war I sat down on the damp moss with my baby on my lap and cried bitterly."

"From her keel to her taffrail . . . disease and death were wrought into her very timbers." Wrought as well into faces of Patriots wither- ing in the "Old Jersey," most wretched of the prison ships mired in Wallabout Bay near Brooklyn. Captives lived on bilge-tainted meat and wormy biscuit, amid raging pox. A boat took off hammock-shrouded corpses daily. Some 8,500 Patriots died in prisons.

Winter—the perennial enemy that tortured Washington's army in 1777-78—lays siege to Valley Forge once more. While the British snugged down in Philadelphia 18 miles east, bedraggled Patriots limped to these broad slopes, where replicas of Gen. Henry Knox's four-pounder guns remain emplaced. The army and its cause survived, an inspiration through all our winters of discontent.

The Indians also lost heavily. The Patriots were first to seek the Indians' help, and a few—Mohicans, Oneidas, Tuscaroras, and Catawbas—took the Patriot side. But most Indians tended to favor the king, primarily because American settlement threatened their hunting grounds and their way of life. Tribe after tribe joined the British, and the fighting was brutal. Backwoodsmen suffered enormously. But so did the Indians. Patriots thrice ravaged the southern hill country of the Cherokee, and destroyed more than 40 Iroquois villages in New York State. With war's end the power of the Six Nations and the Cherokee was sapped. Many tribes were forced to abandon their homelands, and were pushed westward before an onrushing flood of pioneers.

Atrocities were not confined to frontier fighting. When Charleston fell in 1780, Abraham Buford's Third Virginia Continentals, some 350 strong, were the only organized fighting men left in South Carolina. Col. Banastre Tarleton flew after them—infantry and cavalry riding two on a horse, 105 miles in 54 hours—and routed them. His men continued to kill helpless Americans who had laid down their arms and raised a white flag. And men came to know that "Tarleton's Quarter" meant no quarter. At King's Mountain, South Carolina, Patriot militia slew Tories who had stopped fighting and later hanged others. The slain, carelessly interred, were eaten by dogs and hogs.

Nor were civilians exempt from brutality. British and Hessian, Tory and Patriot ravaged and plundered. From Staten Island, New York, Lord Rawdon wrote in August, 1776: "The fair nymphs of this isle are in wonderful tribulation, as the fresh meat our men have got here has made them as riotous as satyrs. A girl cannot step into the bushes to pluck a rose without running the most imminent risk of being ravished . . . and of consequence we have most entertaining courts-martial every day." Civilians in besieged cities—Boston, Charleston, Savannah—saw their houses burn; many fled. Boston lost half its population. Looters pillaged friend or foe. Patriots even ransacked the home of Lewis Morris, a signer of the Declaration of Independence.

To relatives worried about their fighting men, news was tardy and often inaccurate. In the course of a year one Southern mother received a single letter from her soldier-son and several false reports of his death. Soldiers who could not write had to ask comrades to pen messages for them. Letters often went astray.

Families without menfolk scraped along as best they could, the more easily if they lived on the land. Inflation punished civilian and soldier alike. The blockade made imports such as sugar and molasses scarce. Wheat and flour dwindled in New England as the war cut access to supplies in the middle states. The problem grew as Congress, without financial resources or the power to tax, resorted to the printing press and issued some $200 million in unsupported paper money. Ben Franklin suggested that the decline in value as currency passed from one person to another was not a bad

"But pray, how much liberty left they for us?"

Bitter the taunt, as bitter the fate of Loyalists: banishment, mob assault, families sundered—because they opposed the champions of liberty. While Founding Father Ben Franklin labored to bring forth a new nation, son William (above) stood fast for the king who had named him governor of New Jersey. Imprisonment left him "considerably reduced in Flesh"; by some accounts he rotted for a time in the dank bowels of Newgate, a copper mine at Simsbury, Connecticut, which held the most "obnoxious" Tories. When William later sought reconciliation, Ben wrote him: ". . . nothing has ever hurt me so much."

A year before Bunker Hill, Bostonians mobbed hot-headed John Malcom, a tidewaiter (he collected customs from ships arriving with the tide), daubed him with hot tar and feathers, and forced him to toast the king with tea—then the queen and the royal family, until his stomach turned rebel. Like William Franklin, Malcom sought compensation in England; as evidence of his ordeal, he saved a peel of his tarred and feathered skin.

way to compel each receiver to contribute to the cause. Most of his fellow countrymen disagreed. Those on fixed pay—preachers, teachers, public officials—were hard hit.

Merchants sought ways to escape regulation. Confronted by price controls on rum and sugar, Philadelphia dealers began charging for the containers. On April 19, 1777, a Boston mob celebrated the anniversary of Lexington and Concord by running out of town five merchants who had refused to accept paper money as if it were hard cash. There were profiteers among the Patriots, and men who took legitimate advantage of wartime opportunity. James Warren, a Massachusetts political leader, commented afterward that "fellows who would have cleaned my shoes five years ago now ride in chariots." It is doubtful that many really poor men became that wealthy. But landowners unmolested by soldiers got good prices for their products. And Continental officers, gaining prestige and popularity, often secured public offices after the struggle.

Though Patriot leaders declared that education must be fostered in the new nation, the war set back the cause of learning. An estimated one quarter of the college students —many of them preparing for the clergy—joined Patriot forces. British prisoners were housed at Harvard; there was fighting on the Princeton campus; the College of William and Mary was used as a hospital.

We are told that American morals also sank as a result of the war. Lafayette urged that Continentals be kept apart from French soldiers and their dissolute ways. But Patriot armies, like British ones, had laundresses and other female camp followers. One pernicious effect of the conflict was the increase in dueling. Europeans subscribed to it, and Continental officers acquired an affinity for it with their commissions. In 1777, resorting to the "field of honor," Gen. Lachlan McIntosh killed young Button Gwinnett, a Georgia signer of the Declaration. (The resulting scarcity of Gwinnett's signature has long dismayed collectors of the signers' autographs.)

In the midst of strife, torn by jealousies and divisions among themselves, the Patriots formed an American federacy. From 13 colonies they created 13 states and a national government. Leaders burdened by raising money and troops took time, often in the shadow of advancing British armies, to draw up state constitutions. Legal bulwarks against despotism were built—the writ of habeas corpus, trial by jury, protection against cruel and unusual punishments. Written guarantees of freedom of the press came into being. Democracy and social equality advanced—though not for all.

Some slaves gained freedom by serving the king as soldiers, laborers, and scouts. But blacks were much more helpful to the American cause. Free Negroes of New England, and quite a few of Virginia, carried arms in Continental and militia units. In a party that penetrated British lines in Rhode Island in 1777, a black called Cuffee broke through a locked door and helped capture Gen. Richard Prescott, roused from bed without even his breeches on. Slavery conflicted with the trenchant statement in the Declaration that "All men are created equal," and Patriot leaders almost unanimously condemned the institution. Blacks, however, profited only in minor degree from the war's outcome. Northern states, with relatively few slaves, began to abolish slavery as early as 1780. The Continental Congress forbade it in the great Northwest Territory between the Ohio and the Mississippi. But black servitude continued in the South and in fact began to spread beyond the southern Appalachians during the war.

There was other unfinished business. Many men without property were still unable to vote. In some states only wealthy men could hold higher offices. Roman Catholics and members of other churches continued to suffer discrimination. Women were denied equality in politics and the courts. Thus, while the victorious Patriots could take pride in their new nation, in their system of representative government, in their bills of rights, the American Revolution was far from complete.

★1776★ Birth of the Nation

The most conspicuous fact of life in the New World was growth. Towns grew, counties grew, colonies grew. Families grew too, for American women generally had more children than their European sisters. Through births and immigration—and despite the toll taken by smallpox, diphtheria, yellow fever, and other killers—the colonial population doubled about every 25 years, a rate unheard of in the history of the Old World.

Of the men and women who left the Old World for the New, the largest single group was made up of unwilling immigrants from Africa; they proved as prolific as their masters in producing children after they got here. Blacks constituted perhaps 20 percent of the population in 1776. (The proportion was about the same in 1790, when the first official census counted a nation of 3.9 million.)

Most Germans and Scotch-Irish who came here in the 18th century headed first for the backcountry of Pennsylvania. They then pressed into the valleys behind the coastal settlements of the Southern colonies. By 1776 most of the area east of the Appalachians was occupied and pioneers were beginning to file through the passes to the farther slopes. So rapidly were they moving that in the decade after the Revolution more than 100,000 trekked over the mountains to stake out a new home and a new way of life in Kentucky and Tennessee.

When free men moved out to form new settlements, they expected to enjoy the same rights and liberty as the folks back home. The right to vote and hold office traditionally and legally belonged to landowners. And since the Americans who moved west generally owned or claimed to own the land they settled on, they expected to have a hand in their own government. Easterners who controlled the colonial legislatures might be slow about extending representation to the new districts, but Westerners were not slow about reminding them. Americans, conditioned to growth, usually responded in time to prevent serious friction. Englishmen, however, acted a bit too slowly. When they failed to recognize their prolific overseas progeny as equals, Americans declared their independence—to preserve the liberty they had always enjoyed.

Not all Americans were free, though the Revolution did see the abolition of slavery throughout the Northern colonies. For those without liberty the American Dream was often a nightmare. Yet despite their bondage many slaves managed to retain vestiges of independence. They maintained families, raised children, and by the sheer force of human dignity denied the laws that treated them as things.

Like most other Americans, they worked on the land. And the lives of those who work on the land, whether hired hands, gangs of slaves, or independent farmers, always have been dictated by the rhythm of nature. At harvest time and at planting time that rhythm might require back-breaking toil by freeman and slave alike. But it also furnished welcome intervals when there was nothing to do but sit by the fire and rest, talk, tell stories, play with the children, go to the races, loaf and invite the soul.

Life in 1776 was less frenetic than it has since become. And the simple pleasures of living, along with its pains and perils, are reflected in the objects that have drifted down to us through time. They remind us of what Americans may have had in mind in 1776, when they talked of life, liberty, and the pursuit of happiness.

Up goes a Liberty Pole, exclamation point in early independence celebrations and symbol of the Liberty Tree under which Boston revolutionaries met until the British cut it down.

Life

Wed largely to the land, the daily routine varying only with the seasons and the accidents of life, the family formed the foundation of colonial society. New families took strength from the old, and young people did not venture forth at a callow age. In New England women usually married in their early 20's; men married around the age of 25 to 27.

Parents of the newlyweds helped establish the budding household. From the bride's family came furnishings or money; from the groom's, twice that value in land, housing, tools, and cattle. As land grew scarcer in the 1700's, sons were set up in trade or given cash to move. Not often did several generations crowd together in one household, though an elderly parent might move in with a son, perhaps exchanging money and land for a home.

"Little strangers"

were welcomed into the colonial home by a midwife and neighbors. Some might bring words of welcome on a pincushion, a gift with message and design formed by pinheads. During the month of recovery that followed the blessed event, the new mother often had her own mother staying to assist.

New England ministers did their bit with advice on how to "Prepare a Pious Woman for Her Lying in." Labor pains, woman's curse for Eve's misdeed, said Cotton Mather, should "lead you to bewail your Share in the Sin of your first Parents."

"In general great Breeders,"

commented an English nobleman about colonial wives. Modern historians studying New England town records find that the first baby usually came 15 months after marriage. But by 1750 one-third to one-half the brides in some communities marched pregnant to the altar. Babies arrived at two-year intervals; seven to nine was the average born to a family.

Courtship in New England often included bundling: A couple, fully clothed, lay on or in a bed, usually with an upright board between them. Some clergymen attacked the custom. But one noted in 1781 that bundling, "with so much innocence," had gone on for 160 years, "and, I verily believe, with ten times more chastity than sitting on a sofa."

Brocaded wedding slippers

graced the well-shod bride. The granddaughter of Massachusetts Governor Simon Bradstreet wore this one for her marriage in 1760. A well-to-do young woman was usually wed at home in noontime rites. Guests at a wedding in a humble German home in the Shenandoah Valley would try to steal a bridal shoe during the hearty nuptial meal. Bridesmaids kept watch, though serving food distracted them. Whoever succeeded won a bottle of wine, the bride paying forfeit before she could begin to dance.

Pennsylvania Dutch Fraktur

spells out a baptismal wish in the European tradition: "Oh, dear child, you were baptized into the death of Christ, who purchased you from hell with his blood. . . . Awake to God's honor and your parents' joy, to your neighbors' benefit and bliss." The fraktur took its name from a German handwriting style.

Godparents probably gave this rare gift to Stovel Ehmrich, born January 23, 1771.

"Sucking bottles

for children," advertised by a Philadelphia pewterer in 1764, were relatively rare in a society where most women nursed their babies. Fashionable city ladies, however, gave their infants over to wet-nurses. An observer in Virginia noted in 1774 that "it is common here for people of Fortune to have their young Children suckled by the Negroes!"

Papboats—the one here is silver—served not only babies but also invalids. Soft, pulpy foods were fed from its wide lip.

Disease claimed young lives, but not in the great numbers once thought. Andover, Massachusetts, in the late 1600's saw fewer than 20 percent of its youths under 20 perish; epidemics in the 1700's raised the figure to more than 30 percent. Colonial boosters in Europe claimed the air was healthier on this side of the Atlantic. Records do indicate that children had a better chance of surviving at least in the northern colonies than in most of England and Europe.

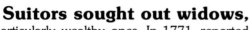

Suitors sought out widows,

particularly wealthy ones. In 1771, reported Williamsburg's *Virginia Gazette,* young William Carter married the Widow Ellyson, "aged eighty five; a sprightly old Tit, with Three Thousand Pounds Fortune."

But scholars such as John Demos now challenge "the old stereotype of the doughty settler going through a long series of spouses." In a sample studied in Plymouth, about two-thirds of those over 50 had been married just once. Only six percent of the men and one percent of the women wed more than twice.

Dressed like adults,

children were expected to act accordingly. Misbehavior could mean a whipping, as disciplinarians sought to "break" and "beat down" selfish natures. Not all parents agreed on the benefits. An English visitor found southern youth "pamper'd much more . . . than Neighbors more Northward."

"Went to the Funeral

of Mrs. Sprague, being invited by a good pair of Gloves," entered Boston magistrate Samuel Sewall in his diary for July 25, 1700. Following honored custom, funeral guests received gifts—gloves, rings, scarves, and spoons like the 7½-inch Dutch-made one below. (In 32 years of service at Boston's North Church, one minister reportedly collected 3,000 pairs of gloves.) Presents of finest quality went to close friends of the deceased and to socially prominent persons.

The cost of food and drink also contributed to mounting funeral expenses. Reaction set in by the 18th century; Massachusetts moved to forbid alcohol and limit gift-giving. Judge Sewall noted in 1721: "Mrs. Frances Webb is buried. . . . I think this is the first public Funeral without Scarvs."

"In Memory

of Mary . . . Who Departed this Life . . . In 39th year of Her age. On her left Arm lieth the Infant Which was still Born." Despite such mute evidence as the Massachusetts gravestone below, with its open-coffin carving and inscription, childbirth may not have been as deadly as scholars once believed. Historian Philip Greven, examining the 18th-century mortality rates for Andover, found that women during their childbearing years had a risk of death no greater than that for men of comparable ages.

New England funeral processions wound through public streets, necessitating patrols to guarantee others free passage. Mourners at the churchyard burial grounds saw tombstones alike in sentiment. The rhymed epitaph for a Tute, a Shute or a Root began, "Here lies cut down like unripe fruit"—even for Gershom Root, plucked at 73.

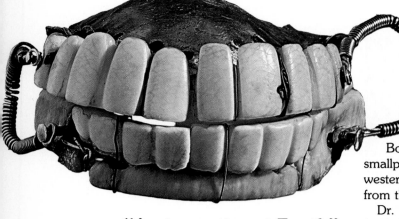

"An impertinent Tooth"

in his upper jaw, William Byrd "contrived to get rid of this troublesome Companion by cutting a Caper." The versatile Virginian simply tied a string between the tooth and a log on the ground, then sprang into the air. The tooth came out "with so much ease, that I felt nothing of it." Others fared less favorably at the hands of "tooth-drawers" and physicians using the popular "turn-key" extractor. Not until the 1760's could a qualified dental practitioner be found in the colonies.

Bad teeth troubled most Americans. George Washington frequently bought toothbrushes, powders, and washes. But by age 22 he had lost a tooth. His denture (above) dates to the 1790's. The teeth, carved of ivory from walrus or hippopotamus, are mounted on a base of hammered gold. The common folk made do with actual teeth from an animal—especially elk—set in plates.

Artists painting Washington limned on his left cheek a blemish, probably the side effect of an abscessed tooth. Gilbert Stuart and other painters complained that they could not capture a satisfactory look about the general's mouth because his denture pushed out his lower lip.

Light flickered

in early Pilgrim homes from rushes or the pith of reeds soaked in tallow or fat, formed into ribbons, then clamped and burned in rushlight holders.

Candles and oil lamps eventually supplanted the often makeshift iron holders. They varied from simple tongs in a wooden base to floor models; a movable slide raised or lowered the light. Some, like the standing one here, doubled to hold candles, which were cleaner burning but also more expensive.

As smallpox

swept Boston in 1721, the Reverend Cotton Mather urged his friend Dr. Boylston to try inoculation, used earlier in Turkey. After successfully testing it on his son and two servants, Boylston inoculated 240 people with live smallpox virus—the first large-scale test in western medicine. Mortality rates dropped from the usual 15 percent to 2 percent.

Dr. Boylston had studied at home under his father. Service as a surgeon's mate in the Revolutionary War helped train Dr. Philemon Tracy, here taking the pulse of a demure lass. Experience was the only teacher for most of America's 3,500 medical men in 1776.

The Plymouth farmer

setting out to harvest his crops in 1650 was his own weather forecaster: "Mists . . . in the vallies . . . promise fair hot weather." He had planted mainly Indian corn, wheat, and rye, and perhaps some oats, barley, or field peas. The corn would yield some 18 bushels per acre, the wheat and rye about eight. Finished in the fields, the farmer tended his livestock—cows, steers, oxen—and pampered his fruit trees: apple, cherry, plum, and pear. "To furnish their pot," his wife put traditional vegetables in their 1/4- to 1/2-acre garden: carrots, melons, artichokes, cabbages, radishes. (No potatoes; suspicious farmers thought eating them every day caused death within seven years.) Herb and flower mingled with onion and parsnip, but very aromatic plants, such as roses, grew in pots—lest their odor spread through the soil and injure the vegetation growing nearby.

"Wett all over

at once" for the first time in 28 years, said a Quaker woman after enduring a therapeutic shower. People usually just sponged off.

City dwellers could take soiled clothes to cleaners. In the *Virginia Gazette* one advertised scouring and spot removal to make garments "look as if they were new."

Sumptuous meal

in mid-afternoon on a southern plantation would be prepared by slaves following recipes read aloud by their mistress. Diners sat down to cuts of boiled or roasted meat—ham, turkey, lamb, or beef—surrounded by heaped platters of fish, small game, and vegetables. For dessert: puddings, pies, cakes, sweetmeats, and fresh fruits.

Ordinary farm families knew no such variety. Indian corn was one of their staples. They boiled or stewed most food, tenderizing tough meat and making eating easy for people with many spoons and rarely a fork.

"My ink freezes so,"

complained one New Englander on a bitter January day in 1716, "that I can hardly write by a good fire in my Wives Chamber." In many early homes the kitchen had the only fireplace. Warming pans like this, filled with glowing coals, took the nip from sheets in icy bedrooms. As settlers cleared the woods around towns, a fuel shortage developed. Kitchen hearths shrank, and Ben Franklin, improving on the fireplace, invented a cast-iron stove. Heat spread more efficiently through its baffles. It's still built today.

Liberty

"The Revolution," John Adams said, "was in the minds and hearts of the people." And the people of the colonies played a much larger role in politics than was the case in the mother country. In England and in the colonies only landowners could vote, but most adult male Americans owned enough land to qualify. The Revolution saw a widening of suffrage. Ben Franklin advanced the opinion that "the franchise is the common right of freemen," and six states did lower the amount of property required or opened the vote to all male taxpayers. It did not occur to anyone to offer the vote to women.

Gathering at the gallows,

spectators heard penitent criminals warn them movingly "on the fatal Consequences attending an early Habit of Vice."

The rattlesnake,

fair in its warning but deadly in its strike, symbolized the early revolutionary spirit. It adorned several flags during the war; John Paul Jones raised one (above). With peace, the serpent vanished, losing out to the red and white stripes of the national flag.

"Lewd and unseemly

behavior" was the charge that sent Captain Kemble of Boston to the stocks for two hours in 1656. The offense? The story goes that he returned on a Sunday from a three-year voyage—and on his doorstep kissed his wife. All colonies had Sunday "blue laws" (possibly named for the blue Puritan emblem or the blue paper they were printed on). New England enacted and enforced the harshest.

Political buttons

appeared in 1789 as Americans selected George Washington to be President of their new nation. Choosing from more than 25 designs offered by firms in New York and New England, citizens sewed the buttons on their coats and trousers.

Voters on election day

gathered at polling places, talking, trading, and drinking with a festive air. Candidates' friends circulated, looking for support.

In Virginia each voter approached a long table where the office-seekers sat. As he announced his preference, shouts of approval—and jeers—burst forth. The lucky candidate, usually a man of wealth and social status, rose to express his thanks: "Mr. Buchanan, I shall treasure that vote in my memory. It will be regarded as a feather in my cap forever." So important was this ritual that when, as a candidate, George Washington could not attend an election, he appointed a stand-in.

The ballot box was not the only place where political disputes were settled. Bitter struggles flared between the Conservatives—moneyed planters and merchants who favored a limited suffrage—and the Radicals. Artisans, laborers, and poor farmers, the Radicals campaigned for a broader-based democracy. Two men died as armed factions fought in Philadelphia in 1779. And in Charleston five years later the militia was sent out to keep the peace during a political battle.

In stocks sat lower-class people; better-bred scofflaws preferred the pillory.

Pursuit of Happiness

Colonists taming the land found pleasure in their work—in hunting and fishing, in helping at a cornhusking, a house-raising, or an apple-paring (for butter, sauce, or drying).

Weary men hauled off to nearby taverns for conviviality and news. They read what might be the only newspaper in town and heard "pretended Politicians" give their views. Few patrons were as thoughtful as newlywed William Ellery of Newport. He gave up his nightly trip to the tavern when he read in his bride's diary about her delight at having him home for a single evening.

On Christmas Day

in 1686, Puritan Samuel Sewall found "Shops open today generally and persons about their occasions." Puritans had nothing to do with "wanton Bacchanallian Christmasses"—or "devilish instruments" like Maypoles. (This one, if they'd been near it, would have been torn down.) They found their kind of merriment at elections, commencements, and training days for the militia. Thanksgiving, a "moveable feast," usually after harvest, united families for turkey and pumpkin pie.

Royal anniversaries sparkled with bonfires, public dinners, fireworks, and illuminations of houses. New Yorkers had 24 such holidays a year when the Crown ruled the calendar.

"They will dance

or die!'' wrote Philip Fithian about the Virginia gentry. In his diary the tutor to the Carter family described Col. Richard Lee's annual ball, where friends gamed, dined, and danced for several days: "For drink, there was several sorts of Wine, good Lemon Punch, Toddy, Cyder, Porter &c.—About Seven the Ladies & Gentlemen begun to dance in the Ball-Room—first Minuets one Round; Second Giggs; third Reels; and last of all Country-Dances; tho' they struck several marches occasionally—The Music was a French-Horn and two Violins.''

During the Revolution a few years later, Americans deftly footed such patriotic country dances as "Burgoyne's Defeat" and "A Successful Campaign.''

Ornaments of life

not to be neglected in a woman's education, wrote Thomas Jefferson, were dancing, drawing, and music. Young ladies preferred to play the harpsichord, dulcimer, spinet, or guitar; gentlemen took up the violin, flute, or French horn. Family members would play the tunes for an evening of dancing. Moravians who settled in Pennsylvania introduced to America the French horn and the music of Haydn.

"Their Silks & Brocades

rustled and trailed behind them,'' noted Fithian, as he watched the ladies dance.

Young hands brought life

to this miniature kitchen (17 inches high), which came to America from Germany—in a ship's hold or the mind of its maker. Such toys taught a girl the art of cookery and the management of a kitchen full of utensils and vessels she would have to know about. She "baked" pound cakes in the fluted copper pan and she learned that puddings belonged in the domed pewter dishes.

Boys valued jackknives

to shape treasures like whistles, windmills, waterwheels, and popguns. But more than one used his blade to carve a "much admired Name, upon a smooth beautiful Beech-Tree."

Girls imitated elders

so realistically when playing house that they would spit on the floor and then vigorously scrub with stick brushes. They also "knit" garters and stockings with straws or "spun" with strings tied to chairs.

Tutor Philip Fithian encountered two of the Carter girls who "by stuffing rags & other Lumber under their Gowns just below their Apron-Strings, were prodigiously charmed at their resemblance to Pregnant Women!"

Rocking horses

have galloped since the 1600's. Chair-makers and carpenters made the fancy steeds. But thoroughbreds also came from home: usually whittled planks with head and tail added.

Dolls to delight daughters

sprang from parents' ingenuity. Colonists fashioned them from cornhusks, rags—and nearly any other material at hand. Young girls from better families expected to own one imported doll, stylishly dressed. Linens, laces, and brocades clothed the Queen Anne doll, so named because of its popularity during her reign, 1702 to 1714.

When Susanna Holyoke and her maid returned home from a ball in Salem in 1795, they dressed her Queen Anne doll (below) in a pink silk gown and hooped skirt and teased the brown wig into a modish hair-do—exactly imitating one of the women at the ball.

A grandson annoyed

diarist Samuel Sewall when he caught the lad "playing Idle Tricks because 'twas first of April; They were the greatest fools that did so. . . . How displeasing must it be to God."

In well-appointed kitchens,

bowls and platters of wood, stoneware, pewter, and earthenware would be arrayed much as they are here in play. Wealthy colonists dined from china dishes and showed off such items as bowls flecked in aubergine purple, a white pie platter adorned with a cross. Pewter basins held vegetables; mugs, from gallon- to gill-size, measured out liquids.

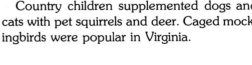

Age-old pastimes

amused youngsters. They flew kites, rolled hoops, and played marbles, hopscotch, leap-frog, hide-and-seek, and blind man's buff. Boys might gather for such ball games as cricket, fives (a kind of handball), tip-cat (which used a bat and a ball), and stool-ball (an early form of cricket in which a player is seated). All enjoyed rounds and singing games: "Here We Go Round the Mulberry Bush," "Little Sally Waters," "London Bridge." Players of every age joined in parlor games that called for paying forfeits of kisses.

Country children supplemented dogs and cats with pet squirrels and deer. Caged mockingbirds were popular in Virginia.

Ice skaters

joined in parties to cut fine capers and break winter's boredom. Shops as far south as Williamsburg advertised either plain or fluted skates. But children sometimes slid about without any skates on frozen rivers and millponds.

On the fall of a die,

on sports events, the weather, politics—colonists at home or tavern called out a bet and looked for odds. In the "seductive arcana of city dissipation," cards and billiards most often parted a man from his money. Women also wagered on card games and, in Virginia at least, even children gambled.

Sport of kings

in genteel Virginia was limited to gentlemanly participants, as tailor James Bullock discovered. He was fined 100 pounds of tobacco for presuming to enter his horse in a race.

Nothing prevented crowds from cheering on their favorites, most avidly in Charleston and New York. After 1763 the *South Carolina Gazette* printed betting odds and detailed accounts about the turf.

Game great and small

fell to hunters' guns as they found sport in gathering food: wildfowl, deer, bear, elk. Animals once plentiful dwindled; Virginia in 1705 declared a closed season for deer.

Fishing rivaled hunting in popularity. "I have . . . spent as much time in taking the Fish off the Hook," wrote one angler, "as in waiting for their taking it." Shad "in great store" and other fish teemed in Virginia. In tidal waters there oysters reportedly reached 13 inches; one crab could feed four men.

Lavish picnics

drew Southern planters to river's edge on sunny afternoons. At first each family brought its own food to the fish-feast or barbecue. As wealth increased, they took turns treating one another. One old-timer complained, "This is our third Barbeque day. . . . an expensive thing." He preferred the old ways, since many now came "only for the sake of getting a good dinner and a belly full of drink." Some Northerners picnicked on exotic fare. Ship captains returning from the Caribbean towed turtles home astern and provided limes for punch. Newport, Rhode Island, spread the most memorable feasts.

Beer, hard cider, applejack,

peach brandy, and the No. 1 drink, rum— young and old downed them all. Pennsylvania alone imported 526,700 gallons of rum in 1752 and distilled another 80,000 locally. Southern planters served foreign wines. Folks drank at baptisms, weddings, funerals—and elections, though laws generally forbade getting votes with food and drink.

The last time this Season several new and surprising Feats of Activity,
Ground and Lofty TUMBLING,
By Mr. M. Sully and Masters C. and T. Sully.

Particularly, Mr. M. Sully will turn in the Air confined in a

SACK:

Likewise will throw a Somerset holding an

Expanded Umbrella.

Master C. Sully will turn twelve times with

FIRE WORKS

Fastened to different parts of his Body.

THE WHOLE TO CONCLUDE WITH AN

EPILOGUE,

By Mr. M. Sully, in character of Harlequin, which finishes by a surprising Leap through a

BALLOON,

Surrounded with

Brilliant Fire-Works.

Doors to be opened at Six o'Clock, and the performance to begin at Seven.
No admittance behind the Scenes.

Glittering acrobatics

entertained South Carolina gentry. Among those appearing with others of the Sully family in Charleston (above) was Thomas, later to win acclaim as a portrait painter. Exhibitions like the one mounted by the Sullys traveled throughout the colonies, giving performances in taverns or as the afterpiece to an evening of serious theater.

Both Shakespearean revivals and contemporary London hits, such as *The Beggar's Opera* and *The Beaux' Stratagem,* drew crowds of wealthy theatergoers in Philadelphia, New York, and Charleston. But it took ingenuity to circumvent the obstructions sometimes raised against plays. One producer in 1762 billed *Othello* as "Moral Dialogues in Five Parts, Depicting the evil effects of jealousy and other bad passions and Proving that happiness can only spring from the pursuit of Virtue." Not a play, at all!

Finish flag waves home the winner on an 18th-century English straightaway track that colonials adopted.

Potent Pamphlet,

Thomas Paine's *Common Sense,* sold in the hundreds of thousands within months after publication in 1776. As instructive literature, it would be read aloud at home. Novels reputedly offended women's delicate sensibilities.

Military hero and Indian

date these playing cards to the time of the Revolutionary War. Earlier decks bore pictures of English royalty. Puritan officials in New England frowned upon what they called "the devil's picture-books," but there as elsewhere people eagerly took to games like whist. By the 1770's Boston had its own Thursday night "Card Assembly."

"Before Service" on Sunday,

Virginians passed the time secularly, "giving & receiving letters of business, reading Advertisements, consulting about the price of Tobacco, Grain &c. & settling either the lineage, Age, or qualities of favourite Horses," tutor Fithian wrote home to New Jersey. "In the Church at Service, prayrs read over in haste, a Sermon seldom under & never over twenty minutes, but always made up of sound morality.... After Service ... strolling round the Church among the Crowd, you will be invited by several different Gentlemen home with them to dinner."

In stern New England, though, worshipers gathered in unheated meetinghouses to hear three-hour sermons and perhaps two hours of prayers. "This day so cold," noted a Puritan on January 24, 1686, "that the Sacramental bread is frozen pretty hard, and rattles sadly as broken into the plates."

During a noon break persons from outlying areas might go to a "nooning house" or a tavern to eat cold baked beans and socialize.

Nimble fingers stitched

a serene Sunday in a small New England town after the Revolution. Citizens of a new nation trod old paths to their church.

The appliquéd quilt is accented with embroidery. Its creator learned her stitches—as well as the alphabet and lessons in good behavior—by sewing samplers in her youth. Quilting called for the longer arms and larger hands of womanhood.

A New World of Learning

Gordon S. Wood

No frills, no flotsam, and two 2's always equaled 4 in the schoolroom of yesteryear. Mid-19th-century children answered "present" at roll call, totted sums, puzzled over hand-me-down textbooks, and left marks of their brief tenancy on desks such as this from a school in rural New Hampshire. Meagerly appointed, classrooms lacked such tools as maps, globes, even blackboards and chalk. Slates and slate pencils, in general use after the Revolution, made handy writing gear; children, saving precious paper, ruled, folded, cut and sewed it into copybooks.

Before steel pens became common about 1850, a first step in penmanship was to make the pen by sharpening a quill with a pen-knife. Students made their own ink at home from powders, dyes, berries, or from the steeped bark of the swamp maple. Ingredients in old ink recipes include salt as mold-retardant and a few drops of brandy as antifreeze—reminders of the sweats and shivers once endured in the atmosphere of learning.

Americans are an educationally-minded people. No nation in history has devoted so much of its resources to educate so many of its young. In a land of diverse peoples—immigrants of different races, origins, religions, languages—where nationality cannot be easily taken for granted, education has been asked to make us a nation, a single people with values in common. Education also has become a key to our great ideal of equality, releasing the individual from inherited chains that might keep him outside the opportunities of American life. Because education underlies all of what we are or would like to become, it inevitably has become an arena for some of the bitterest of our social and intellectual conflicts.

The early English settlers brought to the New World an intense and passionate interest in education, an interest radically different, however, from ours today. An educational revolution was taking place in England; upheavals of the Reformation dissolved the monasteries and chantries that had been the formal agencies of learning in medieval times and broke the ecclesiastical monopoly of education. Rising groups, particularly merchants, started schools not only to sustain Protestant ideals but also to prepare men for positions in the emerging bureaucratic state and in the expanding commercial economy. Renaissance England gave new people access to schooling, multiplying the number of schools until by mid-17th century England had a school for every 4,400 people. It was perhaps the most literate society the world had known.

Medieval Europe had not regarded childhood as a distinct and peculiar period in life, demanding special solicitude by the parents. Children were rarely sentimentalized in writings or art; in portraits they often resemble miniature adults. Parental neglect, ignorance, and indifference were reflected in the rates of infant mortality: one-fourth to one-third dead before the age of one year. Well into the 18th century, in some areas and in some social classes, children under age seven or so simply did not count for much. As one satiric rhymester put it, some English parents ranked young children

> Among their cats and dogs, their bulls and bears;
> Mere animals whose gambols now and then
> May raise a laugh, and turn the rising spleen,
> Ere reason dawn'd, or Cunning Learnt disguise.

At age seven, when "reason dawn'd," parents abruptly plunged the child into the adult world with little anxiety for the youngster's particular feelings or problems. They regarded the process of growing up as a steady and imperceptible evolution—with no recognition, for example, of adolescent storm and stress.

By the time of the first English migrations to America, however, some European parents were paying more attention to children and their peculiarities of dress, toys, jargon, and moral training. Family portraits more and more centered around the children. Although this dawning discovery of childhood by some European gentry stimulated an interest in education that carried over to the New World, it was religion above all that accounted for the colonists' obsession with education.

Reformed Protestantism, or Puritanism, when transplanted to New England, left an indelible imprint on America's educational history. In revulsion against the elaborate icons, colorful vestments, and other attractions to the eye employed in Roman Catholicism and High Anglicanism, the Puritans stressed the ear and mind for acquiring religious understanding. Although they did not think that mere knowledge of Scriptures and of theology could guarantee saving grace, they deeply believed that learning was a necessary part of the preparation for salvation. "The Word Written and Preacht," Thomas Foxcroft, minister of Boston's First Church, explained in 1719, "is the ordinary Medium of Conversion and Sanctification."

The Puritans felt sure that children were born without a fear of God—indeed with an original sinfulness and an obstinate pride that resisted God. They and their stubborn wills, declared John Robinson, the Pilgrims' minister, must "be broken and beaten down; that so the foundation of their education being laid in humility and tractableness," they could be taught a proper awareness of God by parents, clergy, and others. The 17th-century Puritans were obsessed with their children, but they scarcely sentimentalized them. A severe regimen to arm them against the lures of the Devil included family prayers twice a day, daily Scripture readings, and repeated explanations of church sacraments. Most important of all was catechizing—that personal process of questions and answers which formed for colonial children the most constant and everpresent means of instruction in the faith.

Even in many non-Puritan areas outside New England, religion permeated and overawed people's lives and comprised for most settlers the only means of explaining and dealing with the world. Religion blended naturally into all elements of the culture; most colonists had little of our modern sense of sharp separation between church, state, and society. They thought of society not as an aggregation of individuals but as an organic whole with a unified culture, a world of fixed ranks and degrees. As John Winthrop told his fellow passengers in 1630 on the ship bringing them to Massachusetts Bay, "God Almightie in his most holy and wise providence hath soe disposed of the Condicion of mankinde, as in all times some must be rich, some poore, some highe and eminent in power and dignitie; others meane and in subjeccion." Finding one's proper place in this ordered society and understanding the need to stay in that place—all learned within the pervasive preparation for salvation—was thus the be-all and end-all of education, indeed of life. Such a society could never sustain our modern distinction between "private" and "public." Education could only be the responsibility of everyone, a communal responsibility.

Tudor-Stuart England had discharged that responsibility by creating schools. In the wilderness of the New World, settlers at first had to fall back on what had always been the central institution for acquainting the young with the world—the family. Not yet an insular institution, the 17th-century family in America lay open to the world, mixed with the world, sent some members out and brought others in. Of a piece with the larger society, the family did what society did: educated the young, maintained the economy, cared for the sick and aged. Other institutions—church, state, and schools—elaborated

Book of books, the Bible was end and means of education for early Americans. Children learned letters and moral lessons from vivid tales and proverbs, absorbed the cadences of psalms and prayers. The epochal King James version, new in 1611, remained religious and cultural keystone in families like that of the Reverend John Atwood, 19th-century Baptist minister and treasurer of New Hampshire.

Devils and specters

America's colonists believed in the reality of the supernatural, and beheld various "wonders of the invisible world." Sinners who invoked Satan expected to see him and to smell the brimstone that lingered after his appearance. A Dutch visitor to Boston around 1680 reported that he had never heard more talk of witches and witchcraft. In Philadelphia a Lutheran pastor in 1716 recorded the case of a housewife who, in a moment of anger, called upon the Devil. Shortly thereafter she heard footsteps on the stairs and then "perceived a dark human face, making horrid grimaces with mouth wide open and teeth gnashing." Terrified, she begged her husband to read Psalm 21, "which he did, and the face disappeared."

God's providence often took the form of wondrous sights. In 1682 a Harvard tutor noted in his diary that the people of Lynn, Massachusetts, had seen a knight in armor outlined against a dark cloud. Presently the man vanished and in his place appeared a splendid vessel, "the handsomest of ever they saw." North Carolinians reported several apparitions of Sir Walter Raleigh's ship "under sail, in a gallant posture."

The most celebrated spectral ship of colonial times was that described by New Haven settlers in 1648, after the loss of a vessel carrying several leading citizens. All winter the settlers prayed for word from their missing companions. Then, wrote Cotton Mather, after a blinding thunderstorm, "a ship . . . appeared in the air." It was the missing ship and, as townspeople watched, aghast, its masts fell one by one. "Quickly after the hulk . . . overset, and so vanished into a smoky cloud."

on and extended the responsibilities of the family. Affairs of the family, "a little commonwealth," were very much the business of the larger commonwealth. In the 1640's the government of Massachusetts Bay, realizing "the great neglect in many parents and masters in training up their children in learning and labor," empowered local officials "to take accompt from time to time of their parents and masters . . . concerning their calling and impliment of their children . . . and to impose fines upon all those who refuse to render such accompt." Virginia passed a similar law. In addition, Puritan Massachusetts declared parents and masters responsible for children's "ability to read and understand the principles of religion and the capital lawes of the country."

Understanding the capital laws was crucial. In 1649 the Puritan government ruled that any child over 16 who "shall CURSE, or SMITE their natural FATHER, or MOTHER" or act in a "STUBBORNE or REBELLIOUS" manner would be put to death, unless parents had been "unchristianly negligent" in his education or provoked him by "extreme & cruel correction" into protecting himself from "death or maiming." Although apparently no child was executed under this statute, it does show how the community's authority reached into what we would regard as the private sanctuary of the family. Even into the early 18th century, governments continued to intervene in family affairs, putting children found in "gross negligence" — not knowing the alphabet by age six — into other families to be educated. In colonial America parents, even the well-to-do, voluntarily placed their children for training and upbringing in other families.

The apprenticeship system trained most boys — and some girls — for their life's work and position in society. In that tight hierarchical world the parents selected the child's vocation or "calling." As early as age 7 or 8, but more commonly at 12 to 14, children were bound over to masters in other households. A written indenture between parent and master confirmed the placing out of a child as servant or apprentice, usually for seven years or until age 21. The contract made the master in effect the father and often specifically required him to teach reading and writing, as well as a trade. The masters' authority allowed "moderate Correction" or "reasonable Chastisement" of their "children," even the apprentice of 20. Occasionally they abused the right of punishment and had to face a court suit — or search for a runaway.

Some boys having "but a weak body & so not able to follow Husbandry," as one Massachusetts youth complained, convinced their fathers — or their ministers, who often intervened — to let them prepare for a learned career. Girls in early America had no such opportunity. To further both learning and faith, some colonists from the outset wanted to found schools as Englishmen had been doing for decades. Indeed, in the "howling wilderness . . . far removed from the cultivated parts of the world," schools seemed imperative "lest degeneracy, barbarism, ignorance, and irreligion do by degrees break in upon us." In New England and the Chesapeake Bay area, early colonists endowed schools in the English tradition, usually by donating land which might yield rent. But land here was so plentiful that getting tenants was not easy, and most early endowed schools had trouble staying alive. When it became clear that the economy was too primitive and fragile to finance schools in the English way, the colonists turned to direct, regular contributions from the community.

The Puritan stronghold of New England made the most explicit effort. In 1647 the government of Massachusetts Bay, aware of the subtle aims of "that old deluder, Satan, to keep men from the knowledge of the Scriptures," and anxious "that learning may not be buried in the grave of our fathers," enacted what has become the most famous statute in American education. The law required every town of 50 or more households to maintain a "petty" school to teach reading and writing, and every town of 100 families also to support a Latin grammar school to prepare boys for the university — both

A		In *Adam's* Fall / We Sinned all.
B		Thy Life to Mend / This *Book* Attend.
C		The *Cat* doth play / And after flay.
D		A *Dog* will bite / A *Thief* at night.
E		An *Eagles* flight / Is out of fight.
F		The Idle *Fool* / Is whipt at School.

A pupil's progress: from sin to syntax

Learning to read gave babes in the wilderness a head start in a lifelong footrace with the Devil, pious New Englanders believed. Tots of three or four were taught the basics from hornbooks — wooden paddles covered with translucent horn "to save from fingers wet the letters fair." The best-selling *New England Primer* proceeded from alphabet to syllables to readings meant to instill moral precepts. Rhymed proverbs (left) led letter by letter from Adam's fall to Zaccheus' climb, then to a catechism, Bible questions and answers. More than one colonial child grew "tired of having good dinged into 'em" by rote and by rod.

A revolutionary idea, that texts should interest children, eventually shaped livelier stories, maps, and colored illustrations. A period-character named Mr. Stops (below) showed 19th-century Dicks and Janes how correct punctuation makes sense of nonsense.

ROBERT'S first interview with M⸰STOPS

Young Robert, could read but he gabbled so fast,

And ran on with such speed that all meaning he lost

Till one morning he met M⸰Stops by the way

Who advis'd him to listen to what he should say.

Then, entring the house he a riddle repeated

To shew, WITHOUT STOPS, how the ear may be cheated.

M⸰STOPS Reading to ROBERT and his SISTER.

"Evry lady in this land

"Has twenty nails upon each hand

"Five & twenty on hands & feet

"And this is true without deceit."

But when the stops were plac'd aright,

The real sense was brought to light.

"Is it not a cruel fate a master thus to be, Doom'd to teach such naughty boys, such blunder heads as these. . . . letters telling, hard words spelling; Pens a making, boys a shaking, Reading writing scolding fighting, Coaxing on the stubborn ones, and pushing on the lazy." Thus ran the schoolmaster's lament in a song of the 1830's. Little wonder a man so beset felt like rewarding the very diligent pupil.

types to be sustained by local taxation. Because these schools supplemented the family's role in education, attendance was not compulsory for children taught at home.

Other New England colonies copied the law. The financial base of education had shifted from self-perpetuating endowments to continuing dependence on the community, either by taxes or gifts. Since paying fines was cheaper than supporting schools, many New England towns flouted the law. By 1689 Massachusetts had only 23 schools, far more, nevertheless, than any other colony. Pupils also had to pay tuition and fees, which usually limited attendance to children of the wealthy. Later efforts to provide more equal access to schooling did away with tuition. As New England's population scattered, separate school districts were created, and schoolmasters were no longer moved about. During the later 17th century many New England grammar schools began admitting girls and no longer confined their teaching to the classics. Veering far from their original purpose of only preparing boys for college, the grammar schools by the middle of the 18th century had absorbed the mission of petty schools.

The middle and Southern colonies had such a hodgepodge—private tutors, "dame schools," evening schools, boarding schools, religious academies—it was impossible to say precisely what was a school. General taxation was not common in these colonies. Modes of support for schools varied widely: endowments, subscriptions, lotteries, tuition, and taxes. Although there was a sense of communal responsibility, parents bore the principal burden. If they wanted their children to learn more than they themselves could teach, they had to pay. Free schools were rare throughout these colonies.

Some wealthy planters' children went "home" to England for schooling, others to local boarding schools like Somerset Academy on Virginia's Eastern Shore. There, said a 1769 ad in the *Virginia Gazette,* two masters "taught the rudiments of English grammar, orthography, or the art of spelling, and . . . writing," also Latin, Greek, and "various branches of the *arts and sciences,* such as geography, logick, navigation, surveying &c. . . ."

Other Southern gentry, like Robert Carter of Nomini Hall in Virginia, hired private tutors. When 26-year-old Philip Fithian, recent Princeton graduate, arrived at Carter's plantation in 1773 he confronted eight pupils—Carter's sons and daughters plus a nephew. They ranged from 18 and reading the narratives of Sallust in Latin to 7 and just learning the alphabet. The expense of private education meant that most children in the colonial South never had access to formal schooling. Indeed, even in New England, it is doubtful whether most colonial children ever went to school.

Those who did attend school in early America would certainly never have forgotten it. Schooling was a grueling experience. The students' day was long. In the 17th century one New Haven grammar school ran from 6 to 11 a.m. and from 1 to 4 p.m. in winter, to 5 p.m. in summer. Schools usually stayed open all year; students periodically withdrew and returned, depending on the needs of their families. Schoolhouses were primitive and small, roughly 18 by 20 feet. Low ceilings and few windows resulted in poor ventilation and a stifling atmosphere which made it not only hard to learn but, as one 18th-century pupil recalled, "a toil to exist." Heat in the winter came from a single fireplace; the students nearby roasted their flesh while those at a distance had their noses turn blue and their ink congeal. Given the severe conditions, it is amazing that so many students not only survived but went on to college and learned careers.

123

Learning the R's and the "speaking of speeches"

"It would be well if they could be taught everything that is useful, and everything that is ornamental," said Benjamin Franklin, "but Art is long, and their time is short."

Curriculums of colonial schools included at least two R's: reading and writing "a fair hand and swift." One penmanship system among dozens that later developed advocated tying the fingers holding the pen to acquire a "mode of freedom and command of hand." The teaching of the third R often hung on the schoolmaster's ability—or lack of it—as an "arithmeticker." In pace-setting Massachusetts, arithmetic became a legally required subject in 1789, along with English, orthography, and "decent behavior."

Rhetoric was considered so essential a skill of early America's educated man that Harvard students gave it a full day each week. Boys in Latin grammar schools, meant to prepare them for college, memorized long passages from their readers and recited them with broad, stereotyped gestures, also committed to memory: "When the pupil has got in the habit of holding his hand and arm properly, he may be taught to move it," said one reading text. "Never hold any body by the button or the hand, in order to be heard through your story," advised another. There were rules also for listeners: "If thy superior be relating a story, say not, I have heard it before, but attend to it as if it were to thee altogether new; seem not to question the truth of it; if he tell it not right, snigger not."

A defect in the new nation's schools, said schoolmaster Noah Webster, "is the want of proper books." With the zeal of a patriot he produced his blue-backed speller to "diffuse a uniformity and purity of language," a grammar, the first reading text compiled in America, and dictionaries that set standards for today. In his primer, A is for apple pie.

In the lexicon of the roughhewn West, A is for ax, O for ox, familiar objects to millions of Westerners for whom McGuffey's Eclectic Spellers and Readers became bywords. The series, begun in the 1830's, was still popular in 1894, the year of the arithmetic poster at right, which presents problems in terms of plums and peas, cherries and chickens.

Not all lessons came from books. Under the "Apostle's Oak" in Newton, Massachusetts, boys pursue another R—recess. The oak marks a spot where "Praying John" Eliot once taught and preached to the Indians.

"YOU SOULS OF GEESE!"

"OH, DESPAIR!"

"THE WHOLE CREATION . . ."

VERBS.

Active.   *Passive.*   *Neuter.*

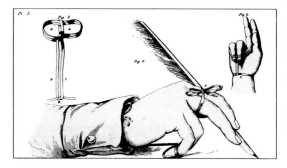

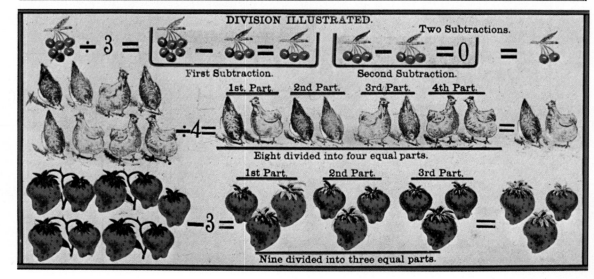

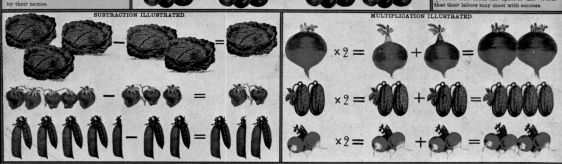

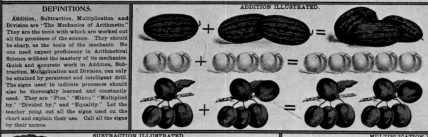

From the beginning, the New England Puritans' religious errand into the wilderness had required the creation of a seminary "to advance learning and perpetuate it to posterity." In 1636, six years after they arrived at Massachusetts Bay, the Puritans established Harvard College. Contrary to English ways, they maintained a degree of community control over the faculty, setting a pattern for American colleges. Virginia in 1693 established William and Mary in Williamsburg for the sustenance of Anglicanism. Yale, founded in 1701, offered more support for Puritanism. Until the mid-18th century, these three were the only colonial colleges.

Avowedly meant to train ministers, these colleges also prepared men for other learned careers. Nearly half of Harvard's 17th-century graduates became something other than clergymen. Because of the expense—equal to a laborer's full pay for two years—colleges generally remained the preserve of the well-to-do. And the gentry, particularly in the South, expected higher education to remain an exclusive mark of a gentleman. As late as 1770 one South Carolinian opposed having a college in his colony because it would make learning "cheap and too common." Harvard and Yale even carried calibrations of the social order into college life. Both ranked entering freshmen according to the social and political dignity of their fathers, especially alumni, and according to their predicted future contributions to the society.

The college faculty and president tended to treat students as children, sustaining authority with rituals and laws, together with faculty-administered punishments: fines, whipping, boxing on the ears, and "rustication" or exile to the country to live with a minister for a time. Rigid rules governed students' lives. They got up, ate, studied, relaxed—all by the clock. Yale students had to be in their rooms by 7 p.m. in fall and winter. Into the early 19th century, Brown allowed no talking during study hour except in Latin. Students resisted the regimen, sometimes in indirect ways: Harvard students in the late 17th century defied college rules by growing their hair long—a "lust" to the Puritans. Student protests grew bolder and more destructive as time went on; by the early 19th century riots were common in many colleges. Between 1800 and 1830 Princeton had six disruptions; half the students were expelled in 1807.

The three decades prior to the Revolution saw six more colleges—present-day Princeton, Columbia, Pennsylvania, Brown, Rutgers, and Dartmouth—added to the original three. That generation produced 3,000 graduates, twice as many as the previous century.

After the Revolution, a mania for making colleges began to spread among the contending religious sects. The result was the creation of nearly 900 up to the time of the Civil War; by 1860 fewer than 200 of them survived. The phenomenal crop of sectarian colleges was scarcely what Revolutionary leaders had anticipated. George Washington, for one, had hoped for a national university, a focus for the intellectual resources of the entire nation. But in the splintered post-Revolution society, the best the federal government could do for higher education was to grant land to the states for each to set up a "seminary of learning." About a dozen weak state universities were created from these grants before the Civil War. Only in the later 19th century would state universities, particularly in the Midwest and West, shape their identity as non-sectarian, popular institutions oriented to the practical.

By the end of the 18th century the impact of a growing population and rapidly developing market economy fundamentally altered American life. As religion loosened its grasp, particularly on the well-to-do, getting ahead and acquiring wealth became popular goals. Said a rhyme in a late 18th-century edition of the *New England Primer:*

He who ne'er learns his A.B.C.   *But he who learns his letters fair*
Forever will a blockhead be,   *Shall have a coach to take the air.*

"To reform mankind, . . . begin with children"

All spit and polish and decorum, the student body of a school in southwestern Montana faces the camera with teacher Miss Blanche Lamont. In 1893 the hamlet of Hecla, clinging like a mural on the wall of Lion Mountain, lived on silver, lead, and copper from mines even higher up. To reach portals where "the rarefied air is rather rasping on the constitution," miners with the aid of a hand cable climbed a slope too steep for snow to stick. They lowered the ore in buckets.

Even in so rough and remote a setting as a Western mining camp, settlers wanted schooling for their children. In the eventful year of 1864, when Montana became a Territory, vigilantes of the gold-mining towns of Bannack and Virginia City hanged 23 outlaws (including a sheriff and two deputies) for 102 murders—and each town started its first school. Said Territorial Governor Sidney Edgerton: "A self-ruling people must be an educated people, or prejudice and passion will assume power. . . . Children are in a sense the property of the public and it is one of the highest and most solemn duties of the state to furnish ample provision for their education."

Other Western states and territories shared the sense of public responsibility and, like Montana, established school systems among their first official acts.

In the West, as in the rest of the country, females teaching in the public schools outnumbered males. Of women in the West listed in the 1890 census as employed in "gainful and reputable" occupations, 12,000—one in ten—were teachers. They were earning slightly more than the national average public-school salary of $256 a year.

As mistress of a one-room school, a girl fresh out of high school or a special teacher-training course at a "normal" might be little older than her oldest pupils. The presence of a sister or brother who would tattle to parents added the reinforcement of home standards to make an unruly pupil toe the line.

More "reputable" than she might have wished, the schoolmarm even into the 20th century often was forbidden to marry, "keep company," or ride in a vehicle with any man but her father or brother. She could not wear fewer than two petticoats, smoke cigarettes, dye her hair, or loiter in ice cream parlors.

Unnamed and unsung in the chronicles, teachers work their wonders, making marks on history through names in the roll book.

For each of the states a "seminary of learning"

Brilliant mathematician Benjamin Peirce (right), having worked out a formula well over the heads of his Harvard pupils, would sometimes stare at his work: "Gentlemen . . . we don't know what it means, but we have proved it . . . it must be the truth."

A gap as wide as that between Peirce and his dumbfounded students kept most American youth from the early elitist colleges, geared to training men for the professions. After 1830, strides of reform narrowed the gulf.

Women, for 200 years left waiting on the porch of America's temples of higher learning, at last got a foot in the door. Oberlin, private coeducational college in Ohio, graduated the first three female "bachelors" in 1841 — and also pioneered in admitting blacks.

Amid strife of the Civil War, President Lincoln signed the Land-Grant Act, endowing colleges in each state. Greatly advancing the cause of mass education, low-tuition land-grant institutions raised the academic dignity of "agriculture and the mechanic arts" without excluding liberal arts and sciences. Women sat up front in science class at Iowa State University (below), which counted agricultural wizard George Washington Carver among its graduates, Class of 1894.

Colleges utilitarian in outlook could also make room for athletics, adding zest to campus routine. Men of Cornell's varsity crew in 1876 synchronized oars on Cayuga's waters — and beat Harvard by a length and a half. Cornell had a women's crew by 1896.

Though not until 1975 would federal rules ban sex discrimination in school athletics, the high-vaulting form of Ina E. Gittings at the University of Nebraska shows that by 1890 the "weak, fragile" American female of men's fancies had already come a long way.

If the 17th-century Puritans could have heard their descendants' shameless hymn to acquisitiveness, they would have turned in their graves.

The family too was slowly releasing its multitude of holds on the society, pulling back in isolation from the larger world, and sentimentalizing itself. As women enlarged their domestic role, the home became a shelter from the vicissitudes of the outside world. Apprentices, no longer "children" in the family, became trainees in a business. New institutions, such as almshouses and asylums, took over social burdens once assumed by the family. Adapting to a new aspiring society, education became less and less an instrument for setting the child into his proper niche in life. Education now became a springboard propelling the child out of his inherited past and sending him to wherever his talents could carry him.

Man now was optimistically considered to be a malleable creature, and America to be "in a plastic state." Benjamin Rush, a signer of the Declaration of Independence and a spokesman of the American Enlightenment, said it was possible "to convert men into republican machines." The stress on education for conversion (to patriots, not saints) echoed the old Puritan tradition. Thus the religious past was linked with the republican future — and both were fulfilled in the 19th-century common school movement. By the 1830's, as society reeled under the forces of industrialization, urbanization, and mass immigration, people listened seriously to the appeals for common education.

Horace Mann and others believed that an America fragmented by differing social classes, religions, languages, and ethnic groups must be republicanized and made homogeneous through common values if the experiment in popular government were to succeed. These mid-century reformers set about creating a school system for everyone — rich and poor; Anglo-Saxon, Irish, German; Baptist, Presbyterian, Catholic.

The family and other private mechanisms could no longer be responsible for education. Children now had to be wrenched loose from their families, their origins, and whatever entrapped them in peculiar and parochial outlooks. The reigning assumption about the nature of the child — far from the Puritans' concept of original sin — was now that of John Locke: "in a great measure passive, subject to such influences as others may choose to impress upon it." Educational reformers held that with such an assumption the world might be made over. The complicated process of acquainting the young with the world was now separated from society and settled within the four walls of the school. Teachers would be the new priests, preparing people for a new kind of salvation. They told themselves they had taken on an awesome burden:

Magnify your office, teacher!   *Are you not the prophet preacher,*
Higher than the kings of earth; —   *To the future giving birth?*

By the middle of the 19th century a remarkable new system had emerged. Education, now almost completely identified with schooling, was rapidly becoming a distinctly "public" enterprise — and in many places, compulsory for all children. Because education was now a science, its emerging structures needed statistics, libraries, centralized administrations, and professional teachers — now mostly women — trained in new "normal" schools with special certifications. School buildings became better lighted, airier, more spacious; curriculums became more utilitarian and less classical, and introduced such "electives" as bookkeeping and chemistry.

Here indeed was a new world of learning, whose main outlines and fundamental faiths were recognizably those of our own day. It was not simply that more schools had been developed or that larger numbers of children were being instructed. Rather, in those first 200 years an entirely new conception of education had been created to fulfill the purposes of a new kind of American society.

From experience all knowledge is founded, said philosopher John Locke. Through a brief 1899 field trip, pupils in Washington, D. C., jotted on the "white paper" of their minds: the iceman's tongs gripping ice and a spring scale weighing it, the cold touch of ice on fingers and tongue, the creak of wagon wheels and clop-clop of hoofs—morsels of education not only of the people but by the people.

Americans on the Move

Ray Allen Billington

Pushed from crowded cities and worn-out farms, pulled by the lure of land for the taking and riches for the finding, pioneers trekked toward the sunset and opportunity. Those who had wagons stocked up on sacks of salt, kegs of bacon, and trunks of clothes, and creaked westward in wagon trains at an ox's plodding pace. In barrels of corn meal, eggs might nestle—luxuries soon enjoyed and fondly remembered when supplies dwindled. A tar pot swung by a strap to silence the dry axle with a dab of tar and tallow, but nothing eased the jounce of strap-iron tires on wagons without springs. A Colt revolver could settle arguments, rout varmints, sound reveille— and, if handled clumsily, add a grave to the hundreds at trailside. When cholera struck, a tin lantern's light could paint a tragic shadow- play on a wagon's canvas top as a mother bent to her child in the prairie night. Despite risk and rigor, generations of settlers stretched their nation's dominion from sea to sea.

Westering ran in their blood. Their grandfathers had moved out from Britain's coastal beachheads, out from Jamestown and Charleston, out from New Haven and Plymouth and Boston, planting their farms first along the fertile river bottoms, then in the lands between, to overrun the coastal lowlands by the end of the 17th century. Their fathers had spread across the hilly piedmont and spilled over into the Great Valley of the Appalachians where they joined with Scotch-Irish from Ulster and Germans from the Rhenish Palatinate to push the frontier to the crest of the mountains. They themselves had breached that barrier to build their log cabins along the Nolichucky and Watauga in eastern Tennessee, or to follow Daniel Boone's Wilder- ness Road into bluegrass country where palisaded "Kentucky Stations" at Boones- borough and St. Asaph's and Harrodsburg marked the first conquest of the interior.

Now, in the waning years of the 18th century, they—and their sons—were eager to be on the move once more. For a generation they had been held back, as a revolu- tionary war was won and the borderlands quieted by military might and diplomatic negotiation. The westward tide was ready to roll again. All the ingredients of a major rush were there. Eastern farms with soils worn thin by repeated overcropping were selling at $14 to $50 an acre, while government lands in the interior were priced so rea- sonably after 1800 that a newcomer needed only $160 in cash to buy 320 acres, with another $480 due over the next four years. In the East old societies were solidifying under the domination of entrenched cliques that seemed to have lost touch with the common folk; in the West new societies were so plastic that any young man of proper skill and ambition might become a leader. And, equally important, the move from East to West was not impossibly difficult, for during the war years roads had been cleared pointing toward the interior. All were crude traces, with brush and small trees hacked away, streams bridged by felled trunks, and impassable swamps "corduroyed" with rows of logs, but they led the traveler to his destination—a better life, economically and socially, than he had known in the East.

So the march began, slowly at first, then gaining momentum as the 18th century drew to a close and the 19th began. The better-off rode in wagons carrying their house- hold goods, with livestock driven behind. The poorer trudged along with all their world- ly possessions strapped to their backs, slogging even through the snow of early spring "because everybody says it's good land." One traveler said 500 wagons passed through Albany, New York, in a single day; others reported the roads across Kentucky and

133

Tennessee so crowded that laggards were pushed from the highway. Everywhere on that new frontier—in western New York and Pennsylvania, in eastern Ohio, in Kentucky and Tennessee—all was bustle and confusion as newcomers slashed away the trees that symbolized the untamed wilderness; even shade trees, windbreaks, and maple groves were sacrificed on the altar of civilization.

"The woods are full of new settlers," wrote an observer in western New York. "Axes are resounding, and the trees literally falling about us as we passed. In one instance we were obliged to pass in a field through the smoke and flame of the trees that had lately been felled and were just fired." By 1810, when the Indian uprisings that merged into the War of 1812 stymied migration, Kentucky and Tennessee and Ohio were states, and Indiana and Illinois had earned territorial status.

With peace in 1815, pioneers hankered to be on the move again. They were spurred now by the realization that the Indians had been mercilessly defeated during the fighting —those to the northwest by William Henry Harrison at the Battle of the Thames, those to the southwest by Andrew Jackson at the Battle of Horseshoe Bend. Surely the tribes could be cowed into surrendering their ancestral lands.

And what lands those were! To the north of the chain of settlements that hugged the Ohio River lay a wilderness paradise, where the countryside had been flattened and enriched by the great glaciers of the Ice Age and where the humus-rich soil was said to be "so fat that it will grease your fingers." To the south lay the fertile bottomlands and plains of Alabama and Mississippi, largely unsettled by whites. Fortunes could be made there by growing that glamorous new crop, cotton, now profitable for the first time because an ingenious Yankee, Eli Whitney, had invented a "gin" to extract seeds from the fibers. The Mississippi Valley, north and south, seemed fated to become the granary and clothier of the world. The fortunate who reached there first would surely find pots of gold at the end of every rainbow.

Overcrowding and worn-out soils at home also helped to spark the "Great Migration" to these lands of promise. First to invade the Lake Plains to the north—the Old Northwest—were small farmers driven off their lands in the southern backcountry by

"O the luxury of a house, a house!" Words of one pioneer woman seem etched in the faces of others as they rest near Colorado Springs, perhaps during the midday respite called "nooning." Only foolhardy pioneers went west alone; many joined trains (opposite) up to three miles long. At a trail fork they might find a red barrel labeled "Post Office" to receive their letters of hope and despair.

expanding cotton plantations. The trip was easier now; like pioneers before them, some bought or built flatboats and drifted down the Ohio. Travelers reported a regular procession of these ungainly craft, a sweating farmer at the sweeps, his wife churning or hanging out the wash, children playing on the deck, cows munching hay in the prow. Others followed the National Road, a broad, gravel-paved highway built across the mountains by the federal government; it reached Wheeling by 1818 and central Ohio by 1833. "We are seldom out of sight, as we travel on this grand track, towards the Ohio, of family groups before and behind us," one traveler wrote. "Old America," observed another, "seems to be breaking up and moving westward."

Most of the travelers camped by the roadside at night, huddling around their flickering campfires for light and warmth. The more affluent patronized the inns that mushroomed along the highway, enduring poor food, the noise of barroom brawls, and the indignity of sleeping two or three to a bed, with teamsters and judges, legislators and herdsmen, assigned indiscriminately to places between the none-too-clean sheets. "A most almighty beautiful democratic amalgam," one Westerner called it. The inns of the frontier made strange bedfellows—and served as living testimony to the fact that, in the West, scarcity and expediency proved all men equal.

Settlers who got there first felt right at home in woodlands like those they had left behind. In southern Ohio, Indiana, and Illinois they found rippling streams to supply them with water, trees to give them wood, groves to shelter game animals; they could even judge the land's fertility by the density of forest on it. But by the early 1830's the wooded hill country had been comfortably filled, turning the tide of latecomers to the level country farther north. Here they faced a new environment: the prairie. To get water a man had to dig a well. To build shelter he had to buy lumber or peel up the sod and stack it into a cubicle. And just to break the sod for a planting he had to hire a huge plow designed for the job, plus three to six yoke of oxen to pull its massive blade through the dense mat of grass roots. This alone cost about two dollars an acre—and that was more than he had paid for the land.

Undaunted, the prairie pioneers moved in. The region became the mecca of Yankees and New Yorkers driven from ancestral farms by a vogue for sheep-growing that swept the Northeast, where burgeoning textile mills were creating a market for wool. Michigan felt the impact first, then northern Indiana and Illinois. "Almost all vessels from the lower lakes are full of passengers," a Chicago newspaper reported in 1835, "and our streets are thronged with wagons loaded with household furniture and the implements necessary to farming." From Illinois the pioneers spilled over into Wisconsin in the late 1830's and into Iowa a few years later. All the upper Great Lakes country was abustle as trees were felled, prairie sod broken, cabins built, and split-rail fences hurried into place to guard planted fields from wandering cattle.

The Old Southwest—the southern backcountry stretching west to the Mississippi—enjoyed an equally remarkable transition between 1815 and the 1840's. Indians had to be removed first, for western Georgia, Alabama, and Mississippi was the home of Indians later called the "Five Civilized Tribes"—Cherokee, Chickasaw, Choctaw, Creek, and Seminole. Some had followed the white man's path so exactly that they operated plantations, owned slaves, had their own cotton gins and grist mills, even published their own newspaper. But the white man's ways were no guarantee of the white man's friendship; the tribes were ruthlessly driven westward to a "permanent" home in the "Indian Territory"—modern Oklahoma minus its panhandle. On their heels as they departed came the invading hordes, drawn largely from the Carolinas and eastern Georgia—where repeated plantings of tobacco had worn and gullied the land—to sweep across western Georgia, then over Alabama and Mississippi into Louisiana.

THE NATIONAL Wagon Road Guide.

In the trail of the Buffalo, followed first the Indian, then the White Man.

"Over the Rocky Mountains' height,
Like ocean in its tided might,
The living sea rolls onward, on!
And onward on, the stream shall pour
And reach the far Pacific's shore,
And till the plains of Oregon."

SAN FRANCISCO:
PUBLISHED BY WHITTON, TOWNE & CO
125 Clay St., corner Sansome.
1858.

"The living sea rolls onward, on!"

Hoofs and wheels beyond counting carved an eloquent autograph where the Oregon Trail labored up a Wyoming knoll. Latecomers found ruts so deep their wheel hubs scraped the sides. With iron bars they hacked the ruts wider lest a hub gather grit that could wear the wheel loose. Such rigors surprised pioneers guided—and often disastrously misguided—by trail books whose deskbound authors may never have seen the routes they detailed. Week after weary week, the "living sea" hymned on one book's cover (above) strewed the trailside with flotsam. Among the debris, as in this sketch by a forty-niner (below), dead animals lay rotting. The graves of their masters averaged 17 to a mile.

First came the small farmers who were on the cutting edge of all frontiers—men of little means, vast ambition, and an unquenchable belief that the next move would reward them with the prosperity that had eluded them before. Not long after they made the first scars on the wilderness an Eastern planter was likely to appear, spying out lands suitable to plantation agriculture, unwilling to gamble his sizable investment of slaves and materials on unproven soils. Finding the right spot, he would buy out the "improvements" of a dozen small farmers (sending them leapfrogging west once more), then return home to sell his worn fields and lead his family westward. They made an imposing procession: the planter and his family in a buggy at its head, wagons filled with chattels, herds of livestock, bands of slaves marching under the watchful eye of an overseer. "It would seem," wrote a newspaper correspondent as he watched them pass, "as if North and South Carolina were pouring forth their population by swarms. . . . The fires of their encampments made the woods blaze in all directions." By the 1840's the "Cotton Kingdom" was established—and the foundations were laid for the bitter sectional conflicts that would later erupt into civil war.

Most of the pioneers who settled the Old Southwest—and a majority of their cousins around the Great Lakes—felt content to develop their holdings and "grow up with the country." But a restless fringe among them yearned to move on almost before they had cleared their first fields and planted their first crops. These were the men with the West in their eyes, the congenital wanderers who led the march westward. "This is a land of plenty," one of them explained, "but we are proceeding to a land of abundance." Let the soil begin to lose its youthful energy, let strangers press within a few miles, let rumors fly of richer lands ahead, and they were off like the wind, never satisfied if a white man was between them and sundown.

In western Pennsylvania empty dwellings stood by the roadsides, abandoned in "the rage for descending the Ohio"; in Ohio half-cleared farms lay deserted by their owners because Illinois beckoned; in Illinois men heard of the new meccas, Missouri and Iowa. The abandoned farm was as symbolic of frontier restlessness as the ghost towns that still dot the West. "He lives and dies in hope," wrote one who knew this manner of frontiersman, and he might have added that the hope was all too seldom realized.

The nation was fortunate that expansion had bred such restlessness, for a mighty compulsion was needed for the next step westward. The lands along the Mississippi posed no great problems to the pioneers. Missouri filled so rapidly that it entered the Union in 1821; Arkansas was admitted in 1836, Iowa in 1846. But beyond their western borders lay a chain of Indian reservations granted the transplanted Eastern tribes for "as long as trees grow and the waters run," and beyond that, the vastness of the semi-arid plains, labeled by early explorers as the Great American Desert, and the Rocky Mountains. To reach more hospitable lands on the Pacific slope, frontiersmen had to hurdle nearly 2,000 miles of hostile country. Here loomed a challenge to test the ambition and stamina of even the most restless pioneer.

The "men of the Western Waters" had learned their frontiering on the banks of the Mississippi. Toughened by rough-and-tumble life in a raw new land where the law was carried in holsters and boot-tops, swaggeringly proud of their country and disdainful of all others, brave to the point of foolhardiness, these were the self-proclaimed "ringtailed roarers, half horse and half alligator," who could outdrink, outspit, outride, outshoot, and outfight any man in all creation. That the lands they coveted were already occupied by Europeans (the Southwest by Spaniards and, after 1821, by Mexicans; the Northwest shared with the British) was to them a challenge, not a deterrent. Their manifest destiny shone clearly; they were to be (in the spread-eagle language of the day) "the benefactors of their race, the founders of a new, enlightened and powerful

"We shall frequently meet with them"

Explorer John C. Frémont's quiet understatement of 1843 holds no hint of hundreds of battles and decades of strife to come as the frontier leaped to the Pacific, then turned to fill the mountains and plains where Indians had lived for uncountable generations. Tribes such as the Crow (opposite) long had hunted amid ample game. To them, wagon trains were at worst a nuisance, at best a source of trade or occasional plunder.

But in desert wastes beyond the Rockies, small bands of Indians lived in delicate truce with a harsh environment, wresting from the land "roots, seeds, and grass, every vegetable that affords any nourishment, and every living animal thing, insect or worm. . . ." To these tribes—derided as "Diggers" because they dug pit houses and grubbed for food—the passing wagons spelled hunger as game fled or fell to the gun, cattle ate the browse, and encampments ringed the water holes. Desperate Diggers turned to preying on each summer's bounty of tasty cattle and horses, a last-straw torment to travelers already exasperated by peril and privation. Too late the Diggers' brothers on the Plains awoke to the threat of encroachment; bloody wars and tenuous treaties boxed them all into reservations.

Mormon emigrants might seem to draw their handcarts with jaunty gait (below), for they had somewhat less to fear from Indians than did "Gentile" pioneers. Mormon writ saw Indians as Lamanites, a Lost Tribe of Israel; this perspective on Indian ancestors helped win the red men's respect and even some conversions. Many whites were "Amerikats" to be hated and feared—but Mormons came into the Indians' midst as friends.

"We will suffer greatly"

Not even the prophesy of a Paiute chief fore-told the miseries Indians would endure on reservations: hunger, shame, dependence on conquerors. But another Paiute, the prophet Wovoka, preached a religion of hope to leaders such as Sioux Chief Kicking Bear (above). To restive Sioux crowded onto reservations like Pine Ridge in South Dakota (left), Kicking Bear taught Wovoka's rites, vowing that a great landslide would bury the intruders and restore the Indians to a land reborn. Whites called the ritual a "Ghost Dance" and, fearing bloodshed, banned it, though it forbade violence. Enforcing troops slew some 200 Sioux in a last Indian "battle" —the massacre at Wounded Knee in 1890.

state," the lusty visionaries who would bear the "blazing light of civil and religious liberty" to the "now wild shores of the great Pacific."

The usual precursors of expansion—fur trappers and missionaries—led the way in the 1830's. Before long the Mountain Men all but put themselves out of business by their relentless trapping of fur-bearing animals; within a decade the Rocky Mountain country had been so thoroughly trapped out that, as one trapper lamented, "lizards grow poor, and wolves lean against the sand banks to howl." But they explored the West almost down to the last square inch, blazing trails and noting where the good lands lay. And they had weakened the Indians with liquor, disease, and the subtle undermining of Indian self-sufficiency. They and the zealous missionaries brought back tales to make a pioneer's soles itch.

At the same time a pulse-stirring propaganda campaign, launched by self-appointed evangelists of empire, painted the Far West in irresistible colors for all who could read or listen. So potent was the barrage of superlatives that listeners soon began parroting what they had been told: California, said one prospective immigrant, offered "such fascinations as almost to call the angels and saints from their blissful garden and diamond temples in the heavens." Malaria, the "shaking ague" that was a universal affliction in the Mississippi Valley, was reputedly unknown in that paradise. The only Californian said to have a chill was considered such a curiosity that people came from miles around to watch him shake. In Oregon "rain seldom falls, even in the winter season; but the dews are sufficiently heavy to compensate for its absence." There beets grew three feet in diameter, turnips five feet around, and wheat with seven heads to the stalk and stems as thick as walking sticks. "They do say, gentlemen," avowed one speaker in

"Gold! Gold! . . . Thousands are going"

New Yorker Philip Hone didn't exaggerate; in 1849 some 85,000 fortune-seekers fell on California for a share of the "color" first spotted in John Sutter's millrace the year before. Back East, every leaky hulk that could float swallowed a glut of passengers and raced to San Francisco. Once there, even the crews lit out for the diggings, leaving the bay littered with ghost ships, some with cargo still aboard. Many were dragged ashore and used as living quarters; others just sank. So did the hopes of all but a lucky few of their passengers.

Gold in his eyes but only dreams in his sack, Minnesota schoolteacher George W. Northrup posed with tools for reaping a fortune—and pistols for holding onto it. Perhaps solace waited in the jug, for he never left Minnesota; Indian arrows felled him at 27.

"Gold must be had," wrote a forty-niner who reached California only to die in his twenties; like so many, he had been "willing to brave most anything in its acquisition."

Missouri, "they do say that out in Oregon the pigs are running about under the great acorn trees, round and fat, and already cooked, with knives and forks sticking in them so that you can cut off a slice whenever you are hungry." Why would anyone want to stay at home when such abundance beckoned?

The movement began, slowly at first, with small parties plodding westward over the Oregon and California trails. Not until 1843 did the tide gain momentum. That spring about 1,000 persons gathered at the jumping-off point near Independence, Missouri. They knew they would be venturing beyond the pale of the law, so they resorted to democratic procedures. A constitution with an elaborate preamble was adopted ("Whereas, we deem it necessary for the government of all societies, either civil or military, to adopt certain rules and regulations. . . ."), a captain chosen, a Council of Ten elected to settle disputes and try offenders for any acts "subversive of good order and military discipline." But scarcely had the march begun when a dispute arose and generated such heat that the party split; those with no cattle pushed on rapidly, and a "cow column" followed more slowly. Both reached Oregon's Willamette Valley in October. One emigrant wrote in his diary, "Friday, October 27.—Arrived at Oregon City at the falls of the Willamette. Saturday, October 28.—Went to work."

Over the next few years the Oregon and California trails guided a steady stream of wagon trains westward. At first a typical train mustered from 50 to 75 men with their families, for experience showed that parties of this size were formidable enough to discourage Indian attack and small enough not to exhaust pasturage. When large parties proved unwieldy, trains shrank to eight or ten wagons. Large or small, each train elected a captain and each adopted rules that pledged obedience to his orders—and the

"The gold is here sure enough"

Though "in rags, almost barefooted, without provisions and almost without tools," Isaac Wistar and his fellow forty-niners rejoiced at journey's end, "for we . . . can raise the color ourselves everywhere, even on this very creek." In those early gold rush days a lone prospector could hunker down by an icy stream, pan up water and gravel, and watch for a glint of gold as he swirled with numbed fingers for ten minutes or so—carefully, lest the gold slosh out with the lighter grit.

Despite skimpy yields, aching bones, and hands turned leathery by the chill of snowmelt streams, loners still dip their pans and hope for the fortune that—who knows?—may someday pan out.

Wistar and his party were already too late for "crevice mining," the method of early prospectors, who had only to gouge the gold from dry gulches with any handy tool, even a teaspoon. Most of the later arrivals, finding even stream beds panned clean, banded together to sink pits and tunnels and build long sluice boxes that, like the prospector's pan, combed color from dross.

Miners in Idaho (opposite) shovel ore into a "long tom." Sluices stretching up to 50 feet were lined with cleats or heavy rocks to stop the gold but let the waste wash away—a prodigal process that lost perhaps as much as it found. Without a handy stream to divert into the tom, some crews had to build flumes to tap creeks far upslope.

Hopeful hordes soon ended the heyday of placer mining—a term that rhymes with "passer" and refers to deposits at or near the surface. Then prospectors became true miners, tunneling ever deeper for ore.

Aiming to get rich and get out, miners threw together slapdash settlements and bore discomforts with lusty good humor. No ocean lapped "Ocean Grove" near Piñon, Colorado (below), a mining camp whose signs for ladies and tourists cheered lonely men who rarely saw either. When ore petered out, so did most of these villages of caves and canvas and packing-crates. But cities born in such squalor and dreams live on throughout the West.

Folk in finery flood the streets of Cripple Creek, Colorado, on Independence Day, 1893. Soon to outstrip all its era's goldfields but one, "Cripple" had already outgrown the shacks of its founders—but not their earthy pastimes: three-day poker binges, dance-hall brawls, wenching here on Bennett Avenue. Cowtowns boomed too; in a Dodge City store, "endless variety" awaited all who prospered.

right to displace him whenever he exceeded his authority. Travelers often drove scaled-down versions of the Conestoga wagons that had been used for freighting since the early 18th century. More commonly, they journeyed in covered "emigrant wagons," sturdy farm vehicles pulled by oxen or mules (horses were unable to endure the long haul), each loaded with 1,500 to 2,500 pounds of food and goods. Such travel allowed few comforts, but at least these peripatetic democracies were usually safe; only when travelers took untested routes, left too late to avoid winter snows, or set out in a caravan too small to deter Indian attack was there any great threat to life.

As the settlers' numbers grew, so did their demands for a stable government. "Where the highest court of appeal is the rifle," said the Oregonians in droll understatement, "safety in life and property cannot be depended on." By 1846 some 5,000 Americans shared the Oregon Country with a sprinkling of British settlers and the Hudson's Bay Company. The Americans were bent on winning the region for the United States, but the company stood in the way. Its officials must have tossed through many a sleepless night behind their log stockade at Fort Vancouver, wondering when those rambunctious Americans might storm across the Columbia River with guns and torches to carry out their oft-repeated threat. The presence of those truculent frontiersmen, all skilled in the use of "the Bowie knife, Revolving Pistol and Rifle," convinced the Hudson's Bay Company at last that its destiny lay elsewhere; a diplomatic settlement in 1846 awarded the entire region south of the 49th parallel to the Americans.

By then only about 1,000 Americans lived in the Sacramento and San Joaquin valleys of California. Openly disdainful of their Mexican overlords, the settlers stirred up a revolution in the spring of 1846, hoisted over the plaza at Sonoma a flag bearing the figure of a bear, and declared their independence. The Bear Flag Revolt merged into the larger war between Mexico and the United States that began later that year. With peace in 1848 not only California but all the Southwest was transferred to the United States. Americans on the move had carried their nation's boundaries to the Pacific.

Some of the best-prepared pioneers ever to cross the Plains had recently set up a community by the Great Salt Lake in present-day Utah; soon they would apply for statehood. Members of the Church of Jesus Christ of Latter-day Saints—the Mormons—had endured intense persecution in the East, fleeing from one community after another, until in 1844 their Prophet, Joseph Smith, was murdered by a mob as he languished in an Illinois jail. Their only escape, they had decided, was to move again, this time to lands no one else wanted where they could at last be left alone.

Smith's mantle of leadership fell to 43-year-old Brigham Young, an early convert. Young had trusted the accounts of Western explorers, and in them had read that the most isolated region in the West was the valley of the Great Salt Lake, bastioned by mountains on the east and vast, broiling deserts on the west. Snowmelt coursed down the mountainsides, assuring life-giving water supplies to a haven of "good soil and good grass, adapted to civilized settlements," as one account described the valley.

During the next year the Mormons sold their belongings (usually for a pittance), abandoned their neat, substantial brick homes, and started westward, to rendezvous in the autumn of 1846 at Winter Quarters, near modern Omaha. Young spent the cold months instructing the Saints in plains travel, urging courage in the face of hard work, disease, and winter storms that together claimed 600 lives. In April, 1847, a "Pioneer Band" of 143 men, three women, and two children set out, blazing a new "Mormon Trail" along the north bank of the Platte River to avoid contact with the "Gentiles," who were crowding the Oregon Trail along the south bank that year.

The Mormons' objective was complete isolation in a remote stronghold that would provide them with the necessities of life. But the vista that greeted them when they crested the mountains and descended into the valley of the Great Salt Lake was hardly inviting: "a broad and barren plain," as one account describes it, "hemmed in by mountains, blistering in the burning rays of the midsummer sun. No waving fields, no swaying forests, no verdant meadows... but on all sides a seemingly interminable waste of sagebrush... the paradise of the lizard, the cricket and the rattlesnake." Brigham Young, abed with a fever in one of the wagons, realized they had reached their destination. "This," tradition reports him as saying, "is the place."

The Mormons had found isolation; now they must persuade the desert to sustain them. They began to till the soil—and the sun-baked earth shattered their plows. Irrigation was the obvious answer, for experiments showed that the land yielded to the plowman and bore bountifully when watered. But this took time, and the 1,800 Saints who reached Utah that summer were to endure great hardship before spring came, most of them with only their wagons to ward off the icy blasts, and only thistles, sego-lily roots, and oxhide soup to keep them from starvation.

Brigham Young's genius and the willingness of the Mormons to subjugate their

"There is a good deal of sin and wickedness"

"Stealing, lying, swearing, drinking, gambling and murdering," howled a shocked New Englander in a boomtown of the West. An 1854 account agreed, for "dust was plentier than pleasure, pleasure more enticing than virtue." And when an Eastern writer damned Cripple Creek's street of bawdy houses, the town retaliated by naming "the line" after him; conveniently, his name was Julian Street.

When a pinch of gold would fetch a drink, maybe two, a miner with a sackful could choose his solace from a week of toil. In Telluride, Colorado, he could belly up to the Cosmopolitan Saloon's mahogany bar (below) for a snort by the marshal's elbow. To the click of a wheel or the slap of an ace, he could double his stake—or lose it.

And when his gaze drifted to the beauty clad only in a picture frame, he knew where to find the perfumed original. Like the prostitute who posed, nameless and shameless, for an early photograph (opposite), she might cost $400, even $600, a night; she might answer to "Pussycat Nell" or "Big Flossie"; she might be booked up until tomorrow. But she would make him bathe, shave—and behave. In subtle ways she too helped tame the West.

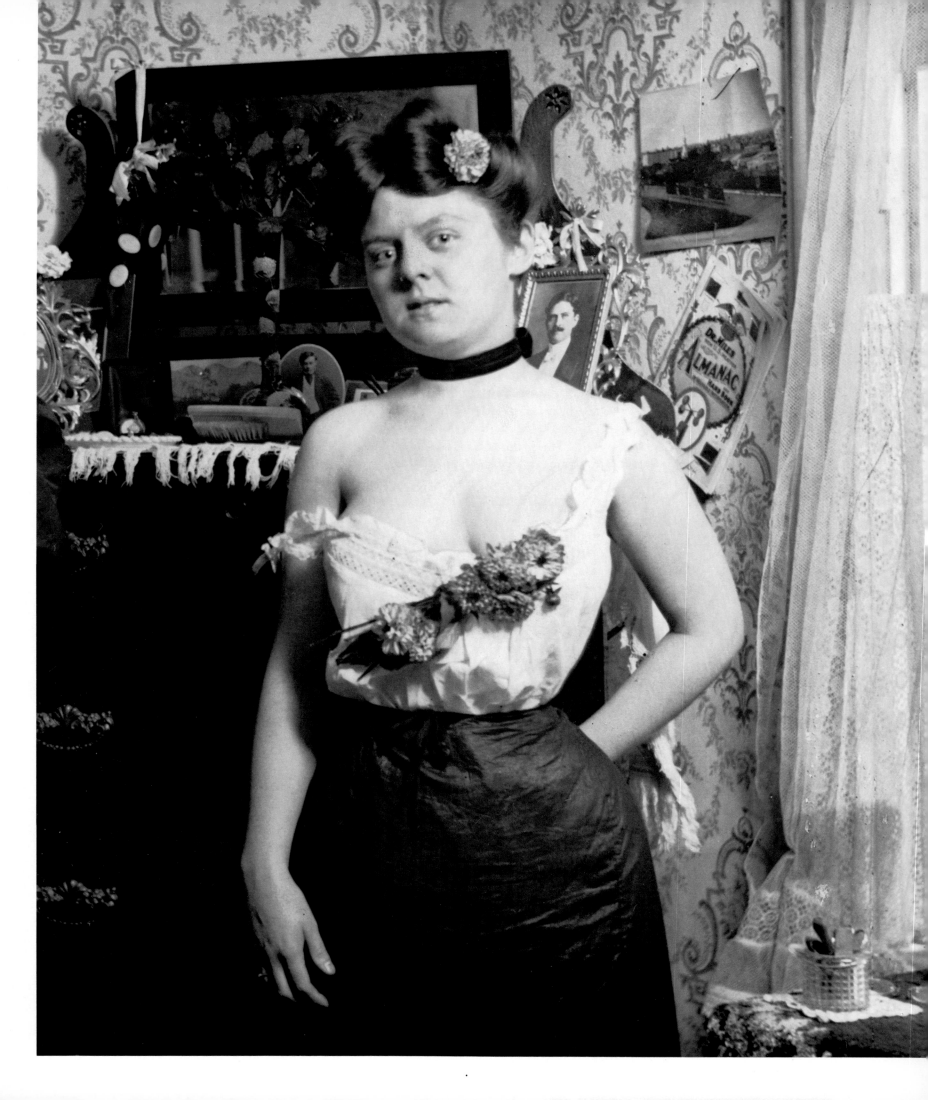

Battling with boasts

As the nation surged westward to the Mississippi, the hinterland rivers and forests gave rise to new types of frontiersmen — keelboaters and backwoodsmen whose antic brags and prodigious feats reached an apex with the legendary adventures of men like Mike Fink and Davy Crockett.

The classic yarn of the frontier, calculated to shock and awe Easterners, describes a brawl between two backwoods bully boys. Always in these encounters, the preliminary verbal sparring includes extravagant boasts and rhetoric salted with backwoods expressions.

Nimrod Wildfire, feeling "wolfy" after ten days without a fight, rudely awakens a dozing keelboatman. The two exchange insults. At length the riverman proclaims: "Mister, I'm the best man — if I ain't, I wish I may be tetotaciously exflunctified! I can whip my weight in wildcats and ride straight through a crab-apple orchard on a flash of lightning — clear meat-ax disposition! And what's more, I once back'd a bull off a bridge."

"Poh," counters Nimrod, "what do I keer for that? I can tote a steamboat up the Mississippi and over the Allegheny Mountains. My father can whip the best man in Old Kaintuck and I can whip my father. When I'm good-natured I weigh about a hundred-seventy, but when I'm mad, I weigh a ton."

They rush into each other "like two steamboats going 60 miles an hour."

"He was a pretty severe colt," recalls Nimrod, "but no part of a priming to such a feller as me. I put it to him right droll — tickled the varmint till he squealed like a young colt, bellowed 'enough' and swore I was a rip staver. Says he, 'Stranger . . . if you'd stand for Congress, I'd vote for you next 'lection.'"

ambitions to the welfare of the group allowed the development of a cooperative social order that functioned with admirable efficiency. Salt Lake City was laid out, irrigation ditches were dug, each person was allotted the land he could cultivate most effectively, and new communities were sited wherever streams gushed or veins of iron and coal were discovered. By 1849 the Mormons were established firmly enough to draft a constitution for the State of Deseret (a term denoting the industrious honeybee, borrowed from the *Book of Mormon*). Their petition for admission to the Union stirred a controversy for many years before Utah became a state.

Scarcely had the Saints sunk their roots when their isolation was doubly threatened, first by the transfer of their territory to the United States after the Mexican War, then by the discovery of gold in California in January 1848. For a time the nation took this news calmly; promoters had too often "humbugged" frontiersmen with fake tales of riches. Then President James K. Polk, anxious to justify his grabbing of California from Mexico, reported in December that "accounts of the abundance of gold in that territory are of such an extraordinary character as would scarcely command belief were they not corroborated by the authentic reports of officers in the public service." These words from on high, bolstered by the spectacle of a tea caddy in the War Office laden with 230 ounces of California gold, evaporated all skepticism.

Overnight the nation went mad. Newspapers outdid each other's extravagances: "The Eldorado of the old Spaniards is discovered at last," crowed one. "We are on the brink of an Age of Gold," exulted another. Tales of fabulous finds crowded their columns: a stream bed of solid metal being chipped out with pickaxes . . . a claim that paid $20,000 in six days . . . Indians who threw away their arrows and stuffed their quivers with precious metals. All who could read — or just listen — caught the fever; everywhere once-rational men danced to the "Gold Diggers Waltz" or sang

Oh, Susannah, don't you cry for me,
I'm gone to California with my wash-bowl on my knee.

"The coming of the Messiah or the dawn of the Millennium," reported one newspaper, "would not have excited anything like the interest."

Perhaps 25,000 left the East by sea that winter, bound for Panama and the hazardous journey across the isthmus or for the equally dangerous voyage around Cape Horn. Others spent the cold months organizing "mining companies," transforming the farm wagon into a "prairie schooner," poring over the dozens of guidebooks that appeared miraculously, and dreaming of the bags of dust and nuggets that would be theirs when they reached the "diggings." With the first hint of spring the forty-niners overflowed the embarkation towns along the Missouri River — Independence, Kanesville, Westport, and St. Joseph — to jam every room to capacity and strip the stores of shovels, picks, washing pans, and miscellaneous nonessentials, most destined to be discarded along the trail. Even before the prairie grass began to green they set out, on foot and in small caravans of wagons. Some starved, more died of the cholera that pursued them westward. But most reached the Mother Lode country after hardships that toughened them for the even more rigorous ordeal ahead. As many as 55,000 emigrants may have followed the overland trails that summer of 1849.

Nearly all faced tragic disillusionment, for by the time they arrived the good mining sites had already been appropriated. Some turned tail for home, but most stayed on to work old diggings or prospect for new, sustained by the dream of the fortune to be found in the next washing pan. Theirs was a miserable life, working long hours standing knee-deep in icy streams; subsisting on coarse bread, greasy pork, and beans; drinking coffee "strong enough to float a millstone"; sleeping in brush shanties or drafty tents.

"We are out of 'life' just now"

"Life" meant whiskey in the Silver City *Avalanche* of February 3, 1866. Soon wagons would bring more to this Idaho boomtown where hip-high stacks of silver bars waited in the street for shipment. A kerosene lamp and iron stove added elegance to the Idaho Hotel, whose 50 rooms still welcomed tourists a century later. But life, like whiskey, had run out with the ore.

A swayback bunkhouse in nearby De Lamar (left) dreams of days when it too was called a hotel—as was anything from haymow to whorehouse. Ghost towns by the thousand—Kansas alone once counted over 2,500 —dot West and East alike, relics of the restless spirit that chooses opportunity over permanence. Each is heir to Jamestown, America's first "permanent" town—a ghost by 1722.

From green gold under the miner's boot grew empires beyond his dreams. Cattlemen found grama and buffalo grass, free for the grazing, that could feed vast herds on drives to faraway markets. Americans ate beef as only Europe's wealthy could. In the 1870's barbed wire cut homesteads from open range — and faceless men took clippers and law in hand as the sodbuster and the cowboy warred.

In ramshackle mining camps named Whisky Bar or Hangtown or Hell's Half Acre or Red Dog, the streets lay boot-deep in dust and littered with old bottles and sardine tins. Illness and death visited the mining camps regularly, and homesickness took an emotional toll almost as frightful as the physical.

Every new camp attracted a swarm of desperadoes, gamblers, harlots, and "claim jumpers" who threatened the lives, property, or well-being of the law-abiding majority. So the miners in each camp arranged mass meetings, organized the area into a "mining district," drafted a "mining code" to regulate the size and working of claims, and elected a sheriff, district recorder, and other officials needed to enforce the laws they had made. When this machinery proved ineffective, the usual answer was a vigilante committee to warn undesirables away and hang those who refused to take the hint.

But the all-too-frequent miscarriages of justice perpetrated by these extralegal bodies offended the strong urge of American frontiersmen for responsible law enforcement. Though the mining districts had no more legal authority than the vigilantes, at least they rested on a solid democratic base, mirrored the will of the majority, and served as a provisional form of government until the federal structure could be extended westward. This was universally desired. "Congregate a hundred Americans anywhere beyond the settlements," wrote an observer at one mining camp, "and they immediately lay out a city, frame a State constitution and apply for admission into the Union, while twenty-five of them become candidates for the United States Senate."

The "majorities" who grasped the reins of government refused to grant either rights or protection to the "minorities" among them. Few native peoples have suffered as did the California Indians at the hands of the forty-niners; within a decade most of the tens of thousands who had lived in relative peace for generations were either exterminated or driven from their lands. Nearly all mining codes were marred by clauses barring Asians, Mexicans, and Latin Americans from operating mines, with the oft-repeated justification that "coloured men were not privileged to work in a country intended only for American citizens." In camp after camp non-whites were murdered, driven out by mobs, heavily taxed, or allowed to work only "tailings," the scattered mounds of ore abandoned as worthless. The 1,000 blacks who had reached California by 1850 avoided similar treatment just by staying in the cities where prejudice was slightly less

virulent. Frontiering mothered democracy, but a democracy that was sadly restricted.

As surface wealth was skimmed off and shafts had to be sunk to gold-bearing rock far below, thousands of prospectors faced a choice: Should they assure themselves security by working as tunnelers or quartz-mill operators—or should they invest in a mule and outfit to continue their search elsewhere? To many, the answer was easy; the true prospector could no more resist the excitement of questing than he could a faro game. Wrote one who knew the breed: "What a clover-field is to a steer, the sky to the lark, a mudhole to a hog, such are new diggings to a miner."

From California, prospectors fanned out over the West in search of new diggings. Most wandered away their lives. When one of them did strike it rich, a rush followed as prospectors and miners, gamblers and saloon-keepers, merchants and outlaws hurried off to the favored spot. Like as not the boom quickly fizzled; like as not another find was reported not far away. Overnight the whole population would be off once more, leaving homes and furniture and even clothing. Better to lose a few possessions than miss out on a fortune! The laggard was the loser; the first on the scene skimmed off the cream. The American "go-ahead" spirit was nowhere better expressed than on the exploding mining frontier.

In that feverish search for sudden wealth the prospectors peopled much of the Far West. Most of their placer mines were soon exhausted. Scattered ghost towns remain today as monuments to the enterprise—and bad luck—of their founders. But now and then a truly spectacular find was made. In Nevada the famed Comstock Lode yielded $300 million in gold and silver. In the Pike's Peak country a series of strikes laid the basis for Colorado's economic growth. In the Black Hills of South Dakota the nation's last major rush spawned Deadwood and other wide-open towns, where the "Wild West" made its last stand against the tides of law and order. Less spectacular discoveries in the Pacific Northwest, in Montana and Idaho, in Arizona and New Mexico, lured farmers and tradesmen who moved in to cater to the needs of the hard-rock miners. The West was building its first permanent population.

California boasted only 380,000 inhabitants when the Civil War began, New Mexico 95,000, and all the other territories beyond the Rockies fewer than 100,000. But the frontiersmen were a vocal crew, and they wanted one thing above all else: better communication with the "States." They thirsted for letters, newspapers, merchandise, a sense of belonging to a homeland temporarily forsaken. They needed a bond more reliable than the occasional wagon train, more rapid than the ships that took months to round the Horn. Railroads were untested and expensive. The answer: stagecoach service subsidized by the federal government, for the distances were so great and profits so problematical that private enterprise was not interested.

The Butterfield Overland Express Company was awarded a $600,000 annual grant with the stipulation that it provide mail service twice a week between St. Louis and San Francisco, completing each run in 25 days or less, following a 2,812-mile route that dipped south to El Paso. Service began in September 1858, when a handsome Concord coach swept away from San Francisco and another from Tipton, Missouri (reached by rail from St. Louis). For 24 days they traveled day and night, changing horses and drivers at way stations along the route, until on October 9 and 10 cheering crowds welcomed them to their destinations. All the nation celebrated the forging of a new link between East and West. "I cordially congratulate you upon the result," President Buchanan lauded John Butterfield, a massive, square-jawed man with many years of stagecoaching under his belt. "It is a glorious triumph for civilization and the Union."

The stagecoach was more glamorous than effective as a bond between East and West, and the railroad would soon take its place. Once more government subsidies were

"We were without law"

One pioneer summed up the solution for folk beyond the reach of courts: They made their own law. In the rush for riches, few men had time to sit on juries, few towns had money for jails. So, when warnings went unheeded, out of camps and boomtowns galloped vigilantes to head off the desperado, hold a kangaroo court, and lay on the lash or "stretch hemp." Such a spectacle quieted many a rowdy.

East and West reveled in nickel magazines and dime novels that told wild tales of lawmen and badmen larger than life.

No. 577   NEW YORK, JUNE, 1. 1912   5 CENTS

The BUFFALO BILL STORIES
Devoted To Far West Life

BUFFALO BILL AND the SILK LASSO   OR PAWNEE BILL'S MASQUERADE

BY THE AUTHOR OF "BUFFALO BILL"

STREET & SMITH
PUBLISHERS
NEW YORK

Suddenly the tables were turned, and the masked outlaw found himself
underneath the famous scout and looking into the ominous
barrel of Pawnee Bill's revolver.

"So that every poor man may have a home"

With these words President Lincoln endorsed the Homestead Act that in 1862 gave a settler 160 acres if he worked it five years. Thousands thronged to the Great Plains and there formed "claim clubs," akin to the miners' vigilance committees, to keep order and thwart claim-jumpers. Hardy homesteaders sank roots, sweated, prospered—and posed for the itinerant photographer. John Curry and his wife (right) emptied their Nebraska sod house of all its status symbols: sewing machine, Christmas wreath, and a caged bird to soften the silence with a homey chirp.

Drought, insects, loneliness drove many a 'steader out. And so did the same laws that lured them here, laws made back in the wooded and watered East where 160 acres could support a family farm. Not here; the plains had long been called the Great American Desert. "The government is willing," said one writer, "to bet the homesteader 160 acres of land that he'll starve to death on it in less than five years." Unless the 'steader bent the law, he could lose the bet.

A claim had to have a house with a window. Some built with only a door and "installed" a window frame on a nail inside. Couples held two claims by raising one house, half on hers, half on his. One cabin sufficed for many if built on wheels and rolled to a claim on the day the claimant swore a cabin was there. And a rule requiring a 12-by-12 house did not say feet; a 12-inch house (below) sheltered its ingenious owner from nothing but the law.

"The solution of all poverty's problems"

That was homesteading to optimistic Elinore Stewart, a Denver laundress gone to Wyoming. "But," she hastened to add, "persons afraid of coyotes and work and loneliness had better let ranching alone."

The work began the moment the wagon wheels stopped turning. As the propagandists had promised, many a plowman found in the grasslands no stump or rock to cuss. But that also meant he found no wood or stone to build a home. Families fell upon their wagons —once proudly painted, now patched and battered—and improvised what shelter they could from the otherwise useless rig. And out of the land rose the house of sod, snug in the cold and cool in the heat of perhaps half a dozen prairie years. If plastered and whitewashed, a "soddy" could last a century.

For millenniums the roots of buffalo grass had knit the topsoil into a tough, dense pad several inches thick and endless miles wide. Peeled up in blocks (opposite, upper) and stacked like bricks, it made sturdy walls—but a bad roof that dripped inside for days after a rain and sometimes caved in from its own weight. Roofs of dugouts gouged from a hill might collapse under a different burden: a cow ambling onto the roof from the hillside.

The cow could be forgiven, for its blundering was outweighed by its gifts—among them the "cow chips" that fueled cookstoves for Kansas 'steader Ella Sly (lower) and thousands like her in the wood-poor plains. There were few alternatives: kindle corn cobs, twist hay into "cats," trek 40 miles or more to chop firewood. Hard, dry buffalo droppings littered the ground; they burned rapidly but well. And when they ran out, the family cow kept up a small but steady supply.

At first women picked them up with sticks, then a rag, then an apron corner. "And now?" asked a Kansas newspaper in 1879. "Now it is out of the bread, into the chips and back again—and not even a dust of the hands!"

Wealth from wood blessed the family of Harvey Andrews of Nebraska (right); cedar from his Cedar Canyon claim made fencing for his neighbors' lots, ridgepoles for their soddies, firewood for their stoves. But wealth could not stay the raging blizzard, turn away the plague of grasshoppers, put out the racing grass fire, nor speed the day-long ride to a doctor perhaps 60 miles away. Under the sod of the Andrews farm lay their Willie, who survived such rigors for only 19 months.

essential; Congress, realizing this, in 1862 chartered two companies to build from east and west to a junction point, promising each company generous loans to ease construction costs and 10 (later 20) square miles of adjacent land for each mile of track built. Thus was launched one of the most dramatic races in American history, for each was determined to outbuild the other to win the loans and land grants. Armies of Irish laborers, hired by the Union Pacific to work westward from Omaha, pushed their way across the plains, grading and bridging and hammering down the rails, four to a minute, in a mighty anvil chorus; in California 7,000 Chinese laborers hacked their way across the Sierra Nevada, then sped eastward across Nevada and into Utah. Finally, in the spring of 1869, the rails met at Promontory, Utah, as the nation cheered again. "Chicago made a procession seven miles long; New York... fired a hundred guns... Philadelphia rang the old Liberty Bell; Buffalo sang the 'Star-Spangled Banner.' " Within 15 years, four twin bands of steel spanned the continent and opened the vast province of the Great Plains to the march of the frontiersmen.

Cattlemen appeared first on the scene, attracted by thousands of square miles of unfenced grasslands that could be appropriated free of charge and held against intruders by holster law. During the 1860's and 1870's ranches spread from western Kansas and Nebraska over Colorado, eastern Wyoming, Montana, and the Dakotas as the "Cattle Kingdom" took shape. Grass was like gold in that giant pasture, and profits were stupendous. Longhorns could be bought in Texas for a few dollars, driven north, crossed with Eastern bulls to improve the quality of the meat, and allowed to multiply on free government land.

Ranchers, like the miners, soon found that self-regulation was necessary to stop rustling and range wars. Their answer: "cattlemen's associations" that registered "range rights," recorded brands, and supervised the twice-a-year roundups in which cattle were sorted out and calves branded. The reign of the cattlemen was brief, for overgrazing ruined pasturage and an uncommonly cold winter in 1886-87 littered the landscape with frozen longhorns, just as overproduction toppled prices disastrously. Ranchers responded by buying government land, fencing fields, and growing grain for winter feeding. The open range was no more.

The agricultural invasion of the Great Plains had been delayed until technological know-how supplied the tools needed for the conquest of that vast, semi-arid, treeless area: barbed wire for fences, not to enclose the cattle and keep them in but to enclose the crops and keep them out; gang plows and reapers to allow a few men to do the work of many; mechanical threshers; well-drilling equipment and windmills to supply water. Above all, the invasion needed railroads to open up markets and supply the many necessities unavailable on the grasslands: lumber for homes, wood and coal for fuel; furniture and clothing and food. By the early 1870's, most were available; the advance over the "Last Best West" could begin.

Population pressures had been building for a generation in the Mississippi Valley. The sodbusters arrived in droves from the East, from Germany and Scandinavia, from adjacent states. Some came by rail, attracted by the extravagantly romantic advertising of the land-grant railroad lines with millions of acres for sale. More came by wagon, for a few months' journey was worth the convenience of arriving with draft animals and farm implements. All dreamed of the 160 acres of free land granted under the Homestead Act of 1862. Even though most found that the best sites had to be purchased from railroads or speculators, "Free Land for the Homeless" was a compelling magnet.

So they came, moving westward with the railroads that were being built across Kansas and Nebraska; in the two years after 1870 the frontier advanced a hundred miles. Competition for land was so keen that homesteaders sat in the doors of their sod houses, shotguns in hand, to warn off would-be "jumpers." One wrote that "the whole country is full of persons rushing hither and thither in search of homes." Kansas gained 432,000 inhabitants between 1880 and 1890; Nebraska swelled by some 600,000. To the north the Dakotas boomed, growing at the rate of 400 percent a decade, and reaching 539,500 settlers by 1890. Even distant Wyoming and Montana attracted their quota of 'steaders as irrigation transformed arid valleys into farmlands. Wyoming boasted 62,555 inhabitants by 1890 and Montana mustered about 142,900.

By then good lands were less easy to find. "In order to get claims," wrote one settler, "we must push on and on." Finally Congress began piecemeal to open the Indian Territory to homesteaders—the last major area in all the West that had not been settled by whites. Land-office administrators expected a heavy demand, but no one was prepared for what followed. On April 22, 1889, the 1,920,000-acre Oklahoma District was opened; 100,000 "Boomers" crowded the borders, wheel to wheel in wagons, buggies, carts, bicycles—anything that would speed them to the promised land. Troops held them back until noon when shots signaled the opening. Pandemonium erupted as wagons and horsemen raced in all directions; the successful hammered in their stakes, and the unfortunates purpled the air with curses. Within three hours the district was settled; by nightfall Oklahoma City had a tent population of 10,000 and Guthrie, 15,000.

The cornucopia of free lands, which had nurtured expansion since the birth of the nation, was nearing exhaustion. The Director of the Census only confirmed the obvious when he announced in 1890 that "the unsettled area has been so broken into by isolated bodies of settlement that there can hardly be said to be a frontier line." This pronouncement of the closing of the frontier was decidedly premature; good lands still awaited the plow and more were to be brought into production by improved agricultural technology, irrigation, and the expansion of the transportation network. Four times as many acres were homesteaded after 1890 as before, and twice as many since 1910 as in the prior half-century.

Yet no seer was needed to recognize in 1890 that the nation's future would differ from its past. No longer could the landless, seeking opportunity and self-betterment, count on finding unexploited natural resources along the frontiers. The movement into unpeopled space that had helped sustain the country's economy for three centuries, and that had stamped its people with many of their distinctive traits, had ended.

Oklahoma! Land-hungry latecomers wanted it, Indians owned it. The 'steaders won. More than 100,000 of them lined the Cherokee Strip on September 16, 1893. Guns barked at noon—and in they thundered. Wagons overturned, horsemen fell. Some sneaked in early —the "Sooners." Empty crates became land and law offices as 40,000 claims were staked by sunset in America's last great land rush.

Tying the Nation Together

William H. Goetzmann

From Maine to Baltimore by stagecoach and sailing vessel; on to Pittsburgh by train, canal barge, and stage; next, to St. Louis by steamboat; then on across Missouri on horseback — thus, in two weeks or so, a mid-19th century traveler could span America's settled East. Far behind him, the sleek side-wheeler Francis Skiddy *chuffed along the Hudson in 1849, whisking passengers between New York and Albany at a breathtaking 23 miles an hour. And in 1857 the elegant* Phantom — *whose builder felt locomotives should "look somewhat better than cookstoves on wheels" — sped riders along one of a hundred lines that served the East. But from his saddle, the cross-country traveler in Missouri saw only rutted trails vanishing into the West. Thousands had ventured down those trails and tens of thousands would follow; not for long could such rude roads suffice as links to folks and factories they left behind. Rail, steamer, stage, and telegraph became nerves and bloodstream as America came of age.*

"We rush like a comet into infinite space!" Former Congressman Fisher Ames of Massachusetts was dismayed when he learned in 1803 that President Jefferson had purchased Louisiana. Seventeen disparate states loosely joined in a Union that stretched 1,800 miles along the Atlantic Coast and into the backcountry of Ohio, Kentucky, and Tennessee — that was bad enough. Germans and Scotch-Irish had already inundated the frontier regions, and not even Noah Webster could yet make the nation speak with one voice. There wasn't an established church, just a collection of denominations and sects — and evangelists inventing more.

That fragile Union, so carefully nurtured by Federalists such as Ames, was about to be pulled apart, flung across the Mississippi and the "Stoney Mountains" to infinity by a President who prattled on about "sister republics" spanning the continent. The mind reeled; disappointment and anger welled up. Now, barely into the 19th century, it was clear there would never be a *United* States.

Fisher Ames had a point. Louisiana was a vast, unknown land that neither Spain nor France had successfully held. Many Americans feared it would draw even more of their countrymen out of the seaboard towns and cities, perhaps to disappear forever into the barbarism of the backwoods or fur hunters' dens in the mountains, beyond the reach of civilization and its bulwark, the law. No real communication across that immense territory seemed possible; the pioneers would have only the Indians to imitate. Civilized social intercourse would be nil; commerce would surely die. The Union's only memorials might be weed-grown wagon traces and isolated fishing villages along the coast.

Unlike the Federalists, however, most Americans were optimistic. To them, as to Jefferson, the frontier was the future. A sense of national pride and cultural solidarity developed early in the 19th century. There was, after all, a national government in the new capital city of Washington, based on a specific national document, the Constitution, which was already an object of veneration. The people's representatives — senators from every state, congressmen from every district, however remote — assembled in the capital city to determine the course of the nation. Political parties tying these representatives together in common interests had begun to emerge. A Supreme Court under Chief Justice John Marshall had clearly established lines of federal authority. And the national role of the Presidency had been incalculably enhanced by George Washington, man and symbol. Both parties — Federalist and Democratic-Republican — and most regions of the country were agreed upon a common currency and a national bank, as

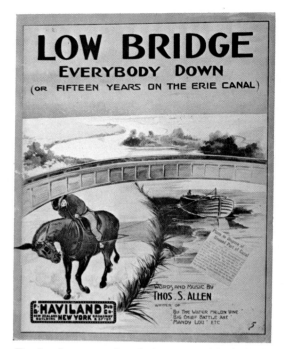

well as the need for roads and a national defense. A military academy had been established, and a Geographer of the United States was busy mapping the country.

Poets and orators, preachers and educators proclaimed the ties that bound Americans together as "one people under God," while the nation's schoolbook writers addressed the coming generations in similar terms. Thus the process of tying the nation together was as much political, intellectual, and symbolic as it was technological.

Nevertheless, in a way perhaps unprecedented in history, technology played a crucial role in the development of a new nation. Technology's task was nothing less than subduing a continent, much of which was still a wilderness. Many inventions, or the principles behind them, came from Europe; some were brought to America by immigrants, others were conceived by Americans living in Europe. But most machines, gadgets, and techniques took on a peculiarly American style: lighter, cheaper, faster, easier to build, more specialized, and not designed for permanence. While manufacturing was a growing interest in 19th-century America, ingenuity from all regions focused on the problems of transportation and communication.

On the earliest trails—many of them enlarged backwoods Indian paths—travel was difficult and dangerous. It was practically impossible to transport a heavy load, especially across the Appalachians to the "western" settlements. It took a man on horseback nearly three months to struggle from Massachusetts to the Carolinas—if he made it at all; gangs of bandits preyed on lone travelers along the gloomy forest trails. Many people had no choice; horses, wagons, and stagecoaches carried the itinerant peddler,

Earthy boatmen bawled unprintable ballads to a mule—which "blushes like a gal," said the laundered lyrics of this Tin Pan Alley hit.

the mail or post rider, the traveler, the circuiting preacher, lawyer, doctor, judge. Nearly every rural family depended on the horse, and a fine one became a status symbol.

Stagecoaches took some of the risk and discomfort out of overland travel and added a measure of speed. "We were rattled from Providence to Boston in four hours and fifty minutes," wrote one traveler in 1822. "If anyone wants to go faster he may send to Kentucky and charter a streak of lightning!" But roads were almost uniformly bad; as late as 1904 only 7 percent of public roads in the United States were surfaced.

The bulk of traffic went by sea. Sloops and schooners plied the coastal lanes, sometimes turning inland up Chesapeake Bay, the Potomac, the Cooper, or the Hudson to stop at scattered river towns or planters' wharves, take on cargo, and deliver the news. Beyond the mountain barrier, traffic also moved on water, but shortest distances weren't always straight lines. To trade with the East on any large scale, settlers had to ship their goods down the Mississippi, across the Gulf of Mexico, and up the Atlantic Coast. They felt they needed transmountain roads, and they blamed Eastern capital and the government for keeping them in thralldom by ignoring repeated demands.

From the beginning American entrepreneurs and statesmen foresaw the West as a great inland market and source of raw materials. Like Jefferson, and even Fisher Ames, they realized the precarious nature of a Union cut in half by the Appalachian Mountains. In 1806 Congress finally authorized a National Road from Cumberland, Maryland, to Wheeling, then in western Virginia; it was completed in 1818. But when Congress approved federal funds in 1817 to connect Washington with the Southern states and

"That's fine travelling; that's what I like"

Footsore and saddlesore, bone-weary of the jouncing wagon and stagecoach, traveling Americans took to the new canals with the gusto of a New York innkeeper of 1832. "You push along so slick, there's no chance of getting one's neck broke as there is aboard those stages on the rough turnpikes; if the boat sinks, one's only up to one's knees in water." An editor called passenger craft "fairy palaces in miniature"; proud owners used horses, not mules, and dubbed boats the *Hero*, the *Frolic*, the *Civility*, the *Truth*.

Walk-in-the-Water bore an apt name, for a speed limit held Erie canalmen to a plodding four miles an hour. Egged on by passengers, some captains hitched up extra horses and let men help pull towropes as they raced rivals at ten miles an hour. At a lock the skippers would slap down $10 fines and race on.

The Erie eventually had 83 locks; early ones measured 15 by 90 feet. Thus a big packet crammed its 100-plus passengers into an 80-foot length, and it took a deft helmsman to ease its 14-foot beam into a lock with only inches to spare.

Dandies doze or chat with the ladies as a packet glides into this view of the Delaware and Hudson Canal. Here on deck the breezes play, but round the bend a bridge waits to exact its homage from the deck set. Bridges by the hundred rejoined severed roads and farms; builders found it cheaper to lower the passengers than raise the spans. High arches demanded only a nod; others prostrated the traveler and scraped overboard any who failed to heed the yell: "Low bridge!" Boatmen bet on who would get knocked down — and sometimes shouted slogans like "All Jackson men stand up!" The gullible who did were promptly vetoed by an oncoming span.

At bedtime the "fairy palace" turned to a "horrible hencoop." All were moved to tiers of 18-inch-wide bunks against the cabin walls, there to swat bedbugs and mosquitoes, gag on stale air, toss and turn to the snores of the hardy few who found sleep — and crash to the deck for rolling over unskillfully.

Fares of about five cents a mile included such berths (Charles Dickens mistook them for bookshelves) and meals. He saw "salmon, shad, liver, steaks . . . ham, chops" at each repast — and perhaps new faces. Wily walkers on the towpath would flag down a packet at mealtime, gorge for a mile, then hop off and hike away, pounds heavier, pennies poorer.

165

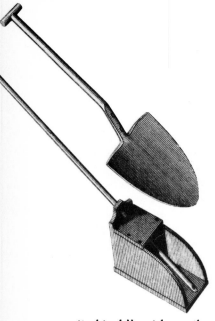

aid in other "internal improvements," President Madison vetoed what he thought was an undue extension of federal power. By then most Southerners agreed with the President; if the government subsidized roads, it would likely get the funds through a tariff system that would raise the price of foreign goods exchanged for Southern cotton. Many Northerners agreed too; their own roads were relatively good, and they feared losing even more of their population if emigration became easier. Many a desperately needed federal road bill was detoured forever by sectional rivalries and constitutional debate.

Thus most road-builders had to risk their own capital. In 1794 a 62-mile toll road was completed between Philadelphia and Lancaster, Pennsylvania—"wch was very much wanted," noted one observer, "as the Old one is very bad, indeed." The new one was America's first macadamized road—"a masterpiece of its kind," said another writer, ". . . paved with stone the whole way and overlaid with gravel." Its success helped touch off a turnpike craze as builders laid ribbons of gravel or plank, or a rough corduroy of logs, along some crucial route. But this one was among the few that made money. Maintenance was expensive, and toll gates (where, upon payment, an attendant turned a pike that barred the way) were too easily circumvented. In the 1830's the boom fizzled. It had produced some rather wretched roads—"a series of alternate swamps and gravel pits," grumbled Charles Dickens in 1842—but even these had been a boon to travelers.

Very early, Americans began to think of building canals that would connect the heads of Atlantic-flowing rivers with streams in the heart of the continent. In 1784 Thomas Jefferson, sensing the Western settlers' mounting anger, supported a plan to improve the upper Potomac and the Kanawha rivers so as to route western trade through Alexandria, Virginia, rather than through the Great Lakes and the Hudson in the North, or the Mississippi and New Orleans in the South. "Nature then, has declared in favor of the Potomac," he argued, "and through that channel offers to pour into our lap the whole commerce of the Western world." But funds could not be raised, and the Hudson and the Mississippi eventually made New York and New Orleans the principal ports and markets of antebellum America. Alexandria remained a sleepy village.

As early as 1804 Simeon DeWitt, surveyor-general of New York, became intrigued with the possibility of connecting the Hudson River with the Great Lakes via a canal through the Mohawk Valley. He asked James Geddes, a state assemblyman, to report on the feasibility of the plan. By 1810 a New York State Canal Commission was established. In 1817, thanks to strong support by DeWitt's cousin, Governor DeWitt Clinton, the New York Assembly authorized construction of the Erie Canal.

A handful of self-taught engineers, including Geddes, directed work on the canal's three major segments. They drew the plans, designed the locks and aqueducts that carried "Clinton's Ditch" over obstructions, and supervised every detail of construction. Thousands of English, Welsh, and Irish immigrants earned their living digging the Erie Canal. Completed in 1825, it was more than a remarkable engineering project. It was a cultural event of the first magnitude. The canal opened up remote western New York, facilitated travel on the Great Lakes, and launched settlement on their shores as far west as Green Bay, Wisconsin, and Chicago. The canal brought settlers west, and spawned a wild, polyglot boom in the towns along its banks. Rome, Troy, Utica, Lockport, and Buffalo became wild-west towns of

"The very rocks rend to welcome me"

Lafayette was impressed. Since 1823 men had filled the air around Lockport, New York, with a booming "Look out!" followed by a jarring blast and a rain of rubble as they punched the Erie Canal through a rib of rock. Now, in June of 1825, they linked a long line of blast holes with trails of gunpowder and greeted the touring hero of the Revolution with a thunderous tattoo.

The canal itself might have spoken the old marquis's words. For nearly eight years crews had been digging the great waterway, hefting dirt with shovels and boxlike scoops, moving mountains piecemeal in shallow wheelbarrows, inching ever closer to completion. But at Lockport loomed the greatest hurdle: the Niagara Escarpment, the same jut of rock that formed nearby Niagara Falls.

"Twelve Dollars a month and found" — pay plus meals and lodging, promised ads in 1821. For that, some 1,200 Irish laborers channeled as deep as 30 feet in stone, hauling out debris by hand, then by ingenious horse-powered cranes whose 70-foot-high spoil heaps still loomed over the city a century later. At Lockport, then a rattlesnake-infested wilderness, crews built double locks to lift boats over the scarp in five giant steps. Town founders raised houses on streets laid out in the woods, then leaned uprooted trees against them to ward off fist-sized fallout from blasting. Lockport survived, and so did one set of locks; the other was obliterated by the New York Barge Canal.

Towns all down the Erie readied for a gala opening in October 1825. But would the canal be ready? Officials posted a keg of whiskey at intervals ahead of the diggers. When they reached it they drank it, then barreled along to the next — and a timely finish.

167

the day — and eventually the prime target for preachers whose fire and brimstone inspired the nickname, the "Burned-over District." The Erie Canal channeled the trade and emotional allegiance of the Old Northwest into New York City, making it the nation's largest port. The city rapidly assumed a commanding role in finance, in commerce, in Atlantic shipping, and, by the 1840's, even in literature and other forms of culture.

The success of the Erie Canal caused a canal-building boom across the country. By 1840 canals joined Boston and Lowell, Providence and Worcester, New Haven and Massachusetts' Northampton. The Chesapeake and Ohio Canal finally linked Cumberland, Maryland, and Alexandria. Richmond tapped the West via the James River and Kanawha Canal. The Delaware and Chesapeake bays were connected, and a mainline canal, complete with inclined planes and a portage railroad over the Alleghenies, flowed all the way from Philadelphia to Pittsburgh. The Ohio River was joined to Lake Erie, and an even longer waterway flowed from Toledo, Ohio, to Evansville, Indiana. Infant Chicago reached out to the Mississippi with a canal to the Illinois River. Hundreds of smaller waterways served as feeders to the great canals.

Travel by canal boat was slow, but far less arduous than driving heavy wagons over rivers of mud. By 1840 Americans had built 3,326 miles of canals — but because of financial collapses and increasing competition from railroads, canal-building had all but ceased. Many states defaulted on bond issues, and boomtowns along the towpaths became backwash country villages. Only a few canals continued in heavy use. The Erie, for example, did not reach its peak until the 1880's.

Even before the building of the Erie Canal, there appeared on the Hudson an invention that would revolutionize water transportation: the steamboat. In August of 1807 Robert Fulton proved the commercial value of his craft, popularly called the *Clermont*, by taking passengers from New York to Albany in 32 hours; sailboats might take four days. Fulton did not invent the steamboat. But from his shallow-draft designs, drawn with an eye to Western rivers, emerged an ideal vehicle for tying the country together.

Fulton saw the steamboat as a "cheap and quick conveyance to the merchandise on the Mississippi, Missouri, and other great rivers which are now laying open their treasures to the enterprise of our countrymen." His company proved its practicality on Western waters in 1811 when the *New Orleans* steamed from Pittsburgh down the Ohio and Mississippi, bound for the boat's namesake city. In Missouri those on board suddenly found themselves in the midst of the great New Madrid earthquake, the worst ever observed outside a volcanic region. As they watched in horror, riverside bluffs caved in, islands were swallowed up, great waves rose and fell, and the channel was utterly

"Wooding up," Princess buys four-foot logs from a farmer whose bonfire led the pilot to his woodyard, one of thousands along the Mississippi. Now and then a steamboat got fooled instead of fueled as looters' fires decoyed it into shipwreck or ambush. Many more were lost when boilers blew or woodwork blazed; 50 died with New Jersey in 1856, 200 in 1859 with the fast, elegant Princess.

Steamboats still crowded New Orleans in 1895. A hint of scrollwork here, a dapper captain there, recalled a heyday when sounders yelled the depth—"By the mark, twain!"— and gave a name to Samuel Clemens. In 1858 Capt. John Klinefelter (opposite) asked him to pilot the Pennsylvania, but young Sam demurred and took to shore. Four days later the boat blew up, killing Sam's brother Henry.

obliterated. Ashore the ground rippled and cracked, trees flailed like buggy whips, buildings fell in splinters. The shocks continued for two weeks. The *New Orleans* steamed right through it all. Three years later she hit a stump and sank, but by then she had pioneered regular service on the Mississippi. And in 1815 a rival company took its *Enterprise* down to New Orleans and back up to her home port 50 miles above Pittsburgh, thus establishing competition on the river.

A revolution had taken place. The West began to control its own economic destiny and draw closer to the East via the river roads. "Steam navigation colonized the West," wrote former Senator James H. Lanman of Connecticut in 1841. "Steam is crowding our eastern cities with western flour and western merchants, and loading the western steamboats with eastern emigrants and eastern merchandise. It has advanced the career

of national colonization and national production, at least a century!" Another American declared that the steamboat would "give to the republic one national heart, and one national mind." And still another rhapsodized that "A steamboat, coming from New Orleans, brings to the remotest villages of our streams, and the very doors of the cabins, a little Paris, a section of Broadway, or a slice of Philadelphia. . . ."

Some 740 riverboats steamed on Western waters by 1850. In that year St. Louis alone logged 2,897 steamboat arrivals from the upper and lower Mississippi, the Ohio, the Illinois, and the Missouri. The hooting steamboat, with its flat bottom and shallow draft, seemed able to go anywhere; skippers boasted they could navigate on a heavy dew. Even in far-off California steamers chugged up the Sacramento River to the goldfields in 1850. And in 1857 Lt. Joseph C. Ives steamed up the Colorado almost to the Grand Canyon in an iron-hulled boat fittingly named *The Explorer*.

The Western steamboat probably evolved from the flat-bottomed, square-ended river barge. The barges, or flatboats, usually made of light, cheap lumber, were knocked together upriver, loaded with bulky goods, and floated to New Orleans; there they were broken up, and lumber and goods were sold. Square-ended Western riverboats also were quickly and cheaply made. Neither type seems to have been built from extensive plans; few if any plans of the pre-1850 Western riverboats exist today. At first engines followed British designs, but the more practical — and hazardous — high-pressure engine developed in America by Oliver Evans soon was common on Western rivers. Jerry-built to last perhaps five years, most steamboats averaged less. As a South Carolinian explained to Alexis de Tocqueville, "I asked the builders of steamboats . . . why they made their vessels so fragile. They answered that, as it was, the boats would perhaps last too long because the art of steam navigation was making daily progress."

Frail as they often were, some steamboats looked like floating palaces — "an engine on a raft with $11,000 worth of jigsaw work," quipped one wag. Western steamboats, snorted another critic, "are built of wood, tin, shingles, canvas and twine, and look like a bride of Babylon. If a steamboat should go to sea, the ocean would take one playful slap at it, and people would be picking up kindling on the beach for the next eleven years." Even at home on Western rivers, the steamboats faced a gamut of perils. Between 1811 and 1850, some 44 collided, 166 burned, 209 blew up, and 576 hit obstructions and sank. They were monuments to a kind of ingenuity, symbols of those grand days full of life on the Mississippi, floating democratic amalgams of merchants, planters, Indians, gamblers, immigrants, soldiers, and ubiquitous American con men.

If steam worked well on water, why not on land? Inevitably, men began to try it. As early as 1804 Oliver Evans chugged around the Philadelphia landscape and riverscape in a strange, watertight wagon dubbed *Orukter Amphibolos*. Rigged with a paddle-wheel astern, Evans' "amphibious digger," intended as a river dredge, was America's first steam-driven land vehicle. In 1825 John Stevens built the first American steam locomotive. It was a toy that rattled to nowhere on a circular track at his Hoboken, New Jersey, estate, but it fueled a growing interest in railroads. Four years later, Horatio Allen, with no previous experience, demonstrated an English locomotive called the *Stourbridge Lion* on a hair-raising three-mile run through the woods of Pennsylvania.

"Thus," he wrote, "on this first movement by steam on railroad on this continent, I was engineer, fireman, brakeman, conductor and passenger." Apparently unnerved by the experience, he never drove a locomotive again.

In 1830 Peter Cooper built and ran the *Tom Thumb,* first locomotive to pull a load of passengers in America. The little one-and-one-half horse-power rig even outran a horse and carriage until a belt slipped and it lost the much-publicized race. It ran on tracks of the newly formed Baltimore and Ohio, one of five railroad companies organized by then. That same year the South Carolina Railroad Company, with Horatio Allen now chief engineer, unveiled America's first scheduled steam railroad train. The *Best Friend of Charleston* drew the train between Charleston and nearby towns for six months, then blew up when a fireman sat on a safety valve to silence its irritating hiss. And that too was a landmark: the first accident in the annals of American railroading.

Public reaction to the new invention was mixed. Emily Dickinson liked "to hear it lap the miles, and lick the valleys up"; Henry David Thoreau grudgingly admitted that "when I hear the iron horse make the hills echo with his snort like thunder, shaking the earth with his feet, and breathing fire and smoke from his nostrils . . . it seems as if the earth had got a race now worthy to inhabit it." But in 1830 a newsman, with tongue only partly in cheek, warned that railroads "will set the whole world a-gadding. . . . Grave plodding citizens will be flying about like comets. . . . it is a pestilential, topsy-turvy, harum-scarum whirligig. . . ." Critics, though, were few; railroads captured imaginations—especially, it seemed, of inventors.

The earliest trains rolled on wooden rails surfaced with long straps of iron. The straps tended to work loose and curl up under the weight of a passing train, sometimes thrusting up through the floor of a coach—to the consternation of its passengers. Then Robert L. Stevens designed the T-shaped iron rail, safer, stronger, easier to lay. A uniquely American technology began to take shape—from the ground up. Europeans laid rails on granite blocks, but Americans quickly switched to wooden ties; they were cheaper and gave a softer ride. American railroads often routed *(continued on page 178)*

"Think of that," marveled Mark Twain, "for perishable horse and human flesh and blood to do!" On horses bred and fed to outrace Indian ponies, daring Pony Express riders sped across the West in 1860-61. Indians caught only one; his horse delivered the mail alone. First mail and freight, then plucky passengers rode sturdy stagecoaches of the West—robbed as much in fact as in folklore.

"21,000,000 strokes and this...marvel will be done"

Reporter William A. Bell watched in awe as Irishmen, Indians, Chinese, Mexicans, and drifters of every stripe stretched tendrils of the Eastern railroad web into the West. Crews with shovels and buckets readied the roadbed. Teamsters reined up wagonloads of ties, then giddapped back for more as gangs thumped ties and plates into position.

Sweating men laid the rails with drill-team precision. At a command, two grabbed a rail from a waiting wagon and hefted it forward. Two more took hold, then two more, until 12 were trotting to the ties with some 30 feet of iron. "Halt!" barked a boss, like as not an ex-Union army officer; "Down!" and the rail found its home. Spike drivers locked it to the ties, three blows to a spike, ten spikes to a rail. "On with another!" and four rails a minute clanged down in a brawny ballet.

Rails for tomorrow roll in on those laid today, and behind them, the ungainly box-cars with bunks where tired gandy dancers—railroad laborers nicknamed for tools they used—could dream of a golden spike.

"It will shake the . . . stoutest hearts"

One look at a bridge like this, and a San Francisco newsman knew that more than the trestle would tremble "when they see that a few feet of . . . timbers and seven-inch spikes are expected to uphold a train in motion." But railroads rushing to completion had no time for tunnels and earthworks; those could be added later. Across plunging chasms and frothing streams, construction gangs wove webs of wood—adjustable as the newly-cut timbers shrank—and did without amenities in the race to finish. One crew ate in shifts from plates nailed to a table and swabbed out with a mop between sittings. In moments of rest the railroadman distilled fatigue, loneliness, and myriad ills into song:

I found myself more dead than alive
From working on the railway.

Perched on a spidery span, men of the Northern Pacific pose with visiting families high in the Cascade Mountains of Washington. Here in 1886 Chinese laborers laid a switchback route that tested the mettle of locomotives pulling in pairs up a climb of 296 feet per mile of track—and of crews whose lives rode the brakes down the other side. In winter snow-bucking trains coupled a plow at each end lest they be stalled by drifts ahead, then trapped by slides behind.

By 1888 the route—and this span over Mosquito Creek—lay abandoned as trains labored through the two-mile-long Stampede Tunnel. But inside the smoke-choked bore, crewmen—some in gas masks—yearned for the air and scenery on the old route's rickety trestles. One yearned no more; in "Stampede Hell" in 1912 he was asphyxiated.

The old route's jackstraw bridges trembled, but none tumbled—as did many others, even some of iron. A decade earlier, in 1876, an 11-car train rolled onto a span near Ashtabula, Ohio, then crashed with it into a 75-foot gorge. Wooden cars became infernos, torched by their pot-bellied stoves; as many as 92 may have died in the disaster. Another 200 spans, most of them railroad bridges, crumpled between the fall of Ashtabula's and the rise of Mosquito Creek's; in the 1870's perhaps one bridge went down for each four that went up. And in North Dakota the Northern Pacific crossed the Missouri River on no bridge at all; ferries in summer took the trains over, and in winter stout-hearted passengers rode rails and ties laid right on the yard-thick ice.

tracks along lines of least resistance, with many twists and turns to climb mountains or dodge obstacles. Some of the turns proved too tight for heavy, fixed-axle British locomotives. So in 1831 John B. Jervis developed an idea to mount the front wheels in a truck that swiveled to take the sharpest curve. Passenger cars began as single coach bodies, then grew to several end-to-end on an elongated frame; the private compartments thus created became Europe's standard. But by the mid-1830's English actress Fanny Kemble found Americans riding in cars with end doors and "a species of aisle in the middle for the uneasy . . . to fidget up and down, for the tobacco chewers to spit in, and for a whole tribe of itinerant fruit and cake sellers to rush through. . . ."

The American car with its boxlike interior made it difficult to segregate passengers into class accommodations. Elite Europeans disliked this innovation; association with the common people, their pets and small livestock—odors and all—was considered vulgar. But Americans had no time for niceties. They were in a hurry to get where they were going—especially to get on with exploiting a continent.

The government, now less wary of "undue extensions" of its power, was willing to assist the railroads. The Illinois Central, completed in 1856, was first to receive a land-grant subsidy: six alternate sections of land per mile of track, a section being 640 acres. Soon this became common practice in inducing the railroads to cross the empty plains, the Rockies, and the deserts of the West. The railroads, which in turn could sell the granted land, launched a massive campaign to lure immigrants out West to build up commerce along the tracks.

The government also tried to help by using the army to locate routes. In 1853 the United States Corps of Topographical Engineers conducted the most extensive railroad reconnaissance ever made. Four parties crossed the West, each on a different parallel, in search of "the most practicable route for a railroad to the Pacific." Scientists went along to catalog the flora, fauna, geology, and natural resources of the West in a great national inventory. When the first transcontinental railroad was built, however, it followed none of the army's routes, but rather one touted by Col. Grenville Dodge, who became head of construction for the Union Pacific as it labored westward from Omaha. At the same time, the Central Pacific inched its way eastward from California. In Utah the two lines' grading gangs built right past each other, hoping to lay claim to land ahead of the track crews. Finally Congress chose Promontory Point, Utah, as the spot where a golden spike would tie the nation together. On May 10, 1869, the spike was hammered home in a great outpouring of speeches and strong drink. The whole country celebrated. "California annexes the United States!" a San Franciscan trumpeted. Promontory Point would soon revert to desert as the line was re-routed through Ogden, but the drama of its shining hour would never be duplicated.

With astonishing rapidity, railroads laced America; they drove most of the canals out of business and rivaled or complemented the steamboats. In 1860 the United States was crisscrossed with 30,626 miles of railroads; by 1890, there were nearly 200,000 miles. Railroads made possible the great cattle industry of the Western plains as railheads reached out to meet Texas cattle trails in such Kansas towns as Dodge City, Ellsworth, and Abilene. Railroads made great marketplaces of Kansas City, St. Louis—where James Eads' monumental steel truss bridge across the Mississippi replaced train-carrying ferries—and Chicago, which became an immense inland port, the place where railroad and steamboat met the Great Lakes and eventually the sea.

The railroad had indeed linked America. It transported people to all parts of the country. It carried the mail and, through Montgomery Ward catalogs, the city's products into the country, gradually connecting country life with city life and reducing the importance of the one-street country town. It forever altered the Indian's way of

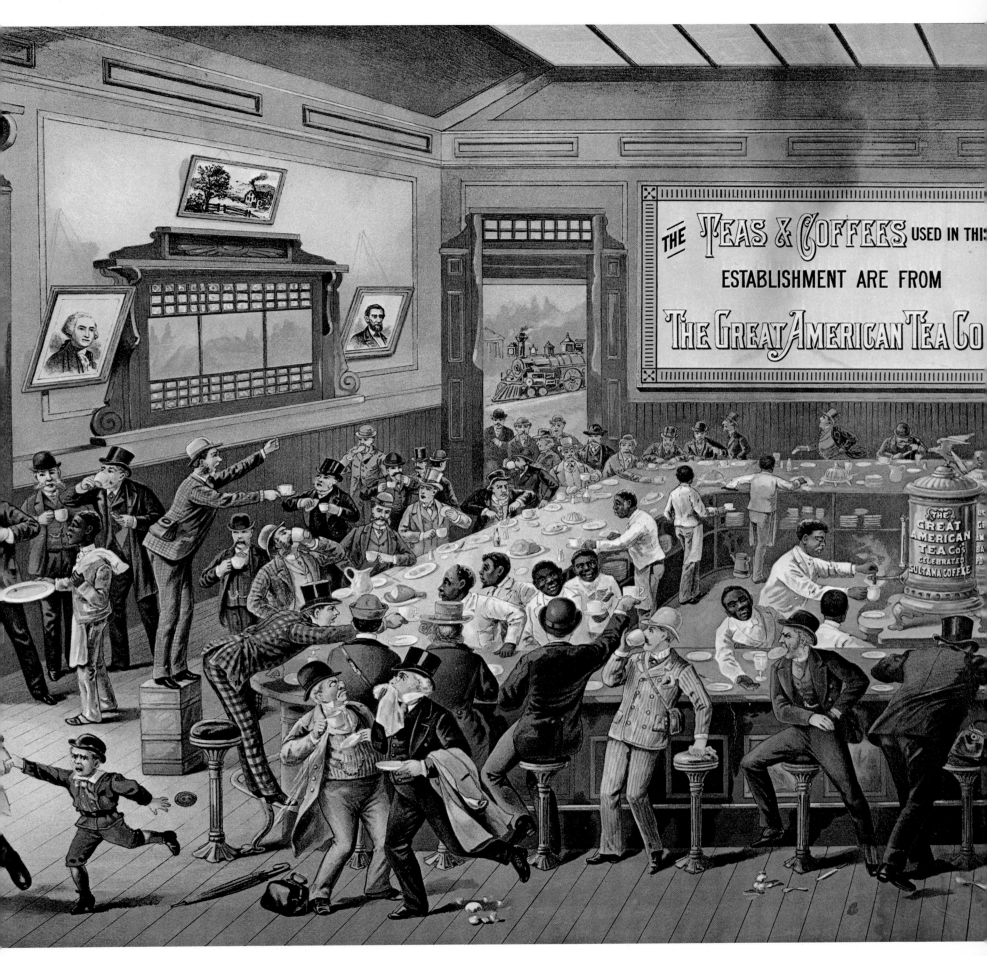

Uneasy riders by the trainful gulp and run at a depot lunchroom in this 1886 cartoon. In days before dining cars, hungry hordes spilled from braking trains to bolt bad food in a race against the boarding bell. Stops lasted 20 minutes, often 10—sometimes less when lunchroom owners bribed trainmen to leave early so food paid for but uneaten could be resold to the next clamoring crowd.

"As though sitting in their parlors"

Thus would Americans travel in trains to come, said a seer of the 1860's; they would "sleep and eat on board of them with more ease and comfort than . . . on a first-class steamer." Soon George Pullman fulfilled the prophecy with the "Pioneer A," a plush passenger car with hinged seats and upper berths that made it a sleeper by night. The Pioneer joined Lincoln's funeral train and wafted President Grant homeward; a later model joined other plush Pullmans to pamper elite guests on the first through train from coast to coast. Competitors withered as Pullman built dining cars, parlor cars, vestibule cars—and the town of Pullman, now part of Chicago. Everywhere, station platforms and tracks too wide or narrow for Pullmans were rebuilt to a gauge now standard nationwide.

A convertible sleeper like this one "becomes your home," said a guidebook of 1884. "Here you sit and read, play your games, indulge in social conversation and glee." But beyond the Missouri River, "there is often an indescribable mixture of races in the same car." At night the angled panels overhead will lower, seats will fold flat, and the ladies—there are gentlemen present—will slip into curtained berths to writhe out of voluminous dresses in privacy. By day they all can walk from car to car, shielded from elements and accidents by accordion-pleated vestibules of steel and elastic. In rolling restaurants that added a new meaning for "diner" to the language, they will enjoy "the best style of culinary art," at a price to make their grandchildren sob.

Travelers on the Santa Fe sampled the finest meals on wheels and gave thanks to Fred Harvey, who spread the tables with Irish linen, Sheffield silver, and fine cuisine. Harvey did for the hungry what Pullman had done for the sleepy. To upgraded depot restaurants he brought bright and comely "Harvey Girls"; in the process he brought some 5,000 brides to lonely Westerners.

Comfort had been long in coming. In 1842 Charles Dickens called an American railroad "a great deal of jolting, a great deal of noise, a great deal of wall, not much window, a locomotive engine, a shriek, and a bell." He might have mentioned a great deal of sparks, as did a woman in 1836 who ended a short ride with 13 holes burned in her gown. For meals, some pre-Pullman riders packed box lunches and endured flies and odor all day. At dusk some slept on boards across the seats, others in bunk-lined sleepers with scant privacy. One woman lamented that "young girls should have to be thus familiarized with that unattractive object, a sleepy and unwashed man. That trial should at least be postponed until marriage has rendered it inevitable."

life by inundating his land with settlers. It made far-off California feel more a part of the Union, though discrimination in freight rates—charging more for one commodity or locale than another, and more per mile for short hauls than for long—made the South feel less so. The railroad created great companies and concentrated great wealth as railroad magnates gobbled up small lines, rigging rates and fares. At the turn of the century, a railroad official was asked how his rates were set. "To be perfectly honest, we get all we can," he replied, "and even that is too little."

Most important, the railroad was a dramatic, visible symbol of national union. After 1869 a citizen or even a foreigner could travel anywhere, through all the states and territories, coast to coast, north or south, without passing through customs or a passport or visa check, as one did in Europe. There was no better evidence of union.

Even in the heyday of developing transportation systems, a startling idea came to fruition: the notion of the message arriving *before* the messenger. In 1832 the young American painter Samuel F. B. Morse, with sketchy knowledge of electromagnetism, became convinced that messages could be sent over wires for long distances. But his first instrument could span only a short distance before its signal petered out. By 1837, aided by the discoveries of Princeton physicist Joseph Henry, Morse had invented a system of relays to reinforce the fading pulses; now he could telegraph a message accurately over any distance. After years of persuasion, Congress in 1843 voted $30,000 to build an experimental line—a wire strung on poles, with glass drawer knobs as insulators—between Baltimore and Washington. On a spring day in 1844, couriers sped to the capital by train with the news that the Whig convention in Baltimore had nominated Henry Clay for President. But via Morse's wires and relays the message beat the messengers by more than an hour.

The possibilities of Morse's invention were quickly grasped. Henry O'Rielly, an outspoken Irish-born promoter, built 8,000 miles of telegraph line through communities all the way to the Mississippi and the Great Lakes. Newspapers began transmitting dispatches from the front in the Mexican War over what O'Rielly called "the lightning wire." In 1848 newspapers, banding together for collective use of the wire, formed the Associated Press. Eight years later all the different telegraph systems joined in one monopoly called Western Union. In 1861 a telegraph wire was strung from New York to San Francisco, reducing the time between the coasts from days to seconds—and the Pony Express, inaugurated only a year before with daring messengers riding through Indian country, was rendered obsolete.

The telegraph became a new tool for commerce. Reports of railroad shipments could be relayed ahead. The price of gold on the San Francisco Stock Exchange, of grain futures in Chicago, of cotton at the New Orleans Exchange—all this and more could be instantly flashed around the nation, making the country a true national market.

At the Centennial Exhibition in Philadelphia, the giant Corliss steam engine (page 224) seemed the most dramatic exhibit. But on June 25, 1876, a visitor, Dom Pedro II, Emperor of Brazil, picked up a strange device, which had been patented only a few months earlier. He put the instrument to his ear and suddenly exclaimed, "I hear, I hear!" With Alexander Graham Bell's telephone, the message again preceded the messenger, but now in the message one could hear and feel the very presence of the sender. A new age of instantaneous, personalized communication had begun.

The transportation and communications revolutions seem to have linked people together, but whether this is really the case is still an open and important question. Transportation also split people apart, spreading Americans all across the continent, dividing families and ethnic enclaves, effacing local memories, promoting a kind of endless transiency that replaced lasting relationships with tangential and temporary

181

ones. Person-to-person relationships characteristically became, to borrow a phrase from Daniel J. Boorstin, "pseudo-events." Herman Melville shrewdly grasped this idea in his riverboat novel, *The Confidence Man,* in which one by one the various transients on a riverboat are victimized by a con man, yet neither the reader nor anyone on the boat knows who he is. He may be any one of them, since they know so little about each other. Such estrangement hardly ties a people together.

In antebellum America, improved transportation fostered specialization. The interests of other sections of the country became far less important than one's own. New York, dominating the flow of commerce via the Erie Canal, reigned over a majority of states that were subservient to industrial interests. And this alarmed the South.

Increased communications pointed up the traditional stereotypes and caricatures of North and South. As propaganda and prejudices reinforced—and then hardened— moral positions, a "non-negotiable" situation became almost inevitable. As Fisher Ames had warned, we rushed like a comet into space—and our course led to the firing on Fort Sumter and civil war.

After the tragic conflict, the transportation revolution split the country in other ways. It promoted the growth of large cities and an eventual clash between urban and rural values that still continues, long after the Populist Crusade of the 1890's. Industries grew to giants, concentrating factory workers in cities where every day they could see about them the stark contrasts between wealth and poverty. The great railroad strikes of the 1870's sounded a strident warning of social conflict. The rise of the farmer against the railroads spurred the enactment of the Granger laws for "just, reasonable, and uniform rates" and resulted in the creation of the Interstate Commerce Commission in 1887, the first such federal regulatory body.

On September 15, 1896, a railroad official with the beautifully apt name of William Crush tried to bring Texas farmers and railroaders together. Some 50,000 people mobbed the temporary "town" of Crush, boozing, jostling, straining for a better view. Two locomotives—one painted red, the other green—touched cowcatchers, backed their empty trains two miles apart, lurched ahead as crews jumped clear, and rammed each other at full speed. Unexpectedly, both boilers exploded; three people were killed and dozens injured by flying iron. For one day the feuding factions had been drawn together by railroad trains, if only to watch their spectacular destruction. But when the steam cleared, the old divisions that those trains had fostered still remained.

Like the crash at Crush, the profound social process of tying the nation together had been an ambiguous exercise that also seemed to drive it apart. Resolving this cultural paradox remains a major social question of our time.

"Goodbye, old Pal"

There she sat, an old steam loco off on a rusty spur, her boiler chalked with a poignant farewell. The track ahead led to the scrapman's torch; after World War II diesel gradually replaced steam even as airliners, trucks, and cars sapped the lifeblood of the railroads. But behind lay a century-long heyday.

And what a heyday! There were railroads before there were locomotives; oxen and even sails had drawn the cars along. In 1830 Peter Cooper's locomotive steamed down the Baltimore & Ohio tracks with old musket barrels for boiler tubes; a century later there were about 65,000 steam locomotives on America's rails, some of them grown to giants with 20 drive wheels. Crack liners such as this Pennsylvania Limited lured passengers with baths, barber shops, stenographers, maids, valets, and sumptuous observation-car platforms for "enjoying the dissolving views."

Wrecks could be awesome—and awesomely entertaining. In Texas in 1896 William Crush staged one (below) for 50,000 onlookers, among them a cameraman later known as One-Eye Deane; a bolt felled him as the engines blew up.

Once "tank towns" sprang up every 40 miles or so, where water awaited the thirsty locos. Locals recognized each engineer by the way he made his whistle "talk." Now only air horns blare as diesels streak through. But sophisticates still call the hamlets "jerkwater." Dinah still blows her horn in song; Casey Jones keeps his hand on the throttle in folklore; countless kids fall asleep as the little engine snorts "I-thought-I-could, I-thought-I-could." And behind the last of the steam locomotives, excursionists still pile into bright-hued wooden cars to hiss and hoot down the high iron to yesteryear.

The People's Choice

William V. Shannon

Politics "is the only pleasure an American knows," said Alexis de Tocqueville in 1832. Handed down by generations of voters, campaign relics recall the political pleasures of yesteryear. German-Americans, who marched in a torchlight parade for Lincoln holding the flame aloft in this cloth-covered box, read campaign ads and news in their own language —and "Old Abe" boned up on German grammar. Though the Know Nothing Party sang anti-immigrant songs, politicians in the know aimed flyers at the bold and eloquent Irish, who quickly found their way into City Hall. Party bosses made voting easy by printing a "ticket" for the voter to slip into the box, which was easily "stuffed." Southern Democrats' 1860 ticket goes into this New York box.

President Grant's meerschaum pipe and a McKinley ashtray portend smoke-filled rooms to come. The two-faced mug gave the drinking voter a choice: McKinley (shown) or Bryan—the gold standard or silver. Asked which he was for, a Tammany boss replied, "I'm in favor of all kinds of money."

The generation that fought the Revolution and founded the Republic was dying. But the Founders' system of "gentry politics," which had produced a succession of aristocrats for President, lingered on. Leading men arranged nominations privately and informally by exchanging letters and visits; they shared power with Congress by meeting in caucus. An Electoral College, some of whose members were elected by state legislatures, not directly by the people, chose the President and the Vice President. Political parties had little formal structure.

Four candidates chosen by congressional caucus vied for the office of President in 1824. Gen. Andrew Jackson, hero of the Battle of New Orleans that marked the end of the War of 1812, led the other three in popular and electoral votes; but because he lacked a majority the election went to the House of Representatives. John Quincy Adams, the runner-up, won. This outcome dismayed the people of the West. By then, one American out of three lived beyond the Alleghenies, and Jackson was their man. The General himself was outraged. Unscrupulous politicians had made a "corrupt bargain," he thundered, cheating the people of their will. For the next four years his campaign, led by Martin Van Buren of New York, hammered away at this issue, which would help elect "Old Hickory" President in 1828.

Jackson's Presidency ushered in an earthy, democratic style of politics. Although he was not the uncouth backwoodsman depicted by his enemies, the craggy Tennessean was a self-educated man lacking in the polished style and upper-class background of previous presidents. "When he comes," Daniel Webster predicted, "he will bring a breeze with him. Which way it will blow, I cannot tell." Jackson's followers believed it would blow for their benefit; on Inauguration Day in March 1829, they streamed into the Capital by the thousands. "Persons have come five hundred miles to see General Jackson," Webster marveled, "and they really seem to think the country is rescued from some dreadful danger." The new President rode to the White House on horseback, a great multitude surging along behind him. When the backwoods spilled over into the White House reception, one witness called the spectacle "a regular Saturnalia." Thronging the East Room, the crowd fell on the refreshments, breaking china and smashing furniture. To clear the room, tubs of punch were placed on the lawn. "The reign of King Mob," wrote Justice Joseph Story, "seemed triumphant."

In the new era of the common man, our modern two-party system emerged. Some Jeffersonian Republicans transformed themselves into Jacksonian Democrats. Others, led by Senators Henry Clay and Daniel Webster, organized an opposition party, the Whigs. The name derived from pre-Revolution Whigs who had resisted Royal power; the new Whigs resisted the power of "King Andrew." Whigs and Democrats differed on economic issues, such as the role of the federal government in banking. The Jackson administration encouraged loyalty by giving government jobs to backers. "To the victor belong the spoils of the enemy," boasted Democrat William L. Marcy; opponents called it "the spoils system." In practice the Jacksonians fired only about one officeholder in ten, but most victors found the purge distasteful. When President Jackson was urged to replace the postmaster in Albany, an old soldier, he refused: "By the Eternal! I will not dismiss the old man. Do you know that he carries a pound of British lead in his body?"

Restrictions limiting the right to vote to those who held property or paid taxes faded away in the democratic atmosphere of the 1820's. The people voted directly for Presidential electors in three out of four states by 1824. All secret organizations became suspect, including the Society of Freemasons—a group that claimed both Washington and Jackson as members. But the Masons lost favor, and an Anti-Masonic Party took shape. To dramatize their belief that all political decisions should be made openly, the Anti-Masons held the first national nominating convention in 1831. The idea caught on, with Jackson's approval—here was a way to mobilize popular support. By 1844 both parties had adopted platforms at conventions. A ritual of American party politics had arrived. Through the years the nominating convention grew into an extravaganza that H. L. Mencken would call "gaudy and hilarious . . . melodramatic and obscene . . . exhilarating and preposterous."

Statistics on voter turnout reflect an explosion of political activity and interest. In 1824 only 27 percent of those eligible to vote participated in the Presidential election. In 1828 it was 58 percent, and by 1840 a whopping 80 percent. The rate remained high to the end of the century, never falling below 70 percent. The nation's population more than doubled between the administrations of Jackson and Lincoln—a propitious time for the new politics of propaganda, patronage, and intensive organization pioneered by the Jacksonians.

The Whigs won the first national election to turn on what we now call "image-making." It all began with a blunder by the opposition. Commenting on the Whig nomination of William Henry Harrison for President in 1840, a Baltimore newspaper sniffed that he would be perfectly content to sit in a log cabin with a barrel of hard cider for the rest of his days. Whig strategists seized on this condescending remark, and promoted log cabins and free cider as symbols of their candidate, who was presented to the public as a two-fisted, plain-spoken Westerner. Instead of formal public meetings the Whigs staged colorful parades and invited voters to barbecues and clambakes; they set up log cabins in town squares and distributed thousands of miniature cabins as well as medals showing Harrison wearing a coonskin cap.

To discredit President Martin Van Buren—a tavern-keeper's son—the Whigs attacked him as an aristocrat who lived in the White House in royal splendor. Andrew Jackson had been called "Old Hickory"; Whig publicity men (and a young editor named Horace Greeley) dubbed Harrison "Old Tip." Paraders chanted a campaign song:

> Farewell dear Van, To guide the ship
> You're not our man, We'll try Old Tip.

The "log-cabin" candidate was, in fact, the son of an aristocratic Virginia planter who was a signer of the Declaration of Independence. As a youth, Harrison migrated to Ohio and began a long but undistinguished career in state politics. In 1811 he led the militia against Indians in a bloody battle near the village of Tippecanoe. Linking the

"Coming of the green" to freedom's abundance

Pushed from his potato patch and shadowed by famine, the poorest of the poor in a feudal society, an Irish Catholic peasant marveled at news from America. "This is the best Country in the world it is easy making money," an Irish girl wrote from New York in 1848. Heeding the call, thousands packed meager possessions in knapsacks, and, dressed in tattered swallowtail coats and knee breeches, trekked dusty roads to Dublin (opposite) and other ports. There cargo ships laden with timber and cotton unloaded and then set sail, ballasted with Irishmen, for the return trip to Canada, a waystop for "Paddy," who walked or sailed south to the United States.

Sharpies pounced on Irishmen who debarked in Boston or New York, "the dew of Galway" still on them. The sharpies led them to boardinghouses that fleeced the bewildered newcomers of their scant resources. Yet most Irish stayed in the city, where they could find a church—and perhaps a saloon—nearby and hear the soft brogue of their countrymen. Emigration's living chain was lengthened by each immigrant who saved money and sent for a relative. From 1848 to 1861 the Irish sent home $60 million. Few returned to Ireland except for a visit—and surely their dapper duds and tales of gold-paved streets lured more wearers of the green to America's shores.

"The time has come . . . every breeze says change"

At a festive Whig rally for William Henry Harrison in 1840, Daniel Webster's ringing words evoked an issue of the times: the destiny of a lusty young nation heading west. But the Whigs' rip-roaring campaign buried issues in ballyhoo. Huge rallies heard Harrison praised as a homespun hero and his opponent, Martin Van Buren, vilified as a corseted dandy who perfumed his whiskers and drank wine "from his coolers of silver." Mile-long parades rolled through cities, the log-cabin symbol mounted on bandwagons (opposite, in Philadelphia), "banners waving and mottoes flashing," abundant free cider dispensed on street corners "with good effect." A rally at Tippecanoe battleground in Indiana attracted "15 acres of men" and "6,000 females." Campaign souvenirs flooded the country: canes, snuffboxes, and cabin-shaped whiskey bottles; Tippecanoe Shaving Soap and Log Cabin Emollient; ties and bandannas (below).

General Harrison took to the stump, a term harking back to colonial days, when frontier orators harangued the crowd from tree stumps. Backing him in Illinois was the "best stump speaker in the West"—a 31-year-old Whig, Congressman Abraham Lincoln. His speech in Carlinville was "abruptly terminated" by a "log-cabin float drawn by nine yoke of oxen." The Democrats were trounced. Harrison got 234 electoral votes to Van Buren's 60. The loser's explanation: He'd been "lied down, drunk down, and sung down."

Packaged and sold as a "log-cabin" candidate, Harrison was born at Berkeley, a Tidewater Virginia plantation. But five successors really were cabin-born: Fillmore, Pierce, Buchanan, Lincoln, and Garfield.

long-forgotten skirmish with Harrison's running mate, John Tyler, the Whigs popularized the first Presidential campaign slogan: "Tippecanoe and Tyler too!"

Harrison won a clear victory, only to die of pneumonia a month after taking office, leaving the Presidency to a man best remembered as the second half of that great slogan. The only other President the Whigs elected was another elderly general, Zachary Taylor, in 1848. But they perfected the techniques that—until the arrival of radio and television—would dominate political campaigning for the next hundred years: the torchlight parades, the razzle-dazzle public rallies, the badges, buttons, and gimmicks, the humorous songs and catchy slogans.

The Whigs demonstrated that propaganda was a political weapon available to both parties. But the Democrats—who were not burdened with the grab bag of opposing interests that bedeviled the Whigs—won five of seven national elections between 1832 and 1856. Although the Democrats split into Northern and Southern factions in 1860, they survived the war as a national party, while the Whigs disappeared. The secret of the Democrats' survival is tied to a drama that began to unfold in the years from 1830 to 1860—the steady influx of immigrants from Europe, their concentration in the cities, and their devotion to the Democratic Party.

The census of 1860 showed that of 31 million people in this country, 4,136,000 were foreign-born. The overwhelming majority of them lived in the Northeast and the Middle West. Very few of them settled in the South, except in the ports of Baltimore and New Orleans. The two largest groups had emigrated from Ireland and Germany; a third group came from England, Scotland, and Wales. The rest were emigrants from Canada or from less populous European countries, such as the Norwegians who went to Wisconsin and Minnesota and the Dutch who found homes in Michigan.

Although most immigrants were farmers, many of them chose to stay in the city in America, where their labor was needed to build houses, factories, transportation lines, and water and sewer systems. Uprooted German craftsmen and peasants readily found work as tailors, cabinetmakers, printers, brewers, and carpenters; the Irish, who came from a depressed rural society, drifted into unskilled, lower-paid jobs—longshoremen, teamsters, laborers, waiters. Irish women worked as domestic servants and seamstresses. A good wage for a working man in those days was a dollar a day; housemaids earned as little as a dollar a week.

"Little Dublins" appeared in factory towns of the Northeast. At first, competition for jobs prompted employers to post signs: "No Irish need apply." But by the eve of the Civil War, Irishmen had begun to replace native farm girls in the woolen and cotton mills of New England. Some Irishmen left their wives and children in the East to find jobs on riverboats and in railroad construction gangs; others settled in new railroad towns—Albany, Buffalo, Chicago, St. Paul, or Omaha—and sent for their families. "There are several sorts of power working at the fabric of this Republic," a newspaper commented in 1847, "waterpower, steam-power, horsepower, and Irish power."

With the rising tide of immigration, almost every sizable city in the East and Middle West became a network of immigrant enclaves. Like the original Dutch settlers, the Irish in New York congregated on the Lower East Side. In the Bowery to the north the softly spoken *"Ja, mein Herr,"* mixed with accented English that visitors heard in the streets, signaled the beginning of *Kleindeutschland*—Little Germany—where two-thirds of the city's 100,000 Germans lived before the Civil War. German restaurants and beer gardens, German churches and schools, a German theater and library served the community. Similar enclaves existed in Cincinnati, St. Louis, Chicago, and Milwaukee. Scandinavian writer Frederika Bremer, traveling in the United States, described Milwaukee's German Town of the 1850's. Lively music and dancing, good beer

John Adams (shown) and
James Madison, limned on
porcelain, may honor the
Constitution, c. 1795.

Ratchet noisemaker boosts Cleveland, who
won a second (nonconsecutive) term, 1892.

Cast-iron doorstop, probably
from Jackson's 1828 campaign

Every four years, a carnival of democracy

To elect a President, Americans stage a jamboree. It all began in the rollicking politics of the 19th century—recalled by a wondrous array of vote-for-me gadgets. The Founding Fathers took a more somber view. "The spirit of party . . . kindles . . . animosity," observed George Washington, the "people's choice" with no dissenters. So early makers issued only commemorative pieces, such as the Adams-Madison jar. By the time the partisan frog croaked for Andy Jackson, families in wagons bumped for days over rough roads to hear a politician's vows. An 1845 law put elections in November's first week, after harvest and before roads became impassable. Whigs in 1840 as a stunt went from city to city to "keep the ball rolling"—and coined a phrase.

Stephen A. Douglas hired a train with a cannon to announce his arrival, and President Andrew Johnson (left) politicked by rail. As railroads spread, "whistle-stop" campaigning began. In 1884 "Mugwumps"—an Indian word for "chief"—entered the political lexicon when it labeled top Republicans who bolted the party to support Grover Cleveland, foe of Tammany. Voters ignored the disclosure that he had fathered an illegitimate child. Mrs. Belva Lockwood ran on the Equal Rights ticket, but only men could vote. Outweighed in 1888, Cleveland won in 1892, the year his voice was heard on the newfangled phonograph. The new century began with a "full dinner bucket" pledge; by 1960, candidates could "promise the moon and mean it."

McKinley-Roosevelt celluloid button, 1900

Maryland Whigs rolled a 12-foot paper ball for William Henry Harrison, 1840.

Toy scale weighs Benjamin Harrison (left), and Grover Cleveland, 1888.

191

and good food distinguished the residents "from the Anglo-American people, who, particularly in the West, have no other pleasure than 'business.' "

For most Irish and German immigrants, however, community life centered around the church. To be Irish and Catholic was practically synonymous. Many of the Germans were also Catholic, the rest were Lutheran or belonged to other Protestant denominations. If they were to have churches, the newcomers had to sacrifice and scrimp, contributing their pennies each week. As the new churches rose brick by brick, city officials and Catholic clergy clashed over the use of Protestant materials, such as the King James Bible, in the public schools. As a consequence, in many communities Catholics began building their own parochial schools.

The controversy exploded into a political issue when proponents of the public-school system confronted those who favored church schools. In New York, for example, the Catholic bishop, with the governor's support, argued for state funds to support Catholic schools, arousing the ire of Whigs and Democrats alike. A compromise gave each ward its own school commission with power to allocate funds. In other cities there were no easy remedies, and riots erupted.

Every city organized volunteer fire companies and armed militia. Since the established units made the immigrants feel unwelcome, they formed their own. Irish Rifles, Emmet Guards, and Hibernia Guards drilled once a week and would, in theory, defend the country in time of war. In practice they were more social than military, marching on the Fourth of July in splendid uniforms and celebrating St. Patrick's Day with more pomp than it had ever been observed in Ireland. A German company, the Von Steuben Guards, commemorated the illustrious baron's role in the Revolution.

From these immigrant neighborhoods, with their churches, schools, volunteer fire companies, militia units, beer gardens, and saloons, emerged a new style of urban politics. And though the Germans were politically active, the Irish were naturally political. Their first leaders had been sports heroes, orators, and revolutionary activists. John "Old Smoke" Morrissey, a flamboyant gambler and prizefighter, was elected to Congress from a Manhattan district in 1866. Born in Tipperary, he had emigrated as a child. Old Smoke earned his name in a barroom encounter when he kicked over a stove and fell backward into the burning coals. He rose, coattails smoking, and knocked out his adversary. Morrissey made a fortune in Wall Street and founded a fashionable gambling salon in Saratoga Springs, New York.

Gradually, people like William Marcy "Boss" Tweed emerged to organize Irish political strength into disciplined machines. Tweed, not himself an Irish Catholic, started out as a young tough in "Company Six" of the volunteer firemen. From 1865 to 1871 he and his associates, Richard "Slippery Dick" Connolly and Peter Sweeney, controlled New York's Democratic organization, Tammany Hall. The Tweed Ring and men like them in other cities worked behind the scenes to manipulate the elected regime.

Machine politics were plain and practical. The poor had no social service agencies, no unemployment compensation or social security. A man looking for a job, a family facing eviction, a widow—all needed immediate help. Through ward heelers in every block and clubhouses in every district, the political machine provided help in exchange for votes. Tammany's power stemmed from its control of jobs on public works projects and with private utilities and transit companies. With 12,000 jobs and a 12 million-dollar payroll, Tammany rivaled the Carnegie iron-and-steel works in the 1880's.

Money poured into machine coffers from bribes and kickbacks—forms of extortion called "dishonest graft" by Tammany ward boss George Washington Plunkitt, who carefully distinguished it from "honest graft." If a machine insider knew what land was slated for public improvements and profited by buying it up in advance—that was

Tammany: the house that graft built

New York after the Civil War struggled in the embrace of Tammany Hall, the city's Democratic political club. To a *Puck* cartoonist it was a lecherous tiger sporting a shamrock, for Irish pols had made Tammany their vehicle for political power. Schooled in neighborhood politics and street-gang violence, a succession of bosses dipped deft fingers into the public till. Richard Croker, a near-dictator of New York from 1886 to 1902, died on his Irish estate in 1922 with a fortune of $5 million.

"The Society of St. Tammany" began as a harmless fraternal order named for a Delaware Indian chief. Members paraded on the Fourth of July and "Tammany Day"; a Philadelphia patriot received the invitation opposite in 1773. But the club faded away except in New York, where it took a political turn: Aaron Burr, perhaps Tammany's first "boss," used its clout to become Vice President.

Tammany Hall's most infamous boss, William Marcy Tweed—a great, hulking Scotch-Irishman—plundered the city for six years; estimates of his take range from $30 million to $200 million. The Tweed Ring (boss, mayor, a "fixer," and a collector, or "bag man") took bribes and kickbacks from construction contracts. A $250,000 courthouse, for example, cost the city $12 million. A thief who lived like a king, Tweed wore a cherry-size diamond stickpin and built an estate with stables framed in mahogany. His lavish charity silenced much criticism and bought votes. At a Tammany headquarters (right) patrolled by tough Irish "bhoys," tickets marked "Please naturallize the bearer" were handed to immigrants. Cooperative judges obliged 41,000 times in 1868—and the *Tribune* mocked: "Judge McCunn has issued an order naturallizing all the lower counties of Ireland, beginning at Tipperary and running down to Cork." To those demanding reform, Tweed retorted, "What are you going to do about it?"

An answer came from a crusading cartoonist, Thomas Nast, whose drawings in *Harper's Weekly* marshaled public opinion by holding the Ring up to ridicule. As the empire began to crumble, an insider—"Slippery Dick" Connolly—gave evidence to investigators. It was "everyone for theirselves," and Nast drew the beleaguered Ring as roosting vultures in a storm; the caption said, "Let us prey." Boss Tweed had heard his last hurrah. Imprisoned in 1873, he was asked his religion. "None," he replied. "Occupation?" "Statesman."

War on the immigrant

The Plug-uglies—thugs hired by the Know Nothings to "plug" unfriendly voters—terrorized Baltimore in the 1850's. A secret society whose members replied "I know nothing" when asked their beliefs, it opposed "Popery," saw the Irish as "grog-shop rowdies" and the Germans as "lager-beer loafers" who took jobs away from the native-born. The Know Nothing Party nominated Millard Fillmore for President in 1856, pledging to bar the foreign-born from office and extend the naturalization wait to 21 years. Lincoln said if they won he would emigrate to a country "where despotism can be taken pure . . . without the base alloy of hypocrisy." But the party faded on the eve of the Civil War.

honest graft. "I'm gettin' richer every day, but I've not gone in for dishonest graft . . . I seen my opportunities and I took 'em," said Plunkitt, summing up his philosophy.

The machine corrupted the police and reached into the courts, influencing the enforcement of gambling and prostitution laws. Sometimes it had the power to "fix" cases and arrange suspended sentences. "The city government is rotten to the core," New Yorker George Templeton Strong noted in his diary. But for the immigrant poor, the machine functioned not only as a social service agency, but also as a pressure group, providing jobs and recognition. Despite recurring scandals and intermittent reforms, the machines that appeared before 1860 survived and flourished many decades.

Immigrants arriving in the United States before the Civil War allied themselves with the Jacksonian Democrats. Not for nothing had the party championed universal male suffrage and the wholesale naturalization of foreigners; a party representing the people in opposition to banking and business interests had no difficulty appealing to impoverished newcomers. The cities' immigrant-based political machines, deriving their energy from local issues, could survive even though the Democrats were out of power at the national level—a fate the party did suffer after the Civil War.

While the immigrants struggled for a foothold, politicians grappled with the central issues of the day: economic growth, "manifest destiny," and slavery. James K. Polk, elected President in 1844, had won the Democratic nomination as a virtual unknown—the nation's first "dark horse" candidate—defeating the party's front-runner, ex-President Van Buren. Polk's election inspired a popular new "Polka," which the Whigs described as "one step forward and two steps back." But Whig pessimism was ill-founded, for Polk emerged as a strong Chief Executive. During his administration, the nation annexed Texas and fought a short war with Mexico, acquiring New Mexico and California. At the same time, a treaty with England settled competing claims in the Northwest, consolidating American control of Oregon.

Despite periods of economic depression, this was a time of prosperity and rapid industrial development. The task of building railroads through newly won territories began, and slave-owning planters expanded cotton, rice, and sugar production. Although many Americans happily concentrated on moneymaking, others unceasingly pressed the country to think about the "great moral, social, and political evil" at the heart of national life—the dark and troubling question of human bondage. Could slavery be squared with the words of the Declaration of Independence that "all men are created equal and are endowed by their Creator with certain unalienable rights"?

A few voices had always protested slavery, but the time had come to move against the "monstrous scourge." Abolition became the "reform of reforms," although it was not the only moral question under scrutiny. During these years Dorothea Dix campaigned for enlightened care of the insane, Samuel G. Howe for better education of the blind. Others crusaded for improved public education, women's rights, and temperance. The energy for moral crusades came from the missionary zeal of American Protestantism. Though it took different forms, the religious impulse that brought the Pilgrims to Massachusetts in 1620 persisted during the next two centuries. As Americans moved west, religious revivalism and moral concern guided their journey. Bulwarked by an unshakable faith, the abolitionists battered down layers of public apathy and hostility. Believing the emancipation of the slave was God's will, they spoke to a people accustomed to obeying it.

Their leading spokesman was a Massachusetts editor, William Lloyd Garrison. A grandson of immigrants, Garrison had been raised by a pious mother in terrible poverty. His early education was reading the Bible, and he grew up a stern, self-righteous young man, deeply religious and determined to become famous and do good. "O Lloyd," his

On the block, a people without a choice

The auction hammer's steady beat sent slaves to toil on cotton plantations, in rice and cane fields of the Deep South. Banned by England, then by act of Congress in 1807, the African trade went underground—and flourished. Domestic traders could advertise openly (below) or visit plantations, searching for bargains in border states, where slave labor was unprofitable and prices low. The purchased blacks were shipped south by sea or land, linked in coffles and "handcuffed in pairs with iron staples and bolts." Housed in slave pens, the chattels awaited the dreaded auction block and an unknown future. Former slave Solomon Northrup described a New Orleans sale: "Customers would feel of our bodies . . . make us show our teeth . . . as a jockey examines a horse."

Just before the Civil War a prime field hand went for $1,800, a blacksmith, $2,500. In Lexington, Kentucky, "handsome mulatto women sitting at their needle"—concubines—brought $2,000 or more. From 460,000 in 1770, the number of slaves rose to nearly four million by 1860, half the number of whites in the South. Yet only 12 percent of owners held more than 20 slaves. Living on her husband's Georgia plantation with 700 slaves in 1839, English actress Fanny Kemble denounced the "unmitigated abominable evil"—from the paternalism shown house slaves, "that maudlin tenderness of a fine lady for her lap dog," to "flagrant acts of cruelty" inflicted on labor gangs. But compared with a master degraded by slavery, she wrote, "the wretchedest slave . . . is worthy of envy."

$1200 TO 1250 DOLLARS ! FOR NEGROES !!

THE undersigned wishes to purchase a large lot of NEGROES for the New Orleans market. I will pay $1200 to $1250 for No. 1 young men, and $850 to $1000 for No. 1 young women. In fact I will pay more for likely

NEGROES,

Than any other trader in Kentucky. My office is adjoining the Broadway Hotel, on Broadway, Lexington, Ky., where I or any Agent can always be found.

WM. F. TALBOTT.

LEXINGTON, JULY 2, 1853.

mother wrote, "shun the appearance of evil for the sake of your soul as well as the body." Like his mother, he believed that no matter how desperate the prospects, God would come to his aid. Fate had cast him in the role of peace-loving fanatic.

Apprenticed to the editor of the *Newburyport Herald* in Massachusetts at the age of 13, Garrison began to find himself. He read widely, nourishing his eager mind. From the back files of the *Herald* he learned the New England view of the nation's history and acquired a taste for fierce, polemical journalism. Garrison was never the kind of newspaperman who believed there were two sides to a story. He founded a newspaper of his own that failed, then drifted about New England as editor of party-backed newspapers during political campaigns, studying the issues of the day. The antislavery cause soon captured his attention.

On January 1, 1831, Garrison printed the first issue of his abolitionist paper, the *Liberator,* with an editorial that would become famous: "*I will be* as harsh as truth, and as uncompromising as justice. On this subject, I do not wish to think, or speak, or write, with moderation. . . . I am in earnest—I will not equivocate—I will not excuse—I will not retreat a single inch—AND I WILL BE HEARD."

Only 400 copies of that issue were printed, and not all of them sold. Three years later the *Liberator* still had only 400 subscribers, but it was already becoming famous. Garrison shrewdly exploited his enemies by sending the unsold copies of each issue to Southern editors. Offended and outraged, they quoted his most provocative remarks to show their readers what diabolical things the Yankees were saying. Northern editors, indifferent to abolition but interested in a good fight, reprinted these exchanges, adding comments of their own. Then Garrison reprinted the original article and all the comments in the *Liberator,* with more high-voltage prose of his own. In this way Southern editors unwittingly helped him keep the pot boiling.

Garrison organized groups of free Negroes in several Eastern cities who sent voluntary contributions in support of abolition, but this was not the only source of revenue. He and a few like-minded believers formed the Antislavery Society, of which Garrison long served as corresponding secretary. Help came from scattered individuals. John Greenleaf Whittier, the shy young Quaker poet from Massachusetts, contributed poems. Arthur Tappan, a wealthy New York silk merchant, and his brother Lewis sent Garrison money. James and Lucretia Mott and other prosperous Philadelphia Quakers joined the crusade. The Motts boycotted products raised and produced by slaves, serving only "free" rice and sugar, and wearing clothes made from "free" cotton. Even the candies they made and sold bore antislavery couplets:

> *If slavery comes by color, which God gave,*
> *Fashion may change, and you become the slave.*

Lucretia Mott spoke against slavery in churches and on lecture platforms—wherever she could find an audience. "The infidelity I should dread," she once said, "is to be faithless to the right, to moral principle, to the divine impulses of the soul, to a confidence in the possible realization of the millennium now."

Wendell Phillips, a wealthy descendant of one of Boston's original Puritan families, also interested himself in Garrison's work. A graduate of Harvard Law School, Phillips at 24 seemed destined for a successful career in law and politics. But one afternoon, looking out his office window, he saw a mob dragging the defenseless Garrison toward City Hall. The crowd, angered by recent abolitionist activity, considered Garrison a disturber of the peace, though they eventually released him unharmed. Shortly after he witnessed the incident, Phillips met Garrison and became a valuable recruit for the antislavery cause. A meeting in Boston's Faneuil Hall in 1837 to protest the mob-killing of Elijah Lovejoy—an Illinois editor who printed antislavery articles in defiance of Southern opinion—was the occasion for Phillips' first notable public address against slavery. From then until the outbreak of the Civil War, the abolitionist cause, once a lonely crusade, gained irresistible momentum.

National politics reflected the furor over slavery. Antislavery voters had strongly opposed the war with Mexico and the annexation of vast new lands, fearing their exploitation by "King Cotton" and his slaves. The issue became so heated that it temporarily threatened party unity. Martin Van Buren, who had lost the Democratic nomination to Polk in 1844, agreed in 1848 to lead a third-party movement, the Free Soilers. With the slogan "Free soil, free speech, free labor, and free men," the party opposed the extension of slavery into the territories.

A few years later a bitter struggle over the question of slavery in the Nebraska Territory gave rise to the modern Republican Party. When the Kansas-Nebraska Act, passed in 1854, decreed the territory open to slavery if the settlers voted for it, Southerners were pleased, the Northern abolitionists in an uproar. Stephen A. Douglas, who supported the bill, remarked that he could have traveled all the way from Boston to Chicago by the light of his own burning effigies. Insistent demands for a new party in which Free Soilers, antislavery Democrats, and Whigs could all feel at home culminated in a meeting at Ripon, Wisconsin, in 1854. The new organization, strongly opposed to slavery, would be called the Republican Party.

During this stormy interlude, Irish and German immigrants abruptly entered national politics—as scapegoats. With slavery the irrepressible issue, politicians in the dying Whig Party tried to distract the voters' attention by attacking immigrants as a danger to the American way of life, and their religion—Catholicism—as a threat to Protestant supremacy. In Massachusetts and a few other states, the Know Nothings, as the anti-immigrant party was popularly called, swept to power. But their rule was brief. The agitators lacked the skill and commitment of the abolitionist leaders.

For the immigrants, the Know-Nothing agitation had divided political consequences. Liberal Germans rallied to support the new Republican Party and oppose slavery. More conservative Germans voted in 1860 for Democrat Stephen A. Douglas and maintenance of the Union. The Irish, already Democratic, remained loyal to the party. Many felt hostile to the abolitionists, particularly in New York where the Irish competed with free Negroes for jobs as longshoremen and laborers. But when war came in 1861, patriotism won out, and the sons of Erin enlisted in the Union Army in droves.

Most Northerners focused more and more of their attention on the slavery issue and its implications for the preservation of the Union. Abraham Lincoln, no abolitionist, spoke the growing conviction of many when he reluctantly concluded, "A house divided against itself cannot stand." The South, had it been patient or still willing to compromise, probably could have withstood the changing drift of opinion in the North. In 1860, only 40 percent of the electorate voted for Lincoln and the Republicans' pledge to permit no further expansion of slavery in the territories. But a "go-it-alone" spirit had come to the fore in the South. Garrison had always been willing to see the North secede if that was necessary to break the constitutional compact with the slaveholding South. Now he would see the slaveholders try secession, and the North sadly decide to go to war to prevent their leaving.

As the guns boomed at Fort Sumter and President Lincoln appealed for 75,000 volunteers, the abolitionists could look back on a 30-year struggle to emancipate Negroes. In the beginning, majority opinion had been everywhere overwhelmingly against them. But in their deep religious faith that their cause was just and one day must prevail, they believed in Wendell Phillips' words: "One, on God's side, is a majority."

"Shall our own brethren drag the chain?"

In three-cent copies the Antislavery Society sold John Greenleaf Whittier's 1835 poem of protest, illustrated by a fettered captive (above). Chains of oppression, forged in Africa, enslaved ten million Negroes in the New World from the 16th to the mid-19th century. Captured inland and marched to the African coast in stout iron shackles, the victims boarded ships for the so-called "Middle Passage"—second leg of a trading cycle that brought guns and trinkets to Africa in exchange for slaves, who were sold in America for cotton and tobacco, products salable in Europe for cash. Some on the jammed slave ships resisted servitude by "leaping with crazy laughter to the waiting sharks."

The voice of black protest—in insurrection and in sagas of life in bondage written by former slaves like Frederick Douglass—would be heard for years to come. By 1804 the states north of Maryland had taken steps to abolish slavery. But in 1850 the Fugitive Slave Act, which required citizens of free states to turn in runaways, aroused the North "like a firebell in the night." Emerson called it a "filthy enactment," and abolitionist Theodore Parker penned a warning to Negroes (opposite) after runaway Thomas Sims was dragged out of Boston and publicly whipped in Savannah. As a war measure in 1863, Lincoln freed the slaves in secessionist states; but rebels who surrendered in 90 days could keep their slaves. "It is my last card," he said, "and I will play it and may win the trick."

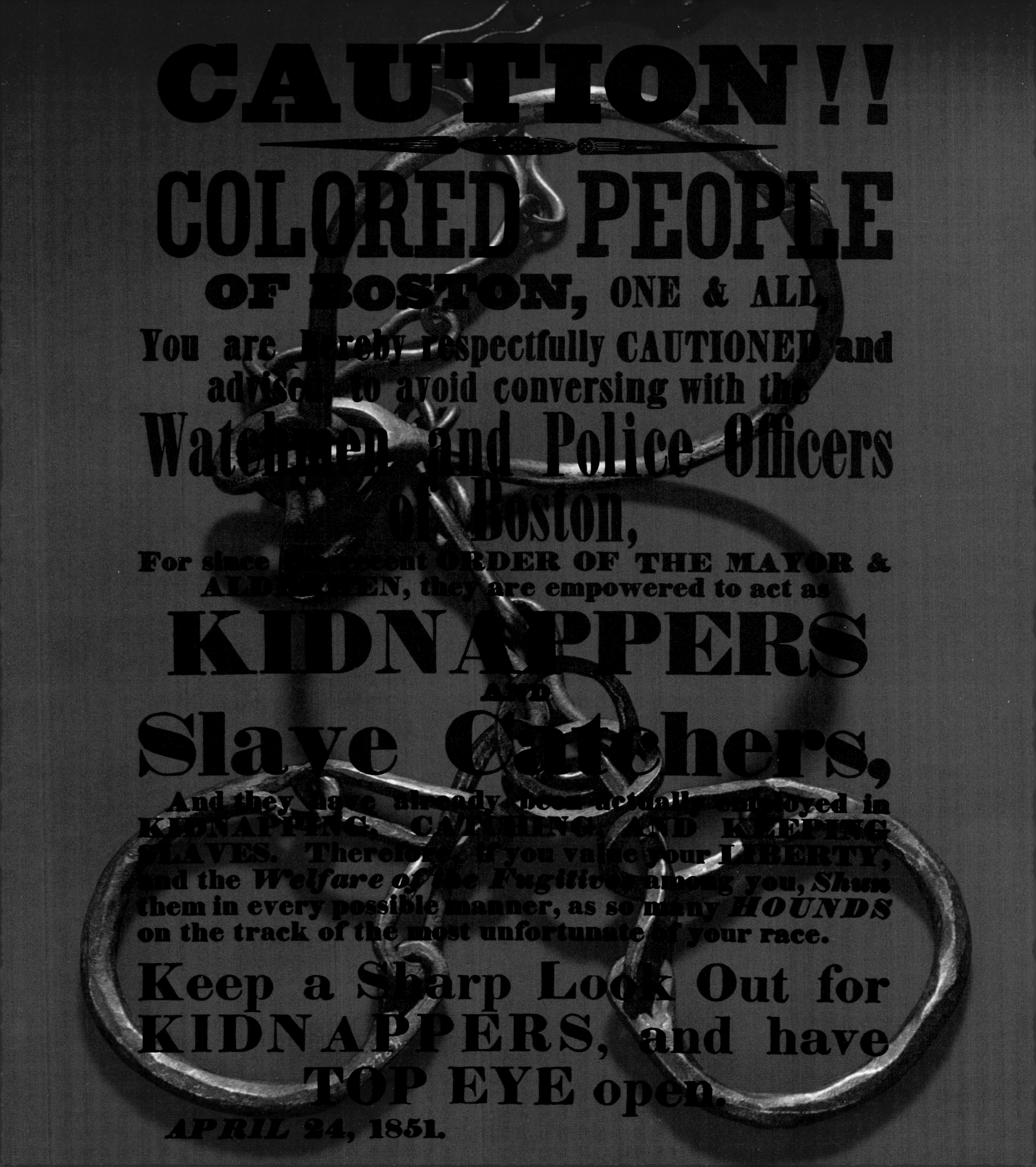

CAUTION!!

COLORED PEOPLE

OF BOSTON, ONE & ALL,

You are hereby respectfully CAUTIONED and advised, to avoid conversing with the

Watchmen and Police Officers

of Boston,

For since the recent ORDER OF THE MAYOR & ALDERMEN, they are empowered to act as

KIDNAPPERS

And

Slave Catchers,

And they have already been actually employed in KIDNAPPING, CATCHING, AND KEEPING SLAVES. Therefore, if you value your LIBERTY, and the *Welfare of the Fugitives* among you, *Shun* them in every possible manner, as so many *HOUNDS* on the track of the most unfortunate of your race.

Keep a Sharp Look Out for
KIDNAPPERS, and have
TOP EYE open.

APRIL 24, 1851.

Living Through a Civil War

David Herbert Donald

To blare of bugle and roll of regimental drum—sounding for camp's dull routine or battle's dread thrill—Johnny Reb and Billy Yank marched to civil war. Theirs was a contest of unequal odds. A Confederacy with a white population of 5.5 million faced a Union with 20 million. Eight out of ten of the sundered nation's factories hummed on the Northern side. It had 70 percent of the railroad mileage and most of the money. Yet the war was joined—with all its glory and valor, its tragedy and muck, its toll of more than 600,000 dead. Most who fought were young; one authority estimates two-thirds of the Federals joined before 22. Many an under-age lad evaded enlistment rules by hiding the number 18 in his shoe, standing on it, and swearing he was "over 18." In dewy-faced freshness soldiers posed before "daguerrean artists" for "shadows" to send home. Identities might be lost, as with the Reb and Yank here, but all had one thought: "The differance between dyeing to day and to morrow is not much but we all prefer to morrow."

"So Civil War is inaugurated at last," George Templeton Strong wrote when he learned that the Confederates on April 12, 1861, had attacked the Union garrison at Fort Sumter, in the harbor of Charleston, South Carolina. "GOD SAVE THE UNION, AND CONFOUND ITS ENEMIES. AMEN," the New Yorker prayed. When news of the firing on Sumter reached Georgia, it aroused a different emotion in the heart of the Reverend Charles Colcock Jones. "All honor to Carolina!" he exclaimed. "I hope our state may emulate her bravery and patriotism—and *her self-sacrificing generosity....* The conduct of the government of the old United States towards the Confederate States is an outrage upon Christianity and the civilization of the age...."

Neither Strong nor Jones could conceivably be considered typical of the civilian population of their hostile sections. The New Yorker—son of a prominent attorney, an honors graduate of Columbia College (later Columbia University), and a partner in a profitable Wall Street law firm—was too conservative in politics, too fastidious in taste to be representative of anything more than a tiny section of the New York elite. Jones, for his part, was an equally exceptional Southerner. His ownership of three plantations, with some 3,600 acres and 129 slaves, in Liberty County along the coast south of Savannah, made him one of the wealthiest men of the area. Even less typical was his career as a Presbyterian minister. A product of seminaries at Andover and Princeton, he could have had his choice of Southern pulpits. Instead, he elected to spend most of his active years as missionary to the slaves of his region.

But if Strong and Jones were exceptional men, their responses nevertheless fairly captured the reactions of their rival sections to the outbreak of a war so long anticipated, so long feared. The written records left by these men, together with other members of their families, provide a comprehensive view of life behind the lines in both the Union and the Confederacy. Strong's account consists chiefly of the entries he made in an extraordinarily detailed and voluminous diary. Jones kept no such diary, but he and his family were prodigious letter writers. Two sons and a daughter, and a number of close relatives, kept in constant touch from their scattered homes and through their travels, penning a letter every three or four days, giving all the news.

Both Strong and Jones recorded the remarkable, if temporary, unanimity of sentiment that developed in the North and in the South after the hostilities began. Gone now were the doubts, the divisions, the differences that had plagued both sections for more than a decade. In the North loyalty to the Union, a sentiment that had seemed to

languish during the long years of sectional strife, welled up. The streets of New York, like those of most Northern cities, were thronged with volunteers. Stopping one young recruit, the son of a farmer who lived near Rochester, Strong asked why he had hurried to join the army. "I voted for Abe Lincoln," the lad told him, "and as there is going to be trouble, I might as well *fight* for Lincoln." Seeing flags displayed everywhere, Strong felt they symbolized the popular mood of "perfect unanimity, earnestness, and readiness to make every sacrifice for the support of law and national life."

Southerners too were ready to make every sacrifice. Secession, the organization of the Confederacy, and the outbreak of war put an end—at least temporarily—to local divisions. Now it seemed clear that advocates of Southern separatism had all along been right. The war made it easy to see, as Jones put it, that "we are two people distinctly and politically now—what we have been in fact for the last 10 or 15 years."

Confederate citizens rushed to enlist. "The anxiety among our citizens is not as to who shall *go* to the wars, but *who shall stay at home,*" noted the Georgia politician, Howell Cobb. In the Jones family it was plain that Charles Colcock Jones, Sr., a 56-year-old minister with impaired health, must remain at home, but he encouraged both his sons to join the army. His physician-son Joseph, with skills needed by the civilians of Augusta, nevertheless concluded "that he could not reconcile it to his conscience to remain quietly in professional pursuits when his country was imperiled; that the reflection in the future would be disagreeable when all would be over and he never to have borne any part in so good a cause." His brother Charles, who was mayor of Savannah when the fighting broke out, and could easily have avoided military service by accepting another term, decided that he must also enlist "as a matter of personal duty and of private example. . . . The service will be arduous, involving sacrifices great in their character; but I am of opinion that my duty requires it, and I will go."

Whether in the Union or the Confederacy, those unable to enlist wanted to assist the soldiers in every way they could. Sometimes such volunteer efforts were largely of symbolic value, as when some 30 New York society ladies met at the Strongs' house to sew havelocks—"white coverings for the military cap and for the back of the neck as a protection against heat," as Strong explained in his diary. It is doubtful that any Civil War soldier ever found these objects anything but a nuisance, but, as Winslow Homer depicted the scene in a widely published drawing, the dedication of the young women to the cause was impressively sincere.

Civilian efforts usually were more practical. Mary Jones, wife of the minister, pledged that she and her household slaves at Montevideo, the Joneses' 941-acre plantation on the North Newport River, would supply complete uniforms for four Confederate volunteers. With the blessing of Mayor Jones, the women of Savannah held a fair in May 1861 and raised several thousand dollars for the benefit of Confederate soldiers. The mayor's cousin in Marietta, Georgia, teamed with other women to provide uniforms for Cobb County volunteers. Some bought the cloth and thread, others cut patterns, the rest sewed. "It is incredible how many garments can be made by machine and otherwise," she reported. "We furnished three companies [300 men] this week. . . ."

Far more extensive and highly organized were the exertions of Strong and his New York associates. The recent experience of the Crimean War had shown that, without proper sanitation and supplies, deaths from disease would probably exceed those from combat. But well-informed Northerners realized that the tiny medical bureau of the United States Army, headed by a doddering surgeon general, was wholly unprepared to cope with the impending problems. So a group of prominent New Yorkers formed a volunteer auxiliary association which became known as the United States Sanitary Commission; it undertook to supervise the diet, hygiene, and hospital care of Union

"WAR—Exsurgat Deus"

When New Yorker George T. Strong, stirred by the fall of Fort Sumter, called for God to rise up, he viewed the conflict as "a religious war"—more important to mankind than any "since the Saracen invasion . . . was beat back by Charles Martel." In Georgia, Charles C. Jones saw it as "a national judgment" that "comes from God . . . to accomplish given ends." Such thoughts reflected the tenor of a divided, but devoutly Christian, populace.

Invoking God in Southern anthem or Northern "Spirit of '61" poster, citizens rallied—as at Union Square in New York (opposite) where 200,000 greeted Sumter defender Maj. Robert Anderson "with roars that were tremendous." The flag he had struck on April 14, 1861, graced Washington's statue. In four years to the day Anderson would raise the flag again over the recaptured fort.

John R. Strong (left) and George T. Strong, Jr.

Ellen Ruggles Strong

George Templeton Strong, Sr.

In four years of war "we . . . lived a century"

Taught by a doting mother and encouraged by a lawyer-father who spent hours with him at evening lessons, George Templeton Strong was reading at four, studying astronomy, botany, and Latin at seven, and browsing for fun through Sophocles in Greek at 12. At 14 he entered college and at 15 began the diary that—40 years and some 4.5 million words later—became a rich legacy for posterity.

Strong was a prominent Wall Street attorney of 41 when the war thrust him into a key role with the U. S. Sanitary Commission. The volunteer organization sought to relieve the war's horrors for troops whose "line of march is traceable by the deposit of dysenteric stool." The Commission recruited nurses, planted vegetable gardens at hospitals to improve diets, supplied drugs, dispensed "fifty thousand pounds of anti-scorbutics . . . daily to an army that has begun to shew symptoms of scurvy." Almost every day Strong's diary noted some Commission chore.

His wife, Ellen—a "heroine" he married in an 1848 rite followed by a "soirée dansante, all very jolly and brilliant"—also labored for the Commission. She ran fairs, acted in plays to raise funds, and served as a nurse on a hospital ship in Hampton Roads. Strong lauded her "call" to patriotic work—"a loud call, of two hundred trombone power"—yet in typical male fashion worried about "the little woman" and thanked Heaven her exertions did not leave her "broken down and . . . ill."

Strong crowded "a century of common life" into his war years—helping choose a rector for Trinity Church, aiding the law school and new school of mines at Columbia College, saying no to a suggestion that he become a candidate for the college presidency. Still, he found time for such things as helping his children "ignite certain crackers" on July Fourth or playing chess with ten-year-old Johnny.

"What a time it has been," he wrote of the war years. Yet they took their toll. Illness and postwar economic conditions harried him. He died in 1875. Among the mourners in packed Trinity Church: President U. S. Grant.

Mary Jones Jones

Mary Jones Mallard

Charles Colcock Jones, Sr.

Joseph Jones

Charles C. Jones, Jr.

"Write . . . regularly," admonished Charles Colcock Jones, and members and relatives of the close-knit Georgia family heeded—with some 6,000 letters that paint an intimate picture of Southern life and the war. Few details escape: a prosaic remark ("stormy today") or a vivid account of collapsing in a dentist's chair "from nervous exhaustion and loss of blood" after having nine teeth pulled.

A tidewater missionary and planter, Jones won recognition even in the North as "Apostle to the Blacks" for his evangelism among slaves. He married his first cousin—"my love, my sweet Mary"—in 1830; it was she who took special interest in collecting the family letters. Their firstborn, Charles Jr., a Princeton- and Harvard-trained lawyer, spent the war as

an artillery colonel irritated by "mosquitoes and fleas" and a diet of " 'sobby corn dodgers' and antiquated beef." His brother Joseph won degrees from Princeton and the University of Pennsylvania medical school; as a wartime major assigned to medical research he once visited Andersonville prison to study "the most dreadful diseases amongst those infamous Yankees." Daughter Mary—a "sprightly, intelligent" product of a Philadelphia finishing school—married at 21 before the war's outbreak. All survived the conflict except Charles Jones, Sr. When he died in 1863 from an old ailment, slaves at his graveside (left) recalled his Christian ministry: "Our dear master has not left any of us poor," said Sue, a house servant.

troops. In June 1861, at the second meeting of the Commission, Strong was named treasurer. For the rest of the war he spent at least half his time at the Commission's headquarters on Broadway. As branches sprang up across the country, his responsibility was to coordinate their fund-raising drives and to see that the money contributed was prudently and honestly spent. By the end of the war Strong had approved disbursements totaling $4,925,000; no hint of fraud or jobbery ever touched his office.

Thanks in considerable measure to Strong's exertions, the Sanitary Commission was able to supply to Union troops those necessities the incompetent army administration neglected. An admiring reporter listed some items stocked at depots close behind battle lines: "Stockings, shirts, drawers, trowsers . . . pillows for the head and for stumps of limbs, slings of various sizes, paper, envelopes, pencils, sponges . . . towels, brooms,

buckets, bed-pans, crutches, drinking cups, matches, tobacco, pipes, liquors of different kinds, oranges and lemons, spoons, soft bread, oatmeal . . . farina, dishes of different kinds, tents, bedticks, shoes, slippers, beefsteak . . . canned fruits and vegetables, dried fruits, pickled onions . . . candles, soap, canes, fans."

No mere clerk, Strong frequently had to go with other Commission members to Washington to cut through red tape so these supplies could reach the fronts. The Commission forced the retirement of the ill-qualified head of the army medical bureau and promoted the appointment of brilliant, if irascible, William Hammond as surgeon general. Utterly dedicated to relieving soldiers from needless suffering, Strong and his colleagues judged Washington officials by their willingness to work with the Commission. Strong found Lincoln's chief of staff, Henry W. Halleck, a foot dragger and concluded he was "weak, shallow, commonplace, vulgar." Secretary of War Edwin M. Stanton, who had taken a dislike to the Commission, struck him as "not a first-rate man morally or intellectually." But Gen. Ulysses S. Grant, who consistently favored the Commission's work, "talks like an earnest business man, prompt, clear-headed, and decisive, and utters no bosh."

Visiting the Army of the Potomac during Gen. George B. McClellan's 1862 thrust toward Richmond on the peninsula between the York and James rivers, Strong was horrified to discover that army doctors were "utterly and disgracefully unprovided" for their duties. Strong saw "men . . . lying on bare hospital floors and perishing of typhoid who could be saved if they had a blanket or a bed, or appropriate food and . . . hospital clothing instead of their mud-encrusted uniforms." He vowed he would help correct this situation, even if he had to neglect his law practice and lose half his income. Before the end of the war he could take rightful pride in the success of the Commission. "I believe," he recorded, ". . . that we have saved more men than have been lost in any two days' fighting since the war began. Thank God that a miserable, nearsighted cockney like myself can take part in any work that . . . helps on the national cause."

Devotion to the national unity was not, of course, confined to men. Northern women — like those in the Confederacy — freely contributed time, energy, and money to the cause. Strong's wife, daughter of one of the wealthiest and most aristocratic lawyers in New York, felt the same impulse to serve as did her husband. In 1862 she volunteered to help nurse the wounded from the disastrous Peninsular Campaign, and,

A puny U. S. Army of 16,000 in 1860 swelled with war's outbreak into "watch-fires of a hundred circling camps." Blue forces at Cum-berland Landing in the 1862 campaign against Richmond covered "Twenty square miles" with "a solid mass of tents and artillery and wagons." Drawn to war were men of 80 — and boys. Johnny Clem (opposite), a drum-mer at nine, rose in peace to major general.

"... such stuff as dreams are made on"

The ad offered "PHOTOGRAPHS, RICH, RARE, AND RACY" that the Civil War soldier could buy for 50 cents. And buy he did. Pinups papered camp huts and went into knapsacks of Reb and Yank. Some were "actress cards." This one of a leggy charmer came from France—where Louis Daguerre's 1839 invention was snapping nudes by 1840. The commonest were fashion drawings cut from magazines. Showing mainly hoops and ruffles, they still delighted "the boys . . . most of whom have forgotten the appearance of the female form divine," a lieutenant noted.

Magazines and dime novels bought from sutlers, and meatier books from home, helped pass the tedium of camp. So did gambling. "Nine out of ten play cards for money," a soldier wrote—though before a battle Bibles often displaced decks. Favored gaming ran to poker and dice, but men even bet on races and fights staged with lice.

"Fancy ladies" flocked to cities near the front. In Washington so many roamed one area that soldiers—with a play on the name of a Union general—called it "Hooker's Division." Ribaldry extended into song, with both sides hurling taunts in verse across the lines.

No other U. S. war has produced so many songs. By the thousands they poured out— Northern publishers even sending ballad sheets through the blockade. Some stirred dreams of an Aura Lea, others sentiments of flag and home. A favorite—or a well-known hymn—might set enemy camps singing in unison. Oddly, "Dixie" was written by a Northerner; "Battle Hymn of the Republic" stemmed from a Southern air.

to her husband's considerable surprise, found that she enjoyed the "Bohemian life" of a nurse. Her superiors commended her "cordial acquiescence in drudgery."

Not all women were willing to play the traditional roles that conservative males like Strong expected of them. Indeed, the war considerably accelerated the women's rights movement. Organizing the Women's Loyal National League to promote the twin causes of Union and emancipation of slaves, Susan B. Anthony and Elizabeth Cady Stanton achieved a degree of political influence they had never had before; their wartime activities greatly strengthened the woman's suffrage cause after the war. Working independently of the Sanitary Commission, Clara Barton—later to found the American Red Cross—did heroic service in getting medical supplies to the front and in ministering to the wounded. After a day in an army hospital following one of the major battles, she wrote, "I wrung the blood from the bottom of my clothing before I could step, for the weight about my feet." Less conspicuous was the work of Abigail W. May; as chairman of the New England Women's Auxiliary Association of the Sanitary Commission, she helped raise nearly one million dollars and, to Strong's disgust, insisted upon having a say in how it was spent. Strong recorded that she "invited us to invite her attendance" at meetings, where her presence put a considerable constraint upon the male members —in addition to preventing them from smoking their favorite cigars.

O f course not even the most dedicated civilian, whether in the North or the South, could devote all his time and energy to supporting the national cause. Even in the midst of death and desolation, people worked and ate and slept; family life revolved in the familiar cycles of marriages, births, and deaths. Especially in the North—except in the small portion touched by Confederate invasions—everyday life for civilians went on at much the usual pace. George Templeton Strong, for example, found that his work for the Sanitary Commission still left time for his many other interests: "energizing in Wall Street with reasonable diligence," serving as vestryman for Trinity Church and as trustee of Columbia College, going to monthly meetings of the Century Club where he enjoyed the company of such men as George Bancroft, the historian, Francis Lieber, the political theorist, and Abram S. Hewitt, the industrialist. And only the most desperate emergency could keep him from regularly attending the opera and the Philharmonic concerts, for he was passionately devoted to music.

Still, the war did make a difference. Secession and the outbreak of hostilities precipitated a sharp depression in early 1861. By September Strong declared he was "resigned to speedy and total insolvency. War, taxes, and cessation of business will have done their work before long." In early 1862 when the Union government, unable to finance the war, issued unredeemable treasury notes (promptly dubbed "greenbacks") to pay its bills, Strong felt the financial pinch even more sharply. As the notes depreciated in value, debtors rushed to pay off their mortgages and to redeem their bonds; the man who had borrowed a dollar in gold in 1861 could pay his debt with a greenback that by 1864 was worth only about 63 cents. Strong, who had invested heavily in bonds and mortgages, found the effect "disastrous."

Strong's view of the economy was unnecessarily pessimistic. By the middle of 1862 the North as a whole began to prosper. His father-in-law, Samuel B. Ruggles, who made a railroad tour of the Middle West that summer, better understood the temper of the times. Telling Strong of the huge wheat and corn crops he had seen, Ruggles said he was confident "of our national wealth and ability to feed the world." He predicted that he would live to see "King Cotton dethroned and King Breadstuff crowned as his successor." Buoyantly optimistic, Ruggles was always ready to invest in new projects. He tried to interest his son-in-law in the newly chartered Union Pacific Railroad, and he forecast that, once it linked with the Central Pacific pushing east, it would prove

Through soldiers' eyes

Little but the name is known of the Confederate artilleryman who painted the swirl of battle around Elkhorn Tavern in the South's defeat at Pea Ridge, Arkansas. Or of the Massachusetts sergeant whose sketches dramatize camp punishment. A man could be spread-eagled to a gun-carriage wheel for kicking a horse or getting drunk—perhaps, wrote a Yank, on whiskey made from "bark juice, tar-water, turpentine, brown sugar, lamp-oil and alcohol." A soldier could be told to perch on an open barrel with weighted knapsack or made to parade in a "wooden overcoat"—for swearing at an officer. Courts-martial, recorded in explicit detail, reveal that Rebel and Union soldiers blued the air with epithets familiar to GIs of yesterday and today.

enormously profitable. The fast-growing petroleum industry, which sprang up after Edwin L. Drake successfully drilled for oil near Titusville, Pennsylvania, in 1859, also fascinated Ruggles. He gave Strong 10,000 shares of Kenzua Petroleum Company stock, but his son-in-law failed to catch his enthusiasm. "My stock has cost me nothing, so I have nothing at stake," Strong wrote, "and any oil of gladness that may flow therefrom, if only half a pint, will be so much clear gain."

Strong, suspicious of quick profits, viewed disdainfully the extraordinary prosperity evident throughout the North by 1863. He held himself aloof from the newly wealthy "shoddy aristocrats"—so called because some had made their fortunes by selling the government uniforms made of shoddy, the sweepings from floors of woolen mills and cutting shops. Held together with glue, the stuff made passable cloth until exposed to the first rainstorm. Strong was disgusted by the contrast between the deprivation he witnessed on the battlefield and the conspicuous consumption exhibited by "the crowds of gents and giggling girls" who flocked to the newly opened Central Park on Sundays to display their expensive clothing, jewels, and carriages. He shared the censorious view of the *New York Independent* which railed in June 1864: "Go into Broadway, and we will show you what is meant by the word 'extravagance.' Ask Stewart [a noted department store owner] about the demand for camel's-hair shawls, and he will say 'monstrous.' Ask Tiffany what kind of diamonds and pearls are called for. He will answer 'the prodigious,' 'as near hen's-egg size as possible,' 'price no object.' "

Failing to share in this prosperity, Strong, though wealthy, sympathized with those who were hurt by wartime inflation. Until the end of 1864 wages failed to keep up with prices, and laborers suffered. Women workers were particularly hard hit, especially those whose husbands were in the army and could contribute little to support their families. As more and more women sought employment, their wages fell. In 1861, for instance, the government paid women employees at the Philadelphia Armory 17½ cents for making an army shirt. Three years later, when prices were at their peak, it paid only 15 cents—and private contractors paid only 8. Inequity and deprivation gave life to the nearly defunct labor movement, and newly formed unions often threatened work stoppages to get higher wages. With tolerance exceptional in a man of his background, Strong noted on November 12, 1863, "Workmen and workwomen of almost every class are on strike (and small blame to them). . . ."

Strong's tolerance, however, was not broad enough to extend to workers who challenged the government's war policies. With total lack of sympathy he witnessed the New York City draft riot of July 11-13, 1863, the worst of a series of such eruptions across the Northern states. To workingmen, the administration in Washington appeared uninterested in their problems while it showed profound concern about those of blacks in the South. Lincoln's Emancipation Proclamation of January 1, 1863, seemed to many white laborers in the North less a humanitarian act than an invitation for more and more freed slaves to pour into the cities and compete for jobs.

Discontent became open disaffection when the Lincoln administration resorted to conscription in order to maintain the armies in the field. The initial draft produced an explosion in New York. A mob first attacked the enrollment officers who were drawing the names of draftees, then turned on the police, and further diverted itself in what Strong called "cowardly ruffianism and plunder" of stores and warehouses. Toward the blacks of the city the mob exhibited its most fearsome hostility. After sacking and burning a Negro orphan asylum, the rioters hunted down any blacks unwary enough to appear on the streets and hanged to lampposts those they were able to catch. Loathing this "Irish anti-conscription Nigger-murdering mob," Strong urged that it be "put down by heroic doses of lead and steel."

More than Northerners, civilians of the South found that the war affected every facet of their daily lives. Almost from the beginning Confederates began to feel the pinch of the shortages. Theirs was an agricultural society, primarily devoted to raising cotton and tobacco. When the war closed Northern markets and the Union blockade cut off those in Europe, bales and hogsheads piled up. Confederate authorities urged farmers to grow grain instead. Having the utmost confidence in Jefferson Davis, "our worthy President (at once soldier and statesman)," the Jones family willingly responded to this appeal. Cotton planting at 2,000-acre Arcadia, largest of their plantations, was limited in the 1862 season to one acre for every field hand. Wrote Charles C. Jones, Jr., approvingly: "Every bushel of corn and blade of grass will be greatly needed for the support of our armies."

But the transformation of Southern agriculture could not prevent food shortages in the Confederacy. With so many men in the army, there were not enough hands to till crops, and the creakingly inefficient Southern rail system made it impossible to distribute fairly what food there was. As early as August 1861 the Joneses' cousin in Marietta complained of the "high price of bacon, corn, and coffee." With amazement she announced, "Rice is three pounds to the dollar and very scarce."

Soon such prices would be considered astonishingly low. The Confederacy, even before the Union, turned to the printing press to finance the war, issuing paper money in an endless stream. Nobody knew just how much was printed. A Southern humorist claimed that when the Secretary of the Treasury was asked "to say bout how much he thought war in sirkulation . . . he said . . . akkordin to the best of his rekelekshun, thar war six hundred miliyuns or six thousand miliyuns — he warent sure which." A Confederate treasury note with a face value of one dollar was worth but 29 cents in gold by 1863, only 1.7 cents by early 1865. As the value of money fell, prices soared. "Living is ruinous, and exceedingly scarce," reported Mrs. Jones's brother from Rome, Georgia. "We have not had a piece of meat on our table for five days." Skyrocketing prices made Charles C. Jones, Jr., a beggar, and he wrote his parents "to send us *anything to eat* which you can spare from the place."

Nevertheless, the Joneses were comparatively fortunate. Those Southerners who had no country relatives to draw upon for food, and particularly those who lived on fixed incomes in the cities, fared worse. The situation in Richmond, capital of the Confederacy, was most critical of all. Overflowing with officers and civilian officials and their families, this sleepy Southern town grew into a city overnight. But public services were virtually nonexistent; housing was scarce and expensive; food, regularly diverted from the capital to the nearby army, was in short supply. The chief of the Confederate Bureau of War, Robert Kean, complained that Richmond prices made his $3,000 salary worth about what $300 would ordinarily buy, and by October 1863 his family was reduced to eating only two meals a day. J. B. Jones, a clerk in the department, reported in May 1864 that shoes sold for $125 a pair, potatoes for $25 a bushel, and flour for $275 a barrel. "Such is the scarcity of provisions," he declared, "that rats and mice have mostly disappeared, and the cats can hardly be kept off the table."

Until 1864 the Jones family in rural Georgia suffered comparatively little. Of course they missed luxuries like tea, which had to be smuggled through the Northern blockade, but, as Mrs. Jones asserted, "We will endure privations joyfully rather than yield an inch to the vile miscreants that are now seeking our destruction." More serious was the shortage of salt, for without it they could not preserve and store meat. As increasing numbers of Georgians trooped to the coast to boil sea water and produce their own salt, they began to chop down trees and steal firewood from Maybank, the Joneses' 700-acre plantation overlooking the mouth of the Medway River. Early in the war the Joneses needed clothing and blankets for their slaves. Since the few woolen factories in the

"They peopled Hades," a journalist wrote of artillerymen handling cannon like these 12-pounders in a Union battery drilling before the *battle of Chancellorsville. Basic field gun for both Blue and Gray, the muzzle-loaders could fire three rounds a minute: solid balls with a* *range of 1,500 yards or shot-filled canisters that at 200 yards sprayed a deadly hail on troops advancing shoulder-to-shoulder.*

"... the last full measure of devotion"

The immortal tribute to the war's "honored dead" rang out in Abraham Lincoln's two-minute address at Gettysburg. There had flared the costliest battle of a conflict that took some 360,000 Union and 258,000 Confederate lives. The exact toll may never be known; sketchy Federal records and a Richmond fire leave historians sifting estimates. But this is sure: More men died in the Civil War than in any other the nation has fought.

The war also saw unprecedented suffering. Both sides were slow to gear for handling casualties. After the first battle of Bull Run men with bullets in their legs had to walk 20 miles for treatment. At Seven Pines the wounded lay for hours in a cold drenching rain. "Many died from this exposure, and others prayed for death to relieve them from their anguish," an observer wrote.

Even after field hospitals and trained ambulance teams became common, the wounded still faced fearsome trials. Medical knowledge was slim. Flaxseed and bread served as poultices; opium and morphine were indiscriminately used in liquids, pastes, pills, and plasters. One man, shot through the abdomen, "rallied after free exhibition of whiskey and Morphia," a physician reported.

Soft lead bullets shattered bone, and every battle left amputees like these at Chancellorsville. Risk of infection was great. "We knew nothing about antiseptics," a surgeon would recall. Anesthesia in operations had begun in 1846, and ether and chloroform were given more than 80,000 times in the war. Yet many doctors believed "surgical shock" valuable and so opposed anesthesia; thousands of patients did without. At Gettysburg a general described how surgeons, "their bare arms ... smeared with blood, their knives not seldom held between their teeth," worked amid "pools of blood and amputated arms or legs." With the wounded bandaged by rags, or carried in manure-littered railroad cars that had just hauled horses, little wonder more men died from wounds than were killed in action.

Disease took even more. "They hev Been 11 Died with the fever ... and 2 died that was wounded so you now See that these Big Battles is not as Bad," a Carolinian noted.

Typhoid and dysentery rampaged because of poor sanitation and contaminated water. Camps pitched in swamps invited malaria; not until the century's end did science prove that insects carried disease. Lice roasted from clothes at campfires reminded soldiers of "popping corn." Fleas formed "in companies ... for the purpos of carrying us off."

Men who fell in battle usually were buried on the spot, with a blanket for a casket and a pencil-marked scrap of wood for a headboard. Where the sweep of battle left no time for niceties, as at Cold Harbor (right), months might pass before interment. Embalmers—like these displaying bodies in coffins at a wreath-draped "office" near Gettysburg—served anyone willing to bear "the cash cost of caring for a dead comrade."

Despite the grim statistics, notable advances in medicine could be counted. From the war came the pattern for the modern hospital; medical specialties developed; a system of case reporting began; the nurse was transformed from pesthouse attendant to respected professional. Thus, for more than the Union's preservation, those "who here gave their lives" did not die in vain.

The black role in "a white man's war"

Hardly had Sumter fallen when black students at an Ohio college leaped to enlist. Their state rebuffed them; "We were told... this was a white man's war," one recalled. Prejudice ran deep—"I don't think enough of the Niggar to go and fight for them," a Union soldier said. Attitudes eased as the view spread that, to destroy the Confederacy, its slavery prop had to be toppled. Blue columns drew trails of liberated slaves. "We bring in some 500 prisoners... and about ten miles of Negroes," a general reported.

Blacks at first found service overseeing refugee camps. But by mid-1863 recruitment for regular regiments zoomed. Eventually some 179,000—three-fourths of them from slaveholding states—enlisted. Most did garrison or fatigue duty, though some saw combat. A number, like this sergeant little known but by name, won noncommissioned rank. Their officers usually were whites; a chance at a lieutenant's pay was "no small temtation" to serve in an all-black unit.

When Federals advanced, Southerners moved field hands to "safe" plantations. But, as Charles Colcock Jones put it, "no reliance can be placed *certainly* upon any." Yet the alacrity with which slaves seized freedom when the opportunity came surprised most owners. The Confederacy in March 1865 finally turned to enlisting blacks, but by then the war already was lost. In North and South, the donning of the uniform had opened avenues to far-reaching social change.

South were busy with orders for uniforms, Mrs. Jones undertook the hard labor of weaving her own blankets, and her husband proudly reported that she "clothed most of the people" on the plantation as well.

The fate of these "people"—Southern planters rarely spoke of "slaves" but called them "the servants" or "our people"—was a matter of growing concern to the Joneses. Far more than most Southern families, they took a paternalistic interest in their slaves. Mrs. Jones treated them—especially the house servants she knew best—almost as members of the family. In 1864 when Elvira chose a husband, she received a regular wedding at Arcadia, where "wreaths of China brier were festooned over the doors and around the room, and on the mantelpiece stood two bottles filled with large bunches of dogwood flowers." Slave bridesmaids and groomsmen attended at the ceremony, which under Georgia law had no validity at all, since slaves were chattels.

A large portion of the Jones family fortune was invested in slaves. Along the Georgia seacoast, where without risk Federal gunboats could push up the hundreds of inlets and rivers almost to the doors of plantation houses, slaves were a particularly vulnerable sort of property. As early as July 1862 Jones learned that some slaves in Liberty County had run away to the Union boats. "The temptation of change, the promise of freedom and of pay for labor, is more than most can stand," he judged tolerantly.

That tolerance diminished after Lincoln issued the proclamation that made freedom for slaves an official war aim. Viewing Lincoln's emancipation announcement as "a direct bid for insurrection, as a most infamous attempt to incite flight, murder, and rapine on the part of our slave population," the Joneses began to look for a plantation in central Georgia, presumably safe from Union raids. At last they found one in Burke County, near Waynesboro, to which they sent most of the field hands.

Those whites who, like the Joneses, remained in the coastal area began to feel isolated and frightened. Since two-thirds of the voting population of Liberty County had enlisted and since most of the slaves had been moved inland, the countryside looked deserted. Sam, a faithful retainer, reported to the Joneses' cousin: "Liberty County *done*—the people *'most all gone 'way.'"* After the death of her husband from "wasting palsy" in 1863, Mrs. Jones was almost alone in the plantations at Montevideo and Arcadia, with "not a white female of my acquaintance nearer than eight or ten miles."

Mrs. Jones, however, fared better than her daughter, Mrs. Robert Quarterman Mallard, whose husband in 1863 accepted a call to a church in Atlanta. Believing, as did

"No one who has not seen the train of an army in motion, can form any just conception of its magnitude," a Union officer wrote. So Southerners marveled when Federal supply wagons streamed into captured Petersburg in 1865. Here was war in a new way—vast armies, masses of matériel. And, noted a historian, if God willed that the Union won, He was "on the side with the heaviest battalions."

Charles C. Jones, Jr., that "when peace and happiness are again restored . . . the future of this city will be very bright," Mallard and his family were just getting settled as Gen. William T. Sherman began his campaign to capture that bustling rail hub. Soon the city filled with refugees. Wounded soldiers poured in until stores and public buildings had to take the overflow from hospitals. For several months Mallard preached to the soldiers and left tracts at the hospitals, and his wife nursed the gravely ill. But when it became clear that Atlanta was going to fall, they fled to Montevideo.

After capturing Atlanta, Sherman turned from its smoking ruins and began to cut a swath across Georgia to the sea. The first Union troops, belonging to Gen. Judson Kilpatrick's cavalry, descended upon Montevideo on December 15. Arresting any able-bodied white males they found and enticing blacks to leave the plantations, soldiers went from house to house, ostensibly searching for weapons but actually seizing anything valuable they came across. They poked through every room at Montevideo, forcing Mrs. Jones to open cupboards and unlock trunks, and they made off with clothing, jewelry, and souvenirs. The soldiers stripped the storeroom of its sparse supply of corn-meal, bacon, and potatoes; they told Mrs. Mallard that "they meant to starve us to death." When Mrs. Jones begged the soldiers to leave enough food for the women and children, they laughed scornfully and dumped a quart or so of meal on the floor.

The Union troops made life at Montevideo a nightmare for three weeks. When not ransacking the big house, they prowled around the slave quarters, picking up what few valuables they could scrounge and making sexual advances toward the black women. The Jones household slaves proved clever at outwitting the succession of invaders. The young cook, chased into the big house by three lustful white soldiers and a Negro, locked herself in the kitchen to gain enough time to disguise herself as "a sick old woman, with a blanket thrown over her head and shoulders, and scarcely able to move." "Gilbert," Mrs. Mallard reported of another slave, "keeps a sling under his coat and slips his arm into it as soon as they appear; Charles walks with a stick and limps dreadfully; Niger a few days since kept them from stealing everything they wanted in his house by covering up in bed and saying he had *yellow fever.*"

Not all slaves, even on the Jones plantation, remained devoted to their masters. "The people are all idle . . . seeking their own pleasure," Mrs. Jones complained. Disillusioned by what she considered faithlessness on the part of so many of the slaves she had treated indulgently, she turned against them bitterly. "I have told some . . . that as they were perfectly useless here it would be best for me and for the good of their fellow servants if they would leave and go at once with the Yankees."

By mid-January 1865, as Sherman's army moved north to devastate the Carolinas, most of the Union soldiers in the Georgia coastal region disappeared, but the chaos and disorder they brought remained. If a planter left the area, vandals immediately stripped his house of everything movable. If he stayed on, he had to deal with surly and insolent blacks. In either case he was forced profoundly to alter his habits of thought. He had not merely to recognize that slavery was dead; he was forced to admit that his whole mythology about slavery as a benevolent institution, with which the blacks themselves were content, had been a tissue of lies. Living unprotected and almost alone at Montevideo, Mrs. Jones captured the mood of the Southern whites: "Clouds and darkness are round about us; the hand of the Almighty is laid in sore judgment upon us; we are a desolated and smitten people."

Absorbed in their own private and partial experience of the Civil War, most civilians, North and South, exhibited surprisingly little interest in the great problems of the period that have fascinated historians. Of course, educated families like the Joneses and the Strongs read in their newspapers accounts of campaigns and battles, followed the arguments over the merits of rival generals and strategies, or weighed alternate praise and condemnation of Presidents Lincoln and Davis. But the voluminous records kept by the Joneses and the Strongs—like those preserved by so many other civilians during the war—give remarkably little attention to those matters.

Not a member of the Jones family ever questioned the merit of the Confederate cause which, as Charles C. Jones, Sr., wrote, "exceeds in character that of our first [i.e., 1776] revolution." None ever doubted that it must be supported against "our malignant, unscrupulous, and determined enemy." Mrs. Jones spoke for her united family when she wrote: "I believe we are contending for a just and righteous cause; and I would infinitely prefer that *we all* perish in its defense before we submit to the infamy and disgrace and utter ruin and misery involved in any connection whatever with the vilest and most degraded nation on the face of the earth."

Similarly George Templeton Strong gave his unqualified support to the government in Washington. At the outset of the war he was put off by Lincoln's appearance and manner: "Decidedly plebeian. . . . his laugh is the laugh of a yahoo, with a wrinkling of the nose that suggests affinity with the tapir and other pachyderms; and his grammar is weak." But after seeing the President several times, Strong judged him "a most sensible, straightforward, honest old codger" and rated him "the best President we have had since old Jackson's time, at least." In December 1863, when most Northern politicians were sniping at the President, Strong intuitively understood the mood of the Northern people: "Uncle Abe is the most popular man in America today. The firmness, honesty, and sagacity of 'the gorilla despot' may be recognized by the rebels themselves sooner than we expect, and the weight of his personal character may do a great deal toward restoration of our national unity."

T hese civilians felt that in God's good time peace would come and, along with it, a new sense of nationhood—separate for the South, as Confederates hoped; one united country, as Northerners expected. Paradoxically, both goals were to some degree realized. The war did much to enhance the American sense of nationality. The victory of the North meant that the nation's territorial integrity would never again be challenged. During the war the functions of the government were enormously expanded, and the Chief Executive exercised power greater than that ever before entrusted to a single American. Even while the fighting raged, such things as establishment of a national bank, chartering of a transcontinental railroad, opening of public lands to homesteaders, and creation of land-grant colleges put government closer to people's affairs and strengthened the attenuated bonds of national unity.

But even as the war promoted American nationalism, it solidified the persistent sectionalism that had led to the conflict. After four years of war, Southerners and Northerners could not easily accept each other as members of a common country, or even as men and women sharing common human traits. Just as Southern whites came to think of pillaging and marauding Union soldiers as devils incarnate, so many Northern soldiers developed a fierce hatred for the South and its inhabitants. "Everything looks as if it is going to the devil," one Michigan volunteer reported of the South, "& I know the citizens ought to, & I have faith they will."

In March 1865 Strong wrote what he would never have said four years earlier: "I almost hope this war may last till it become a war of extermination." And in all the wartime Jones correspondence there is nothing like the hatred a daughter-in-law expressed when she learned of Lincoln's assassination: "One sweet drop among so much that is painful is that he at least cannot raise his howl of diabolical triumph over us."

Decades would pass before old rancors would fade, old sectionalisms meld in an expanding nation whose "new birth of freedom" Lincoln predicted at Gettysburg.

"I can make the march, and make Georgia howl"

The whole South howled when Gen. William T. Sherman made good his pledge to his chief, Gen. U. S. Grant. The two had agreed to a "burnt country" drive from Atlanta that would split the South, destroy resources needed for fighting, and hurry an end to the war.

Leaving Atlanta's factories and warehouses smoldering, Sherman marched to Savannah almost unopposed. His 60,000 men cut a swath 60 miles wide. With bonfires of crossties they heated ripped-up rails to wrap around trees—"Sherman's neckties"; chimneys of burned buildings stood as "Sherman's sentinels." His army lived off the land, picking farms so clean "there was not even a chicken" to eat the few "grains that Sherman's horses had left." Foragers harassed families; at the Reverend Jones's plantation their "wild halloos and cursing" sounded beneath a window while Mary Jones Mallard bore a daughter.

From Savannah Sherman turned north, skirting already shell-torn Charleston (opposite). Refugees fled his path. The war uprooted Southerners by the tens of thousands. Chasing a will-o'-the-wisp safety, many moved repeatedly, sometimes living on soup "made from half a Cow's head." "War is cruelty," said Sherman, "and you cannot refine it."

★1876★
Centennial!

William Peirce Randel

The Fourth of July comes every year, but '76 arrives only once in a century, once in a lifetime—the Fourth of July all year long. Americans planned to make the most of 1876, a grand time to refurbish old heroics, bind up sectional wounds, renew faith in the democratic process, beam with pride at a hundred years of progress. Scholars might contemplate sober appraisals, but the people—40 million strong—welcomed the Centennial Year with unparalleled exuberance, confident that it would prove forever memorable.

In January, less than a dozen years after Appomattox, the House of Representatives resolved not to disturb the present harmony "nor wantonly revive bitter memories of the past." A bill was introduced restoring full civil rights to the few former Confederates not included in the general pardon of 1872. But when debate began, James Blaine of Maine offered an amendment to exclude Jefferson Davis. An arrant opportunist, Blaine knew his action would split the Democratic majority and perhaps bolster his chance to win the Republican nomination for President. National harmony would have to wait.

Faith in the democratic process was the next casualty. Orville Babcock, President Grant's confidential secretary, went on trial for complicity with the Whiskey Ring, a conspiracy of distillers and tax officials. Instead of firing Babcock, Grant named him Inspector of Lighthouses.

A greater shock to the nation was the exposure, early in March, of Secretary of War William Belknap, a grafter who sold army post traderships and contracts for cemetery headstones. Impeached and tried, Belknap was acquitted because many Senators felt they lacked jurisdiction after Grant accepted Belknap's resignation. It set a bad precedent. Vermont Senator Justin Morrill observed, "The doctrine of resignation and avoidance . . . fritters away all the power there is of real substance in the Constitution relating to impeachments. . . ."

Other Cabinet members proved corrupt, and by midsummer Grant's administration was near collapse. Loyalty to friends, even when they grossly betrayed his faith, was Grant's undoing.

The nominating conventions in June offered some basis for hope. The Republicans ignored both Grant and the rascal Blaine, choosing instead Ohio's governor Rutherford B. Hayes. The Democrats named Governor Samuel Tilden of New York. Both were men of integrity, committed to reform; either would restore respect for the office of the President. But the election results were disputed and not settled until the eve of inauguration the next March. The protracted uncertainty plunged the nation back into despair. The year closed in a darkness as palpable as the bright hopes of its dawn.

Fortunately for the nation, diversions from harsh reality were plentiful. Horse racing led among spectator sports, and baseball was gaining ground. Melodramas like *East Lynne* and *The Octoroon* packed Broadway theaters and the "opera house" in many a remote small town. Young John Philip Sousa was touring the country as conductor of a variety show band. Comic opera was widely popular; favorites were Jacques Offenbach's *La Vie Parisienne* and *La Jolie Parfumeuse,* conducted by the French composer himself, one of the year's many eminent visitors from abroad. Vacation resorts—Saratoga Springs, the Poconos, San Diego—thrived in spite of

At the Independence Hall that brought forth the first Fourth of July, fireworks, bells, and torches hail a Centennial Fourth only a minute old.

the financial slump. People were reading John Habberton's syrupy *Helen's Babies* and Mark Twain's *Tom Sawyer*—which was banned by some libraries. Bayard Taylor, reigning as leading poet, was applauded for his parodies of Walt Whitman.

The major diversion of the year was the Centennial Exhibition, with 249 structures on 285 acres of Philadelphia's Fairmount Park. The Exhibition was officially opened by President Grant on May 10. Dom Pedro II, Emperor of Brazil, the one foreign head of state attending, joined Grant in starting the great Corliss Engine in Machinery Hall, and the Empress Theresa opened the Women's Pavilion. In the next six months millions of city and country Americans and visitors from abroad passed through the turnstiles (admission 50 cents) to admire fire engines and Pullman Palace Cars, totem poles, Swedish stoves, Benjamin Franklin's venerable hand press, cascading industrial pumps, etchings by Queen Victoria, a coat, vest, and breeches that George Washington had worn, stuffed birds, silkworms, popcorn machines, Japanese screens, Yale locks, canned oysters, and more paintings and sculpture than most visitors knew existed.

The Exhibition's architecture proved as fascinating as the exhibits themselves. The art gallery, Memorial Hall (which alone survives of the five major buildings), was the first large American structure in the neoclassic Beaux Arts style. Horticultural Hall's Moorish design included horseshoe arches of red, cream, and black brick. Agricultural Hall, an outsize barn, sported silo turrets. The two largest buildings, Machinery and Main, resembled factories except for their extensive decoration. All five buildings were admirably functional, the exhibits well displayed.

Technology was on the march in 1876, but in the prevailing complacency such portents of things to come as typewriters and the Otis safety elevator—soon to make skyscrapers feasible—were largely ignored. Alexander Graham Bell's telephone, on display in Main Hall, could not be demonstrated in the general hubbub and endless concerts, but it won a commendation from astonished judges at an after-hours demonstration.

The summer of 1876 was the hottest in 60 years. Only with cooler days did the Exhibition draw the crowds it was well able to accommodate. William Dean Howells, editor-in-chief of the *Atlantic Monthly,* was a frequent, enthusiastic, and perceptive visitor, but he sought in vain for a unifying principle in the kaleidoscope of displays. Other critics in the years since have decried the Exhibition's materialistic emphasis and motley architecture. But objective modern judgment must consider it a success. The variety of buildings faithfully reflected contemporary eclectic taste, while material progress was, next to independence itself, what most Americans believed they should be celebrating. The Exhibition not only bolstered national pride but also broadened Americans' awareness of many foreign cultures.

The crowning event of the year, on July 4, was not at the Exhibition but at Independence Square. A vast parade passed in review before Gen. William Tecumseh ("Uncle Billy") Sherman, commander of all United States armies. Guests included Prince Oscar of Sweden and General Saigo of Japan. The low rumble of spectator

On opening day at the Exhibition, 100,000 people and countless umbrellas jostle in front of Memorial Hall. "The first day," said a Japanese observer, "crowds come like sheep; run here, run there.... rush, push, tear, shout... say damn great many times." The 2,500-horsepower Corliss steam engine (opposite) provided power for saws, lathes, presses, pumps, and mills in Machinery Hall.

German cannon and an iron obelisk give a martial air to Machinery Hall, which had more sewing machines than artillery. The cap pistol (opposite) and other souvenirs went home with visitors — some of whom may have worried about their health. To ward off the 10 million Centennial tourists, some misanthropic Philadelphians posted signs on their houses warning of smallpox.

excitement competed against a reading of the Declaration of Independence and the formal speeches. Everyone noticed President Grant's absence and many condemned it. But relatively few in the vast crowd noticed the day's chief incident. In the midst of the festivities, five women headed by Susan B. Anthony mounted the platform and handed the startled master of ceremonies a "Declaration of Rights for Women." As they retreated, these five pioneers of women's liberation scattered invitations to a meeting at a nearby church, where a large audience cheered the new song, "A Hundred Years Hence," predicting a government no longer exclusively male.

The decision not to open the Exhibition on Sundays was less a concession to piety than recognition of the Sabbath suspension of railroad travel. Railroads in 1876 were the principal means of transportation and essential to industry. Competition for their control had become fierce and ruthless. For the richly rewarded winners 1876 was the last year of unchallenged complacency; 1877 brought a railroad strike—the first general strike in American history—and the birth of effective union power.

The indulgent public made folk heroes of financial wizards, just as they did of Western badmen, who were motivated by the same dream of wealth, though far less successful in attaining it. Jesse James's raid on a Northfield, Minnesota, bank on September 7, 1876, failed so dismally that his gang was never again a potent threat. But to the civilized East, the lawless and picturesque West was an exciting distraction from political debacle. Dodge City, only four years old, had already earned a reputation for vice and violence when Bat Masterson arrived there as U. S. marshal in 1876. The Black Hills town of Deadwood, with a hundred saloons and one church, was a strong rival for notoriety. There, on August 2, retired marshal Wild Bill Hickok was fatally shot while playing poker. His occasional companion, Calamity Jane, one of the frontier's many fascinating women, was on the federal payroll in 1876 as a scout in Custer's command. She was ill on June 25 and missed the action now known as "Custer's Last Stand." The massacre caused a major sensation when news of it reached the East on July 5. Only a few people questioned the cause Custer died for.

Scattered through the federal government were men of enlightened outlook, distinguished scientists dedicated to public service. George Davidson, noted for his achievements in the use of astronomy for a navigational survey of the Pacific Coast, spoke for all such men when he boasted, in 1900, of having worked Sundays and holidays for 45 years "because I believe I can add something to human knowledge."

Such words, however meaningless to venal Cabinet members, were understood on the college campus. Farsighted educators were adding practical studies and research to traditional classical studies. As one university president put it, the curriculum should range "from hog cholera to Plato." Such radicalism aroused strong opposition from sectarians fearful that science would undermine religious faith and from those who insisted that a good education must include heavy doses of Greek and Latin—"the Latin fetish," as England's T. H. Huxley, the world's best-known scientist, called it.

News that Huxley would visit the United States in 1876 exhilarated scientists and outraged religious fundamentalists. Huxley lectured on evolution, but more significant was his address at the new Johns Hopkins University. Discussing the American future, Huxley said that size and wealth do not make a nation; what matters more are the uses to which these things would be put. "You and your descendants," he said, "will have to ascertain whether this great mass will hold together under the forms of a republic. . . ." Huxley concluded that "the one condition of success, your sole safeguard, is the moral worth and intellectual clearness of the individual citizen." If no other relic of the Centennial survived, this challenge with its undiminished relevance would make the year memorable.

LIFE

The Centennial era: It was an age that inaugurated apartment houses and national parks, linoleum and oleomargarine, riveted Levis and Hires Root Beer, football and dime stores. It was the Gilded Age of Jay Gould and Horatio Alger. It was a time of energy and inventiveness, of expansion and mobility— and change. In Texas you could still buy land for 50 cents an acre, and travelers roared over the rails from San Francisco to New York City in six days and twenty hours. Americans seemed to be building a new civilization on what awed them the most: the machine and mass production.

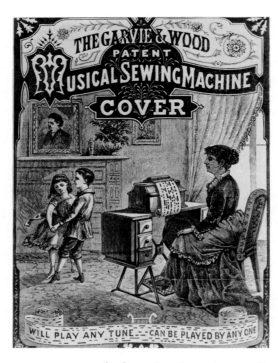

THE GARVIE & WOOD PATENT MUSICAL SEWING MACHINE COVER

WILL PLAY ANY TUNE — CAN BE PLAYED BY ANY ONE

Machines of note

devised in this great age of invention included the dual-purpose musical sewing machine cover, patented in 1882. The sewing machine treadle operated the musical rollers, which in turn produced melodies. The era also ushered in the telephone, phonograph, electric light, carpet sweeper, cash register, automatic milking machine, and the first safe can opener (it used a cutting wheel instead of a bayonetlike blade). An observer at the Exhibition noted that Americans displayed more labor-saving devices than "articles of beauty and elegance."

A final photograph

before burial was a common practice; often the family gathered around the casket. Sometimes a photographer would be summoned to a deathbed to make a last portrait—living or dead. Fewer than half the infants born survived beyond ten years. Children's books dwelt on death. In an age that knew little of bacteriology or preventive medicine, friends comforted parents with the adage: "'Tis virtue makes an early grave."

Art for the masses

meant one or more of John Rogers's plaster "groups" in the parlor; "a few statuettes," said *American Woman's Home*, ". . . will give a really elegant finish to your rooms." Mass-produced by the thousands and sold chiefly by mail (free glue was included for repairs), the table-top sculptures cost from $6 to $25. The scenes of family and village life were as respectable as the equally popular Currier & Ives prints. Sentimental art had much greater appeal than the works of some contemporary American artists, such as Thomas Eakins, generally condemned for being too realistic.

Flaunting improprieties,

photographer Frances Benjamin Johnston in a self-portrait symbolizes rebellion against a society that forbade women to smoke, touch alcohol to their lips, or exhibit their limbs. A French visitor of the 1880's saw some contrasts: The unmarried girl was "independent. . . . When the fancy strikes her, she travels with a gentleman . . . talks of love. . . . After marriage she is a mother annually; is alone all day; hears at night nothing except discussions about patent machinery. . . ."

At home on the range,

two-thirds of the population still lived in rural areas in 1900, model year of this Home Comfort stove. The salesman, peddling in Midwestern farm country, proves his stove is rugged by whacking it with a hatchet —a kitchen tool. Wood fired many stoves still cooking in the 20th century.

"Money is power.

You ought to be reasonably ambitious to have it. . . . because you can do more good with it than you could without it." The words are from a popular lecture of the day, "Acres of Diamonds," delivered more than 6,000 times by Philadelphia clergyman Russell H. Conwell.

"Tomatoes

have always been favorites here," wrote John Lewis, a transplanted Englishman. "They generally require a person to be educated to them. . . . They . . . are eaten in every possible way, mostly however cut up alone or with cucumber, or stewed & used as a sauce. They want *character*, but many like them raw to allay thirst. . . . Large quantities of 'ketchup' are made from them, that being indeed the national 'Sass.' "

Three square meals

in the 1870's, as reported by Lewis: a breakfast of steak, fried potatoes or fried hominy, and hot bread, followed by pancakes topped with molasses. The noon meal included a roast and vegetables, with pie or pudding for dessert. The breakfast menu was repeated at suppertime. Lewis, who worked for a wholesale grocer in New York, described the meals of city people, many of whom ate in restaurants. In his favorite one he usually paid a quarter for a meat dish and pie.

Words from the lovelorn:

E. J. B. — For God's sake, tell me, how could you do as you have done to me, or for what reason. Tell me. SUSAN

Will lady who formerly lived in West 21st St and who in May last, in company with a gentleman, bought a goldfish on 6th Ave., send her address to Lyman.

B. — Have tried every day, but could not see you; am half wild; send me word where and when. Y.

"PERSONALS" FROM THE *NEW YORK HERALD*, 1876.

"Unmentionables"

was the polite word for trousers (also called "unwhisperables") in the American Victorian age. Women were told almost nothing about sex before they were married. Children believed that babies arrived in the doctor's bag. Birth control was unmentionable—and the idea of family planning was denounced as immoral. The 1873 Comstock Law prohibited circulation of birth-control information through the mail. Nevertheless, the birth rate for the middle class and upper class was dwindling. And some gynecologists reported that they were spending more time on post-abortion problems than on maternity cases.

Patent medicines,

unregulated by law, abounded in those days of home remedies (Dr. Rupert Wells's Radiatized Fluid for Cancer, Dr. Raphael's Cordial Invigorant for the Wonderful Prolongation of the Attributes of Manhood). Most medicines were liberally spirited—up to 44 percent alcohol in some—and many contained large doses of opium, morphine, or cocaine. Infants became addicts from opium-based cough syrup, used to quiet crying spells as well as coughs. One physician estimated in 1876 that there were 100,000 opium addicts in the country. Once addicted, the victim could turn to Sears Cure for the Opium and Morphine Habit. Dr. Oliver Wendell Holmes, one of the few skeptics, said all medicines then in use should be "sunk to the bottom of the sea."

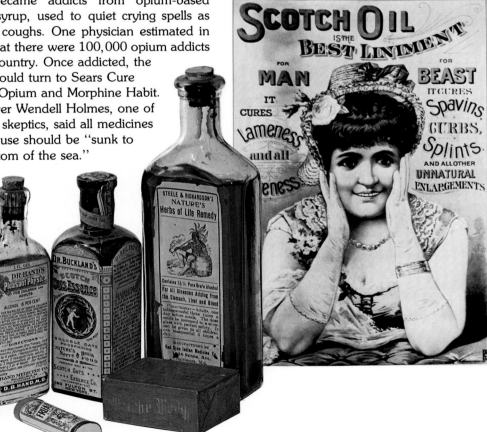

LIBERTY

Though the age was Victorian and outwardly proper, a flabby morality prevailed. In politics, cronyism became known as Grantism, and the acrid odor of corruption swept the land. As Americans, young and old, rich and poor, found that the rights of one were not the rights of all, the post-Civil War complacency was eroded by undercurrents of discontent. Women, farmers, factory workers, blacks, and Indians challenged the status quo.

A German immigrant

who became a U. S. Senator from Missouri, Carl Schurz hailed the Centennial Year: "Our generation has to open the second century of our National Life, as the Fathers opened the first. Theirs was the work of independence, ours is the work of reformation."

"The best system

is to have one party govern and the other party watch," said Congressman Thomas B. Reed in a speech in the House in 1880.

Symbol of freedom,

a full-scale model of the arm and torch of the unfinished Statue of Liberty was displayed at the Centennial Exhibition. Also known as Bartholdi's Electric Light, for the statue's French creator, the model stood 40 feet high and could support a dozen people standing around the rim of the torch. Plans for the statue itself provoked mixed reactions. Some critics attacked it as expensive and useless. The *New York Times* even hinted at fraud: Wasn't the proper place to begin a statue at the feet rather than at the arm?

"The women-folk

are dabbling in politics," chortled the *Chicago Tribune* in a typical male response to the campaign for female suffrage. Although in 1869 the Wyoming Territory passed a bill allowing women to vote, national enfranchisement still stood another half-century away. Yet the battle raged. Some women refused to pay taxes or obey the laws of "a hateful oligarchy of sex." One male argument: If women were allowed to vote, they would crowd all the men out of office, and men would be obliged to stay at home and take care of the children.

50,000 jobless marched

in New York City in August 1876, carrying signs that demanded "immediate employment for the unemployed of this city" and "Government protection and provision to all from the cradle to the grave."

"The Indian Question"

was raised and answered by Helen Hunt Jackson, novelist and poet who investigated the government's dealings with tribes. She sent her report, *A Century of Dishonor,* to every member of Congress. "There is not one among these 300 bands of Indians," she wrote, "which has not suffered cruelly at the hands either of the government or of white settlers. The poorer, the more insignificant, the more helpless the band, the more certain the cruelty and outrage to which they have been subjected."

Rural revolt,

fueled by inflation, the expense of farm machinery, and the high cost of transporting crops, led to the founding in 1867 of the National Grange (Patrons of Husbandry). By 1875 there were 15,000 local granges and 800,000 members. The Grange, fighting for government regulation of exorbitant railway freight charges, won a significant victory in 1876 when the Supreme Court ruled that state legislatures had the power to restrict the rates charged by public utilities.

"An American

can see only one Centennial, so we decided to make the most of it," said one celebrant of that patriotic year. "Away with the themes of war!" wrote Walt Whitman. "...I raise a voice for far superber themes...." Centennial fervor, which lingered past the turn of the century, inspired commemorative songs, books, and paintings; tricolored hair ribbons; and this all-American doll.

Capital punishment

was abolished by the Maine legislature in 1876. Despite arguments that the lack of executions would produce a rash of murders, there were no murder indictments in the state that year. Similar bills failed to pass the Kansas and Iowa legislatures in 1876.

"I can retire to private life

with the consciousness that I shall receive from posterity the credit of having been elected to the highest position in the gift of the people, without any of the cares and responsibilities of the office," said Samuel J. Tilden when informed that, although he had won the popular vote for President in 1876, he had lost the electoral college vote. The Republicans' rooster strutted over the Democrats' donkey after the disputed election went to Hayes. Cartoonist Thomas Nast drew an elephant to represent Republicans in 1874; the Democrats' donkey appears as early as 1837.

The freed slave statue

at the Centennial Exhibition was, ironically, in the Austrian exhibit. Though emancipated in 1863, black Americans were not enfranchised until 1870. In that year, Hiram Revels became the first black U. S. Senator. The second, Blanche K. Bruce, elected in 1875, asked not for new laws but for "enforcement of those that already exist." But in 1875 Tennessee adopted the first "Jim Crow" laws separating blacks from whites in public places. And in 1890 poll taxes and literacy tests were enacted to disfranchise thousands of blacks.

John D. Rockefeller

in 1879 formed a "trust" of 27 oil companies that controlled 90 percent of the industry. Steel, sugar, tobacco, and other trusts also emerged. The monopolies fixed wages and prices and wiped out competitors. State laws offered little relief. Finally in 1890 Congress passed the Sherman Antitrust Act.

Baby-kissing candidate

Rutherford B. Hayes stumps in Steubenville, Ohio, during his successful 1876 presidential campaign. His administration was known as the "cold water regime" because First Lady Lucy Hayes served only non-alcoholic beverages at the White House. As one guest remarked, "The water flowed like wine."

231

PURSUIT OF HAPPINESS

Once they called it idleness. Now they talked of leisure. After long years of war—and with growing industrial prosperity—Victorian Americans could think about play. Strict observance of the Sabbath faltered, and Sunday became "free day." Farm families still made social gatherings of such chores as cornhusking and quilting. But in the city times were changing as the workday shortened and as variety spiced life: concert halls, amusement palaces, bowling alleys, melodrama in cheap theaters. (In wicked New York City, nine out of ten theaters were burlesque by the 1890's.) And the outdoors got organized in 1876 with the formation of the Appalachian Mountain Club.

Phineas Taylor Barnum

sold his Hippodrome, his American Museum (See the Feejee Mermaid!), and his menagerie (11 camels! 4 giraffes!) to concentrate on one major project in the Centennial Year: his traveling circus, "surpassing anything before attempted in this country." Each circus day began with a 13-cannon salute and ended with fireworks. Barnum had begun his traveling circus in 1872. By 1885 there were 50 circuses in circulation. P. T. Barnum, though, had the greatest show on earth. And a motto: "Every crowd has a silver lining."

"Come to the woods,"

John Muir said in 1875. People did, for the fun—and with a new awareness that the wilderness needed to be preserved. Yellowstone National Park was established in 1872, Yosemite in 1890, the Adirondack State Forest Preserve in 1885, the first national forest reserves in 1891.

Sports history

was made at Hill's Theater in New York on March 16, 1876, when Miss Nell Saunders and Miss Rose Harland met in the first public female boxing match. Miss Saunders won. The prize was a silver butter dish.

AN INTERESTING MOMENT DURING THE PERFORMANCE THREE RINGS SIMULTANEOUSLY OCCUPIED BY EQUESTRIENNES AND ARENIC EXPERTS EXECUTING THR

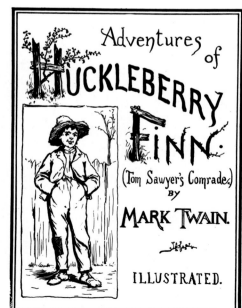

Adventures of HUCKLEBERRY FINN. (Tom Sawyer's Comrade) BY MARK TWAIN. ILLUSTRATED.

Best sellers of 1876

included George Eliot's *Daniel Deronda,* Jules Verne's *Michael Strogoff,* and Ann Eliza Young's *Wife No. 19,* an exposé of Mormon plural marriage. Literature of the day was often moralistic and seldom true to life. Dime novels featured Wild West heroes or Horatio Alger's rags-to-riches tales.

Tom Sawyer, published in 1876, was Mark Twain's first solo venture into the novel. He copied his manuscript on a typewriter, later claiming to be the first to use this new invention for literature. *Tom Sawyer,* though successful, was criticized for its "bad English" and disrespect toward institutional piety. Even before its publication, Mark Twain had begun work on a sequel—*Huckleberry Finn.*

BAILEY ON EARTH

IN THE MAIN PAVILION.
HOSTS OF DAINTY
LING AND DARING FEATS.

Health and leisure

resorts—old favorites Saratoga, New York; Long Branch, New Jersey (where President Grant summered); and Hot Springs, Arkansas —lured the rich and not-so-rich. A new spot, Jacksonville, Florida, was becoming popular. Southern California vaunted solar therapy. Said a New Year's Day, 1876, editorial published in a small town called Los Angeles: "The health-giving powers of our climate are attested by many of us, more or less invalids, being capable of working in the open air almost every day in the year. . . ."

"Baseball,"

said Mark Twain, "is the very symbol, the outward and visible expression of the drive and push and rush and struggle of the raging, tearing, booming nineteenth century."

Harness racing

was a properly utilitarian sport: The two-wheeled carriage raced on Sundays, went to business on weekdays. Jockey races were less popular, but Churchill Downs was built in 1875, year of the first Kentucky Derby.

Antique hunting

captivated those who did not "have things that came over in the Mayflower." An art critic in the 1870's advised them that "the best places in which to look . . . are . . . the henyards, the closets and drawers having for years been given over to the fowls."

Croquet

was so popular that wickets came equipped with candle sockets for playing at night. By day, there was tennis or lawn bowling.

Holiday customs

and some of the holidays were born in our Victorian era. Thomas Nast's 1862 sketch of Santa Claus first depicted him as a jolly, bearded fat man. Halloween became a youngster's holiday; Thanksgiving grew beyond its New England boundaries to become a national feast day; President Hayes inaugurated the Easter egg roll on the White House lawn. Memorial Day was launched in 1868, Arbor Day in 1875. But in 1880 *Harper's* magazine mourned the demise of a holiday—the over-commercial, impersonal St. Valentine's Day.

Party decoration

Valentine greeting

Easter candy box

Christmas seal

New Ways of Working

Elting E. Morison

American pacemakers, ingenious new things of metal, keyed a vibrant age of making and doing. Flip a switch; light the dark. Call a number; span a thousand miles.

The year 1900 saw 24 million bulbs carrying out Edison's promise of electric light so cheap "only the rich . . . burn candles." Dawn to dark no longer limited man's productive hours. After Alexander Graham Bell's fateful "Mr. Watson, come here," the telephone's wire web set vibrations of big deals and small discussions ringing over the land — to 600,000 subscribers in 1900. One Christopher Sholes and partners, having devised a typewriter, sold it to Philo Remington, who had a firearms factory and no war. The "little joker" clicked, eventually, making a place in the office for new waves of women.

Thus by gears and cams and unseen pulses, "the art advances, the artisan recedes" in offices and factories, mills and mines. And the moving finger of the time clock writes IN OUT COME GO — tallying the paid-for hours of a worker's day, handing back the rest.

To get a sense of the new ways of working that developed in this country after the Civil War, we should know something about the old ways. Consider, for instance, several days in the life of Matthew Patten, farmer and Justice of the Peace in Bedford, New Hampshire. On January 29, 1760, he bought a mare for $12. On the first of February he asked his neighbor James Houston to come to the farm to set the shoes on his new horse. He gave his friend a little coal and a few small iron bars. Houston built a fire, heated the bars, and then pounded the metal into thin strips that became, with further pounding, a set of horseshoe nails. He was doing what is called forging, and he was doing it the way the Romans had done it 1,700 years before.

That same day the Widow Nimock came to the farm. Some months before, Matthew Patten had sheared his sheep and had taken the fleece and some cotton to Widow Nimock. She had cleaned the raw wool, picked it, and spun on her own wheel "3 spinle and 4 Cutts" of yarn. Next day he took two bushels of "indian Corn" to Colonel Goffe's mill to be ground. Two days later Archibald Maccollum came to the house to stay. He was given the skin of a calf Patten had butchered and that his neighbor James Ayers had tanned. From this leather Maccollum put together with twine and wooden pegs "a pair of shoes" for Patten, a pair for his son Jonas, and "a pair of pumps."

For each product — nails, yarn, flour, shoes — Patten had supplied his neighbors with raw material. He paid these friends mostly in cash, but he also paid them with his own time and skill. Better with wood than most, Patten could hew, quite precisely, a beam out of a log; he could make sleighs, ox yokes, pine panels, and saddletrees. He was often at a neighbor's house busy with his ax, saw, drawshave, and hammer.

This way of working entailed a considerable division of time, place, goods, services, raw materials, and skills. Matthew Patten spent a good deal of his time negotiating fair exchanges of wool, wood, iron, money, and hours of labor. At Colonel Goffe's mill, waterpower turned the granite millstones to make flour, but nearly everything else was hewed out, cut up, hammered down, picked clean, or spun by human hand. Manufacturing meant what it said, making by hand. In those days, a man worked quite directly for his living — to get the food, clothing, shelter that he needed to stay alive. His living — what today people would call his life-style — was the way he worked.

Such conditions continued for a long time. In 1835 — 75 years after Houston set the shoes on Matthew Patten's new mare — Thomas Houthers, a blacksmith in Parkesburg, Pennsylvania, worked at his trade in a somewhat more sophisticated atmosphere.

Customers now came to him. In his shop he had his own raw materials and tools: four forges, as many anvils, a lathe, a small drill press, and a set of taps and dies for cutting screws. With this equipment he could fix wagons, put iron tires on cartwheels, and hammer out small, simple parts to repair machinery in the nearby grist and textile mills.

But he still had to do most of the essential things himself. He had made the drill press. And when he wanted power to work the press and to turn the little lathe, he built with his own hands and out of his own ingenuity a six-horsepower steam engine. He put this together alone—made the forgings, hammered out the boiler plate, cast the gears and "fit the work all up, without tools, except makeshifts."

In 1857, nearly a century after James Houston shod Patten's mare, John Fritz, Thomas Houthers' onetime apprentice, constructed an ironworks in Johnstown, Pennsylvania, from the ground up: buildings, furnaces, rolling mills, squeezers, cranes. He designed all the machinery himself, using as working drawings his memory of ironworks where he had labored as a young man. Fritz and his fellows—young men off the surrounding farms—made all the separate elements with not much more in the way of tools than hammers and cold chisels. And the way John Fritz worked in the iron trade in 1857 was closer to that of the Biblical Tubal-Cain than to the ways of any laborer in a mill in Gary, Indiana, today. Tubal-Cain was "an instructor of every artificer in brass and iron" (Genesis 4:22).

Men like John Fritz were often called "artists," and there was a good deal of truth in that old term. Men labored within the conditions of art; they worked for the most part on their own, and they worked to complete a whole from all the parts, whether the finished whole was a shoe, a barn, or a steam engine. An artist, says Noah Webster, is one who practices a calling "in which conception and execution are governed by imagination and taste." Such virtues were forced upon these earlier makers of things. They knew next to nothing in a systematic way about the strength of materials, the composition of metals, or the characteristics of the natural forces they were seeking to shape and organize. They had to play it all by ear, to fill, by the dictates of their imagination and taste, the gap between what they knew and what they wanted to do. The art that governed both conception and execution in those days stands out obviously in things like the chairs of Duncan Phyfe or the houses of Charles Bulfinch. But art also was at work as a concealed force in the design and fabrication of more humdrum artifacts: the bridge trusses of William Howe, the canal locks of Loammi Baldwin, the railway trusses of John Jervis. The times and the state of the art required that a man who was making something put a great deal of himself into it. So from the thing that was made one could tell a good deal about the man who made it.

Given such conditions of manufacture—so personal, so individual—it is not surprising that objects that were made often seemed to have a character, a personality, all their own, even when made in quantity. Take stagecoaches. In the first half of the 19th century in a town not far from Matthew Patten's farm, the firm of Abbott and Downing made the great Concord coaches famed in this country (page 173) and around the world.

In Concord before the Civil War about 100 men were making these coaches out of ash, poplar, and basswood, and leather and "iron of the best Norway stock." Each coach was built from the ground up as a thing by itself—its own wheels, springs, axles, and body—by three or four men working together. Downing inspected each part of each coach as it was built. He smashed any part "with the smallest flaw before the eyes of the workmen, which was the most emphatic and cheapest argument he could produce to let his workmen know that no sham work was allowed in their shops." Painting and decoration "was an art not a trade." Each coach had its own color scheme, its own ornamentation, and its own name. When the vehicle went through the shop door, it was

Vulcanic glare suffuses an 1895 steel mill where workers "teem," pouring molten metal from a ladle into ingot molds. A Bessemer converter blazes — "half a furnace and half a cyclone" during a "blow" as air-intensified combustion purges the metal's impurities. In demonic heat and din men toiled 12 hours a day, once a fortnight earning a 24-hour respite that "ain't no Sunday."

"The entire human race desires to ride"

When a body meets a chassis coming through a 1914 Ford assembly line, another newborn Model T "glides out into the world," already sold for cash. Autocrat Henry Ford had hit upon a basic little black car most anyone could love $500 worth and was mass-producing 1,000 a day, 600 at this Highland Park, Michigan, plant. Ford's secret? No secret: machinery, the "new Messiah." And method. Inside the plant, lathes hum, hammers tap, presses thud, drills whir, shapers clack, reamers and milling machines creak and groan. Fifteen thousand sturdy metal servants closely spaced in sequence, linked by gravity chutes and conveyor belts and human workmen standing elbow-to-elbow.

Ford first used the epochal moving assembly line in 1913 to make flywheel magnetos (opposite). To put together this part of the ignition system from its pile of pieces had taken one skilled worker 20 minutes. The job was dissected into 29 tasks by 29 men spaced along a moving belt; this cut the average time to 13 minutes, 10 seconds. Raising the work height to a less-tiring 35 inches and adjusting the belt speed to an optimum 44 inches a minute further cut the man-minutes to 5. Shaved time saved money. The system spread.

By building only the Model T, Ford could afford costly specialized machines: one to drill 45 holes at once from four directions; a bolt-holding brace ("assembler then has both hands free to run the nut home"). Complex machines might do multiple tasks. Human hands usually did one or two, as on one 45-station chassis-assembly line:

Step 5. Two men. Place nuts on truss-rods. Place and fix control-lever rock-shaft.

Step 6. One man. Fixes front spring, tightens nuts, and puts in 4 split pins . . .

Such tasks could be done, the company said, by operators "who have nothing to unlearn . . . and will simply do what they are told to do, over and over again, from bell-time to bell-time." Simple repetition built speed, but if "routine . . . is broken, he must inevitably call his brain into action . . . and must lose some time." Mesmerizing monotony could cause accidents. Gates and railings screened workers from speeding belts and whirling flywheels. One sign said: TO STOP THIS MACHINE PULL PLUG. Unheard-of wages — $5 for 8 hours — kept early Fordmen "absolutely docile" and put millions of Americans on the road to automobility (p. 303).

"a resplendent and proud thing . . . of beauty and dignity and life . . . as inspiring to the stage-faring man as a ship to a sailor." Stephens Abbott had constructed the first of these coaches in the six months from Christmas Eve 1826 to July 1827, and 40 years later it still required about three weeks to turn out a finished product.

About 90 years after Abbott made the first Concord coach, another kind of conveyance was being built in Detroit, Michigan, in the following way: Separate parts for the chassis of this vehicle were put on a track — an assembly line — that moved one foot every ten seconds and passed in front of a row of men. At each step each man did something to the accumulation of parts in front of him. There were 45 separate stops or stations. "The first men fasten four mud-guard brackets to the chassis frame; the motor arrives on the tenth operation and so on in detail. Some men do only one or two small operations, others do more. The man who places a part does not fasten it. . . . The man who puts in a bolt does not put on the nut; the man who puts on the nut does not tighten it." By this process one Model T Ford chassis was put together in one hour and 33 minutes. Each car as it rolled out of the factory was exactly like every other Model T. And, as all the world now knows, each Model T was painted black.

Between the first Concord coach and the debut of the Model T, a great many things had happened to change the way Americans made things and to change the ways of working. At the bottom appear to be two causes: common sense and a bright idea.

Somewhere near the end of the 18th century it began to dawn on people that a Matthew Patten made things the hard way. He took his sheep shearings to one house to get them picked and cleaned and spun into yarn; took the yarn to another house to get it woven into cloth; and then he brought the cloth home for his wife to cut up and sew into clothes. To simplify this process, men designed machines that would do much of the work. Most of this invention was done in England, but by 1800 instruments for spinning yarn and weaving cloth by waterpower had been built in this country. The next step was to bring the machines into one place so that people could work together through every stage of the process from raw wool to finished cloth.

In America this total concentration of effort — the common sense of the factory system — began in the textile industry. After several preliminary installations in various New England towns, the first model for a complete factory was created at Waltham, Massachusetts, in 1813. Soon all along the rivers of New England there were mill buildings where people picked, cleaned, spun, wove, fulled, and dyed wool and cotton textiles. Usually, most of the workers were women. Men did the heavier work of shifting materials and repairing machinery. Children often did the lighter kinds of work.

The early mill owners usually had a genuine concern for their employees' physical and spiritual well-being. They built solid structures for the help to live in and often required workers to attend church on Sunday. Boardinghouses were needed because in the early days there were no other houses near the mills where laborers off the farms could live. Whether the people who lived in these company structures liked them and whether they enjoyed the work in the mills is not altogether clear. But the boardinghouses and apartments were no worse than the cold attics of farmhouses, and the work, though monotonous, was not as wearing physically as the daily tasks on a New England farm. In either place they worked hard from sunup to sundown — and beyond.

Never before had there been a more efficient way to make things. In the second half of the 19th century the owners of the Amoskeag Mills in New Hampshire made the astonishing claim that they were producing a mile of cotton fabric a minute. Not surprisingly, the makers of other kinds of products soon began to use the factory system. The best example — the one that had the most profound effect upon the nation's economy and way of life — is found in the iron and steel industry.

"It is their station to work. And they do"

An early glow of paternalism faded from New England's model factory towns when immigrants outnumbered local "rosy-cheeked farm girls" in mills along the Merrimack. And later owners, often out of touch with employees, met hard times by requiring more work for less pay. Women usually got one-third to one-half the wages paid to men for doing comparable jobs. Shoe factory women in Lynn, Massachusetts (right), were paid three to five dollars weekly in 1895.

Each amount on the pay envelopes below represents a week's work in one of the textile mills of Lawrence, Massachusetts, in January 1912. The next week, the meager wage was reduced 32 cents—the price of ten loaves of bread. Factory owners, required by a new state law to limit the hours of women and minors to 54, speeded up the pace of production to make up the deficit and also cut wages. Angry mill hands—25,000 men, women, and children—took to the streets in protest.

"There is no strike in Lawrence, just mob rule," one owner said of the spontaneous walkout. The radical Industrial Workers of the World, which had a small local, succeeded in organizing the textile workers—despite their 25 nationalities. "Among workers there is only one nationality, one race, one creed," said a youthful organizer. After 63 days of hunger, harsh words, an aborted dynamite plot, and police brutality, the dramatic strike ended. The workers won.

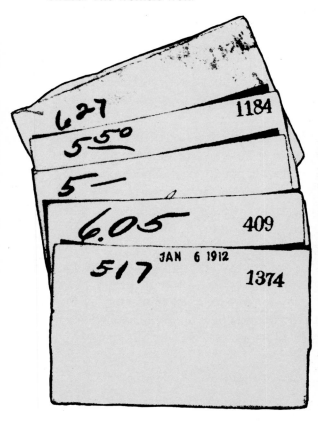

Until the Civil War this industry was centered in the Middle Atlantic states, especially in Pennsylvania, where there were sufficient supplies of iron ore and coal and timber for charcoal. But the industry was scattered around the countryside: a blast furnace here, a forge there, a rolling mill in some other place. Soon after the Civil War things began to change, basically because of the discovery that large quantities of steel could be made quickly by simply blowing a blast of air through a batch of molten iron. Also, enormous amounts of steel were suddenly needed to make rails for the railroads that were tying the parts of the vast country together. Men were forced to think out a way to increase the flow of the indispensable metal from the point of origin as iron ore to the finished products of rails, ingots, castings, and plates.

The man who thought the best was Alexander Holley, a remarkable man who knew as much (which wasn't much) about the chemistry of steel as anyone of his time. He

also understood the structure of machines—locomotives, Bessemer converters, reverberatory furnaces, cranes, rolling mills—and most of all he had a great feeling for mechanical systems. He figured out how to put all the mechanisms together into what was called the fully integrated steel mill. His mill could take iron ore and move it through a system that turned out steel in a hundred different shapes, in great quantities, very fast. Consider the effect: In 1867 this country produced 20,000 tons of steel ingots and castings; in 1899, it produced 10,640,000 tons.

Working with the metal in those days was backbreaking, dirty, sometimes suffocating, and quite often dangerous. Steel is heavy, measured in tons, and in the making goes from the hard and cold to the liquid and hot as fire. Much of the work was still done by hand— puddling; feeding great sheets of metal through the rollers of the mill; moving heavy castings around the mill floor. Such machines as there were often broke down in ways that not only slowed up the job for several hours but also put life and limb at hazard. In one shop, for instance, twice in six months a 30-foot flywheel slipped off its axle and flew 40 feet before it slammed against the mill wall. A churchman from Hungary who came to study conditions in the steel mills concluded, "This scarcely is work for mankind." The accident report in the Pittsburgh district for the months from July 1, 1906 to June 30, 1907 states that 195 men were killed. Five died by asphyxiation from hot gas; 22 by explosions of hot metal; 10 in the rolling mills; 42 by traveling cranes; 24 by falls from high places—some into molten slag; 7 electrocuted; 8 crushed; 77 by other causes. Pittsburgh, said Lincoln Steffens, looked "like hell with the lid off." At the beginning of this century men—and boys of 10 and 12—worked in that hell 12 hours a day, six days a week and sometimes on the seventh day, for 14 cents an hour. But out of the inferno came all those tons of ingots and metal plates.

The common sense that brought together all the parts of a manufacturing process in one place—the factory system—was the first cause for the profound change in the ways

Matron and misses, miles from a city emporium, let their fingers do the walking through a catalog. Aaron Montgomery Ward's mail order wish-book, sent at first to Granges, grew from a one-page list in 1872 to 1,036 pages in 1899. The next year Ward's "Cheapest Cash House in America" was topped in sales by upstart Sears, Roebuck and Company, "Cheapest Supply House on Earth."

"The very latest. . . . all the newest wrinkles"

As America's torrent of mass-produced goods overflowed the cornucopia, aggressive salesmanship spurred mass consumption. Advertisements in such widely read magazines as *McClure's* offered free catalogs, a 30-day free trial, money back if not fully satisfied. And if you didn't have money, you could buy some items on the installment plan—introduced nationally to sell Singer sewing machines.

Pictures, trademarks, catchy slogans proclaimed the marvelous: Thomas Edison's "talking machine," George Eastman's Kodak. Early photography's glass plates were as clumsy as the phonograph's cylinders. So in 1888 Eastman put film in his first Kodak and told amateurs: "You press the button, we do the rest." For $25 you got the small, fixed-focus camera, film for 100 photos, and its processing. You sent the loaded Kodak to his Rochester, New York, factory and got back prints, camera, and, for $10, another roll. Not until the "Gramophone" and its records of the late 1890's did "mechanical music" boom—and stop sounding like "a partially educated parrot."

Universal, which sold women on the idea that to make bread you need a dough kneader, then convinced them they needed choppers—and a durable kitchen gadget was born. But for the real drudgery of housework, the silent servant of the future, electricity, was already plugged into city homes. "Back and forth goes the tub, washing the clothes for dear life. . . . mere child's play to run it."

Mail-order buying, a convenience for city folk, proved a godsend for many rural people, especially after the advent in 1896 of rural mail delivery. The ponderous Ward's or Sears, Roebuck catalogs offered goods from Abdominal corset to Zulu gun (a shotgun for "general purposes"). Thumbing well-filled pages, much of America mulled over purchases of housewares and harness, corsets, collars, shirtwaists and cheviot suits, bicycles, buggies, gimp tacks, parlor organs.

Indoor plumbing so proudly hailed in cities was not yet a farm necessity. Sears could supply a pump and pipe wrenches to install it at well or cistern, a japanned tin bathtub with wooden handles, and even a cable-and-pulley exerciser that added "luxury and pleasure" to the city bath. But most farm folk still bathed by the bucketful and trod with tradition down the back-door path to the outhouse and last year's catalog.

244

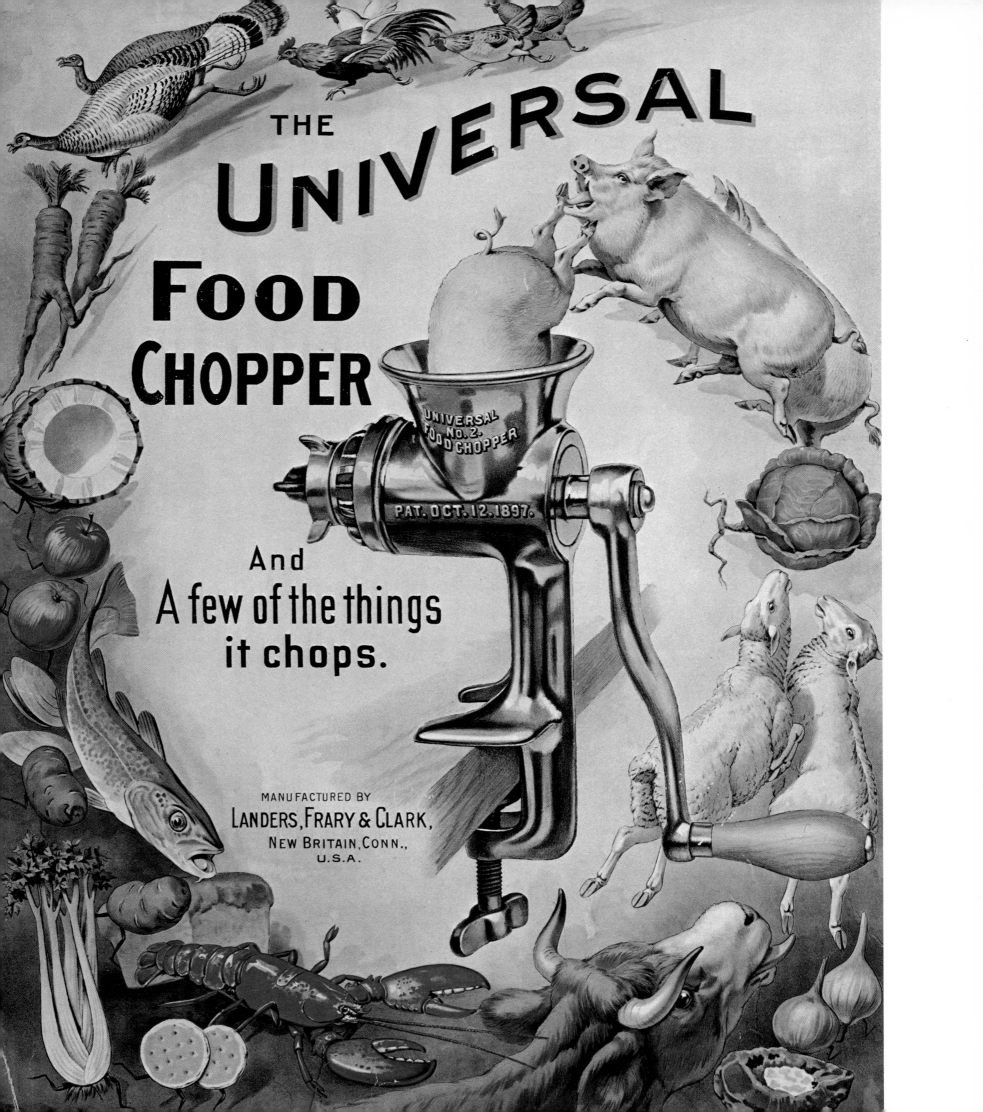

Pigs going to market in 1880 toil up ramps to a packing plant's top floor and a disassembly line. Workers hoist porkers by the feet, slit throats, scrape, gut, cure, grind, render, can, and label. Refrigerated cars to transport fresh meat made the nation's rail hub, Chicago, "hog butcher for the world." Foodstuffs and by-products from fertilizer to bristle brushes used "everything but the squeal."

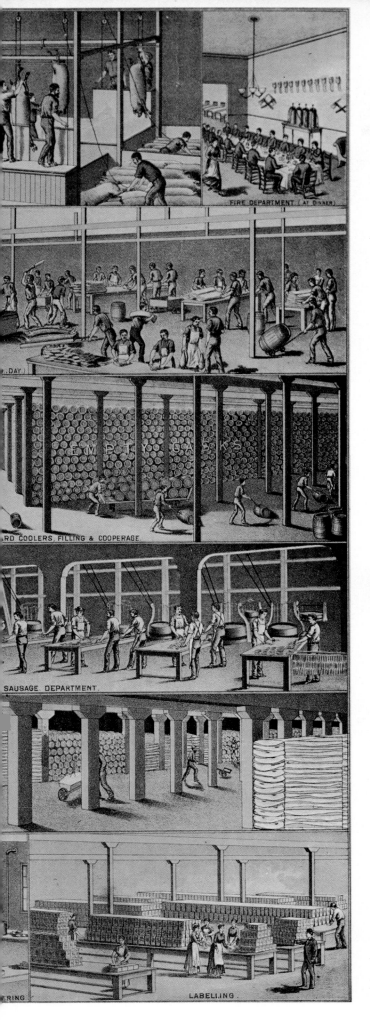

FIRE DEPARTMENT (AT DINNER)

...DAY)

...RD COOLERS, FILLING & COOPERAGE.

SAUSAGE. DEPARTMENT.

...ERING

LABELLING.

of working. The second cause, a bright idea, had occurred to Eli Whitney in the first days of our national history, but not much had been done with it for half a century. In 1798 he had taken a contract to make muskets for the United States Army. At that time muskets and rifles were made by gunsmiths—artists—who made each part of the weapon with great skill. After carefully shaping and judiciously filing each piece, they fitted the parts together. It was a difficult and elegant art, requiring as it did the precise mating within a single unit of all the components. No musket was exactly like another musket. The individuality of the gunsmith was reflected in each one.

Whitney began with the idea of a great many guns built from parts made by machines. He would construct one machine to make trigger guards, another to make lock plates, and so on. These machines would, as only machines can, eliminate the variations created by human hands. Each trigger guard would be just like every other trigger guard. Whitney said his tools would be "similar to an engraving on copper plate from which may be taken a great number of impressions perceptibly alike." From all these separate carbon-copy pieces would come a set of identical guns. What Whitney called the "uniformity system," or the principle of interchangeable parts, led in time to the assembly line and mass production. Just as integration of the mills enabled the steel industry to turn out heavy ingots and large metal plates in quantity, so the uniformity system enabled industry to turn out all kinds of products—very big and very small, from jackknives to automobiles—in great quantities and all alike.

The system did not happen all at once or indeed for some time. New devices—called machine tools—had to be created for the making of parts. A labor force had to be built up and trained. Men and machines had to be linked so that all these parts could be put together into finished products on a constantly moving assembly line. And markets had to be created for the mass of varied things that could be produced. But by 1900 we were pretty well along with the process.

What the refinement of this system has achieved, reckoned in terms of goods produced, is a kind of miracle. Consider the accumulation of things—toasters, shoes, television sets, cookstoves, cars, jet engines, plastic plates, and so on and on. And because things can be made in such quantity—one car in about one hour—they can be sold cheaply enough so that almost everyone can buy. It is almost as though we Americans have created a new kind of reality for ourselves out of the things we have made. Yet even miracles have an underside. Making a toaster or a jet engine in our times is not as exhausting or backbreaking a job as making steel was in 1885. But modern work has its drawbacks. Just as the gun was split up into separate parts by the uniformity system, so was the gunsmith. In the new way of working, each man often does only one small thing ("the man who puts on the nut does not tighten it") again and again and again. And often a machine does much of his job for him. A man, for instance, may feed into a gear-cutter a tape that tells the gear-cutter what size gears to cut for the next four hours. When this happens, the machine also cuts the man down considerably below his true size; there is a lot of man left over that is not used.

Dull work reduces the total competence in any single human being to a thin slice of habituated technique, locks a person into the confining logic of machinery, conceals from him the fact that whatever small thing he does has something to do with all the other small things that become in time a finished product. Dull work is dehumanizing, and in the end as dangerous to the spirit as the spill of molten steel was to the body. Such things have been said over and over again for the past 75 years.

What else is there to say? First, that, given a choice, ever since the girls came out of the hills of New Hampshire and the meadowlands of Massachusetts to go into the mills of Lowell, Americans have chosen, more often than not, to leave the farm for the

Before Dial O

The smiling customer may get a pain in the ear, not a cooing "Number, please?" Early operators were male — and surly often enough to warrant a switch at the boards. Girls might sniff smelling salts when calls got hectic. But neither earthquake nor fire kept them from plugging away at San Francisco's improvised exchanges in 1906 (opposite). Eight years later linemen upped a last pole and, West Coast to East, people shouted "HELLO" at the strange gismo, then read the sign: "Don't talk with your ear, nor listen with your mouth."

factory. Perhaps, as the Bible suggests, daily bread is always earned in the sweat of the face; perhaps the choice can only be between the bad and the worse. But throughout our history the bad has gotten better. Working conditions are safer, cleaner, and not as backbreaking. Wages are higher; days are shorter. Still better conditions, still shorter hours, still more money, however, does not get at the problem of work itself. Work simply becomes something to do as little of as possible, so there will be more time and cash to do something else — such as riding ski lifts or snowmobiles, or flying jets to faraway places in the sun.

The new ways of working have been extended far beyond the factory walls — to mining, agriculture, the building trades, the care of the sick, the handling of materials, and the transport of people. Almost everyone today works within the boundaries and definitions of some kind of technical system. The management of these systems has produced all kinds of new jobs having to do less with the shaping of materials than with the control of words, numbers, ideas, and people. Instead of working with turret lathes, drill presses, cranes, or gear-cutters, now a great many employees use desks, tape recorders, computer consoles, and office intercoms. In such pursuits there is a lot of talk and thought — how much thought is hard to say, but before divestiture Ma Bell was one of the five largest companies in the country. Much of the world's work today is done in offices, moving about words, policies, and thoughts. In this way of working, reality becomes more a matter of abstractions than of objects. There is not so much sweat, but it is often harder for one to know at the end of a day exactly what he or she has done.

If the country's earlier growth derived from the increasing power to organize men and then machines into effective systems, the source of our more recent development has been the increasing power to organize ideas — especially ideas obtained from science. A good many people now are employed not in factories or in offices but in laboratories. This is a new way of working that, in turn, profoundly affects the kind of work that those outside the laboratories do. The demand in the 19th century was for more of the same kinds of products. In the 20th century the demand has been for a wider variety of new things. At the heart of this concept lies the systematic production and organization of ideas — what we now call research and development. A considerable history lies behind the refinement of this process.

The men who built the Concord coach did not need new information or new ideas. The tools they used had come down to them from previous generations; the properties of the materials they worked with — mostly wood — could be learned by experience. They could proceed to build a vehicle by following hallowed procedures, rules of thumb. What was true for them was true for most workers until the latter 19th century.

But by 1875 the invention of new tools, the acquisition of new materials, the development of new kinds of energy, and most of all the expansion of knowledge about the natural world put most people who made things into unfamiliar surroundings. They had to proceed not so much by standard practice and rules of thumb as by their wits.

Electricity offers the most obvious example. Here was a novel energy — more subtle, more intricate than wind or falling water or even steam. By 1840 men knew something about electricity in a theoretical way. But they still had much more to learn, even in theory, and no one had clear ideas of how electricity could be put to common use. The story of its development, fascinating as intellectual history, can be suggested by a brief description of how men came to build an electric lamp.

In 1840 William Grove demonstrated in England that an electric current passed through a filament, or thread, inside a glass gave off light. He had an interesting idea but he was a long way from making a lamp that would sell. First men had to figure out how to create a reliable vacuum in a glass bulb. Twenty-five years passed before Hermann

"We take them as soon as they can stand up"

The Southern mill manager may have been exaggerating—but not by much. Children at the turn of the century did go to work at remarkably tender ages. Child labor, an old appendage of industrialization, was encouraged by employers trying to boost profits and accepted by working-class parents trying to make ends meet. Boys and girls even looked forward to working. "Factories will not take you unless you are eight," a youngster in Syracuse, New York, complained in 1904.

Work, many elders argued, kept children from "idleness by which they are corrupted." And what if they earned but a pittance at their hard jobs? Andrew Carnegie boasted that such industrial titans as John D. Rockefeller, George Westinghouse, Marshall Field, and himself had "trained in the sternest but most efficient of all schools—poverty."

The census of 1900 counted 1,750,000 "gainfully occupied children aged ten to fifteen." Among the nation's textile workers, a third were "lively elves" whose nimbleness and acceptance of discipline and drudgery made them preferable to adults, a mill owner said. Tykes were sought for agriculture because, being short, they could "pick tobacco leaves, cotton and cranberries without being fatigued." Mines, canneries, jute mills—plant after plant employed "mere babies."

Their exploitation rivaled that exposed by Charles Dickens's pen in England during the 1840's. Striplings toiled at spinning machines from 5:30 a.m. to 5:30 p.m. without a break for lunch. Dashes of cold water "by the vigilant superintendent" kept youngsters awake; shifts ran to 2 a.m. in a New York cannery. Ten-year-olds tied stoppers on 300 dozen bottles a day in glass factories, or hunched daylong over hot molds. "Breaker boys" of eight or nine bent backs from 7 a.m. to dark picking slate from chutes of dusty, tumbling coal—for wages of $1 to $3 a week.

An accident rate three times that of adults; exposure of such conditions as the boarding of shop windows so children couldn't be seen working on Sundays; and photographs (far left) of tiny mill workers and grimy young miners by Lewis W. Hine—a "conscience with a camera"—stirred the nation. States passed laws limiting daily hours to ten (but exempting orphans, extra work with parental approval, and "voluntary" overtime). Not until New Deal reforms of the 1930's, however, were the evils of child labor erased.

Pittsburgh steelmen in T-rail formation hail the first billion-dollar corporation, U. S. Steel, in 1901. Andrew Carnegie, not present, had just abdicated the throne of steel for a life of play and good works on a pension that rumor set at $40,000 a day. An era of laissez-faire and no taxes saw big companies gobble weak ones, justifying it by citing "social Darwinism" — the fittest survive and get rich.

Sprengel invented a pump that would do this. Then it was found that most filaments were made of material that burned out in a very few minutes. It took 15 more years before Thomas Edison in New Jersey came up with a possible solution.

Edison by the middle 1870's was well on his way to his definitive reputation as the "wizard of Menlo Park." No scholar, no diver into nature's deepest mysteries, he cared next to nothing for the advancement of man's knowledge and even less for acquiring this world's goods. The pattern of his genius was to become absorbed in making something well enough for it to make money. In the general field of telegraphy, he had devised, among other things, a machine to count votes, a stock ticker, and a system for carrying four messages simultaneously on the same wire. Once a device of his passed the test of the marketplace, Edison forthwith became absorbed in making something else. In 1877, he turned his attention to the incandescent light bulb.

The thing that was needed most was a filament that would burn in a vacuum for an extended period without clouding the inside of the glass bulb. Edison's program was to try one material after another until one worked. He tried dozens of different things — including a fishline, a blade of grass, and a hair from an assistant's beard. He discovered that a charred or carbonized sewing thread would do the job. Beginning during the night of October 21, 1879, the thread burned for 13½ hours. Edison experimented further and found that carbonized bamboo of a certain type made the best filament. Even with a good bulb, a reliable vacuum, and a usable filament there was still a link needed for a stable electric lighting system to serve the man in the street and at home — a new circuit that would produce an even flow of current at the needed voltage to every lamp in the system. On New Year's Eve that year a great crowd came to Menlo Park to see strings of lights burning brightly in and around Edison's laboratory.

Amid wild public excitement Edison began designing generators and supplementary engineering equipment to make electricity in quantity and distribute it through the system. He and his associates built the pioneering Pearl Street power plant in lower Manhattan. When it came into service in 1882, the plant served 60 subscribers.

To put anything together in the old days — Patten's piece of cloth or Edison's electric light — a great deal of time had to be spent fitting small pieces together. The light bulb required knowledge of physics, the invention of some new tools, experimenting with many kinds of materials, and the creation of novel engineering structures. It soon became evident that the process would go faster and more easily if all its parts — and all the men involved — were assembled in one place. The sensible next step was to build a laboratory in a factory. The General Electric Company built the first industrial laboratory in Schenectady, New York, in 1900. At the outset, the story goes, three men from GE — Edwin Rice, Albert G. Davis, and Charles Steinmetz — traveled to Lynn, Massachusetts, to discuss the proposed laboratory with Elihu Thomson, a founder and guiding light of GE's formative years. The three delegates represented quite different interests in the company. Rice as technical director was primarily concerned with achieving reliability and uniformity in the things GE produced. Davis, manager of the patent department, brought a sense of urgency; he hoped to find a way to make better light bulbs before a competitor, Swan, in England did. The third, Steinmetz — a brilliant German scientist who worked for GE in independent splendor, doing just what he wanted to do — joined the discussion out of intellectual curiosity.

Like Edison, Elihu Thomson was partly a product of those great attic and cellar classrooms in the homes of America where boys heat test tubes, construct batteries, fool around with crystal sets, and sometimes come upon a vocation. In 1879, the year Edison set the midnight bulbs burning in Menlo Park, Thomson had constructed a complete arc-light system for a Philadelphia bakery. Afterward for several years he

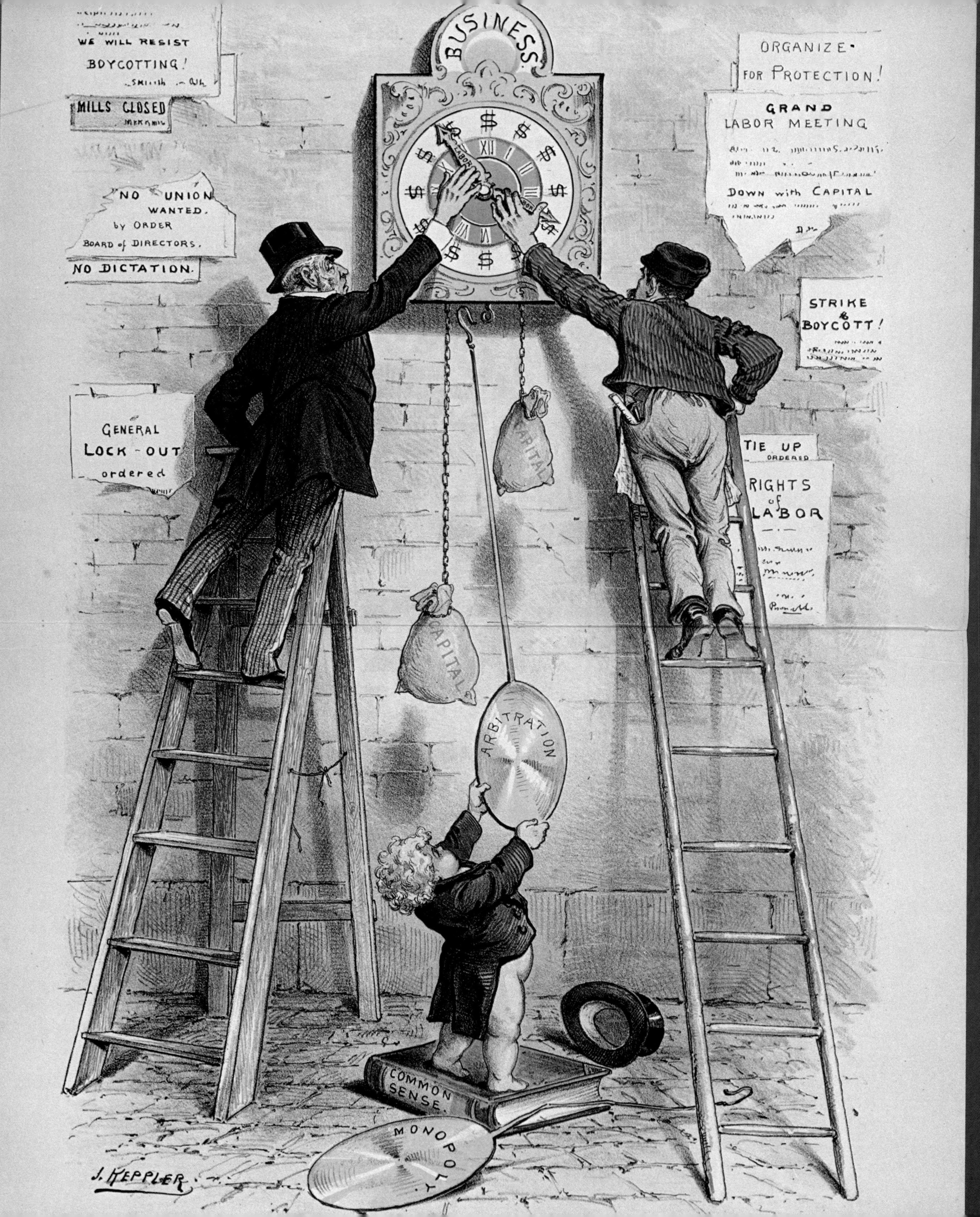
BUSINESS
WE WILL RESIST BOYCOTTING!
MILLS CLOSED
NO UNION WANTED. by ORDER BOARD of DIRECTORS.
NO DICTATION.
GENERAL LOCK-OUT ordered
ORGANIZE FOR PROTECTION!
GRAND LABOR MEETING
DOWN with CAPITAL
STRIKE & BOYCOTT!
TIE UP ORDERED
RIGHTS of LABOR
LABOR
CAPITAL
CAPITAL
ARBITRATION
COMMON SENSE.
MONOPOLY.
J. KEPPLER.

"Eight hours for work, eight hours for rest"

And "eight hours for what we will" — workers sang it in union rallies and blazoned it on placards hoisted in the first Labor Day parade, on September 5, 1882, in New York City. A dozen years of strife and strikes ensued before labor's day became a national holiday.

Federal workers won the 8-hour day in 1868, but most of the nation still toiled 10 or 12 in 1890. Free-enterprise employers set wages and hours — take it or leave it. Unions, gaining power with numbers, urged workers to leave it en masse and force concessions. A third interest — the public — often required government to take a hand when rival clock fixers could not agree on the time of a day.

A FEW THOUGHTS FOR

A FEW THINKERS

provided intellectual energy for an enterprise that successfully invaded virtually every sector of the rapidly expanding electrical field, and that later grew into GE. When the company shifted its headquarters to Schenectady, Thomson had chosen to stay at his laboratory in Lynn, still wielding a force as a part-time consultant for GE.

Thoroughly sympathetic to the need for fundamental research in physical science, Thomson told the three they could do no better thing than to create within the company a laboratory separate from all operations and commercial pressures, where men could "ask whatever questions of nature they could devise."

The new laboratory, headed by Willis Whitney, started out in a barn behind Steinmetz's house. Surrounded at first only by interesting problems, Whitney began to gather men able to deal with those problems and to create conditions in which they could do their best work. Once a month in the early years, Thomson went to Schenectady to discuss with Whitney the kind of work the laboratory might do. Each trip ended the same way. The two went to Keeler's Restaurant in Albany. Each ordered a Manhattan cocktail and a mushroom omelet. And then, as Whitney recalled, they would "deal in the materials of the universe." Then Thomson took the night train home.

On an early trip Thomson had suggested taking a look at filaments, and one of the first structures Whitney had built was a small, high-temperature furnace for testing materials. When he tried carbonized cellulose, then used as filament in the incandescent lamp, he found that intense heat, in effect, metalized it. In that form it could convert electrical charges into light more efficiently, using only 2.5 watts per candlepower instead of 3.1 watts — a 19 percent saving in the lamp's use of energy. At a cost of one million dollars, General Electric in 1906 built a new plant to make these better lamps. But even before the new plant came into production, Whitney and his colleagues had begun studying the next improvement. If a metalized filament worked such an improvement, then why not real metal? Into the project Whitney lured physical chemist William D. Coolidge from the faculty of the Massachusetts Institute of Technology.

At Schenectady, Coolidge began to investigate the possibility of using tungsten, which has the highest melting point of any metal: 3410° C. The problem was to produce tungsten that was ductile — that could be "drawn out permanently" into a thread. The search seemed to Coolidge "very unpromising." Tungsten was so hard that it broke files and at ordinary temperatures it was very brittle. Beyond that, "it belonged to a family of metals no member of which had ever been brought into a ductile state." What supported him were three things. He knew, as any old-time blacksmith did, that most metals increase in ductility as they approach the pure state and as they are intensively "worked" or pounded. He knew how to put order and system into an investigation. And, finally, every day Willis Whitney came into the laboratory to look into the state of the search and to ask, "Are you having fun?" Fun was a favorite word of Whitney's. Those in the laboratory came to realize that his question meant, "Are you still working on that problem no one else has found the answer to?" which in turn meant, "Are you still engaged in the most exciting exercise there is in life?"

In pursuit of such fun, Coolidge proceeded to find out more about tungsten than anyone had learned in the 150 years since it had been identified. He subjected the metal to gradually increasing heat. At each stage he took samples and worked them by rolling, by drawing through small holes, by swaging, or beating — 10,000 machine-dealt blows a minute. After each systematic beating and working, he carefully analyzed the sample and noted changes in chemistry and structure. As the records of observation grew, so grew the knowledge of tungsten. Then Coolidge began mixing tungsten with other substances. Again a long series of tests with more records, more analyses. Ultimately, he had what he wanted — a ductile tungsten thread-filament.

The lamp that came from these endeavors got the efficiency up to one watt per candle and extended bulb-life—it was claimed—27 times. The work of Irving Langmuir and 25 other men over the next few years doubled the efficiency and tripled the life.

Consider again the results. For 21 years before 1900 the incandescent lamp had been stabilized at a point of interesting, promising inefficiency. Then in half that time the life of the lamp had been extended 400 percent and its efficiency (reckoned in candle-power per watt) improved by 700 percent. As supplementary fallout, General Electric gained a competitive advantage that amounted almost to a monopoly.

The point of the demonstration was not lost on the American industrial scene. By 1920 Dupont, Standard Oil, Kodak, and U. S. Rubber had all established laboratories. By 1950 there were 2,000 industrial laboratories in the nation. Many of these, seeking small, temporary advantage in the market, often simply test and tinker with existing products. A number confine their deeper researches to narrow channels set by the nature of the things their parent companies make. A very significant few devote a large part of their resources to the investigation of first causes, creating the laboratory conditions where men could ask "whatever questions of nature they could devise." Quite often the answers they discover make fundamental contributions to our understanding of how nature works—and quite often they lay the foundation for new products.

Making an institution of the process of converting ideas into goods has had extraordinary effects on production in the United States. Scientific findings provide the modern base for making things. Since the path of scientific thought is always forward, its ideas are always changing; therefore the ideas applied—engineering—are always changing. Production, in turn, is geared toward the making of new kinds of things and, therefore, toward new ways of working.

There is no question that this systematized push of ideas into production has transformed the life of the American at work. Industry today is far more interesting and exciting than it was when volume rather than variety was the dominating concept—when the principal decision a man might have to make was whether to hire a hundred more men or to light off another open hearth furnace. Now the search is constant for improved means and for new products. In a process that rests on ideas, the need to know, to think, to imagine new possibilities—these are the great imperatives. The life of the mind penetrates far more deeply into the corporate structure than it used to. An important new way of working, therefore, is the way one uses one's head.

All these remarkable changes in our industrial development raise questions, of course. Do we need all the new things? Can we stand the rate of change produced in our ways of living and working, changes forced upon us by the rising tide of new things? Can we manage wisely the new technical systems we all work in? As Irving Langmuir observed 45 years ago, the tandem marches of science and engineering have enabled us to solve a problem "where . . . it was not even suspected that there was a problem." It is not so clear as it used to be that the problems solved—and the endless stream of new artifacts made—coincide nicely with the fulfillment of needs in men and women.

There seems, in other words, to be a developing mismatch between our extending knowledge of what we can do with the materials and forces in the world around us and our older, but less certain, understanding of what we have to do to be ourselves. And in this mismatching—such is the power in the machinery we work with and such is the confusion about our real needs—we are likely to come away losers, ground down, blown up, twisted out of shape, crammed into computer-designed compartments, bored to death. To find some saving order—where all the things our work can make or do can be brought within the range of our understanding and put in the service of our needs, purposes, and affections—would seem to be the next order of business.

Making headway in a crusade for fair treatment as workers and as citizens, women showed their solidarity in a march down New York's Fifth Avenue in May 1912. The parade started on time. The 15,000 demonstrating for woman's suffrage ranged from society matrons to sweatshop seamstresses (above) still incensed by a tragic factory fire, and—more cheered than jeered—some 600 men.

The World Enters America

Ann Novotny

The Statue of Liberty took her stand in New York harbor just as the United States opened wide the golden door. Nearing the "coveted shore" at the turn of the century, millions of immigrants gazed on the beckoning torch. It lit the path to haven—and a new homeland. In five years the certificate of naturalization, granting citizenship, could be theirs.

Frédéric Bartholdi's creation, presented to the nation in 1884 by the people of France, inspired an embarrassing apathy among local citizens asked to pay for the statue's pedestal. Not enough money came from gala benefit dinners and sales of mementos like this six-inch replica of the 152-foot-tall colossus. But when immigrant Joseph Pulitzer appealed to readers of his New York World, $100,000 in nickels and dimes poured in. Not until 17 years after the dedication ceremony in 1886 would Liberty find her voice in the words of Emma Lazarus affixed to the base: "Give me your tired, your poor, Your huddled masses yearning to breathe free. . . ."

As the ship steamed through the Narrows into New York harbor, the passengers crowded the small steerage deck. Everyone pushed to the rail, straining to see the amazing view. People jostled each other to get a better look, and mothers lifted small children in the air to see. There on the left rose the towering statue of "Liberty Enlightening the World," and next to it, on Ellis Island, stood the vast complex of red brick buildings with ornate towers and white limestone trim. Many on deck broke into tears, crying and laughing at the same time, slapping each other on the back in joy and relief. One word was the same on all tongues: "America!"

A message of almost magical appeal had reached even the remotest villages of Europe by the end of the 19th century—the news that there was work to do in America, that hands were needed to hammer railroad tracks, to load cotton and wheat and tobacco on the docks, to slaughter cattle and pack meat in Chicago's stockyards, to fell giant trees in the Northwest, to mine coal in Pennsylvania, to manufacture the clothing and machinery demanded by the growing nation. Lured across the Atlantic by tales of work, food, and opportunity for all, 32 million men, women, and children emigrated from Europe to the United States in a scant hundred years, beginning about 1830. The story of these courageous and energetic immigrants—as they were called when they reached their destination—is the story of America's growth.

They came in such astounding numbers that in some city districts it became unusual to meet a native-born adult. By 1890, more than four out of every ten residents of New York, Chicago, and other industrial centers were foreign-born; German and Polish immigrants made up about the same proportion of Milwaukee's population. The Massachusetts mill towns of Lawrence, Lowell, and Fall River grew heavily foreign. By 1890 half the country's coal miners had been born abroad, and nearly half its lumbermen. A decade earlier, in Pittsburgh, the Irish, British, and German steelworkers and ironworkers about equaled the native Americans. In New York by 1890 four out of every five laborers, half the draymen, more than half the tailors and dressmakers, three out of every five carpenters and domestics, two out of every three masons, bricklayers, and tradesmen, were immigrants. Of the city's 1.5 million inhabitants, only 300,000 had been born to parents who both were native Americans.

The statistics kept soaring as the 19th century turned into the 20th and the biggest mass movement in history began: One million immigrants landed in the United States in 1905, another million in 1906, and more than a million and a quarter in the peak

"Our eyes beheld the Promised Land"

Steerage passengers crowd the deck of the German liner S. S. *Patricia,* an immigrant's "Mayflower" of 1906. Passage to a new life cost about $30 from Hamburg, as little as $12 from Italy. Their Plymouth Rock was Ellis Island, where one observer saw "sun-browned faces . . . lit up with hope and fear, joy and sorrow. . . . Hope for success in the new land to which they are voluntary exiles; fear of the unknown future; joy that the long-dreaded voyage is over; and sorrow at the memories tugging at their heart strings."

From 1892 until the depot closed in 1954, more than 16 million immigrants passed through Ellis Island, named for an 18th-century owner. The original buildings burned down in 1897, and a new, turreted complex replaced them. Ellis Island served as barrier as well as gateway; those too old or too weak to support themselves were turned back from what they called the "Isle of Tears." In 1911 about 13,000—some 2 percent of the year's 650,000 arrivals—made the bitter voyage back to the lands they had forsaken.

Emmanuel Goldenberg treasured a far different memory: "At Ellis Island I was born again." He arrived in 1903, tortured by memories of pogroms that had sent his family out of Romania into exile. Reborn here at the age of ten, he achieved fame and fortune as an actor named Edward G. Robinson.

year of 1907. On one busy day in April of that year nearly 12,000 steerage passengers went through Ellis Island; 3,500 a day was not unusual. Russian Jews, southern Italians, and the various nationalities from within the Austro-Hungarian Empire accounted for most of the arrivals during those years.

Clustered in industrial centers populated with their own countrymen, the newcomers had little need or opportunity to learn the language of their new homeland. In 1910 some 3 million of the country's 13 million foreign-born adults spoke no English. Most of the jobs they found were dirty and dangerous—and required muscle or manual dexterity rather than the ability to communicate in English. Russian Jews became peddlers, tobacco workers, and above all, garment workers in the city's sweatshops. Italian construction gangs dug tunnels and subways, built railroads and skyscrapers. Poles and Slovaks worked in coal mines and steel mills. Greeks opened small coffee shops and restaurants; many Germans were butchers and bakers.

After the Civil War, when the United States faced a desperate shortage of labor, American manufacturers sent agents all over Europe to recruit workers with special skills—Welsh and Cornish miners or Italian stonemasons, for example. Sometimes all the strong young men of a village succumbed to the tempting offers and sailed together as a ready-made work crew. To keep out cheap labor and thwart strike-breaking, American unions in 1885 forced passage of the Contract Labor Law, which banned this kind of recruiting. But the practice continued in a clandestine way. In Greece or southern Italy a steerage ticket cost a relatively small amount, though for the average peasant it might equal a year's wages. How was a poor man to raise the money unless he bound himself to a *padrone?* Under questioning at Ellis Island, he had to remember to deny that he had accepted a specific job in exchange for his passage.

The almost insatiable demand for unskilled and semi-skilled labor could never have been met by the native population, no matter how rapidly farmers' sons abandoned the land and flocked to work in the cities. Immigrants often took the blame for lowering wages, breaking strikes, and aggravating the problems of the city slums. But they were basically responsible for America's prosperity. As they settled down to raise their families, their need for services and products of others' work became a major factor in

"We were . . . swamped by that human tide"

An interpreter on Ellis Island in 1907 remembered not only endless, bewildered crowds but also strained facilities: One night 1,700 people tried to sleep in a dormitory that had 600 bunks. Stewed prunes and bread made a meal three times a day, served up by a profiteering concessionaire. Reform brought new dormitories, a mess hall, and a varied diet. Diners (below) got thick stews and hearty soups at 11:30 a.m. In the Registry Hall (pages 264-265) an inspector might judge the "right to land" of 400 to 500 newcomers a day.

A Russian-Jewish girl's haunted eyes mirror the immigrants' ordeal. The uncertainty they faced at Ellis Island grew through the years as the U. S. enacted restrictive legislation. Backed by some labor unions and "America for Americans" groups, the Quota Law of 1921 imposed a ceiling of 358,000 immigrants a year, the total from any one nation not to exceed 3 percent of its people in the United States in 1910. Since no one counted them by nationality as they left Europe, a human tragedy began. Shiploads of immigrants arrived, unaware that quotas had been filled. One group of 500 southeastern Europeans screamed and smashed up the waiting room when told they were inadmissible. Such scenes of anguish ceased when a revised law in 1924 required visas before departure. A new immigration act in 1965 abolished the national origins quota system.

the national growth. During the 20 years of heaviest immigration, the population of the United States rose by half, from 63 million in 1890 to 90 million by 1910.

Many immigrants sailed to America with the dream of working their own farms. Agents in the 1870's and '80's scoured the villages and towns of Europe, seeking passengers for the Western railroads and settlers for states that urgently needed people. A typical recruiter trudged the rounds of Bremen's shipping offices and emigrant boardinghouses, hammering up posters and thrusting rhapsodic pamphlets into any receptive hand. The state authorities of Minnesota, Nebraska, Wisconsin, and Iowa also distributed leaflets describing the free, 160-acre homesteads, the climate, soil, and crop yields, the wages. The leaflets told of the railroads built and building, of the schools, churches, and newspapers that would cater to an immigrant in his own language.

Immigration statistics always showed a close relationship to the fluctuations of the American economy. By the 1880's, bad news traveled so fast that people could respond and postpone their plans until better days arrived. The financial panic of 1893, combined with a cholera scare the year before, caused a sudden drop in American immigration. In the years of most drastic depression, a steady trickle of immigrants packed up and returned home, discouraging their countrymen from attempting the journey. Others emigrated in the face of the gloomiest warnings, declaring that the worst year in America had to be better than normal times at home.

Those who decided to set sail shared one overriding emotion: They wanted the best of the news from America to be true. They desperately needed a golden land to believe in, for things at home were not good. Europe in those decades was undergoing deep change. Food shortages brought on by overpopulation and poor harvests sent millions of Italians across the sea to the United States. Because of the simple difficulty of earning a living, more and more peasants in the far-flung Austro-Hungarian Empire concluded that America was the only land of hope for them; factory-made products, some imported from industrialized countries, were rapidly replacing their traditional handicrafts. Poverty, famine, and oppression brought death and despair to the Irish people. Agents for absentee landowners sublet potato fields and wretched hovels at high rents to as many tenants as they could squeeze on the land. When farms were consolidated for more efficiency, thousands of Irish peasants were evicted from their tiny plots, and faced the choice of becoming paupers—or emigrants.

Oppressive, corrupt governments aggravated the struggle to earn a living. In Germany the Revolution of 1848 sent to U. S. shores thousands of disillusioned liberals and nationalists. Czarist Russia shook with revolutionary agitation, police terror, assassinations, and organized massacres called pogroms. It became a crime to form any group resembling a labor union, where opposition might ferment.

Minority ethnic and religious groups emigrated in numbers much larger than their proportion in the general population. Some, like the Christian Greeks living in Moslem Turkey, fled to save their lives. The Jews in Russia, living within the designated "Pale of Settlement," suffered severe economic restrictions. They were forbidden to own land, and quotas barred most of them from higher education. In the 1880's a wave of pogroms spread across southern Russia. Soldiers and police looked on grinning as peasant mobs attacked Jews and wrecked their homes and shops. The ordeal stimulated the first great exodus of Russian Jews.

In 1892 during a pogrom in the Siberian village of Temun, the house of Rabbi Baline went up in flames. Huddled in a blanket beside the road, the rabbi's four-year-old son, Israel, watched the fires blazing. Next morning the family set out on a long journey to safety, arriving at Ellis Island in 1893. The Balines began life anew on New York's Lower East Side, where Israel worked as a newsboy and (continued on page 269)

At the golden door, the rites of passage

Scrutinized, prodded, and tested, immigrants ran a medical gauntlet created by an 1891 fitness law. Those who failed could be deported; those showing symptoms of smallpox and other contagious diseases were quarantined, then admitted. Medical teams checked for tuberculosis (opposite), leprosy, and favus, a scalp disorder. They snapped back eyelids to spot trachoma, a blinding illness responsible for more than half the medical detentions. The trachoma virus later was isolated by a Japanese immigrant. On the coats of two out of every ten aliens the examiners chalked letters—H for heart trouble, F for a suspicious rash, E for eye problems; a letter meant segregation in a wire pen for further examination. In 1913 came intelligence tests, including puzzle-solving timed by stopwatch; 1,200 a year were sent away as mental defectives.

The testing ended with a wait on a bench, but not all families passed together. Children over ten were on their own; some who failed returned to the old country—alone.

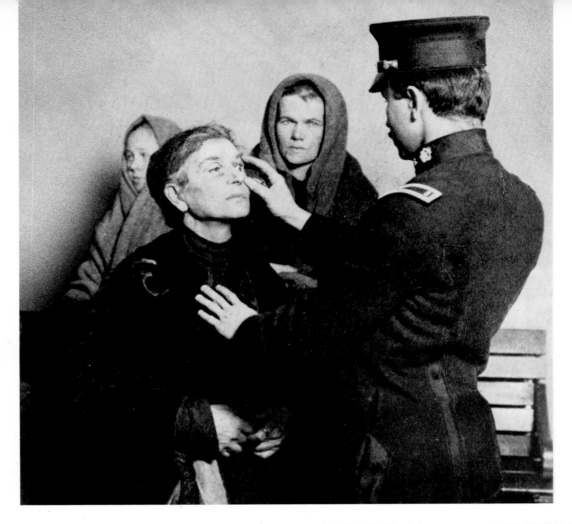

A brave new world within their grasp, hopeful immigrants arrive at Ellis Island, clutching their few possessions and precious papers.

Already they rush in tempo to a guidebook's advice for new Americans: "Run, do, work, and keep your own good in mind." A family,

eyes on Liberty (opposite), awaits the last leg of the long journey—a 30-minute ferry ride from the island to a New York dock.

singing waiter. He also started writing songs—including "Alexander's Ragtime Band," "White Christmas," and "God Bless America," under the name of Irving Berlin.

The trip to America was a frightening experience for simple rural people who had never been to a crowded town, who had never seen a train or a steamship or the ocean, and who had never been humiliated by strangers shouting orders in an incomprehensible language. In their villages they had known how to act; they had formed family ties, and they had solved problems in traditional ways. Now they were on their own, doing something new and dangerous, with no friends or standards to guide them. The ocean terrified them, especially if they sailed in winter aboard a small ship. One youth from the Balkans remembered "the howling darkness, the white rims of the mountain-high waves speeding like maddened dragons toward the tumbling ship. . . ." Only their despairing certainty that they must leave home—and their almost religious faith in the promised land—gave them the strength to embark.

The journey often began with farewell scenes of mingled sorrow and excitement. Emigrants leaving a Croatian village went to confession and Mass, received a special blessing from the priest, then made a round of farewell visits. The entire able-bodied population of the village escorted them to the railroad station, though the nearest might be many miles away. Sicilians solemnly visited family graves, then danced through the night before departure. Irish villagers held a wake, an all-night session of drinking and singing, laughing and dancing, with ritual lamentations and blessings the next morning as the emigrant party left. To look back was to weep. Brothers and sisters might follow them across the Atlantic, but most emigrants left their native soil knowing they would never see their parents or their birthplace again.

By the last quarter of the century, a network of railroads linked almost every region of Europe with the large ports. Most emigrants from Russia, Germany, or the Austro-Hungarian realms headed for the German port of Hamburg. There they were shepherded into the shipping company's modern, barracks-like emigrant station where 4,000 people at a time could be housed, fed, washed and disinfected, medically examined, and questioned for the official passenger lists, while baggage and clothes were fumigated. The center's electric lights, showers, and steam radiators seemed to the country people as marvelous as anything they had heard about the United States. A special dining hall served kosher food. There were churches, a synagogue, even a

clothing shop and daily band concerts on the lawn. Those who passed through other ports—Bremen, Antwerp, Rotterdam, Le Havre, Liverpool, Glasgow, Southampton, Copenhagen, Piraeus, Trieste, Palermo, Genoa, Messina, Constantinople—found a variety of conditions. In the smaller ports they slept in dirty boardinghouses with little to eat but hard bread and soup. Sometimes they waited three weeks for a ship.

Aboard at last, the emigrants settled down for a long voyage. On sunny days they crowded on deck, trying to enjoy the fresh air in spite of cinders from the smokestacks. Sometimes there was a moment of excitement—the sighting of a whale or a distant iceberg—but time passed slowly. Occasionally a newborn baby was baptized by the captain; more often, a baby died and was buried at sea with brief ceremony. A young sport might start a game of cards or dominoes, whirl a girl around the deck, pick a fight, play tunes on a tin whistle or harmonica; single girls giggled at the compliments of the young men who so greatly outnumbered them. Older men sat stolidly smoking pipes; their wives sewed. The few who knew how to read thumbed through guidebooks or missionary-society leaflets about the United States. Children playfully pushed in and out of the crowd. Mostly the travelers talked of the future, remembered the past, and stared at the sea until bad weather drove them below.

When wind and chilling rain kept them in steerage for several days, the foul air became stifling. Only the newest liners had sitting space or even room in the passageways for more than a few people. A mid-century law decreed that each passenger must have a berth 6 feet by 18 inches. There were too few toilets, no facilities for washing with fresh water. Although the steerage area was whitewashed and disinfected in port, it quickly became filthy, reeking of old food, vomit, and unwashed humanity. During the stormy season some passengers lay in their bunks for days (fully dressed under two rough blankets), unable to face meals of stringy boiled beef, salt herring, and thick slices of stale black bread. Children cried incessantly. There seemed to be no room, no air to breathe, no way to fall asleep. The odor—they called it the smell of "ship"—permeated every possession; it would last for months.

The Serbian-born physicist Michael Pupin made the voyage in 1874, when he was a boy of 15. To raise the steerage fare he sold his books, his watch, and, most unfortunate of all, his sheepskin coat. Having seen pictures of half-naked American Indians, he believed the United States was a hot country where warm clothes would not be needed. It was March on the Atlantic, and, crying with cold, he kept himself from freezing at night by standing on deck hugging the warm smokestack.

After the endless nights and days, a morning would come when a sudden change in the ship's motion signaled the end of the voyage. The harbor pilot from the Ambrose Lightship was coming aboard. If the U. S. Public Health Service cleared the ship, she sailed safely past the quarantine hospitals on Hoffmann and Swinburne Islands, and the enormous harbor came into view. Other transatlantic ships, small tugs, and paddle-wheeled ferries crisscrossed in every direction. There stood the Statue of Liberty—and there, after 1892, the place of judgment, Ellis Island.

The federal government had been in control of admitting immigrants since 1882, the year of the first national immigration law applying to all ports of entry. The law excluded Chinese "coolies," prostitutes, and "any convict, lunatic, idiot, or any person unable to take care of himself or herself without becoming a public charge." The law also required shipping companies to pay 50 cents per passenger to cover the cost of administering receiving stations and hospitals. From 1855 on, immigrants entered New York through Castle Garden, at the tip of Manhattan Island. But the facilities in the old circular fort were hopelessly inadequate for the millions who came after 1885. The result was a new federal station built on Ellis Island.

The joke's on them

The ethnic tale told in dialect is a distinctively American form of humor, for perhaps nowhere else have people of so many nationalities mingled. Their children, raised in this country and keenly aware of Old and New World cultural differences, have proved adept at mimicking the verbal eccentricities of their European-born elders.

New York's Lower East Side throbbed with life at the turn of the century (opposite). It became a prolific breeding ground for Jewish dialect stories, many of which ultimately entered the nation's fund of humor by way of vaudeville, burlesque, and the legitimate theater.

Anecdotes involving the rabbi, the *schnorrer* (beggar or cadger), and the *shadchan* (marriage broker) circulated widely within the community. So did jokes about people who had changed their names. In one story an immigrant petitions the court for a new name. The judge asks what his name is.

"Vell, my name iss Abraham Stinker."

"Abraham Stinker! I certainly can't blame you for wanting your name changed. And what would you like to have it changed to?"

"Allen Stinker."

America's image as a land of milk and honey also inspired much ethnic humor, especially in the late 19th century, when thousands of impoverished immigrants streamed to these shores. Many of them expressed their hopes and dreams with anecdotes like this one, which was told about various nationalities.

A Montenegrin from the rugged hills of southwestern Yugoslavia arrives in New York. He is soon strolling along Fifth Avenue, admiring the skyscrapers and shop windows. Suddenly he sees a ten-dollar bill on the pavement. He stoops to pick it up, hesitates, then straightens up. "My first day in America," he mutters. "Why should I work?"

The "endless workroom" called the sweatshop

"Take a Second Avenue Elevated and ride to the sweater's district. Every open window of the big tenements . . . gives you a glimpse of . . . men and women bending over their machines or ironing clothes. . . . The road is like a big gangway through an endless workroom." In such words and in vivid photography (opposite) Jacob Riis, himself an immigrant, chronicled the era when New York became a city of many nations, its population swelling from one million in 1875 to 3.5 million in 1900. One-third of its people were foreign-born, and the sweatshop and the tenement were their fate. Unskilled, they competed for jobs and drove down pay scales. Italian families did piecework at home; the pay was one cent for seven paper roses. An impoverished Italian mother sent her younger children to steal coal from the railroad yards, for the older ones could be prosecuted. She reasoned "with the cunning of the poor," novelist Mario Puzo wrote of his mother.

Most immigrant Jews stayed in New York. But many from an earlier wave had braved the frontier, often as peddlers who carried goods in packs, and, if they prospered, in wagons. One roamed gold camps, then settled down as a merchant in Arizona. His grandson, Barry Goldwater, became a U. S. Senator.

Most Jews from a Russian or Polish *shtetl* — village — worked in sweatshops of the garment trades. They were paid piecework rates so low that it could take 90 hours' labor in a stifling tenement to earn $15. Workers were fined 25 cents for giggling, 50 for looking out a grimy window. Children struggled under heavy loads, delivering bundles of precut clothing parts to be sewn together in the garment district's numerous shops.

David Dubinsky, a Polish Jew who had escaped Russia by "stealing the border" — bribing a guard to look the other way — earned $3 a week as a cloak cutter in 1911, the year of the fire in the "fireproof" Triangle shirtwaist factory, where 146 workers — most of them girls — died in the flames or jumped to their deaths. Dubinsky, stunned by the tragedy, joined the International Ladies Garment Workers Union, rose through the ranks, and became president in 1932. The I.L.G.W.U., backing labor law reform and stricter building codes, saw the end of the sweatshop. As the ready-to-wear industry grew, union membership rose, topping 400,000 in the 1970's.

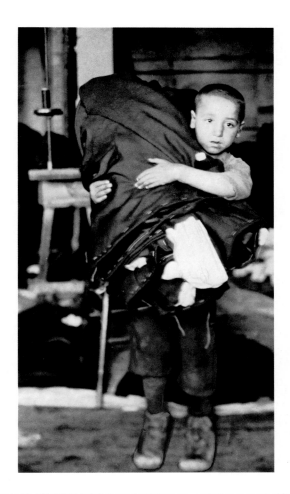

Making the grade as a new American

Ben Franklin grumbled that the influx of Germans into Pennsylvania would contaminate the English language. About a century later the country wondered how to assimilate one million foreign-born, most of them illiterate. But education's alchemy would turn immigrants into Americans. Massachusetts opened a night school in 1870 with classes in mechanical drawing. Courses in English and hygiene (opposite) and the manual arts sprang up in the nation's school systems and factories. When a 1906 law required spoken English for naturalization, educators taught immigrants words needed in everyday situations — such as getting breakfast. The earnest air — and fractured English — of a citizenship class was captured by Leo Rosten's *The Education of Hyman Kaplan*. Hyman speaks: "When people is meating on the boulvard . . . one is saying, 'I am glad I mat you,' and the other is giving answer, 'Mutual.'" Public schools claimed the children. Many proud parents escorted their children on the first day "as if it were an act of consecration."

"America is God's Crucible, the great Melting Pot where all the races of Europe are melting and reforming!" exclaimed the hero of a popular play in 1908. But the melting pot was only a myth; ethnic variety enriched American life. Meat-and-potatoes Yankees adopted goulash and chili, ravioli and frankfurters, bagels and Danish pastry. Transplanted institutions — German kindergartens, Yiddish theater, Scandinavian 4-H clubs — flourished in their new land and helped to transform America into a nation of nations.

In the spring of 1891, as construction was in progress, the government enacted a stricter immigration law which excluded polygamists, people with prison records for crimes of "moral turpitude," and "persons suffering from a loathesome or a dangerous contagious disease." Year after year, reasons for deportation multiplied.

Immigrants sailing into New York harbor at the turn of the century felt nervous and uneasy, for they had heard unhappy rumors about people being shipped home. As their vessel swung into the Hudson River and Ellis Island's red brick buildings slid past the port side, it seemed, miraculously, that they had passed by the place of danger. But when the ship docked in Manhattan, only the first- and cabin-class passengers walked down the gangway and disappeared into the sheds. Guards shouted at the immigrants in several European languages: "Hurry along there! Don't dawdle!" Pushed into a roped enclosure at the end of the dock, the crowd milled around restlessly, wondering what would happen next. Then they boarded ferryboats and barges, and, wedged together, began the ride back down the river. For an hour they had stood on American soil; now at Ellis Island they would find out if they could stay.

As they landed and entered the sprawling complex, guards separated them according to numbers on big tags tied to their coats. An interpreter called out these numbers in German, Polish, Hungarian, Italian, and Russian, and groups of 30 people at a time moved forward until they were standing in the great Registry Hall — probably the largest room they had ever seen — filled with a throng of men and women, children and babes in arms. The market square in their village, even the busiest streets of Hamburg or Le Havre, had been nothing like this. Everyone was talking at once, a few people were crying, and above the general noise the newcomers could hear shouted the names of people from every corner of the Old World: "Ella Jogar! Antek Milkowski! Dimitri Petrov! Giuseppi Policano! Anna Zavachan!"

There was no time to stop and stare. Hurried along an open passageway framed by iron railings, the immigrants passed their first test almost before they were aware of it: A few yards away stood a doctor in the smart blue uniform of the U. S. Public Health Service, watching them carefully as they approached. Small children were taken from their mothers' arms and made to walk. As each person reached the doctor he peered hard at the immigrant's head and hands, and with an interpreter's help asked a simple question or two — "Name? Age? Work?" — to test for feeblemindedness or deafness. Other doctors were waiting to look for specific diseases.

The lucky ones escaped back into the Registry Hall, where they sat on long rows of benches, talking anxiously, rehearsing for one last time their answers to probable questions about money, work, and friends. The waiting time, an hour or two on busy days, seemed endless; some people leaned on their bundles in nervous exhaustion and attempted to sleep. Half a dozen inspectors tried to determine in less than two minutes whether each immigrant was "clearly and beyond a doubt entitled to land." They could do little more than verify the most important information. "What work do you do? Do you have a job waiting for you? Who paid for your ticket? Is anyone meeting you? Where are you going? Can you read and write? Have you ever been in prison? How much money do you have? Show it to me, quickly."

About one immigrant of every six would be detained — some for their own protection. Officials refused to send single women alone into the streets, nor would they release the elderly or the penniless until relatives, friends, or someone from an immigrant aid society came to take charge of them. A few from each group might be held for the Board of Special Inquiry, for cross-examination about their ability to earn a living, their religious or political beliefs, or possible violations of the Contract Labor Law. In a busy year 70,000 such cases would be heard; five out of six were finally admitted.

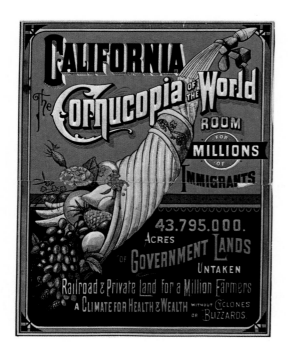

"And to the Republic for which it stands"

Children in New York City's Mott Street Industrial School recite the Pledge of Allegiance. A classroom ritual since 1892, it became a special part of the immigrant pupil's education. The Polish-born writer, Mary Antin, recalled the thrill of claiming the Stars and Stripes as her own flag, for the flags in Russian Poland had inspired fear. "As we had no country, so we had no flag to love," she wrote. "Naturalization may mean more than the adoption of the immigrant by America; it may mean the adoption of America by the immigrant."

Many Europeans journeyed far beyond Mott Street; to them America meant "the west and the wind blowing." Alluring posters tacked up in every corner of the Old World promised free farmland in the Golden West. The railroads, owners of 181 million acres along rights-of-way, schemed to attract immigrants. The Burlington line sent a crop exhibit on European tour—and offered free lodgings at its Immigrant Home in Lincoln, Nebraska. Norwegians and Swedes flocked to the northern plains; Czechs sought homesteads in Nebraska, Russian-German Mennonites, in Kansas. The posters had not told of grasshopper plagues, Indian attacks, or loneliness. Some committed suicide, went insane, or headed home. But nearly all stayed and gloried in frontier democracy with the Swede who wrote, "Neither is my cap worn out from lifting it to gentlemen."

Detained immigrants and deportees lived in dormitories with tiers of iron bunks reminiscent of steerage, and ate in a dining hall whose manager had trouble finding menus that were universally acceptable. All immigrants would eat kosher beef, but Scandinavians wanted dried fish, Italians grumbled about the absence of wine; and one group of Moslem dervishes, forbidden to eat anything over which the shadow of an infidel had passed, would swallow nothing but boiled eggs. There were two hospitals, a children's playground, and sometimes band concerts. But in spite of the best efforts of the commissioners, Ellis Island was never a happy place. An uncounted number of deportees killed themselves there or disappeared into the dark waters of the harbor rather than submit to being shipped back to Europe.

The fortunate majority received a nod and a landing card from the inspector who first questioned them. After only three or four hours on the island, they were free to leave. They stopped at the money exchange, perhaps at the small post office to send the good news home at once, then went downstairs to claim trunks from the baggage room and maybe to buy a box lunch for their continuing journey (sandwiches 4 cents each, bologna 13 cents a pound, apples 2 cents each). In the Railroad Room they could line up to buy a ticket, to anywhere in the country, from 12 agents who together sold 25 tickets a minute on their more frantic days. But the pace slowed while the agent pondered where the immigrant really wanted to go. "Pringvilliamas" was one Italian's version of Springfield, Mass., and "Linkinbra" a German's distortion of Lincoln, Nebraska. An agitated Hungarian woman waved a scrap of paper reading "Szekenevno Pillsburs," which turned out to be Second Avenue, Pittsburgh.

A great many travelers went no farther than New York, landing in Battery Park, where a waiting crowd of friends and relatives let out sudden shrieks of recognition, and tears of happiness streamed down almost every face. Then piles of baggage were loaded onto horse-drawn wagons while the immigrants were pulled along, with gasps of amazement, to the elevated trains that rumbled overhead. So the citizens-to-be set off into the New World, gaping at the tall buildings, staring at such wonders as an automobile or a small black child. They were taken to a tenement room on the Lower East Side, probably, to enjoy an evening of good food, talk, and laughter, as more and more neighbors crowded in to welcome the newcomers. Then came the much-needed chance to wash, and to sleep for a night on a mattress that no longer rolled with the waves. The next morning life in America began with an introduction to a sympathetic boss or construction foreman, who was usually foreign-born himself.

To make the New World seem more hospitable, immigrants surrounded themselves with companions, objects, and rituals from the Old. They spoke their native tongue at home and read foreign-language newspapers years after they had raised grandchildren who spoke only English. They clustered in ethnic neighborhoods: Genoa, Calabria, and Sicily placed their distinctive stamp on specific blocks in New York's Little Italy. Jews gathered together according to their origins. (Rivington Street was jokingly referred to as a suburb of Minsk.) Roman Catholics from Austria, Poland, or Italy barely recognized the Irish churches as of their own faith.

Most of the children went to school, though they were expected to get up as early as 4 a.m. to help earn the family's income. Because they learned English quickly, they acted for their parents as a bridge between the Old World and the New. In school they rattled off the names and dates of American history, celebrated national holidays with patriotic poems, and saluted their flag. The adults suffered from a sense of alienation; even when they prospered, they often felt they did not belong. Clinging to ties in Europe, they winced as their children spoke the words that their own tongues could never utter: "At home here in America . . . back there in the old country."

Cities in the Machine Age

Blake McKelvey

The rambunctious American town flexed its muscles during the industrial revolution and grew into a city. Fed by old skills and new technology, the city bulged out, then up after the Civil War. With the traditional tools of their art—triangle, T-square, brass compass, ruler for measuring in reduced scale— architects and planners blueprinted a new look for the city. And a structure peculiarly American began to scrape the sky.

Elevators let New York's 260-foot, clock-towered Tribune Building strain upward. But the alchemy that changed iron to steel let buildings soar. When the Bessemer converter and the open hearth furnace lowered steel prices from $150 to $45 a ton, skeletons made of I-beams became practical. Walls once held up buildings. Now they became curtains enwrapping the building's inner strength. The sky was the limit! And the appetite for sky-scrapers would help fire the foundries that launched the United States into the 20th century as the industrial leader of the world.

Cynics dubbed it "Powers' Folly." But Daniel Powers, a banker in Rochester, New York, wasn't worried. The Civil War had just ended, and he chose for his Powers Block a site at the city's central Four Corners. The history of the site exemplified the growth of Rochester, spurred by the Erie Canal from a frontier hamlet in 1812 into one of America's first boomtowns. The corner had seen five successive structures come and go—a log cabin, two frame taverns, a brick hotel, and a stone bank. Now, in 1865, Powers began raising a five-story, "fireproof" cast-iron building. Faced with iron panels that simulated cut stone, floored with marble, and served by a gracious wrought-iron staircase as well as the first elevator in upstate New York, this imposing commercial structure would have 160 offices and 15 street-level stores. Skeptics said tenants would never fill them.

Shortly after construction was completed in 1870, Powers left on a trip to Europe, where he purchased a large painting for his office. A dealer persuaded him that it would cost no more to ship four paintings than one, and Powers returned to Rochester with more works of art than he could hang in his office. He added another floor to the Powers Block, providing ample room for an art gallery and a library, a hall for receptions and dances, and several studios. Soon most of the offices and stores were rented, and the hall was leased by a dance instructor; the cotillions and assemblies there highlighted the social scene. Streams of visitors, disembarking from horsecars at the Four Corners turntable or arriving by excursion trains at nearby stations, hastened to board the "verti-cal railroad" for their first ride in an elevator, a lift by hydraulic power to the fifth floor. There, many paid 25 cents to see their first art show.

Surrounded by cast iron and marble, Powers felt safe from the recurrent fires that still worried most merchants even after the introduction of horse-drawn steam fire engines in the 1860's. But as an added precaution he installed a water tank atop the building, at the same time assuring his friends in the tax league that Rochester did not need and could not afford a water system. When news of the Chicago fire of 1871 flashed eastward, Powers learned that cast-iron buildings had been destroyed in the flames along with those of wood, brick, and stone. He hastily resigned from the tax league and organized a committee to demand not one but two water systems.

Years passed and neighboring structures rose to challenge the Powers Block, but the banker kept adding floors to retain the loftiest building in town. By the combination of a key location, a dynamic businessman, and a melding of technology and architecture,

The ill wind that untangled New York

In an American cityscape of the early 20th century, New York displays what urban evolution had temporarily produced: tall buildings and uncluttered streets—wide enough for horse and gas buggy to pass in peace. The wedge-shaped Flatiron Building towers over a Madison Square free of the wires that had enmeshed Lower Manhattan (below).

Telegraphs, telephones, and electric lights made midtown hum, but their wires wrapped the center of the growing metropolis in a cocoon. Then, in March 1888, a blizzard struck. Gale winds blew down poles and snapped wires, cutting off power, fire alarms, and communications. Messages to Boston—battered, as were Baltimore and Philadelphia—went by cable via London. Hansom cabbies fed their horses whiskey and threaded 20-foot snowdrifts. New Yorkers tunneled from their houses and dug out frozen corpses. The marooned bedded down in Macy's department store or played euchre in Grand Central Depot. Life began to return to normal a few days later. And those overhead wires were soon buried in underground conduits.

The ordeal revealed an indomitable spirit, one that Walt Whitman recognized. "The human qualities of these vast cities," he wrote, "is . . . heroic, beyond statement."

the Powers Block became a symbol of urban growth in the Industrial Age. It still stands.

Rochester itself was typical of the changing American city. In the mid-1850's many old residents thought Rochester was past its prime. Flour milling, which had boomed at the falls of the Genesee River, moved west to the new wheat fields. Restless sons of the pioneers pulled up stakes too, lured by the discovery of gold in California and by opportunities to plant new towns in new territories. But if Rochester's advantages had palled for some folk, other people—"huddled masses yearning to breathe free"—saw their value and found them attractive. Slowly community leaders, who like Powers had stayed behind, discovered the city's chief asset was no longer the Genesee River or the Erie Canal or the commerce they carried. It was the stream of newcomers, who brought untiring energies, fresh skills, and eager hopes for the future.

Transit facilities provided a catalyst for growth in the American city. New transportation systems transformed "walking" towns into highly mobile cities with clearly defined residential, commercial, and industrial districts. Horsecar lines, introduced before the Civil War, played a limited role in the transformation, for most people still walked to work, to shop, and to worship in their own neighborhoods. With the mounting tide of immigrants, joined by ex-farmhands from increasingly mechanized rural areas, the demand rose for something faster than horsecars to move workers from the spreading residential areas to the business districts. Horses were not only slow but also subject to infirmities. An equine flu epidemic in 1872 killed so many horses that idled transit drivers in some cities pulled cars by hand. Healthy horses generated a different problem—pounds and pounds of manure a day. Along with the pigs, cows, chickens, and geese that were tolerated members of the community, horses contributed a bucolic aroma to even the largest cities.

To the rescue came the speedier, non-polluting cable car, introduced in 1873 in San Francisco, where most hills were too steep for horses. Andrew Hallidie, a wire rope maker, borrowed an idea from England where coal cars were hauled by cables on colliery railways. He built a stationary steam engine to run an endless cable below the pavement. A "gripman" on the car would operate a clamp extending down through a slot in the roadway to grip or release the moving cable. On the trial run, the gripman looked down the 12 percent grade of Clay Street into San Francisco Bay, quailed, and resigned on the spot. Undaunted, Hallidie took the controls and made the run.

As it turned out, the cable car did not rescue every city. The high cost of installing the tracks and underground cables discouraged its wide acceptance. But most cities welcomed the electric trolley after Richmond, Virginia, opened a line for regular service in 1888. Motors on the cars received power from an overhead wire by means of a "troller," or wheeled carriage, at the end of a flexible pole. Soon, though, trolley car congestion threatened to block all movement at "rush" hour. Gradually the cities discovered that technological advances brought major problems and sometimes created petty annoyances. When it snowed, for example, horsecar lines could simply switch to sleighs. With trolleys, companies had to clear the snow from the tracks, often clogging adjoining roadways. Snow battles erupted when merchants or highway crews shoveled the snow back onto the tracks. Eventually the city had to haul the snow away as trash.

Railroads, carrying commuters and commerce, penetrated most cities. Not without hazard. In the Chicago of the Gay Nineties, English journalist William Stead found that the "railroads which cross the city at the level in every direction . . . constantly mow down unoffending citizens at the crossings." Many cities elevated trolley lines and railroads, sometimes on embankments that segmented the community—Philadelphia had an embankment known as "the Chinese Wall." Finally, rails went underground when Boston, New York, and Philadelphia built subways at the turn of the century.

"Give us . . . speedy . . . and cheap transit"

A familiar cry in today's crowded cities, but it dates from an 1867 *New York Times* editorial deploring the slow motion of the horse-drawn omnibus and the horsecar (opposite). When the horsecar arrived in 1832, it seemed a heroic improvement over the venerable omnibus. The new carrier hitched the horse to an iron-wheeled car that averaged five mph on iron rails. New York hailed the innovation as "the greatest achievement of man," one that "will make Harlem a suburb of New York."

The love affair didn't last long. "People are packed [in the cars] like sardines in a box, with perspiration for oil," went one pungent complaint. Pickpockets thrived, and one disgusted rider advised passengers to "carry bowie knives and derringers."

Rapid transit finally appeared in 1868 with elevated trains pulled by stubby locomotives. They hit speeds of 15 mph and charged a ten-cent fare that dropped to a nickel at rush hour. But they spread smoke, cinders, and noise, scared horses, and shook buildings as they passed by. At New York's Greeley Square, where hansom cabs line up in 1898 beside the statue of the *Tribune*'s editor, vibrations from the El nearly danced Mr. Greeley off his base. He had to be fastened down.

The course of transit lines and the rising land values downtown helped shape the cities. As artisans' shops grew in size, they moved their locations from lofts and back rooms in the central district and clustered as factories along water and rail transport arteries. Midtown residents sold out and moved to less congested areas on the outer reaches of the transit lines, away from the obnoxious odors of stockyards, soap factories, breweries, and foundries on the "other side of the tracks." Enterprising businessmen converted the vacated residences to more productive commercial use—as offices, banks, hotels, theaters, department stores. Almost unnoticed, the expanding city gobbled up irregular plots of vacant ground where once children had played and parents had planted truck gardens or pastured a cow.

Of all urban problems, streets produced the most persistent headaches. Increased traffic by cart, wagon, and carriage pulverized early surfaces of macadam, or crushed stone, which had to be sprinkled with water to lay the dust. Resurfacing with expensive cobblestones or bricks brought strong opposition from adjoining property owners charged with part of the cost. Then in 1870 Edward De Smedt, a Belgian immigrant, introduced the first crude asphalt by paving a road in Newark, New Jersey. Developed and refined, asphalt made a smooth, durable covering. It soon became popular.

On some streets, such as affluent East Avenue in Rochester, carriage owners complained that asphalt could cause a horse to slip and break a leg. But asphalt proved a boon to the growing host of bicyclists who "scorched" about, terrifying buggy drivers in the 1890's. Asphalt was much preferred in crowded tenement districts, the *New York Times* noted. "That material can be kept clean so easily that the health of a neighborhood is appreciably affected by its use, and, besides, danger of an epidemic which might spread to wealthier parts of the city is averted."

Tearing up the streets time and again called for the coordinating of municipal services. Gas companies had laid mains for street lamps as fast as the cities erected them. When this operation paralleled the laying of water mains, it saved the city money. But the completion of water systems led to widespread use of new flush toilets, developed in

Bargain hunters of 1897 throng Siegel Cooper's New York department store. Lured by newspaper advertisements, free deliveries, and giveaways like the fan opposite, shoppers shuttled downtown on trolleys and rode elevators to floor upon floor of lavish displays. A typical store spread wares along six miles of counters. Its 650 feet of showy plate glass created a new pastime — window shopping.

England by 1870, and made it necessary to tear up the streets again for sanitary sewers.

When Cleveland lit up a public square in 1879 with arc lamps (a continuous spark arcing between two carbon rods), other cities hastened to place them on busy streets. In 1880 arc lights brightened New York's Broadway, the first gleam of the "Great White Way." With the development of Edison's incandescent lamp, electricity displaced gas lighting in homes and office buildings. Power and telephone companies planted poles and strung wires in every direction. By the late 1880's the festoon of wires overhead created such a hazard, especially for firemen, that New York placed the wires underground. Once again the streets had to be torn up.

America was growing so fast during these decades that urgency stamped every need for public services. Out of that urgency rose the political boss. A man with connections in business and local government, a man who controlled votes with patronage and favors, the boss could get things done—sometimes at a staggering cost, as in New York where Boss Tweed swindled the treasury of millions (page 192). Private investors competing to set up gas, electric, telephone, and transit companies were not above bribing city officials with graft or "boodle." This widespread practice led journalist William Stead to write that the city, "instead of being governed in the interests of the citizens, was practically farmed out to corporations."

Despite such corrosive defects, the cities thrived. Their many conveniences and vitality astonished Londoner G. W. Steevens, who characterized America in the 1890's with the title of his book, *The Land of the Dollar*. In New York, "the most magnificent embodiment of titanic energy and force," Steevens could be whisked around for a nickel on the El, cable car, or ferry. The bustle of building captivated him. "Everything centres in hard utility," he wrote. "It is the outward expression of the freest, fiercest individualism. The very houses are alive with the instinct of competition, and strain each one to overtop its neighbours." Wherever he went in America, Steevens found burgeoning cities. Denver, reached after a journey across lonely prairies, surprised him as a civilized place of brick homes on paved streets, with such amenities as electric lights and trolleys.

All very gratifying. But as the cities grew, so grew their pockets of deterioration. After a New York tenement house ordinance of 1879 banned windowless rooms, five- and six-story tenements rose on deep, narrow lots. Each building provided windows opening into air wells midway on both sides, in compliance with the law. In time these "dumbbell" dwellings (named for their shape on the blueprint) gave one Manhattan district an unrivaled density of 986 people to the acre. Improved transit facilities, once envisioned as an answer to congestion, now spread the contamination. Elevated trains, spewing smoke, cinders, and noise, helped blight endless miles of new dumbbell tenements. In the late 1860's New York numbered 15,000 tenement houses; two decades later they had doubled in number and housed more than one million residents. Often two or more low-income families crowded into a single apartment. Air spaces became convenient trash chutes, cesspools of filth—and fire hazards.

Makeshift sweatshops thrived in tenements. Degenerate offspring of the age-old master-journeyman system, the sweatshop had its strongest hold on the clothing industry, which had been inundated by successive waves of German, Jewish, and Italian

High-style fashions suit urban shoppers

Vast emporiums, gay as bazaars with a "perennial air of festival and excitement," put ready-to-wear clothing within reach of city shoppers. Electric lights, cash registers, and inter-department telephones sped the proliferation of "consumers' palaces" —from Jordan Marsh in Boston to I. Magnin in San Francisco.

By 1910 every item of feminine apparel, from "Paris-imported bonnets to pink-satin boots," could be bought ready-made in palatial department stores. Abundant high-quality textiles, a large immigrant labor force, cloth-cutting machines, and gas and electric pressing irons made production fast, easy, and cheap. Tailor-made garments were similarly reasonable.

Swathed in silks and satins (up to 20 yards in an afternoon gown), city ladies went shopping, paid calls, or formally received guests at home. Few well-dressed women dared venture out-of-doors without a fancy bonnet and gloves. These wasp-waisted women, cinched by whalebone and "rust-proof" steel, achieved breathtaking svelteness. Corsets formed the foundation of the fashionable "S" curve—dubbed the "kangaroo bend"—and trimmed up to 15 inches from a female midriff. Flounced petticoats, swishing with an enticing "frou-frou," enhanced the hourglass effect; embroidered silk stockings and high kid shoes added a glamorous footnote.

Ready-to-wear for women and men came in sizes to fit every shape and purse. Men could buy suits "at all sorts of prices" without the "costs and inconveniences of a custom tailor." Detachable collars of paper or celluloid let a man wear a white shirt two or more days. Colored, soft-collared shirts marked workers until the 1890's, when gentlemen donned them for summer. Pants lacked belt loops and needed suspenders. Armbands governed sleeve length until measured sleeves were introduced in 1911.

Warner's Rust-Proof

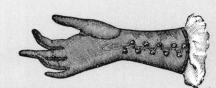

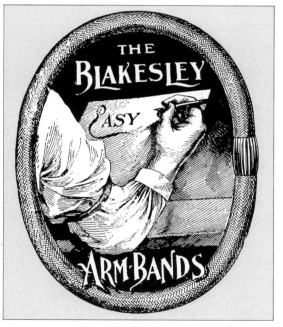

"Two Miles of Millionaires!"

That boast near the turn of the century characterized New York's upper Fifth Avenue, where industrial and financial giants—"robber barons," some were called—flaunted wealth in flamboyant mansions and life-styles. The turreted Vanderbilt chateau at 58th Street covered half a block and housed 30 servants. "The Breakers," a 70-room Vanderbilt "cottage" at Newport, Rhode Island, cost at least $4 million to build.

This was the Gilded Age (there was no income tax) when matrons like Mrs. George Jay Gould—wearing a $500,000 necklace (above)—married their daughters to impoverished European noblemen, when "Bet-a-Million" Gates lost $400,000 at cards in one evening, when "Society" was *The 400*—the number of guests who fit into Mrs. William Astor's ballroom. The nation counted about 4,000 millionaires, 1,100 of them in New York; an Astor observed that "a man with a million dollars is as well off as if he were rich."

Gazing on the wealthy, the middle class saw living proof of a booming economy—and shared with the rich some of the finer things in life: electric lights, a telephone, perhaps a new white porcelain bathtub.

immigrants. Poverty—and lack of skills—had compelled each group to battle for economic and social position by accepting reduced wages and progressively worse living conditions.

"The unsanitary conditions of many of these tenement houses," reported one observer of Chicago in the 1890's, "and the ignorance and abject poverty of the tenants, insure the maximum probability of disease; and diphtheria, scarlet-fever, smallpox, typhoid . . . have been found."

Some industrialists as well as wage earners sought escape from the ills of congestion. In 1880 George Pullman, the railroad sleeping car magnate, began converting a swamp south of Chicago into a company town of 1,400 dwelling units, with factories to employ some 4,000 workers who rented the houses. A landscaped square, a playground and athletic area, a generous planting of trees, plus an arcade, a hotel, church, school, and theater—but not one saloon—made Pullman, Illinois, according to a newspaper in 1883, "the most perfect city in the world." Yet all its advantages did not forestall the 1894 Pullman strike when the company cut wages but not rents. A forerunner of today's planned towns, Pullman was soon swallowed by the encroaching metropolis of Chicago. But as a community—and a National Historic Landmark—it lives on.

Pullman's use of landscaping and a small park was in step with another trend: urban park planning. Pre-Civil War cities had cherished their cemeteries as informal parks where families picnicked on sunny Sundays and laid flowers on the graves of loved ones. The rich had their estates and resorts. A new movement toward large municipal parks for all classes had begun with the work of landscape architect Frederick Law Olmsted, who saw the need for "a simple, broad, open space of clean greensward" surrounded by enough woods "to completely shut out the city." In 1858, with Calvert Vaux, Olmsted designed New York City's Central Park. A commissioner described the southern part of the proposed 800-acre park as a "filthy, squalid and disgusting" suburb of "wretched hovels, half hidden among the rocks" and polluted "by heaps of cinders, brick-bats, potsherds, and other rubbish." Factories and "numerous swill-milk and hog-feeding establishments" had to be removed before the land was transformed into a sylvan retreat of winding paths, green meadows, lakes, terraces, and trees.

Olmsted designed other "greenswards," including Brooklyn's Prospect Park and

Tenement life: "The sunlight never enters"

To most people, the immigrant poor lived invisibly, though their slums had been spreading for decades after the Civil War. But Jacob Riis, a Danish immigrant, saw them with a police reporter's eye as he covered New York's Lower East Side. On notorious Gotham Court, a "packing-box tenement," he focused camera (opposite) and words: "I knew . . . the well-worn rut of the dead-wagon and the ambulance to the [court] gate, for the tenants died there like flies." In "the foul core of New York's slums," where a woman lived by selling stale bread and where children shared a gutter with a dead horse awaiting the offal cart, Riis stalked apathy: "The battle with the slum began the day civilization recognized in it her enemy." His crusade spurred young Police Commissioner Theodore Roosevelt and others toward reform.

Warrens of disease and despair, the worst slums had communal toilets and hallway washtroughs. Lack of ventilation made the air foul and sickening. In three years, 61 of the 138 children born in Gotham Court died— most of them in their first year.

Crowding created the horror. Riis told of five families—20 people—living in one 12 by 12-foot room with two beds. Such conditions led to degradation and depravity, fostered prostitution, spawned "Street Arabs"—waifs who "didn't live nowhere"—and gangs of murderous, thieving toughs.

Some people simply gave up. Riis anguished over a hardworking young husband and wife who lived for a time in an attic cubbyhole with a single window. They were "tired," wrote Riis. That's why they took poison.

"The grocery-man's inhumanity to man"

"Look before you eat," advised *Puck,* whose 1884 cartoon of adulterated food (opposite, lower) contained little humor but sound advice. The pictorial weekly charged that grocers "fortified" sugar with sand, tea and coffee with dust, and butter with renderings from animal carcasses. Soon, *Puck* predicted, it would be necessary "for every citizen to carry with him a stomach-pump and an emetic."

Bakers added alum and sulfur of copper as preservatives; consumers found surprises like oven ash and grit from machinery in their staff of life. Swill milk, sold in bulk from carts, came from city cows fed on distillery mash. Dealers increased their milk supply by adding water, then improved color by stirring in chalk, plaster of paris, or molasses. A water shortage, one cartoon suggested, "would put the milk-man out of business."

Gastronomic danger lurked everywhere. Soldiers in the Spanish-American War died from eating "embalmed beef"; in the early 1900's some European countries banned American meat. After Harvey W. Wiley, Chief Chemist of the Department of Agriculture, set up a "Poison Squad" and found formaldehyde, boric acid, tetanus spores, and other "reprehensible substances" in many canned foods, President Theodore Roosevelt in 1906 signed The Food and Drugs Act.

Cities fought other health hazards. Rags, trash, and ashes from stoves overflowed curbside barrels, adding their pollution to the stench from animal excrement. When New York City set up a Board of Health in 1866, sanitation workers, as one of their first tasks, collected 160,000 tons of horse manure from neighborhood lots alone.

For decades garbage had been sold to farmers who fed it to swine. But pigs could not eat the paper, glass, and tin containers produced by new technology in packaging and discarded by an exploding population. Cities buried their refuse, burned it, even dumped it in ocean, lake, or river. That only spread the pollution. In 1885 New York built one of the country's first incinerators on Governors Island. But incinerators could not solve the entire problem; the residue of ash and non-combustibles had to be disposed of. Dumps and landfills—including even canyons—became scarce as cities sprawled across the countryside. For decades the trash piled up. And then the system that began with pigs—recycling—returned as a new idea.

Detroit's Belle Isle, and laid out Riverside, a model Chicago suburb. Carefully planned with an eye for beauty, Riverside departed from the conventional grid layout and provided generous house lots fronting on curved streets that led to small parks. One of Olmsted's greatest accomplishments after Central Park was his landscape plan for the 1893 World's Columbian Exposition in Chicago. For millions of visitors from across the country the fair revealed what city planning could do, even for turbulent Chicago, a city of which Rudyard Kipling later wrote, "Having seen it, I urgently desire never to see it again. It is inhabited by savages." That may have been Chicago outside the fair, but inside stood the White City. Its gleaming buildings, lagoons, fountains, and boulevards sent fairgoers home imbued with a new vision of what the American city could be. All over the country a City Beautiful movement began to spread. Even in the depths of the financial panic that ran from 1893 to 1896, the Cleveland Architectural Club prepared plans for a new civic center around a man-made lagoon.

The City Beautiful movement did more than beautify. It brought recognition to struggling urban institutions. In the search for structures worthy to adorn civic centers, citizen committees sought a public library, an art gallery, or a science museum, and pressured local philanthropists to donate funds for their construction and support.

The panic of 1893 frustrated some ambitious schemes to refurbish the cities, but in the last decades of the 19th century astute builders, engineers, and architects had already combined resources to develop the skyscraper. In the 1870's steam-powered as well as hydraulic elevators helped make seven- and eight-story buildings practicable. A decade later, speedier electric elevators with safety brakes stimulated the rise of still taller buildings, though heavy walls limited height.

Architects took a first step toward the skyscraper by placing iron bars in masonry piers for reinforcement. Chicago's 16-story Monadnock Building, designed in 1891 by Daniel Burnham and John Root, was called the triumph of commercial architecture in the age of masonry—even as the age was passing. Another Chicago architect, William Le Baron Jenney, had earlier employed a skeleton of iron and steel in his ten-story Home Insurance Building, completed in 1885. To it he attached stone and glass walls as a covering, not as a weight-bearing element. The all-steel frame, 135-foot Wainwright Building in St. Louis, completed by Louis Sullivan in 1892, accented vertical lines and influenced skyscraper design for years to come.

The skyscraper symbolized a successful city. It proclaimed the community's economic vitality, the ability to generate enough business to fill its offices. It testified to a transit system that could deliver workers and clients to its doors, a telephone system to facilitate communication, and sanitary sewers adequate for all floors.

If the skyscraper was the symbol of the business district, the public school was the focal point of the neighborhoods, especially those absorbing immigrant families. The need for schools to teach children of varied backgrounds inspired a state teacher's college in Oswego, New York, to launch a new technique: teaching teachers to communicate more effectively by replacing traditional memory drills with instruction focused on familiar objects. Francis W. Parker introduced art and manual training to poor Irish youths in Quincy, Massachusetts, in the late 1870's. And St. Louis, with its large number of Germans, opened public kindergartens and offered elementary science courses. The variety of these new approaches enlivened classwork.

As an increasing number of pupils continued into the upper grades, cities responded with more high schools. Unfortunately, they attracted only a fraction of eligible youths. Some authorities acted to compel attendance of all children until their 16th year, partly to remove them from the labor market. But truant officers usually proved ineffective; poor parents, needing the income their children provided, seldom cooperated.

293

"Grandest Spectacle of Modern Times"

Palatial white buildings, mirrored in lagoons and Venetian canals, gleamed under the morning sun on May 1, 1893, in South Side Chicago. President Grover Cleveland pressed an electric key, and the World's Columbian Exposition—a year late in commemorating Columbus's discovery of America—throbbed to life. Dynamos hummed. Machinery rumbled. Fountains gushed. Flags skittered up poles. A 5,000-voice choir sang and 150,000 people cheered. The Age of Electricity, the World of Tomorrow, the White City had arrived. It would light up America.

A dazzling spectacle of monumental Old World architecture housing marvels of science and industry and art, the fair drew 25 million visitors before it closed in October. From farm and town and foreign capital they poured in. "Sell the cook stove if necessary and come," wrote one awestruck spectator to his parents. "You *must* see this fair." Another assured his wife that the visit had been worthwhile, "even if it did take all the burial money."

What did they get for their money? A vision of the wondrous future, especially at night when the new magic of electricity blazoned palaces like the Agriculture Building (right), and colored searchlights painted electric fountains in rainbow hues. It was so beautiful it hurt: The old couple with the cookstove did come—and they shed "tears of joy . . . almost as poignant as pain."

Electricity drove the elevated train that circled the fairgrounds, supplying power by means of a third rail, the world's first. Electricity coated metal with gold, it carved designs on glass, it worked stoves, fans, even crude dishwashers. With a thousand bulbs the Tower of Light (page 296) seemed to blink out the message of a brighter tomorrow. Edison's Kinetoscope transmitted "scenes to the eyes as well as sounds to the ear." A "miniature ammonic ice-plant" promised to cool an entire house. A telephone hookup brought concerts from New York.

Visitors gasped at the weird, the wacky, the wonderful: an early zipper, model tenements, cured meats, French tapestries, a ten-ton Canadian cheese, Venus de Milo molded in chocolate, a life-size mounted knight made of dried prunes. Germany, one of 77 participating nations, trundled in a giant coastal gun that could hurl a one-ton shell 16 miles.

The Woman's Building, designed by a female graduate of the Massachusetts Institute

of Technology, showed off a model kitchen featuring a tile floor and a gas stove. Mrs. Potter Palmer, Chicago's social queen, praised the mechanical household gadgetry and declared, "Women as a sex have been liberated." Princess Eulalia, representing her nephew, King Alfonso of Spain, proved it — she smoked cigarettes in public.

At the mile-long Midway, visitors rolled on wicker chairs into exotic worlds: a parade of African "cannibals" (right), medieval villages, South Sea Island huts, camel drivers and donkey boys, a Moorish palace, an Egyptian temple. Men drank beer in Old Vienna, and bowler-topped dandies stroked their mustaches at Little Egypt (above) gyrating the hootchy-kootchy, "the genuine native muscle dance." And they tapped their toes to a new and catchy kind of music by blacks from Mississippi River towns — ragtime.

Everyone rode G. W. Ferris's wheel, 250 feet in diameter, built to rival the Eiffel Tower. They packed in, 60 to a car, for the high point of their visit. From the top of the wheel they could see outside the White City to a suffering gray city. In the financial panic of 1893 breadlines lengthened, and 2,000 homeless men a night slept in the corridors of City Hall.

When the fair closed, the *Chicago Tribune,* speaking for the millions who had seen it, wistfully bade goodbye to "a little ideal world, a realization of Utopia . . . in which this splendid fantasy of the artist and architect seemed to foreshadow some far-away time when all the earth should be as pure, as beautiful, and as joyous as the White City itself."

296

Although the schools were unable to hold on to all children of the poor, the new facilities proved otherwise useful to the community. Auditoriums and laboratories provided lecture halls for adult forums and workbenches for scientific societies. Classrooms opened at night for immigrant men and women eager to learn English. Gymnasiums in a few progressive high schools offered room for exercise and showers, and newly built playgrounds encouraged organized sports at the turn of the century. That New York City did not build a municipal children's playground until 1899 appalled journalist Jacob Riis. In *A Ten Year's War,* published in 1900, Riis lamented, "It is not two years since a boy was shot down by a policeman for the heinous offense of playing football in the street on Thanksgiving Day."

In some states schools offered basic lessons in personal hygiene and banned the public drinking cup. New York in 1892 directed health officials to inspect the sanitary facilities of all schools once a year. Boston followed by appointing 50 physicians to examine all school children for communicable diseases. To promote cleanliness among adults as well as youths, many cities built public baths. Some were free, others charged as much as five cents for soap and a towel. Here a citizen could actually wash his entire body in a shower stall or a bathtub. That could be a novel experience if you lived with 2,000 other people in a New York tenement that contained not one bathtub.

For decades the city dweller had accepted an increasing mortality rate as natural to urban growth. In big cities, the death rate of 28 per 1,000 from 1815 to 1839 had risen to 30 per 1,000 from 1840 to 1864. A drop to 25 in the two post-Civil War decades demonstrated the results of improved water supplies and the use of sanitary sewers. But the service did not reach everyone. In the 1890's some households relied on the indoor earth closet, a toilet that deposited a layer of soil as an absorbent covering after each use. Even as late as 1900, Baltimore still had some 90,000 backyard privies.

The problem was not simply one of financing the necessary public works. It was a matter of knowledge—or lack of it. The germ theory, advanced by Louis Pasteur in the 1870's, finally began to win acceptance. Sanitary engineers experimented with chemical and biological treatment of wastes; in 1893 at Brewster, New York, chlorine was used for the first time to treat sewage in the United States.

The germ theory alerted health authorities to other hazards—milk from tubercular cows and diseased meat from uninspected slaughterhouses. Checking for watered milk no longer sufficed; now barns came under government inspection. Minneapolis even secured authority to destroy tubercular cattle on farms outside the city.

The plight of children and the poor attracted the concern of private groups as well as public authorities in the late-19th century. In many cities there appeared church-supported orphan asylums, homes for the friendless, recreation centers, sectarian hospitals, and relief societies that sent slum children off on farm vacations. Their appeals for support from charitable residents became so persistent that a move to coordinate efforts resulted in the systematic organization of private charitable activities. By the late 1880's, in several of the nation's largest cities, reform impulses began radiating from a new social institution, the settlement house.

Patterned after Toynbee Hall in London, the settlement house operated on the principle that the best way for concerned clergymen and college graduates to serve slum residents was to live and work with them as friends and neighbors. Jane Addams of Hull House in Chicago and other early social workers put in 20-hour days organizing and operating day nurseries, clubs for children, adult education courses, gymnasiums, and employment bureaus. They pressed for effective building codes and housing inspections to maintain standards of sanitation and population density. And they helped spark reform movements that brought a new civic vitality to many cities. The reformers had a

Rescuing the cities with steam and steel

A steam pumper thunders down a New Haven, Connecticut, street in 1910 during the waning days of glory for horse and steamer. The engine fought fire with fire: An engineer in the rear shoveled in coal to heat the boiler that powered the pump that drove a stream of water 300 feet. Developed in the 1860's, steamers ended a romantic era. Once rival companies of boisterous volunteers, pulling hand pumpers and hose carts, raced to a fire, then battled for possession of cistern or hydrant. Often as not the building burned down before the victors began to pump.

Every city lived under a fiery threat. Periodically fires consumed slums—but there was at least some hope that the next housing might be better and even escape urban blight. After its 1871 holocaust, Chicago rose from its ashes like a phoenix, reborn in skyscrapers typified by the steel-skeletoned Reliance Building (above), completed in 1895. A Chicago Architectural Landmark, it still stands.

lot to overcome. Vice and crime had grown up with the city, baffling the generally poorly trained police, who frequently were political, not professional, employees.

In the mid-1860's fewer than a dozen cities could boast of a uniformed police force. But as the century drew to a close, the police multiplied to meet growing labor unrest, the violence of roving gangs, and mounting offenses against property. In immigrant neighborhoods, where strange tongues bewildered the police, the situation became so serious that merchants bought protection from the dominant ethnic gang.

Corrupt police might provide similar "protection" for a price, looking the other way in return for tribute from shady saloonkeepers and madams. Despite restraining regulations, brothels proliferated—Philadelphia topped an 1880 federal census with 517 bawdy houses. Temperance leaders also met frustration. In their drives they attempted to limit saloon activities with Sunday closing laws and bans on music, games, and women bartenders. But when New York banned Sunday liquor sales, many saloons became makeshift brothels. The older custom of handing out fines for violations evolved into an informal license system that allowed illicit bars to operate with police "cooperation." (People in the Gay Nineties called these places "speakeasies," a word that would appear again during Prohibition.) In 1896 some 4,000 New Yorkers who paid federal taxes on liquor sales held no local saloon licenses. The boodle thus made available to obliging officials helped to corrupt administrations and entrench boss rule. But the corruption got so bad it finally brought a wave of citizen reaction.

Reformers found their most effective weapon in the new popular magazines. To attract more readers, *Cosmopolitan* and *McClure's* published sensational articles by social activists and muckrakers, writers like Ida Tarbell and Lincoln Steffens who exposed misconduct, vice, and corruption. Reaction against blatant corruption also came from reform politicians. After Hazen S. Pingree won as the businessman's candidate for mayor of Detroit in 1889, he insisted on improved street pavements, a better sewage system, an end to school board patronage, and toll-free roads. One of the mayor's biggest tasks was to force the city railway, dominated by several of his backers, to switch from horsecars to trolleys. Pingree also pushed for adequate gas, telephone, and electric services at lower rates. Although these issues brought him into conflict with old friends, he received increased backing from ethnic groups and labor. Pingree and "good government" mayors like Samuel "Golden Rule" Jones in Toledo and Tom Johnson in Cleveland inspired other reformers.

In St. Louis, Joseph W. Folk, a young attorney promoted by Democratic boss Ed Butler as a "safe" candidate for prosecutor, won election in 1900 and launched a dogged battle against the men who helped vote him into office. The issue again involved a street-railway franchise and wholesale bribery. Folk's crusade came at an inopportune time, for the promised transit improvements were needed for the upcoming Louisiana Purchase Exposition in 1904. But Folk proceeded to submit the names of nearly 100 citizens to a grand jury anyway, secured confessions and indictments, and laid bare the boodle dealings of men both high and low.

Lincoln Steffens felt that "bribery is not a mere felony, but a revolutionary process . . . going on in all our cities." After he heard of Folk's investigations and published his muckraking article on "Tweed Days in St. Louis" in *McClure's,* urban residents all over the country took a closer look at their local administrations.

Millions of those concerned urbanites flocked to the St. Louis fair. As the time approached, they booked passage on steamboats and bought tickets on excursion trains. And some venturesome "sports" even made the trip in that newfangled contraption, the automobile. Those pioneer motorists didn't realize it then, but as they chugged onto the scene, they brought with them a whole new set of urban problems to add to the old.

Trolleys seemed to be one answer to mass transit problems, but they also contributed to the paralysis of downtown commerce: Witness this tangle in the Chicago Loop around 1910. When an electric streetcar finally did get moving, it menaced pedestrians. This led harried Brooklynites to style themselves the Trolley Dodgers, a name that later rubbed off on the local professional baseball team.

The Automobile Arrives

Bernard A. Weisberger

Rambling flivver of song and lore, a 1910 Model T poises in gleaming miniature atop a roster of states. The porcelain-enameled iron plates, handsome relics of "automobiling," identified some of the millions of nomadic Americans who took to the road from 1901, the year state auto registration began, to 1918, the year almost half the cars sold in the United States were Model T's.

Earliest markers were homemade, often with brass house numbers riveted to a wooden shingle or a leather pad. New Jersey shows a manufacturer's seal on a state-issued plate. Over the years boosterism led to a profusion of state slogans, mottos, and emblems — the Georgia peach, Louisiana's pelican, Wyoming's bucking bronco. By 1916 most states used embossed metal. In World War II Illinois tried a soybean compound, which dogs and cows sometimes ate. Today's plates, standardized and reflectorized, show our safety consciousness. Yet, in a bumper-sticker era, variety and plate-spotters endure.

The automobile and the American people met in the 1890's, a portentous moment for the encounter. Infatuated with national growth, with speed, and with the productive miracles of applied science, the United States was on its way to industrial leadership of the world. In less than a Biblical lifespan the locomotive had conquered the enormous spaces of the continent and woven the provinces of seacoast and lake, mountain and plain, into a single market — a cohesive community with no major center more than a few days from another.

Savoring this triumph, most Americans expected that any further breakthroughs in transportation would also yield wonders. The gasoline buggy vibrated with the right, exciting potential. The automobile promised to make Everyman his own engineer, choosing his own routes and timetable, ensconcing his family in its own private coach. This prospect alone guaranteed that when the inventor-matchmakers introduced the car to America, romance would blossom quickly.

The love affair produced a perplexing and paradoxical array of results. Among them: prosperity for the glass, steel, rubber, and petroleum industries, but a precarious dependence on auto sales for their continued health; the breakdown of rural isolation, but the disintegration of cities through flight to an exploding suburbia; easier access to our national parks and our other natural splendors, but erosion of that beauty through overuse. Today, as we take a new, critical look at the social costs of the automobile, we see it in nearly every thread of the pattern of our lives. We and the automobile have forged the mobile American culture. And what 90 years of history have joined together cannot easily be put asunder.

In America, in the beginning, were the backyard tinkerers, building on foundations laid in Europe as early as 1860. Significant native developments awaited the early 1890's, when a bicycle craze put hundreds of thousands of Americans behind handlebars and spurred demands for hard-surfaced roads. As the number of roads increased, so did the interest in long-distance highway travel — and with some form of power less fallible than a pair of pumping human legs. Automotive pioneer Hiram Percy Maxim later said, "A mechanically-propelled vehicle was wanted instead of a foot-propelled one, and we know now that the automobile was the answer."

On September 21, 1893, a single-cylinder "motor carriage" coughed its slow way down a street in Springfield, Massachusetts. Its builders, Frank and Charles Duryea, were bicycle mechanics. So were many other early car makers in the United States and

303

Europe—and so were the men who raised the bike to another level, the Wright brothers. On the Fourth of July, 1894, along Pumpkinvine Pike in Kokomo, Indiana, a man with the apple-pie name of Elwood G. Haynes drove a car of his design, which had been built by two fellow mechanics. Soon after this, Hiram Maxim yoked a gasoline engine to a tricycle and, in 1895, with the Pope Manufacturing Company of Hartford, Connecticut—bicycle makers—he began manufacturing cars, first electric, then gasoline.

New England and the Midwest took the lead in early experiments. Charles B. King showed Detroit its first car in March 1896. A few months later Henry Ford, a self-taught engineer at the Detroit Edison Illuminating Company, unveiled his quadricycle, built by hand in his spare hours. Ransom Eli Olds, of Lansing, Michigan, and Alexander Winton, of Cleveland, also demonstrated cars in the mid-'90's. Another pair of brothers, Francis and Freelan Stanley, put out a steam-driven car in Newton, Massachusetts, in 1897; an electric auto had already been built in Des Moines.

Around the turn of the century, the two questions Americans were asking about the automobile—how fast will it go, and for how long?—were being answered in well publicized races. Frank Duryea registered an average five miles an hour over 55 miles of icy Chicago streets on Thanksgiving Day in 1895. Two years later a Winton made an 800-mile "dash" from Cleveland to New York in ten days. Running time was just under 80 hours. Ahead were steady gains in speed and endurance.

Makers of steam autos and electric cars muttered in alarm about the perils of the gas buggy. Col. Albert Pope doubted that people really wanted to "sit over an explosion." Another advocate of electricity warned that the exhaust pipes of gasoline-powered cars spewed a "continuous stream of . . . thick smoke with a highly noxious odor." Steam and electricity were popular, quiet, smooth riding, but problems of weight and maintenance handicapped them. City residents found gasoline fumes a less offensive prospect than streets reeking with horse manure and buzzing with flies. And farmers welcomed a means of locomotion that did not get sick or go lame. The taste for progress made acceptance of the automobile inevitable, and within a dozen years of the Duryeas' first ride hundreds of hopeful investors had joined auto manufacturers. The era of the inventor yielded quickly to the era of the entrepreneur.

From about 1910 to 1925, shrewd business leaders welded large-scale engineering to new marketing techniques. Auto-making became an industry whose success outran all reasonable probabilities. Forces that were transforming American economic life—high-speed production, rigorous cost control and cost shaving, the consolidation of many processes and firms into a few huge corporations, and widescale, relentless salesmanship—all these focused on the auto with spectacular results.

The early autos were almost literally horseless carriages—some equipped with sockets for whips! Engines were mounted haphazardly under the body; steering was often by tiller; the gearing and drive systems were exposed to the elements; wheels bore unmistakable resemblance to those of buggies and carryalls. But bit by bit a new style emerged. In the many makes and models before 1920, a gradual standardization appeared, aimed at comfort and power. Within only a few years the basic "modern" automobile had arrived. Improvements took some of the adventure out of being an "automobilist," but they were indispensable to mass acceptance of the car.

To put the nation on privately owned wheels, prices had to come down. The most relentless warrior against high automobile costs was Henry Ford. Eccentric, opinionated, oddly gifted, and sometimes lucky, Ford became the ultimate symbol of mechanization and efficiency. (In Aldous Huxley's 1925 satire, *Brave New World,* the deity of a dehumanized and programmed society is known as "Our Ford.")

In 1908 Ford ordered his company to concentrate on the single vehicle which grew

"Down the road of life we'll fly . . .

. . . Automobubbling, you and I. . . ." So went the song of the jaunty Curved Dash Oldsmobile. Tune and auto won American hearts. The world's first mass-produced car, it made a landmark appeal to "automobile girls" in a *Ladies Home Journal* ad in 1903. With a firm hand on the tiller, this couple in their runabout might "scorch" along country lanes at 12 mph. In 1905 two of the little buggies, Old Scout and Old Steady, made the first coast-to-coast auto race: 48 days, New York to Portland, Oregon. In the same year a White Steamer chuff-chuffs through Pennsylvania mud (opposite). These typical motor tourists spent perhaps $100 a month to maintain their car, which cost $2,500.

Enthusiasts sang automobile songs—"Let's Have a Motor Car Marriage," "Just Get Out and Walk," and hundreds more. They read pulp fiction like "Motor Matt's Red Flier—or on the High Gear," in which a crack motorist foils a counterfeiter. Theatergoers gasped at melodramas starring actual automobiles which, via stage machinery, "raced" each other and challenged speeding locomotives. In *Horseless Age,* one of many motoring magazines, drivers exchanged "Lessons of the Road" and were told that "motoring requires a costume as distinctive as does yachting and other sports." Women and men contested in tours and rallies. All fought dust, wind, rain, and cold, in a practical yet bizarre array of goggles, veils, dusters, and furs.

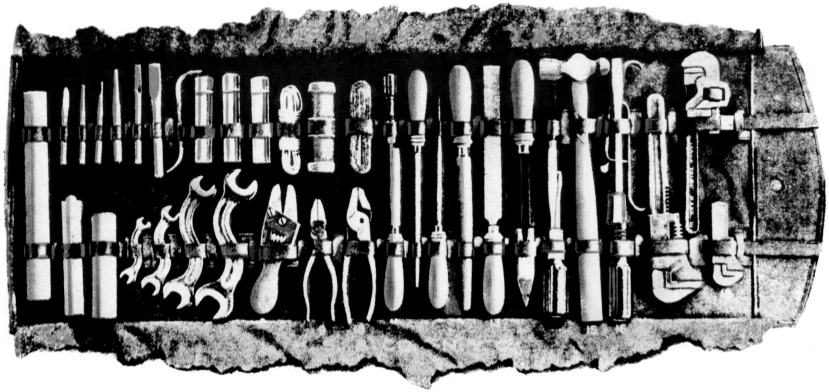

Get out and get under (and over and inside)

America's early horseless years brought forth mechanical critters as fragile and contrary as Old Dobbin had ever been. But heroic autoists solved the mysteries of the motorcar and made do-it-yourself mechanics an art as noble as horsemanship.

In 1906 Hammacher, Schlemmer and Company sold this 18-pound collection of files, cold chisels, pliers, and other tools. Even ten years later, *Motor Magazine* recommended more than 60 items, including mastic to seal leaks in the gas line; extra hoses, wire, spark plugs; towing cable, oil, grease; and a can of gasoline with funnel and chamois for straining. Road dust and flying rocks imperiled exposed parts. Bolts cracked. Axle nuts jarred loose. Springs broke. Sometimes a motoring party endured a surprise vacation while awaiting a part ordered by telegraph; the well-prepared driver then installed it himself.

Tires were a plague. Earliest drivers jolted along on solid rubber. Though pneumatics made the ride easier, they were delicate: on a bad day, a puncture every 10 or 20 miles! "Clincher" rims, integral with the wheel, held tire and tube in a death grip. Crowbars, sledge hammers, and strong language loosened them for patching. But even a motorist who set out with extra casings, tubes, hand pump, and portable vulcanizer might still rumble home on a bare rim or a tire stuffed with grass or hay. Rims were demountable

by 1915. Rubber improved so that tubes did not balloon, and tire life increased. The first two decades brought such improvements as the H-slot manual gearshift and the left-side steering wheel—the better to see the road. The electric starter arrived in 1912; it eliminated the dangerous job of hand-cranking. (A back-firing engine could make the crank a whirling weapon that shattered bones.) Each year, as *Motor World* said, drivers found new ways to master "the steel muscles and the fiery heart" of their clanking steeds.

Elegant pioneers in the Maxwell (opposite) make their uncertain way through the night by glowing kerosene side lamps and acetylene head lamps. The smelly acetylene, generated by dripping water onto calcium carbide, traveled through copper tubing from a tank on the running board. The tool kit's cold chisels and cleaning wires removed lime deposits from the burners. By 1915 electric systems gave better illumination but maintenance included frequent cleaning and "oiling of the ball bearings of the dynamo."

Auto lovers had long cited primitive roads, not machinery, as their chief source of woe. Drivers endured ruts, rocks, sand, blinding dust in dry weather, axle-deep muck in wet. Some prudently carried an ax to cut a pole for leverage when the wheel dropped out of sight. Until the 1920's only a brave soul would dare to take an auto very far from home.

"Road!" sputtered one veteran of a 1902 transcontinental trip. "Were no such things as roads in them days. We followed the Santa Fe Trail!" Later he would have encountered a

bewildering rainbow of telegraph poles banded to mark routes colorfully named (Blue Grass, Cannonball) but hard to follow. Advertisers and motor clubs printed cherished guides which enlightened the motorist on unfamiliar territory both inside and outside his auto—everything from the riddle of a leaky tire valve to the "law of the road." Best loved were the Official Automobile Blue Books. They gave detailed routes and described services found (or not found) along the way. In 1910 a driver bound from Milton to Sulphur, Kentucky, set his trusty odometer at zero, consulted with his sharp-eyed navigator, and warily proceeded:

Route No. M 67.
MILTON TO SULPHUR—19 Miles.
(Via Bedford.)
Macadam and gravel roads.

.0	Milton, south, ford rocky creek bed; pass one-story frame store; turn sharp to right;
.5	Cross small wooden bridge;
1.6	Up long winding hill, turn to left and pass toll gate (20c to Bedford);
4.5	Cross small wooden bridge, turn sharp to right;
5.6	Turn sharp to right, passing road on left; pass Lee Ports small country store;
7.6	Callis Grove country store;
9.6	Toll gate; follow telephone poles;
10.8	BEDFORD, pass through, pass cemetery; follow telephone poles, turn to left, pass toll gate (25c to Sulphur);
12.3	Turn to right;
13.7	Down long hill;
14.2	Turn to left, then right, cross small wooden bridge, jog 300 feet to right, following stone fence;
14.4	Turn to left and cross wooden bridge;
14.8	Jog 150 feet to right, turn left, cross long iron bridge;
15.7	Cross wooden bridge;
16.4	Toll gate; follow telephone poles down grade, turn left and right;
18.9	Ford creek, pass between saw mill and frame cottage, jog to left 200 feet;
19.0	Cross railroad, SULPHUR.

Cranked and revved-up, supercharged engines roar at the start of the 100-mile Indianapolis Speedway race in 1909. Winner Louis Strang, driving his Buick, No. 33, averaged 64 mph on the gravel track. The first Indy 500 was run in 1911, on the newly paved "Brickyard." Early racing gave us the rearview mirror, modern spark plugs, balloon tires, aluminum pistons, and streamlined styling.

into the celebrated Model T, affectionately named "Tin Lizzie." Through most of its 19 years, the Model T stood out uncompromisingly against the trend toward styled comfort. It was high, square, and open. It lacked a gas gauge, shock absorbers, and a fuel pump. Its planetary gears were worked by two pedals. Its four-cylinder engine had to be hand-cranked into life before yielding up its 20 horsepower. At first Model T's were red, pearl gray, or Brewster green—the last ones offering a competitive range. But from 1912 to 1925, as Ford himself said, they came in any color, so long as it was black. Ford guessed that Americans would buy a utilitarian vehicle that was easy to repair and able to go almost anywhere, if it were cheap enough. Seldom has a hunch been more rewarding. Ford drove the cost down from an initial $850 to a low of $290 in 1924. Sales soared from some 10,000 in 1908-1909 to almost 1 million in 1921.

Ford cut costs by assembly-line construction, the naked chassis accumulating parts as it rolled along, and each worker having a specific, repetitive task of attachment. Ford adapted the assembly line from other industries (meat-packing, for example), but contributed by refining the process again and again. He hired time-study experts to whom a few seconds of eliminated waste-motion were as precious as rubies, and engineers who gloried in shaving a superfluous ten-thousandth of an inch of metal off a part, thereby saving a fraction of a cent. The mini-seconds and micro-inches added up, over thousands of hours, to cheaper, faster, and better quality production. There were human costs on the line; the workers, in their frenetic—though well-paid—dance of monotony, seemed to become almost indistinguishable from their machines. But the miracle of mass manufacture was dazzling enough to blind society to its flaws.

The principles of "Fordism" also included control of the materials that went into a car. Ford poured his multimillion-dollar profits into perfecting a system "where steel from Iron Mountain, and miles of glass from Minnesota and . . . tires made of Brazilian rubber . . . all arrived . . . at the instant when Henry Ford needed them." The Ford operation emerged as the pacesetter of the industry, and the industry as the pinnacle of technological progress. Yet Ford's reign over auto-making came to an end in the mid-1920's when General Motors surpassed him in sales. GM represented other approaches —mainly variety production and aggressive marketing—which completed the job of turning the United States into an automobile-saturated nation.

General Motors was the creation of the freewheeling William Crapo Durant. Self-supporting at the age of 16, Durant entered carriage manufacturing at 20, and by 1900, though not yet 40, was a millionaire. In 1904 he moved into the auto world with the purchase of the company founded by David Buick, a plumbing merchant and inventor. Durant hoped to unite several car firms, each catering to a different taste—for luxury, speed, comfort, utility. Part of Durant's motivation was a shrewd notion that diversification meant corporate safety. But part was also a simple delight in the game of acquisition and combination. He tried to buy several concerns, including Ford's. (Ford, apparently willing to sell, asked more cash than Durant could muster.) Finally, in 1908 he incorporated GM by uniting Buick with the company that made Oldsmobiles and another that produced the Oakland (later the Pontiac). In 1909 he brought Cadillac into the fold. Next he bought out makers of motors, spark plugs, and other components and accessories. By 1910 he had run GM deeply into debt. Billy Durant, it was said, could create but not administer. A banking syndicate bailed out the corporation, at the price of participation in control of GM—and the ouster of Durant.

Undaunted, he went into partnership with Louis Chevrolet, a Swiss-born racing driver, who was marketing a car of his own design. The Chevrolet was a huge success. Durant unobtrusively traded Chevrolet stock for GM stock, until the triumphant September day in 1915 when he announced to a board meeting that he held the controlling

"No hill too steep
No sand too deep"

Catchy slogans sold cars. Advertisements-on-wheels succeeded too, for fans swarmed to automobile shows, races, and reliability runs. From her fencepost perch, photographer Alice Austen documents a 1910 road race on Staten Island, New York. Heights challenged machine and driver in the early days. At the 1912 Easter Sunrise Service on Rubidoux Mountain near Riverside, California, hundreds of cars lined the looping trail. In 1920 one visitor from the East advised, "A powerful car can jog upward most of the way on 'high.'" By then, Easter dawn traffic jams were so bad that worshipers could not park on the road. As of old, they climbed on foot.

Delighted Americans discovered their country, and motor-gypsying became a craze. Wretched roads in national parks did not deter eager travelers. Naturalist John Muir welcomed the "useful, progressive, blunt-nosed, mechanical beetles." In 1913 cars began to climb Yosemite's rocky routes. Horse-drawn traffic had right-of-way: Autos halted at the road's edge until the skittish teams had passed. Soon park visitors found garages, one an open-sided tent. These 1922 roisterers in the overburdened Studebaker honor a custom older than the automobile: to be photographed in mock-peril on Overhanging Rock at Yosemite's Glacier Point. (A Locomobile first made it in 1900.) Today rules and a railing discourage such stunts.

interest once again. With him this time came not only the Chevrolet Company but also the chemicals tycoon, Pierre du Pont, whose company would invest heavily in GM.

Once again Durant went on an expansionist binge, buying firms that supplied automotive elements. Into GM's structure came Delco, which furnished electrical equipment; the Hyatt Roller Bearing Company and its hard-headed young president, Alfred P. Sloan, Jr.; the Fisher Body Company. Durant even added Frigidaire, which he picked up because he saw a future for refrigerators and could not resist a good buy, no matter how incongruous. He defended his purchase by saying that both a car and a refrigerator consisted of a motor in a box. Such purchases laid the foundation for GM's later economic strength. But there were also disastrous transactions—overpayment for an eventually worthless tungsten lamp patent, for instance, and the acquisition of an unprofitable tractor division. Moreover, in time Durant's high-handedness angered and drove away subordinates like Charles Nash and Walter P. Chrysler, who founded rival firms. Finally Durant overextended himself again and in 1920 was forced out for good. The du Ponts and J. P. Morgan stepped in to repair the financial damage.

In the reshuffle which followed, Alfred P. Sloan emerged as head of GM. Sloan, son of a wealthy tea and grocery wholesaler, had an engineering degree from MIT, a consuming dedication to growth, and an unshakable belief in American free enterprise. But the prizes were to be won by self-denial and sweat. "Sooner or later," wrote Sloan, "we must realize that only by more work and still more work—always efficiently used—can we capitalize our unlimited opportunities." He himself practiced an almost monastic

Wheeling and dealing— the Florida land boom

Automobile-borne, Florida land-fever erupted in the mid-1920's. Tourists riding in an ingenious yoking of Model T's were the vanguard of millions who poured south and east on new cross-country highways. Promoters bused in prospects from as far away as San Francisco, greeted them with hoopla, free crockery, friendly elephants, beauty contests, Paul Whiteman's jazz band at poolside, and William Jennings Bryan declaiming from a floating platform. Tin-Can Tourists (named for their portable larders) jammed the Dixie Highway. Land changed hands fast and often fraudulently, hawked by "knickerbocker boys"—salesmen in plus fours—and their scouting "bird dogs." Customers stood in line for hours to buy Davis Islands lots, then still under water. Pumping dredges created the three new pieces of real estate out of sand from the bottom of Tampa Bay.

simplicity, speaking little, rarely laughing, seldom entertaining guests, and disdaining recreation. He once bought a yacht at his associates' urging, but gave it up without ever having used it much. Everything about him, said a business magazine article, "has gone into the job." Thanks to such concentration, at age 48 Sloan was able to put in force his ideas for corporate organization of the auto industry. One idea was to make the various divisions of the company autonomous and independently responsible for profit. The divisions' efforts would be coordinated by a kind of general staff, and their pricing policies would reflect accounting formulas rather than hunches.

Sloan thought Ford was wrong, that the future did not lie in constantly cheapening the basic car which had won acceptance with the public. Instead, Sloan believed in creating varieties of that vehicle, relentlessly advertising them, and even helping customers finance their purchases. It was Sloan's concept to have each of GM's constituent companies produce a car in a different price range. It was Sloan who devised the annual model changeover. He brought a director of styling into the company in 1927 and aggressively increased the number of GM dealerships.

Sloan gave the dealers a growing variety of features, gadgets, and dreams to sell. Sometimes the yearly "innovations" were improvements, such as four-wheel brakes, electric windshield wipers, and heaters. Sometimes the innovations were cosmetic: GM cars could be ordered in any one of many colors—the products of du Pont paint laboratories. And sometimes the "options" were useful or pleasant, but had little to do with transportation—radios, clocks, ashtrays, or cigarette lighters.

The race went to Sloan. GM crept steadily up on Ford, bypassing other competitors on the way. In spite of improvements to the Model T, Henry Ford conceded in 1927, after 15 million of them, that Lizzie had had her day. The company shut down, retooled the great River Rouge plant, and proclaimed the Model A to a clamoring public. But GM's Chevrolet took the lead in the low-priced field, almost never to be beaten thereafter. All auto manufacturers—whose numbers had been steadily shrinking, from more than 100 in 1923 to 44 in 1927—fell into line, offering cars with more cylinders, more interior appointments, more extras (such as spare tires).

Emma Rothschild, critic and historian of the auto industry, says that its two shaping energies were Ford's quest for ultra-efficiency in manufacture, and Sloan's discovery of the possibilities in what he called perpetual improvement and elaboration. Between them, they had accomplished an automotive revolution in the 35 years since the Duryeas' first horseless ride. In 1929 American manufacturers produced 4.6 million cars and 771,000 trucks, 85 percent of world production. In 1920 there was one passenger car registered for every 13 Americans; in 1930, two for every 11. By the late 1970's, auto density had increased to just over one car for every two people.

Behind this advancing wave came a new array of industries. The Americans whose livelihoods were directly linked to the automobile included owners and employees of garages, service stations, auto parts stores, roadside restaurants, and the "tourist cabins" which eventually acquired sophistication and became motels. The Automobile Age also generated a formidable expansion of the petroleum, rubber, steel, and glass industries, which led the way to the boom of the 1920's. Before reaching its fortieth birthday in the United States the automobile had become probably the dominant element of the American economy.

Federal, state, and local government gave priority to highway construction, forever transforming the national landscape. In hamlet after hamlet rural isolation was wiped out at a 40-mile-per-hour clip. The auto sped through the countryside, exposing it finally—and fatally—to the modernist influences of the city. The city itself sprawled outward. Suburbia was no longer confined to strips along commuter rail lines. Speculators bought cheap land within an hour's drive of downtown centers and planted rows of bungalows, Cape Cods, and "ranches." Small towns, whose Main Streets had long been nurseries of American social habits, became bedroom communities for former city dwellers.

The creativity of advertising men soared on the wings of enticing automotive copy. Crude facts of horsepower and gear ratios became less important than the intangible ego satisfactions of ownership. "There's a savor...about that car," ran a trend-setting ad of 1926; "of laughter and lilt and light—a hint of old loves—and saddle and quirt. It's a brawny thing—yet a graceful thing for the sweep o' the Avenue." Hidden desires for status, power, sexuality, and rebelliousness were coaxed into the open and promised gratification through the properly styled machine. Like movies, auto ads

As the tourist trade expanded in the 1920's, so did the imagination of roadside vendors — and their stock of lures. At this New Jersey rookery of the signpainter's art, the weary traveler could take a dip, fill his pipe, or pacify the kids with pop or ice cream. Highways bloomed with "tea shoppes," Brooklyn diners in the Midwest, and lunch stands in Los Angeles resembling derbies, jailhouses — and dogs.

HIS TENOR VOICE

SHE THOUGHT DIVINE

TILL WHISKERS

SCRATCHED

SWEET ADELINE

Burma-Shave

'TWENTIES TOURISTS
WASHED THEIR HAIR
NEATH TREES 'N TARP
AND OPEN AIR
Ramblers Rave

THE BRIGHT RED SIGNS
WE USED TO SEE 'EM
BUT NOW THEY'RE GONE
TO THE MUSEUM
Jingles Brave

FROM '25
TO '63
WE RODE AND READ
THEN CAME TV
O Changing Wave

NOW ADS ON TUBES
ARE SIGNS OF TIMES
BUT HOW WE MISS
THOSE FUNNY RHYMES
O Burma-Shave!

pandered to the fantasies of men and women caught up in a mechanized world. Paradoxically, the ads promised individuality through mass consumption.

To purchase cars, families broke the old Puritan taboo against personal debt. The high cost and the care of cars could keep people in debt for most of their productive lives. Yet car ownership was a bondage willingly assumed. A small-town banker observed in 1925: "The paramount ambition of the average man a few years ago was to own a home and have a bank account. The ambition of the same man today is to own a car . . . whatever the reason, the result is . . . debt, debt, debt, for a costly article that depreciates very rapidly and has an insatiable appetite for money." And yet he concluded, "I still drive one myself. I must keep up with the procession."

A new morality and a new set of manners drove into American life with the car. It took families out of church on Sunday and put them on the highways. It also took young people out of the home — and far beyond chaperones — for their courtship rituals. The auto alone could not be blamed for changing sexual patterns. But great-grandparents today remember their cars, above all else, when they recall that era of joyrides to roadhouses, petting in the rumble seat, and bootlegged bottles. Whether the Jazz Age really meant liberation, license, or loneliness, it rode on wheels.

The bursting of the prosperity bubble in 1929 shocked the auto industry. New Deal relief measures somewhat eased the plight of the unemployed; yet effects of the Depression remained even after slumping auto sales rallied in the mid-1930's. Auto workers had accumulated grievances over the years, among them irregularity of employment, a lack of advancement opportunity, and the iron discipline of the assembly line. Driven to militancy by hard times, they organized and fought. The winter of 1936-1937 brought to General Motors a wave of crippling strikes. Members of the United Auto Workers occupied the factories; the tactic was called a sit-down strike.

For 44 bitter winter days the battle went on. Sloan and other company officials saw Bolshevism rampant and were outraged when Michigan Governor Frank Murphy refused to use the National Guard to recapture the properties. It was a curiously peaceful "revolution." The sit-downers regularly cleaned up the plants and set up patrols to prevent sabotage. And the management supplied brooms and paper towels. Except on one brief occasion, company guards made no effort to shut off heat and utilities or to prevent union deliveries of prepared meals to the occupiers. In the skirmish that followed the one attempt, union men drove off police and were not again molested.

GM finally capitulated and signed a union contract. Chrysler, Ford, and other companies followed. As the UAW grew in size and strength its bargaining techniques became more sophisticated. By the 1960's, the union was deeply involved in the future of the industry. Through periodic negotiations for contract renewals the UAW had won for its members impressive packages of benefits, including health insurance and company-paid pensions. The union had become a major voice in Democratic politics in Michigan and part of the institutional machinery which kept autos rolling off the lines.

The Depression, while gathering the auto workers into the UAW, also swept away all but a handful of the hundreds of companies born in the heyday of the Auto Age. Even during the 1920's many names had faded away. More vanished in the Crash and its aftermath, joining an honor roll of fallen cars that Americans had once held in affection: Franklin, Pierce-Arrow, Locomobile, Stutz, Cord. But Nash, Hudson, Willys-Overland, Packard, and Studebaker hung on, ironically to disappear in the better times after World War II. The Big Three — Ford, Chrysler, and GM — survived with scars. GM did best, largely because of its diversified operations in the manufacture of refrigeration units, diesel locomotives, and aircraft engines. (Later the Anti-Trust Division of the Department of Justice would rebuke such activities.) The Depression in the long run

The phantom rider

No legend enjoys wider circulation in the United States than the account of the vanishing hitchhiker. The story has been traced back to the days of horse-drawn vehicles. Invariably it takes place in a specific locale and is told with an air of conviction. The hitchhiker usually is a young woman, but in the tale's most recent incarnations the wanderer is a young man — a bedraggled hippie. This traditional version, recorded in 1969, takes place in North Carolina:

"While I was in Bath High School, the students began telling the story of the ghost . . . seen by a man a few nights before. It was a very foggy night. It seems that it was in the wee hours of the morning [and] the man was returning home from a business convention.

"As he started under a certain underpass at Greensboro, he was flagged . . . by a young girl dressed in a white formal. He stopped and asked if he could help her. She answered that he could take her home. . . . She gave him her home address in Greensboro. It was on a dimly lighted street [that] the home was finally located.

"The man drew the car to the curb and got out to open the car door for his passenger. When he reached the other side . . . he found no one there. Thinking that she may have gone in, he rang the doorbell to make sure she was safe. After a time an old lady answered. . . .

"He told her he had brought her daughter home and wanted to make sure that she had gotten inside safely. The lady began to cry and told him, 'My daughter was killed . . . just outside of Greensboro twenty years ago tonight on her way home from the high school dance. Tonight is not the first time that she has since tried to get home.'"

Even in a modern "filling station" in 1923 many a motorist could recall the days when autos were few and gas was where you found it—often in a barrel behind the smithy or livery stable. Until 1920 hardware or general stores and groceries sold half the nation's gas. But mobile pumps roamed, charging motorist and motorcyclist what the traffic would bear: in 1911, about 12 cents a gallon.

accelerated the concentration of manufacturers. Since 1964 four concerns have produced almost all American-made passenger autos: the Big Three and American Motors, formed from a merger of the Hudson and Nash-Kelvinator corporations.

The year 1941 began a spectacular rebound. Even before Pearl Harbor, purchasing agents from the United States and British armed forces were placing orders for trucks and military vehicles. Federal officials were also investigating the possible use, as in World War I, of automotive production machinery, leadership, and experience for general wartime manufacturing. When war came, civilian car-making gave way to herculean productive accomplishments. Auto companies alone turned out some 4 million engines of all types, nearly 6 million guns of various kinds, just under 3 million tanks and trucks, and 27,000 aircraft, as well as an extraordinary array of miscellaneous military hardware—helmets, fire extinguishers, buckles. American industry's quick convertibility had a large share in winning the war. It was no accident that the director of production for the War Department was the president of GM, William S. Knudsen.

War's end brought a surge in the demand for cars; registrations soared from 25 million in 1945 to 40 million in 1950. Re-converted assembly lines labored for a growing population which again had money to spend. If the 1920's had seemed a golden age to auto builders, the 1950's were beyond their wildest dreams. Annual sales reached a record 8 million in 1955. The acceleration of automobile growth is displayed in one surprising statistic. In 1967 the number of cars built in the United States since the Duryeas' day was 200 million. It had taken 59 years, until 1952, to produce America's first 100 million automobiles. In the following 15 years the next 100 million were produced.

Suburbia continued to grow. The second car became a family necessity. Shopping malls ringed the cities, with parking lots so huge that unwary customers often wandered amid the massed, nearly identical ranks, in forlorn search of their lost cars. Prosperous parents succumbed to pleas and bought the coveted "wheels" for their teen-agers. Youngsters with less affluent or more resistant parents could, in a booming economy, earn the few hundred dollars that would buy one of the used cars that seemed to beckon from every corner lot. High schools had to create student parking areas. For young people the car was a passport to some kind of self-realization. They cruised about, casually eating up hundreds of miles, in search of mates, music, causes, and kicks—or, like the beat characters in Jack Kerouac's 1957 novel *On The Road*, simply to get away from whatever seemed to confine them.

The cars of the 1950's were the culmination of extravagant styling. They blazed with chrome; their seductively upholstered interiors echoed to high-fidelity music; as many as 300 horses crouched under their hoods; power mechanisms helped to brake and steer them or activated their windows; currents of filtered air created comfort no matter in what climate or season the car might roll. As prices rose and the national economy fluctuated, the companies had to plug their products harder, but the bullishness of Detroit remained strong in the Eisenhower years.

On a lonely road when the wheels had stopped

Footweary in an automobile culture, migrants trudge a deserted Texas highway. This family, flooded from Arkansas farmland, walked 900 miles to work Rio Grande cotton fields.

The hungry '30's saw the auto worker emerge as a pivot in the economy. Employed, he was a consumer. And bound to his fortunes were some 5 million Americans whose jobs depended on car-related industries, which by 1931 were hard hit. For half the workers in Detroit's factories were jobless.

The dynamic Motor City, whose assembly lines had been a tourist attraction, now became a showcase for the nation's misery. A line worker's weekly pay envelope held about $20. He spent about a third of it for food,

another third for housing. One of the new cars he himself made would have cost half his yearly wage. If he had a car—one in every two families did—it was probably an old one. He drove it carefully because the tires were bad, and he stayed close to home because vacations were expensive. In 1932 the auto market hit bottom. Depressed North Carolina farmers, too poor to buy gasoline or tires, hitched mules to their idle vehicles and began calling them Hoovercarts.

Hard times or not, Americans eagerly visited yearly auto shows across the nation, where they saw freewheeling, power brakes, synchromesh transmission, radios—and lower prices. Automakers opened the 1935 shows optimistic that they would begin "a new era of prosperity." They did. Americans in that year bought 2.8 million new cars—almost three times as many as they had in 1932.

Meanwhile the highway network grew and grew. In 1921 only 387,000 miles of United States roads had been surfaced. Over the next 20 years surfaced mileage tripled. The Depression era especially had stimulated highway construction, as the federal government assisted impoverished state and local authorities. Engineers designed highways to accommodate the swelling flow of high-speed vehicles. The Pennsylvania Turnpike, begun in 1938 on New Deal funds, pioneered modern highway design. Utilizing railroad tunnels built 60 years earlier, it incorporated easy curves, limited access, and other safety-oriented features of future long-distance highways.

In 1944 Congress authorized $1.5 billion for comprehensive national highway improvements. States were to provide matching funds. In 1956 the Interstate Highway Act committed the federal government to assume 90 percent of the cost of a 41,000-mile network of superhighways. These, along with toll roads and turnpikes built by the states, made it possible to race across the country at a mile a minute, seeing everywhere the same panorama of four, six, or eight lanes, divided by a median strip and beaded with clusters of gas pumps, fast-food restaurants, and motels. The money for the national highway system would come from a trust fund of gas and other automotive taxes, making Washington the custodian of gigantic sums dedicated to the greater glory of the auto. And the voice which guided that stewardship was a powerful highway lobby, representative of all the industries that thrived on road use and construction.

The interstates and turnpikes slowed when they came to cities. Expressways carried them over or around urban street grids, with convenient exits for downtown business districts. To make room for these elevated highways, bulldozers leveled whole neighborhoods, often taking away housing that inner cities desperately needed.

Life with the automobile had become a paradox. People were always moving, farther than ever before, fulfilling an American compulsion that went back to Daniel Boone's trailblazing and Huck Finn's raft. But this freedom of movement was enslaving Americans; the automobile was changing society. Hidden costs would someday have to be paid. The years since about 1960 have been a time of adding up these costs.

In the 1960's, when so many American institutions were being assessed, trouble had already come to the auto industry. First there was a sudden invasion of imports. Between 1955 and 1960, sales of foreign-made cars in the United States rose from 58,000 to 499,000, equal to about 7.5 percent of domestic production. Many of these were not luxury or sporty cars. They were versions of the unlovely but lovable, humble but hardworking Volkswagen. The size and high prices of American cars had driven customers to look for a reincarnation of the Model T, at least for a second car—a plain and unfrilled

We kept changing our mind—and our cars

"We want the man who buys one of our products never to have to buy another," Henry Ford philosophized in 1922. But we Americans swung to-and-fro in pursuit of automotive novelty, utility, and style. First we drove open cars. In 1919 only 10 percent were closed; a decade later only 10 percent were open. The 1930's brought back convertibles—their popularity peaked in 1965, then nosedived. Size waxed and waned. Fragile carriages of the first decade gave way to heavy touring cars. Gradually the auto lost its luxury image and lighter vehicles won favor, most notably the Model T. But cars began growing again. The early 1940's saw the launching of post-war monsters which, in the '50's, held small cars to 10 percent of the market; by the '60's, compacts were 40 percent.

Early cars were tall, boxy, with vertical windshields and radiator grilles. Designers explored the functional logic of streamlining and, in the '30's and '40's, decreed curved lines, slanting grilles, inclined two-piece windshields, lower silhouettes. By the mid-'50's stylistic and engineering innovations brought back angles. Interests changed. In the 1960's the fidelity to traditional passenger cars faded as Americans, as if to show they were individuals, shopped their way through a variety of specialized and recreational vehicles.

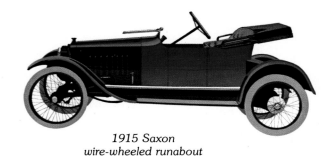

1915 Saxon
wire-wheeled runabout

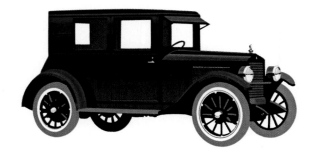

1922 Essex
first inexpensive sedan

1924 Chrysler
four-wheel hydraulic brakes

1925 Chevrolet
successful competitor of Model T

1932 Ford
low-priced V-8, rumble seat

1934 DeSoto Airflow
pioneer of aerodynamic styling

1947 Kaiser
unusual slab-sided styling

1958 Rambler
compact station wagon

1935 Plymouth
best seller in Depression

1949 Cadillac
beginning of tailfin fad

1958 Chevrolet Impala
new series, sculptured lines

1939 Plymouth
its "ragtop" power-operated

1949 Buick
pillarless hardtop

1958 Thunderbird
restyled from 1955 T-bird

1940 Oldsmobile
genuine "woody," Hydra-Matic

1956 Packard
deluxe Clipper model

1961 Pontiac Tempest
intermediate size, 4 cylinders

1946 Studebaker
trend-setting post-war design

1957 Oldsmobile
protective bumpers, more glass

1964 Mustang
four-seater semi-sports car

The game's over, and the cheers and the music. It's hamburger time around prized wheels from Roosevelt High: a '39 Ford. After World War II teen-agers and cars merged. Along came custom-painted, souped-up dragsters, sectioning-channeling-chopping hot rodders. And the driver's license became the badge of a kind of adulthood — by the 1970's, a badge worn by almost as many girls as boys.

Feature attraction of the drive-in society

Movies and motorcars, two American institutions which were born about the same time and grew up over the same years, finally met at the drive-in theater. The time was June 1933; the place, Camden, New Jersey. Depression and wartime economies only slowed the growth of an irresistible idea—30 years later some 4,000 drive-in movies dotted cities, small towns, and cow pastures from one end of the United States to the other. Charlton Heston spreads Mosaical arms against the evening sky of Salt Lake City, Utah. The rows of shiny, beetle-backed autos, noses tilted screenward, might be anywhere. Over the years of driving-in to banks, restaurants, laundries, churches—even the barber and the justice of the peace—Americans have shown that they like sit-down mobility.

At early theaters a booming sound system angered neighbors. In-car speakers solved that problem—and in-car heaters kept patrons warm in winter. The drive-in became a way of life: Meals, fetched afoot or fetchingly carhopped; a place to do the laundry between features; heaters to warm baby's bottle—the family trade sustained many drive-ins. Parents could bring the kids, turn them loose at the swings, and remember dates at the passion pit and movies they didn't watch about beach parties and teen-age werewolves.

small vehicle for short trips. The Beetle filled the breach as Tin Lizzie had 40 years before. Behind the Volkswagen assault wave came fresh contingents of other small cars made in Sweden, France, Italy, Germany, Great Britain, and Japan. Detroit responded with its own small cars. But still inspired by the principles that Sloan had originated, the cars were larger than their foreign competitors and were usually laden with "options" as they emerged from the showrooms.

A second challenge came with Ralph Nader's 1965 *Unsafe at Any Speed.* (Like John Keats' earlier assault on the industry, *The Insolent Chariots,* the book bore a title that itself was a pungent criticism that stuck in the mind.) The annual highway death toll had long been blamed on driver carelessness—or, in the industry phrase, on "the nut that holds the wheel." But Nader pointed to brakes, steering linkages, and other parts that failed under stress and caused fatal crashes. While Detroit's leaders denounced "Naderism," they began to examine their products more carefully—and to recall hundreds of thousands of cars annually for the correction of defects.

Urban critics of the car launched a broader attack. They argued that the car, by creating suburbia, had drained the city of its most affluent people—and of many of the places where they spent their money. The cars that did enter the city were driven into the city's heart; they clogged the streets, transformed precious land into parking lots, befouled the air, and, like a cancer, destroyed the tissue of city life. Urban designers called for pedestrian malls from which cars would be barred. Pressure groups battled in city halls, in courtrooms, in newspapers, and before television cameras to prevent the razing of old buildings for parking lots or expressways. In their eyes, it was a fight for "people-space" against "machine-space."

Gasoline shortages in the 1970's led to a realization that the nation's supply of energy was limited, that it could not indefinitely light cities, run factories, and power public and private transportation without a system of priorities. Choices would have to be made, possibly allocating more money to mass transit, less to highways. Just as Americans were shocked to discover in the 1890's that free land was running out, so 80 years later they were challenged by the possibility that the fuel supply was exhaustible. Was the auto doomed to extinction as the prime creation of a passing era? Was it a scapegoat for an avaricious society? There was a plaintive note in the comment of Henry Ford II that his industry had been wrongly "blamed for causing a host of . . . problems—including, to name just a few, air, noise, and visual pollution, unplanned suburban sprawl, the decay of central cities, the decline of public transportation, and the segregation of minorities in urban ghettos."

The automobile is neither an innocent victim nor a potential fossil. It has wastefully consumed national wealth and changed our old ways. But it has also created wealth and built institutions. It still employs and sustains millions of people and pays a substantial share of the national tax bill. When assembly lines shut down and several hundred thousand auto workers were laid off in the 1970's, the nation relearned in a melancholy way how much America depends on the automotive industry. GM advertisements, urging the purchase of a new car as a way to "keep our economy rolling," pointed out that the automobile "accounts for one-sixth of our Gross National Product. Thirteen million jobs—one in every six—and 800,000 businesses, from steel companies to the corner service station, depend on the automobile."

The problems of the automotive age will not be solved by eliminating the automobile. Disenchantment does not mean absolute abandonment: We still have railroads. And it seems unlikely that grass soon will grow over silent superhighways. If the love affair between car and country is destined to become more calculating, it appears also destined to endure. America's future seems bound to the machine—especially the marvelous escape-machine that was, and is, the auto.

"When you drove a Buick, a big, yellow Buick"

César Baldaccini's crushed-auto sculpture, "Yellow Buick" (below), embodies the view that the automobile as love-object is dead. Polluted cities, paved-over countryside, and gorged highways show some of the cost it has exacted. American poet Karl Shapiro's "Auto Wreck" describes the highest price:

*. . . The ambulance at top speed floating down
Past beacons and illuminated clocks
Wings in a heavy curve, dips down,
And brakes speed, entering the crowd.
The doors leap open, emptying light;
Stretchers are laid out, the mangled lifted
And stowed into the little hospital. . . .
And the ambulance with its terrible cargo
Rocking, slightly rocking, moves away,
As the doors, an afterthought, are closed.*

In the late 1960's we smashed into each other over 20 times a minute, 24 hours a day. From 1961 to 1973 traffic accidents killed over 14 times as many Americans as died in Viet Nam. But the gasoline shortage in late 1973 produced the 55 mph speed limit, which began to save lives. In the decade following 1976 the death rate per miles traveled dropped appreciably. We buckled up; we got engines that saved fuel. We drove less on rural roads, more on safer interstates with guardrails, crash cushions, median barriers. Could the Automobile Age be growing up?

Americans at Play

Russell Lynes

The game is Remember When, and it's your turn. Start at the baseball: real horsehide, made priceless by immortals. Roll the dice and go directly to poker, according to Hoyle the national card game of the United States. This full house could have smiled on Warren G. Harding; he owned these cards and chips and, like Presidents since Washington (a whist fan), he tried his luck.

Take the pencil with its bidding guide for bridge-whist and jot down your score. It's your bid: What would you do with this hand against a bid of seven spades? Harold S. Vanderbilt, father of contract, bid seven no-trump — and made the contract in one of bridge's boldest moves.

White tiles recall Mah-Jongg, a Chinese import that swept the United States in the 1920's, then faded in the '29 Crash. Made-in-America Monopoly, born of the Depression, let anyone play real-estate tycoon. After 80 million sets, players are still going to jail, but houses and hotels, once made of wood, have become tokens of the plastic age.

There was a time in the 1880's when throngs of tightly corseted women, men in bowlers and frock coats (or gartered shirt sleeves), and children in knickers and cotton stockings gathered in the summer on the shores of Chautauqua Lake in upstate New York. They lived in rustic cottages and even in tents, and they came for campfires and "hymnsings," for fishing, culture, and uplift. There, in a wooden amphitheater or under the stars in "God's Temple," as they called it, they listened to famous opera singers or to concerts by a symphony conducted by Walter Damrosch. They heard solemn and frothy lectures by novelists and philosophers, bishops and humorists. Indeed, they occasionally sat at the feet of a President of the United States, for such was the wholesome reputation of Chautauqua that it attracted the mighty as well as the humble. On one occasion in 1880 James A. Garfield, the last President to be born in a log cabin, posed a question we are still trying to answer.

"We may divide the whole struggle of the human race into two chapters," he declaimed. "First, the fight to get leisure; and then the second fight of civilization — what shall we do with our leisure when we get it."

In the 1880's the fight to get leisure for more Americans than just the rich was beginning to be won. On a visit 40 years earlier Sir Charles Lyell, a distinguished Englishman of driving energy, devoted to geological exploration and popularization of science, looked about him in America, and with wonder and some skepticism said: "I had sometimes thought that the national motto should be, 'All work and no play.'"

Indeed, people never seemed to stop working. Their days started before the sun was up and ended after it had set — in winter long before and long after. In the country relaxation itself was work: a quilting bee or a cornhusking or a logrolling to clear the land or the raising of a rooftree for a barn — necessity made into an excuse for social high jinks. Work done, the evening relaxed with a feed of gargantuan proportions and then erupted with song and dancing. In towns the center of social life was the church for the fastidious and the pool parlor and saloon for the godless. With whiskey only 25 cents a gallon, even men of the cloth were known to succumb.

To countrymen, cities were centers of sin where rich young men raced their carriages over cobblestoned streets and the toughs brawled and whored and terrified the gentlefolk who thought it expedient and proper to stay at home in the evening behind closed shutters. There in the company of a few friends they might indulge in charades, "living statues," or card games. But never on Sunday, when card-playing was synonymous with sin. In most cities there were theaters where "respectable" people could go with prudence and watch such famous thespians as Fanny Kemble or Edwin Booth. Or there was a concert hall where they could hear Jenny Lind, "The Swedish Nightingale," who first enthralled Americans in the 1850's.

She had been brought to America by P. T. Barnum, the great entrepreneur of hocus-pocus whose museum in New York, with its freaks and exotic animals and wax figures, its dabs of horror and driblets of culture, was the distant but nonetheless distinct spiritual forebear of today's Disneyland and Disney World. Barnum's museum may have been lowbrow in some eyes, it may have offended sensibilities now and then, but it was as moral as Pear's Unscented Soap. So are the Disney lands.

The work ethic was the only ethic, or so most citizens — except those who had clearly gone to hell — firmly believed. "True Recreation," admonished a book on parlor games, "must not interfere with our duty; must not injure health; must not waste money; must not waste time" — and "ought to improve the mind and the heart." Fun for fun's sake, play for the joy of playing, were considered naughty self-indulgence or worse. In Philadelphia in 1827 the work day for journeymen carpenters was cut back to 10 hours from the usual 12 or 14, but only to provide them "a sufficient time in each day for the cultivation of their mind and for self-improvement."

Obviously such loftiness went unfulfilled in practice. Work was a way of life which took its toll. America was producing, critics said, "a pale, pasty-faced, narrow chested, spindle-shanked, dwarfed race" such as "never before sprang from loins of Anglo-Saxon lineage." Something had to be done. One answer was organized sports.

Baseball caused a revolution in the nation's attitude toward outdoor organized play. In the beginning baseball, which evolved from the English game of rounders, was a fashionable pastime for fashionable young men. The first team, the Knickerbockers, organized in New York in 1845, played in straw hats and blue woolen trousers and white flannel shirts. The game was presided over by an umpire wearing a stovepipe hat who sat on a chair just outside the first-base line. The pitcher threw underhand, the players were barehanded, and nobody called balls and strikes or fouls. In 1869 the first admittedly professional team, the Cincinnati Red Stockings, took on all challengers in a national tour without losing a game. By then the magazine *Galaxy* could report: "It is a mania. Hundreds of clubs do nothing but play, all summer and autumn. . . . Since the war, it has run like wildfire. Young soldiers, full of vigor, and longing for comradeship and manly exercise, found them in this game." Baseball was, moreover, not just fun to play but fun to watch, to give one's loyalty to, and, of course, to bet on. Soon there were teams of workingmen who did not hesitate to play or practice, as a team of Boston truckmen did on the Common, at 5 a.m. so they could get to work on time.

To counteract a wave of public disapproval of gambling and payoffs associated with games, Chicago businessman William A. Hulbert in 1876 organized a number of teams into the National League of Professional Baseball Clubs, and public respect was soon regained. By 1890 baseball had become the big business it has continued to be. Baseball is the only organized sport that matured in the 19th century which is essentially today what it has been for a hundred years.

Sweet sixteens-or-so and their wing-collared beaux gather round the piano, center of many an 1890's home. Not even the newfangled talking machine could drown out hometown chorales or parlor soloists warbling minstrel tunes and favorites like "In the Gloaming." Varied voices—tenor, lead, baritone, and bass—blended in lusty barbershop quartets; foursomes still harmonize as Granddad did.

"Whoop la, out of the way"

So sang Americans in 1869 as stalwarts took to the marvelous iron-tired wooden bicycle—

*We come with lightning speed,
There's nothing like the rattling gait
Of the flying velocipede.*

How to ride it? "Straddle a Saddle," said one writer, "then Paddle and Skedaddle."

It took courage to straddle the big wheel of an "ordinary"; a sudden stop sent a rider head-over-handlebars. Then came the chain-driven safety bicycle—and a rash of races as new and old models vied for public favor. Perhaps the high-wheelers won this contest in St. Paul in 1891; only a year before, one zoomed a mile in 2 minutes 29 seconds. But the new bike swept the nation off its feet.

A surefooted few tried the pedespeed, "skating" off with wheels on their heels and a look-no-hands flair. Millions joined bicycle clubs, took outings, and cheered for professional racers. On New York's Riverside Drive, an ideal bikeway for "scorchers" to flaunt speed and skill, these women flaunted little of either. But they showed a glimpse of ankle as hems rose, bloomers blossomed, and woman-kind rolled toward a freer 20th century. "Cycling," said a magazine in 1896, "builds up their feeble frames" and cheers up "their dull and sordid thoughts."

Church and cycle vied for people's Sundays; a wag offered the solution below. One cleric was not amused: "You cannot serve God and skylark on a bicycle," he harrumphed.

Football, by contrast, first played between colleges in 1869, was just a heave-and-shove contest, a game as static as it now is fluid, all violence and little flair, and restricted to the polite colleges of the East. It quickly grew into a spectator sport, though it remained for decades a game for the "classes," not the masses. In 1873 at the first Yale-Princeton game several thousand spectators stood along the sidelines to watch; by 1893 there were about 40,000 in the bleachers.

But it was not sunny afternoons in the wooden bleachers that would transform the pale and the pasty-faced. They would be saved by something that drove away sciatica, headaches, insomnia, and dyspepsia; something that gave "a vigorous tone to the whole system." Not in 200 years, said a prominent New York physician, had any invention "done so much for the human family." The new tonic was the bicycle.

It bumped and rattled its way into widespread popularity with the appearance in the 1860's of a wood-framed contraption with pedals on the front wheel. Formally it was the velocipede, familiarly the "boneshaker"—and an immediate hit. Young men bought bicycles by the thousand, and songs and poems were written to celebrate the velocipede. Then in 1876 at the Centennial Exhibition in Philadelphia appeared a new bicycle from England. Its 60-inch front wheel and tiny rear wheel were as unequal in size as the two coins that gave it a nickname, the penny-farthing. Despite its over-the-handlebars dangers, it inspired the organization of hundreds of bicycle clubs. In 1882 some 20,000 of these "new machines" were in use—the vanguard of the one million on dirt roads and sidewalks 11 years later.

The "safety bicycle," with its equal wheels, chain drive, pneumatic rubber tires, and "drop frame" for women, intensified the craze. Through the 1890's safety bicycles sold for an average of $100 to $125, the rough equivalent of $800 to $1,000 today. By 1899 more than 300 bicycle factories hummed in America. Clothiers and liquor dealers and piano manufacturers were furious because everyone seemed to be saving to buy "wheels." One desperate hat maker even tried to get Congress to pass a law requiring every bicycle owner to buy at least two felt hats a year. Diamond Jim Brady, as notorious a spendthrift as he was a famous philanthropist, was said to own a dozen gold-plated bicycles with silver spokes and sparkling with diamonds and rubies. Even so, the jewelry business was off 50 percent.

According to the *Twelfth Census of the United States,* taken in 1900, "few articles ever used by man have created so great a revolution in social conditions as the bicycle." By no means the least of these was its liberating effect on women. Here was a form of recreation that men and women could enjoy together as they had enjoyed no outdoor sport before. Off they could go on their individual bikes or tandems—the "bicycle built for two"—sometimes by themselves, sometimes in groups with their picnic baskets, for country outings. Certainly there was little likelihood that a chaperone would be puffing along behind. *Outing* magazine called cycling "a step towards the emancipation of woman from her usually too inactive indoor life."

The bicycle craze began to collapse just before 1900, and by 1905 more than three-fifths of the manufacturers had gone out of business. What had been a delightful toy for adults and children continued to be a child's toy, and in many cases one that gave boys and girls their first taste of freedom. For adults who had no other means of transportation, the bike was merely a tiresome necessity. After three decades of bicycle doldrums, adults began to take it up again in the 1940's—but without the headlong enthusiasm of the late 1960's and early 1970's. In the peak year of 1973, 15 million bicycles were sold. In 1980, there were some 95 million bikes in use.

At the turn of the century, the bicycle was overwhelmed by the popularity of that other phenomenon of the day, the trolley car. It made its horse-frightening debut in

All out for fun at the end of the line

Where the trolley stopped, the fun began for these Baltimore picnickers headed for Gwynn Oak Park. Most turn-of-the-century cities had a trolley park, perhaps with band concerts, merry-go-round, roller coaster, Ferris wheel, baseball diamond, swimming spot, zoo, even a racetrack. Magnets for millions on any day off, the parks were what one writer called "the great breathing-places for . . . people in the city who get little fresh air at home." Here they got excitement, and nowhere more than at Coney Island in Brooklyn.

"If Paris is France," wrote 17-year-old George Tilyou in his own newspaper, "then Coney Island, between June and September, is the world." For beach crowds he later built a world of fun in Steeplechase Park. Success begat competition, until the five-mile-long island blazed with more electric lights than some entire states could muster. Dreamland alone turned on a million bulbs.

And in Luna Park, showmen conjured up a dreamscape of plaster towers, ersatz waterfalls, and eye-popping thrill rides (opposite). "Ah, God," mused a visitor, "what might the prophet have written in Revelation, if only he had first beheld a spectacle like this!" What indeed, if he had beheld the electrocution of an elephant, staged by showmen to draw a crowd to Luna? Or the cockroach races that Luna ran during the Depression? Or Luna's own death in a 1949 fire?

Nothing like "the good old summer time"

Vaudeville star George "Honey Boy" Evans said it on a New York beach in 1902, and people have hummed it ever since—but Americans had known it for years longer. Summer by summer they shed taboos against leisure, reveling instead in a newfound love of the outdoors and longer vacations.

Proper dress and decorum prevailed as tourists of the 1880's viewed the Wisconsin River's famed Dells; parasols kept the ladies' skin milky, and only the oarsmen showed shirt sleeves. But soon costumes began to fit both form and function, even baring the arms and ankles—pardon, "limbs"—of swimmers at Coney Island. Swimmers? In ten yards of wet flannel, most could only hold the safety rope and bob up and down. "Oh! ye happy waves," one newsman gushed, "what a blissful destiny is yours, when you can enclasp and kiss such lovely forms." More joys awaited ashore. On Coney Island, Nathan's sold treats for pennies. His best was his wurst; here the five-cent hot dog was born.

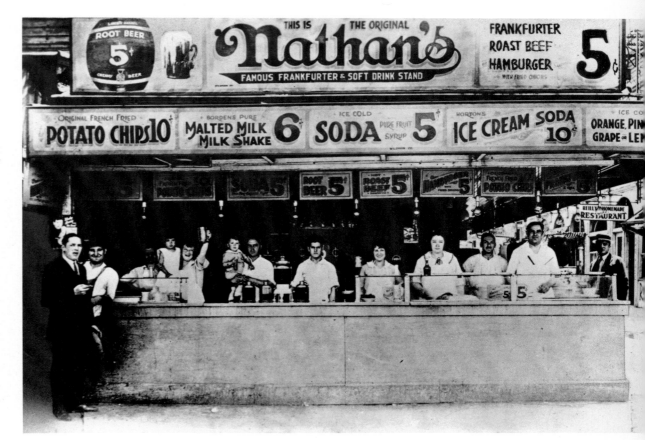

As dapper on ice as on the avenue, young blades of the 1890's watch a bustled belle cut a fine figure with her beau in New York's Central Park. Generations strapped on iron-edged wooden skates. Then Jackson Haines, a ballet master from New York who fostered figure skating, pioneered steel blades in the 1850's. During the Civil War he went to Europe, where he put ballet on ice.

1888, and, some 40 years later, became at least a temporary victim of the automobile on the paved roads which were first built at the insistence of the bicyclists. The trolley's initial excuse for being was not pleasure but practical transportation. Farmers and shoppers and businessmen rode from rural areas to towns and from towns to cities, with what then seemed the speed of lightning on what was known as the "inter-urban," and it quickly became everybody's delight. Families crowded the cars for excursions to town parks on Saturday evenings to hear the band concerts that filled the air with marches by Sousa and Viennese waltzes and popular ballads. Or on Sundays townspeople escaped to find a cool and shady place not too far from the tracks to spread their baskets and empty the picnic hamper, packed with cold chicken and hard-boiled eggs and ham and lemonade and delicious surprises. Or they rode the cars just for the thrill of racing through the countryside or to get a breath of fresh air on hot days in the open cars that were one of the treats of summer.

But it was frequently "the end of the line" that lured most passengers. The traction companies, or street railways, were chiefly responsible for the creation of amusement parks. They put them out in the country—even though the country might be within city limits—and charged special excursion fares to entice the use of the trolley cars over weekends, especially on Sundays. There young lovers, and parents clasping the hands of their children, and boys and girls with a whole dollar for an evening spree found a fantasy world of roller coasters and Ferris wheels festooned with strings of electric bulbs in days when they still had the magic of novelty. There were shoot-the-chutes and bump-the-bumps, and the air was filled with the smell of frying fat and roasting peanuts and popcorn and hot dogs, which a surprised visitor to Coney Island described when he first encountered one as "a weird-looking sausage muffled up in two halves of a roll." There was the watery piping sound of the merry-go-round with its gilded chariots for the grown-ups and its gloriously carved and painted horses canter-ing on their pumping brass poles for the would-be cowboys, while the sports leaned way out from the rim to snatch for the brass ring that would give them a free ride. There were the wheels of chance, and the shooting galleries with their snapping .22's, their targets that rang like gongs, and their endlessly moving rows of little white ducks, and the cries of the hawkers and the shills.

Thousands of families traveled far beyond the trolley park. They packed their spacious wardrobe trunks to head for vast wooden hotels with wide verandas in the mountains, on the lake, or by the sea. There they dressed in their best summer dresses or their white flannels and blazers and sat in rockers or swings or ham-mocks. Occasionally they roused themselves to stroll around the garden or down a woodland path. They went for a drive in a carriage or were pushed in a rolling chair along the boardwalk. Or, goggled and swathed in dusters, they went motoring. After tea on the veranda or, in bad weather, in one of the innumerable sitting rooms, they changed for dinner and ate their way through eight or nine courses. The gentlemen then retired to the smoking room for their coffee and brandy and cigars (no smoking, of course, in the dining room). Later, a game of cards might occupy both gentlemen and ladies until bedtime. Some gentlemen, however, retired to the billiard room or, though not openly in "respectable" houses, to the poker table.

Auction bridge evolved from whist around the turn of the century and remained the standard game for polite society until the late 1920's. Then it was superseded by con-tract bridge, a game so exacting that by 1931 half a million Americans were paying professionals to teach them how to play.

During the 1920's in hotel card rooms, as in living rooms from Bangor to Santa Barbara, hundreds of thousands of men and women—and children—were pushing

"A New Game" made to order

It might have been named "boxball." Boxes were what James A. Naismith wanted, but two peach baskets were what the janitor found. So they were nailed to the railing of the running track above the gymnasium floor. And in December 1891, at the YMCA Training School in Springfield, Massachusetts, the first trial game of basketball was played. Eighteen students, surprised by their own enthusiasm, ran back and forth until William R. Chase sank history's first basket to end the lung-bursting experiment. Score: 1 to 0.

They didn't know they had started what some would call America's most popular team sport. Naismith, a Canadian physical educa-tion teacher, simply sought an exciting way to help students keep fit during the slump be-tween football and baseball. "A New Game" was all he called it, and he had hardly written his 13 rules when changes began.

An early one cut the bottom out of the bas-ket and brought the referee down from his ladder, where he had perched to retrieve the ball after a score. Another change added a backboard—not for bank shots, but to keep fans from leaning over to tip their team's shots in or bat the foe's away.

America went hoop-happy. Barnyards, suburban driveways, and city playgrounds all sprouted backboards—and would-be Nat Holmans, Hank Luisettis, Wilt Chamberlains. Nowadays some 34 million American adults take part in basketball activities, and high school games alone draw 300 million fans a year. Naismith might be awed by the spectac-ular three-digit scores of today's giants. But he did live to see his "New Game" become a top sport, the only one entirely made in America.

Last game of the first World Series of Base-ball: October 13, 1903. Boston, home team and tops in the new American League, leads *Pittsburgh, champion of the venerable National League, 3 runs to 0, and 4 games to 3. Swarming fans twice stop the game. Finally,* *"Big Bill" Dinneen winds up, lets the spheroid fly—but there is no joy in Pittsburgh . . . mighty Honus Wagner has struck out! Upstarts win!*

What's a three-letter word for a craze?

That's easy: F-A-D. Crossword puzzles, Mah-Jongg, miniature golf, and a feast of fads swept America between world wars. Were they uplifting amusements or just trivia triumphant? Who cared? They were fun.

Crossword puzzles did expand the devotee's vocabulary; fans met Egypt's sun god Ra and newly knew the gnu. But mostly the puzzles banished ennui as they spread like Etna's aa. As sure as an em is two ens, crosswords became a national obsession. A railroad provided puzzle dictionaries in its club cars, college teams matched wits in tournaments, and a preacher cast his sermon in crosswords for his flock to solve during the service. The world knew you were addicted when you strapped a tiny lexicon to your wrist and went about with aardvark to zygote on your carpus.

"Kung!" wasn't in the book, but it was on the nation's lips as players by the million called out their moves around a Mah-Jongg set. Akin to dice and dominoes, China's ancient game spawned endless rule changes — and more than 20 American rule books to keep up with them. Production experts hurried to China to set up assembly lines; Chicago slaughterhouses shipped over their beef bones when Chinese tile-carvers ran out of the traditional calf shins. The sets, of 136 or 144 tiles, outsold radios in 1923 — and boomed the sale of oriental robes. Wearing one was half the fun; a few fanatics wouldn't touch a tile without donning Chinese garb.

No one could touch a golf ball without a healthy bank account; bags of clubs, greens fees, caddy tips, and country-club memberships were par for the course. Then Garnet Carter built his "Tom Thumb Golf Course" in Florida in 1929, and by the summer of 1930 miniature golf sprouted everywhere — even inside a New York City apartment building (opposite). Half an acre could hold all 18 holes; small change could cover all the costs of a ball, a putter, and an hour or two on the links. Players roamed "greenswards" made of dyed cottonseed hulls, dodged sand traps and water hazards, and putted through pipes, over bridges, into mouseholes in pursuit of par. A year later the fad popularized driving ranges, where duffers hooked and sliced a bucket of balls while boys scurried about under umbrellas to retrieve the shots. Some hoped the 125-million-dollar industry might cure the Depression. It didn't — but it outlived those doldrums and still helps us out of ours.

around little ivory or bone tiles marked with colored circles, Chinese characters, or bamboo designs, saying Chinese words, and speaking knowingly of Winds and Dragons. They were playing Mah-Jongg, a game not so much of skill as of luck — appealing because it sounded pleasant as the tiles clicked against each other and looked pretty on the green baize cover of the card table. The Mah-Jongg fad lasted five or six years, about as long as the fad for Canasta did in the late 1940's and early 1950's. Scrabble, a word game also played with little tiles — only these were made of wood — enjoyed a vogue for about as many years, though it still has its ardent partisans.

It was also in the 1920's that the crossword puzzle swept America. It had first appeared in the *New York World* in 1913 as a feature of the Sunday supplement. But not until 1924 did the columnists Franklin Pierce Adams (known as F.P.A.) and Heywood Broun take up the idea and make much of it. In that same year a new publishing house, Simon & Schuster, issued the first crossword puzzle book. The puzzle killed Sunday hours. It was the opiate of the commuter on subways and buses and trains. The crossword was said to have caused suicides from frustration. Men were trotted off to jail because they refused to budge from restaurants until they had finished filling the last little square. It put words like *lo* and *ai* and *en* into the vocabularies of clerks and bank presidents, countermen and headwaiters, stenographers and congresswomen. And more than 60 years later it is still doing the same kind of thing. There is hardly a daily or weekly paper in the nation without a crossword puzzle.

At the summer hotels, the less sedentary young were sometimes joined in their games of croquet by their elders. Or they met them on the tennis court or at the beach — girls in their serge bathing dresses and black stockings and men in dark woolen trunks and striped tops. The picnic seems to have been least subject to changing fashion, though its elaborateness has varied with time and place. A picnic at fashionable Newport, Rhode Island, in the 1890's might involve not only tables and napery, silver and champagne, butlers to precede the picnickers to a beach or a shaded lawn to prepare the way, and all manner of delicacies, but even a temporary dance floor. A New England clambake, with its smoldering fire in a pit of sand and the smell of roasting corn and clams and seaweed, was a quite different matter — as different as the Western barbecue is from the cookout on the patio, a recent ritual at least partly inspired by the disappearance of the servant class.

Many summer hotels had ballrooms where Saturday night dances ended at midnight sharp with the playing of "Good Night Ladies." Compared with what it has become in recent years, social dancing at the turn of the century might almost seem to have been a sedentary pastime. It was formal, performed in prescribed steps. The energetic waltz and polka were thought to be not quite nice by ladies who sat like pouter pigeons in their lace collars along the sides of the room.

Ragtime helped to change all that. Its popularity spread in the 1890's and 1900's, and by 1911, Irving Berlin's "Alexander's Ragtime Band" — rollicking, if not real rag — seemed to Alexander Woollcott to "set the shoulders of America swinging with syncopated jubilance." The older, straitlaced generation was appalled that the young threw themselves into such shocking intimacies as the Bunny Hug and contortions like the Turkey Trot. Then it was time for another craze, one that captured all generations. The high priest and priestess of the dance were the Castles, Vernon and Irene. The Castle Walk, the maxixe, and the tango were for the sophisticated willing to take lessons, while the one-step was the basic figure for Dixieland jazz, which superseded ragtime. By the 1920's the fox-trot became the standard for dancing slowly to the "Indian Love Call" from *Rose-Marie* and "What'll I Do?" from the *Music Box Revue of 1923* or briskly to George Gershwin's "Fascinating Rhythm" or Ray Henderson's "Button Up Your

Overcoat." Those were the days when nightclubs, roadhouses, and speakeasies were at their peak, when Paul Whiteman played for tea dances at the Biltmore in New York with Bix Beiderbecke or the Rhythm Boys, one of whom was Bing Crosby. The Charleston had a brief if violent fling in the 1920's, followed in the 1930's by the Big Apple and the far more durable Lindy Hop, elements of which linger in the shuffling, groin-pumping, and hip-twisting of the discotheque and rock era.

By the late 1920's, more adventurous Americans accepted an even greater challenge than the Charleston to staying on their feet: skiing. A group of Norwegian settlers in Minnesota organized one of the earliest ski clubs in this country in 1883, but skiing did not catch on until the 1930's. So, during the Great Depression, when thousands were standing in breadlines, a surprising number of Americans were lining up for the ski trains and buses that took them to the slopes of New York, New England, Colorado, California, indeed to any high country. Tennis and golf shops suddenly became ski shops as well, and the costumes for skiing—heavy, patterned sweaters, baggy pants, parkas and caps—became as crucial as skis and boots and poles. A few department stores gave ski instruction to neophytes on indoor slides covered with borax. Après-ski was as important as skiing to many. It was the rousing gaiety by the open fire in the imitation Swiss chalets, the hot toddies, the songs, the talk of stem turns and trails and powder snow and ski wax, for which many young women saved their wages. After World War II, ski lodges sprang from formal summer hotels and became more and more elaborate, with heated swimming pools, indoor skating rinks, and fancy bars.

"Athletics is today the religion of the United States," wrote John R. Tunis, a philosopher of American sports, in 1932. "To this religion of sports then, the American turns naturally. For sports come to him instinctively . . . [He] is taught to hit, kick, and throw balls of all kinds, baseballs, footballs, golf balls, tennis balls, basketballs, and so forth, from his earliest youth. His boyish heroes are never soldiers, sailors or explorers as in other lands; they are athletes, airmen, champion football or golf players. . . . No wonder, therefore, that the American nation, trained to think, play, and compete in athletics, is sport mad." At about the same time Stephen Leacock, the great Canadian humorist, wrote of Americans trying to have fun: "They can't play. They try to but they can't. They turn football into a fight, baseball into a lawsuit, and yachting into machinery."

Since then, Americans at play have changed, just as they had changed in the half century before 1932. In that year the standard workweek was five-and-a-half days; the weekend started with Saturday half over. During the Depression, when country clubs were failing because their members couldn't afford the dues, the number of public courses grew rapidly, and golf, which like tennis had once been a game of the wealthy, became a sport for all classes. Professional football, then professional basketball came of age as television added a nationwide audience to the fans in the stands.

When more than a fourth of the population watches the Super Bowl game, it is easy to say that this reflects the intellectual and physical norm of the nation. But what about the fishermen who whip our streams, the hunters who track our woods? The company softball teams? The bowling leagues? And the individuals playing their own games—especially tennis, which boomed in the 1970's as a professional and amateur sport. New courts started appearing at the rate of 1,000 a month. By 1975 the number of players was 34 million, including 2 million under the age of 11.

Every weekend we see Americans at play—or heading for play: families in cars with canoes or skis on the roofs, or bicycles strapped onto rear bumpers, or motorcycles or boats on their trailers. They are all heading for freedom, trying to escape from being a captive audience. In this land where the professionalization of sports has reached manic intensity, they are, in the full sense of the word, amateurs.

Solid—and in the groove

If you're *In the Mood*, take a *Sentimental Journey* down the *Street of Dreams* to years when *Boogie Woogie* put *Star Dust* in hepcats' *Green Eyes*. Gather at the *Juke Box Saturday Night;* for nickels this one blared the hits:

A-Tisket A-Tasket. *Chick Webb and his Orchestra with Ella Fitzgerald. 1938.*

Chattanooga Choo Choo. *Glenn Miller and his Orchestra with Tex Beneke and the Four Modernaires. 1941.*

Mister Five by Five. *The Andrews Sisters with Vic Schoen and his Orchestra. 1942.*

Bésame Mucho. *Jimmy Dorsey and his Orchestra with Bob Eberly and Kitty Kallen. 1943.*

My Old Flame. *Benny Goodman and his Orchestra. 1944.*

Sioux City Sue. *Bing Crosby with The Jesters and Bob Haggart and his Orchestra. 1946.*

For Sentimental Reasons. *The King Cole Trio with Nat "King" Cole. 1946.*

One of the prime movers that caused a revolution in our recreation, manners, and social attitudes — the bicycle — today is riding the crest of a spectacular revival. Young people with cameras and skillets and tents and sleeping bags wheel off for the woods and the upland meadows, and middle-aged city-folk pedal in parks, hoping to trim their waists and tone their hearts. Cities like New York, which regularly closes portions of Central Park to automobiles, have recognized the bike as a socio-political fact of life.

There's a boom too in the building of what we call cultural centers. Every major city and every ambitious minor one must have its own version of New York's Lincoln Center, with its opera house, concert halls, and theaters. Municipal, state, and federal support of the arts, a feeble trickle in the early 1960's, has increased. Elected officials have discovered the political importance of concertgoers — concert attendance has doubled in the last 20 years — and of opera and dance fans, devotees of experimental theater, and people who like to go to museums. Politicians know that culture, like bicycling, is good for you — and them. And entrepreneurs, aware of how well it pays to encourage Americans to play, are giving us stadiums, racetracks, gambling casinos, and a new and different kind of amusement park — the theme park.

The theme park was invented by Walt Disney, who conceived it to be as wholesome as Snow White and that frightening witch, no more and no less. Disneyland in California opened in 1955 and is still world famous. Disney World — a resort complex near Orlando, Florida, with a theme park called the Magic Kingdom — followed in 1971 and launched its ambitious Epcot Center in 1982. Disney World's Magic Kingdom is a compendium of slick nostalgia, even slicker "future shock," extremely sophisticated urban planning, business acuity, and larger-than-life animated bears, pirates in caves, plastic jungles filled with plastic rhinos, snakes, elephants spouting water, and spotlessly clean and clean-cut young men and women attendants. One is not supposed to confuse anything in the Magic Kingdom with reality. What is projected for the future has all the plausibility of the "Little Nemo" comic strips of 1905, and what is meant to be American nostalgia may be comforting, but it is cosmetic history.

What would they think of our answers — Sir Charles Lyell, who wondered if the national motto should be "All work and no play," and President Garfield, who said that the second fight of civilization is "What shall we do with our leisure when we get it." One answer is that a great many of us are still compulsive workers, and that a great deal of what passes for play is work. We feel we have to be doing things — making things, assembling things, going places, improving our minds, slimming our bodies, hardening our muscles, or, if we are young, fighting "the system" and frightening our parents. But many of us are content to sit still and let others work to entertain us — professional athletes, comedians, singers, musicians, actors, dancers. We gape at their prowess, and we forget them for new heroes.

In fact most of us are some of each — actors and spectators, doers and done-bys. We have nearly won our freedom from the Puritan ethic with its motto: "The Devil finds work for idle hands." We have rid ourselves of at least some of our guilt for wasting time. We are a different breed from our Victorian forebears — physically (we're much bigger), morally (we're much more permissive), and socially (we're much more relaxed). We have, moreover, made sports democratic; once an upper-class prerogative, they are now everybody's. While many sports have become increasingly professionalized, the crowds of fans have vastly increased. But so have the numbers of amateurs who work hard at playing for the fun of it. If we are becoming a nation of amateurs in the games we play, the travels we take, the objects we collect, the things we make, we will have indeed answered Sir Charles Lyell. But I am not so sure that we have yet given a satisfactory account of ourselves to President Garfield.

American leisure: the pursuit of fun and fantasy

Say "cheese!" Mickey Mouse clicks with yet another fan, this time as a camera with its own smile. And the smile is well-deserved; Florida's Disney World, which includes the Magic Kingdom theme park shown here and Epcot Center, draws double Florida's population in visitors each year. An explosion of make-believe radiates around Cinderella Castle: dancing bears, talking Presidents, scowling ghouls, pistol-packing badmen, rides into myriad worlds ranging from under the ocean to beyond the moon. In its first full year, 1972, Disney World and its older California cousin, Disneyland, attracted 21.6 million visitors, nearly twice as many as went that year to all the games of the National Football League.

The Disney never-never lands reign supreme among theme parks. Some 50 major ones dot the country. They lure tourists into such divertissements as a land of lions, a park-sized Polynesia, or a grand ol' uproar of fiddle and banjo — to the tune of a billion dollars in gate receipts a year.

How much do we Americans spend on fun in all its endless guises? No one can say, for who can define fun? But if fun can be put in figures, here's how we adults and teenagers spend outdoor time in an average year. Some 50 percent of us take one or more trips to a zoo, fair, or amusement park. Fifty-three percent swim, or walk for pleasure, and 48 percent say they enjoy a drive. Ants or no, 48 percent also try at least one picnic, and 24 percent camp out. Thirty-four percent of us try our hand at fishing and 32 percent go biking. Among boaters, 8 percent tote canoe or kayak to rivers, while 19 percent hop into motorboats and zoom past the 6 percent who sail as skipper or crew in the U. S. pleasure-craft fleet.

Gone to the Movies

Richard Schickel

"The magic empire of the twentieth century. The Mecca of the world." In the subtitle of The Last Command, a 1928 silent movie about making movies, Hollywood gave itself that accolade. But more than magic put images on film. From the era of the hand-cranked camera (this one dates to 1925) to the dawn of the wide-screen vista, technology shaped an art. Born mute in black and white, movies grew up on innovations. One fulfilled what early lobby posters promised: stars in living color. Tinting—sometimes by hand, a frame at a time—evolved into Technicolor, introduced by Walt Disney in 1932 in a short made with animation—artful technology.

For a Pickford or a Rin-Tin-Tin—later, a Bogart or a Monroe—to become a household word, technology allied with talent: director, cameraman, writer, stuntman, set and costume designers. And if there was magic, it touched the flickering light and shadow between projector and screen, making images that became lodgers in our memories.

James Agee's autobiographical novel, *A Death in the Family,* begins with a recollection of going to the Majestic as a child, of finding the way to seats "by the light of the screen, in the exhilarating smell of stale tobacco, rank sweat, perfume and dirty drawers, while the piano played fast music and galloping horses raised a grandiose flag of dust. And there," he remembered, "was William S. Hart with both guns blazing and his long, horse face and his long, hard lip, and the great country rode away behind him as wide as the world." The year was about 1915, when movies as an institution were little older than Agee himself. Most of the first three pages of his Pulitzer Prize-winning book are devoted to a vivid recollection of the Chaplin comedy which shared the screen that night with the Hart Western.

It is hard to imagine a writer of today—say, one born after 1940—writing about his own moviegoing with such intensity. Looking back to the innocent exhilaration, the awed expectation and fulfilled wonder that the simple act of going to the movies had for people, one cannot help but reflect on what we have lost.

Today's film audience, that human odd-lot that erratically turns up at the movie houses, is radically different from the Great Movie Audience which existed until about the end of the 1940's. During the 40 years or so when movies were the dominant instrument of mass entertainment—the only dramatic entertainment for millions—no ineptness on the part of director or actors, no vulgarity on the part of a script writer, could loose the ties that bound audience to medium. "I remember pausing on my way out of Loew's Sheridan in New York City some years ago, after having submitted to a real stinker," social critic David T. Bazelon has said. "I shook my fist at the screen: 'You win this time, damn you! But I'll be back!' "

Why did the people go back again and again? Another critic, Robert Warshow, suggested an answer from his own experience: "because I am attracted to Humphrey Bogart or Shelley Winters or Greta Garbo; because I require the absorbing immediacy of the screen; because in some way I take all that nonsense seriously." Warshow added that he had seen many bad movies, "but I have rarely been bored at the movies; and when I have been bored, it has usually been at a 'good' movie."

To be sure, other critics—especially those owing allegiance to a competing art form—disparaged the innocent delight of the multitude in the upstart medium. In 1935, when the American movie industry was in a golden age of creativity, the drama critic George Jean Nathan declared that for "a person of the slightest culture and experience" an

outstanding film could not satisfy as the theater could "even in its lesser flights." Wolcott Gibbs delivered a more scornful commentary in the pages of *The Saturday Review:* Ninety percent of the movies exhibited in the United States could not be written about "in any publication not intended to be read while chewing gum." Always tender to criticism, producers reacted to this kind in part by making high-flown adaptations of classic (or at least classy) literary and theatrical works, such as *Romeo and Juliet, The Good Earth,* and *Carmen* (which has been turned into a movie 14 times, by actual count). A few classics were well rewarded at the box office. If most were not, moviegoers did not begrudge the medium its cultural aspirations; they would cheerfully sit through these earnest endeavors while waiting for the *real* movie.

What we responded to were certain conventions of plot and characterization that took root in film: the gangster movies as Edward G. Robinson and James Cagney made them; the numberless Westerns with their rugged stars, beginning with Hart and continuing through his artistic heirs, John Wayne, Joel McCrea, Gary Cooper, Randolph Scott, and the rest; the endlessly imperiled virgin heroines, as played in silent films by Mary Pickford and Lillian Gish; the bright, fast-talking girls of slightly more recent vintage, such as Carole Lombard in *Twentieth Century* and Rosalind Russell in *His Girl Friday.* Even in the 1950's, the years of decline, the American cinema developed a new archetype suited to the times—the sullen, rebellious, inarticulately troubled anti-hero, epitomized by Marlon Brando in *On the Waterfront.* The successful conventions—those that lured us into the theater in the largest numbers—were repeated and repeated until we were conditioned to expect, then demand the repetition; having learned to love Cagney as a gangster or Cooper as a Westerner, we wanted them to remain so, celluloid world without end. "If it has been good once, it's good another time," director Howard Hawks once said of the similarity of some of the scenes in his movies. He was pleased when people told him they'd caught him repeating himself "because if they can remember that long, the scene must be pretty good."

Many a parent (at least, where I lived) thought our habitual attendance of no moral, spiritual, or intellectual benefit and a waste of time. They hoped we would outgrow the movies, or at least feel a decent puritanical guilt about our intense involvement with the on-screen lives of Bogart, Tracy, Gable, et al. Much effort was expended to explain that life was not the way the movies showed it to be; that our chances for heroic adventure were far slimmer than *The Plainsman* or *Air Force* might lead us to think; that noble renunciation, as in *Casablanca,* was simply not experienced in the humdrum routine of the real world. I assume that little girls were similarly warned: that their chances of finding mates as attractive as movie leading men were nearly non-existent; that suffering would not be as glamorous as Bette Davis made it seem in *Dark Victory;* that courtship would not be as graceful as Astaire and Rogers made it look; nor marriage the barrel of fun tapped by Powell and Loy.

But of course we knew all that—we really did, just as we knew that when actors died in movies they didn't really die. Without the words to express it, we understood that movies selected from reality and exaggerated it to create their visions of life. They did offer escape, as their moral critics insisted. But there was more to it than that. In retrospect we see that movies were offering us high-relief paradigms of human behavior. Most of us would not be called upon to stand up for principles and against majority opinion and the machinations of the power elite as, for example, James Stewart did as a Senator in *Mr. Smith Goes to Washington.* But it was possible in little ways, at school board meetings or in business conferences, to pattern ourselves on his model. That such lessons could be taught by attractive people in an exciting medium seemed to me then, as it seems to me still, simply wonderful.

"They grow everywhere"

Lurid posters drew young and old to what one critic called "the blight of the nickelodeon"— makeshift theaters whose 10-cent admission belied their name. They grew from nickel-in-the-slot devices like Edison's Kinetoscope that showed "living pictures" of a man sneezing. In its brief heyday before 1918 the nickelodeon offered an hour-long miscellany of comedy, adventure, and fantasy. Lantern slides between reels preached niceties to a largely immigrant audience, daringly showed ads of corseted ladies, flashed lyrics for sing-alongs. Silent films were never silent. Even the humblest of theaters hired a pianist or violinist whose tempo suited the action.

Camera! Action! Ice! — the art of realism

Ice cakes, sawed and set adrift by dynamite, perform on cue for director D. W. Griffith (in fedora) as his cameras grind away on *Way Down East,* an epic potboiler. Heroine Lillian Gish floats off and hero Richard Barthelmess, slowed by his enormous overcoat, leaps awkwardly from floe to floe. The star may have used such standard ploys of the silent era as the heavenward gaze. But Griffith's demand for realism put her in actual danger; she nearly lost her outflung right hand when a chunk of ice grazed her. Griffith got cast and crew in condition with cold baths and long walks, then took them to White River Junction, Vermont, for filming. His studio was in a New York City suburb.

Movies started in the East. Until the 1920's companies filmed in such places as Saranac Lake, New York, and Providence, Rhode Island. Hollywood was hardly more than a citrus grove in 1913 when Cecil B. DeMille and actor Dustin Farnum, lured by its sunny days, selected it as the site for *The Squaw Man,* the first major film produced there.

The development of movies was terribly accidental and very American in the pragmatic adaptation of talent to a new and exciting technology. Abroad, film was recognized from the start as a new form of artistic expression; European movies tended to reflect cultural traditions or the current preoccupations of intellectuals and artists. Only in America was the basic model for development *industrial;* the unspoken desire was to treat movies as product, not art, and to devise forms that could be handled in mass-market style. In effect, the movies, not unlike Detroit, offered a limited number of makes and models which were restyled just enough every year to give moviegoers an illusion of novelty without upsetting their expectations.

This method of organizing the market represented a considerable improvement over the situation in the decades surrounding the turn of the century, when the motion picture camera and projector were being perfected. The first captains of the industry were inventor-entrepreneurs, far more interested in the profits from manufacturing their machines and selling or licensing them than in the programs the machines were capable of creating and exhibiting. Rational, sensible men, they took as their model not consumer trade but heavy industry. They were content to provide the public with scenic views and newsreels, confident that the novelty of their inventions themselves would assure profitability. But that novelty soon wore off and the movies became commercially moribund. Mostly they were shown in vaudeville houses, usually relegated to the role of "chasers" — presentations after the live show and so lacking in appeal that they encouraged one audience to decamp so that another one could sit down.

At this critical time Edwin Porter produced two documentary-like one-reel photoplays. A cameraman in the studios of Thomas A. Edison (one of several inventors who held patents for movie machines), Porter was bored with turning out picture postcards that moved. He studied the new films by a Frenchman, George Méliès — charming fantasies like *A Trip to the Moon* which knitted a few scenes into a simple story. Porter set out in 1903 to make a movie as realistic as Méliès' were fantastical. Rummaging through the Edison files, he collected shots of fires and firemen. He hired actors: a fire chief, a mother, a child to be rescued from a burning building. The first American dramatic movie, *The Life of an American Fireman,* lasting but ten minutes, attracted some modest attention. His second documentary-like production was a sensation. In *The Great Train Robbery* Porter brought to the screen two of its future staples — the Western and the chase — and startled audiences with a closeup of an outlaw firing his pistol point-blank at the camera.

All events seemed to work in film's favor now. In 1903, not long after the making of *The Great Train Robbery,* a strike by vaudeville performers left theater managers with an urgent need for some new attraction. Movies literally filled the bill. A short time later, a man named Thomas Tally decided that his Los Angeles penny arcade would provide nothing but films as amusement. Other people, including many recent immigrants, suddenly saw in movies the opportunity to become small-time capitalists for a minor investment. It didn't take much to rent a store, some folding chairs, and a few films. Many a nickelodeon opened its doors with *The Great Train Robbery,* and many a theatrical empire (Paramount Pictures, to cite one example) was begun by men who acquired their grubstakes nickel by nickel in these little people's theaters. Only five years after Porter produced the first great American "hit," an estimated 8,000 to 10,000 nickelodeons were offering entertainment to the masses. New studios flourished, in response to the demand for films, grinding out perhaps two one-reelers a week, often shooting one entirely in a day.

Plots were simple; usually there were only seven or eight scenes. But the movies were launched. And the man of the hour was someone who *(continued on page 365)*

They "completely let go. They screamed."

When Harold Lloyd slipped into a theater to hear that eruption of laughter, movies were silent—but comedians' fans weren't. Charlie Chaplin was funny munching on a boot (of licorice); Lloyd drew nervous laughs and gasps as he hung from a clock. (Below him were mattress-covered platforms. But a test dummy dropped on one bounced to the street.) Buster Keaton earned laughs by crafting precise stunts: When a house falls on him, an open window safely enframes him.

Stan Laurel, thin man of the English music hall, and Oliver Hardy, fat man of American

vaudeville, had teamed up before talkies arrived; their routine owed little to sound. But in the comic opera *Fra Diavolo* they used the new medium hilariously. Drunk in a wine cellar, they giggle, then laugh, then roar until the audience instinctively joins in.

The Marx Brothers began as a vaudeville act. One sketch, in which Harpo had three lines, worked better when he was silent; he never again spoke on stage or in films. In 1929 they commuted between *Animal Crackers* on Broadway and a sound stage on Long Island to make their first movie, *The Cocoanuts.* Daffy patter became Groucho's forte. He tells a woman to meet him under the moon— "You wear a necktie so I'll know you."

W. C. Fields, who mastered silent and talkie, kicked and choked children for a gag. "The funniest thing about comedy," he said, "is that you never know why people laugh."

356

Risking his life for a laugh, Harold Lloyd dangles 12 stories high in Safety Last *(1923), a "thrill picture" that won him a dislocated shoulder. Right: Buster Keaton gives Kathleen Myers a lift in* Go West *(1925). Opposite: Charlie Chaplin dines in* The Gold Rush *(1925). The Marx Brothers act up* At the Circus *(1939): Harpo and Chico (pointing) fire Groucho. Oliver Hardy and Stan Laurel unbrick a wall in* Blockheads *(1938). W. C. Fields throttles a suspect in* The Bank Dick *(1940).*

357

"Spin a Little Web of Dreams"

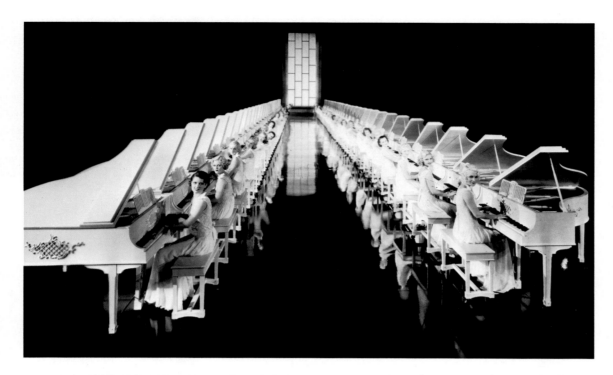

The title of a 1934 movie melody struck a theme of Hollywood musicals: to transport audiences into a fantasy world where troubles are shed by dancing in the street or singing in the rain. Movies had learned to dance and sing when they learned to speak; the first talkie, *The Jazz Singer,* had more music than dialogue because 1927 technology could reproduce instruments better than voice. The first true musical, *Broadway Melody,* came in 1929; *Whoopee* in 1930 marked the film debut of Busby Berkeley. A Broadway dance director, he brightened a drab era with his

extravaganzas, inventively linking pretty girls with "miles of silk, tons of feathers, and gallons of glitter." He filmed chorines from myriad angles, blueprinted dance patterns, and used elaborate props like the pool and the elevating tiered fountain of *Footlight Parade* (opposite); its pumps, pipes, and controls rivaled an ocean liner's engine room.

Musical stars like Ginger Rogers and Fred Astaire (above in *Swing Time*) won millions of fans. "Can't act. Can't sing. Balding. Can dance a little," a studio test report said of Astaire. But the pair produced repeated hits. "He gives her class, and she gives him sex," quipped Katharine Hepburn. And they both made a nation want to dance.

Battery-powered beauties—wired to neon-tubed violins that made glowing patterns in the dark—dance a Berkeley number in Gold Diggers of 1933. Berkeley's Gold Diggers of 1935 (top) had 56 pianists and 56 pianos waltzing—moved by men underneath, in black and following black tapes on a black floor.

Filming a West that never was

The "giddyap business," the scoffers called it—the making of "oaters," "horse operas," cowboy movies. But the Western has been rounding up moviegoers since the early days—when "Broncho Billy" Anderson of *Great Train Robbery* fame did 376 of them in 376 weeks. Lack of faithfulness to the real West seldom stirred concern; old plots were re-hashed, stock footage re-used. Yet they filled theaters, for they satisfied a hankering for a vanished frontier whose rough justice "kept women indoors, men in line and bad men in Boot Hill." And the hero might be you.

Stars of the silent screen often were real ranchmen like steely-eyed William S. Hart (above), who spoke Sioux at six, or Tom Mix, who could, if the script required, shoot off suspender buttons so an actor's pants would drop. With sound came the singing "cowboys," among them radio's Gene Autry, who disliked riding horses, and Roy Rogers (right), who became a franchised name. Epic Westerns were built around superstars, such as John Wayne (opposite), and classics became remakes—*The Spoilers* five times, *The Plainsman* twice. (Latter-day versions, opposite.) "When Doomsday finally rolls around," veteran producer Nunnally Johnson commented, ". . . it will undoubtedly catch 500 cowboy actors still galloping through the dust . . . to cut off the outlaws at Eagle Pass."

Roy Rogers hoists hat and Trigger in a typical publicity photo. You're covered (left) by William S. Hart in The Gun Fighter *(1917). Opposite: John Wayne in* Red River *(1948) epitomizes the Western's action—described as a "fight at the start, one in the middle, and a grand finale in the last reel." In* Winners of the West *(1940), stuntman Yakima Canutt (top) performs the leap that became his trademark. Rory Calhoun slugs Jeff Chandler in* The Spoilers *(1955). Don Murray roasts in* The Plainsman *(1966).*

"Mother of Mercy, is this the end of Rico?"

Of Rico, yes. But Edward G. Robinson's Capone-like gang leader was only the beginning. Cashing in on the novelty of sound, Hollywood transformed headline news of Prohibition mobsters and gangland hoodlums into a cacophony of sawed-off shotguns, tire-squealing big black cars, and the rapid-fire tough talk of the underworld.

Crime paid at the box office—some 60 gangster films appeared between 1930 and

1932—but on the screen a typically brutal gunning-down awaited Scarface, another of many film Capones. James Cagney's punk, Tommy Powers (opposite), rose to brief enjoyment of camelhair coats and limousines before being done in by fellow mobsters.

An unlikely path led Cagney to crime—professional dancing. Bogart, Muni, and Robinson achieved film gangsterdom via the New York stage, where Bogie's surly, brooding Duke Mantee first set his style.

Into the 1960's and '70's moviegoers still craved the history and near-history of crime. *Bonnie and Clyde* (1967), *Shaft* (1971), and *The Godfather*, like *Little Caesar* 40 years earlier, each explored the violence of an era.

Edward G. Robinson stops lead in Little Caesar *(1930) and pin-striped Paul Muni (left) sprays some in* Scarface *(1932). Opposite: James Cagney pushes a grapefruit into the face of moll Mae Clarke in* The Public Enemy *(1931); a critic called the scene "one of the cruellest, most startling acts ever committed on film." As bootlegger Tommy Powers, Cagney died at his mother's door, riddled and wrapped. Killer Duke Mantee—Humphrey Bogart—confronts Bette Davis and Leslie Howard (at left) in* The Petrified Forest *(1936). Salvatore Corsitto gets the ear of Marlon Brando, who makes offers people cannot refuse in* The Godfather *(1972).*

362

Ornate showcases, such as Loew's Paradise in New York, appeared in the 1920's. Stars twinkled in ceilings as fake clouds floated by; electricians were cautioned, "Be sure the stars are turned off before leaving." Ushers dressed like hussars—and these "attachés" at New York's Roxy even trained under a retired Marine Corps colonel. Hands signaled available seats—and the approach of bosses.

knew a bit about dramatic construction, someone with theatrical training. Successful actors viewed the movies with disdain. Film robbed them of their greatest gift, a trained voice. And the pay was only about $5 a day. But there are always more thespians out of work than employed, and there were any number of newspapermen and frustrated authors with unfinished plays in their desks and dreams of glory in their heads. On the gifts of such people the movies began to be built. Few were geniuses, few were innovators, few realized the fantastic potential of the new medium.

They turned naturally to the material they knew best, that of the live theater. In the highly fanciful melodramas then in vogue, moral lines were much straighter, much more shining white or deep-dyed black than in real life. The movies simply borrowed the stage's pure heroines imperiled by unparalleled villainy and its upright heroes whose chivalric code hardly permitted even an embrace of the young women they went to such lengths to rescue—with, of course, never a thought of carnal knowledge.

It was D. W. Griffith, unsuccessful actor, failed playwright and poet, who discovered a power in film that all along had been waiting to be released. He went to the Biograph studios on 14th Street in New York in 1908, looking for work as a day-labor actor, and soon replaced a director who was having trouble with both liquor and the new medium. Griffith was 33 years old and must have sensed that he was being given a last chance at the worldly success that had so far eluded him.

In nearly six years at Biograph he made more than 400 films and converted a novelty into a substantial art form. To begin with, he greatly extended film's range of subject matter. Besides conventional melodramas, he adapted fiction as well as poetry to the screen; made semidocumentary films which focused on such topics as gang warfare in the slums; experimented with farce as well as with what we now call situation comedy; and developed the Western, war, and crime genres on new and more spectacular levels. In sum, all the great staples of American movie-making, if not invented by Griffith, were firmly established by him during his Biograph years.

More important, he laid the groundwork for telling stories in cinematic terms. Most film makers kept plot lines linear. Almost without conscious thought Griffith saw that flashbacks and "switchbacks" (as he called cross-cutting) were natural to the screen, that scene changes requiring enormous effort on the stage could be achieved in a wink of the camera's eye or with a snip of the editor's scissors.

Not without difficulty from the front office—which believed that audiences wanted to see the full figures of actors, as if at a play—Griffith moved his camera into the stage area, converting the lens from passive spectator to active participant in the drama. He isolated for the audience the most important element in a scene, providing in a soundless medium the dramatic emphasis playwrights could obtain with the spoken word. Through these closeups he found, as he liked to put it, the power to "photograph thought." It is this power that enables movies to transcend material that, judged on purely literary grounds, is undistinguished, even cheap.

The late director George Cukor, who made popular and unforgettable films from the 1930's on (*The Philadelphia Story* and the Spencer Tracy-Katharine Hepburn comedies), said it was film's business to penetrate to "the reality beyond convention" — to reach the authentic emotions evoked by even the most melodramatically incredible stories. Cukor cited his version of *Camille* with Greta Garbo, made in 1936. Few persons today would be moved by that once-popular stage play. But the film: ah, the film! Cukor spoke of the "wantonness" and "perversity" of Garbo's characterization, observed so intimately by the camera. And he told of her erotic honesty, the boldness of the pleasure she took in sex, communicated not through stripteases or bedroom gropings but through the glitter in the actress' eye, a small gesture, a modest laugh. One can begin to understand the courtesan's ineluctable appeal — how she could lead men to ruin themselves for her. This human reality, intimately glimpsed, does indeed transcend the conventions of a creaky old theatrical property.

Or take the least realistic of all film forms, the musical. Following Fred Astaire and Ginger Rogers in the elegant self-expression of their dances, the camera was again "photographing thought," and by doing so made us not merely accept the highly unrealistic (in real life, no one breaks into dance on a street or in a park) but hunger for it and believe that life not only could be this way but *should* be.

During his last years at Biograph, Griffith chafed at the restrictions of the one- and two-reel length imposed by his corporate masters, who believed that the audience would not sit still — literally — for more. And when the Italians began producing longer, more spectacular films, they challenged Griffith's supremacy as a director. He left Biograph for a firm that promised freer rein for his imagination. The result was the first great spectacle film, *The Birth of a Nation,* based on an enormously popular, and melodramatically racist, novel, *The Clansman.* It turned out to be, with its exciting battle sequences and its suspenseful threats to fair Southern womanhood by lustful blacks in the Reconstruction era, the most successful movie ever made until *The Godfather* came along to probably break its record. (No one knows how much Griffith's movie actually grossed.)

However distasteful its theme, *Birth* was a crude but powerful example of something like ideal form for other directors to follow. It was not only spectacle and suspense that brought the people in; it was the combination of these with intimate, tender scenes of family life under the pressures of war and war's aftermath. Such scenes humanized the film and to some extent canceled out the ugliness of its message. At last someone had balanced and blended the unique, defining elements of cinema: its capacity for unprecedented spectacle and unprecedented intimacy. When the great pioneer died in 1948, a broken spirit ignored by the industry, another director, René Clair, observed: "Nothing essential has been added to the cinema since Griffith."

To some extent he was even responsible for the "star system," though he didn't much care for the fact that mere actors outstripped the director in fame and fortune. Before 1920 one of his discoveries, Mary Pickford, had signed a million-dollar contract. Charlie Chaplin was the only other performer so well rewarded at the time, although other, younger players were paid many times the pittance that the first movie performers earned. The public had begun to single out the anonymous youngsters whom Griffith and others exposed to them week in, week out in their little films. At first the producers refused to identify the players, fearful of the salary demands which

"I'd Love to be a Talking Picture Queen"

That wistful song in *New Movietone Follies of 1930* reflects the fantasies of fans smitten by Hollywood's glamor and eager to emulate its stars. Ringlet-curled Shirley Temple inspired dolls, books, nursery furniture — and look-alike contests. Manufacturers, quick to cash in on movie-spawned fads and fashions, even offered faithful copies of chic outfits worn by "confession" film heroines. Any woman could don the burgundy velvet dress Loretta Young wore in *Born to Be Bad.* Tortoise-shelled tots publicized comedian Harold Lloyd, whose lensless frames sparked the popularity of these new "horn-rims."

Movies could turn off sales too. In *It Happened One Night* Clark Gable showed Claudette Colbert and his fans that he did not wear an undershirt — and sales tumbled. In *A Streetcar Named Desire,* though, Marlon Brando made the torn T-shirt a he-man badge.

Italian-American comedian Cassio eats spaghetti offensively in Who Am I? Such scenes could keep a movie out of Italy. Censors' stitchery changed Maureen O'Sullivan's attire from scant in Tarzan and His Mate (1934) to modest in Tarzan's New York Adventure (1942). Johnny Weissmuller's brief costume stayed the same. The movies' morals code of the 1930's banned the straying kisses Don Alvarado ardently demonstrates on Lili Damita in The Bridge of San Luis Rey (1929).

See no evil: watching the morals of movies

Hollywood's first censor—the Hays Office—coaxed and bullied movie makers in a crusade for pure films. Was Tarzan's mate wearing an indecent costume? Was a kiss too ardent? Was crime paying? Submitted scripts were combed for double entendres—even in marginal directions: "Filmy negligee" became plain "negligee." And a censor, after reading "From off-stage, we hear the scream of a naked woman," reportedly deleted "naked."

Off-screen scandals of several stars inspired the Motion Picture Producers of America to appoint Will Hays, a Presbyterian elder and former postmaster general, as morality czar in 1922. The Hays Office exercised some suasion over movie content until the 1930's, when Mae West provoked complaints with her swinging hips and sexy quips. In her first movie, *Night After Night* (1932), an admirer remarks, "Goodness, what beautiful diamonds." And she replies, "Goodness had nothing to do with it." Some feared that Hollywood would slip back to its spicy past. (A single scene in the 1920 film *Man, Woman, Marriage* displayed eight nude women.) The Legion of Decency was formed to pass judgment on films for Catholics. And Hollywood decided to enforce its previously voluntary production code so that "the sympathy of the audience shall never be thrown to the side of crime, wrong-doing, evil or sin." The code banned: "Excessive and lustful kissing, lustful embraces, suggestive postures and gestures." Profanity and "vulgar expression" were forbidden, as were *alley cat, bat,* or *broad* "applied to a woman" or *tom cat* to a man.

Other nations added prohibitions on movies they imported. English censors abhorred acts of violence—or a man and woman, including married couples, in a double bed. (To save on refilming bedroom scenes, Hollywood adopted twin beds.) Mussolini barred movies linking Italians and spaghetti for comic scenes. Mexico objected to outlaws who looked as if they came from south of the border.

When the mass audience deserted movies, many taboos vanished. And in 1968 the industry shifted from censoring to classifying. The ratings ranged from G ("suggested for general audiences") to X ("persons under 16 not admitted"). No censors kept Dustin Hoffman and Mia Farrow out of bed in *John and Mary* in 1969. It had been a long time since the days when Mia's mother had to worry about what she wore as Tarzan's mate.

individual popularity and recognition would bring. But when the producers at last allowed player credits on the screen, a wondrous phenomenon asserted itself: Merely by putting popular actors and actresses into a movie, no matter what the movie's quality, you could guarantee it would be profitable. Stars thus took some of the guesswork out of movie-making. It might be difficult to predict what new sensation would thrill the public, but when a star was hot you could reasonably predict for the short term (five, perhaps ten years) what his or her films would gross.

Players from the live stage—for example, Sarah Bernhardt and John and Ethel Barrymore (whose brother Lionel had not been too proud to work for Griffith in the early Biograph days)—now discovered there was much to be gained by working in movies, especially financially. Some actors also found out that the artificial styles they had developed to reach and move the last row of the balcony were ludicrous on screen. Success in movies usually went to young people like Lillian Gish, whose limited theatrical experience had not petrified into unbreakable habit. Young players learned that screen acting consisted largely of behaving in a natural manner, that you could speak volumes with your eyes or a gesture, that art here was all artlessness. Quite ordinary people, who were sometimes actually discovered, as legend would have it, on the drug store stool (Lana Turner *was* discovered there), proved to have some inborn ability to communicate through a camera's lens, while others, more gifted in the classical theatrical talents, were failures. The camera simply "likes" some people, director Howard Hawks has noted. "And the people it likes can't do any wrong."

In the 1920's, as the American film industry converted from the classic free-enterprise model (hundreds of small suppliers) to the more common 20th-century oligopolistic model (a handful of large suppliers), the master industrialists of the one-industry town of Hollywood became unduly self-censoring. They feared that the occasional visionary film would gum up what was turning out to be a smoothly functioning assembly line, regularly delivering an extremely narrow range of products to theaters (also in those days controlled by the studios—or was it vice versa?). They were rich enough and skillful enough to have been more experimental, to have indulged the more artistic whims of the talent they held under such tight control. Artistic possibilities were being explored in the expressionistic movies of Germany, the revolutionary spectacles of Russia, and the soberly probing psychological dramas of Sweden. The visions these films offered—to cite a notable example, Sergei Eisenstein's *Potemkin,* a story of the aborted 1905 revolution in Russia—were highly subjective, highly stylized, and, depending on your point of view, quite disturbing or quite stimulating. Some cinema purists believed this was the direction in which all film, even the benighted American product, must go. As they pointed out, without the dimension of sound the movies could not hope to move in the direction of realism.

There were, to be sure, some excellent American silent "art" films: *The Crowd,* a study of the frustrations of urban life by the most sophisticated silent director, King Vidor; Victor Seastrom's *The Wind;* Karl Brown's *Stark Love;* and the handcrafted work of the comedians, after Griffith possibly the greatest American innovators.

Charlie Chaplin's breakthrough as the most popular screen star about 1914 did much to pave the way for other comedians who mined the possibilities of surrealism. Chaplin's makeup, costume, and mannerisms were hardly lifelike, and neither were the predicaments in which he eventually found himself. But these predicaments usually began as perfectly sensible attempts to solve commonplace problems and took place in settings as familiar as the sidewalks in front of our houses (except for *The Gold Rush*). The same was true of the uncannily emotionless yet otherwise entirely recognizable Buster Keaton, routinely fouling up such tasks as building a boat or shoeing a horse.

And of Harold Lloyd, that extraordinarily ordinary looking youth who kept finding himself clinging to the ledges of skyscrapers or to some flimsy handhold on a runaway vehicle. What happened to them was fantastic, entirely unreal. But they themselves were as real as real could be—completely identifiable projections of the audience.

"Speech has been a success for thousands and thousands of years," John Barrymore is said to have remarked as the movies began to talk at the end of the 1920's. "And now they are testing it." Newsreel coverage of Lindbergh's triumphal return to America after his solo flight across the Atlantic proved sound's commercial potential. The same year, 1927, Warner Brothers created a sensation with *The Jazz Singer,* starring Al Jolson, a silent film save for music and a little dialogue. Hollywood, thrown into momentary panic, turned to Broadway for carloads of writers, directors, and players experienced with the spoken word. Cameras had to be housed in soundproof booths, inhibiting flexibility, so their whir would not be picked up by the microphone. Sound technicians temporarily eclipsed directors in importance.

Lillian Gish lamented that "the movies married sound instead of music." The rumor that John Gilbert's voice did not "mike" well ruined his career, though he probably could have survived the transition if Louis B. Mayer (the second M in M-G-M) had not wanted to use this excuse to rid himself of a blithe but troublesome spirit. Another leading man, John Bowers, committed suicide by walking into the ocean (providing the inspiration for a memorable scene in a later movie, *A Star Is Born*). Sight gags no longer sufficed for comedians; sound nearly drowned Buster Keaton and Harry Langdon, who was all but forgotten by the public until James Agee rescued his reputation in a famous essay on silent comics. But few real stars vanished from the screen because they could not meet the requirements of the added dimension.

Career and technical problems were temporary; the great permanent consequence of sound was a greater sense of realism. Speech produced a realistic rather than a purely romantic identification between movies and audience. Actors and actresses seemed more real in talkies and were cast in more realistic settings and situations; they were propelled in this direction by technology and the mood of the Depression, which began almost as sound was ushered in. Cagney as a fast-talking gangster in *The Public Enemy* (1931) seemed as real as life itself. So did Claudette Colbert and Clark Gable in the tacky tourist-court room they shared in *It Happened One Night* (1934).

Hollywood was soon at ease with sound. Stanley Kauffmann aptly described dialogue, especially as it was directed by Hawks, Cukor, Frank Capra, Preston Sturges, and others who came to the fore in the early years of talkies: "Every scene is played faster than necessary, including love scenes, as if the speed knob on the phonograph had been turned ahead slightly, and all the dialogue written in tight-packed wisecrackese which *sounds* like life but really is the 20th century American theater's equivalent of blank verse. For it is not realism but real speech distilled and heightened. . . . It is an American convention, an abstraction."

Alfred Hitchcock, a master of such suspense films as *North by Northwest* and *Psycho,* cared little if we emerged blinking into the light of the lobby and pointed out fallacies in the construction of one of his stories. What was it those German spies were after in *Notorious,* the Ingrid Bergman movie he made during World War II? Hitchcock suggested to his producer that they sought uranium 235 to make an atomic bomb. "Oh, that's a bit far-fetched," the producer answered. (Remember, this was pre-Hiroshima.) Hitchcock then suggested that industrial diamonds would do as well. He coined a name, "the macguffin," for the object the people of his films so passionately pursue. "The macguffin is the thing the spies are after, but the audience *doesn't* care. It could be the plans of a fort, the secret plans of an airplane engine. . . ."

"One hundred and fifty dollars—in gold"

Just as dashing Rhett Butler bid top price at an Atlanta charity ball for a dance with newly widowed Scarlett O'Hara, producer David O. Selznick spared no expense in filming *Gone With the Wind.* Margaret Mitchell's Civil War novel was "brought to the screen" in the best Hollywood style—and in the tradition of epics drawn from another best seller, the Bible. The final cost, about $4.2 million, included a two-year search for the perfect actress to play Scarlett and a $5,000 censorship fine so Rhett could say, "Frankly, my dear, I don't give a damn" when he walked out on her.

Selznick persevered through leading lady Vivien Leigh's makeup poisoning and leading man Clark Gable's threat to quit rather than cry when his role called for tears at his daughter's death. (He wept.)

At the Atlanta premiere, outside a theater rebuilt to resemble the plantation house Twelve Oaks, 150,000 cheered the stars. One paper called it "the most important event since Sherman marched to the sea." In worldwide release since 1939, GWTW has earned $841 million (in 1987 dollars), proving Selznick's belief that Hollywood style is pure gold.

Selling escapism in 80-minute packages

For a quarter—or less when specials were on—you could buy admission to Hollywood's make-believe and forget the Depression outside theater doors. And Americans did. By the late 1930's about 17,000 movie houses, some showing as many as 400 films a year, were playing to 85 million people a week.

To meet the demand, Hollywood ground out a smorgasbord: swashbucklers, crime movies, comedies, films based on literary classics. George Arliss played so many biographical roles teachers worried lest students grow up thinking all historical figures looked

like him. Walt Disney produced his first full-length cartoon, *Snow White,* with the help of 570 artists. Other artists made Boris Karloff 18 inches taller and 60 pounds heavier for his role in *Frankenstein.* And wizardry with photographs of a pliable, 18-inch model of rubber and sponge, superimposed on shots of buildings, jungle, and people, created the beast charmed by beauty, *King Kong.*

Movie hits brought follow-ups. Did fans like *Charlie Chan?* Hollywood turned out 46 more. Was lovable *Andy Hardy* a smash? Two decades saw another 15. *Frankenstein* had sons, daughters, ghosts. In tough times escapism, not social comment, was box office.

Savoring the stills: King Kong (1933) protects Fay Wray from an ornery pterodactyl. Errol Flynn (at right), in title role in The Adventures of Robin Hood *(1938), crosses swords with villainous Basil Rathbone. Judy Garland and Mickey Rooney sip sodas in* Love Finds Andy Hardy *(1938). Charlie Chan (Sidney Toler) and No. 1 son (Victor Sen Yung) examine a gun with Chief Souto (Harold Huber) in* Charlie Chan in Rio *(1941). Dwight Frye frightens monstrous Boris Karloff in* Frankenstein *(1931). And Spencer Tracy, playing a vielle, sings a sea chanty to young Freddie Bartholomew in* Captains Courageous *(1937).*

What Hollywood was after in its golden years was "a little magic," to borrow a phrase from Vincente Minnelli, director of such musicals as *An American in Paris* and *Meet Me in St. Louis.* "If you get involved and if the picture haunts you a little bit afterwards, then you have created a little magic." Directors nearly always sought a wide audience. Raoul Walsh admitted to inserting scenes "for my own gratification," but mostly he sought to "play for the public, because that's what kept us alive." Most directors were content to put a new twist on one of the well-established formats, a new wrinkle on a character or a situation; familiarity with these conventions bred contempt in neither creators nor audience. The directors many of us have come to admire most in retrospect—the "action" directors like Walsh (*High Sierra, They Died with Their Boots On*) and Hawks (*The Dawn Patrol, Red River*)—made films which, as critic Manny Farber noted, were not "experimental, liberal, slick, spectacular, low-budget, epical, improving, or flagrantly

commercial. . . ." These men accepted "the role of hack," he said, so they could "involve themselves with expedience and tough-guy insight in all types of action. . . . The important thing is not so much the banal-seeming journeys to nowhere that make up the stories, but the tunneling that goes on inside the classic Western-gangster incidents and stock hoodlum-dogface-cowboy types."

Gangster movies, for example, traditionally depicted hoodlum heroes as the products of flawed society. When that vein played out, Walsh's marvelous *White Heat* gave us our first psychopathic mobster, a melodramatically malevolent example of Freudian theory in antisocial action. *The Gunfighter,* instead of presenting Gregory Peck as just another fast draw, made him a killer who wanted to quit—but could not because every punk in a bar was determined to test him. One could endlessly extend the list of tunneling activity, especially as the movies of the late 1940's searched desperately for new gimmicks to compete with television's product, which was basically B-picture material from the past.

But always the movie makers sought the "reality beyond convention," sought to combine, as Edgar Morin, a French student of mass psychology, put it, "the exceptional with the ordinary, the ideal and the everyday, ever more intimately and diversely." This permitted—no, encouraged—the public to identify with the heroes and heroines of film, to believe that the situations in which they found themselves actually mirrored life and to believe that life might sometimes be as pleasingly, idealistically, and morally resolved as the movies were. In isolated scenes, in a bit of business, a snatch of dialogue, a sudden revelation in characterization, we knew we were somehow involved with recognizable human truths. What we did not realize until too late was that those shadows on the screen were making a vast nation into a community, that our feelings for "all that nonsense" bound us together then and, indeed, bind some of us together now through an intense, shared memory—far richer than the term "nostalgia" signifies.

The movies, in their great days, were only occasionally art as it is traditionally defined, but they were much less often the trash that many people insisted they were. They were something like life, yet something better, something that weekly reaffirmed its

Fans surged to the fore in Hollywood's hey-day. They strained at the barricades at the premieres; they could make or break stars at the box office. They relished fan magazines' mild disclosures—and in letters to their favorites asked for more: Greta Garbo's shoe size (6AA), Joan Crawford's bust size (37). And often they wrote for souvenirs, such as the wishbone of Fred Astaire's Christmas turkey.

best possibilities and let all of us share values — of right and wrong, of truth and beauty.

And now the Great Movie Audience has broken up. In 1948 some 3.4 billion tickets were sold at the nation's box offices; in the 1960's the number of admissions stabilized at about 1 billion. Two-thirds of the old crowd wandered off somewhere, to return for only a few films, perhaps two or three a year — *The Sound of Music, The Godfather, The Exorcist* — which promised something like the old-fashioned combination of spectacle and intimacy, novelty and tradition, reality and romance, delivered under some sort of high emotional pressure. For the most part the modern movies are big, dumb, and slow — over-rich fare for an over-rich society, lacking the cheeky qualities that made the films of the '30's and '40's so pleasurable.

We cannot blame the situation entirely on television or the growth of other competing leisure-time industries. We cannot even blame it entirely on the temper of our times. The fact is that the people who made movies began, in the panic that followed the first great defections of their audience, to believe their critics — which was easy enough to do, for Hollywood has rarely known, really known, what it was doing. The old industrial system of production was phased out; with demand cut by two-thirds, there was no longer a need for it. Grown fat and lazy off the profits of the war era, when any movie could make money, Hollywood was ill-prepared to adjust to changing times. Instead of seeking new conventions which generally would be embraced by a large audience — or at least trying seriously to update the old ones — the industry offered to the mass audience such tired and inept pastiches of the original as *Airport* and *Love Story.* A knack had been lost.

We do have powerful examples of film art that appeal not to the masses but to an elite audience; *Five Easy Pieces* is a good example. We also have been given movies that invited us to wallow masochistically in our sense of individual alienation from the community *(Midnight Cowboy),* which reflected our galloping urban paranoia *(Death Wish),* and which played on the great schisms between races *(Super Fly)* and classes and age groups. These films exacerbated our wounds; they did not heal them. They were part of our problem, not part of our salvation. Some few productions from the new generation of movie makers, such as *A Woman Under the Influence,* were interesting and intense, revealing aspects of our life and times that the old films could not help us penetrate. In Mel Brooks and Woody Allen we discovered highly individual comic talents to rank with, say, W. C. Fields and the Marx Brothers. But most new movies "interest" us without really involving us — or without making us feel sanguine as we warily approach the box office the next time we decide to take a flyer on a film.

The trouble is, as Farber once said, that movies aren't movies any more. The conventions that sustained them, the conventions that were responsible for the "movie-ness" of movies, that differentiated them from all other forms of art and entertainment, have disappeared. In tone, in style, in the narrowness of their appeal, they are too often like every other art form in the waning years of the 20th century: confused, spiritless, depressing, and for the most part powerless to induce the emotional response, the sheer pleasure, that they once induced at some level for everyone. They have none of the sudden giddy spells of a Busby Berkeley or Vincente Minnelli musical, none of the sudden bursts of exquisitely choreographed action once provided by a Hawks or a Walsh, not even the honestly felt, if crudely expressed, emotion of the great weepers like *Now, Voyager* — can anyone remember the last time he or she cried at a movie? And they don't have the thrills, the warmth, the sheer silly good feeling about ourselves, our fellow patrons, and the medium itself that once came naturally in the comforting darkness. The movies have passed into history. We are left to live uneasily, touched by pangs of nostalgic longing, with something called film.

In war, patriotism writes the scripts

Within two months of the Japanese attack on Pearl Harbor, Hollywood fired the first salvos of its own counteroffensive, sending Barry Nelson off to battle in *A Yank on the Burma Road.* As the barrage continued, films portrayed the face of the enemy: the Japanese in *Bombs Over Burma* (above), Nazis in *Berlin Correspondent* (opposite).

The quickie war-movie tradition went back to 1897. Within hours after the United States declared war on Spain, two enterprising film makers cranked out a flickering one-reeler, *Tearing Down the Spanish Flag.*

World War I audiences sat through *The Kaiser — Beast of Berlin, To Hell with the Kaiser,* and *A Little Patriot,* in which child star Baby Peggy encouraged fellow moppets to spit on daddies who were slackers. Between wars, *Wings,* a 1927 epic of World War I aerial dogfights, became the first movie to win an Academy Award; an anti-war film, *All Quiet on the Western Front,* won in 1930.

Donald Duck *(Der Fuehrer's Face)* and Bugs Bunny *(Herr Meets Hare)* enlisted in World War II. And escaped convicts in *Seven Miles from Alcatraz* risked recapture to foil the Nazis, explaining, "We may be rats, crooks, and murderers — but we're Americans!"

I WANT YOU
FOR U.S. ARMY
NEAREST RECRUITING STATION

JAMES MONTGOMERY FLAGG

On the Home front

Frank Freidel

Twice in 25 years the United States sent its sons overseas to fight in global conflicts. In World War I, James Montgomery Flagg's stern-visaged Uncle Sam pointed a judgmental finger from posters and inspired young men to line up at recruiting offices. In the wide-brimmed campaign hat, doughboys sailed to "kick the Kaiser." A generation later, in the visored cap of World War II, GIs (for Government Issue) marched off to battle the Axis of Hitler, Tojo, and Il Duce.

World War II borrowed a phrase from World War I — "home front," the battleground for civilians who stayed behind. Some became Civilian Defense workers, a white helmet their symbol of authority. They learned first aid, got everybody off the streets in air-raid drills, and patrolled the night during test "blackouts," making sure no light showed around shrouded windows and doors. Some civilians cheered up lonesome GIs at USO (United Service Organization) centers. And many gave a part of themselves: More than 13 million pints of blood were collected by that old-timer from World War I, the Red Cross.

Americans entered the first World War with the idealistic fervor of medieval Crusaders setting forth to redeem Jerusalem. They swept aside dissenters as unpatriotic and extolled sacrifice to attain victory. Their enthusiasm echoed the cheering that had swept Europe when war broke out between France and Germany in August 1914. Three years of holocaust had burned out the optimism there, but now it flared anew in the United States.

A soft spring rain was falling the evening of April 2, 1917, when President Woodrow Wilson arrived at the Capitol to ask Congress to pass a war resolution against Germany. A cavalry escort shielded him from the crowds of both enthusiastic supporters and pacifist demonstrators. It was a noble address, holding forth the promise that American intervention would transform the deadlock in Europe into a war to make the world safe for democracy. A war to end war, it would be called.

For the American nation the year and a half of participation in the conflict created an era of intense patriotic display. Ellen Maury Slayden, pacifist wife of a Texas congressman, noted that Washington, D. C., was flaming with flags even before the declaration of war on April 6, and that the clergy were afire with war spirit. "The churches are bedizened with flags over the doors, in the vestibule, the chancel, and carried in the processional. . . ." Two young Frenchwomen, Madeleine and Jacqueline de Bryas, arriving in New York from a somber, blacked-out Paris to speak at war rallies through the summer of 1918, were dazzled by the profusion of bunting, banners, and posters: GIVE TILL IT HURTS . . . FIGHT THE HUNS . . . PERSHING'S CRUSADERS. "Fifth Avenue looked so bright under its gay-colored flags," they wrote, "that the town seemed decked out as if for some great victory."

Few people dreamed at the time Congress voted war — and a blank check to wage it — how massive American intervention would be or how much the nation would be changed. Many visualized little more than sending additional supplies to the Allies and a naval war against *Unterseeboots* — German U-boats. If an army went overseas, people thought it would be voluntary, as in the Spanish-American War; former President Theodore Roosevelt, though aging and ill, vainly sought permission to lead a volunteer force as he had in Cuba. But the Allies grew so desperate, not only for ships and supplies but also for fighting men, that the United States resorted to conscription to raise an army of millions under Gen. John J. (Black Jack) Pershing. When the draft bill was debated in Congress, Speaker of the House Champ Clark protested that in his state of Missouri people regarded a conscript as little better than a convict. But the bill went through. The nation mobilized.

The figures that the Wilson administration began to write on Congress's blank check seemed staggering. The government built an army that eventually totalled four million. The navy numbered 600,000 more, and the Marine Corps nearly 80,000. Cantonments were hastily thrown together to turn civilians into soldiers. All-out production went into building a "bridge of ships" to carry these men, together with munitions and food for the Allies, across the submarine-infested Atlantic. Cargo ships were needed to replace heavy losses to the British merchant fleet, and the navy required squadrons of escort vessels for convoy duty. By the end of the war, U. S. ship production had reached ten million tons. The greatest of the shipyards, at Hog Island near Philadelphia, thrilled the De Bryas sisters, who were taken to the top of a fire lookout tower to gaze over expansive shipways where 23,000 workers labored.

Over-all war production figures ran spectacularly high, due in part to Liberty Loan rallies at factories that helped intensify workers' pride in a historic achievement—the greatest industrial output the world had ever known. When Jacqueline de Bryas spoke before 7,000 workers at a plant in Chester, Pennsylvania, the men sang the "Marseillaise," the French national anthem, and shook her hands so often that her light-colored gloves turned black. The workers apologized, but she replied gaily, "It will seem as if I, also, were making munitions for the boys."

To meet the quotas of manpower, munitions, and food, the government enlisted the entire economy. Volunteer efforts proved enormous, but the government could not trust to voluntarism alone. So Congress conferred wide powers upon the administration, which established war agencies. Soon there was a War Industries Board, a Fuel Administration, a Food Administration, and a War Labor Board. The Railroad Administration leased all the railroads and ran them as a single line. Altogether, some 5,000 war agencies, large and small, directed American economic activity. Personnel came from law offices, college faculties, and industry; a number of executives took leave of absence from their companies and served for a dollar a year. Many young staff members were women, and hundreds flocked to Washington from all over the country.

Mrs. Slayden was little impressed with any of them, scoffing at the professors and quoting newspapers as saying that the dollar-a-year men were "earning fully 99 cts. of it." As for the government girls, in the fall of 1918 she helped care for a number of them convalescing from the influenza then ravaging the globe. They ranged from "illiterate little shop girls to graduates of Smith and Wellesley," and she tried to convince them that their duty was to leave Washington and go home. Her tart disapproval of all those serving the government cast suspicion over her and her husband.

In its total war effort, the Wilson administration launched a vigorous mobilization of the minds of the American people. The Committee on Public Information turned out patriotic press releases and pamphlets by the millions, and from a roster of 75,000 provided speakers for every occasion. These speakers, called "Four-Minute Men," seldom achieved the brevity their title implied but did much to stimulate public enthusiasm. Excitement reached a crescendo during the Liberty Loan drives. At a motion-picture show, the touring De Bryas sisters were diverted by a Four-Minute Man who offered to punch a hole in his new straw hat if someone would subscribe to a thousand-dollar bond. " 'A thousand,' shouted a man's voice from the balcony. And the speaker . . . thrust his closed fist vigorously through the crown of his straw hat, shooting it straight toward the generous subscriber."

War frenzy, fed by anti-German phobia, carried over into punishment of those who were thought to be disloyal. Congress and state legislatures passed harsh statutes,

"We shall fight . . . for democracy"

President Wilson's call to arms in April 1917 captured the spirit of a nation unprepared for total war. Everyone seemed to be seized by patriotic fervor. Boy Scouts paraded Old Glory down New York's Fifth Avenue; George M. Cohan wrote his pulse-quickening "Over There" to spread the word that "the Yanks are coming"—and 24-year-old Norman Rockwell illustrated the sheet-music cover. Movie celebrities, like Douglas Fairbanks standing under the benevolent hand of George Washington on Wall Street, exhorted huge rallies to buy Liberty Loan bonds. The drives reaped some $21 billion.

The Selective Service Act, passed May 18, registered men 21 to 30, later reached those 18 to 45, and eventually drafted nearly three million. It was a well-groomed army. Clean faces, General Pershing believed, boosted morale, and for the first time in U. S. history soldiers were issued razors. Early inductees had to drill with broomsticks until America's growing war machine supplied the first of three million rifles. Meanwhile, the vanguard sailed to France. In Paris on July 4, 1917, beside the grave of the French hero of the American Revolution, a Pershing aide, Col. C. E. Stanton, uttered the stirring words, "Lafayette, we are here!"

At home, civilians abstained from wheat on Mondays and Wednesdays, all meat on Tuesdays, and pork on Thursdays and Saturdays. Some swore off beer because many brewers had German names; sauerkraut became "liberty cabbage," hamburger "Salisbury steak," and dachshunds "liberty pups."

Heatless Mondays saved coal. As an energy-conserving measure, the nation adopted daylight-saving time, an idea recommended by Benjamin Franklin 150 years earlier.

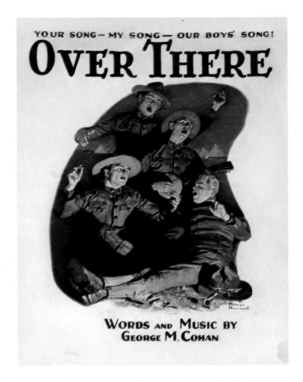

YOUR SONG—MY SONG—OUR BOYS' SONG!

OVER THERE

WORDS AND MUSIC BY
GEORGE M. COHAN

The war to end war comes to an end

A limping army aviator and friends parade in New York City on November 11, 1918, the first Armistice Day (now celebrated as Veterans Day). Of the two million men who sailed to France, 53,000 died in combat and 204,000 were wounded. Rehabilitation of the maimed led to advances in plastic surgery.

Total commitment at home by women and children helped keep the casualty count from going higher. Girl Scouts (below) collected peach stones; when heated and turned into charcoal, the pits went into gas-mask filters. Women assembled bombs in defense plants, learned to repair cars, carried the mail, directed traffic, and worked as trolley conductors. The navy recruited 11,000 women yeomen for shore duty, some as wireless operators; one of the women opposite wears the greatcoat and campaign hat of a Marinette, one of 269 enlisted to serve as stenographers and clerks in the Marine Corps.

And then it was over. Or was it? President Wilson, addressing Congress on November 11, announced: "Armed imperialism . . . is at an end. . . . Who will now seek to revive it?" Only ten months later in Bavaria, the small German Workers Party attracted a bitter war veteran named Adolf Hitler. In 1921 he took over the party, changed its name, and unleashed Nazism on the world.

YOU SAVE PEACH SEEDS THEY WILL SAVE SOLDIERS LIVES

and there were more than 1,500 arrests for making seditious remarks. Members of the radical Industrial Workers of the World suffered both in the courts and at the hands of mobs. And a telegram from President Wilson stating that Democratic Representative James L. Slayden had not "given support to the administration" led Slayden, despite his 22 years in Congress, to withdraw from the 1918 election.

For many Americans, however, the war brought benefits as well as problems. There was full employment and high wages. Farmers enjoyed a 25 percent jump in real income; they sold their mules to the army and plowed up pastures with their new tractors. Income of workers in industry, transportation, and mining climbed 20 percent. Moreover, the demand for workers, made more acute since the war had cut off immigration from Europe, for the first time provided opportunities in Northern factories for large numbers of blacks from the South. Thousands made their way north where, the Negro newspaper *Chicago Defender* told them, a man could be a man. They suffered from discrimination and endured race riots, but they found a higher standard of living.

For women especially, the war brought new opportunities. Their energetic efforts at doing a man's work helped make ridiculous the assertion that their only rightful realm was the home and that they must be sheltered from the ballot. By the end of the war, women were winning their long struggle for suffrage. "The greatest thing that came out of the war," said Carrie Chapman Catt, a leader in the struggle for passage of the 19th Amendment, "was the emancipation of women, for which no man fought."

In the aftermath of the Armistice on November 11, 1918, the American people wished to return as rapidly as possible to their prewar way of life. They were weary of government restrictions and tired of 18 months of patriotic exhortations. But everyday life would never entirely get back to earlier patterns. Women's skirts, shortened by wartime directives to save cloth, grew even shorter. Government regulations had taken the steel out of corsets, and soon corsets all but disappeared. The image of doughboys in the trenches relaxing with a smoke gave a new popularity to cigarettes. To conserve grain, a restriction had been placed on alcoholic beverages — a measure to be followed after the war by Prohibition.

Removal of wartime controls brought rising prices and sudden unemployment. White-collar workers and others whose incomes had not gone up felt the double pinch of higher taxes and the rising cost of living. In the 12 months after July 1, 1917, prices rose 17 percent. Then the ending of the war terminated government industrial contracts just as millions of servicemen poured back into the labor market.

The war brought major changes as well as many small alterations in the American way of life. It demonstrated the enormous potential productivity of the United States and the way in which that productivity could improve living conditions through more buying power. Government supervision had been repugnant, but it had worked. In future times of crisis, whether depression at home or threats from abroad, there would be pressure to return to federal controls like those of 1917-18.

Toward other nations there continued a feeling of responsibility that took the form of widespread relief to famine-stricken areas. Then disillusionment became predominant — a feeling that the leaders of Western Europe were self-serving, and that Eastern Europe carried the threat of Bolshevism. The Senate rejected U. S. membership in the ill-fated League of Nations and thus rejected the assumption of responsibilities for collective international security.

America's isolationist interlude would last little more than a score of years. Ultimately, what came out of the experience on the home front in World War I was the ideal of a better standard of living and of greater opportunities for all. After World War II, America would try to extend that ideal to the rest of the world. *(continued on page 406)*

Interlude: the bittersweet decades

Over here, over here . . . surely a smiling land of opportunity beckoned its heroes. The mood turned stale while welcoming cheers still hung in the air. Jobless veterans found war workers in silk shirts, Jack Dempsey shielded from the draft in shipyard jobs. On July 4, 1919, Dempsey battered Jess Willard to become heavyweight champion of the world.

The ol' home town? Stifling, wrote Sinclair Lewis in *Main Street*, a 1920 best seller. Small-town America withered his worldly heroine: "When Carol had walked for thirty-two minutes she had completely covered the town . . . and she stood at the corner of Main Street and Washington Avenue and despaired."

With prices soaring and wages lagging, some four million workers struck in 1919. When Boston police walked out, looters panicked the city; armed war veterans guarded the streets. The strikers lost. Among the winners: Massachusetts Governor Calvin Coolidge, hailed for his antistrike stance. A year later he won the Vice Presidency.

Race riots wracked 26 cities. And the Ku Klux Klan, buried along with Civil War hatreds, was back. Reborn in 1915—the year the film *The Birth of a Nation* exalted the old Klansmen—the Klan spread racism and xenophobia far beyond the South. Hooded Klansmen here flaunt the colors to celebrate July Fourth in Long Branch, New Jersey. "Many a bum show," George M. Cohan once noted, "is saved by the American flag."

Bolshevism roused fear. Anarchists, foes of all government, took to violence—"propaganda by the deed." At Attorney General A. Mitchell Palmer's home a bomber blew himself up in 1919; pieces of him fell on the nearby lawn of Assistant Secretary of the Navy Franklin Roosevelt. In 1920, while Palmer and young J. Edgar Hoover rounded up "Reds," Nicola Sacco and Bartolomeo Vanzetti were accused of a robbery murder in Massachusetts. The case dragged on for seven years; then they died in the electric chair. To the trial judge the two were "anarchist bastards." To millions the "good shoemaker and . . . poor fish peddler" became martyrs of the working class, their plight a damper on the decade that roared with gaiety.

Gopher Prairie: small town, small minds—and mighty proud of it

Smiling Chicago steelworkers grew bitter as their strike failed.

The Passion of Sacco and Vanzetti, portrayed by artist Ben Shahn

Flapper era frees the "new woman"

Raccoon coat and snug-fitting cloche hat were the "bee's knees."

A Pulitzer Prize Novel

SO BIG
EDNA FERBER

Best-selling novel of prairie life garnered fiction honors in 1925.

Hemlines rose, necklines plunged. Brassieres were in, corsets fading fast. The waistline was still slender. And so was everything else. The hourglass had turned into a boyish stick figure —when it wasn't hidden in a fashionable raccoon coat. Garter buttons drew men's eyes to knee caps—and rolled, flesh-colored silk stockings. The satin "Betty Boop" button (right) displayed the painted lips and lashes associated with the whoopee years.

Yet there was more than met the eye in the finger-snapping, hip-waggling insouciance of the devil-may-care era of the flapper (a young woman who kicked off constraints). "Nice" girls were smoking, drinking, and even necking. One of F. Scott Fitzgerald's heroines asserted, "I've kissed dozens of men. I suppose I'll kiss dozens more." Guardians of morals lashed out at flappers who danced "cheek-to-cheek and loin-to-loin with their boyfriends."

In a decade obsessed by consumer goods, advertising companies aimed campaigns at women. The cosmetics industry netted $141 million in 1925; between 1918 and 1928 cigarette production doubled. In New York City, women in 1929 puffed "torches of freedom" on Fifth Avenue to launch smoking in public.

Though women had voted in Wyoming since 1869, the 19th Amendment enfranchised women across the land. Miriam (Ma) Ferguson became governor of Texas in 1925; Margaret Sanger preached birth control; and temperance crusaders battled bathtub gin and hip flasks. Edna St. Vincent Millay, one of many perceptive emerging writers, heralded flaming youth with a confession:

My candle burns at both ends;
It will not last the night;
But ah, my foes, and oh, my friends—
It gives a lovely light!

John Held's cover-girl flapper sways to the beat of American-born jazz. The saxophone, Jazz Age symbol, imitated "the yowl of a cat, the moo of a cow . . . a yawn, a grunt, a belch." The U. S. Navy helped spread this "folk music of the machine age": After navy pressure closed Storyville, New Orleans' red-light district, as a 1917 war measure, black jazzmen drifted up the Mississippi, speeding the migration that had already begun.

Chicago police fight "indecent exposure" in 1922—the year after 16-year-old Margaret Gorman became the first Miss America.

In 1920, for the first time, all women could vote in a Presidential election.

"I do"

LUCKY STRIKE CIGARETTES

"It's toasted"

Advertising makes a subtle pitch to the woman smoker.

"The saloon is as dead as slavery!"

Giddy with victory, enemies of Demon Rum hailed the day in January 1920 when the 18th Amendment to the Constitution took effect, prohibiting liquor traffic across the land. To rural preacher, feminist reformer, and sober industrialist, a dry nation would tighten family bonds, purify sinful cities, reduce absenteeism on the job. But neither law nor moral suasion could quench a hard thirst.

Soon rumrunners threshed coastal waters; contraband poured down from Canada by truck and boat. "You cannot keep liquor from dripping through a dotted line," said a former federal agent. Illegal stills sprouted like weeds; home brewing revived. The law allowed wine-making for personal use; in six years California grape growers increased their acreage some 700 percent. Grape concentrate was sold in bricks—along with a warning against following the accompanying instructions for making wine! Gunmen warred for bootlegging territories worth millions; scarcely a week went by in Chicago without a gangland killing. Licensed saloons gave way to illegal speakeasies, where even top-hat clientele waited for peephole identification.

With Utah's vote on December 5, 1933, the 21st Amendment was ratified, repealing the 18th. The "Noble Experiment" was over.

Gen. Smedley Butler won battles in Philadelphia but lost the war.

Do-it-yourself vintners turned grape concentrate into wine.

Prohibition campaign buttons vied for voters' hearts and minds.

USE A LITTLE WINE FOR THY STOMACH'S SAKE
I TIMOTHY 5th CHAPTER 23rd VERSE

Wet paraders in New York bolster their cause with a Bible quote.

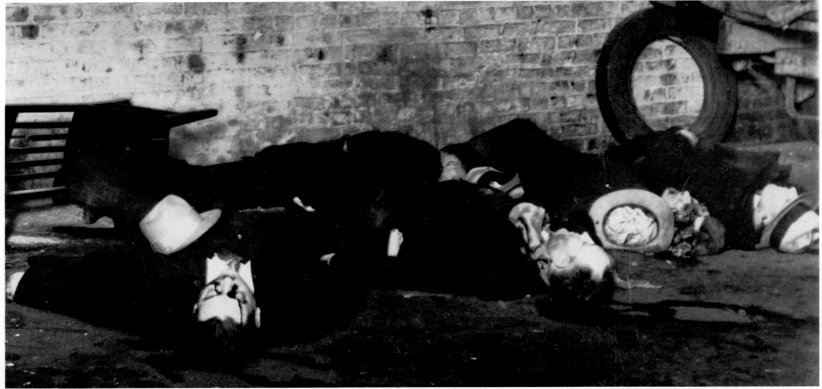

St. Valentine's Day, 1929: Machine-gunned mobsters sprawl on a garage floor. Seven died in the massacre, climax of Chicago's gang wars. The winner: "Scarface" Al Capone, king of bootleggers.

"The will to worship never flags"

"The typical American . . . is led by cheer leaders, press agents, wordmongers, up-lifters," sneered H. L. Mencken in 1922. Weary of Great Causes, the nation took up a succession of small ones, even found a pedestal for iconoclasts like Mencken who hacked away at *boobus Americanus* and his idols.

The arts of ballyhoo puffed and spangled each passing fad. Edward L. Bernays, a pioneer of public relations, came to see himself as a "creator of events." The flicker of lime-light could catch English Channel swimmers, visiting royalty, marathon dancers, lurid crimes, or the discoverers of King Tut's tomb. In Baltimore, Alvin "Shipwreck" Kelly sat on a flagpole for 23 days, seven hours, and the public had a new record to cheer.

White-robed Aimee Semple McPherson spread the Gospel according to Hollywood; in a church topped by a brilliant cross visible for 50 miles, storm-tossed virgins were saved by Sister Aimee while a brass band blared. In 1926 she vanished for a month. Kidnaped, she said; a lovers' romp, the evidence revealed. Headlines echoed her fall from grace.

Fundamentalism suffered even more at the "monkey trial" of 1925, a test of Tennessee's ban on the teaching of evolution. In the back-woods town of Dayton, William Jennings Bryan's faith in the literal truth of Scripture underwent a withering assault by the great trial lawyer Clarence Darrow. Bryan, three times a Democratic candidate for President, died a week later, his wounds still fresh.

New styles of journalism sharpened the daily drama for a larger audience than ever before. The tabloid *New York Daily News,* born in 1919, promised a handy size for sub-way straphangers, short stories, "the best and newest pictures." Soon it outsold every paper in the land. In 1928 a photographer strapped a camera to his leg and snapped the execution of Ruth Snyder, killer of her spouse; the *News* sold 150,000 extra copies.

On May 21, 1927, "something bright and alien flashed across the sky"—a simple deed of courage and meaning. When Charles A. Lindbergh returned after the first transatlantic solo flight, New York went wild. (He sits hat-less in the lead car.) The nation showered him with love; the press stalked his every step. From an authentic American hero, he became, reluctantly, a media celebrity—"a person," Daniel J. Boorstin has written, "who is known for his well-knowness."

Pole sitter Kelly lured crowds to theaters, hotels; disk, stirrups steadied him.

"World's most pulchritudinous evangelist": Aimee in Los Angeles

"The most remarkable exclusive": Ruth Snyder dies in Sing Sing.

"To protect the word of God": Bryan preps for the monkey trial.

Two-a-day: "Hello, audience!"

Al Jolson in blackface, on bended knee . . . theatergoers everywhere knew that pose, that big voice full of "pathos and soft slurring tones." Now, in 1927, they saw him—and *heard* him—on film. Ending one song, he ad-libbed, "Wait a minute! You ain't heard nothin' yet!" He was right. The 291 words of synchronized dialogue in *The Jazz Singer* were the first drops of a storm that never stopped. In the deluge, vaudeville, battered by silent movies and radio, went down, bobbed briefly in the '40's, and finally sank. By midcentury, live vaudeville—the mix of singers, dancers, comics, jugglers, leaping dogs, fighters—lay in the nation's memory bin beside the gas lamp and the horse and buggy.

Vaudeville had enjoyed a glorious run. It had come out of the "dime museums" of the late 1800's with their freaks and pickled fetuses, out of minstrel and medicine shows, its name somehow derived from the satiric *vau-de-vire* songs sung in the 15th century in Normandy's valley of Vire. From the first, vaudeville aimed at "straight, clean, variety"—family fare—though the box-office lure of a sizzling Salome dancer tempted many an impresario. By the turn of the century, pioneer B. F. Keith booked acts for 400 theaters east of Chicago; Martin Beck's Orpheum Circuit controlled two-a-days (matinee and evening shows) west to California. Into the big time Beck brought Harry Houdini, King of Handcuffs. Though hidden keys often freed him, his wizardry remains a wonder. "Jailed" naked, he escaped. Chained, he dove from a plane into a river—and lived.

Clumping onstage in 1905 on a horse shod in felt, Will Rogers twirled his lariat into top-banana billing. But it was that Oklahoma drawl, twitting high-and-mighty pols, that made him a revered folk philosopher. Will claimed he never met a man he didn't like, including W. C. Fields, who once said of him, "I'll bet a hundred dollars he talks just like anybody else when he gets home." For a decade Rogers graced the Ziegfeld *Follies;* his last stint in 1925 capped 20 years in New York. Fabulous Florenz Ziegfeld tolerated comics and loved the chorus line. *Show Boat* in 1927 blended his "glorified girls" with Jerome Kern's score and Edna Ferber's story. By then Broadway had bid goodbye to the schmaltz and blarney of *Abie's Irish Rose* after a record run of 2,327 performances. And Wall Street was about to lay an egg.

Young Houdini: A locksmith apprenticeship unlocked an art.

Horseplay from the '25 Follies: Will Rogers ropes Ray Dooley.

Star-crossed lovers of Abie's Irish Rose *held Broadway's endurance record until* Tobacco Road *came along in 1933.*

Show Boat *gave the medium of musical comedy the new message of a serious theme. The haunting "Ah gits weary . . ." of "Ol' Man River" lingers on.*

Al Jolson's "voice with a tear" was joined to film in The Jazz Singer—*and show business was never again the same.*

"Advanced Vaudeville" filled the bill with top-flight talent.

"What's the meaning in these faces...?"

Suddenly it soured—the Jazz Age, the Roaring Twenties, Coolidge Prosperity. The most exciting of all the fun and games was the first to end. Anyone could play: With a little cash and a lot of credit you bought shares in a company, and you waited for the stock to rise. Then you could cash in. But the factories were humming; everybody was bullish on America. Who could resist such a game?

"Black Thursday"—October 24, 1929—popped the bubble; stock values shrank by billions. Wall Street panicked. Factories closed. Banks failed. Increasing millions lost jobs, homes, farms. What to do? You could sell apples on the street. You could line up for a handout of bread, soup, a night's lodging, the rumor of a job. (In 1931 Communist Russia advertised 6,000 skilled jobs; 100,000 Americans applied.) You could hop a freight train and ride to—where? Or, in this land bulging with food, you could starve.

There were murmurings of revolution. Poet Florence Converse studied the grim faces— "Full of eyes that will not meet"—for signs of a spark. "It needs but one," she warned:

> "One to start a funeral pyre,
> One to cleanse a world by fire."

STOCK PRICES SLUMP $14,000,000,000 IN NATION-WIDE STAMPEDE TO UNLOAD; BANKERS TO SUPPORT MARKET TODAY

Otto Soglow cartooned Wall Street's plunge in October 1929. Reginald Marsh etched the aftermath in "Bread Line" (upper).

Faces of want, from sidewalks of New York to San Francisco (right), where Dorothea Lange recorded "White Angel Breadline."

"Families . . . dusted out, tractored out"

The furrowed brow of a barren hill, the farmer bowed in defeat—to industrial depression was joined the retribution of exhausted land. On baked Southern slopes gullying streams ran red with silt. On dry Western plains a decade or more of boom-time sod-busting for wheat unbound the soil; drought and wind brought in the bitter harvest. In 1933 "black blizzards" spilled Dakota farms on Chicago, on Albany. Dunes drifted across Oklahoma; a Dust Bowl spread across the heartland, from Texas to Canada.

And then, wrote John Steinbeck, "the long staring silence that had gone out to the fields, went now to the roads, to the distance, to the West. . . . from Kansas, Oklahoma, Texas, New Mexico; from Nevada and Arkansas families, tribes, dusted out. . . . They streamed over the mountains, hungry and restless—restless as ants, scurrying to find work to do—to lift, to push, to pull, to pick, to cut—anything, any burden to bear, for food." By the tens of thousands the Okies poured into California, bedsprings and babies bouncing on groaning jalopies, to become migrant laborers, northing with the harvest season from California's Imperial Valley to the apple orchards of Washington.

In Iowa farmers burned grain for fuel; it cost less than coal. In South Dakota a county elevator offered *"Minus* three cents a bushel" for corn. When milk went down to a penny a pint, New York dairymen dumped it. A newspaperman heard of woodsmen torching forests in Washington State to get work as fire fighters. In Seattle women scavenged garbage heaps beside a market. In Oregon buzzards feasted on slaughtered sheep.

For more than three years Herbert Hoover presided over the spreading misery and took the brunt of public wrath. He had succored victims of the Boxer Rebellion in China, fed starving Belgians in World War I, fought famine in postwar Europe and the ravages of Mississippi floods in 1927. Now, in the climactic challenge of his life, he was shackled by principle: The "spirit of charity and mutual self-help" must relieve America's suffering. He would unlock the federal treasury only as a "last resort." So the epithets grew: The homeless clustered in shacktowns—"Hoovervilles"; they slept under newspapers—"Hoover blankets"; Texans ate armadillos—"Hoover hogs." He was already a defeated man when the people resorted to the polls.

Iowa Christmas, 1936: Children of a tenant farmer gather round for the holiday dinner of cabbage, potatoes, and pie.

U. S. 99, 1937: "They scuttled like bugs to the westward."

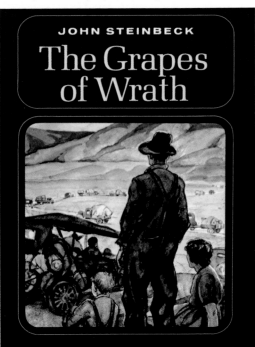

JOHN STEINBECK
The Grapes of Wrath

The Pulitzer Prize novel of 1940 portrayed the ordeal of the Okies.

Harvard, Illinois: Farmers spill milk, hoping to boost prices.

"But above all, try something"

To Depression-benumbed Americans, Franklin Delano Roosevelt took the Presidency as an apostle of action. He had confidently promised a "New Deal." He had said that if one expedient didn't work, what matter; try another. But *try*. Now with jaunty assurance that "the only thing we have to fear is fear itself," he began a four-term administration that put the guiding hand of government into previously untouched corners of national life.

Fresh from his March 4, 1933, inauguration, Roosevelt closed the nation's banks, beset by depositors' runs. Reopened banks, he told Americans in the first of his "fireside chats" by radio, would be a safer place for money "than under the mattress." Here was a simple truth, but it brought out a billion dollars in hoarded currency. A helpless public wanted reassurance. And action. And got it.

Into Congressional hoppers the administration poured bill after bill. Out came a stream of agencies that headlinese squeezed into an alphabet soup of initials—AAA, CCC, NRA, TVA, SEC, FDIC, FCC, WPA. The Civilian Conservation Corps put youths into olive drab and army tents at $30 a month digging ditches, building firebreaks, or planting 127 million trees as shelterbelts on the Great Plains. The Agricultural Adjustment Administration paid farmers to slaughter pigs or plow under cotton in hopes of limiting supply and raising prices. Patriotic fervor akin to that of 1917 greeted the National Recovery Administration's codes setting minimum wages and maximum hours while letting industries fix prices and rules for competition; the NRA's blue-eagle symbol appeared even on suntanned backs. Works Progress Administration funds poured into relief projects—some 600 airports, 100,000 bridges, 500,000 sewers; theater, art, and writing programs. And trivial tasks that gave a new meaning to the old handicraft term "boondoggle."

New Deal spending put money into pockets and boosted confidence—though unemployment remained as widespread in 1937 as it had been in 1931. Other measures—creation of the Tennessee Valley Authority, stock market regulation, Social Security, strengthening of labor unions—brought enduring change. "That man in the White House" stirred bitter denunciation and lavish praise. But, in the words of a British historian, FDR's New Deal left "the existing system reinforced, underwritten, and remarkably resilient."

A 1935 act put Social Security into FDR's panoply of reforms.

Movie starlets do their part for NRA's slogan and emblem.

Cincinnati airport mural, one of some 400,000 WPA art works

Joe, Jesse, Diz, Red, Babe . . . the greats

We see them now in snippets of gray film that move too fast, mocking their grace, reassuring generational chauvinists who worship idols of instant replay. But not so long ago. . . .

An urban Huck Finn named George Herman Ruth came out of Baltimore with power in his arm and in his bat. Baseball needed that bat; the game had become one of tight defense, crafty hitters, bunters—"The Dullest Sport in the World," a writer carped. Then came the Babe, swinging "big, with everything I've got." What a joy to see him swat a towering homer ("a pop fly with a brand-new gland," wrote Heywood Broun). Baseball read the omens, produced a lively "rabbit" ball, moved fences in. Soon the Babe was leading a "Murderers' Row" of New York Yankees clad in pinstripes that gave the billowing Ruthian torso a svelte look. In 1927 he hit an astounding 60 home runs, a new record.

By then, pro football had taken off—mainly on the flying heels of Red Grange. He had become a household name since that day in 1924 when he scored four touchdowns for the University of Illinois against Michigan— the first four times he carried the ball.

Babe Ruth slammed his last homer—No. 714—in 1935. The year before, Dizzy Dean, his gift for gab and blazing fast ball at their peak, predicted that "me and Paul" would win 45 games for the St. Louis Cardinals. Diz took 30; Daffy—brother Paul—won 19. Looking to the World Series against Detroit, Diz announced, "Me and Paul can beat 'em all." They did, pitching two wins apiece.

As Berlin prepared for the 1936 Olympics, a Nazi pamphlet prattled, "Among inferior races, Jews have done nothing in the athletic sphere, and are surpassed even by the lowest Negro tribes." U. S. trackmen took a dozen gold medals; Cleveland's "Tan Streak," Jesse Owens, won the 100- and 200-meter sprints and the long jump, and led the 400-meter relay winners. Theories of a master race had collided with a fact: a master racer.

Two months earlier Germany's pride, Max Schmeling, had knocked out Joe Louis. Boxing fans thought Louis, with his stinging left jabs and paralyzing rights, invincible. But Schmeling saw an opening for his own right smash and exploited it. Louis got up—to win the heavyweight championship, to erase Schmeling in a return bout, to defend his title 25 times. Braddock, Galento, Pastor, Conn, Baer, Walcott . . . remember?

The Brown Bomber evens the score against Max Schmeling with a one-round knockout in Yankee Stadium, June 22, 1938.

Jesse Owens keeps shipshape en route to Olympic glory in 1936.

Got any cards to trade? What'll you give for a Dizzy Dean?

Harold (Red) Grange, Galloping Ghost of the Illini, turns it on.

Those daring young airpersons

On January 9, 1793, President Washington and a crowd of Philadelphians witnessed America's first manned "air voyage." Jean Pierre Blanchard lifted off in a blue-and-gold balloon, and landed some 15 miles southeast near Woodbury, New Jersey, displaying a "passport" signed by the President.

It took another century before man could voyage through the air upwind, and several more decades before the surprise wore off. Crowds still gawked in the 1920's when a "flying circus" buzzed a town, luring the folks to a field where as little as a dollar bought a taste of the daredevil's life. At Steubenville, Ohio, one day Bill Brooks made 490 trips with dollar rides in a single span of daylight. Anything for a payday. Stuntmen hopped from plane to plane; lashed to a wing, they pantomimed a tennis match. Bowser Frakes specialized in crashing planes. He smashed up 98, usually beyond repair; only once did he suffer serious hurt.

Barnstormer "Slim" Lindbergh flew the Chicago-St. Louis mail route in 1926. Lost in a stormy night, he would run the gas tanks dry so the mail wouldn't burn in the crash, then parachute to earth. He searched out the wreck, retrieved the mail, and delivered it to a post office. A New York-Chicago line in the late '20's took one passenger per trip—but he might be bumped by more mail. Will Rogers, wild about flying, would weigh in at package rates and sit with mail sacks piled on him.

With Lindbergh's Atlantic crossing, air travel boomed. Cabins of tri-motored Fords and Fokkers began to look like club cars. To avoid night flights, early coast-to-coast passengers flew by day, entrained at night.

Schedules, safety, profit and loss. But the spacious sky still had room for heroes—and heroines, insisted Amelia Earhart, social worker turned aviatrix. To the argument that tensions of the menstrual cycle handicapped women as pilots, she replied with opposing biological evidence—and common sense: The same claim could apply to women trapeze artists. And she flew—across the Atlantic as a passenger in 1928, then alone in 1932. She flew the first successful Hawaii-to-California solo in 1935. Two years later she and her navigator Fred Noonan vanished in the Pacific on a round-the-world flight. Deeds like hers, wrote Walter Lippmann, prove we are not merely dust, but "also fire, lighted now and then by great winds from the sky."

Luxury liner of the late '20's hauled eight on Miami-Havana run.

"We" — the Lone Eagle and his Ryan monoplane — made history.

Amelia — ready to race her Lockheed across the country in 1933

A new 30-center marked the debut of scheduled crossings in '39.

"But we like it, and it's distinctly ours"

No other country in the world, said Will Rogers, could understand the American political convention—whose noise and emotion and hoopla amounted to "Those that are in are trying to stay in, and those that are out are trying to get in."

His wit found grist in political events—15 men in a smoke-filled Chicago hotel room picking Warren G. Harding as the 1920 Republican convention's nominee, Democratic delegates battling through 102 ballots in New York in 1924 before factions backing Alfred E. Smith and William G. McAdoo compromised on candidate John W. Davis.

Eight years later Franklin D. Roosevelt broke convention tradition by flying to Chicago to make his acceptance speech as the Presidential nominee. Before, candidates had waited weeks for formal notice, pretending surprise when it came. This campaign also saw radio emerge as a powerful political tool. The medium reached people at home, remote from crowd psychology, and put new demands on speech writer and speaker. Roosevelt's rich, intimate voice contrasted with Hoover's heavy seriousness. In office, FDR's fireside chats made him a household confidant—bringing a 500,000-letter deluge to a White House where until then one aide could handle all Presidential mail.

The New Deal forged a coalition of city machines, laborers, and farmers; in 1936 it swamped Kansas Governor Alfred M. Landon. The Sunflower State nominee won only Vermont and Maine; bumper stickers noted that "Sunflowers die in November." The *Literary Digest* had predicted a Landon win; its postcard poll took names from phone books and auto registries—where FDR's "forgotten man" was unlikely to be found.

In 1940 Roosevelt, breaking a precedent that began with George Washington, sought a third term. Use of campaign buttons set a record: Democrats 21 million, the GOP 33 million. The army captaincy granted FDR's son Elliott became an issue as a peacetime draft loomed. Wendell L. Willkie's dynamic image captivated a GOP convention tired of "old pro pols." He stumped 34 states, stirring zeal with 550 speeches in 51 days. But the Nazi surge in Europe and Roosevelt's magic tipped the vote to the Democrats. In '44, with the nation at war, Roosevelt defeated Thomas E. Dewey. Said FDR: "Dr. New Deal" had become "Dr. Win-the-War."

When wind delayed FDR's July 2, 1932, arrival in Chicago, convention managers stalled proceedings so he could address delegates. His fireside chats (1938 above) always began "My friends." Opposite: Willkie fans overflow an October 1940 rally in Buffalo, New York.

When the Japanese attack on Pearl Harbor plunged the United States once more into war, Americans marched off to battle not so much with flying flags and patriotic oratory as with a grim, realistic determination to fight for the survival of the nation and its allies. Earlier, at the outbreak of war in Europe in September 1939, there had been little division of sympathies, as in 1914. Americans abhorred the aggression by Germany in Czechoslovakia, by Italy in Ethiopia, by Japan in China. Yet, remembering the dread years of 1914-18, people overwhelmingly sought to avoid direct involvement. Debate flared between isolationists and interventionists when German armies, in the spring of 1940, took France and threatened Britain. But a sizable majority of citizens cheered President Franklin D. Roosevelt as he undertook to transform America into an "arsenal of democracy," extending material aid to the British and, after the Nazi thrust eastward in June 1941, to the Soviet Union. Step by step the nation moved closer to outright war with the Axis. By the fall of 1941, the United States was tightening economic restrictions against Japan and waging a naval war against German submarines in the North Atlantic.

At this point, debate and hesitation came to an end. The December 7 attack on Pearl Harbor united the American people as never before in the formidable task of building an armed force capable of winning the war.

Reactions of anger, fright, confusion, and determination on that Sunday of shock carried over into the following days. Thousands of reservists donned uniforms and headed for mobilization centers; millions of others sought to enlist or waited for "Greetings" from their draft boards. From a nation of civilians, the United States once again turned into one of warriors and war workers.

Americans had shuddered at newsreels depicting the horrors of the Nazi blitz in the Netherlands and Belgium and the Japanese incursions into China. Now they feared devastation similar to that of Amsterdam or Nanking might be wreaked on their cities and homes. Throughout the land Civilian Defense wardens conducted practice "blackouts" and memorized the silhouettes of enemy aircraft. Soldiers guarded key bridges and installations against saboteurs. On the Pacific Coast, barrage balloons hung over shipyards, and sandbags were piled around telephone exchanges, as though the next Japanese thrust might be against the mainland. An alert triggered an air-raid alarm in Los Angeles, and antiaircraft guns pounded against a nonexistent invader. But the somber news from the Pacific was all too real: American ships and planes in Hawaii had suffered major damage. American soldiers, sailors, and marines had died.

In the months that followed, blow fell upon blow as the Axis advanced in both hemispheres, the Japanese into New Guinea threatening Australia, and the Germans almost to Cairo and the Caucasus. Allan Nevins, a historian of the Civil War, compared the mood of the nation—"the most discouraging in American memory"—with that of the North during 1861. Yet, during that grim first year, statistical experts on America's productive capacity remained optimistic, certain of ultimate victory. Even in December 1941 the United States was producing almost as much war matériel—for the Allies and our own defense buildup—as Germany and Japan combined.

Just as it had a generation earlier, the role of arms and food production dominated life on the home front. Americans were bombarded with advertisements that proclaimed the significance of the manufacturers' products, ranging from tanks and airplanes and ships to combat boots, wire fasteners, and air conditioners. At times the advertisements, claiming that victory was being achieved through this or that product, seemed ludicrous, but they helped America mobilize. And the fact that the United States could produce landing craft, weapons, and ammunition in overwhelming quantities would not only tip the balance on the battlefield but also lessen the cost in American lives. In 1944, soldiers advancing along narrow country roads in France

"A date which will live in infamy"

Japan's surprise attack on the U. S. fleet at Pearl Harbor, Hawaii, on December 7, 1941, provoked President Franklin D. Roosevelt's memorable phrase and once more set a vast stage for tearful goodbyes.

It also touched off a West Coast hysteria against Japanese Americans, both the older, foreign-born Issei and their native-born offspring, the Nisei. They numbered some 125,000, most along the Pacific Coast, and though two-thirds were citizens by birth, all were seen as potential subversives by neighbors and officialdom alike.

Harassed, assaulted, denied food, clothing, and jobs in their communities, many moved inland. In 1942 the government made evacuation mandatory from the "strategic area" of California, Oregon, and Washington. Ordered to relocation centers, evacuees large and small (above) took only what they could carry and moved into wire-enclosed compounds of tar-paper barracks. There they set up self-governing communities, established hospitals, tilled fields, and made camouflage nets for the army. Depending on the job, they received $8 to $19 a month. Later, as hysteria subsided, the government relocated them to the "outside."

Despite suspicion and mistreatment, Nisei servicemen fought bravely in battle. In Europe their 442d Regimental Combat Team distinguished itself as the most decorated outfit in the war—18,000 citations.

NO TIME TO LET LOOSE!

It's a Fight to a Finish!

Works of war

SBD Dauntless dive bombers, part of an army-navy aerial armada that numbered 300,000 planes, wait for navy wings at a Douglas Aircraft plant. For five years, war production roared along in three shifts to turn out weapons. Women, donning kerchiefs and long pants, made up a third of the factory force. "Slacks," wrote one commentator, "have become [their] badge of honor."

Posters spurred war workers (above) and warned against loose talk of ship and troop movements that might cost lives (below). Families that lost a member in the war proudly displayed the gold-star flag.

...because somebody talked!

were able literally to spray trees with machine gun bullets to flush out German snipers. "To the Americans," wrote British political scientist Denis W. Brogan, a long-time commentator on the American scene, "war is a business, not an art."

Nevertheless, Washington administrators and business leaders slowly had to relearn how to operate the industry of war. In the two years before Pearl Harbor, two million troops had been trained and the level of aircraft production had reached 25,000 planes a year, but there was still confusion among the war agencies in Washington and in defense installations across the country. Agency succeeded agency like a rescrambling of anagrams, from the OPM (Office of Production Management) to the WPB (War Production Board) in January 1942; from the OES (Office of Economic Stabilization) to the OWM (Office of War Mobilization) in May 1943. Gradually, the agencies developed workable techniques and, as in World War I, finally regulated the entire economy. These offices decided on priorities of production, allocated scarce raw materials, channeled manpower, settled labor disputes, encouraged farm production, fixed prices, rationed consumer goods, censored the news, and shaped the minds of the people.

Quarrels among agency heads, as well as between the administration and Congress, received headlines sometimes rivaling those from the battlefronts. Author Agnes Meyer, in *Journey Through Chaos,* a series of dispatches on conditions throughout the nation, reported: "Whether it be management or labor or businessman or farmer, everyone has told me the same story of distress concerning their relations with Washington. . . . I often wondered during my trip whether the Washington war lords realize what the daily reports in the newspapers concerning their quarrels and indecisions, their . . . complicated directives and contradictory statements are doing to the country?"

But these were the noises of democracy at war. Despite all the confusing and onerous directives, the democratic machinery was still in operation, and in the end proved effective—much more so than that of the totalitarian enemies. Manufacture of automobiles and other durable consumer goods gave way to machine guns, cargo ships, and a thousand accouterments of war, in quantities and with an efficiency the world had never seen. Shipyards, for example, turned out 64,500 landing craft; the sturdy, slow Liberty ship, which in 1941 took nearly a year to build, by the end of 1942 was being completed in 56 days. Annual American production at the close of the war in 1945 nearly doubled what it had been in 1939.

In contrast to the public activity of administrators and industrialists, scientists and engineers labored in an atmosphere of secrecy, racing to beat the Germans in the development of ingenious devices like the proximity fuse, and of new and more powerful weapons. Above all it was the atomic bomb they worked on intensely, fearful of the consequences for the world if Hitler got the bomb first. Jonathan Daniels, a White House assistant, remembered the "recurrent coming and going . . . [of the] scientific gentlemen. They had not looked like the planners of the atomic bomb. They were college professors in a Washington in which college professors have often been made to seem much more comic than Congressmen." Yet out of their brilliant teamwork came the weapon that would alter permanently the course of world history.

Throughout the war, factories, fields, and armed forces required an immense mobilization of manpower. Once again America faced a shortage of workers, this time following a decade of Depression unemployment when at least a fifth of the work force had been always idle. The armed forces eventually took 15 million men from the labor force; when military needs had become really acute, the draft drew off skilled workers that it had taken industry months to train. "Help Wanted" signs appeared everywhere, and few applicants were turned away. Even those previously considered unemployable because they were too old or too young found jobs. In sections of the country where schools paid salaries well below those of war industries, teachers joined their students in leaving schools for factories. Sex and race barriers fell, and those who had eked out a near-starvation existence in rural areas moved to city jobs. The South became transformed as underprivileged whites and blacks alike moved from the countryside to war plants and shipyards. Population also shifted to the Pacific Coast, where heavy industry rapidly grew.

Especially for blacks, who had been crushed by the Depression, war jobs offered a chance to move ahead in society, though not without struggle. Two million obtained employment in war plants, but problems with transportation—segregation on public transit down South and harassment up North—often made it difficult to get to work. In Detroit, where blacks crowded in with whites who also were migrants from the South, tensions exploded into a riot in June 1943, and 25 blacks and 9 whites were killed.

White-collar workers, to supplement salaries that seldom kept up with prices, sometimes took on part-time jobs in war plants, in canneries, or in fields harvesting crops. One California professor, who kept it quiet, later confessed that without his war work in a cannery he could not have balanced the family budget.

All war workers enjoyed paychecks far beyond anything dreamed of during the Depression. The tendency of some, who had been long unemployed, was to spend the money freely and foolishly—and anyway they expected their prosperity to last only as long as the war. Others felt disappointed, after years of want, to find that good pay did not solve all their problems. Four families out of ten either could not save or would not save. The other six families heeded the exhortations of the government and saved billions of dollars in war bonds, creating a reservoir of wealth that would help launch a postwar consumer boom—and a concurrent, spiraling inflation.

There were widespread appeals to women to take jobs. One advertisement picturing a woman war worker bore the caption, "My husband's in the Army. I'm in a shipyard. . . . We're in the war together." Once again on the home front it became a women's war as industrialists rediscovered that women could fill almost any kind of job. Not only did Rosie the Riveter work on Flying Fortresses, she learned welding and soldering and a multitude of other grimy mechanical tasks. Some of the women were well educated and took the jobs primarily out of a desire to help the war effort. Edsel Ford employed 600 women college graduates in his Highland Park, Michigan, plant. For servicemen's wives, there were not only financial and patriotic motives but the need to keep busy while their husbands were away.

Although mothers sought to make up for the absence of fathers, and nursery schools provided child care for working women, many children suffered from splintered family life and exploitation. In families with fathers away or both parents employed, children often worked part-time. A 14-year-old boy in Wichita, Kansas, whose parents were aircraft workers, held a job at a drugstore soda fountain from 5 to 10 p.m. on weekdays, and from 10 a.m. to 11 p.m. on weekends—for little more than ten cents an hour! Children sat in movies or wandered the streets until a parent came home from working a late shift. Some children lived in housing so crowded that they had to wait until their parents went to work before getting into bed. A social worker asked a 13-year-old girl what she was doing sitting in a California beer hall late at night. "I'm just waiting for 12 o'clock," she replied. "My bed isn't empty until then." Juvenile delinquency, a term then gaining currency, went up 56 percent, and newspapers lamented the prevalence in amusement areas of teen-age girls—bobby-soxers, who wore anklets with loafers or saddle shoes—and of teen-age boys wearing bizarre zoot suits.

Despite the dislocation of large numbers of war workers, most Americans remained in their old homes at their old occupations, touched only by the departure of fathers,

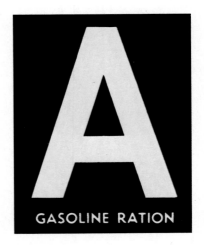

GASOLINE RATION

"Don't you know there's a war on!"

Every salesman said that to every customer who tried to buy something temporarily or permanently gone. When stocking material —silk, rayon, and the new synthetic, nylon— went to war in powder bags and parachutes, these women found a substitute: liquid leg makeup. Some even painted on seams.

Wartime austerity offered only one abundance—jobs. The appetite of battle consumed everything else. To control inflation, the federal government set prices and rationed a variety of consumer goods, including gasoline. The "A" stamp, affixed to the windshield, allowed the owner three gallons a week—and no joyriding permitted. Gas rationing helped create the car pool.

Food was rationed by points; to buy a pound of ham for 51 cents (below), a housewife also had to spend 8 points.

It was a time of standing up in crowded trains, of sleeping in hotel corridors, of waiting at gas station and butcher shop. Mostly it was waiting for the war to end.

husbands, sons, and brothers for training camps and by the inconvenience of consumer shortages. It wasn't much more of a women's war in the military than it had been in World War I; only a quarter million women enlisted. But those who remained at home observed an intriguing change come over American life.

Paul Gallico, journalist and author, wrote of the home front in 1942: "That was the spring when women took to wearing slacks in the streets (a great blow to the human race), old toothpaste tubes had to be turned in for new ones, men's trousers were commanded to be cuffless, and a radio comedian named Bob Hope began to play soldiers' camps around the country. . . . That was the spring we first heard about sugar rationing, with gasoline rationing to come. Ice cream was reduced to ten flavors, and civilian suffering really hit its stride when the War Production Board banned the use of metals for asparagus tongs, beer mugs, spittoons, bird cages, cocktail shakers, hair curlers, corn poppers, and lobster forks. New York blacked out, and for days we talked about how beautiful the great city looked stark and naked, silhouetted against the moon. . . . Sex reared its pretty head in factories as an occupational hazard. Girls were requested to quit wearing sweaters, peekaboo waists, halters, and other revealing garments. The boys were rubbernecking themselves into too many accidents."

As the war progressed, shortages of merchandise grew. In the Depression era, the customers had always been right; now they were always wrong. The quality of goods deteriorated as prices inched upward, although the Office of Price Administration succeeded in holding over-all inflation to a 3.3 percent increase during the war. Meat, coffee, canned goods, and shoes were rationed, in addition to sugar, tires, and gasoline. Housewives became expert in handling ration stamps, each worth ten points—red for meat, cheese, and fats, blue for processed foods—and the small round tokens (made of a soybean compound) given as change for points. Cigarettes, unrationed, disappeared from the counters, and like most other scarce items showed up on the black market.

Much of the task of helping housewives, organizing salvage, and maintaining community services came under the Office of Civilian Defense. In the first frightening days of the war, OCD had recruited men and women who had grimly gone about their duties during test blackouts as though they were on guard in London against German fire bombs. One exasperated woman civic leader scribbled a note during an OCD meeting complaining that the speaker "looks on an Air Raid Warden as some sort of vestal virgin." As the tide of war turned in late 1943, however, volunteers shifted their energies toward more mundane but useful services remembered from World War I—the sale of war savings stamps and the planting of victory gardens.

By 1944, newspapers and radios more and more often brought word of American and Allied successes, and the nation, tired of war, looked ahead toward victory and reconversion. Congress enacted legislation providing benefits for the returning veterans, the GI Bill of Rights. There was bitter debate over whether wartime taxes should be raised still higher, whether industries running out of war orders should be allowed to switch back to consumer items, whether wages and prices should be allowed to rise. In the Presidential race, a weary, ailing Franklin D. Roosevelt, seeking a fourth term, once again campaigned with fire and humor to edge out young Governor Thomas E. Dewey of New York. The following April, Roosevelt died; the nation mourned his passing and, ready or not, entered a new era.

A month later, on May 7, 1945, Germany surrendered. Limited victory brought a heady VE Day celebration. But in August, when Japan gave up after atomic bombs devastated Hiroshima and Nagasaki, crowds poured into the centers of cities in wild rejoicing. The American people had survived a second world war. They deserved the fleeting joy of victory and peace. Tomorrow they would face a nuclear world.

Home from the war to brave a new world

Atomic bombs over Japan snuffed out the last flames of war in 1945 and changed some 15 million GIs back into eager civilians with dreams of the future. Norman Rockwell's joyous homecoming scene captured what many a fuzz-faced lad had missed most— Mom and the bobby-soxed girl next door.

Veterans, happily shedding uniforms for civvies, were not always understood by loved ones, as cartoonist Bill Mauldin knew (below). To help readjustment, some states gave cash bonuses; the government's GI Bill of Rights provided college and vocational training, and guaranteed loans to buy a home (at 4 percent interest!) or start a small business. Some vets just drifted, buoyed by the "52-20 Club," which paid $20 a week unemployment compensation for a year.

America seemed much the same, yet the war wove changes into the fabric of life: pay-as-you-go income taxes; miracle drugs like penicillin and sulfa; imitation rubber for tires and shoes. The 1940's hastened development of other man-made substitutes, creating a world of synthetics: plastic clothes, furniture, boats, even hair. Technology came forth with electronics, computers, nuclear energy. Industry churned out television sets, garbage disposers, and automatic dishwashers. And American couples produced, from Pearl Harbor to the Korean conflict in 1950, a baby boom of 30 million brand-new citizens.

"I was hoping you'd wear your soldier suit, so I could be proud of you."

norman rockwell

In Everybody's Living Room

Erik Barnouw

Television's "glistening scene, replacing the hearth, has become the focal point of the home," writes author Erik Barnouw. TV's eye glows in a setting reminiscent of pre-World War II living rooms. This 1940 RCA Victor radio-television combination has a five-inch screen and sold for $350. Only a few of the 10,000 sets built before the war survive — most of them museum pieces like this one.

On the screen Edward R. Murrow reports on the "alarm and dismay" caused by Senator Joseph R. McCarthy's anticommunist crusade. A videocassette preserves the telecast of March 9, 1954. The glowering senator later called Murrow "the cleverest of the jackal pack" — and a nation tuning in on TV began to realize the impact of a new social force. Murrow's pioneering documentary series, See It Now, *started in 1951 with a split-screen view of the Golden Gate and Brooklyn bridges. The spanning of the nation by television soon evolved from symbol to reality. Today 98 percent of American homes have at least one set.*

For many Americans television provides a window on reality that at times seems more real than their own lives. Millions of youngsters spend more hours gazing through that picture window than in any other waking activity — more than they spend in school. Even for some adults six hours a day constitutes an average televiewing stint. For a majority of Americans television is the main source of news, and has been for more than two decades. For some it is the *only* source of news. The view from the television window, in living color, more alive than life, carries an authority that tends to make other events irrelevant, even nonexistent. Having witnessed the Kennedy funeral pageantry, the murder — live on television — of his accused assassin, and scenes from battlefields and riot-torn cities, people feel that they have been front-row spectators in the arena of modern history. What appears on the tube exists. What one reads or hears about, but does not actually see on the screen, seems remote and abstract.

The result, especially as it applies to news programming, has been a ceaseless eruption of what Daniel J. Boorstin calls "pseudo-events" — press conferences, summit meetings, marches, and demonstrations planned and staged expressly for television cameras. Businessmen, politicians, and leaders of causes long have recognized that the struggle to survive in today's world often means a fight for visibility on the tube.

How did it all begin? The history of television intertwines with that of older, related media: telegraphy, telephone, film, radio, and the recording arts. Like theirs, television's key developments stemmed principally from the work of individual experimenters. All these inventions were at first regarded as toys, hobbies, fairground curiosities. Yet their patents soon became assets of corporations and the subject of patent wars and monopoly litigation. Each medium, in turn, was felt to have a pervasive and unsettling social impact, not readily definable.

As early as 1884 Paul Gottlieb Nipkow, a German inventor, patented a crude television system that used a perforated scanning disk to transmit images — still pictures as well as moving ones. For many years Nipkow's disk served as the basis for image-transmission experiments on both sides of the Atlantic.

In 1927 Secretary of Commerce Herbert Hoover appeared in an experimental demonstration conducted by the American Telephone and Telegraph Company. The following year General Electric broadcast television's first melodrama, *The Queen's Messenger*. Company technicians watched on screens measuring four inches wide by three inches high, the size of a file card or snapshot. Radio station WGY in Schenectady,

New York, broadcast the sound elements; experimental station W2XAD beamed the picture. Three cameras, all motionless, all taking closeup shots, were used. General Electric later telecast a science-fiction production that dramatized a guided missile attack on New York City. As far away as Pittsburgh a radio "ham" picked up the experiments. The images, though little more than silhouettes, seemed to augur a new epoch.

In Hollywood, meanwhile, the success of a partly talking film that opened in 1927, *The Jazz Singer,* produced an upheaval in the movie industry. Silent-film actors and actresses with squeaky voices found themselves cast adrift by their studios. Hollywood frantically imported Broadway dramatists. The mood of change quickly communicated itself to the broadcast world. As movie films moved to sound, broadcasters reached for the picture. Within five years, predicted one industry official, television would be "as much a part of our life" as radio had become. But he was wrong.

"WALL STREET LAYS AN EGG," proclaimed the headline in *Variety* on October 30, 1929. The financial bubble had burst. The stock market plummeted. Paralysis gradually gripped the nation. Innumerable projects were shelved — television included.

Though momentarily slowed by the Depression, radio broadcasting actually benefited in the long run. As theater and movie audiences shrank, home audiences grew. Radio won an almost irrational loyalty among listeners. Social workers reported that destitute families driven to give up icebox, furniture, or bedding clung to their radios as the last link with the outside world. At the same time, the decline of theater and vaudeville brought a surge of talent to the airwaves: Eddie Cantor, Rudy Vallee, Fred Allen, Jack Benny.

At Last!
Six Tubes With *One* Control *Price* $140

Then in the summer of 1930 a young inventor named Philo T. Farnsworth won a patent that would galvanize the television industry. Farnsworth, a member of a large Mormon family, had first encountered electricity at the age of 14, when his father bought a generator to power the family farm on the upper reaches of the Snake River in Idaho. A few years later the youth astounded his high school science teacher by proposing to transmit images electronically with a system that would supplant the mechanical wheels and disks then used by experimenters. Eventually he met a backer who set him up in California, and in 1927 he succeeded in transmitting graphic designs that "jumped out at us from the screen." In August 1930, at age 24, Philo Farnsworth was granted his patent. Television as we know it was taking shape.

In April 1935 the Radio Corporation of America announced a million-dollar appropriation for television demonstrations. A studio in New York's Radio City was converted to television. Actors began to appear in hallways and cafeterias with green face makeup and purple lipstick. Two years later television's first mobile unit — two enormous buses crammed with equipment — was ready to take to the streets. At last the moment seemed ripe for television's commercial debut. RCA picked a target date and site for the unveiling: the 1939 World's Fair in New York.

On February 26 a test pickup from the unfinished fairgrounds featured an *Amos 'n' Andy* telecast with actors in blackface. On April 30, the formal opening, Franklin D. Roosevelt became the first President in office to appear on television. RCA sets with five- and nine-inch picture tubes went on display at the fair, followed later by sets with twelve-inch tubes. Prices ranged from $199.50 to $600. Crowds stared at the flickering

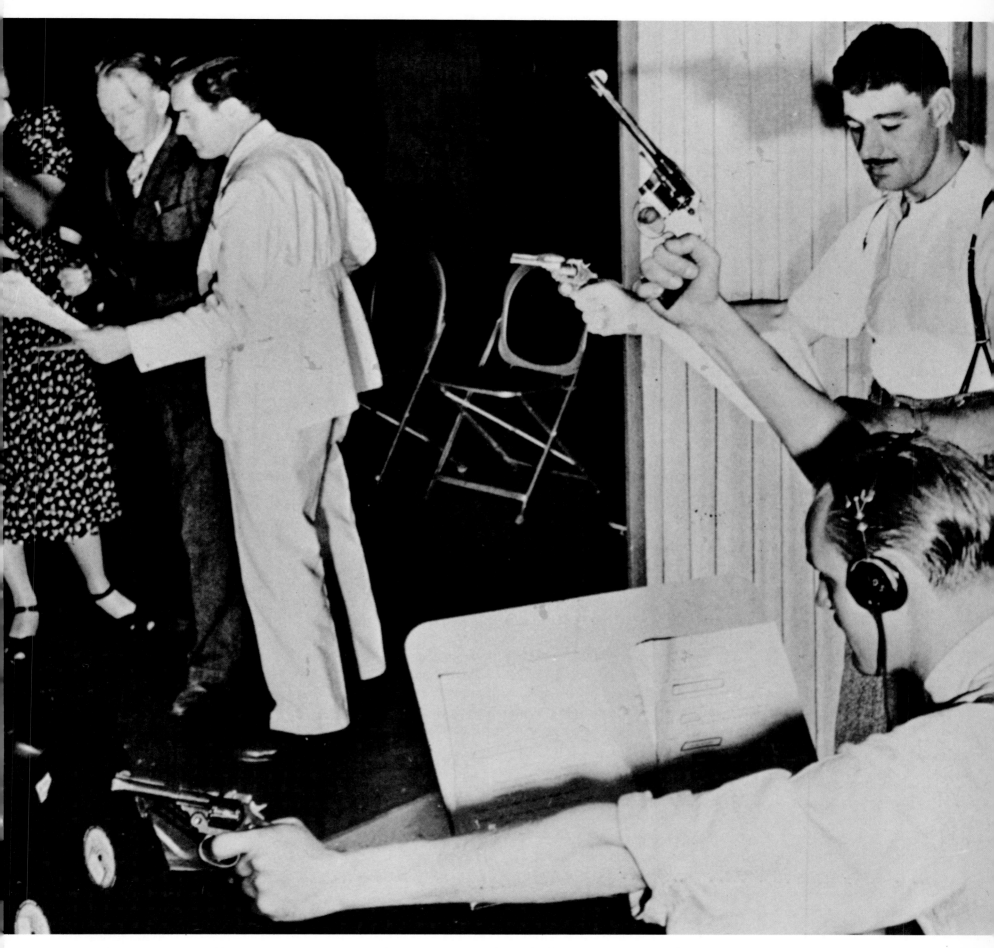

Sound technicians "come on like gangbusters" in the cops-and-robbers radio drama that inspired the simile for sensational entrances. Popular in the 1930's and '40's, Gangbusters opened with the chatter of machine guns, the wail of sirens, and the tread of convicts in lockstep. A 1924 ad for radios (opposite) stresses ease of operation—an improvement hastened by the military needs of World War I.

scenes: plays, snatches of opera, kitchen demonstrations; comedians, singers, jugglers, puppets. But by now the world was on the brink of holocaust, and as the United States geared for World War II, television gradually faded from the public eye. Most of the 23 stations in operation during May 1940 went off the air. Sets disappeared from the market. A few went into police stations to be used as training aids for air-raid wardens.

At war's end, America indeed was ready for television. In June 1946 a National Broadcasting Company telecast of the Joe Louis-Billy Conn championship fight impressed the *Washington Post:* "Television looks good for a 1000-year run." By July the Federal Communications Commission had issued 24 new licenses. As sets appeared, bars and taverns rushed to acquire them. In January 1947 the opening of Congress was televised for the first time. That summer the Zoomar lens, unveiled in a Columbia Broadcasting System telecast of a baseball game between the Brooklyn Dodgers and the Cincinnati Reds, revolutionized sports viewing. The camera's ability to leap from a long shot of the entire field to a closeup of the pitcher working his wad of chewing tobacco caused a stir. Children watched a new series, *Howdy Doody,* in the New York area, and in Chicago they saw *Kukla, Fran and Ollie. Meet the Press,* a longtime radio fixture, made its first televised appearance.

This was commercial television's formative period, the years during which its program patterns, business practices, and institutions took shape. Radio had blazed the way in the late 1920's by establishing a nationwide network structure linked by cables and supported by advertising revenues. Now television followed in radio's footsteps.

In late 1948 the FCC, having issued about a hundred television licenses, declared a "freeze." Interference problems had to be studied. The outbreak of the Korean war two years later became a reason for keeping the freeze in effect. Thus, 1948-52 became a strange period for television—a testing period. New York and Los Angeles, each with seven stations, saw television in full operation. Other major cities such as Houston, Milwaukee, and Denver, had no television at all, or only one station. Because of this spotty distribution, advertisers seeking national coverage continued to sponsor their network radio series. But they watched the "television cities" closely, and soon the portents were eloquent: Lipstick maker Hazel Bishop, doing a $50,000-a-year business, took to television in 1950 and saw sales zoom to $4,500,000 in two years. Areas with ample television coverage in 1951 reported a 20 to 40 percent drop in movie attendance; theaters closed in waves. Most television cities noticed a sharp decline at sports events, although wrestling, a prominent television feature, did well. Restaurants and nightclubs felt the impact. A variety series starring Sid Caesar and Imogene Coca became a Saturday-night terror to restaurateurs. Diners rushed home early to catch the show. Many cities reported drops in taxicab receipts. Jukebox earnings sagged. Some libraries, including the New York Public Library, noticed a slump in book circulation, and many bookstores recorded drops in sales. Radio listening declined sharply in television cities. TV took the blame.

During this period many television drama programs consisted of "episodic series," in which one or more major characters appeared in each episode. Some, like the *Aldrich Family,* were family series, but most fell into the law-and-order category: *Man Against Crime; Martin Kane, Private Eye; Mr. District Attorney.*

Man Against Crime, starring Ralph Bellamy, premiered in 1949 and soon achieved high ratings. In the radio tradition, the show was produced by an advertising agency. While following the radio pattern, *Man Against Crime* and other dramas faced problems unique to television. In radio the length of a play could be gauged by counting words— 140 to 150 a minute. Television timing, because of action intervals, proved considerably more treacherous. In 1949 all such programs were produced live, and the timing varied

Listening to a place they called Radioland

Most radio stars of the 1930's and '40's had started out being seen—in vaudeville and musical comedy. But they broadcast themselves so well that listeners could somehow conjure them up: Charlie McCarthy making a dummy of Edgar Bergen; Jack Benny hesitating when a holdup man demands his money or his life; Fred Allen in Allen's Alley; Kay Kyser in his "Kollege of Musical Knowledge"; Kate Smith and the moon coming over the mountain.

Fictional folk became real. Kids joined Little Orphan Annie's Secret Society or, with decoders and glow-in-the-dark rings, plunged into adventure serials. Radio could stoke elders' imaginations too. In 1938, when Orson Welles "interrupted" a program to dramatize an invasion by Martians, numerous listeners panicked. Switchboards jammed in police stations and newspapers; sailors were ordered back to their ships; drivers sped out of New York and Philadelphia; people saw Martians.

Radio, which began as "wireless telegraphy," found its voice on Christmas Eve 1906, when shipboard wireless operators on the Atlantic heard a woman singing, a violin, and a man reading passages from Luke. Such experiments continued until, by World War I, so many amateurs were on the air that they hampered military communications and had to be silenced. In 1920 trailblazing KDKA of Pittsburgh broadcast returns of the Harding-Cox election. Two years later more than 500 stations were on the air. Radio had arrived.

Toppered Charlie McCarthy clowns with Orson Welles (left) and Edgar Bergen.

Bandleader Kay Kyser's program combined quiz show, music, and comedy.

A one-day composite of some of the most popular radio shows of 1939 and 1940. Times listed are actual.

9:00	Don McNeill's Breakfast Club
10:00	Marriage Clinic
10:30	Just Plain Bill
10:45	Houseboat Hannah
11:00	Betty Moore: Home Decorating
11:15	Lorenzo Jones
11:30	Big Sister
11:45	Road of Life
12:00	Mary Margaret McBride
12:15	Her Honor, Nancy James
12:30	Helen Trent
12:45	Our Gal Sunday
1:00	The Goldbergs
1:15	Life Can Be Beautiful
1:30	Right to Happiness
1:45	Betty and Bob
2:00	AMA Health Dramas
2:30	American School of the Air
2:45	Betty Crocker: Cooking Hints
3:00	Orphans of Divorce
3:15	Ma Perkins
3:30	Pepper Young's Family
3:45	Ted Malone: Between the Bookends
4:00	Backstage Wife
4:15	Stella Dallas
4:30	Vic and Sade
4:45	Girl Alone
5:00	Dick Tracy
5:15	Terry and the Pirates
5:30	Jack Armstrong
5:45	Little Orphan Annie
6:00	Edwin C. Hill: News
6:15	Hedda Hopper
6:30	Bill Stern: Sports
6:45	Lowell Thomas
7:00	Amos 'n' Andy
7:15	Jimmy Fidler
7:30	Eddie Cantor Program
8:00	Charlie McCarthy Show
8:30	Burns and Allen
9:00	Texaco Star Theatre
9:30	Death Valley Days
10:00	Bob Hope Show

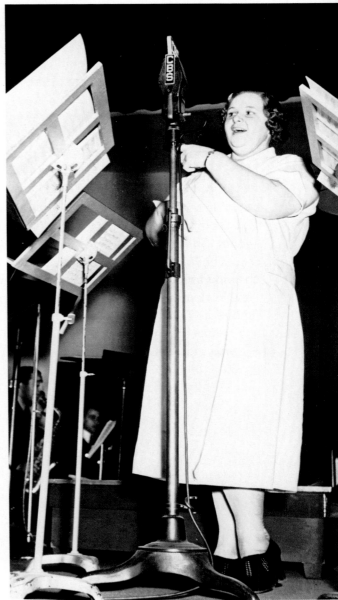

Kate Smith's "Hello, everybody!" greeted 16 million fans on Thursday nights.

Fred Allen, clutched by Jack Benny's wife, Mary Livingstone (right), menaces Jack, held back by Fred's wife, Portland Hoffa. Other hoked-up "feuds" featured Bing Crosby and Bob Hope, Charlie McCarthy and W. C. Fields.

wildly from one rehearsal to another. On *Man Against Crime,* a "search scene" near the end of each program solved the timing problem. A signal told Bellamy how long to search. If time was running short, he could go straight to the desk to find the hidden clue; if he had to stall, he could digress by first touring the room, looking under sofa cushions, or even tearing them apart.

Violence, if on-camera, could be staged only briefly. Prolonged physical struggle was hardly feasible amid flimsy sets. Although many kinds of crime might be used as plot elements, arson was not one of them: it might remind the viewer of fires started by the sponsor's product—cigarettes. Nor could anyone cough on *Man Against Crime.*

The year 1951 saw the entry of Lucille Ball and her husband, Desi Arnaz, onto the television scene. Their series *I Love Lucy,* filmed in a fringe Hollywood studio, became a leading favorite of television audiences by the following year. Within months another filmed entry, *Dragnet,* challenged its leadership, and that same year—1952—*Man Against Crime* switched over to film. The production crew moved to a studio in the Bronx built by Thomas Edison in 1904. Here actors found relics of Mary Pickford, Richard Barthelmess, and Thomas Meighan, stars of the old days of silent film.

Television's shift to film had several advantages: It relieved brutal pressures on actors

and production crews who previously had only the briefest time for rehearsals. It reduced timing problems, permitted a wider choice of scenery, and cut down the chances for error. It also opened up a new market—the sale of programs overseas.

As 1952 drew to a close, droves of actors and other personalities rushed into television. Bishop Fulton J. Sheen appeared in a weekly series opposite Milton Berle and his Texaco program. Quipped Berle, "We both work for the same boss—Sky Chief." Violent roller derbies won a wide following. Gorgeous George, the wrestler with marcelled hair, made periodic television appearances. *Information Please* provided an erudite touch. Walter Winchell, wearing his hat like a 1930's reporter, shouted scoops in a gravelly voice. Dr. Frances Horwich talked to preschool children on *Ding Dong School.* The *Today* series began, partly newscast and partly variety show. Its purpose at first baffled reviewers, and it won neither audience nor sponsor until the arrival of J. Fred Muggs, a young chimpanzee. Producer Gerald Green described what happened after Muggs became a *Today* regular: "Women proposed to him; advertisers fought for the right to use his photo in their supermarket flyers; Chambers of Commerce sought his good offices; actresses posed with him; officers of newly commissioned vessels demanded that he christen them."

By now some 15 million television sets glowed across the land, and throughout 1953 stations linked by coaxial cables and radio relays made their debuts. National networks took shape. Sponsors made their moves. Schedules expanded. Senator Joseph R. McCarthy was in the headlines with his search for "Communist infiltrators."

Though episodic series had come to television from the radio world, and were now being taken over by film makers, another kind of drama began pushing to the fore—the anthology series. Unlike the formula-bound episodic series, the anthologies emphasized diversity. The play was the thing. Its length was specified and it had to be produced as a live program in a gymnasium-size studio. Aside from these technical considerations,

Brash and zany Milton Berle reigned for eight years as "Mr. Television." His Texaco Star Theatre, an hour-long comedy-variety extravaganza, debuted in 1948 and soon made Tuesday evening "Uncle Miltie night" across the nation. Farm children in their Sunday-best (opposite) sit spellbound before another longtime favorite: Ed Sullivan, whose variety series closed in 1971 after 23 years.

TV's golden oldies

Humor, action, drama; songs, celebrities, something for the kiddies—the formula for TV entertainment changed little after its development in the 1950's. But some memories linger from that formative era: Rod Steiger and Nancy Marchand in Paddy Chayevsky's *Marty* (May 1953); Sid Caesar's spoof of *From Here to Eternity* (September 1953); the ballyhooed birth of Lucy's baby—in real life and on pre-recorded film—on January 19, 1953; *Dragnet*'s Jack Webb as the cop who said, "All we want are the facts, ma'am."

A decade later, what was golden were commercials: More than 20 an hour bombarded daytime viewers. Production costs soared to $20,000 or more per minute—ten times the per-minute cost of the shows they interrupted.

Lucille Ball announces a blessed event on I Love Lucy.

Howdy Doody shares a secret with Buffalo Bob Smith.

America meets the Beatles on the Ed Sullivan Show in 1964.

James Arness marshaled Gunsmoke's 21-year run.

J. Fred Muggs and Dave Garroway mark Today's fifth year in 1956.

Moderator John Daly quips with What's My Line *panel of the 1950's.*

Sgt. Joe Friday gets his man on Dragnet, *begun in 1952.*

Jack Paar chats with Elsa Maxwell on his late-night show (1957-62).

Free-wheeling mayhem erupts on Roller Derby, *a 1949 entry.*

Carl Reiner bends Sid Caesar's bugle on Your Show of Shows *(1949-54).*

Marty *is presented by the Goodyear Television Playhouse (1951-55).*

The whodunit shows
produced by Congress

In 1950 American television audiences reveled in the madcap comedy of Milton Berle, Jackie Gleason, and Sid Caesar and Imogene Coca, or ogled the celebrities and plunging necklines displayed by Faye Emerson.

Then, in May, another kind of spectacular burst upon the screen—congressional television. In his six-city probe of organized crime, Senator Estes Kefauver opened the hearings to television. Viewers saw a parade of gravel-voiced mobsters, buxom molls, and city officials allegedly on the take. As the hearings reached a climax in New York City, more than 20 million people tuned in. Kefauver acquired a following that, in the words of one TV critic, "even Howdy Doody might envy."

When reputed gangland boss Frank Costello took the stand, his lawyers barred camera shots of his face. America saw instead the revealing drama of his writhing hands (above). Plagued by dwindling matinee audiences, movie houses like the New York theater opposite lured passersby to big-screen viewing.

In 1954 Senator Joseph McCarthy—here muffling the microphone as aide Roy Cohn whispers—took on the U. S. Army. The tempestuous hearings gave voters and colleagues vivid views of "McCarthyism" and led to a 67-to-22 Senate vote condemning him.

writers could write as they pleased. And they responded. So did actors from Broadway and "off-Broadway." It was to be, in retrospect, a golden age of television programming.

Anthology programs included *Goodyear Television Playhouse, Philco Television Playhouse, Kraft Television Theatre, Studio One, Robert Montgomery Presents, U. S. Steel Hour, Revlon Theater, Medallion Theatre.* And later there were *Motorola Playhouse, The Elgin Hour, Playhouse 90,* and others. These dramas helped launch such unknowns as Kim Stanley, Paul Newman, Joanne Woodward, and Sidney Poitier.

Anthologies, in contrast to the episodic series, stressed the closeup. The human face became the stage on which drama was played. To this closeup drama, live television brought another element that had almost vanished from film—"real time," the flow of events at a lifelike pace. Film had long been dominated by its own kinds of time, made by splices at the cutting table. The tempo and rhythm generally were created not by an actor but by a film editor. The manipulation of "film time" had so beguiled editors that they had virtually abolished "real time" from the screen. Now it was back.

The anthologies held consistently high ratings. But advertisers hated them. Most advertisers sold magic. In the world of the commercial, solutions to problems could be achieved as easily as the snap of a finger—with a new pill, deodorant, toothpaste, shampoo, shaving lotion, car, girdle, coffee, or floor wax. But anthology writers took human problems and made them seem complicated—convincingly so. And *that* made a mockery of the commercial. Harassment by sponsors and advertising agencies inevitably doomed the anthologies, which in 1954-55 began a rapid decline. The death of live anthology was Hollywood's gain; television's trend to film quickened.

During this period the showpieces of network television news included the NBC-TV *Camel News Caravan,* featuring breezy, boutonniered John Cameron Swayze, and the CBS-TV *Television News with Douglas Edwards.* Both ran for 15 minutes in the early evening. Viewers were not particularly aware of shortcomings, but for presenting *the* news, crews and stringers in a few dozen cities were ludicrously inadequate. A favorite pronouncement of the day was that television had added a "new dimension" to newscasting. The truth of this concealed a more serious fact: The camera, as arbiter of news value, had introduced a drastic curtailment in the scope of the news. Footage of Atlantic City beauty contest winners, shot at some expense, became more valuable than a thousand pictureless words from Eric Sevareid on mounting tensions in Asia. Near the end of each *Camel News Caravan* telecast came the moment when John Cameron Swayze exclaimed, "Now let's go hopscotching the world for headlines!" What followed was a grab bag of items that, regrettably, had taken place without benefit of camera. Each seemed to need only a sentence.

Then came the quiz-show extravaganzas and the dawn of "adult" Westerns filmed for television by major Hollywood studios. Warner Brothers' *Cheyenne,* ushered in during the 1955-56 season, led the rush for previously unrecognized gold. The series derived from a comparatively unknown full-length movie and starred an even less-known actor, Clint Walker. Most of the episodes took five days to shoot—with many economy measures. For scenes of cattle drives or stampedes, Indian battles, and even barroom shots, the producers drew on leftover footage from old movies. "If you see more than two characters," went a Hollywood joke, "it's stock footage."

These were boom times for television. More than 500 stations now dotted the land. Some 40 million television homes watched an average of five hours of programming a day. Tens of thousands of sponsors supported the programs at a cost of almost a billion dollars a year. By the end of 1957 more than a hundred series of television films—telefilms—were on the air or in production. Almost all were produced in Hollywood, and most were of the episodic series type. The various family-comedy series that had followed *I Love Lucy* now began to be swamped by "action" films. These came in several surges—a crime surge based on the *Dragnet* series, an international-intrigue surge, and a mighty surge of Westerns—30 of them on prime time by 1958.

Normal processes of justice seemed inadequate for the new action telefilms. Producers felt that they needed supplementary individual heroism—and that only film could take full advantage of what has been called the "pornography of violence." Violence exploded on screens all over America. Voices of concern were largely unheeded.

Then, in 1958, the roof fell in on the quiz shows. Rumors of scandal had circulated for months within the industry. And when contestants and other witnesses began publicly revealing that programs had been rigged, the networks quickly decided to unload them. Action telefilms, such as *Shotgun Slade, Johnny Staccato, The Detectives,* and *Bonanza,* hastily filled programming gaps.

The big news for telefilms in 1960 was the meteoric rise of *The Untouchables* on the American Broadcasting Company network. Introduced in October the year before, by mid-April it pushed toward top position. A network executive combed through each script to make sure it contained enough action. An early script was described in reassuring terms: "Many exciting scenes. Opens right up on a lot of action—a running gunfight between two cars of mobsters. . . . Three killed. Six injured. Three killed are innocent bystanders." Five to eight million juvenile viewers saw each program.

ABC-TV's concentration on action was rivaled at CBS-TV. One CBS staff member characterized his network's action films as "broads, bosoms, and fun." NBC-TV, unwilling to leave the field to its competitors, jumped into the fray with *Whispering Smith,* one of television's bloodiest programs. The effects of all this violence were not known. With juvenile delinquency on the rise, some conjectured that television was a factor. Others said that television only mirrored an increasingly violent world.

The 1960's would become a decade of turmoil and violence—real violence—an era that would bring the abortive invasion of Cuba, assassinations of respected public figures, the escalation of war in Southeast Asia, riots, marches, demonstrations and counter-demonstrations. By now, approximately half the people in the United States depended primarily on television for their news. Few realized that the networks through which foreign news came had only the thinnest channels of information.

In 1962 television soared into the space age. Lt. Col. John H. Glenn, Jr., became the first American to orbit the earth. In July, Telstar I, a communications satellite, was thrust into orbit—an event comparable to the laying of the first Atlantic cable. David Brinkley, honoring the feat with a telecast from Paris, indulged his puckish humor by announcing solemnly "via Telstar" that there was no important news.

The following year brought a historic milestone for television: Now, for the first time, according to pollsters, more people relied on television for news than on any other medium. And on that November Friday when an assassin's bullet struck down President John F. Kennedy, nearly nine out of ten sets were tuned in within an hour of the shooting. Throughout the next three days, past and present mingled. At Arlington Cemetery on Monday, even as the television eye gazed at the flag-draped coffin, the nation heard the voice of John Kennedy at his inauguration. By Monday night he had become legend.

The "instant replay" used to re-run scenes of the Lee Harvey Oswald murder also figured in the rise of football as television viewing fare. While one camera showed the over-all action "live," other cameras followed key players close up. Within seconds after a play, its crucial action could be re-examined, or even unfolded in startling slow motion. Brutal collisions became ballets, end runs and forward passes became miracles of human coordination. Football, once an unfathomable jumble on the small screen, fascinated ever-increasing audiences. Football games, often "blacked out" in cities

From Chicago streets to the Sea of Tranquillity

Television news began in 1945 with a paltry budget and an $8,000 camera "liberated" from the Office of War Information. For two years this camera was the mainstay of NBC-TV's news operation—often a hodge-podge of filmed events from various sources, including the Army Signal Corps. Gradually, network executives became convinced that televised news had a future. They increased budgets and in 1947 began to hire movie newsreel camera crews. By 1948 viewers in some cities had a choice of two major evening newscasts: John Cameron Swayze on NBC or Douglas Edwards on CBS.

In June 1953 America saw its first royal spectacular: filmed "kinescope" recordings of Queen Elizabeth's coronation. NBC and CBS competed to get the first view of the pageant on screen. Both chartered special airliners, and NBC, working with the Massachusetts Institute of Technology, devised high-speed film processing. But ABC-TV, a fledgling noncontender, won by minutes, relaying the BBC telecast cabled to Canada.

At 12:40 p.m. on November 22, 1963, the CBS serial *As the World Turns* vanished, and Walter Cronkite appeared to report that President Kennedy had been shot. The serial then resumed. But within minutes sustained coverage began. Two days later, while honor guards prepared to escort the President's body to the Capitol, the accused assassin was slain—by a shot seen round the world.

"Instant replay," which repeated the shot again and again, was also used in televising the Army-Navy football game a few weeks later and within months became a standard technique in covering sports events.

TV also pulled viewers closer to war and riot. Vietnam entered the living room—and so did the Democratic convention of 1968. When antiwar protesters battled Chicago police, author Barnouw recalls, "film and tape arriving at the television control room suddenly began to look like slaughter. Networks threw it on the air as fast as they could. Viewers saw a dizzying kaleidoscope: nominating speech, head-cracking, speech, tear gas, shouting crowd, wounded, paddy wagons, balloting, ambulances, speeches."

And TV news presented moments of triumph. When Neil Armstrong stepped out of *Eagle* onto a ladder, a camera watched, and 1.3 seconds later the image reached earth, where millions saw man arrive on the moon.

Newly crowned Elizabeth II rides away in her coach, June 2, 1953.

Edwin Aldrin, Jr., descends from spacecraft Eagle to the moon, July 20, 1969.

Jack Ruby guns down Lee Harvey Oswald in Dallas, November 24, 1963.

Colt meets Redskin at Washington's Kennedy Stadium, November 18, 1973.

Chicago policeman clubs a demonstrator in Grant Park, August 28, 1968.

An American soldier dives for cover in Vietnam, August 6, 1966.

Keeping an eye on the Presidency

"We wouldn't have had a prayer without that gadget," said John F. Kennedy of the television cameras that helped edge him to victory over Richard M. Nixon in the 1960 election. Kennedy appeared at the first of that year's "Great Debates" fit and tanned from a campaign swing through California. He exuded confidence and vigor. Nixon, recovering from a brief illness, seemed wan and haggard.

A majority of the 75 million Americans who watched the televised debate (right) gave the contest to Kennedy. But radio listeners weren't so sure. To them, neither candidate had

clearly won. Historian Henry Steele Commager, like Rube Goldberg in a cartoon (above), pondered the implications. Did television glorify traits that were irrelevant to the Presidency? Both felt that George Washington would have lost a similar debate.

Since 1952, the year Dwight Eisenhower defeated Adlai Stevenson, politicians have relied increasingly on television to sway public opinion. The Chief Executive has power his opposition lacks. He can present his case by pre-empting prime-time viewing hours and by controlling televised news events.

But television also can record his agony. The cameras had focused on Watergate hearings, on impeachment debates. And then, on the night of August 8, 1974, crowds gathered (right) near the White House to witness—via television—President Nixon's resignation. The scene they viewed glows on the monitor screens (opposite) of Washington's Public Broadcasting System station WETA.

428

where they took place (to ensure attendance at the stadium), produced a new social phenomenon: weekend migrations to motels within reach of other stations. Thus games played in New York brought a boom to motels in Connecticut.

By 1966 television had been the principal news medium for most Americans for four years. For the young, especially, it served as the chief source of information about the world. Most children were heavy television viewers, watching mainly entertainment telefilms, into the high school years. But between the sixth and tenth grades a curious split occurred. Some children remained heavy viewers; others became very light viewers and turned to print for entertainment and information. Sociologists were puzzled. Could it be that television provided a satisfactory representation of the world only until — and unless — the child gained a foothold in the real world?

During 1966-68, at the height of antiwar unrest, most Americans did not demonstrate or riot. Most performed their jobs and relaxed in front of television. In homes with children the set was likely to be on 60 hours a week. The breadwinner watched after dinner. Except for occasional documentaries, evening television confirmed the average person's view of the world. It presented the America he or she wanted and believed in. It was alive with handsome men and women and symbols of the good life. It invited and drew the viewer into its charmed circle. If the circle was threatened, surely it was not because of flaws within, but because of outside evildoers.

Then came Watergate — the "third-rate" burglary attempt at Democratic Party headquarters on the night of June 17, 1972 — and the agonizing months that followed. When the Senate announced in March 1973 that it would hold hearings, noncommercial public television decided to carry them — live by day, repeated via tape at night. The response was staggering. The hearings gave public television, then on a starvation budget, a new lease on life. Some of its stations gained the highest ratings in their history.

Commercial television carried the hearings too, rotating live coverage among the three networks to minimize financial losses. Network executives were somewhat discomfited to find that Watergate outpolled top-ranking daytime serials and game shows. Watergate became an obsession with many viewers. Some watched live hearings all day, taped repeats at night. Senator Sam Ervin, chairman of the investigative committee, became a folk hero. Then came the climactic moment on August 8, 1974, when President Richard M. Nixon appeared on television to announce his resignation.

Sixty hours a week — for millions of Americans television has merged with the environment. Psychically it *is* the environment. What does it all mean? In a few decades television has grown from a toy to a popular diversion, to a pipeline to millions. It is admired, often trusted beyond other sources of news and information, accepted as *the* world — without a sense of what might be missing, because the tube itself defines *the* world. Such trust can be dangerous, especially because the omissions are almost never mentioned — at least not on the tube itself.

Those in television who take seriously the role of watchman on the ramparts, wonder. They feel they must report unequivocally on problems facing society. Among the problems, uneasily felt at many levels of the industry, is commercial television itself, a prime promoter of extravagant — even wasteful — living. Television's success has been that it has, in so few decades, brought an era to full fruition. But for new needs in a world beset by problems of hunger, pollution, energy, and inflation, the kind of television we have known is perhaps less brilliantly suited.

A welter of media developments confronts the television world: cable TV, fiber-optic systems, "wireless cable," videocassettes. Are they sufficiently regulated in the viewer's interest? What changes will future technology bring? We have lived through an astonishing, dizzying era. Others will be sure to follow.

Real and unreal intermingle as closed-circuit television surveys a basketball game at the Capital Centre near Washington, D. C. Fans *follow the action in real time, as seen here; in instant replay; or in slow-motion playbacks. Spectators in the Television Age, they become* *one with the inhabitants of Plato's cave, who took shadows on the wall to be real and, in sunlight, beheld reality as fantasy.*

An American Inventory

Ben J. Wattenberg

Power to the people—electric power—meant power to burn and power to cool, energy transformed from roaring waters or fossil fuels and sent racing along wires to relieve the wearisome drain on human energies. In 1900, electricity meant lighting; most power companies supplied current only after dark. Three years later Earl H. Richardson, superintendent of a California power plant, began promoting his improved electric iron. He persuaded his superiors to generate power all day Tuesday, the traditional day for ironing. The revolution in home appliances had begun.

General Electric patented both this iron and porcelain-based toaster in 1908; the iron resembles the old flatiron it succeeded—but it did not have to be hefted from stove to ironing board and back again. The GE desk fan of 1890 has four more blades than pioneer models of 1882. The Samson United waffle iron of the early 1930's crisps hand-mixed batter. Today electric power, more versatile than ever but getting costlier, will keep prepack waffles frozen until you're ready to pop them into a toaster that pops back.

Through history, the American standard of living has been extolled as a model for the world, condemned as wastefully extravagant, sought eagerly by generations of immigrants, cited in the 1970's as a forthcoming casualty of disappearing natural resources, and mourned in the 1980's as a victim of rapacious international competition. But what exactly is the "American standard of living"? An ambiguous phrase, it has a different meaning for a social scientist than it does for a family on the economic front lines. One thing is certain: Its hallmark is change.

The dramatic turnabout of the standard of living in the United States in the last half century translates into realities to a family: What once was Mom's apple pie now comes frozen from the supermarket ready for microwaving. A vacation trip, once perhaps a long weekend at a lake cabin, has become a deregulated super-saver flight. Today, a middle-class American family may come home to a gentrified townhouse rather than a rural homestead. Even "the family" itself is hard to measure. It may be a childless Yuppie couple in a condominium watching a rented movie on a videocassette recorder.

A "standard," though, ought to deal with something that is measurable. One of its indices, money, is comparatively easy to measure, but a standard should encompass more than money. Fortunately, statisticians and economists are constantly measuring other indicators as well. The United States Bureau of the Census produces about 3,000 statistical reports every year. Numbers pour forth from other government agencies and from trade associations, from industry, from colleges, from research institutions. Armed with such data, we can now try to portray the outlines of the American standard of living through numbers. And that is what this chapter is about: numbers, living numbers.

First, let's take a look at the typical American family as it suffered through the grimmest economic trauma of the century—the Great Depression. In recent years—particularly since October 19, 1987, Black Monday, when a soaring Wall Street market dropped 22.6 percent in a single day—Americans have been looking anxiously over their shoulders to see if the 1930's might return. To older Americans who remember the thirties, the combination of recession and inflation in the 1970's and 1980's seemed at times to call up old scenes of economic disaster. Yet what we saw did not come close to the debacle of the 1930's. Depression images of breadlines and shanty towns create a vivid picture underscored by the numbers. Consider unemployment: It was 3 percent in 1929. By 1933, with almost 13 million Americans out of work, the unemployment rate had soared to 25 percent. In contrast, the 1987 rate was 6 percent.

A crowd of panicked depositors starting a run on a bank is another familiar Depression image. Almost 10,000 banks failed from 1929 through 1933. Millions of people lost their life savings. The shock was so great that half a century later some people still "don't trust banks."

We saw this distrust surface in the mid-1980's as depositors lined up outside the savings and loan associations of Ohio and Maryland, and their withdrawals threatened to wipe out insurance funds. The difference from the 1930's was that the associations *were* insured—in some cases privately, but most of our savings institutions are insured by the Federal Savings and Loan Insurance Corporation.

We learned hard lessons from the Depression and made many changes in laws regulating financial institutions. Today the Federal Deposit Insurance Corporation guarantees commercial bank deposits up to $100,000. The Federal Reserve System promotes financial stability. The Securities and Exchange Commission regulates stock market trading—although analysts agreed after Black Monday that those regulations needed updating and strengthening. We have created a financial safety net, and most economists do not believe that we can suffer another 1930's-style economic collapse.

Without these modern safeguards, the economy hit bottom in 1933. A gradual, halting upturn began. But recovery was so slow that eight years would pass before the nation's production surpassed the 1929 level. At the next census, taken in April 1940, the statistical scars of mass poverty still showed, and median income was no higher in 1940 than in 1928. Then came an economic revolution that would sweep through our way of life.

Between 1940 and 1970 our population grew from 132 million to 205 million. Let's consider what happened to the typical American family—as seen through the lenses of social and economic statistics emphasizing income, education, jobs, and consumer goods.

"We are both black and white, old and young, poor and relatively affluent, producers and consumers. We are all the things that are in contention today. We cannot rush to the barricades of zealotry for any faction, without meeting ourselves coming down the street.

First, we need to define poverty. Economists today have reached general agreement about what constitutes the "poverty line" figure, below which families live in poverty. On the rough assumption that one-third of a poor family's income goes for food, the figure equals the cost of a nutritionally adequate food budget multiplied by three. Official poverty statistics date from 1959, when the rate was 22 percent. By 1970 it was down to 12.6 percent. Using current definitions, recent estimates for 1940 reveal rates of about 60 percent—what we today call poverty was the way most people lived in 1940!

The median family wage over this 1940 to 1970 period shows a dramatic rise. Measured in 1987 dollars adjusted for inflation, it nearly tripled from $9,977 in 1939 to $28,416 by 1969. America has often been cited as the first nation with a majority of citizens enjoying a "middle class" standard of living. But what is middle class? Economists and sociologists have debated the question for decades. One way to define it is to ask how the public characterized it in the period from 1940 to 1970: "Middle-class people," we were told, owned their homes, lived in the suburbs, worked at good jobs, owned one or maybe two cars, insisted that their children finish high school and encouraged them to go to college, took vacations, and had the financial ability to retire in their mid-60's. That describes just what happened to tens of millions of Americans.

Look at education. This newly affluent middle class was quick to buy it. College enrollment surged from 1.5 million in 1940 to a staggering 7.4 million by 1970. Part of that booming enrollment was due to changing demographics—the postwar baby boom provided more college-age people by 1970. But it was not just higher numbers. Greater *rates* of young Americans enrolled in college: in 1940 only 16 percent of Americans from 18 to 21 were in college; in 1970 it was 44 percent.

The job structure in America changed radically during the mid-century years. In 1940 almost half of male workers were farmers, or semiskilled or unskilled laborers. One of the major female occupations was "domestic service worker"—a maid. By 1970 only 31 percent of American males were working on farms or at semiskilled and unskilled jobs. The proportion of women working in domestic service dropped from 18 to 4 percent. New technology, customs, and attitudes were altering the pattern of employment.

Household appliances such as washing machines, dryers, dishwashers, freezers, and vacuum cleaners became more commonplace. Supermarkets carried a wide variety of frozen and canned goods. More women graduated from high school and went to college. All these factors made it easier for a woman to run a household in less time and, in addition, to qualify for professional, technical, skilled, or semiskilled occupations. The number of women in the labor force rose from 25 percent in 1940 to 42 percent in 1970.

Ambitions changed too: In 1940 Hollywood pictured a typical woman worker as a secretary whose ambition was to marry the boss and become a housewife. By 1970 she was more likely to have her eye on an administrative or professional job.

Men's jobs also changed dramatically. With advances in agricultural technology, fewer farmers raised more food. With mass production and automation, fewer factory workers produced more goods. Where did the surplus labor go? Up the occupational scale. The data show huge rises in the number of workers in professional, technical, administrative, and sales jobs. Did the displaced farmer become a professional man? Probably not. He may well have become a mechanic, though, and his son may have gone to college and become a mechanical engineer. That jump in occupational status, of course, also yields a jump in income.

Yes, incomes went up, but when we measure the American worker's rewards for labor, we should go beyond money to at least two other major benefits: security and leisure. In 1940 when Social Security programs were new, the census showed

"*Suburbia. . . . By day . . . a village of women. They trundle mobile baskets at the A&P, they sit under driers at the hairdressers,* *they sweep their porches and set out bulbs and stitch up slipcovers. . . . summer waters are full of [children], gamboling like dolphins.* *The lanes are alive with them. . . . They . . . make rich the dentist and the pediatrician.*"

The Province of the Heart *by Phyllis McGinley.*

that 42 percent of men 65 and older were still in the labor force—at a time when jobs were scarce—because they couldn't get by on the retirement income they had, or because they had none at all. In 1970 that rate was down to 25 percent. In addition, private pension plans became quite common. Back in 1940, the estimated value of private pensions was less than $2 billion. By 1970 it was $151 billion.

But long before retirement, workers by 1970 felt more secure in their work because they were insulated to a degree from the sometimes harsh cycles of the free market. Before World War II all that most workers had to show for their labor was money in a pay envelope. An accident on the job, illness, or a layoff could stop all income. By 1970, a mixture of federal, state, and private programs provided health insurance, unemployment insurance, and workman's compensation for job-related accidents and sickness. Labor union membership rose from 9 million in 1940 to 19 million in 1970. The federal minimum wage law covered only about 40 percent of the labor force in 1940. By 1970 the figure was 74 percent.

Leisure, a word that used to be associated with "the idle rich," had become an important part of the way of life for most Americans by 1970. Collective-bargaining agreements produced a surge in vacation allowances from the late 1940's to the 1960's. The standard work week—with extra pay for overtime—shrank from 44 hours in 1938 to 40 hours in 1945.

Prospering families look for a new way to live, and Americans turned to the suburbs. By 1970 the suburbs accounted for 76 million people—37 percent of the population. And home ownership went up from 44 percent in 1940 to 63 percent in 1970. As the suburbs multiplied, so did the number of cars. In 1940 there were 27 million cars registered in America; by 1970 there were 89 million.

Americans were quick to convert increased pay and more free time into fun and games too. In 1940 they spent some $4 billion a year on recreation; by 1970 the figure reached $43 billion. Visits to national parks shot up from 7 million in 1940 to 46 million in 1970, and major league baseball attendance almost tripled. These increases far outstripped the 55 percent population growth.

More families could now afford to buy the consumer items produced by the new technology. The television set is the typical example. In 1940, census takers did not even bother to count the few families who owned TV sets. By 1970 nearly all American homes had at least one set.

The new standard of living allowed more and more people to enjoy a way of life once reserved for the well-to-do. It was a remarkable success story. After World War II many Americans had worried that the Depression might re-ignite, or more accurately re-deflate. Instead, there was a sustained boom for a quarter of a century, the likes of which the nation had never seen before.

But the economy, like life itself, is full of tricks. As America entered the 1970's, the economy began to falter. There were recessions coupled with high inflation rates that averaged 6.7 percent from 1970 to 1975. Economists once believed this combination of recession and inflation—"stagflation"—to be impossible. A contributing factor was the steep rise in oil prices. Set in motion by OPEC, a cartel of oil-producing nations, oil prices rose from $3.18 a barrel in 1970 to $31.77 in 1981. OPEC's actions caused chaos in the marketplace, and motorists formed long lines at gasoline pumps. From 1978 to 1981 the consumer price index climbed at an almost unheard-of average rate of 12 percent. Prices soared, and wage increases could not keep up.

We Americans began hearing that we couldn't compete with foreigners, that our manufacturing jobs were disappearing, that we had exhausted our natural resources and polluted our air. Economists told us that progress had stopped, that children wouldn't live better lives than their parents, and that we would become a nation with a service economy characterized by low-paid jobs in fast-food joints. Some reports claimed that we were no longer making headway against poverty, that family income had stagnated, that the middle class was being squeezed out and couldn't even afford children any more — that the American Dream was over.

In 1982 there was a huge recession, the biggest since the Great Depression. The unemployment rate rose to 9.7 percent. By the mid-1980's the economy was haunted by "double deficits," huge budget and trade shortfalls, as well as what seemed to be a free-falling dollar — engendering yet new arguments among economists. Then in October 1987 came Black Monday's stock market crash with its loss of 22.6 percent. That was almost double the Black Thursday landslide of 1929 — the one that signaled the beginning of the Great Depression. People said it was "the end of an era," that "America was in decline."

There has indeed been a dislocation of the American economy. Some of our great midwestern industries, such as steel and automobiles, have taken hard knocks from foreign competition. So, too, have the textile and shoe industries in New England. Americans lost their jobs. There was real personal tragedy. A broad geographical swath of the United States, once prosperous and proud of its billowing smokestacks, came to be known derisively as the "Rust Belt." In the mid-1980's, hard times hit the farm and Sunbelt states as agricultural and oil prices dropped sharply, causing major regional recessions. High interest rates kept the value of the dollar high, harming our export industries and yielding big foreign trade deficits.

In short, economic tumult.

Did the American inventory stop appreciating during these admittedly turbulent times? Based on our national data bank and the opinions of many leading economists and social scientists, the answer is an emphatic "no." The times have certainly been volatile, but we have made progress over a bumpy path through the 1970's and 1980's. To see how, let's revisit some of those numbers we left hanging at 1970 and examine some new ones as well.

The actual number of manufacturing jobs in America has not gone down in the last twenty years. It has stayed around 20 million. Some of our manufacturing industries are still world leaders — passenger aircraft and pharmaceuticals, for example, and products from new technologies such as biogenetics and lasers. And, while the number of workers has remained nearly constant, greater productivity has propelled the real dollar earnings of our manufactures from $507 billion in 1970 to $812 billion in 1986.

Our manufacturing sector has not shrunk, but our service economy has grown along with our population, which reached 243 million in 1987. "Service worker" is a much maligned term, usually applied to low-paying jobs. In fact, the U. S. Bureau of Labor Statistics classifies jobs from chambermaid to brain surgeon under service industries. That well-paid lawyer up the street is a service worker. The man who repairs the robotic machinery used to manufacture automobiles is a service worker. So is the very well-paid actor or the incredibly well-paid rock star.

There has been much talk about how the hard-driving Japanese captured the market for videocassette recorders. True enough. They make the hardware. But what is played in those millions of machines around the world? Mostly tapes of American movies and musicians — just as American movies dominate foreign movie screens and American television programs dominate foreign television. American entertainment is a vastly profitable export earner. Everywhere in the world today people listen to American music, watch American movies and sitcoms, read American books, magazines, and newspapers. It is a peculiar time to make the case that our nation is "in decline."

To me it also seems strange to claim that we've stopped making economic

"His participation in the life of the community was so vigorous that he must have been left with almost no time for self-examination. He

headway. I believe that the evidence simply does not support the idea that we're stagnating. We've been moving ahead.

In 1970 the official poverty rate was 12.6 percent. By 1986, after fluctuations, it was 13.6 percent, but many observers believe the level should read lower than the official figure. Since the late 1960's a variety of federal noncash programs have been instituted to help the poor. In 1986 about $59 billion was given to poor people in noncash transfers such as public housing, rent supplements, medicaid, and food stamps. The stamps, to take an example, are not officially cash, and hence not counted in official census poverty-rate data. But if you go into a supermarket with food stamps, you can buy food that would normally be purchased with cash. The Census Bureau calculated that when these programs were counted in, the true poverty rate in 1986 was actually about 9 percent. Now, 9 percent was still plenty of people—about 22 million, with a large proportion of blacks and Hispanics. And far too many children live in poverty. That's our number-one social problem. Still, a 9 percent poverty rate is well below the 12.6 percent rate of 1970.

With lower poverty rates came a decline in the high school dropout rate. It fell from 45 percent in 1970 to 25 percent in 1986. At the same time the college graduate rate went from 11 percent in 1970 to 19 percent in 1986. Employment figures reflect the higher graduation rate. The four Census Bureau job categories that require the most education are "professional," "technical," "managerial," and "administrative." From 1972 to 1986 the rates of Americans employed in those jobs increased from 22 percent to 27 percent. The increase was spectacular for women: The rate of women in those jobs went from 34 percent to 44 percent. For blacks too, the rate rose from about 4.5 percent in 1972 to 6.3 percent in 1986.

Hispanics and other minorities also made steady progress. Most remarkable were the advances made by Asian Americans, many of them recent émigrés. A

was everywhere: he was at the communion rail, the fifty-yard line, he played the oboe with the Chamber Music Club, drove the fire truck, served on the school board and rode the 8:03 into New York every morning...."
The Housebreaker of Shady Hill *by John Cheever.*

new item became a staple on TV news shows: Vietnamese high school valedictorian arrived in America penniless, speaking no English, got straight A's, now going on to M.I.T. to study computers.

Home ownership remained about the same from 1970 to 1986, ending up at 64 percent. Interestingly, those were just the years when it was being said that "people can't afford to buy a house any more." The average house size also increased—from 1,500 to 1,825 square feet—even though family size was coming down.

On the negative side, since 1970 median family income has not gone up much—by 6 percent. But per capita income has gone up by 30 percent from 1970 to 1986. Pessimists wring their hands over the family income figures. I think, with the optimists, that the per capita figures are far more realistic. Why?

Because what has changed in "family income" is mostly "family" not "income." Owing to increased life expectancy, more of our families today are elderly. More, too, are headed by young adults of the baby boom generation. Both elderly and young families are less likely to earn big paychecks because peak earning years are those of middle age.

Higher numbers of divorces, marital separations, and out-of-wedlock births have created more female-headed households. Families headed by women pull down the family income *median,* even though the combined income of the two new households created by a divorced couple may be as much or more than the total income prior to divorce.

Despite the irregularities in the economy, living conditions have progressed. Consider just how much more we have and do today compared to 1970.

In 1970 there were 89 million cars registered in America; by 1986 there were 136 million. In 1970, 5 million Americans traveled overseas—in 1986 the number was 12 million. Visits to national parks have gone up by 52 percent since 1970, while population has only risen 18 percent. Today Americans gobble up every-

thing from concert tickets to designer jeans, spend millions on the latest ski and tennis equipment, invest in vacation homes, and clog the nation's waterways with pleasure boats.

To lure consumer dollars, huge new shopping malls tailor their hours to the free time of working parents. Whole families shop and eat together there, and go to the movies. Consider some of the things they buy—with a wallet full of credit cards easing the purchase. In 1970 there were no personal computers; by 1986 there were 18 million computers in people's homes. As recently as a decade ago American householders owned virtually no videocassette recorders. By 1987 an estimated 49 percent of American households had VCR's and 2.3 billion videotapes were being rented each year. The newest hot item since 1985 is the personal "camcorder," a sound television camera, with an average price of $950.

By all conventional measures, Americans are better off today than they used to be: less poverty, more education, more income, better jobs. Most of the world envies our goods and services. But we have surely learned that the nice suburban house, the second car, the VCR, better medical care and jobs, do not necessarily yield happiness. America today has big problems. We can hardly think everything's fine when polls tell us that drugs are Americans' number-one personal concern; when we see homeless people on the streets; when we agree that our schools aren't educating our children well enough; or when we worry about epidemics of hardly fathomable diseases.

But the essence of American progress has always been ways of concentrating effort on correcting our problems: child labor, sweatshops, rural and urban poverty, unemployment, illiteracy, disease, economic depression, war. That's what a democratic society like ours does best: We cope—not perfectly, not immediately, but relatively quickly and efficiently—and my guess is that we'll continue to do so.

"... 'brand name' called attention to the private ownership of a certain trademark, to the fact that one firm alone was authorized so to designate its product. But the much newer expression 'name brand' makes the name and not the product the center of attention. This is quite a natural way to distinguish commodities in the age of the celebrity...."

The Image by Daniel J. Boorstin.

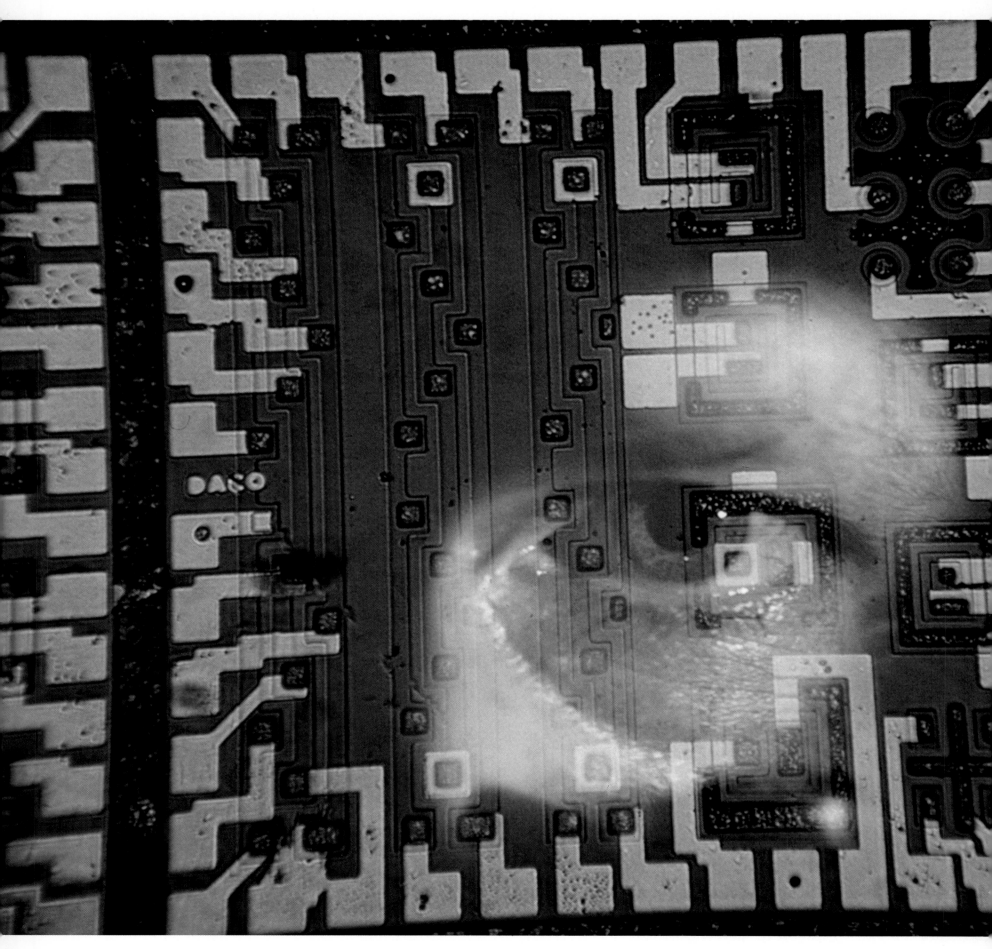

Eye to the future, a technician examines the microscopic circuitry of a computer's logic chip. From relatively simple designs in the 1960's, silicon chips have evolved into complex circuits, some containing millions of transistors. Used in electronic devices ranging from digital wristwatches to supercomputers that help us explore the universe, the chip has ushered in a new era of the machine.

Epilogue: The Fertile Machine

Daniel J. Boorstin

The beauties of the Land have long been praised and sung, for the Land is the proverbial source of strength. We still can see truth in the Greek myth which recounted that the giant Antaeus was invincible so long as he could touch Mother Earth. Hercules finally overcame him by lifting him in the air. Our own Thomas Jefferson put his faith in the people who live closest to the land. "Those who labour in the earth," he wrote in his *Notes on Virginia,* "are the chosen people of God, if ever he had a chosen people, whose breasts he has made his peculiar deposit for substantial and genuine virtue." Living close to the land, Jefferson added, kept a people strong and virtuous, because it kept them independent.

"Corruption of morals in the mass of cultivators," he wrote, "is a phaenomenon of which no age nor nation has furnished an example. It is the mark set on those, who not looking up to heaven, to their own soil and industry, as does the husbandman, for their subsistance, depend for it on the casualties and caprice of customers. Dependance begets subservience and venality, suffocates the germ of virtue, and prepares fit tools for the designs of ambition." Observant Americans have been impressed not merely with what people here could do with the land, but also with what intimacy with the land did to people.

Having moved into the Age of the Machine, we must take the same rounded view. We must reflect with pride and hope (if also with some caution) both on what man has done with the machine, and on what the machine has done—and may do—to man. By contrast with the Land, the Machine has had a bad press. Jefferson himself expressed his strong "moral and physical preference of the agricultural, over the manufacturing, man." "It is questionable," John Stuart Mill observed, "if all the mechanical inventions yet made have lightened the day's toil of any human being."

A literary chorus declares the menace of the machine. "Men have become the tools of their tools," warned Thoreau. Matthew Arnold declared that "Faith in machinery is . . . our besetting danger." "The world is dying of machinery," George Moore diagnosed in 1888, "that is the great disease, that is the plague that will sweep away and destroy civilisation; man will have to rise against it sooner or later." So modern a thinker as Bertrand Russell called machines "hideous, and loathed because they impose

443

slavery." But, then, men of letters—at least until they came to live by the typewriter—were never too tolerant of innovations that enlarged the life and eased the path of the ordinary man. In the beginning, learned men had their doubts about the printing press, which would put reading matter into the hands of the great mob.

The Machine is the great witness to man's power. The Land was there at the Creation. But every machine is the work of man. The power of the Machine is man's power to remake his world, to master it to his own ends. This must be a source of pride in humankind. And it may also be a source of the sin of "pride" in the special Puritan sense. It may tempt us to overlook our limitations and put ourselves in the place of God. There are some strange—even occult—features of the Machine. By inventing Machines, human beings bring into the world exotic new species—tools and weapons, metal and plastic contraptions never before imagined. We have produced a chemical defoliant that outdoes any insect in its power to consume vegetation; a miraculous laser beam that excels the slicing power of any natural stone or metal and acts across vast distances; a vehicle which defecates into the atmosphere—and makes the pollution of horse dung seem trivial; a calculator that outperforms any living being in arithmetic and in applying complicated formulas.

Every inventor is a Pandora. No one has ever discovered a way to *uninvent* a machine. Once mankind has created a printing press, a musket, a cotton gin, a telephone, an automobile, an airplane, a television set, each of these takes on a life of its own. Biologists before Darwin mistakenly believed that no species of plant or animal could ever become extinct—because that would suggest an imperfection in God's original plan. But every machine actually has some of the qualities of an inextinguishable species. There are a few examples of machines that were forgotten for centuries before being found again. But these are rare—mere historical curiosa.

Communities, like men, find it much harder to forget than to remember. Once a machine has entered the warehouse of memory—once it has become an item of everyday use, has been described in letters, in books, and in advertisements, has been recorded in patent offices—then it requires a not-yet-invented form of magic to erase it from human experience and recollection. Even to throw it on the junk heap may prove to be a way of adding it to the future archeologist-historian's record. And, because machines commonly have been made of inorganic materials that are not biodegradable, the carcasses of machines remain strewn across the landscape. As our automobile cemeteries show, machines are hard to bury and not easy to cremate.

Normally when a machine enters the life of civilizations, it spawns other machines, along with novel enterprises and institutions. The machine has bizarre powers to crossbreed, to become a host, a parasite, or a saprophyte living on dead matter. Radios and air-conditioning devices find new habitats within the automobile. Enormous compacting machines come into being to give a new form to deceased automobiles—and small compacting machines arrive to make neat packages of household trash. Machines for increasing and diffusing knowledge are also fertile. The printing press made possible public schools and public libraries, along with publishers and authors who could live by their writing. The automobile brought suburbs, networks of highways, and the Drive-In Everything.

Rarely does a machine, once invented, actually disappear. It tends rather to be forgotten or to be displaced by another machine which does the job more speedily, more economically, or more interestingly. The telephone was not extinguished by the radio (although some early objectors to radio forecast that result), and radio was not extinguished by television. The daily newspaper has survived them all. The motorcycle did not obsolete the bicycle. While the automobile and the airplane seem to have won

New masterworks in the art of healing

Americans born after the nation's 200th birthday had before them a record life expectancy of over 73 years, due in part to a decreasing death rate from strokes and heart disease. Miraculous surgery became routine, implanting in the heart an artificial ventricle (opposite) or an electronic pacemaker that stimulates a regular beat. And, taken from death, a transplanted heart could bestow new life.

Fantastic instruments detect and prevent trouble throughout the body. Infrared scanners can reveal varying temperatures of tissue by displaying them as a colored thermogram (above), which can disclose possible cancerous areas. Computerized X-ray scanners can explore a cross section of the body in 20 seconds. An ultrasound device, using high-frequency sonic beams as a kind of sonar, can portray a fetus in the womb.

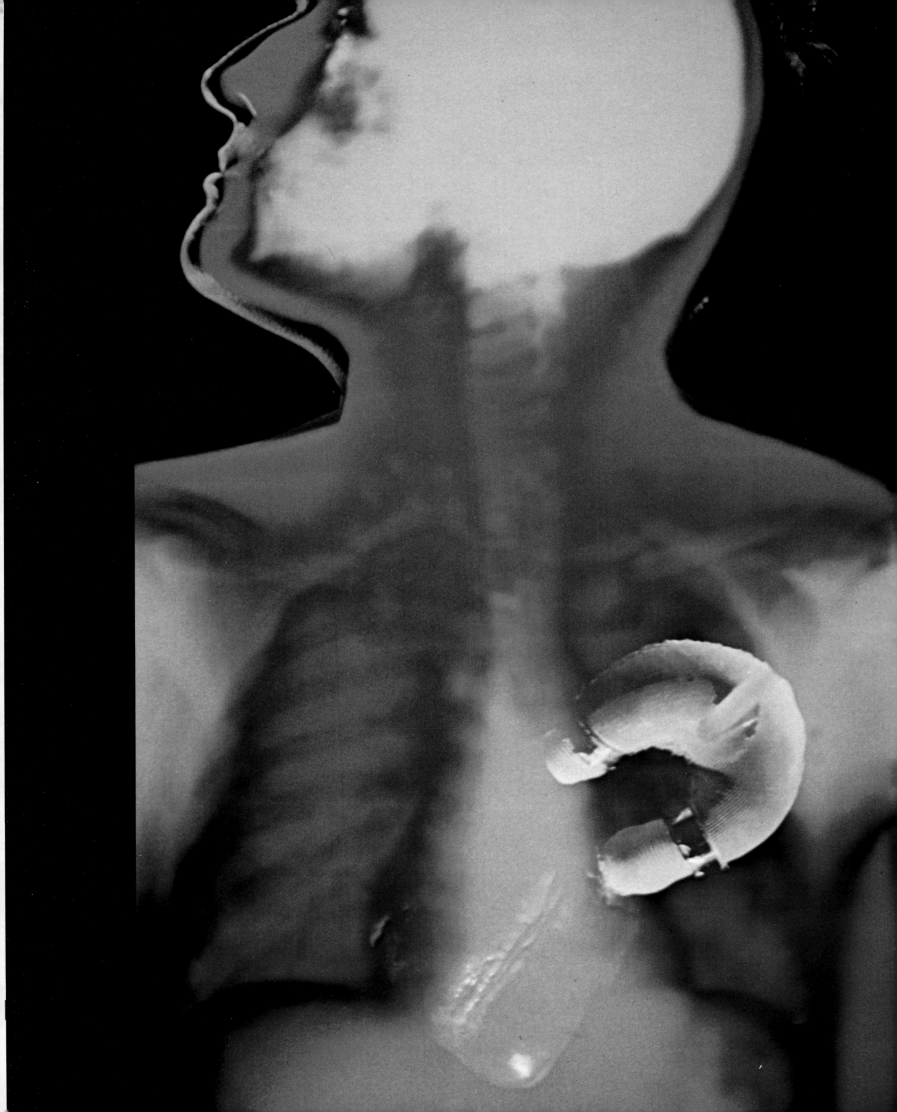

Stepchild of the automobile, Los Angeles sprawls across 464 square miles between the San Gabriel Mountains and the blue Pacific.

Without cars its clustered suburbs could not exist. County residents own nearly 6 million cars. More than a quarter of the city's area is devoted to the auto — streets, freeways, and interchanges; bridges, ramps, and overpasses; gas stations, garages, and parking lots.

the struggle for survival against the railroads, still the railroads have proved so indispensable that we make costly efforts for their resuscitation. The lives of machines are accurately suggested in the new jargon of computers, when we speak of their first, second, or third "generation."

Bringing a new machine into the world, then, like bringing a child into the world, is a serious matter, with incalculable consequences. The power to make machines is a power to accomplish more than we can imagine, in ways we cannot predict. While tyrants and totalitarian governments may try to inhibit the inventor's imagination and can limit his resources, there has never been found an effective mode of mental contraception, nor any permanently effective machine for mind control. No pill has yet been discovered to inhibit the birth of inventions. But governments and other institutions can promote the marriages of minds and can raise the inventive birthrate.

No inventor can know an invention's precise period of gestation or the time required to bring an invention to maturity. Nor can an inventor even begin to imagine the outcome of his success. Eli Whitney surely was not trying to make a Civil War. Cyrus McCormick was not intent on depopulating our farms. Henry Ford had no desire to turn choice city property into parking garages. Inventing a machine, like conceiving a child, is also motivated by personal purposes and private passions, and the act is similarly momentous and irreversible.

We have only begun to realize the Machine's occult powers. And only slowly do we discover that however difficult it has been to govern this Nation of Nations, it may be even more difficult to govern a Nation of Machines. We have had little success in disciplining the automobile. And we are finding the airplane not much more governable. Twentieth-century American civilization, more perhaps than any other in history, is a cumulative product of innumerable passionate, thoughtless, visionary (and sometimes casual) acts of inventive conception. Our cities are a machine-made product.

Yet we have hardly begun to tell ourselves the story. We know the names of a conspicuous few inventors—the Eli Whitneys, the Cyrus McCormicks, the Alexander Graham Bells, the Henry Fords, the Thomas Edisons. These are only symbolic. Just as our celebrated political and military heroes—our Adamses and Jeffersons, our Washingtons and Grants, our Lees and Eisenhowers—serve as reminders of the thousands in the ranks of citizens and soldiers.

Like those heroes, our celebrity-inventors should awaken our interest in the ranks of the common inventors who reshape our lives. Those who have most influenced everyday America—those who transformed our food, shelter, and clothing, our entertainment and information sources—those who first made a paper bag, a rotary press, a folding box, a cellophane wrapper, a picture tube, a calculating machine, or a transistor—they rarely appear in our history books.

Makers of everyday machines that remake our everyday lives have remained anonymous, partly, of course, because the inventor's work is so often collaborative, so often slowly incremental or accidental. Walter Hunt worked earnestly and with little immediate effect at inventing a sewing machine, but somehow casually in a few hours he invented the indispensable safety pin. And inventors also remain anonymous because their feats are not performed on a public platform or on the battlefield, but in attics and garages and closely fenced laboratories.

Perhaps the greatest danger in a machine-dominated America is the temptation to believe that our world is more predictable than it really is. Each triumph of our technology tempts us to redraw the geography of our imagination. We move from the world of romance and adventure into the prosaic territories of what-we-already-knew.

447

From an open world of Mystery into a world fenced by Margins of Error. In 1961 Isaac Asimov announced that we had "entered the age into which science-fiction authors 'escaped' a generation ago. The front pages of the newspapers read like some of the highly imaginative stories of the Thirties. The President of the United States can call for a concerted effort to place a man on the moon and be greeted with a soberly enthusiastic response. But science fiction suffers a malady no other branch of literature does. Each year sees possible plots destroyed."

The increasing quantities of technical knowledge and the growing number of specialties do threaten to fence in our imagination. In *Profiles of the Future,* Arthur C. Clarke notes some technological problems which the most respected experts confidently declared insoluble. What the experts saw as impossible turn out to be the spectacular technological achievements of the 20th century—from splitting the atom to landing on the moon. When an expert (especially an aged and distinguished one) tells us that something can't be done, Clarke concludes, we must not believe him.

We ordinary citizens, the democratic citizenry of a technologically triumphant America—more than any other people before us—have come to take for granted everyday violations of yesterday's common sense. We accept that pictures can fly through walls and reach instantaneously over thousands of miles, that climate can be controlled, that the human heart can be repaired or replaced. In exploring the invisible atom, we do not even require as much persuading as did Ferdinand and Isabella—to invest a million-fold what they invested. We became so accustomed in the 1960's to men walking in the heavens that when there was a new performance on our television sets, most of us didn't even bother to watch. If we have lost some of our wholesome sense of wonder, it is wholesome too that we no longer see an opaque wall separating us from the impossible.

In our expert-ridden world, a democratic citizenry has a newly crucial role. When the expert tells us that it's impossible, *we* don't believe him! The layman's vocation is to preserve the spirit of hopeful skepticism. This is a motive to adventure, a catalyst to the imagination. "Error of opinion," Jefferson declared in his First Inaugural, "may be tolerated where reason is left free to combat it." Similarly, we need never fear the extravagance of our imagination so long as reason is left free to be its tonic and the marketplace of thought is kept open for the competition.

As our nation advances into its third century, we properly emphasize its common faith: the axioms of the Declaration of Independence and the Constitution. We have, happily, shared this faith with others. In the later 20th century the American survival of that faith is remarkable. Our nation has seen the greatest technological cataclysm in history and heard a chorus of the most seductive ideologies and panaceas. The more volatile, more impatient Old Societies say we have not been courageous but simply obstinate.

For more than two centuries now we have, on the whole, kept the faith proclaimed in the Declaration of Independence and the Constitution. We continue the experiment begun in the 18th century. We have refused to be discouraged by the most respectable naysayers. Never before, they tell us, has there been a Nation of Nations. Our strenuous quest for equal opportunity, we are told, is futile. But if we are more earnest than any nation before us to uncover our defects—and more adept at advertising them to the world—this too attests our belief that *every* generation of Americans must find its own ways of experiment.

We began as a Land of the Otherwise. Nothing is more distinctive, nor has made us more *un*European than our *dis*belief in the ancient well-documented impossibilities. Every day we receive invitations to try something new. And we still give the traditional, exuberant American answer: "Why not!"

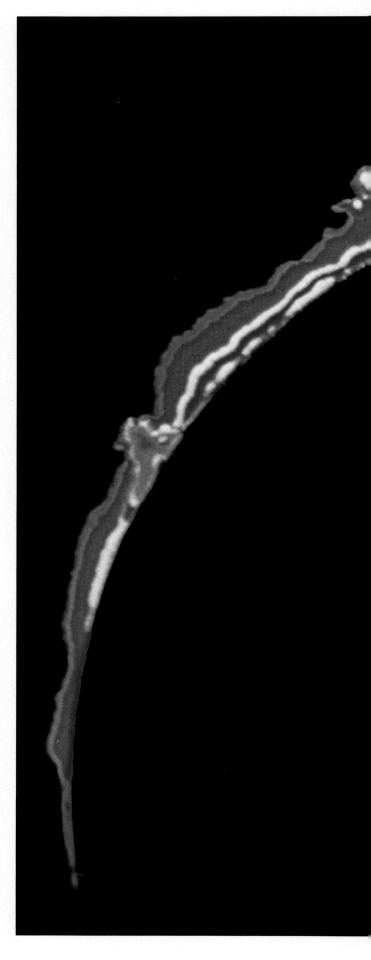

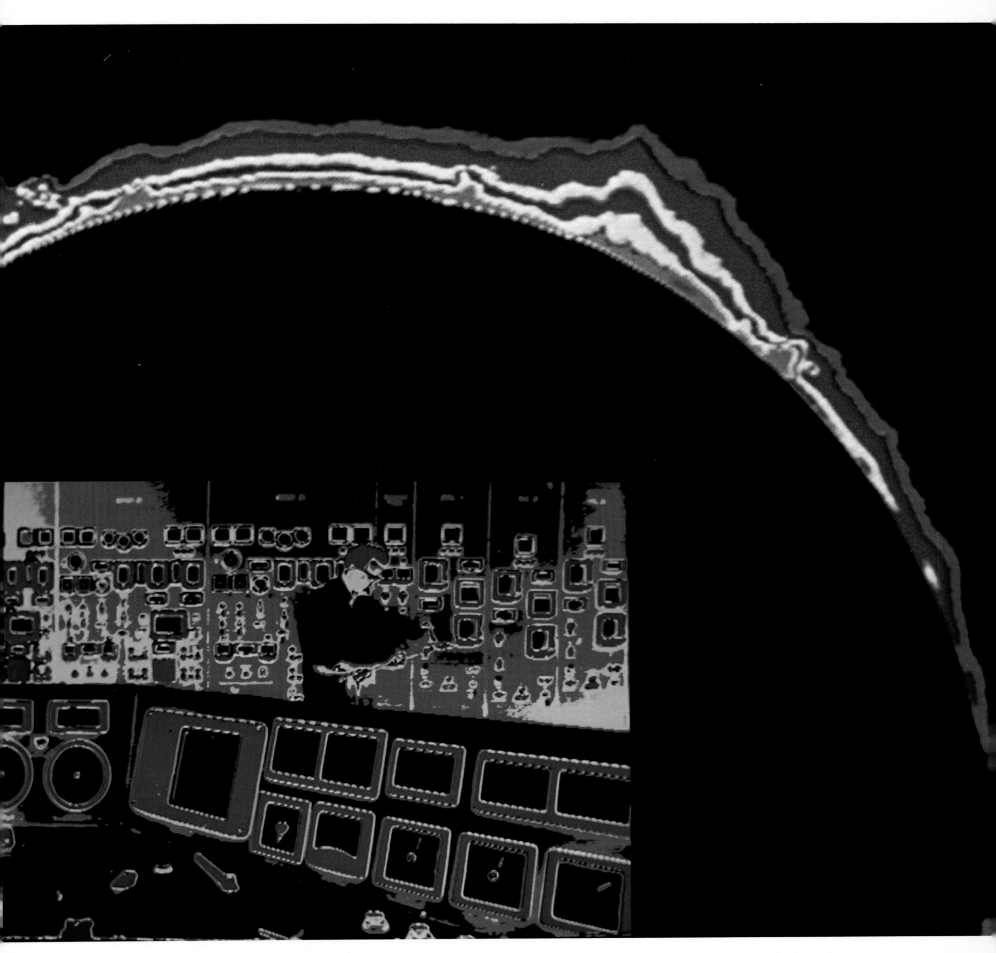

The sun's fiery corona, caught in eclipse, arcs above a control-room scene in the Los Alamos Scientific Laboratory, birthplace of the atom bomb. Color coding indicates levels of brightness in both photographs. The question for the future, says Daniel J. Boorstin, is whether we who ride the gathering momentum of an awesome technology will be able to master and not be mastered by the machine.

Picture Credits

Picture sources are separated from left to right by (;) and top to bottom by (–).

The following abbreviations are used in this list:

Brown – Brown Brothers
Culver – Culver Pictures
LC – Library of Congress
MCNY – Museum of the City of New York
MMA – Metropolitan Museum of Art, New York
NYHS – New-York Historical Society
NYPL – New York Public Library
SI – Smithsonian Institution
T-LPA – Time-Life Picture Agency
UPI – United Press International

2,3-Fred Otnes. 4,5-Harlan A. Marshall. 8-Mr. and Mrs. John Byerly. 9-Matthew R. Isenberg. 10-LC. 11-David R. Phillips. 12, 13-Erwin E. Smith Collection, LC. 14-David R. Phillips. 15-International Museum of Photography at George Eastman House. 16-Missouri Historical Society. 17-Dorothea Lange, LC. 18-Alfred Eisenstaedt, T-LPA © Time Inc. 19-Paul Schutzer, T-LPA © Time Inc. 20,21-Bruce Dale, NGS. **From the Land to the Machine:** 22,23-"The Changing West," by Thomas Hart Benton, 1930, New School for Social Research. 24-by William Gropper, 1939, Courtesy A.C.A. Galleries on loan to the MMA. 25-Neil A. Armstrong, NASA. 26,27-Nebraska State Historical Society. 28,29-James P. Blair, NGS. 30,31-Brown – David Hiser. 32-© Rube Goldberg, King Features Syndicate 1975. 33-Bruce Dale, NGS. 34,35-from "Modern Times," 1936, Museum of Modern Art. **Voyage to Eden:** 36-Fred J. Maroon, map-LC, instruments and model-Museum of American History, SI. 38-Radio-Times Hulton Picture Library. 39-Ron Helstrom. 40-John White, c. 1585, British Museum. 41-Theodore de Bry, *America,* Part II, 1591, NYPL. 42-Theodore de Bry, *America,* Part II, 1591, NYPL – John White, c. 1585, British Museum. 44-Folger Library. 45-*Puck,* September 11, 1889. 46,47-David Alan Harvey. **Working the American Land:** 48-Fred J. Maroon, tools-Museum of American History, SI, vegetables-Turkey Run Farm, National Park Service, and Farm-women's Market, Bethesda, Md. 50, 51-Martin Rogers, Turkey Run Farm. 52, 53-David Hiser; British Museum. 54-NYPL. 55-Peabody Museum of Salem. 56, 57-"Sea Captains Carousing in Surinam," by John Greenwood, c. 1758, St. Louis Art Museum. 58,59-David Hiser. 60-Bettmann Archives. 61-David Hiser; Victor R. Boswell, Jr., NGS, SI. 62 through 67-David Hiser. 68-LC. 69-Library Company of Philadelphia, 70, 71-David Hiser. **The Planting of Cities:** 72-Fred J. Maroon, map and fire engine-Museum of American History, SI, cobblestones-Mr. and Mrs. William McCormack Blair, trumpet-Insurance Company of North America. 74-NYPL. 75-Worcester Art Museum. 76, 77-Massachusetts Historical Society; LC. 78-Bettmann Archives. 79-MCNY – David Hiser, Boston Museum of Art; Insurance Company of North America; Friendship Firehouse, Alexandria, Va. 80-"Night Life in Philadelphia," by Pavel P. Svinim, 1811, Rogers Fund, MMA. 81-Nathan Benn. 82, 83-Nathan Benn. 84, 85-by Thomas Leitch, 1774. Museum of Early Southern Decorative Arts, Winston-Salem, N.C. – SI – LC. 86-Collection of Mrs. Cornelius Boardman Tyler, MMA. 87-"Tontine Coffee House," by Francis Guy, c. 1799, NYHS. 88-Victor R. Boswell, Jr., NGS, Museum of American History, SI. 89-LC – SI – LC. 90, 91-by William Walcutt, 1864, Collection of Gilbert Darlington. **Living Through a Revolution:** 92-Fred J. Maroon, artifacts-Museum of Science and Industry, SI. 94-Massachusetts Historical Society – MMA. 95-LC. 96, 97-American Antiquarian Society; LC. 98-All Anne S. K. Brown Military Collection, Brown University Library, except far right-Musee National de Blerancourt. 99-Anne S. K. Brown Military Collection, Brown University Library – National Gallery of Canada, Ottawa; Anne S. K. Brown Military Collection, Providence, R.I. 100, 101-LC; by John Trumbull, Fordham University, Frick Art Reference Library. 102, 103-Nathan Benn. 104-Mrs. J. Manderson Castle, Jr. – Connecticut Historical Society. 105-by Phillip Dawe, 1774, John Carter Brown Library, Brown University. **1776: A Nation at Birth:** 106-Engraving by John C. McRae after a painting by F. A. Charman, LC. 108-American Heritage Collection; Essex Institute, Salem, Mass. – The Henry Francis du Pont Winterthur Museum. 109-MMA; "Children of Garret & Helena DeNyse," by John Durand, c. 1768, NYHS – NYHS – David Hiser. 110-SI – Cooper-Hewitt Museum, New York; "Dr. Philomen Tracy," c. 1780, Collection of Edgar William and Bernice Chrysler Garbisch; The Henry Francis du Pont Winterthur Museum. 111-Connecticut Historical Society; Culver; University of Hartford Collection – NYPL. 112-Radio-Times Hulton Picture Library; NYPL. 112,113-MMA; NYHS – Colonial Williamsburg – Wenham Historical Association & Museum. 114-Kenneth M. Newmann, The Old Print Shop; The Charleston Museum, S.C. – Charles Towne Landing Photograph Collection. 115-National Park Service, Nathan Benn; Greenfield Village and the Henry Ford Museum. **A New World of Learning:** 116-Fred J. Maroon, artifacts-Museum of American History, SI. 118, 119-by H. F. Darby, 1845, Museum of Fine Arts, Boston. 120-NYPL. 121-NYPL; Free Library of Philadelphia – LC. 122, 123-American Antiquarian Society; SI. 124-"The Apostle's Oak," by George Harvey, 1844, NYHS. 125-from *The Franklin Fifth Reader and Speller,* 1875; American Antiquarian Society – Dartmouth College Library – Reprinted by Permission from *Lithopinion* No. 11, © 1968, Amalgamated Lithographers of America. 127-LC. 128,129-Historical Collection, M.I.T. – National Association of State Universities and Land Grant Colleges. 129-Cornell University – University of Nebraska, Lincoln. 130, 131-Frances Johnson, LC. **Americans on the Move:** 132-Fred J. Maroon, artifacts-Museum of American History, SI. 134, 135-Association of American Railroads; Western History Department, Denver Public Library. 136-David Hiser. 137-Denver Public Library – Henry E. Huntington Library. 138-from *The Rocky Mountain Saints,* by T.B.H. Stenhouse, 1873. 139-Edward S. Curtis. 140,141-LC; SI. 142, 143-Minnesota Historical Society – SI. 144-Natural History Museum of Los Angeles County – Denver Public Library. 145-F. Jay Haynes, Haynes Foundation. 146, 147-Denver Public Library; Kansas State Historical Society. 148-Amon Carter Museum of Western Art. 149-Providence Public Library. 150-NYPL. 151-David Hiser. 152, 153-Erwin E. Smith Collection, LC; Solomon D. Butcher, Nebraska State Historical Society. 154-Glenn E. Miller – State Historical Society of Colorado. 155-Denver Public Library. 156, 157-from *Beyond the Mississippi* by Albert D. Richardson; Denver Public Library. 158-Solomon D. Butcher, Nebraska State Historical Society – Kansas State Historical Society. 159-Solomon D. Butcher, Nebraska State Historical Society. 160, 161-Western History Collection, University of Oklahoma; Oklahoma Historical Society. **Tying the Nation Together:** 162-Fred J. Maroon, models-Museum of American History, SI. 164, 165-New York State Library, Albany – "Before the Days of Rapid Transit," by E. L. Henry, 1891, Chicago Historical Society. 166, 167-NYPL; "Lockport, New York," by J. Buiford, 1836, NYHS – NYPL. 168, 169-from *A History of Transportation in America,* by Seymour Dunbar, 1915; "Wooding Up on the Mississippi," lithograph by Currier and Ives, 1861, MCNY. 170, 171-The Historic New Orleans Collection; Cincinnati Public Library. 172, 173-Pony Express Museum; "Stagecoach Past Mt. Shasta," Wells Fargo Bank History Room, photo by Ivan Essayan. 174, 175-University of Washington, Seattle; Burlington Northern Railway. 176, 177-University of Washington, Seattle. 178, 179-LC. 180, 181-Lucius Morris Beebe Memorial Foundation; UPI. 182-*Dallas Morning News.* 183-Collection of Roderick Craib. **The People's Choice:** 184-Fred J. Maroon, artifacts-SI. 186, 187-NYHS. 188-Franklin D. Roosevelt Library. 189-Grouseland. 190, 191-NYPL – University of Hartford Collection; Ladies Hermitage Association; University of Hartford Collection; LC; University of Hartford Collection. 193-*Puck,* November 1, 1893, NYPL; Library Company of Philadelphia; Culver – Princeton University Library. 194, 195-Maryland Historical Society. 196-"An American Slave Market," by Taylor, 1852, Chicago Historical Society. 197-Cincinnati Historical Society. 198-NYPL. 199-Adam Woolfitt; overlay-LC. **Living Through a Civil War:** 200-Fred J. Maroon, drum and bugle-SI, picture frames-Mr. and Mrs. Howard W. Helfert, portraits-LC, Herb Peck, Jr. 202-NYHS. 203-Collection of Catherine McCook Knox – LC. 204-NYHS. 205-Collections of Georgia Maxwell Seago Fischer, Mary Seago Brooke, Dorothy Wilson Seago, and Robert Quarterman Mallard Seago. 206, 207-Herb Peck, Jr.; LC. 208-Lester S. Levy – NYPL; Institute for Sex Research, Indiana University. 209-*Frank Leslie's New Family Magazine,* 1859. 210-Kean Archives. 211-by Hunt P. Wilson, 1885, Confederate Museum at Richmond. 212, 213-LC. 214, 215-National Archives; American Heritage Collection – Collection of Pearl Korn. 216-Chicago Historical Society. 217-NYHS. 218, 219-LC. 220, 221-LC. **1876: Centennial!:** 222-*Harper's Weekly,* July 22, 1876. 224, 225-MMA; Free Library of Philadelphia. 226-Free Library of Philadelphia. 227-Free Library of Philadelphia; Almar 1876 Inc. 228-NYHS; SI; LC – State Historical Society of Wisconsin. 229-David R. Phillips – SI; NYHS. 230-Free Library of Philadelphia. 231-MCNY; University of Hartford Collection; from *Frank Leslie's Illustrated Historical Register of The Centennial Exposition 1876* – Bettmann Archives. 232, 233-NYHS; LC – John Noble, MCNY; John Noble; Detroit Historical Museum. **New Ways of Working:** 234-Fred J. Maroon, artifacts-Museum of American History, SI. 236, 237-"Bessemer Converter," by S. B. Shiley, 1895, Bethlehem Steel. 238-Courtesy of the Ford Archives, Dearborn, Michigan. 240, 241-from *A Pictorial History of American Labor,* by William Cahn; LC. 242, 243-Sears, Roebuck & Company; David R. Phillips. 244-*McClure's,* 1898-1900. 245-LC. 246, 247-Chicago Historical Society. 248-American Telephone & Telegraph Company. 249-LC – American Telephone & Telegraph Company. 250, 251-LC; Brown. 252, 253-Carnegie Library of Pittsburgh. 254-*Puck,* March 17, 1886. 255-from *A Pictorial History of American Labor,* by William Cahn – M. B. Schnapper. 256, 257-Brown. **The World Enters America:** 258-Fred J. Maroon, artifacts-Museum of American History, SI. 260-262-LC. 263-NYPL. 264,265-Allan Sherman, U. S. Department of Interior. 266-Brown. 267-LC – Brown. 268,269-American Heritage Collection; Brown. 270-*Puck,* October 17, 1894. 271-National Archives. 272-Jacob A. Riis, MCNY. 273-International Museum of Photography at George Eastman House. 274,275-National Geographic Society Collection. 276-NYHS. 277-Jacob A. Riis, MCNY. **Cities in the Machine Age:** 278-Fred J. Maroon, artifacts-U. S. Steel, American Institute of Architects, SI, and National Geographic Society Collection. 280-Feininger, MCNY. 281-Norman Thomas and W. W. Rock. 282-from *Camera Work,* No. 36, Plate XV, International Museum of Photography at George Eastman House. 283-MCNY. 284, 285-Byron Collection, MCNY; Warshaw Collection, SI. 286-*McClure's,* Vol. 32, 1908-09 – Warshaw Collection, SI; Courtesy Warnaco, Inc. 287-*McClure's,* November 1898-April 1899; Men's fashions-*Puck,* 1898-1901. 288,289-Culver; MCNY. 290-Jacob A. Riis, MCNY – LC. 291-Jacob A. Riis, MCNY. 292-Bettmann Archives – *Puck,* March 12, 1884. 294,295-MMA. 296,297-MCNY; LC; Wide World. 298-Brown. 299-*Architectural Record,* July 28, 1894. 300,301-Chicago Historical Society. **The Automobile Arrives:** 302-Fred J. Maroon, license plates-Collection of John D. Garst, model-Long Island Automotive Museum. 304-Sy Seidman. 305-Automotive History Collection, Detroit Public Library. 307-309-Motor Vehicle Manufacturer's Association. 310,311-Staten Island Historical Society; DeWitt V. Hutchings; National Geographic Society Collection. 312, 313-Courtesy of the Ford Archives, Dearborn, Michigan – Strozier Library, Florida State University. 314, 315-Alexander Wiederseder; Brown. 316-Denver Tourist Bureau. 317-Tibor Toth. 318, 319-Brown. 320,321-*Automotive Trade Journal,* July 1, 1931; LC. 322, 323-Dennis Luczak. 324, 325-Edward Clark, T-LPA © Time Inc. 326,327-Allan Grant, T-LPA © Time Inc.; J. R. Eyerman. 328-Museum of Modern Art. 329-Herbert Loebel. **Americans at Play:** 330-Fred J. Maroon, games-Museum of American History, SI, baseball-Mrs. Joseph Judge. 332, 333-Sy Seidman; New York State Historical Society, Cooperstown. 334, 335-F. Jay Haynes, Haynes Foundation; Bettmann Archives – Byron Collection, MCNY – *Puck,* 1895. 336-Peale Museum of Baltimore. 337-LC. 338, 339-H. H. Bennett; Nathan's Famous, Inc. – Brown. 340-Photoworld, Inc. 341-Basketball Hall of Fame, Springfield, Mass. 342, 343-Wide World. 344-UPI – Clifton Adams and Edwin L. Wisherd. 346-SI – LC. 347-Bob Landry, T-LPA © Time Inc. 348,349-Jonathan S. Blair. **Gone to the Movies:** 350-Fred J. Maroon, camera-Audio Optics, Inc., artifacts-Museum of American History, SI. 352, 353-Brown – Bettmann Archives; Sy Seidman. 354, 355-Culver; Collection of John W. St. Croix. 356-Culver; Museum of Modern Art – Collection of William K. Everson. 357-Culver. 358-Museum of Modern Art. 359-Museum of Modern Art; Culver. 360-Museum of Modern Art; Collection of William K. Everson. 361-Culver; Bettmann Archives – Collection of William K. Everson – Bettmann Archives. 362, 363-Culver; Museum of Modern Art – Culver – Collection of William K. Everson – Culver. 364, 365-Ben Hall Collection, Theatre Historical Society. 366-Culver – Museum of Modern Art. 367-The Archives of Labor and Urban Affairs, Wayne State University – Culver. 368-Museum of Modern Art; Culver – Culver. 370-from the MGM release "Gone with the Wind" © 1939 Selznick International Pictures, Inc. Copyright renewed 1967 by Metro-Goldwyn-Mayer. 371-Atlanta Historical Society. 372-Walt Disney Productions; LC. 373-Museum of Modern Art; Culver – Culver; Museum of Modern Art – Culver. 374, 375-from *Naked Hollywood,* by Mel & Weegee Harris, Farrar, Straus, & Giroux. 376-Collection of William K. Everson. 377-The Kobal Collection, London. **On the Home Front:** 378-Fred J. Maroon, artifacts-Museum of American History, SI. 380, 381-Underwood & Underwood. 380-National Archives. 381-LC, by permission of Leo Feist, Inc. 382-*The New York Times.* 383-Bettmann Archives. 384, 385-Harcourt, Brace & Jovanovich, Inc. – UPI – "The Passion of Sacco and Vanzetti," by Ben Shahn, 1932, Whitney Museum of American Art; Brown. 386-Culver. 387-LC; Doubleday & Co., Inc. – UPI – Brown; American Tobacco Co.; from *Buttons,* by Diana Epstein. 388-Culver; SI – Underwood & Underwood; Bettmann Archives – UPI. 389-Pierre Brissaud, *Fortune,* June 1933, © Time Inc. 390, 391-Brown; Culver; UPI – SI – LC. 392,393-LC; Theater Collection, NYPL – Culver; Brown – Brown; Will Rogers Memorial Commission, Tulsa. 394-"Bread Line-No One Has Starved," by Reginald Marsh, 1932, Whitney Museum of American Art – Granger Collection, headline-*The New York Times;* Wide World. 395-Dorothea Lange, The Oakland Museum. 396,397-LC; LC – The Viking Press, Inc.; UPI. 398, 399-UPI; Social Security Administration – Culver – National Archives. 400-*The New York Daily News* – Wide World; Collection of Kenneth A. Villani – Wide World. 401-Brown. 402, 403-UPI; Pan-American Airways – Brown – UPI – SI. 404-UPI. 405-Franklin D. Roosevelt Library – University of Hartford Collection – SI – Keystone Press Agency. 406-LC. 407-Alfred Eisenstaedt, T-LPA © Time Inc. 408-Douglas Aircraft Company. 409-LC. 410-Warshaw Collection, SI – LC. 411-Walter Sanders, Black Star. 412-© 1947, United Feature Syndicate, Inc., reproduced by courtesy Bill Mauldin. 413-Reprinted with permission from *The Saturday Evening Post* © 1945 The Curtis Publishing Company. **In Everybody's Living Room:** 414-Fred J. Maroon, television set-Museum of American History, SI, artifacts-Mrs. Oliver Schaeffer and Mrs. Catherine Starrett. 416, 417-Collection of Irving Settel. 418-Collection of Ernest Trova. 419-NBC – NBC; Culver – NBC. 420, 421-Ed Clark, T-LPA © Time Inc.; Culver. 422, 423-CBS; Culver; Arthur Shulman and Roger Youman – Arthur Shulman and Roger Youman; CBS; NBC; George Skadding, T-LPA © Time Inc. – CBS; NBC; NBC; Culver. 424-Michael Rougier, T-LPA © Time Inc. 425-Alfred Eisenstaedt, T-LPA © Time Inc. – Wide World. 427-UPI – UPI; Dick Darcey, *The Washington Post* – UPI. 428-© Rube Goldberg, King Features Syndicate 1975; UPI – Nathan Benn. 429-Kathy Andrisevic and Rich Shulman. 430, 431-Joseph H. Bailey, NGS. **An American Inventory:** 432-Fred J. Maroon, appliances-Museum of American History, SI. 434 through 441-Fred Otnes. **The Fertile Machine:** 442 through 445-Howard Sochurek. 446, 447-William A. Garnett. 448, 449-Howard Sochurek.

Biographical & Reference Notes

JOHN R. ALDEN is a James B. Duke Professor Emeritus of history at Duke University. A Guggenheim fellow, he was a Commonwealth Fund lecturer at University College, London and a Donald L. Fleming lecturer at Louisiana State University. He is the author of *A History of the American Revolution, The South in the Revolution,* and *Pioneer America.* For further reading: *The Spirit of 'Seventy-Six* by Henry Steele Commager and Richard B. Morris and *American Revolution: Mirror of a People* by William Peirce Randel.

ERIK BARNOUW is editor-in-chief of the forthcoming *International Encyclopedia of Communications* and professor emeritus of dramatic arts, Columbia University. A former editor and writer for CBS and NBC, he produced the film "Hiroshima-Nagasaki, August 1945." In 1971 he received the Bancroft Prize for his book *The Image Empire,* the final volume in his series on broadcasting. His other works include *Documentary: A History of the Non-Fiction Film* and *Tube of Plenty: The Evolution of American Television.*

RAY ALLEN BILLINGTON was senior research associate of the Huntington Library. A Guggenheim fellow, he was a professor of history at Northwestern University and at Oxford. His many books include *The Far Western Frontier 1830-1860, The Genesis of the Frontier Thesis, America's Frontier Heritage,* and *Westward Expansion.* His biography of Frederick Jackson Turner was awarded the Bancroft Prize in 1974.

DANIEL J. BOORSTIN was Librarian of Congress from 1975 to 1987. Former senior historian of the Smithsonian Institution, he has served internationally as a visiting professor of American history and held the first chair in American history at the Sorbonne. He edited *An American Primer* and the 30-volume series *The Chicago History of American Civilization* and wrote *A History of the United States* (with Brooks M. Kelley). Among his other books are *The Americans: The Colonial Experience* (awarded the Bancroft Prize); *The Americans: The National Experience* (awarded the Parkman Prize); and *The Americans: The Democratic Experience* (awarded the Pulitzer and Dexter Prizes).

DAVID HERBERT DONALD is Charles Warren Professor of American History at Harvard. He formerly taught at Columbia, Princeton, and Johns Hopkins universities. He received the Pulitzer Prize for biography for *Charles Sumner and the Coming of the Civil War.* His other books include *Civil War and Reconstruction* and *Liberty and Union.* Suggested further reading: *The Confederate States of America* by E. M. Coulter, *Life in the North During the Civil War* by George W. Smith and Charles Judah, and The National Historical Society's series *The Image of War: 1861-1865.*

RICHARD M. DORSON, former Distinguished Professor of History and Folklore and director of the Folklore Institute at Indiana University, edited the Institute's journal and the Folktales of the World series. Three times a Guggenheim fellow and twice an American Council of Learned Societies fellow, he was a Fulbright professor of American Studies at Tokyo University. He has written widely on history and folklore: *American Folklore, America in Legend, Buying the Wind, Bloodstoppers and Bearwalkers, American Negro Folktales, Folklore and Fakelore, America Begins, America Rebels,* and *Jonathan Draws the Long Bow.*

FRANK FREIDEL is professor emeritus at Harvard University and at the University of Washington, and president of the Organization of American Historians. The author of a multivolume biography of Franklin Delano Roosevelt, he also wrote *Over There, The Splendid Little War,* and *America in the Twentieth Century.* For further reading: *The Glory and the Dream* by William Manchester, *Great Times* by J. C. Furnas, and *War and Society: The United States 1941-1945* by Richard Polenberg.

WILLIAM H. GOETZMANN is Dickson, Allen and Anderson Centennial Professor in American studies and history at the University of Texas. He received the Pulitzer and Parkman Prizes in 1967 for his book *Exploration and Empire: the Explorer and Scientist in the Winning of the American West.* He worked on the recent television series *The West of the Imagination* and coauthored a book by the same name. For further reading: Oscar Winter's *The Transportation Frontier 1865-1890* and Louis Hunter's *Steamboats on the Western Rivers.*

RUSSELL LYNES is a former contributing editor and managing editor of *Harper's* magazine, a trustee of the New-York Historical Society, and past president of the board of trustees for the Archives of American Art. He is the author of *The Tastemakers, The Domesticated Americans, Good Old Modern, The Art-Makers of 19th-Century America,* and *The Lively Audience.* For further reading: *A History of Recreation* by Foster Rhea Dulles.

BLAKE McKELVEY, author and educator, was a founder and first president of the Urban History Group within the American Historical Association and a pioneer in the study of urban development. As City Historian of Rochester, New York, he compiled a four-volume biography of that city and three summary reports. He also wrote *The Urbanization of America, 1860-1915; The Emergence of Metropolitan America, 1915-1966;* and *The City in American History.* For further reading: *Cities in the Wilderness 1625-1742* and *Cities in Revolt 1743-1776* by Carl Bridenbaugh; *City Life 1865-1900* edited by Ann Cook and others.

EDMUND S. MORGAN is Sterling Professor Emeritus of history at Yale. His many books include *Virginians at Home, The Puritan Dilemma, American Slavery—American Freedom: The Ordeal of Colonial Virginia,* and *Inventing the People.* For further reading: *History of Agriculture in the Southern United States to 1860* by Lewis C. Gray and *American Husbandry,* edited by Harry J. Carman.

ELTING E. MORISON is Killian Professor Emeritus at the Massachusetts Institute of Technology. His books include *Men, Machines, and Modern Times,* which received the McKinsey Award; *Turmoil and Tradition,* awarded the Parkman Prize; and *From Know-How to Nowhere.* Further reading: *American Heritage History of American Business and Industry* by Alex Groner; *Ford Methods and the Ford Shops* by Horace Arnold and Fay Faurote; and *Work in America: Report of a Special Task Force to the Secretary of Health, Education, and Welfare.*

ANN NOVOTNY, a former writer, editorial consultant, and director of Research Reports in New York City, wrote *Strangers at the Door, Alice's World,* and *Images of Healing.* Suggested further reading: Carl Wittke's *We Who Built America,* Oscar Handlin's *The Uprooted* and *Pictorial History of Immigration,* and Bernard A. Weisberger's *American Heritage History of the American People.*

WILLIAM PEIRCE RANDEL is a former professor of English at the University of Maine and author of *Edward Eggleston, The Ku Klux Klan, American Revolution, Centennial: American Life in 1876,* and *The Evolution of American Taste.* For further reading: *The Glorious Enterprise* by John Maass and the Paddington Press facsimile edition of *Frank Leslie's Illustrated Historical Register of the United States Centennial Exposition 1876.*

RICHARD SCHICKEL, staff contributor for *Time* magazine, was film critic for *Life.* A Guggenheim fellow, he wrote, produced, and directed the television series, "The Men Who Made the Movies." He is the author of a book by that title and several other studies in film history, most notably *The Disney Version* and *D. W. Griffith: An American Life.* Further reading: George Pratt's *Spellbound in Darkness;* Kevin Brownlow's *The Parade's Gone By.*

WILLIAM V. SHANNON is University Professor and Professor of History and Journalism at Boston University. He served on the editorial board of the *New York Times* and as U. S. Ambassador to Ireland. His books include *The American Irish* and *They Could Not Trust the King.* Suggested further reading: *History of American Presidential Elections* by Arthur M. Schlesinger, Jr., and F. L. Israel and *From Slavery to Freedom* by John Hope Franklin.

BEN J. WATTENBERG, author, editor, newspaper columnist, and political advisor, is a senior fellow at the American Enterprise Institute and coeditor of AEI's *Public Opinion* magazine. He has written and hosted a series of television documentaries. He is vice chairman of Radio Free Europe/Radio Liberty, coauthor of *The Real Majority,* and author of *The Real America, The Good News Is the Bad News Is Wrong,* and *The Birth Dearth.*

BERNARD A. WEISBERGER is a writer, a former professor of American history at Vassar College, and former fellow of the American Council of Learned Societies. His books include *The New Industrial Society* and *The Dream Maker.* For further reading: *The American Automobile* by John B. Rae, *Ford* by Allan Nevins and Frank E. Hill, and *Treasury of the Automobile* by Ralph Stein.

GORDON S. WOOD is professor of history at Brown University and a former fellow of the Institute of Early American History and Culture. His books include *The Rising Glory of America, 1760-1820* and *The Creation of the American Republic, 1776-1787,* awarded the Bancroft Prize in 1970. For further reading: James Axtell's *The School Upon a Hill* and Bernard Bailyn's *Education in the Forming of American Society.*

LOUIS B. WRIGHT, former director of the Folger Shakespeare Library, was vice chairman of the Council on Library Resources, Inc., life trustee of The Shakespeare Birthplace Trust, and a director of the Truman Library Institute for National and International Affairs. His books include *Middle-Class Culture in Elizabethan England, The Atlantic Frontier, Cultural Life of the American Colonies,* and *Gold, Glory, and the Gospel.* For further reading: *The Discovery of North America* by W. P. Cumming and others and *The European Discovery of America* (two volumes) by Samuel Eliot Morison.

Index

Illustrations appear in **boldface** type

Abie's Irish Rose **392**
Abolitionists 195, 197-198
Adams, John 83, 111; memento **190**
Adams, John Quincy 185
Addams, Jane 299
Advertising **114, 147, 228, 229, 244-245,** 285; automobiles 310, 314, 317, **320,** 328; Burma-Shave **316;** cigarettes **387;** circus **232-233;** clothing **286-287;** land 313; "personals" 229; radios **416;** slave sales **84,** 197; television 418, 420, 422, 425, 439-440; vaudeville **393;** World War II 406
Agee, James 351
Agriculture: colonial 50, 53, 55-56; folklore 60; Indians 49, 53; livestock 53; mechanization 27, **28-29,** 159, 435; methods 53, 55-56; tools **48,** 55; see also Farmers
Air conditioning 33, 80, 294, 444
Airplanes **402-403,** 447; World War II **408**
Alcoholic beverages 112, 114, 151, 228, 300, 331 see also Prohibition
Alger, Horatio 228, 232
Algonquians (Indians) **40**
Allen, Fred 416, **419**
Almanacs **68, 69,** 89; maxims 69
American Red Cross 379; founder 209
American Revolution 93-105; atrocities 103, 104; battles 93, 100, 103; blacks **98,** 104; boycotts 68-69, 94; British blockade 99, 103; craftsmen's role 62, 65, 66; Indians **99,** 103; Loyalists 100, 103, **104, 105;** militiamen 93, 98; navies 99; prelude 68-69, 93, 94; prisoners 99, **100-101,** 104; see also British Army; British Navy; Continental Army
Amusement parks 336, **337,** 341; theme parks 348, **349**
Amusements 330-349; Centennial era 223-224, 232, 233; colonial era **112-115;** see also Movies; Radio; Television
Anarchists 384
Anthony, Susan B. 209, 227
Anti-Masonic Party 186
Antislavery Society 197, 198
Apprenticeship system 49, 86, 89, 120, 130
Architecture, urban **278,** 279, 293, 299
Armed forces: world wars 380, 383, 409, 412; see also Continental Army; U. S. Army
Army-McCarthy hearings **425**
Asimov, Isaac: quoted 448
Assembly lines **246-247;** automobiles **238,** 239, 309, 317, 319, 320, 328
Astaire, Fred 353, **359,** 366, 375
Astronauts 426, 442; Edwin Aldrin, Jr. **25, 427**
Atlanta, Ga.: Civil War 219, 220
Atom bomb: development 409, 412, 449
Atwood, John, and family **118-119**
Automobiles 300, 302-329, 435, 437, 440, 444, 446, 447; accidents 328; costs 304, 309, 314, 317, 319, 320, 322; financing 313, 317; imports 322, 328; license plates **302,** 303; maintenance 304, 306, **307,** 309, tool kit **306;** manufacture **238,** 239, 304, 306, 309, 312, 313, 314, 317, 319, 320, 322, 328, 438; models 317, 319, **322-323;** motoring manuals 306; races 304, **308-309,** 310; safety features 328; sales 309, 314, 317, 319, 320, 322; service stations 314, **318-319,** 328; steam 304, **305;** tires 306, **307,** 309, 314, 320
Aviation: barnstormers **402-403;** passenger service **403;** transatlantic flight, first 390, 402

Babcock, Orville 223
Ball, Lucille 420, **422**
Ballot box **184**
Baltimore, Md. 89, 90, 299; Gwynn Oak Park 336, trolley **336;** Plug-uglies **194**
Banks and banking 76, 90, 317, 326, 399, 434; national 90, 163, 220
Barbed wire fencing **153,** 159
Barber, colonial **95**
Barnum, Phineas Taylor: circus 232, poster **232-233;** museum 332
Barrels, making of 56, **62-63**
Barrymore, John 369, 371
Barthelmess, Richard 354
Bartholomew, Freddie **373**
Barton, Clara 209
Baseball 223, 233, 400, 437; first teams 332; "immortals" **400, 401,** autographs **330;** television 418; trading cards **400;** World Series 400, first **342-343**
Basketball 341, **430-431**
Beatles **422**
Bed warmer **110**
Belknap, William 223
Bell, Alexander Graham 181, 224, 235
Bellamy, Ralph 418, 420
Benny, Jack 416, **419**
Benton, Thomas Hart: painting by **22-23**
Bergen, Edgar **419**
Berkeley, Busby: musicals **358-359,** 376
Berle, Milton 420, **420-421,** 425
Berlin, Irving 269
Bessemer converter **237,** 242, 279
"Betty Boop" garter button **387**
Bicycles 283, 303, **334-335,** 336, 348
Biograph studios, New York City 365, 366
Birth control 229, 387
The Birth of a Nation (movie) 366, 384
Birthrate 107, 108, 109, 229
Blacks **21,** 107, 231; athletes **400;** Civil War 210, 217, 219, soldiers **216;** economic gains 440; education 128; employment, wartime 210, 383, 410; freedmen **98,** 104; gold rush 153; northward migration 383, 387; politics 231; see also Slaves
Blacksmith **61**
Blaine, James 223
Blizzard of '88: New York City **280**
"blue laws" 111
Boardman, Elijah 86
Bogart, Humphrey 353, **363**
Bolshevism, fear of 317, 383, 384
Boardman, Elijah 86
Books 55, 89, 209; best sellers **384, 387, 397;** Bible 89, **118-119;** Centennial era 224, **232;** colonial era 115; schoolbooks **116, 121, 125,** 126
Boone, Daniel 90, 133, 322
Boorstin, Daniel J. 182, 390, 415, 441
Bootleggers 388
Boston, Mass. 77, 78, 79, 80, 84, 85-86, 89, 90, 93, 94, 96, 99, 103, 104, 118, 120, 280; Common **74,** 77; police strike 384; State Houses **76, 77**
Boston Massacre 74, 94
Boxing: women 232; world heavyweight championship bouts 384, **400,** 418
Boy Scouts: World War I parade **380-381**
Boycotts 197; Revolutionary era 68-69, 94
Boylston, Zabdiel 110
Bradford, William 44, 89
Brady, Diamond Jim 336
Brando, Marlon 353, **363,** 366
Bridges: canals **164-165;** railroad **176-177,** 178
British Army: American Revolution 93-94, 96, 98, 99, 100, 103, officers 94, **95, 99**
British Navy 99
Broun, Heywood 345, 400
Bryan, William Jennings 390; cartoon **391;** presidential campaign memento **184**
Buffalo Bill Stories (magazine) **155**
Buick (auto) **308-309,** 309, **323**
Bundling 108
Bunyan, Paul **24**

Burma-Shave signs **316**
Butterfield Overland Express Co. 154
Buttons: Betty Boop **387;** political **111, 191, 405;** Prohibition **388**

Cabot, John 37
Cadillac (auto) 309, **323**
Caesar, Sid 418, **423**
Cagney, James 353, **363,** 371
Calamity Jane 227
California: annexation of 195; Bear Flag Revolt 147; Drake expedition 43; migration to 142, 143, 147, 150, 153, 154, 396
California Trail 143
Calvert, Cecil, second Baron Baltimore 45
Canals **164-175,** 166, **166-167,** 168, 178
Cannon: Centennial Exhibition **226;** Civil War **212-213;** Valley Forge **102-103**
Capital punishment 84-85, **111,** 231, 384, **391**
Capone, "Scarface" Al 388
Capra, Frank 371
Card games 115, **330,** 341, 345
Carnegie, Andrew 251, 252
Carolinas 40, 41, 46; agriculture 55-56; naval stores 55; settlement 45
Carpenters' Company: Philadelphia 80, 86, Carpenters' Hall **81**
Cartoons **32;** animated 351, **372,** 376; editorial 89, **193,** 231, **254, 292, 335, 391, 394, 412, 428**
Cattle industry 178; cattlemen 159; cowboys **12-13,** 25, **152-153;** range wars 152
Censorship: movies 369; newspapers 89
Census, Bureau of the: statistics 107, 189, 251, 336, 433-441
Centennial Exhibition, Philadelphia 181, 224, **224-225,** 227; bicycle 336; Corliss steam engine 181, 224, **224;** demonstration of the telephone 181, 224; displays 224, **224, 226,** 228, 230, 231; souvenirs **227, 231**
Chancellorsville, Va.: battle 213, casualties **214-215**
Chaplin, Charlie **35,** 351, **356,** 366, 369
Charities 86, 299
Charleston, S.C. 45, 73, 78, **84-85,** 85, 93, 96, 103, 111, 114, 456; Civil War 201, **221**
Charlie McCarthy **419**
Chautauqua Lake, N.Y. 331
Cherokee Strip: opening to settlers **160-161**
Chesapeake Bay, and region 43, 89, 120; wildlife refuge **46-47**
Chevrolet (auto) 309, 314, **322, 323**
Chew, Benjamin 83; country house **82**
Chicago, Ill. 166, 168, 178, 246, 280; fire 279, 299; gang wars 388; Hull House 299; Loop **300-301;** police **387, 427;** skyscrapers 293, **299;** steel strikers **384;** see also Columbian Exposition
Child labor 239, **250-251, 273,** 276, 410
Childbirth: maternal deaths 109
Childhood: attitudes toward 118, reflected in clothing 8, **14, 75, 109;** colonial amusements **112-113,** 114; see also Education
Christmas: colonial era 112; Great Depression **397;** Santa Claus **233**
Chrysler (auto) 317, **322**
Cigarettes 383; advertisement **387**
Circus poster **232-233**
Cities, colonial 73-91, 93; fires 78, **79,** 80, 89; law enforcement 84-85; officials 80, 84; poor 83, 86; public markets 80; streets **72,** 73, 77, 80, **81,** 83, lights 84
Cities, late 19th century 279-301; corruption 192, 285, 300; cultural institutions 293; ethnic enclaves 189, 192, 276; fire fighters 299, steam pumper 279, **298;** government 192, 195, 285, 300; growth of 279-280, 283; mass transit 280, **282, 283,** 285, 301; parks 290, 293; police

300; sanitation 280, 283, 285, 290, 293, 299; streets 283, 285
City planning 73, 77, 78, 80, 290, 293, 348
Civil rights 89, 104, 107, 230, 231; Confederates 223; see also Voting rights
Civil War 8, 200-221; battles **211,** 213, 214; casualties 201, 214, **214-215;** causes 182; civilian war efforts 203, 204, 206, 209, 210; economy 209-210, 212; financing 209, 212; medical care 204, 206, 214; profiteers 210; refugees **220;** soldiers **10,** blacks **216,** hardships 205, 206, 214, pastimes 209, punishment **210,** weapons 213
Civilian Conservation Corps **398-399**
Civilian Defense wardens: World War II 406, 412, helmet **378**
Clarke, Arthur C. 448
Clay, Henry 181, 186
Cleveland, Grover 294; election campaigns 191, mementos **190, 191**
Cliveden (house), Philadelphia **82**
Clothing: children 8, **14, 75, 109;** colonial era 64, 65, 69, **74, 75, 92, 108, 109, 112;** ready-to-wear 273, **286-287;** recreational activities 335, **338-339,** 346; women's fashions **209,** 335, 383, **387,** 409, 412; see also Uniforms
Coal mining: children **250-251**
Coffeehouses, colonial 86, **87,** 89
Cohan, George M. 384; music 381
Colbert, Claudette **366,** 371
Cold Harbor, Va.: Civil War dead **215**
Colleges 86, 104, 126, **128-129,** 220; enrollment 435; graduates 439
Colonies, English 43-45, 48-71; boycott of British goods 68-69, 94; craftsmen **61-67;** farms 49, **50, 51,** 53; fisheries **54,** 56; manufacturing 69; map, contemporary **96-97;** plantations **52-53,** 55; slaves 55; taxes 68; trade 57, 60, 68, restraints 68; see also Cities, colonial
Columbian Exposition, Chicago 293, **294-297**
Columbus, Christopher 37
Computers 440; components **33, 442-443;** evolution 447; X-ray scanners 444
Concord coaches **173,** 236, 239
Conestoga wagons 89, 147
Confederacy 201, 203, 212, 217, 219, 223; anthem **203;** destruction 219, 220, **221;** refugees **220;** soldiers **200,** blacks 217
Congress: television coverage 418, hearings **425,** 428, 430
Connolly, Richard "Slippery Dick" 192
Conscription: Civil War 210, riots 210; World War I 379-380, 381; World War II 405, 406, 409
Constitution 69, 163, 223, 448; amendments 383, 387, 388
Continental Army 94, **98,** 98-99, 103, **103,** 104; food 98, 100; hardships 93, 94, 98-99, 102, **103;** mutinies 99; uniforms 94, **98,** weapons **92,** 94, artillery **102-103**
Continental Congress 69, 83, 94, 96, 99, 104; Declaration of Independence 96, 103, 104; meeting place **81;** paper money **92,** 98, 103-104
Converse, Florence 394
Coolidge, Calvin 384
Coolidge, William D. 255
Cooper, Peter 172, 182
Corliss steam engine: Centennial Exhibition 181, 224, **224**
Corn **48,** 53, 110
Cotton 134, 138, 212
Courtship 108, 109; automobile **304,** 317, 326
Cowboys **12-13,** 25, **152-153;** movies **360-361;** television **422**

Craftsmen 56, 78, 83, 90, 235, 236; blacksmith 61; cooper 62-63; gunsmiths 66-67, 247
Credit 244, 394; cards 440
Cripple Creek, Colo.: main street 146-147
Crossword puzzles 344
Crow (Indians) 139
Crush, William 182
Cukor, George 366, 371
"Custer's Last Stand" 227

Dancing 16, 112, 345-346, 347
Davis, Bette 363
Daylight-saving time 381
Dean, Jerome (Dizzy) 400
Death 58, 215, 228
A Death in the Family (Agee) 351
Debt, personal 50, 317
Declaration of Independence 69, 96, 103, 104, 130, 195, 227, 448
Delaware and Hudson Canal 164-165
DeMille, Cecil B. 354
Democratic Party 185, 186, 189, 195, 198, 223; immigrants 189, 192, 195, 198; nominating conventions 405, 426; symbol 231; see also Tammany Hall
Department stores 284-285, 286; malls 440
Depressions: Civil War 209; Panic of 1893 293, 296; see also Great Depression
De Soto, Hernando 40
Detroit, Mich.: auto industry 239; Belle Isle 293; race riot 410
Dewey, Thomas E. 412; campaign memento 405
Dickens, Charles 165, 166, 180, 251
Diet 33, 43, 83, 98, 110, 114, 133, 150, 229, 275, 276, 293
Disease 40, 43, 46, 98-99, 101, 109, 133, 142, 150, 444; cities 283, 285, 290, 293, 299; Civil War casualties 204, 205, 206, 214; germ theory 299; immigrants 267
Disney, Walt 351, 372; Snow White 372; theme parks 348, Disney World 332, 349
Dix, Dorothea 195
Dodge City, Kans. 146, 227
Dolls 41, 113; Centennial souvenir 231
Douglas, Stephen A. 198; election campaign 191
Douglas, Frederick 198
Draft see Conscription
Dragnet (television show) 420, 423, 426
Drive-in movies 326-327
Drummer boy: Civil War 206
Dubinsky, David 273
Durant, William Crapo 309, 312
Duryea, Frank and Charles 303, 304
Dust Bowl 396

Earhart, Amelia 403
Earthquakes: New Madrid 168, 171; San Francisco 249
Edison, Thomas Alva 20, 235, 244, 253, 294, 353, 355
Education 88, 112, 117-131, 293; colleges 89, 126, 128-129, 201, 204, 227, 293, 435, 439; compulsory 293; financing 120, 123, 128; immigrants 274, 275, 276, 277, 293; religion 118, 119, 120, 121, 126; teachers 122, 123, 125, 127, 128, 130
Eight-hour day 255; poster 255
Elections, national: campaign techniques 186, 189, 191, 231; conventions 223, 405, 426, first 186; mass media 405, 428; mementos 111, 184, 189, 190-191, 231, 405; rallies 188, 404; slogans 189; voting 111, 186, 387
Electoral College 185, 186, 231
Electricity: Columbian Exposition 294, 296-297; household appliances 228, 432, 435; incandescent lamp 234, 288, development 249, 253, 255-256; street lighting 285
Electronics: medical devices 444, 445
Elevated train 273, 280, 283, 285

Elevators 20, 224, 279, 293
Elfreth's Alley, Philadelphia 83
Ellis Island, N.Y. 259-260, 260, 262, 263-269, 270, 275-276
Emancipation Proclamation 198, 210, 217, 231
Entertainment 33, 112, 113-114, 232-233, 330-349, 437, 438, 440 see also Movies; Radio; Television; Vaudeville
Erie Canal 165, 166, 166-167, 168, 182; construction 167, tools 166; locks 165, 167
Evangelists 163; Aimee Semple McPherson 391
Executions 84-85, 111, 384, 391

Fairbanks, Douglas: Liberty Loan rally 380
Fairs; expositions see Centennial Exhibition; World's fairs
False teeth 110
Families: colonial era 107, 108; educational role 118, 118-119, 120, 123, 130; income 434, 435, 437, 438, 440; standard of living 432-441; World War II 410
Faneuil Hall, Boston 80, 197
Far West: settlement 138, 142-143, 147-148, 150, 153-154
Farmers 435, 438; colonial 49, 50, 53, 56, 93, 98, 110; government subsidy 399; Grange 182, 230; Great Depression 396, 397; World War I prosperity 383; see also Homesteaders; Planters
Federalists 163
Ferguson, Miriam (Ma) 387
Ferris wheel 296, 297
Fields, W. C. 356, 376, 392, 419
Fillmore, Millard 189, 195
Firearms 20, 92, 94, 132; manufacture 66-67, 247
Fires 78, 80, 89, 257, 273, 279, 299; fire engines 72, 79, 279, 298
Fishing 54, 56, 60, 77, 114 see also Whaling
Fitzgerald, F. Scott: quoted 16, 387
Flagg, James Montgomery: recruiting poster by 378
Flagpole sitting 390
Flags 4-5; Revolutionary War 111
Flappers 386-387
Florida: colonists 40; explorers 41; Indians 40-42; land boom 312
Flynn, Errol 373
Folklore 24; boasting tale 150; definition 44-45; devils and specters 120; ethnic humor 270; the phantom rider 317; slickers and bumpkins 78; yarns of the soil 60
Food 48, 49, 65, 68, 77, 83, 98, 178-179, 180, 212, 219, 229, 435, 439; adulteration of 293; ethnic variety 275, 276; hot dog 339, 341; meat packing plant 246-247; rationing 410; travelers' 165, 178-180; vendors 80, 290
Food and Drugs Act (1906) 293
Football 228, 336, 400; professional 346, 348, television 346, 426, 427, 430
Ford, Henry 239, 304, 309, 313, 322, 447
Ford, Henry, II 328
Ford (auto) 322, 323, 324-325; Model A 314; Model T 239, 309, 312-313, 314, 322, assembly 238, miniature (1910) 302
Foreigners: observations on American life 109, 165, 166, 178, 180, 185, 189, 192, 197, 225, 227, 228, 242, 280, 285, 293, 331, 346, 374, 409
Fort Sumter, S.C.: fall of 203; flag 202
Forty-niners 143, 144, 150, 153, 154; sketch by 137
Fourth of July celebrations 106, 204, 222, 224, 227, 384-385
Franklin, Benjamin 79, 83, 89, 103, 104, 110, 111, 125, 275, 381; Almanack 68, 69, 69, 89; printing press 88, 224
Franklin, William 104

Free Soilers 198
Freedmen: American Revolution 98, 104; statue 231
French and Indian War: weapon 92
Fugitive Slave Act 198; warning 199
Fulton, Robert 168
Funerals: colonial era 58, 109, 114; gifts 109
Fur: trade 60, 77-78; trappers 142

Gable, Clark 353, 366, 370, 371
Gage, Thomas 93
Gallico, Paul 412
Gambling 114, 209, 332
Gangbusters (radio show) 416-417
Gangsters 388; movies 362-363
Garbo, Greta 366, 375
Garfield, James A. 189, 331, 348
Garland, Judy 373
Garment industry 260, 272-273, 285, 286
Garrison, William Lloyd 195, 197, 198
Gasoline: ration stamp 410; shortage 328, 412, 437; stations 318-319
Gehrig, Lou: autograph 330
General Electric Company 433; Columbian Exposition exhibit 294, 296-297; electric lamp development 253, 255-256; television broadcasts 415-416
General Motors 309, 312-314, 317, 319, 328
George III: statue 91
Georgia: settlement 45-46
German immigrants: community life 189, 192; politics 20, 185, 198, 230
Gettysburg, Battle of 214; embalmers' office 215
"Ghost Dance" ritual 141
Ghost towns 151, 154
Girl Scouts: World War I 383
Gish, Lillian 353, 354, 355, 369, 371
Glass industry 303, 309, 314
The Godfather (movie) 363, 366, 376
Gold: prospectors 144-145
Gold rush 143, 144, 148, 150, 153-154; boomtowns 144, 146-147, 148, 150, 151, 154; mining camps 144, 153
Goldberg, Rube: cartoons 32, 34, 428
Goldwater, Barry 273
Golf 345, 346; miniature golf 344
Gone With the Wind (movie) 370; premiere 371
Goodyear Television Playhouse 423, 425
Gould, Mrs. George Jay 288
Government: federal 69-70, corruption 223, 230, emergency powers 220, 380, 383, 409, New Deal agencies 399, transportation 165, 166, 178, 182, 322; municipal 78, 80, 84, 185, 192, 195, 285, reform 300; see also Laws; Politics
Grange, Harold (Red) 400
Grange 182, 230, 243
Grant, Ulysses S. 180, 204, 206, 220, 223, 224, 227, 233; corruption of administration 223; pipe 184
The Grapes of Wrath (Steinbeck) 397
Gravestones 56, 58-59, 109
Great Depression 8, 317, 320, 322, 346, 372, 394, 396, 399, 416, 433, 434, 437, 438; breadlines 394, 395; farmers 396-397; migrants 8, 17, 321; relief programs 317, 322, 399; sit-down strikes 317
Great Plains 399; settlement of 156, 159-160
The Great Train Robbery (movie) 355, 360
Griffith, D. W. 354, 365-366, 369
Gunsmiths 66-67, 247

Half Moon (ship) 44
Hallidie, Andrew: cable car 280
Hamilton, Alexander 70
Hancock, John 84, 96, mansion 74
Harding, Warren G. 405; playing cards 330
Harper's Weekly: cartoon 193
Harrison, Benjamin: election campaign memento 191

Harrison, William Henry 134; election campaign 186, 189, 190-191, rally 188, souvenirs 189
Hart, William S. 351, 353, 360
Harvard University 125, 126; instructors 120, 128
"Harvey Girls" 180
Hawks, Howard 353, 369, 371, 374, 376
Hayes, Rutherford B. 223, 233; campaign 231; election memento 231
Health: Centennial era 226, 228, 233, patent medicines 229; Civil War soldiers 203, 204, 205, 206, 214; colonial times 107, 109, 110; health insurance 317; see also Disease; Medical care; Sanitation
Held, John: magazine cover 386
Hepburn, Katharine 359, 366
Hessians: British mercenaries 99, 103
Heston, Charlton 327
Hickok, Wild Bill 227
Highways 314, 328; interstate highway system 322
Hine, Lewis W.: photographs by 250
Hitchcock, Alfred 371
Holidays: colonial era 112; mementos 233
Holmes, Oliver Wendell 8, 20, 229
Homestead Act (1862) 156, 160; establishing claims 156
Homesteaders 26-27, 156-157, 158, 159, 220
"Hooker's Division" 209
Hoover, Herbert 396, 415; campaign memento 405
Hoover, J. Edgar 384
Hornbook 121
Horse racing 114, 223, 233; harness racing 233
Horsecars 280, 282
Hot dogs 341; Nathan's stand 339
Houdini, Harry 392
Household implements 50, 61, 64-65, 109, 110, 112-113, 228, 229, 244-245; electrical appliances 432, 433, 435
Houses 314, 320, 322, 433, 440; colonial era 77, 78, 82, 83; log cabins 50-51, 55; mansions 288-289; plantations 52, 55; soddies 26-27, 137, 156-157, 159; tenements 285, 290, 291
Howard, Leslie 363
Howdy Doody (television shows) 418, 422
Howe, Samuel G. 195
Howells, William Dean 224
Hudson, Henry 44
Huguenots 40, 86
Hunt, Walter 447
Hunting 42, 44, 114; rifles 66

Ice skating 114, 340
Ice wagon 131
Immigrants 15, 20, 23, 86, 107, 133, 159, 258-277; denigration of 185, 195, 198; education of 274, 275, 276, 277, 293, 299; folklore 270; inducements 186, 259, 262; jobs 166, 167, 174, 189, 259, 260, 272-273, 285, 286; living conditions 290; nationalities 186, 189, 259, 260, 262, 440; naturalization 259, 275, notable 20, 259, 260, 262, 269, 270, 273; number of 23, 259-260; passage 261, 269-270; politics, role in 185, 189, 192, 195, 198, 230; receiving stations 270 see also Ellis Island; recruitment 178, 260, 262, 276, poster 276; restrictive legislation 260, 262, 267, 270, 275
Indentured servants 46, 50, 55, 120
Independence Square, Philadelphia: Centennial 222, 224, 227
Indian reservations 138, 140-141
"Indian Territory" 137; opened to settlement 160
Indianapolis Speedway (1909) 308-309
Indians 11, 24, 37, 38, 40, 41, 43, 44, 54, 60, 134, 137, 138, 142, 230;

agriculture 49, 53; Algonquian **40;** American Revolution 94, **99,** 103; Crow **139;** "Diggers" 138; Five Civilized Tribes 137; forced migrations 137, 138; "Ghost Dance" 141; hunting **42,** 50, 53; number of 24, 50; railroads 178, 181; Sioux chief **141;** Timucuan **40, 41;** uprisings 134

Indigo 45, 46, 56, 73

Industrial Revolution 70, 234-257; assembly line production **238,** 239; factory system 239, 242; interchangeable parts 247; machine tools 247; machines, specialized 239; manufacturing methods 236, 239; traditional 235, 236; research and development 249, 253, 255, 256

Industrial Workers of the World 240, 383

Industry 90, 234-257; Depression 399; World War I production 380; World War II production 319, 406, 409; *see also* names of industries

Inflation 99, 103, 209, 210, 212, 230, 383, 384, 410, 412

Influenza epidemic 380

Installment buying 244

International Ladies Garment Workers Union 273

Interstate highway system 322

Inventions **32,** 33, 34, 110, 164, **234,** 294, **432,** 444, 447; automobile development 303-304; Centennial era 224, 228; communications media 415, 416; railroad development 172, 178; steamboat 168

Inventors 20, 171, 172, 181, 235, 253, 255, 283, 416, 444, 447 *see also* Bell, Alexander Graham; Edison, Thomas Alva; Whitney, Eli

Irish immigrants 159, 166, 167, 186, 189, 192; politics 185, 192, **193,** 198

Iron and steel industry **236-237;** factory system 239, 242

Isolationists 383, 406

Jackson, Andrew 134, 185, 186; election campaign 185, memento **190**

Jackson, Helen Hunt 230

James, Jesse 227

Jamestown, Va. 8, 37, 43-44, 46, 47, 49, 53, 65

Japanese Americans: World War II 406

Jazz 312, 345, 387

The Jazz Singer (movie) 359, 371, **393,** 416

Jefferson, Thomas 20, 33, 37, 69-70, 96, 112, 163, 165, 166, 443, 448

Jenney, William Le Baron 293

Johnson, Andrew: campaign **190-191**

Jolson, Al 371, **393**

Jones, Charles Colcock, Sr., and family 201, 203, **205,** 212, 217, 219, 220

Juke box **346**

Juvenile delinquency 410, 426

Kansas-Nebraska Act 198

Karloff, Boris **373**

Keaton, Buster **357,** 369, 371

Kefauver, Estes 425

Kelly, Alvin (Shipwreck) **390**

Kemble, Fanny 178, 197, 332

Kennedy, John F.: television 415, 426, **428**

Kitchen implements: colonial era **50, 61;** electrical appliances **432,** 433, 435; food chopper **245;** stove **229**

Klinefelter, Capt. John **171**

Know Nothings 185, 195, 198; Plug-uglies **194;** sheet music **184**

Korean war 418

Ku Klux Klan: march **384-385**

Kyser, Kay **419**

Labor 435, 437; child labor 239, 251, **273,** 276, 410; fringe benefits 435, 437; hours 237, 240, 242, 249, 251, 437; eight-hour day 255; industrial accidents 239, 242, 251, 257; Machine Age 239, 247, 249, **434-435;** wages 210, 239, 240, 242, 249, 251, 273, 320, 383, 384, 410, 437; working conditions 237, 242, 249, 260, 273

Labor Day 255

Labor-saving devices: Centennial era 228; modern **432,** 433, 435

Labor unions 35, 227, 240, 260, 273, 317, 399; Civil War 210; eight-hour day poster **255;** leaders 20, 35, 273; membership 437

Laboratories, industrial 249, 253, 255, 256

Lafayette, Marquis de 166, 381

Land 24, 25, 30, 46, 49, 50, 93, 107, 443; availability 133, 134; Continental Army bounty 94, 99; fertility 134, 137; prices 133, 228

Land grants: railroads 159, 160, 178; schools 126, 128, 220

Land rushes 133-134, 142-143, 147, 156, 159, 160, **160-161**

Landon, Alfred M.: campaign memento **405**

Lange, Dorothea: photographs by **17, 395**

Laurel and Hardy **356**

Laurens, Henry 85

Law enforcement 84, 231, 300; frontier 143, 147, 153, 154

Laws 120, 126, 128, 231, 293, 399; "blue laws" 111; conscription 379-380, 381; Homestead Act 156, 160; immigration 260, 262, 267, 270, 275; labor 240; child labor 251; sedition 383; slavery 198; transportation 182; veteran's benefits 412

Legends *see* Folklore

Leigh, Vivien **370, 371**

Leisure, uses of 331, 332, 339, 346, 348, 437, **438-439,** 440

Lewis, Sinclair 384

Liberator (newspaper) 197

Liberty Bell 96

Liberty Loan rallies: World War I 380, **380**

Liberty Pole 106

Libraries 89, 444, 456

License plates **302**

Lighting: colonial era 110, rush lamp **110;** electric 228, **234,** 249, 253, 255-256, 285, 294; lantern **132;** streets 84, 285

Lincoln, Abraham 128, 180, 185, 189, 195, 198, 210, 214, 217, 220; election campaign memento **184**

Lind, Jenny 332

Lindbergh, Charles A. 371, **403;** parade honoring **390-391**

Little Egypt **296**

Lloyd, Harold **357,** 366, 371

Lockport, N.Y. **166-167**

Lockwood, Belva 191

Loew's Paradise, New York City **364-365**

"log-cabin" candidates 186, 189

Log cabins **50, 51,** 55

Los Alamos Scientific Laboratory, N. Mex. **449**

Los Angeles, Calif. 233, 406; aerial view **446-447**

Louis, Joe 400; championship bouts **400,** 418

Louisiana Purchase 20, 90, 163

Loyalists (Tories) 100, 103, **104, 105**

Lynch, Charles 100

McCarthy, Joseph R. 415, 420, **425**

McClure's (magazine) 300; advertising **244;** cover **386**

McGuffey's Readers 125

Machine Age 30, 32-35, 70, 228, 442-449 *see also* Industrial Revolution

McKinley, William: campaign mementos **184, 191**

McPherson, Aimee Semple **391**

Macy's (department store): advertising giveaway **285**

Madison, James 166; commemorative jar **190**

Magazines 89, **155,** 192, 209, 228, 233, 293, 300, 304, 306, 332, 336, **374, 386**

Mah-Jongg **330,** 345; players **344**

Mail-order buying 178, 228, 243, 244; catalogs 178, **242,** 244

Main Street (Lewis) 384

Manifest destiny 30, 138, 142

Mann, Horace 130

Manufacturing 69, 70, 235, 236, 438 *see also* Industrial Revolution; names of industries

Maps: British Colonies in North America (1776) **96-97;** Western Hemisphere (1705) **36**

Marines: World War I 380; women **382**

Marsh, Reginald: *Bread Line* **394**

Marx Brothers **356,** 376

Maryland: agriculture 53; settlement 45

Masons (Society of Freemasons) 186

Massachusetts Bay Colony 44, 49, 73, 77, 118, 120, 126

Mather, Cotton 46, 108, 110, 120

Mauldin, Bill: cartoon by **412**

Maxwell (auto) **307**

Mayer, Louis B. 371

Mayflower 23, 37, 44; model **36**

Maypole **112**

Meat packing plant **246-247**

Medical care: advances 214, 383, 412, **444, 445,** 448; American Revolution 98-99, 104; Civil War 204, 206, 214; inoculations 98, 110

Mencken, H. L. 186, 390

Merchandising **229;** department stores **284-285,** 286; installment buying 244; mail-order buying 228, 243, 244, catalog **242;** malls 440

Merchants 60, 68, **86,** 89, 90; Revolutionary era 99-100, 104

Mexican War 147, 150, 181

Middle class: definition 435

Migrant workers **17,** 321, 396

Militia 93, 98, 104, 111, 112; immigrant units 192

Millay, Edna St. Vincent 387

Millionaires 20, 309; number of 288

Mills: grist mill **70, 71,** 235; *see also* Steel industry; Textile industry

Miniature golf 345; course **344**

Mining camps and towns **144, 146-147,** 148, **151,** 153, 154; law enforcement 153, 154; schoolchildren **127**

Minnelli, Vincente 374, 376

Minutemen 93

Miss America, first 387

Money, paper: Civil War 209, 212; Continental Congress **92,** 98, 103-104; "monkey trial" 390; cartoon **391**

Monopolies 231

Monopoly (game) **330**

Montgomery Ward's catalog 178, 243, 244

Mormons: westward migration **138,** 147-148, 150

Morrissey, John "Old Smoke" 192

Morse, Samuel F. B. 181

Mott, James and Lucretia 197

Mountain Men 142

Movie theaters **352-353, 364-365;** drive-in **326-327**

Movies 350-377; cartoons 351, **372,** 376; comedies **34-35,** 351, **356-357,** 365, 366, 369, 371, 372, 376; crime and gangster 353, **362-363,** 365, 369, 371, 372, 374; musicals **358-359,** 366, 374, 376; silents 351, **352, 354-355, 356,** 369, 371; talkies, first 359, 371, **393,** 416; war 365, **370, 376, 377;** Westerns 351, 353, 355, **360-361,** 365, 374

"Mugwumps" 191

Muir, John 232, 310

Muni, Paul **362**

Murrow, Edward R. **414**

Music: Civil War songs 209; colonial era 112; concert tours 223, 332; jazz 312, 345, 387; parlor singing **332-333;** popular songs 345, 346; ragtime 296, 345; rock 19, 346; sheet music **164, 184, 203, 208, 304, 332, 381**

Musicals **358-359, 392-393**

Nader, Ralph 328

Nash (auto) 317, 319

Nast, Thomas 192, 231, 233; cartoon **193**

National parks 33, 228, 232, 303, 310, 437, 440

National Recovery Administration 399; emblem **399**

National Road 137, 165

National unity 25, 163-164, 178, 181, 220

Navigation Acts 68

Navigational instruments **36**

Navy: Continental Navy 99; World War I 380; women recruits 383

New Deal 251, 399, 405

New England: colonial era 43, 44, 46, 50, 56, 58, 60, 65, 68, 70, 77, 108, 109, 110, 111, 115; farms 56; fisheries **54,** 56; sea captains **56-57,** 60; settlement 44; textile industry 20, 70, 239, 240; tombstones **58-59, 109;** West Indies trade 57, 60; whaling **55**

New Haven, Conn. 73, 77, 89, 90; fire engine **298**

New Jersey (steamboat) **168**

New Orleans, La. 387; steamboats **170-171**

New Orleans (steamboat) 168, 171

New York City, N.Y. 77-78, **79,** 80, 84, 86, **87,** 89, 90, **90-91,** 93, 96, 99, 168, 192, 195, 203, 210, 232, **256-257, 280-285, 288-291,** 332, **335, 380-382,** 387, **390-391;** Central Park 210, 290, **340;** Civil War rally **202;** El **283;** Flatiron Building **281;** Lower East Side 189, **271;** Manhattan skyline (1906, 1933, 1974) **30-31;** sweatshops **272;** tenements 285, **290, 291;** Tribune Building **278;** Vanderbilt mansion **288-289**

New York Daily News 391

New York Yankees: "Murderers' Row" 400

Newport, R.I. 77, 78, 85, 89, 93, 288; picnics 114, 345

Newspapers 89, **89,** 345, 444, 448; tabloid **391;** wire services 181

Nickelodeons **352-353,** 355

Nixon, Richard M.: television **428, 429,** 430

Northwest Territory: slavery forbidden 104; *see also* Old Northwest

Nursing bottle **109**

Okies **397**

Old Northwest 30; settlement 134, 137, 166

Old Southwest: settlement 137-138

Olds, Ransom Eli 304

Oldsmobile (auto) **304,** 309, **323**

Olmsted, Frederick Law 290, 293

Oregon (territory): annexation 195; settlement 142-143, 147

Oregon Trail **136,** 143

Orpheum Circuit (vaudeville): bill **393**

O'Sullivan, Maureen **368**

Oswald, Lee Harvey 415, 426, **427**

Owens, Jesse **400**

Paar, Jack **423**

Pacifists 379, 380

Paine, Thomas 115

Parks: municipal 290, 293; national 33, 228, 232, 303, 310, 437, 440

Parlor games 331, 332

Patent medicines **229**

Paving **72,** 77, 80, **81,** 283, 303, 322, 341

Pea Ridge, Ark.: Civil War battle **211**

Pearl Harbor, Hawaii: Japanese attack 406

Peddlers 164, 260, 273

Peirce, Benjamin **128**

Penn, William 45, 73, 78, 83

Pennsylvania: settlement 45

Pennsylvania Dutch: baptismal gift **108**

Pershing, John J. (Black Jack) 379, 381
Petersburg, Va.: Union supply train **218-219**
Petroleum industry 210, 231, 303, 314, 328, 437, 438
Philadelphia, Pa. 73, 78, 79, 80, **80-83,** 84, 85, 86, 89, 90, 93, 96, 104, 109, 111, 114, **222,** 280; brothels 300; *see also* Centennial Exhibition
Phillips, Wendell 197-198
Phonograph 191, 228, 244; advertisement **244**
Photographers: Alice Austen **310;** Mathew B. Brady 8; Jacob Byerly **8;** Lewis W. Hine 251; Frances Benjamin Johnston **228;** Dorothea Lange 16, 394; Jacob Riis 273, 290, 299
Pickford, Mary 351, 353, 366, 420
Pilgrims 23, 24, 37, 44, 195
Pillory 84, **111**
Pinups: Civil War **208, 209**
Pioneers 133-134, **134-135,** 137-138, 142-143, 147-148; self-government 143; *see also* Forty-niners; Homesteaders
Piracy 46, 85, 86
Plantations 45, **52-53,** 55-56, 201, 203, 212, 217, 219; workers 46, 55, 61, 62
Planters: education 123, 201, 205; westward migration 138; *see also* Jones, Charles Colcock, Sr.
Playing Cards **330;** Revolutionary era **115**
Plug-uglies **194**
Plumbing: fixtures **244;** flush toilets 283
Plymouth colony 44
Poker (game) 341; chips **330;** full house **330**
Police 300, **387, 427**
Politics 184-199, 223, 230-231; "bosses" 192, 285, 300; city machines 192, 195; immigrants 185, 189, 192, 195, 198; propaganda 186, 189; reform movement 299-300; "spoils system" 186; two-party system 185-186; *see also* Elections; names of political parties
Polk, James K. 150, 195
Pontiac (auto) 309, **323**
Pony Express 173, 181; poster **172**
Poor Richard's Almanack 68, 89; maxims 69
Population *see* Census
Populists 182
Postal service 85, 89, 135, 154, 165, 178; air mail 402, stamp **403;** Overland Mail Company **172-173;** Pony Express 173; post rider **96**
Poverty: definition 435; income 435, 439; living conditions 285, 290, **290, 291;** relief 83, 86, 299
Princess (steamboat) **168-169**
Printing and publishing 65, 68, 89; newspapers 89, **89;** presses **88,** 89, 444
Prisons: American Revolution **104,** prison ships 99, **100-101**
Privateers 85; American Revolution 99
Privies 80, 299
Prohibition 383, **388-389**
Prostitutes **149,** 153, 209, 300
Puck (magazine): cartoons **193, 292**
Pullman, Ill. 180, 290
Pullman cars 180, 224; convertible sleeper **180-181**
Punishments 84-85, **111;** Civil War soldiers **210**
Puritans 24, 44, 58, 65, 73, 74, 86, 111, 112, 115, 118, 120, 126, 130, 444

Quakers 80, 86, 89; abolitionists 197
Quilt **115**

Radio 416, 418, 444; politics 405, 428; sets **414,** advertisement **416;** shows **416-417, 419**
Radio Corporation of America: television sets **414,** 416
Railroads 172, **176-177,** 178, 181, 209, 220, 227, 228, 447; construction 172,
174-175, 177, 178, 189; freight rates 181, 230; government 380, regulation 182, subsidy 159, 178; immigration encouraged by 262, 276; locomotives 172, **174,** 178, 182, model **162;** passenger accommodations 178, **178-181, 183;** transcontinental, first 178, 181; wrecks 177, staged **182**
Raleigh, Sir Walter 43; ghost ship 120
Rathbone, Basil **373**
Recreation 33, **112-115,** 223-224, 232-233, 330-349, 437, 440 *see also* Movies; Radio; Television
Reform movements: municipal government 300; social 195, 290, 299-300; *see also* Abolitionists
Refrigeration 33, 246
Reliance Building, Chicago **299**
Religion 73, 86, 115, 118, 119, 120, 121, 126, 163, 192; devils and specters 120; evangelists **391;** fundamentalism 390
Remington, Philo 235
Republican Party 223, 405; origins 198; symbol 231, rooster **231**
Resorts 223, 233, 341; activities 345
Revere, Paul 90, 93
Revolutionary War *see* American Revolution
Rice 45, 46, 55-56, 62, 73
Richmond, Va. 212; Civil War campaign 206, **206-207;** trolley line 280
Rifles 94; making of **66-67**
Riis, Jacob 273, 290, 299; photographs by **272, 290, 291**
Riots: Civil War draft 210; race riots 383, 384, 410; students 126
Roads 314, 322; colonial 85, 133; National Road 137, 165-166; paving of 303, 322, 341; turnpikes 166
Roanoke Island, N.C. 43
Robinson, Edward G. 260, 353, **362**
Rochester, N.Y. 90, 280, 283; Powers Block 279
Rockefeller, John D. 231
Rocking horse 113
Rockwell, Norman: illustrations by **381, 413**
Rogers, Ginger 353, **359,** 366
Rogers, Roy **360**
Rogers, Will **392,** 402, 405
Rogers groups (statuettes) **228**
Roller derbies: television 420, **423**
Rooney, Mickey **373**
Roosevelt, Franklin D. 384, 406, 416; death 412; "fireside chats" 399, **405;** presidency 399
Roosevelt, Theodore 20, 290, 293, 379; election campaign button **191**
Ruth, George Herman (Babe) **401;** autograph **330**

Sacco, Nicola 384
St. Louis, Mo. 90, 154, 163, 171, 178, 293; Louisiana Purchase Exposition (1904) 300
St. Louis Cardinals: star pitchers 400, **400**
St. Paul, Minn.: bicycle race **334-335**
St. Valentine's Day massacre **388**
Salem, Mass. 77, 89
Saloons 148, 227, 300, 388
San Francisco, Calif. 154, 181, 249, 286; cable car 280
San Francisco Bay: abandoned ships **142-143**
Sanger, Margaret 387
Sanitation: cities 80, 280, 283, 285, 290, 293, 299
Santa Claus 233
Santa Fe Railroad: menu 180
Schools: classes **122-123, 127-129,** field trip **130-131,** recess 124; classroom conditions 117, 123, 130; curriculums 120, 123, **125,** 128, 130; reading **121,** writing 117, **125;** "dame schools" 86; Latin grammar schools 120, 125; paro-
chial 192, state support 192; public 192, 275, 276, **277,** emergence 130; religious purpose 121, 126; reward for diligence **123;** South 123, 126; sports **129;** textbooks **116, 121, 125;** West 125, **127**
Schurz, Carl 20, 230
Science fiction 416, 418, 448
Sea captains, colonial **56-57,** 60
Sea monsters 38
Sears, Roebuck and Company 243, 244; 1899 catalog **242**
Sectionalism 166, 182, 220
Selznick, David O. 371
Settlement houses 299
Sewing machines 244; musical cover **228**
Shahn, Ben: *The Passion of Sacco and Vanzetti* **384**
Sherman, William Tecumseh 219, 224; march to the sea 219, 220
Sherman Antitrust Act 231
Shipbuilding 54, 60, 69; World War I 380; World War II 409
Ships: abandoned: San Francisco Bay **142-143;** Charles Town harbor **84;** French explorers **41;** immigrant **261;** *Mayflower* **36;** prison ships **100-101;** *see also* Steamboats
Shirley (manor), Va. **52-53**
Show Boat (musical) **392-393**
Siegel Cooper's department store, New York City **284-285**
Silk production, attempted 45, 46, 73
Silver 151, 154
Silver City, Idaho: hotel **151**
Sioux: Chief Kicking Bear **141;** Pine Ridge Reservation, S. Dak. **140-141**
Skaters **114;** Central Park **340**
Skiing 346
Skyscrapers 224, 279, **281,** 293, **299;** Manhattan (1906, 1933, 1974) **30-31**
Slater, Samuel 8, 20, 70
Slavery 32, 46; abolition 98, 104, 107, 195, 197-198; Revolutionary era 104
Slaves 8, 40, 55, 85, 107, **205,** 217, **217,** 219; emancipation 209, 210, 217; life of 107, 110; number of 197, 198; relation with masters 205; trade 60, 197, advertisements **84, 197,** auction **196;** warning to fugitives **199**
Sloan, Alfred P., Jr. 312-314, 317, 328
Smallpox: Indians 44; inoculation 98, 110
Smith, Capt. John 43-44, 47, 49
Smith, Kate **419**
Snyder, Ruth: execution **391**
So Big (Ferber) **387**
Social Security 435; poster **399**
Social services 86, 299, 437, 439
Sod houses **26-27,** 137, **156-157,** 159
Soglow, Otto: cartoon by **394**
"Sooners" 161
Sousa, John Philip 223
South 25, 38, 40, 41, 43, 45-46, 53, 55-56, 60, 134, 138, 166, 182, 197; American Revolution 100, 103; education 123, 126, 205; secession 198; *see also* Confederacy
Space shots **25;** television 426, **427**
Spanish-American War 293, 379
Speakeasies 300, **389**
Spinning: hand **64,** 69; machine 20, 70, 239
"spoils system" 186
Sports: Centennial era 223, 228, 232, 233, **233;** collegiate **129,** 400; colonial era **114;** professional 332, 341, **342-343,** 346, 348, celebrities 20, **400-401,** television coverage 418, 420, **423,** 426, **427,** 430, **430-431**
The Squaw Man (movie) 354
Stagecoaches 85, 154, 163, 164-165, **172-173;** manufacture of 236, 239
Stamp Act 68, 89, 94
Standard of living 432-441
Stanley Steamer (auto) 304
Stanton, Elizabeth Cady 209
Statue of Liberty 259, **269;** memento **258;** model of arm **230**
Steam engines: Corliss Engine 181, 224, **224;** railroad locomotives 172, 182, model **162;** steamboats 171
Steamboats 168, **168-171,** 171-172, 178; captain **171;** collisions 172; fires **168,** 170, 172; model **162**
Steel industry 303, 314, 328, 438; accidents 242; factory system 239, 242; mill **236-237;** U. S. Steel 252
Steffens, Lincoln 242, 300
Steinbeck, John 396
Steinmetz, Charles P. 253
Stock market 86; crash 394, 416, 433, 434, 438; regulation of 399, 434
Stocks, 84, **111**
Strang, Louis **308**
Strikes 182, 210, 227, 240, 355, 384, **384;** sit-down 317
Strong, George Templeton, Sr., and family 195, 201, 203, **204,** 206, 209, 210, 220
Stuart, Gilbert 110
Studebaker (auto) **311,** 317, **323**
Suburbs 435, 436, 437; growth related to autos 314, 319, 437, 446
Suffrage *see* Voting rights
Sugar: West Indies 45, 55, trade 57, 60
Sullivan, Ed: television show **420, 422**
Sullivan, Louis 293
Sully, Thomas 114
Sunday pastimes 111, 115, 232, 233, 317, 331, 335, 341; "blue laws" 111
Supreme Court 163, 230
Swayze, John Cameron 425, 426
Sweatshops 260, **272,** 285
"The Swedish Nightingale" 332
Sweeney, Peter 192
Swimming **338-339,** 348

Tammany Hall 185, 191; headquarters **193;** history 192
Tappan, Arthur and Lewis 197
Tar and feathering **105**
Taverns 85-86, 89, 418
Taxes 288, 322, 412; colonial 68, 94; poll tax 231; school tax 123
Taylor, Zachary 189; memento **184**
Telegraph 181
Telephone 228, **234, 248-249,** 288, 294, 444; Centennial Exhibition 181, 224; transcontinental line **249**
Television 34, 374, 376, **414,** 415-416, 418, 420-431, 437, 438, 440, 444, 448; advertising expenditures 422; anthology series 420, **423,** 425; child viewers 415, **420,** 426, 430, shows for 418, 420, **422;** comedy 420, **420-423,** 425-426; crime dramas 418, 420, **423,** 426; episodic series 418, 420, 425; "instant replay" 426, 431; live vs. filmed 420, 425, 426, 430; networks 418, 426; news events, coverage of 415, 425, **425,** 426, **427-429,** 430; public **429,** 430; quiz shows **423,** 425, 426; sponsors 418, 420, 425; sports 418, 420, **423,** 426, **427,** 430, **430-431;** variety shows **420-423;** Westerns **422,** 425, 426; world view presented by 415, 425, 426, 430, 431
Telluride, Colo.: Cosmopolitan Saloon **148**
Temperance movement 300, 387, 388
Temple, Shirley **367**
Tenements 273, 285, 290, **291**
Tennis 345, 346
Texas: annexation of 195
Textile industry 8, 20, 65, 70, 239, 240, 438; child labor **250;** factory system 239; mill **4-5**
Thanksgiving: history 112, 233
Theater 80, 114, 304, 332, 348, **392-393;** record runs 392
Theaters, movie **364-365, 371;** drive-in **326-327;** nickelodeon **352-353,** 355

Thomson, Elihu 253-254
Thoreau, Henry David 172, 443
Tilden, Samuel J.: disputed election 223, memento **231**
Tilyou, George 336
Time clock **234**
Time-motion studies 239, 309
Timucuan Indians **40;** Europeans encounter **41**
"Tippecanoe and Tyler too!" 189
Toasters: colonial **61;** electric **432**
Tobacco 37, 43, 45, 46, 50, 53, 55, 56, 60, 62; label **53**
Tocqueville, Alexis de 171, 185
Today (television show) 420, **422**
Tom Sawyer (Mark Twain) 224, 232
Tombstones 56, **58-59, 109**
Tools **48,** 55, 61, **61-63, 66, 166, 278, 306**
Toys **112-113**
Tracy, Philemon **110**
Tracy, Spencer 353, 366, **373**
Trade: colonial era 53, 55, 57, 60, 62, 68, 77, 85-86, 89; 19th century 165, 166, 168, 171, 178; modern 438
Trademarks **440-441**
Trains *see* Railroads
Transportation 162-183; colonial 85, 89, 90; mass transit 280, **282, 283,** 285, **300-301, 336,** 341; *see also* Automobiles; Canals; Railroads; Stagecoaches; Steamboats
Triangle shirtwaist factory fire 257, 273
Tribune Building, New York City **278**
Trolleys **300-301,** 336, **336,** 341
Trusts 231
Tunis, John R.: quoted 346
Twain, Mark 170; quoted 173, 233; works 224, **232**
Tweed, William Marcy "Boss" 192, 285
Tweed Ring 192, 195; cartoon **193**
Tyler, John 189
Typewriters 224, 232, **234**

Uncle Sam: World War I recruiting poster **378**
Uniforms: American Revolution 94, **98, 99;** World War I campaign hat **378;** World War I Marinette **382;** World War II cap **378**
Union poster **203**
Union Square, New York City: Civil War rally **202**
Unions *see* Labor unions
United Auto Workers: sit-down strike 317
U. S. Army: Civil War: artillery **212-213;**

encampment **206-207;** enlistees 201, 203; hardships 206; march to the sea 219, 220; medical bureau 203, 206; size 207; supplies 206, supply train **218-219**
United States Sanitary Commission 203, 204, 206, 209

VJ Day **18,** 412
Valentine greeting **233**
Valley Forge, Pa. **102-103;** Continental Army 94, 98, **103**
Van Buren, Martin 185, 186, 189, 195, 198
Vanderbilt mansions: New York City **288-289;** Newport, R.I. 288
Vanzetti, Bartolomeo 384
Vaudeville 355, 392; bill **393**
Verrazzano, Giovanni da 38, 40
Veterans: American Revolution 99; World War I 384; World War II 412
Vidor, King 369
Virginia: agriculture 53, 55; exploration of 43; plantations **52-53;** settlement 43-44, 45, 65
Volkswagen (auto) 322, 328
Voting rights 100, 104, 107, 111, 186, 195; blacks 231; women 209, 230, 383, **387,** march for **256-257**

Wages: auto workers 239, 320; children 251, 410; garment workers 273; minimum 437; steelworkers 242; women factory workers 210, 240; World War I 383
Wagon trains 133, **134,** 143, 147
Wall Street, New York City 78, **87,** 394, 416
"The War of the Worlds" (radio play) 418
Warner Brothers 371
Washing machine: advertisement **244**
Washington, George 62, 94, 96, 98, 99, 111, 126, 163, 186, 191, 402; cabinet 70; cartoon **428;** clothing 224; commemorative buttons **111;** false teeth **110**
Water supply 80, 279, 299
Watergate hearings, televised 428, 430
Wayne, John 353, **361**
Webster, Daniel 186; quoted 185, 189
Webster, Noah 125, 163
Weddings 108
Weissmuller, Johnny **368**
Welles, Orson 418, **419**
West: boomtowns **146-147,** 148, **151,** 154; education 125, **127;** lawlessness 153, 154, 227
Western Union 181
Westerns: movies 351, 353, 355, **360-361,** 365, 374; television **422,** 425, 426

Westward movement 20, 25, 90, 132-161, 163; colonial era 107, 133; contributing factors 133, 134, 154, 156, 166, 171; Indians 103, 134; numbers of migrants 133; routes **136,** 137, 143, guidebook **137**
Whaling **55,** 60
What's My Line? (television show) **423**
Wheat harvest **28-29**
Whigs 186, 189, 192, 195, 198; "keep the ball rolling" **190-191;** rally **188**
Whistle-stop campaigns 191
White, John 43
White Steamer (auto) **305**
Whitman, Walt 25, 231, 280; parodies of 224
Whitney, Eli 134, 247, 447
Whittier, John Greenleaf: antislavery poems 197, illustration **198**
Wilderness Road 90, 133
Willkie, Wendell L. 405; rally **404**
Wilson, Woodrow 379, 381, 383
Wine bricks 388
Winthrop, John 49, 73, 77, 118
Wisconsin River: Dells **338**
Witches 120
Women 8, 294, 296, 304, 435, 439; American Revolution **94,** 103, 104; armed forces **382,** 412; Centennial era 227, **228,** 230, boxers 232; Civil War 203, 204, 206, 209, 210; pinups **208, 209;** colonial era **75,** tasks **64-65;** cyclists **335,** 336; education 112, 120, 123, **128-129,** teachers **127,** 130; factory workers 210, 239, **240-241,** 383, 409, 410; migrant workers 8, **17;** 1920's **386-387;** office workers 235, 380; photographers **228, 310;** pilots **403;** politics 191, 387; suffrage 209, 230, 383, **387,** march for **256-257;** telephone operators 248
Women's Loyal National League 209
Work ethic 332, 348
Works Progress Administration: art work **399**
World War I 378-383; anti-German feeling 380, 381; armed forces: size 380, women **382,** 383; Armistice 383; campaign hat **378;** casualties 383; civilian war effort 380, 381, 383; government agencies 380; mobilization 380; pacifists 379, 380; prosperity 383; radio 417, 418; rallies 379, Liberty Loan 380, **380;** recruiting poster 378
World War II 406-413; armed forces 409, women 412; baby boom 412; Civilian Defense wardens 406, 412, helmet **378;**

civilian service organizations 379; civilian war effort 379, 406, 409, 410; government war agencies 409, 412; Japanese Americans 406, **406;** mobilization 406, 409; posters **409;** prosperity 410; rationing 410, 412, gasoline stamp **410;** VJ Day **18,** 412; war bonds 410
World's fairs 416; Columbian Exposition 293, **294-297;** Louisiana Purchase Exposition 300; *see also* Centennial Exhibition
Wounded Knee, S. Dak.: massacre (1890) 20, 141
Wray, Fay **373**
Wright brothers 20, 304
Wyoming Territory: women's suffrage (1869) 230, 387

Yale University 89, 126, 336
Yorktown, Va.: American Revolution 98, 100
Yosemite National Park, Calif.: autos 310; Overhanging Rock **311**
Young, Brigham 147, 148

Zenger, John Peter 89
Ziegfeld *Follies* 392

Type composition by the Typographic section of National Geographic Production Services, Pre-Press Division. Color separations by Colorgraphics, Inc., Beltsville, Md.; J. Wm. Reed Company, Alexandria, Va., Progressive Color Corporation, Rockville, Md.; The Lanman Companies, Washington, D. C. Printing and binding by Arcata Graphics Kingsport, Kingsport, Tenn. Paper by Mead Paper Co., New York, N.Y.

Library of Congress CIP Data

We Americans / [editorial consultant, Daniel J. Boorstin].— [Rev. ed.]
  p.   cm.
  "A volume in the Story of man library"—T.p. verso.
  Includes bibliographical references and index.
  ISBN 0-87044-749-1 (alk. paper).
  ISBN 0-87044-750-5 (Deluxe ed.: alk. paper)
  1. United States—Civilization. I. Boorstin, Daniel J. (Daniel Joseph), 1914- II. National Geographic Society.
E169.1.W312 1988
973—dc19   88-22403
                                                  CIP

You are invited to join the National Geographic Society or to send gift memberships to others. (Membership includes a subscription to NATIONAL GEOGRAPHIC magazine.) For information call 800-638-4077 toll free, or write to the National Geographic Society, Department 1675, Washington, D. C. 20036.

Acknowledgments

The Charles Town Library Society founded the first public museum in the United States in 1773 in Charleston, South Carolina. Now more than 12,000 public libraries, 6,000 museums, and 4,000 historical societies preserve and teach our cultural history and heritage. In the preparation of this book we called upon the resources of many of these institutions. We are especially grateful for the assistance of the curators and staff of the Smithsonian Institution, the Library of Congress, and our own National Geographic Society Library. We also received valuable guidance from staff members at the Colonial Williamsburg Foundation, Old Sturbridge Village, the American Automobile Association, and the American Institute of Architects.

We are indebted to many at the Smithsonian, including Brooke Hindle, former director of the Museum of History and Technology [now National Museum of American History]; Silvio A. Bedini, former deputy director; Warren J. Danzenbaker, and the following: Richard Ahlborn, Sheila Alexander, Edwin Battison, Don H. Berkebile, Vladimir Clain-Stefanelli, Herbert Collins, Bernard Finn, Anne C. Golovin, Craddock Goins, Genevieve Gremillion, John N. Hoffman, Ellen R. Hughes, Carl H. Jaeschke, Donald E. Kloster, James A. Knowles, Lorene Mayo, Mary Ellen McCaffrey, J. J. Miller, Susan H. Myers, Eugene Ostroff, Frank Roche, Rodris Roth, Carl H. Scheele, John Schlebecker, Anne M. Serio, Elliott Sivowitch, James E. Spears, Carlene Stevens, John N. Stine, Robert Vogel, Robert G. Walther, John H. White.

We especially wish to thank Ruth Boorstin for her help. We were also given assistance by Jan Norbye of *Automobile News,* Lynne Leopold of the Insurance Company of North America, James Bradley, of the Automotive History Collection, Detroit Public Library; Ed Jagels, proprietor of the Idaho Hotel in Silver City, Idaho; Edmund B. Sullivan, curator of the DeWitt Collection, University of Hartford; Paul Henderson of Bridgeport, Nebraska, an expert on the

Oregon Trail; Henry Austin Clark, Jr., of the Long Island Automotive Museum, Earl H. Robinson, Jr., of Swanzey Center, New Hampshire, an expert in automotive history; and David Murphy, of the National Park Service. We wish to thank Tom Logan of Culver Pictures, John J. Fletcher of United Press International, Thomas J. Freeman of Wide World, Jerry Kearns of the Prints and Photographs Division, Library of Congress; and Charlotte LaRue of the Museum of the City of New York. We are also grateful to Gordon Green, Mary Henson, Lars Johanson, and Glenn King of the U. S. Bureau of the Census.

The National Geographic Society gratefully acknowledges permission to reprint excerpts from the following: "Upstream" in *Slabs of the Sunburnt West* by Carl Sandburg, © 1922 by Harcourt Brace Jovanovich, Inc., © 1950 by Carl Sandburg; reprinted by permission of the publisher. "America Remembers" from *American Song* by Paul Engle, © 1933 by Doubleday & Company, Inc.; reprinted by permission of Doubleday & Company, Inc. "Let America Be America Again" © 1938 by Langston Hughes; by permission of Harold Ober Associates Incorporated. *The Children of Pride* © 1972 by Robert Manson Myers; by permission of Yale University Press. *Diary of the Civil War 1860-1865* by George Templeton Strong, edited by Allan Nevins, © 1952 and 1962 by The Macmillan Company. *From Know-How to Nowhere: The Development of American Technology* by Elting E. Morison, © 1974 by Basic Books, Inc., Publishers, New York. *The Education of Hyman Kaplan* by Leonard Q. Ross, © 1965 by Leo C. Rosten; by permission of Harcourt Brace Jovanovich, Inc. "Vanishing Hitchhiker" folktale from the Folklore Archive of East Carolina University, Greenville, North Carolina. "Auto Wreck" © 1942 and renewed 1970 by Karl Shapiro, reprinted from *Selected Poems* by Karl Shapiro; by permission of Random House, Inc. "First Fig" from *A Few Figs from Thistles,* Harper and Row, © 1922, 1950 by Edna St. Vincent Millay.

"In Everybody's Living Room" is adapted from *Tube of Plenty: The Evolution of American Television* © 1975 by Erik Barnouw; used by permission of Oxford University Press, Inc.